Computers
AN INTRODUCTION

Cover photo courtesy of Ramtek Corporation.

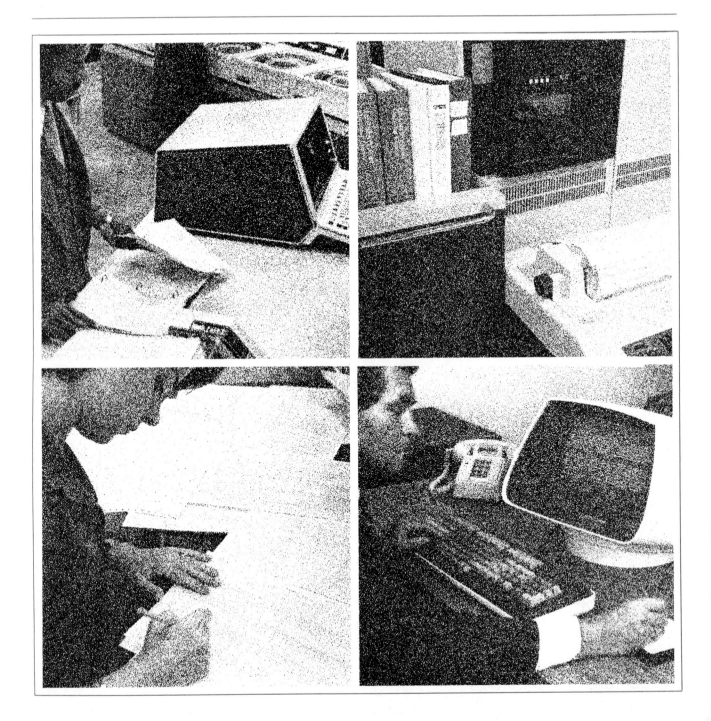

Computers
AN INTRODUCTION

DAVID M. KROENKE
RANDOLPH P. JOHNSTON

MITCHELL PUBLISHING, INC.
Santa Cruz, California

Production: Hal Lockwood, Bookman Productions
Production coordination: Susan Defosset
Cover design and text design: Janet Bollow
Photo essay layout: Michael Rogondino and Pat Rogondino
Manuscript editors: Kate Engelberg, Patricia Cain, and Larry McCombs
Illustrations: Michael Abbey, Pat Rogondino, Barbara Ravizza, and Evanell Towne
Photo research: Syndia Smith
Photographs: Shelly McComas, Chuck O'Rear, Steve Potter, Walt Robinson, Syndia Smith
Chapter opener photographs: Steve Potter
Composition: Graphic Typesetting Service
Color illustrations for *The Chip:* Dave Pauly

Acknowledgments for black-and-white photographs: 1–1, CW Communications Inc., Framingham, MA 01701, reprinted from *Computerworld.* 1–7, 2–3, 6–4, and A–8, Sperry Univac, a Division of the Sperry Rand Corporation. 2–1, 2–2, 2–24, and A–12, Honeywell Information Systems, Inc. 2–7, Inforex, Inc. 2–8, National Computer Systems. 2–19, Cabrillo College, Aptos, CA. 2–21, Basic Four Information Systems. 2–22, Carol Lee/BASF, Wyandett Corporation. 2–23a and 6–12, Verbatim Corporation, Sunnyvale, CA. 2–25, Qume Corporation. 2–27, 6–8, 6–14, A–2, A–4, A–7, A–9, A–11, and E–9, International Business Machines Corporation. 2–30, Apple Computer, Inc. 2–31, Digital Equipment Corporation. 2–32, Cray Research, Inc. 3–20, Unimation. 3–25, Amdahl Corporation. 6–5, BASE Corporation. 8–6, Northern Communication Corporation. 8–11, CODEX Corporation. 8–17, Data General Corporation. 8–18, Hewlett-Packard. A–3, Steve Potter. A–10, Texas Instruments, Inc. A–13, Digital Equipment Corporation. A–14, Intel Corporation. D–1, NASA. D–3, The Boeing Company. D–8, The Technicon Medical Information Systems Corporation. D–11, National Crime Information Center, FBI Headquarters, Washington, D.C. D–12, Barbara Holt, Perkins, Coie, Stone, Olsen, Williams, Seattle. D–15, Congress of the United States, House of Representatives. D–16, SRI International. E–1, Wang Laboratories, Inc. E–10 Xerox Corporation.

Library of Congress Cataloging in Publication Data

Kroenke, David.
  Computers : an introduction.

  Bibliography: p.
  Includes index.
  1. Electronic data processing. 2. Electronic digital computers. I. Johnston, Randolph P. II. Title.
QA76.K746 1984   001.64   83–22130
ISBN 0–938188–13–5

Printed in the United States of America

10 9 8 7 6 5 4 3 2

Each second we live in a new and unique moment of the universe, a moment that never was before and will never be again. And what do we teach our students in school? We teach them that two and two make four and that Paris is the capital of France. When will we also teach them what they are? We should say to each of them: Do you know who you are? You are a marvel. You are unique. In all the world there is no other person exactly like you. . . . You may become a Shakespeare, a Michelangelo, a Beethoven. You have the capacity for anything.

Pablo Casals
Joys and Sorrows, 1970

Contents

Expanded Contents

PART ONE
INTRODUCTION   1

The importance of computer knowledge. The use of a microcomputer at Blake Records provides a lesson in office politics as well. Chuck Swanson, a computer user at TYCON, is asked to assist in a computer project. He doesn't know how.

Establishing the framework for understanding computer systems: the five components. Using this framework to describe an example system: the class enrollment system.

How are computer systems used? A survey from a manager's viewpoint. Characteristics of systems in major functional areas. Kinds of service: transaction processing, MIS, and DSS—the information center.

PART TWO
FUNDAMENTAL COMPUTER SYSTEMS   101

The systems development process has four major stages: requirements definition, alternative evaluation, systems design, and implementation. Illustration of this process at Horizon Artist Supply.

Sequential file systems, one alternative for Horizon Artist Supply. Characteristics of the five components in a sequential system. Application to Horizon's customer master file system.

Direct access file systems, another alternative for Horizon. Characteristics of the five components in a direct access system. Application to Horizon's customer master file system.

Database, a third alternative system. Advantages and disadvantages of database processing. Characteristics of the five components in a database system. Corporate, regional, and personal databases. The relational model.

Harold Johnson, an ambitious and creative employee, is bored and feels unappreciated. He finds a niche as a modern Robin Hood, he thinks. Other examples. Computer crime and what to do about it. Establishing good system controls. How Harold is caught.

Computers as boon and bane. How computers influence business. Application to nonbusiness enterprises. Controlling computer impact through legislation and knowledge.

An electronic typewriter? Yes, and the start of a revolution. Finally, after 400 years, offices are changed, but it's office *augmentation*, not office *automation*.

PART FIVE
COMPUTER
PROGRAMMING   423

Getting started with BASIC. Entering BASIC statements, adding, deleting, and changing statements. Fundamental BASIC statements to build confidence.

The fundamental cycle of programming. Designing from outputs, then inputs, then processing steps. Tools for expressing logic: structured flowcharts and pseudocode.

Preface

Today's computer revolution is rapidly changing the way people think about computers. We know that our perceptions of what computers can do have changed greatly over the last few years. With computers costing less and less while doing more and more, one fact still remains. Computers are the tools of people.

This text is written with you in mind. You are probably just stepping into the world of computing. We hope to explain what computer systems are like and how they are used, so you can begin to build your knowledge about computing. We are going to assume that you have no experience but are eager to learn.

What you are about to read is the sum of many years of experience in the computing field. Experience may be the best teacher, but experience takes a long time to achieve. You can benefit greatly from our experience by carefully learning the material in this book. We wish someone had shared this kind of knowledge with us when we first became interested in computing.

When Dave taught his first "Introduction to Computers and Data Processing" course, he had just left a technical programming job and taught hours and hours of programming to people interested in computers. He also taught hardware. To him at the time, hardware and programs *were* computing.

As he installed more computer systems, he realized that his emphasis was wrong. One situation in particular illustrates this. One of his former students had become manager of a payroll department. She found that the course material was irrelevant to her job. Somehow, knowing two ways of sorting an array of ten numbers in BASIC or FORTRAN did not help her reduce the errors in payroll processing—neither did her knowledge of seven- and nine-track tape drives. What she had learned in Dave's classroom and what she was doing on the job were, at best, loosely related.

Dave decided to change his approach and give attention to the human side of systems as well as hardware and programs. Furthermore, he wanted to bring experience from industry into the classroom to increase the relevancy of the course.

This text reflects this philosophy. It defines a computer system as having five components: *hardware, programs, data, procedures, and people*. When a type of system is discussed (sequential processing, for example), the nature and characteristics of each of these components is defined. In this way, data, procedures, and people were brought into the discussion *along with* hardware and programs. This approach builds a bridge from the technical material on the one hand to people on the other.

Cases, or vignettes, from Dave's experience are also included. These cases are included for two reasons. First, they stimulate student interest. Although students are usually bright eyed when learning programming, their eyes begin to droop when other components are discussed. Students are more interested with the vignettes. Second, the vignettes are helpful illustrations. In a sense they serve the role that program examples serve in a programming textbook.

Today, we believe even more strongly in the need for a balanced approach in an introductory class. Because off-the-shelf software, program generators, and nonprocedural languages have become more prevalent, traditional programming has become less important. The September, 1983, issue of *Computing Newsletter* opened with the following quote of a FORTUNE 500 executive, "Help me with some career-path planning for the 3,000 COBOL programmers who will no longer be needed in my company." There is an increasing demand for graduates who understand the broad fundamentals of computers and can apply those fundamentals to solving problems.

Impact of Microcomputers

The increasing use of microcomputers has generated substantial change in the computer industry in the last three years. Who would have believed that IBM would sell 100,000 personal computers in June, 1983?

The microcomputer boom has increased the importance of studying the five components and learning systems development. First, when users are their own operators, consideration of the procedures and personnel components of a computer system becomes very important. Second, because two-thirds of end-users buy hardware and programs without the assistance of the data processing department, an understanding of the development process becomes crucial. How many times have you been asked, "What micro should I purchase?" by someone who has no idea of his or her requirements?

Finally, end-user purchase of microcomputers has caused us to introduce our systems programs (module I) into our introductory classes. Before the micro, we left operating systems to more advanced courses.

You will see microcomputers throughout this book. In particular, the opening case in chapter 1 concerns the purchase and use of a microcomputer by end-users, and the systems development discussion in chapter 4 considers the acquisition of off-the-shelf programs. The "Micros" photo essay illustrates the acquisition of a microcomputer-based word processing system. Module K presents nonprocedural programming and discusses end-user programming.

Organization

Parts 1 and 2 of this edition introduce computer systems and cover the core content of most introductory courses. Part 3 considers more advanced computer systems.

Parts 4 and 5 consist of modules that are independent of the first nine chapters. These modules contain special topics that may be assigned depending on time available and the orientation of the course. The modules in part 4 can be covered in any order. Programming, presented independently in part 5, may be assigned at any time. The six four-color photo essays are integrated with serious discussions of the conceptual material. They may be assigned independently.

BASIC Programming

While the need to learn traditional programming is diminishing, we agree with many instructors that an introduction to a language such as BASIC is useful.

Consequently, short introductory modules on elementary BASIC and on program design are followed by a more comprehensive treatment of BASIC and advanced BASIC statements.

Appendixes are provided that compare micro BASICs, indicate start-up procedures for different specific systems, and provide a summary of BASIC commands.

Supplementary Materials

An extensive package of supplementary materials has been developed to accompany this text. The materials include an instructor's guide, a comprehensive study guide/casebook, overhead transparencies, a computerized test bank, microcomputer-based BASIC tutorials, and a videocourse.

The study guide leads students through the text. Using this guide, students are able to do more on their own. In situations where many part-time instructors teach this class, use of the study guide will foster consistency. The study guide can become a *de facto* standard.

The videocourse consists of fifteen thirty-minute lessons or programs and illustrates many of the concepts in this text. The documentary-style video programs bring industry into the classroom to demonstrate the application of concepts from this text. Hal Calbom, a professional television journalist, hosts this broadcast-quality series. An excellent student video manual and instructor's guide for the videocourse was prepared by Joe Kinzer of Central State University.

Acknowledgments

Many people have been involved in the development of this book. Much appreciated advice and assistance and many helpful comments were provided by Roy Ageloff, University of Rhode Island; Frank Cable, Pennsylvania State University; Jan Carter, University of Texas; Helene Horger, Lorain County Community College; Tim Trainor, Muskegon Community College; Tony Verstraete, Pennsylvania State University; and Mike Vanacek, North Texas State University. Hugh Bangasser, an attorney with Preston, Thorgrimson, Seattle, provided assistance with statistics on computer crime and instruction regarding computer law.

The production of a four-color book is a major effort. Thanks to Mary Forkner, Publication Alternatives, and to Hal Lockwood, Bookman Productions, for excellent editing on tight schedules. Thanks as well to Roger Howell, Mitchell Publishing, for gathering and analyzing feedback, to Syndia Smith, Mitchell Publishing, for a superb job on photo research, and to Erika Berg, Mitchell Publishing, for her assistance in locating articles for the Profile sections. This text was produced using automated typesetting. Thanks to Nancy Satterberg who inserted the [oq]simple codes[cq] to drive the [it]typesetting[ro] equipment.[pp] (Can you imagine the complexity of the computer program that interprets the above codes as typesetting instructions and not as text?) Finally, a special thanks to *all* of the people at Mitchell Publishing. No author could ask for a more professional, supportive, and enjoyable group with whom to work.

A note from Dave Kroenke: A special thanks to Joe Kinzer, Central State University, Oklahoma, for his advice, support, and friendship over the years. Also, thanks to Glenn Smith of James Madison University for showing me how to be a better teacher. Kathy Dolan, independent consultant, has helped me to shape my ideas on systems development. Thanks as well to Caroline Curtis, Lorain County Community College, for years of helpful reviews and commentary and for her friendship. Thanks especially to Dee Stark, Washington Community College Computing Consortium, for helping shape the study guide that accompanies this text, and to Hal Calbom, KING-TV, Seattle, who wrote and directed the accompanying videocourse.

A note from Randy Johnston: Developing systems is hard work, and Jim Harders has been a patient friend during the time we have developed computer systems together. My parents and relatives have been a great pleasure to me and provided lots of moral support during this project. Thanks, Mom and Dad. The Johnston family (my wife Pam and daughters Sarah and Mary) were very patient whenever I had to take time from our activities to "work on the book." Al Reeve and my best friend, Tim Shook, deserve special mention as influences in shaping the way I feel about people and computing.

Computers are tools for humans. Computers have the potential to remove much drudgery from life. They can perform boring and repetitive work and free humankind for more creative and enjoyable endeavors. As a tool, however, computers have no morality. They can be used to control and manipulate as well. Our request and sincere hope is that knowledge gained from this book will be used, in some way, to benefit humanity.

David M. Kroenke
Mercer Island, Washington

Randolph P. Johnston
Hutchinson, Kansas

A Note on Curriculum Standards

In recent years many concerned educators have devoted considerable time to the definition of curriculum standards for information systems. In a rapidly developing discipline, such standards are very important and at the same time exceedingly difficult to produce. Several groups have done an outstanding job formulating these standards, and this book was developed to conform with and support their efforts.

DPMA   This text provides source material for all of the suggested topics in course CIS-1 of the Data Processing Management Association Education Foundation Model Curriculum for Undergraduate Computer Information Systems. The structure of this text directly recognizes this committee's recommendation that the purpose of this course be to "prepare business majors and others to be intelligent users of computers and to understand the basics of successful computer information systems: programs, procedures, data, people, and computer hardware. . . ."

ACM   This text recognizes the philosophy stated in the Association for Computing Machinery 1981 information systems curriculum report and supports the opinion that "the demand for personnel having a combination of technical and organizational skills is relatively much greater than the demand for solely technical skills."

AACSB   Additionally, this book follows the guidelines set out by the American Assembly of Collegiate Schools of Business, which suggest that students obtain a basic understanding of "management information systems and computer applications."

Both the authors and publisher of this text believe in the necessity and importance of these standards. They will continue to support and work with the many dedicated professionals involved in this important task.

Acknowledgments

Thanks to the following people who have provided helpful comments and other assistance in the preparation of this text.

Roanne Angiello
Bergen Community College

Gary Armstrong
Shippensburg State College

Becky Balestri
Illinois Wesleyan University

Jack Becker
University of Missouri at St. Louis

Thomas Blaney
Bentley College

John Broderick
Bentley College

Bryan Brooking
Simon Fraser University

Evan Brown
Pasadena City College

Sally Burner
James Madison University

Beth Buzby
Jefferson State Community College

Harold Camp
Stephen F. Austin University

Ed Christenson
Calfornia State University, Sacramento

Eli Cohen
California State University, Sacramento

Marilyn Correa
Polk Community College

Marty Cronlund
Anne Arundel Community College

Bill Cummings
University of Missouri

Susan Darst
California State University, Sacramento

Richard Dempsey
Penn State University, Scranton

Doris Duncan
Golden Gate University

Hank Etlinger
Rochester Institute of Technology

Sheila Fay
Solano Community College

Susie Colbrese Floyd
Eastern Montana University

Lee Gilchrist
Greenfield Community College

Ray Graber
Bentley College

Frances Grant
California State University, Chico

Linda Greene
Winston-Salem State University

Chuck Harrington
Metro Tech Community College

Bob Henry
Sinclair Community College

Thomas Ho
Purdue University

Hilary Hosmer
Bentley College

Durward Jackson
California State University, Los Angeles

Gary Jessee
Mountain Empire Community College

Emily Jones
Sinclair Community College

James Jump
Howard Community College

Cheryl Kiklas
Anoka-Ramsey Community College

Mary Kohls
Austin Community College

M. Kresl
Cuyahoga Community College

John Krobock
California State University, Sacramento

Jim LaBarre
University of Wisconsin—Eau Claire

Hollis Latimer
Tarrant County Junior College

Robert Lawrence
California Polytechnic University at Pomona

Ben Lewis
San Bernardino Valley College

Helen Ligon
Baylor University

Olof Lundberg
University of New Orleans

Maureen Martinez
Syracuse University

Mike Michaelson
Palomar College

Judd Miller
Richard J. Daley College

Lewis Miller
Cañada College

Paul Morris
Northeastern University

Tom Mourey
Mesa College

Lewis Myers
California State University, Sacramento

Roy Parkins
Portland Community College

Walter Parrill
Southern Illinois University at Edwardsville

Jim Phillips
Lexington Technical Institute

Jan Pipkin
University of Virginia

Charles Port
Bergen Community College

M. K. Raja
University of Texas at Arlington

Herb Rebhun
University of Houston

H. Terry Reid
St. Peter's College

Olivia Rodriguez
Texas Southmost College

Ruth Schmitz
Kearney State College

Leonard Schwab
California State University, Hayward

ACKNOWLEDGMENTS

Larry Seiford
University of Texas at Austin

Dennis Severence
University of Michigan

Cliff Sherrill
Yavapai College

Bill Smith
Sinclair Community College

Karen Smith
Scott Community College

Steve Suskin
Cleary College

Ken Thompson
Florida Junior College

Dawna Travis
Bentley College

Judy Trujillo
Eastern Montana University

H. Charles Walton
Ball State University

Pete White and Susan White
Catonsville Community College

Craig Wood
Stephen F. Austin University

Bill Wright
Florida Junior College

Sue Zulauf
Sinclair Community College

Photo Essays

The six color sections in this book are unique. Today, you will find many computer textbooks that are full of color photographs. *Computers: An Introduction* contains exciting color photos, too. What makes these photos unique, however, is the way in which they are presented.

Each of the 200 photos was carefully selected to illustrate the content of six essays—essays written on topics of special interest and importance to today's introductory computer student. Thus, the resulting six *photo essays* both entertain *and* instruct. Each photo essay concludes with review questions and enhances the content covered in the text. They may be used in any order or as optional assignments.

This photo essay organizes a look at today's computer hardware into an easy-to-understand format: input, processing, output, storage. It teaches the distinctions between micro, mini, and mainframe environments.

HARDWARE:
More and More for Less and Less

This extension of chapter 4 is unique and practical. It illustrates the value of the systems development process, even at the personal level. The photo essay follows student Jennifer Anderson as she learns the correct process of selecting her own micro software and hardware and developing a personal word processing *system*.

MICROS:
Selecting Your Own Computer

The mystery of today's silicon chip is explained simply, with colorful illustrations and photographs by award-winning *National Geographic* photographer Chuck O'Rear.

THE CHIP:
The Heart of the Computer

COMPUTERS IN SOCIETY:
More Uses, More Users, More Questions

This extension to module D of the text looks at a range of interesting computer applications and asks the reader/viewer to think about their impact—good and bad.

COMPUTER GRAPHICS:
An Art, A Science, A Tool

Graphics is one of the hottest areas of today's computer technology, and this photo essay shows why. It shows graphics as providing something for everyone—from business to the arts and sciences. Illustrations of how simple graphics are generated provide a basis for understanding more complex applications.

THE COMPUTER INDUSTRY AND CAREERS:
Gold Rush of the 1980s

This photo essay offers a current, practical look at a subject of great importance to every student. It includes statistics on salaries and the computer industry that will be updated annually in text reprints. Many useful tips on career planning, both for the future computer professional *and* the computer-literate user, are provided.

PHOTO ESSAY CREDITS
(clockwise by page)

HARDWARE

Opener: Xerox Corporation. Pages 2–3: Hewlett-Packard, Anacomp, Inc., 3M Corporation, Digital Equipment Corporation. Pages 4–5: Inforex, Inc., American Airlines, IBM Corporation, Anacomp, Inc., Hewlett-Packard. Pages 6–7: Apple Computer, Inc., Interdesign, Inc., IBM Corporation, Hewlett-Packard. Pages 8–9: Apple Computer, Inc., Wang Laboratories, Inc., Apple Computer, Inc. Pages 10–11: Digital Equipment Corporation, Amdahl Corporation, IBM Corporation, Paradyne Corporation. Pages 12–13: Anacomp, Inc., IBM Corporation, Hewlett-Packard, RCA. Pages 14–15: Carol Lee/ BASF Wyandette Corporation, IBM Corporation, Verbatim Corporation, Memorex Corporation, AT&T Company.

MICROS

Opener: Chuck O'Rear. Page 2: Syndia Smith. Page 3: Shelly McComas. Pages 4–5: Syndia Smith, Shelly McComas, Chuck O'Rear, Apple Computer, Inc. Pages 6–7: Syndia Smith, Intel Corporation, Shelly McComas, Shelly McComas, Shelly McComas. Pages 8–9: Apple Computer, Inc., Syndia Smith, Syndia Smith. Pages 10–11: Apple Computer, Inc., Syndia Smith, Hewlett-Packard. Pages 12–13: Roland Compu Music/Apple Computer, Inc., Chuck O'Rear, Chuck O'Rear, Apple Computer Inc. Pages 14–15: Chuck O'Rear, Apple Computer, Inc., Apple Computer, Inc.

THE CHIP

Opener: Chuck O'Rear. Pages 2–3: Chuck O'Rear. Pages 4–5: Chuck O'Rear, Intel Corporation, Intel Corporation, Chuck O'Rear. Pages 6–7: Chuck O'Rear, Chuck O'Rear, Chuck O'Rear, Honeywell, Inc. Pages 8–9: Intel Corporation, Intel Corporation, Chuck O'Rear, Intel Corporation, Chuck O'Rear. Pages 10–11: Intel Corporation, Intel Corporation, Chuck O'Rear, Intel Corporation. Page 12: Intel Corporation. Page 13: Apple Computer, Inc., Intel Corporation. Page 14: IBM Corporation, Intel Corporation. Page 15: National Semiconductor Corporation. Page 16: Chuck O'Rear.

Opener: Chuck O'Rear. Pages 2–3: Chuck O'Rear, Unimation, Chuck O'Rear, Ford Motor Company, Chuck O'Rear. Pages 4–5: IBM Corporation, Chuck O'Rear, Chuck O'Rear, Hewlett-Packard. Pages 6–7: Anacomp, Inc., IBM Corporation, Ramtek Corporation, Federal Express Corporation. Pages 8–9: Ramtek Corporation, Chuck O'Rear, Wang Laboratories, Inc., Intel Corporation. Page 10: Fairchild Industries, Gannett Company, Gannett Company. Page 11: Computer Sciences Corporation, Xerox Corporation, AT&T Company, Fairchild Industries. Pages 12–13: Chuck O'Rear, Ramtek Corporation/Digital Productions, NASA, NASA, AT&T Company. Pages 14–15: Chuck O'Rear, IBM Corporation, Chuck O'Rear, General Instrument Corporation. Page 16: Chuck O'Rear.

COMPUTERS AND SOCIETY

Opener: Digital Equipment Corporation. Pages 2–3: Hewlett-Packard, Ramtek Corporation, Ramtek Corporation, Ramtek Corporation, Tetronix, Inc. Page 4: AT&T Company. Page 5: Chuck O'Rear. Pages 6–7: Intergraph Corporation, Intergraph Corporation, Hewlett-Packard, Chuck O'Rear, Ramtek Corporation. Page 10: NASA. Page 11: Ramtek Corporation. Page 12: Ramtek Corporation, Aurora Imaging Systems. Page 13: Chuck O'Rear. Page 14: © Walt Disney Productions, AT&T Company, Ramtek Corporation. Page 15: Ramtek Corporation, Digital Productions, Ramtek Corporation. Page 16: Chuck O'Rear, Ford Motor Company.

COMPUTER GRAPHICS

Opener: Hewlett-Packard. Pages 2–3: Honeywell, Inc., Intel Corporation, Honeywell, Inc. Pages 4–5: Xerox Corporation, RCA, IBM Corporation, IBM Corporation, Hewlett-Packard. Pages 6–7: Hewlett-Packard, IBM Corporation, Intel Corporation, Apple Computer, Inc., Infocom, Inc. Pages 8–9: Hewlett-Packard, Intel Corporation, Hewlett-Packard. Pages 10–11: Hewlett-Packard, Hewlett-Packard, Wang Laboratories, Inc., AT&T Company. Pages 12–13: IBM Corporation, Digital Equipment Corporation, Honeywell, Inc., Walt Robinson. Pages 14–15: AT&T Company, American Airlines, IBM Corporation, Intel Corporation. Page 16: Apple Computer, Inc., Hewlett-Packard.

THE COMPUTER INDUSTRY AND CAREERS

PART ONE

Introduction

The three chapters in part 1 introduce you to computer systems. Chapter 1 tells the story of two companies and their experiences in developing computer systems. The first one turned out very well, and the other one—well, you can read it.

Chapter 2 defines computer systems. You will learn about the five components of a computer system, which will be illustrated by studying an example system that should be familiar to you—class enrollment. Chapter 2 is very important; we will refer to concepts presented in this chapter throughout the text. Chapter 3 surveys the applications of computers. It should help you relate computing to areas that are of interest to you.

CHAPTER 1

Why Study Computing?

Computers are everywhere, from automobiles to zoos. Computers control toys and run factories. They teach arithmetic and schedule airlines. Computers play Defender® and diagnose diseases. In short, computers provide an incredible range of services in our society.

Furthermore, many experts believe that the true impact of the computer is yet to be felt (see figure 1-1). Computers get cheaper and yet more powerful every year, which means that each year a better product costs less money. Even computer professionals are amazed to find they can buy Cadillacs at Chevette prices.

As computers get cheaper, they become affordable to more and more people, and it makes sense to use them for more and more applications. Also, as computers become more powerful, more resources are available to make them friendly and easy to use. Consequently, computers are being applied in new areas, and the demand for computer-knowledgeable people is increasing.

This book concerns the applications of computers to solve problems—how people use computers to help them improve their productivity, pay employees, manage laboratory data, and the like. The book concerns the *integration* of computer technology with organizations of people. As such, it discusses not only computer hardware and programs, but also computer data, procedures for using the computer, and the people involved.

If you have done some programming in high school or elsewhere, you may think you do not need this course. That's probably not true, however. This course involves more than just programming; you will see how to apply the computer to satisfy needs. Programming is just one part of a computer system.

How will knowledge of computer systems help your career? Suppose you and another person are both trainees on a job. Suppose you both have about the same knowledge of the work, but only you have studied the application of computer technology. Whenever computers create problems or are talked about, installed, or used, you will have an advantage.

To illustrate the need for knowledge about computing, we will consider two cases. These cases contain terms that you may not understand. Do not be alarmed by them. You do not need to understand the details of these cases at this point. Try instead to get a feel for what can happen when computers interact with people.

BLAKE RECORDS AND TAPES

"I've had it!" said Ellen Gibson with disgust. "It's ridiculous for the clerks in the sales department to make all these graphs every month. It takes three people 2½ days to do it, and then management changes its mind and wants a different presentation for the board meeting. There's got to be a way to use a computer for this work" (see figure 1-2).

Ellen Gibson is the Manager of Sales Administration for Blake Records and Tapes, a chain of four record stores. Her department handles all the paperwork regarding sales, store inventories, and so forth. Ellen has a B.A. in education; after teaching elementary school for several years, she decided teaching wasn't what she really wanted to do. She returned to college and earned a degree in sales and marketing.

FIGURE 1-1

An advertisement appearing in *Computerworld* (a computer newspaper)

FIGURE 1 - 2

Clerks manually preparing graphs of sales

After graduation, Ellen joined Blake as a salesperson. She became an Assistant Store Manager within a year and six months later was promoted to her present job. She works hard and has a good memory for sales facts. Her manner with people is friendly and easygoing. Ellen is known among sales personnel as the person to call for reliable sales data. Her subordinates think she is a fair and effective manager.

The Need for Computer Assistance

Ellen was upset about the time required to produce graphs of sales data. First, sales data had to be copied from a computer report. Then, the sales totals had to be computed (by hand) in different ways—by store, by record company, and by salesperson. Then, sales predictions had to be calculated (also by hand). Finally, a variety of graphs had to be drawn (see figures 1-3 and 1-4).

Ellen had taken two computer classes in college—an introductory course and a course in systems development. She knew that a computer could save the clerks considerable work and frustration. She thought all the calculations and even the graphs could be prepared by computer, which would eliminate the greatest source of frustration for the clerks—that of doing the calculations and graphs over and over while management decided what it wanted.

> Copy weekly order data from computer report
> Sum data in different ways (by date, record company, salesperson)
> Make calculations on groups of data, generate sales predictions
> Portray results graphically using pie charts, bar graphs, and XY plots

FIGURE 1-3

Tasks performed by Blake's salesclerks

Blake had a computer that was used for accounting and inventory applications. Ellen knew that it could be programmed to perform some of the salesclerks' calculations and to make the graphs. She discussed this use with the Director of Data Processing, Peter Wandolowski. He asked her to fill out a request form, which she had done over a year before. She filled out another request but still received no response. Finally she complained loudly enough that Peter promised to send over a computer systems analyst when he could spare one from other work.

Analysis of the Problem

Two months later, the analyst appeared. His name was Fred Sanchez, and he was superb. He had 12 years of systems-analysis experience, could communicate well, knew data processing inside and out, and had worked with marketing in a previous job. Unfortunately, he was available only on a part-time basis.

In her computer courses Ellen had learned how important it is for computer people to understand requirements. Therefore, she asked Fred to present to her staff his understanding of their requirements when he was finished. She also wanted him to prepare a document summarizing the requirements.

Fred spent the next week with Sales Administration. On Friday he presented his understanding of their requirements to Ellen and the clerks. With a few minor adjustments, they believed, Fred understood their problems very well.

Sample graphs produced by Blake's salesclerks

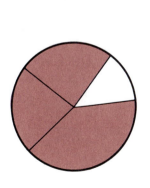 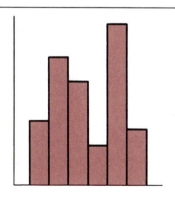 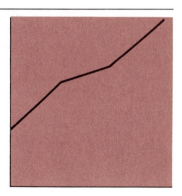

a. Example of a pie chart   *b.* Example of a bar graph   *c.* Example of an XY Plot

As Fred handed Ellen the requirements summary, he said, "Frankly, Ellen, I've got some bad news. If we try to develop these programs in-house, it will be at least a year before we get them done. We've got so much other work, and some of these programs will take some time to develop. We'll need a full-time analyst and a programmer."

He went on to explain that he had put the matter before Peter Wandolowski and had been told that no one was available. They would just have to make do on a part-time basis. Fred candidly told Ellen that this arrangement seemed unfair to all the people involved.

After Fred left, Ellen and her staff stared gloomily at one another. "Well, what will we do now?" Ellen asked.

"Maybe we should try the Yellow Pages," said one of the clerks sarcastically.

"Hey, that's not a bad idea!" said Ellen. "Maybe one of these new microcomputers I've been hearing about can do our job. Let's look into it!"

The Microcomputer System

Over the weekend, Ellen visited computer stores. She gathered information about programs called *electronic spreadsheets* (to be discussed in chapter 3) and about graphics packages. The graphics programs could produce outputs like those in figure 1-4. These systems supposedly would not require programming and could be used by inexperienced personnel with no computing background. "Do you suppose we could run a microcomputer ourselves?" she thought.

The next week was a busy one for the Sales Administration staff. In addition to their regular work, they investigated the possibility of buying a microcomputer. They called several stores and talked with the sales personnel. When they became confused, they called Fred. He came over one afternoon and they asked him questions until 8:00 that night. Figure 1-5 summarizes the conclusions drawn from this conversation.

By the end of the week, Ellen had a good picture of the microcomputer alternative. The advantages were: The computer could run on regular power; it needed no air conditioning. Thus, the micro could be located in their area and controlled by them. Also, it was simple to operate. The electronic spreadsheet and graphics programs would do most of their job, and the computer could be programmed by them in a language called *BASIC* (see figure 1-6).

Disadvantages of the system were: It would cost about $10,000 (although Ellen thought it would pay for itself in labor savings in less than 18 months). Also, the microcomputer would not do their whole job; some work would still have to be done manually. Finally, the graphs would not be as high quality as those the clerks currently produced manually. She thought the graphs would

FIGURE 1-5

Summary of conclusions made by Sales Administration staff

An incredible variety of microcomputer hardware exists
Select programs first, then appropriate hardware
Off-the-shelf programs could perform 70 percent of processing
Remaining 30 percent of programs would need to be written in-house
Several suitable graphics programs exist

Advantages	Disadvantages
1. Can run on regular power and needs no special air-conditioning.	1. Costs $10,000.
2. Can reside in Sales Administration area and be controlled by the clerks.	2. Some manual work required.
3. Is simple to operate.	3. Graph quality not as high as manually prepared graphs.
4. Can be programmed in BASIC.	4. Needs cooperation of Data Processing for input data.

FIGURE 1-6

Advantages and disadvantages of a
microcomputer system

be adequate, however. Finally, in order to do calculations and make the graphs, sales data needed to be input to the micro, but there was far too much data for the clerks to type or key it in. However, Data Processing already had the data in their computer and, according to Fred, the micro could get this data from Data Processing's computer via a communication line (like a telephone line). Fred said he doubted that Ellen would get much cooperation from Data Processing, however.

Ellen thought seriously about this project. On Monday and Tuesday she prepared a proposal for management in which she discussed costs and benefits. She showed that, considering only labor savings, the project would easily justify its cost. Also, she discussed Data Processing's busy schedule and explained how this project would relieve some of the burden on them.

Ellen presented the proposal to her boss, the Vice-President of Sales, and Peter Wandolowski on Wednesday. Pete was vehemently opposed to Ellen's buying a microcomputer. He expressed a dozen or so objections in a 30-minute, emotion-filled meeting.

Resistance from Data Processing

To the Vice-President of Sales, some of the objections seemed rational. Pete believed that Ellen had insufficient and unqualified staff to operate the system and that the system would require much more support than the microcomputer salespeople had said. Also, he was concerned about control of the data. How could Data Processing ensure that Ellen's data was current? Or that her staff would maintain adequate security and control? Or that they would take appropriate backup and recovery actions? He said that Ellen would eventually need professional data processing expertise and that the microcomputer would actually add to the Data Processing burden.

In addition to these concerns, Wandolowski appeared to be threatened. He saw this project as an infringement on his territory. If Sales did this, would Accounting or Purchasing or Shipping be next? If microcomputers started popping up all over the company, would the Data Processing Department be out in the cold? What would happen to his staff? Pete was adamantly opposed.

A Proposal for Ellen

"Well, all right, Pete," responded the Vice-President. "Since you're so opposed to this idea, let's put it before the Vice-Presidents' Council. Maybe we can work out an official policy on these microcomputer systems."

Later, Peter realized that he couldn't let the matter go before the Vice-Presidents. It was simply too risky; suppose their new policy approved users' having their own computers? Would he have any control at all?

By now, Pete had a keen appreciation for Ellen's ability. He had to find a way to provide the service she wanted, or the long range damage to Data Processing would be high.

The next day, Pete made another appointment with Ellen; and he had done his homework. He explained to her the dangers and agonies of running a computer. What would she do when it didn't work? What if the vendor blamed her programming for the malfunction? Who would be responsible for the communication line that linked their computer with the main computer? What did she know about security, backup and recovery, or computer controls?

He asked how much she knew about selecting programs. Was she going to buy the source code? If not, what if the vendor went bankrupt? How could she tell if the programs were any good? What if the programs contained errors? How much documentation would they receive? Would it be complete and accurate? What sort of maintenance agreement was she going to obtain on the hardware? If the hardware failed, how long would it take to get it fixed?

Once he discussed the potential problems, Pete reviewed Ellen's requirements. He had read Fred Sanchez's documentation and knew what needed to be done. He discussed the limitations of the programs that Ellen was planning to purchase and indicated a willingness to add custom programs to overcome those limitations. Finally, he presented a proposal: if Ellen would withdraw her request for a computer, he would make Fred Sanchez available full time. Then, Data Processing would acquire the programs and a microcomputer on Ellen's behalf; Peter wanted Data Processing to maintain control over microcomputer acquisitions.

Ellen considered the proposal. She wasn't overly concerned with the dangers of running a computer. Sure, they might make a few mistakes, but they would learn. On the other hand, did they want to learn? After all, their jobs were in sales, not data processing. She decided that if Pete would do as he promised, she would rather have Data Processing acquire the system than her staff.

"I'll tell you what, Pete," she responded, "I won't cancel my request for a system, but I will postpone it. If Data Processing can acquire the systems we need, on a timely basis, I won't raise the issue again. If you don't deliver, though, I will. And I'll have a document half-an-inch thick on how Data Processing failed."

"We'll deliver, Ellen. I assure you," said Pete, with a relieved sigh.

And they did. Whether from fear or respect for Ellen or a sincere desire to provide better service, Peter Wandolowski ensured that Ellen's department was satisfied. Within three weeks, they had the basic capability. The clerks were relieved of making most calculations. In two months they had an integrated system of programs they purchased and programs developed in-house. The microcomputer resided in Sales Administration and was run by the clerks, all of whom had been trained by Data Processing personnel in the proper procedures for use, backup, and recovery.

Peter was satisfied as well. He had learned that, for some applications, microcomputers could actually save his staff work. Also, because of the success of the project, senior management established a policy that the Data Processing staff would serve as consultants in the acquisition of all future microcomputer systems.

1.1 Why do you think it took more than a year for Data Processing to respond to Ellen's request? What would you do if you were in Ellen's place?

1.2 Fred said it would take Data Processing over a year to develop the programs in-house; yet, as it turned out, only two months' time was required. Why?

1.3 Describe the two most important services that Fred provided to the Sales Administration Department.

1.4 Ellen said she could save more than $10,000 in reduced labor expense if the computer could make sales calculations and draw the graphs. Does that seem reasonable to you?

1.5 List Peter's objections to the microcomputer. Which objections seem reasonable? Which objections seem motivated by his fear?

1.6 Summarize the dangers in having Sales Administration run their own computer.

1.7 Summarize the problems that the Sales Administration Department might have in purchasing their own programs.

1.8 Do you think Ellen's decision to postpone her proposal was a good decision. What would you have done in her situation?

1.9 How did the Sales Administration Department benefit from the cooperation of Data Processing?

1.10 How did the Data Processing Department benefit from this situation?

"Oh, no, not a traffic jam, too!" thought Chuck Swanson as he pulled to a stop behind a long line of cars on the freeway. It was a grey, rainy, early fall day, and Chuck had good reason to be upset. He was in the midst of problems at work, and he needed to be there early.

Chuck was 32 years old and the staff assistant to the Director of Marketing for TYCON Construction Products. His problems had begun nearly two years earlier. TYCON had been experiencing difficulties in processing orders. A rise in construction projects had caused manufacturers' deliveries to TYCON to be irregular, late, and sometimes even canceled. Thus, TYCON's inventory was erratic; customers and sales personnel couldn't depend on prompt deliveries. Furthermore, because some customers' payments were three, four, and five months overdue, marketing wanted to check customer credit before authorizing orders. Unfortunately, since TYCON had over 8000 customers, authorizations were extremely time consuming.

At this time, TYCON had a modest Data Processing (DP) Department that was generally effective. The Data Processing Manager, Tom Jackson, thought he could solve the order-processing and credit-authorization problems with a new, computerized order entry system.

A committee consisting of Chuck, Tom Jackson (as chairperson), an accountant, and a computer programmer was formed to study Tom's idea. Chuck and the accountant told the computer people about the problem and their needs. The committee met five times over a period of three months and created a data processing proposal for management.

In their proposal, the committee recommended the formation of an order entry department with 12 clerks. Each clerk would have a *cathode-ray tube*, or CRT, connected to the computer. (A CRT, which looks like a TV with a keyboard, is shown in figure 1-7.) The clerks would receive orders over the phone and use their CRTs to obtain inventory and credit information from the computer. If the materials were in stock and the customer's credit was good, the order would be approved.

To implement this system, TYCON needed to buy or lease a new computer and related equipment. Several programmers and computer operators also had to be hired. Tom Jackson said the system could be operational in 18 months.

The proposal was reviewed by Chuck's boss and eventually presented to Mr. Art Miyamoto, TYCON's President. (Figure 1-8 shows TYCON's organization chart.) Mr. Miyamoto liked the idea but thought the costs were too high. Because of recent sales successes, however, the company was in a strong cash position, and he approved the proposal but stipulated that the new system had to be operational in a year. Tom said that he could compress the schedule if he could hire one more programmer on a temporary basis. Mr. Miyamoto agreed and the project was on.

The Project Starts

Once approval was granted, the committee stopped meeting, and Chuck Swanson didn't hear much from Data Processing. It was ten months later when Mr. Miyamoto called a meeting with the original committee and Tom Jackson (see figure 1-9). He wanted to know the status of the project.

Tom presented a long list of problems. The new computer kept malfunctioning and two programmers quit and had to be replaced. Their programs had to be thrown out because nobody could understand them. Even worse, during testing they had discovered that two programs didn't fit together, and one had to be rewritten. In addition, Data Processing hadn't known about a new product line and it would take another month or two to incorporate it into the system. Further, order entry personnel still needed to be hired and trained, and procedures had to be developed. Altogether, Jackson reported, it would be another six months before installation.

Mr. Miyamoto was furious. Why hadn't he been informed? Where did the $300,000 go that they had already spent? What were they going to do about the order processing problems for the next six months? Didn't Jackson know that they were losing business and creating ill will? Did Jackson realize that

FIGURE 1-7

Order entry clerks using cathode-ray
tubes (CRTs)

TYCON existed to sell goods and make a profit and not to support every itinerant programmer and computer peddler?

After the meeting, Mr. Miyamoto stopped Chuck in the hall and told him to drop what he was doing. "Chuck," he said, "I have half a mind to cancel this project, but I don't want to lose the money we've invested. Spend some time with the Data Processing people, and send me a memo about what you think we should do."

Chuck spent the next week with Tom Jackson and the Data Processing personnel. They seemed defensive, and they kept throwing terms at him that he didn't understand. They claimed that many of the delays were beyond their control. The programmers also said that the requirements kept changing and

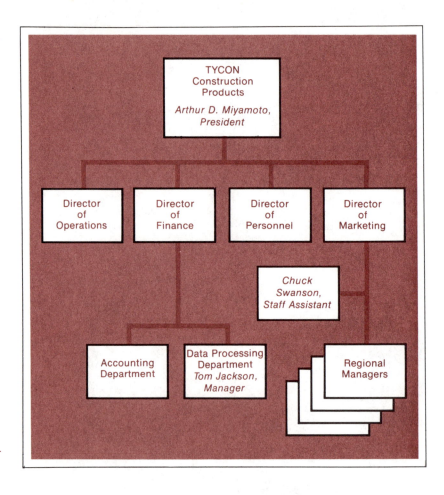

FIGURE 1-8

TYCON's organization chart

they had to redo their work. Chuck tried to find a document describing the requirements so he could see what they meant, but no such document had been prepared.

On the positive side, it was clear to Chuck that the Data Processing personnel were highly motivated. They had worked long hours and were making an exhaustive effort to complete the system. Chuck decided to recommend continuing the project for six more months. His reasoning is shown in the memo in figure 1-10.

Mr. Miyamoto decided to go along with Chuck's recommendation. He asked Chuck, however, to help the project every way he could.

The next six months were as busy a time as Chuck could remember. He and Tom Jackson and most of the Data Processing staff regularly worked 10- to 12-hour days. Chuck was not qualified to help technically, so he tried to remove the administrative burden from Tom.

After five months of this hectic schedule, Data Processing was ready to implement the new order entry and inventory systems. Chuck and Tom checked with Mr. Miyamoto, and he told them to go ahead.

Tom Jackson reporting problems

Problems Develop

At first, the new systems operated well; just a few small problems occurred. One time the computer displayed -5 cases of a siding product in inventory. Another time, several customers were accidentally dropped from the files. But, basically, the system operated well—especially considering the pressure under which it was developed.

At the end of the month, however, disaster struck. The existing computer billing system wouldn't work with the new order entry system! Something was wrong with the order data produced by the new system. The old billing system just wouldn't accept it. Figure 1-11 shows the relationship between the new order entry system and the old billing system.

Tom Jackson and the Data Processing staff worked through the weekend to determine what was wrong. They discovered a major design flaw in order entry. The person who had worked on it misunderstood how the billing system used order entry data. Much of the data needed by the billing system was in the wrong format, and some was simply unavailable.

Data Processing worked furiously to correct the problem. By the end of the next week, it was apparent that another month would be needed to make the

---

TYCON CONSTRUCTION PRODUCTS

MEMO
July 17, 1983

TO: Mr. Arthur Miyamoto, President

FROM: Chuck Swanson

SUBJECT: Order Entry and Billing Systems

I have reviewed progress on the order entry and billing systems as you requested. The following facts are pertinent:

a. The project is definitely behind schedule. However, not all of the problems appear to have been Data Processing's fault. The computer vendor has caused several serious schedule slippages.

b. Approximately $300,000 has already been spent or committed on this project. If we terminate it now, we will be able to recover only about $50,000 of this.

c. Continuing this project for 6 more months will cost from $35,000 to $40,000.

d. There is a significant chance that Data Processing will complete these systems within 6 months. The team members are highly motivated, and their enthusiasm is high.

The cost of quitting now will be $250,000, plus we will still have order entry and inventory problems. The cost of continuing another 6 months will be $40,000, at most, and it is likely we will have a solution to our problems. In my opinion it is worth risking the $40,000 to continue the project.

FIGURE 1-10

Chuck Swanson's memo

billing system operate. Tom Jackson reported to Mr. Miyamoto that TYCON would not be able to prepare bills for four or five more weeks.

Clenching his teeth, Mr. Miyamoto gave Tom a lesson in business. "Tom," he said icily, "if we don't send our customers their bills, they don't pay them. If our customers don't pay their bills, we don't receive any money. If we don't receive any money, we can't pay for our new computer and its staff, not to mention the other incidental expenses involved in running this company. It's called negative cash flow and we can't have two months of it. Go back to the old system!"

"Mr. Miyamoto, we can't," responded Tom. "It will take us three months to reconvert to the old system. All the data has been changed because of the new prices you wanted. We don't have the new prices in the old files."

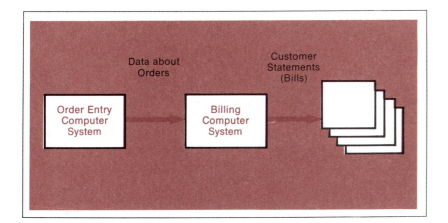

FIGURE 1-11

Relationship between order entry and billing systems

Within a week it was clear to Mr. Miyamoto that Tom was right. They were going to fall six to eight weeks behind in their billing. Mr. Miyamoto had to borrow to cover the short-term loss of revenue. Unfortunately, interest rates were at an all-time high, and TYCON spent over $75,000 on interest because of the error.

At this point, Mr. Miyamoto had had it. He hired a computer consulting firm to investigate the situation. A team of three people spent several days at TYCON talking with Chuck, Tom, the Data Processing staff, users, and customers.

Such was the situation that dreary fall day when the traffic finally started moving as Chuck drove to work. Chuck was analyzing inventory reports when Mr. Miyamoto's secretary called to ask Chuck to come to a meeting. Mr. Miyamoto, Chuck's boss, and the three consultants were present as Chuck sat down at the conference table.

"Chuck," Mr. Miyamoto began, "our consultants have analyzed our order entry project from the beginning and they have given it some very low marks. They feel fundamental principles of systems design were ignored, and they question the professional competency of our Data Processing staff. Further, they believe we should have stopped the project as I wanted to five months ago.

"Consequently, I've decided to return to the old system even though we will lose about $350,000 of our investment plus $75,000 in interest. Furthermore, I have this morning terminated Tom Jackson's employment.

"Frankly, Chuck, I'm disappointed in your performance on this. I know you have limited knowledge of data processing, but it seems to me that you should have known that order entry and billing would be closely related. I think you should have seen this problem developing when you wrote me your memo five months ago. Go back to your staff job and let's not have any more performances like this one."

Chuck felt terrible as he left the meeting. He felt sorry for Tom. He knew Tom had worked long hours to make the system successful. The experience hadn't been good for Chuck, either. Mr. Miyamoto was clearly displeased.

Mr. Miyamoto Acts

Later that night, Chuck tried to discover where he had gone wrong. He decided that the problem was that he just didn't know enough about data processing.

Chuck's Mistakes

What should Chuck have known? If he had taken the course you are currently enrolled in, there is a very good chance that the project would have turned out differently and that TYCON would not have lost the $350,000. First, Chuck would have known how a computer system should be developed. He would have known some of the pitfalls to avoid. He would have insisted on a documented definition of requirements, which by itself could have prevented the billing problem.

Chuck would also have been aware of alternatives to Tom's plan and been certain that Tom at least considered them. He would have seen some of the mistakes that Tom made and had them corrected or recommended that the project be canceled in his memo. Finally, Chuck would have known what users are supposed to do for themselves and what they can in all fairness expect from the Data Processing staff. He would have ensured that the users did their job and that Data Processing was providing appropriate support. He would also have known how important written documentation is during systems development, and he would have insisted on it.

Do not be alarmed if you cannot understand all of this discussion. You will learn about these concepts in this class. This is just a preview. What you should realize, however, is how important knowledge of computing is to every business professional.

QUESTIONS

1.11 Did Chuck have a chance? What could he have done differently before he wrote the memo to Mr. Miyamoto? What would you have done in his situation?

1.12 Do you think the memo in figure 1-10 makes sense? Do you agree with Chuck's reasoning?

1.13 What mistakes did Tom Jackson make? What could Chuck have done about them?

1.14 What mistakes did Mr. Miyamoto make? What could Chuck have done about them?

1.15 Do you suppose it is unusual for one data processing system to be dependent on another, as billing was dependent on order entry? What can companies do to eliminate problems like the ones TYCON had?

1.16 Do you think Chuck should have foreseen the billing problem? Would you have?

1.17 What can Chuck do now? What do you suppose his attitude is toward data processing? Can Chuck be effective on other computer projects?

1.18 Did Mr. Miyamoto really want to cancel the project as he says in the last meeting? Do you think he remembers how he truly felt?

1.19 Suppose Chuck took a data processing class before the disaster. Describe three aspects of data processing he could learn that would help him prevent the disaster.

A COMPARISON OF ELLEN'S AND CHUCK'S SITUATIONS

Do you think that Ellen is necessarily a better employee than Chuck? Did she work harder? No, actually Chuck worked *much* harder than Ellen. Chuck had three disadvantages. First, TYCON's problem was more complex than Blake's. The TYCON personnel had to develop their own programs (at least they thought they did), and they had to coordinate development among more people, as well as with the existing billing system. Second, the supporting data processing personnel at Blake were more competent than those at TYCON. Both Peter and Fred were able to provide Sales Administration with the support they needed.

A third difference between Ellen and Chuck was that Ellen had some knowledge of computing. She had taken two classes in college, and she had some idea of how systems were supposed to be developed. She also knew many of the fundamental terms, so she was less likely to be intimidated by the data processing personnel and by outside experts. Her familiarity with the terminology allowed her to communicate with knowledgeable experts better than Chuck could. In addition, she wasn't afraid to ask questions, challenge people, and do work on her own. She had confidence in her ability and in the ability of her team. Thus, Ellen didn't work harder than Chuck—she simply worked more effectively.

Consider these cases and realize that neither Ellen nor Chuck wanted to work with data processing. However, in the course of their careers, they both were required to. Either of these situations could occur in your career. As you progress through this course, think back to Ellen and Chuck. Remember that the more you know about data processing, the more likely you are to be successful in your career.

A WORD OF ENCOURAGEMENT

If you are like many students, you are uneasy taking this course. You may be fearful that data processing is something you won't be able to understand. That is unlikely. Most students, like Ellen, find that there is no magic to computing and, contrary to popular belief, there is not a lot of math. If you'll invest the time, you'll probably find this course easier than you thought. The experience of hundreds of teachers has been that there are few college students who "just can't catch on." However, it will take time.

SUMMARY

There are important reasons for you to study data processing even if you intend to work in some other field. Computers have changed the world drastically, and some experts believe the greatest change is yet to come. Computers are getting cheaper all the time, so they will see increased use in industry. In the future, many people will be successful because of their ability to incorporate computer technology into their jobs.

A. Speculate on how computers will affect your career. How will knowledge about computing help you?

B. Why are computers becoming so popular?

C. Neither Ellen nor Chuck were data processing professionals, but their ability to perform their jobs depended on their being able to work with data processing. Do you think this situation is rare? Is it becoming more common? Less common? Staying about the same?

D. Think of any two business people in any field; real estate, banking, manufacturing, insurance, selling, and distribution are all possibilities. Suppose both people are well qualified but one has a knowledge of computers and what they can and cannot do. In what ways does the computer-literate person have an advantage over the other? How will their careers differ?*

---

*To answer these questions, you will have to rely on your own intuition and experience. In later chapters, you may need to use additional references.

CHAPTER 2

Introduction to Computer Systems

The term *computer system* will be used throughout this book. In this chapter we will explain its meaning and describe system components. We will first introduce the concept and then examine a computer system familiar to most students, one that does class scheduling. This example will illustrate a computer system and show how its components interact. We will use the definitions of these components many times in the pages that follow. Be sure you understand them.

A *system* is a collection of components that interact to achieve some goal. A *computer system* is a collection of components, including a computer, that interact to achieve some goal. Note the word *including*. A computer system is not just a computer; it includes a computer as one of its components. When the components interact properly, a need is satisfied. For example, some computer systems produce payroll; some compute taxes; some do accounting; and so forth.

Many people are misinformed about the make-up of a computer system. They think it is just a computer and that, if they buy one, their problems will be over. Actually, the computer is only one of *five* components of a computer system. Once the computer is obtained, many problems and considerable further expense remain.

THE COMPONENTS OF A COMPUTER SYSTEM

The five components of a computer system are *hardware, programs, data, procedures* and *personnel*. The presence of all components is required to satisfy a need successfully; take any one of them away and the need cannot be satisfied. Let's consider each of them in turn.

Hardware

The first component that we will consider is computer equipment, or hardware. Figure 2-1 shows a computer used by a bank. It is very large and is actually used to satisfy many different needs, not just one. There is a lot of computer equipment, so it may be helpful if we divide it into categories. *Input equipment* is used to get data into the computer. In figure 2-1, line A points to a cathode-ray tube (CRT); this is one example of input equipment. There are many other types.

Processing equipment does the actual computing once the data has been read in, or *input*. Line B of figure 2-1 points to the *central processing unit*, or *CPU*. You can think of the CPU as the computer's brain.

Figure 2-2 shows a better picture of the CPU. Not very exciting, is it? Inside is a very complex electronic machine, but it's so small you can't see it. Visitors to computer centers are often disappointed with the appearance of the CPU; experienced guides usually spend most of the tour time on equipment such as tape drives. They are more exciting to watch but actually of much less importance.

Another category of computer hardware is *output equipment*. This hardware is used to transfer data from inside the computer to some more permanent form. Line C of figure 2-1 points to a computer printer; this equipment produces wide printouts on paper manufactured with holes in the sides. (In case you haven't seen a printout, an example is shown in figure 2-3.)

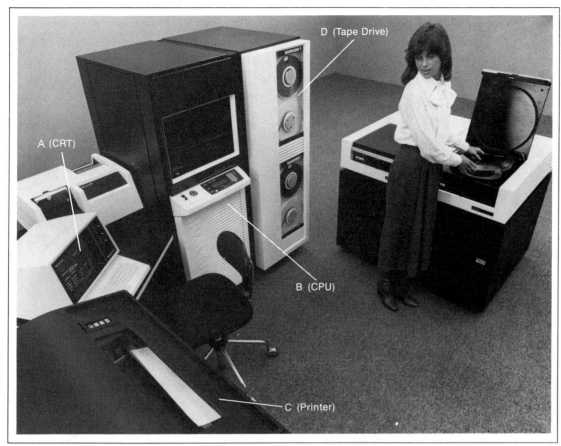

FIGURE 2-1

A computer

FIGURE 2-2

The central processing unit (CPU)

23

FIGURE 2-3

People reading computer-printed report

The fourth and final category of computer hardware is equipment used to store data. An example of this *storage equipment* is the tape drive indicated by line D in figure 2-1. Unfortunately, the CPU (the computer's brain) has a limited capacity to hold data. Consequently, storage equipment is needed to hold data that is not in use. This data is written onto tape and can be read back from tape when required.

To understand the need for storage, compare the CPU to your brain. You may have noticed that you have a limited capacity to hold data (say, for example, when you are grocery shopping). To help yourself, you put thoughts on a shopping list. You read these thoughts into your mind when you need them. In this example, the paper serves as a storage device like the tape equipment in figure 2-1.

Programs

Figure 2-4 summarizes the five components of a computer system and their subelements. We have just discussed hardware. The second component is *programs*. Most computers are general-purpose machines. They can add, subtract, and compare, but they are not designed to satisfy specific needs. A computer

Computer Equipment or Hardware
  Input
  Processing
  Output
  Storage

Programs
  System
  Application

Data
  Input
  Processing
  Output
  Stored

Procedures
  System Use
  System Operation

Personnel
  Systems Developers
  Operators
  Users
  Clientele

FIGURE 2-4

Components of a computer system

must have a program, or *sequence of instructions,* to satisfy a specific need. Thus, a computer with one set of programs might be used to design airplanes. The same computer with different programs could be used to do general ledger accounting or to process insurance claims. You could think of a program as instructions for the hardware.

Figure 2-5 shows a simple program that reads two numbers, labeled A and B, adds them, and prints the result. Figure 2-6 shows a portion of a more complex program used to enroll students in different classes.

Computer programs can be written in a variety of programming languages. Like human languages, these languages differ in vocabulary and structure. They all, however, have the same function: to instruct a general-purpose computer to satisfy a specific need. The program in figure 2-5 is written in the *BASIC* language. The one in figure 2-6 is written in a language called *COBOL*. Although there are several hundred computer languages, only about six or eight of them are commonly used. For one reason or another, the rest have not been accepted. Programming and languages are discussed in detail in part 5 of this book.

FIGURE 2-5

A computer program written in BASIC

```
10  INPUT A,B
20  LET C = A + B
30  PRINT C
40  END
```

```
        IDENTIFICATION DIVISION.
            PROGRAM-ID.  CLASS01.
        ENVIRONMENT DIVISION.
            INPUT-OUTPUT SECTION.
                        .
                        .
                        .

        DATA DIVISION.
            FILE SECTION.
        FD  CLASS-MASTER
            LABEL RECORDS ARE STANDARD.
        01  CLASS-MASTER-REC.
            05 CLASS-NUMBER                    PIC        9(4).
            05 CLASS-NAME                      PIC        X(10).
                        .
                        .
                        .

        PROCEDURE DIVISION.
            OPEN INPUT CLASS-MASTER.
            MOVE 0 TO EOF-FLAG.
                        .
                        .
                        .
```

FIGURE 2-6

Portion of a computer program written in COBOL

There is such a wide variety of programs that they are often divided into categories according to their function. Two categories that are used are *systems programs* and *application programs*. Systems programs control the computer. For example, they cause the computer to start and stop jobs, to copy data from one tape to another, and so on. Application programs are oriented toward a specific need. They perform payroll, do accounting, and so on. The systems programs usually come with the computer, but the application programs do not. Application programs must be developed or acquired separately.

Data

The third component of a computer system is *data*. Before a need can be satisfied, all the pertinent facts must be gathered. This is a special problem for computer systems because all data must be put into some computer-sensible form before it can be read into the computer. Thus data is typed in by means of a keyboard of some type (figure 2-7), or else it is put into computer-sensible form by some other means (figure 2-8).

Complete and correct data is essential for the successful operation of a computer system. Computers are fast, but they have no intuition or judgment. They will work diligently with absolute gibberish and produce outputs of equal gibberish. "Garbage in, garbage out" is an old (30 years is old in this industry!) but appropriate saying in the computer business.

Computer data can be categorized in the same way that we categorized hardware (see figure 2-4). Thus there is *input data* that is read into the computer for processing. There is *processing data* inside the CPU. There is *output data*, or results, that are usually in human readable form. Finally, there is *stored data*. This data is written onto some storage device and saved for later processing.

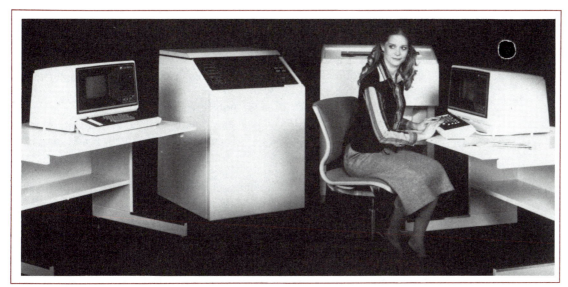

Keyboard data entry device

Mark-sense reader

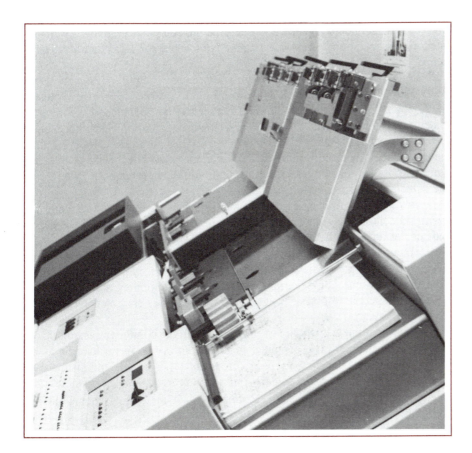

Data can be stored in a variety of ways. It can be recorded on magnetic tape (as on a tape recorder at home); it can be punched on cards; or it can be stored in other ways. The term *storage medium* refers to the type of storage used. Magnetic tape is a storage medium.

People in computing distinguish between data and information. *Data* is defined as recorded facts or figures. *Information* is knowledge derived from data. Thus data and information are not the same. A list of sales made during the past month by 15 sales agents is an example of data. A summation of the sales of each agent, together with the names of the top three, is an example of information.

Procedures

The last two components of a computer system go hand in hand. They are *procedures* and *trained personnel*. Procedures are instructions for people on the use and operation of the system. Procedures describe how people are to prepare input data and how the results are to be used. Procedures also explain what people are to do when errors are created and need to be corrected. Further, procedures explain how people are to operate the computer. They describe what programs to run, what data to use, and what to do with the outputs. Procedures must also describe what to do when the computer fails, or *crashes*, as it is sometimes called.

Personnel

Trained people are the final component of a computer system. People bring the other four components together and integrate the computer system. The major categories of personnel are *systems development personnel, operations personnel, users,* and *systems clientele*.

Systems development people design and produce computer systems. There are two types of systems development personnel. *Systems analysts* investigate needs, formalize requirements, and design all five components of a computer system. Systems analysts work extensively with people, and they need good communication skills. *Programmers* develop and test programs to meet requirements provided by systems analysts. Programmers work less with people and more with the computer. Sometimes an individual performs both jobs. He or she is then called a *programmer/analyst*.

Operations personnel run the computer and related equipment. *Computer operators* control the computer, start and stop jobs, mount tapes, load paper and special forms in the printer, and so forth. *Data entry personnel* key data into computer-sensible form using keypunches and similar equipment. *Data control personnel* are the liaison between operators and users. They accept data from the users, check for completeness, dispatch computer reports, and so forth. These people also serve as tape librarians if tapes are extensively used. (See figure 2-9.)

Users are individuals who interact directly with the computer system. They provide input data and use computer-generated information to do their jobs. Examples are class enrollment clerks, order entry personnel, and airline reservation agents. Finally, the *clientele* of a computer system are people who receive the benefits of the system. Examples of clientele are students having their classes scheduled, customers ordering food or services, and passengers on an airline.

Job Title	Typical 1984 Salary ($) (assuming 3 years experience at job)
Director of Data Processing	45,000 to 75,000 +
Systems Development Personnel	
Systems analyst	25,000 to 50,000
Application programmer	20,000 to 35,000
Systems programmer	25,000 to 45,000
Programmer/analyst	20,000 to 35,000
Operations Personnel	
Computer operator	15,000 to 30,000
Data entry operator	10,000 to 20,000
Data control clerk	15,000 to 25,000

FIGURE 2-9

Computer personnel and typical 1984 salaries

Programmers or other systems development personnel do not have a role during system use. These people design and develop systems, and they make system changes (sometimes referred to as *system maintenance*). However, they have no part in the operation of a well-run system. In fact, as we will discuss in module C in part 4, there are important security reasons why programmers and systems analysts should not be involved in the operation of a system.

To be effective, both operations and user personnel must be trained in the system procedures. They should understand standard procedures and know the location of procedure documentation for unusual conditions or errors.

Once again, the five components of a computer system are hardware, programs, data, procedures, and trained personnel. Without all five components, the computer system will not operate.

How does this information relate to you? You already know more than Chuck Swanson did in the TYCON Construction case. If Tom Jackson presented his idea to you, you could ask, "Tom, where do you propose we get the data?" or "Tom, when are you going to define the procedures and train the users?" You could insist that these questions be answered adequately, or you could protect yourself by withdrawing from the project.

QUESTIONS

This section introduced many terms. The following questions may help you to review them. You should also refer to the word list at the end of the chapter.

2.1 Define a computer system.

2.2 What are the five components of a computer system?

2.3 Describe one type of computer input equipment.

2.4 Describe one type of computer output equipment.

2.5 Describe one type of computer storage equipment.

2.6 What is the CPU?

2.7 What is the purpose of a computer program?

2.8 Name and describe two types of computer programs.

2.9 Name four types of computer data.

2.10 Why is stored data necessary? Give two examples of storage media.

2.11 Explain the difference between data and information.

2.12 What is the difference between procedures and programs?

2.13 Explain three types of procedures needed for a computer system.

2.14 Name three types of systems development personnel. Explain what each does.

2.15 Name three types of operations personnel. Explain what each does.

2.16 What is the difference between system users and system clientele?

THE CLASS ENROLLMENT SYSTEM

Let's now consider the components of a computer system as they apply to a particular application. Specifically, let's consider a system that enrolls students in classes. As you read this application, think about the interaction of the five components. See if you agree that all five are necessary for the system to function.

The Problem

The class enrollment problem is common to all colleges and universities. The various academic departments of the college or university decide to offer one or more sections of a large number of classes. The offerings are published in a class schedule. With the help of their advisers, students select courses from the schedule. They then fill out class request forms and submit the request forms to the administration.

As every student knows, there are conflicts. Some classes are requested by more students than can be accommodated. Other classes are selected by too few students to be taught economically. Consequently, the department

administrators close some classes, add more sections of others, and drop sections of still others.

This leads to a chaotic process known as add/drop. *Students who were unable to enroll in the classes they requested are given an opportunity to wait in long lines to enroll in other classes. Eventually this process terminates. The students finally get acceptable schedules or become so worn out by the system that they decide to take whatever courses they can get.*

The basic functions of the class enrollment system are listed in figure 2-10. Student IDs are compared to a list of valid students to ensure that each requester is officially enrolled and in good standing. Then the requests of each student are examined to determine whether he or she tried to enroll in any classes that meet at the same time. If so, all but one of the conflicting requests are dropped.

Next, students are enrolled in classes as space is available. No classes are to have more than the maximum number of students specified by the department. If a class is closed, the system counts the number of requests for the class

1. Check student IDs against a list of valid students. Ensure that each student is enrolled in the university and in good standing.
2. Check class requests for time conflicts. Eliminate conflicting requests when necessary.
3. Enroll students in requested classes as space is available.
4. Count the number of students enrolled in each class. Close classes when the maximum number have enrolled. Count number of attempts to enroll in class once it is closed.
5. Store student/class enrollment data for later use by add/drop, billing, grading, and other systems.
6. Print students' class schedules.
7. Print a summary report listing each class, the number of students enrolled, and the number of students attempting to enroll after the class is closed.

FIGURE 2-10

Functions of the class enrollment system

after it is closed. Data showing which students are enrolled in which classes is saved for processing by other computer systems. Finally, student schedules and a summary report are printed.

DATA

A computer system is composed of five components: hardware, programs, data, procedures, and personnel. We will now consider each of these components in greater detail. For purposes of discussion, it will be convenient to begin with data. If you want to know still more about computer data after you read this section, turn to module B in part 4.

Computer Representation of Data

The basic building block for representing computer data is called a *bit*. The term *bit* is an abbreviation for *binary digit*. You know what a decimal digit is. It is one of the symbols 0, 1, 2, 3, 4, 5, 6, 7, 8, or 9. A binary digit is similar, but there are only two, 0 and 1.

Bits are used as the basic building blocks for computer data because they are very easy to represent electronically. Bits can be represented by things that are either on or off. For example, we can say that a light represents a 1 when it is on and a 0 when it is off. Figure 2-11 shows a panel of light switches. If we define up as 1 and down as 0, then this panel represents the *bit pattern* 1101. Computers are not composed of panels of light switches, but they do have the capacity to represent large amounts of data by using a variety of devices that are either on or off.

Bits are represented in various ways in different parts of a computer system. In the CPU a bit is represented by the direction of flow of electricity, or by the voltage at a particular location. On magnetic media such as tape, a bit is represented by the direction of magnetization; one direction represents a 0 and the opposite represents a 1. On a punched card, a bit is represented by the presence of a hole (1) or by the absence of a hole (0).

Now, in the simplest terms, patterns of bits are used to represent *characters*. A character is one of the letters A-Z, one of the digits 0-9, or one of the special

31

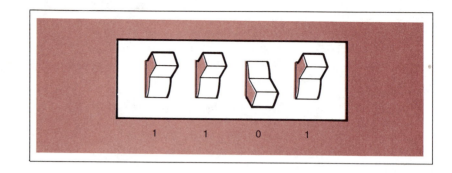

F I G U R E   2 - 1 1

Panel of light switches representing bit
pattern 1101

symbols, such as $, #, *, and so forth. For example, the pattern 000001 might
represent an A; the pattern 000010, a B; and so forth. The word *might* is used
here because there is no single code. The code used varies depending on the
type of computer system and the type of equipment.

Punched-Card Data Representation

Although punched cards are infrequently used in the computer industry today,
we will consider them here because they provide a good vehicle for understanding data representation. The methodology for representing data on tape and
disk is similar to that described here. The essential difference is that magnetization, rather than the presence or absence of holes, is used to represent the
1's and 0's.

Figure 2-12 shows a punched card. This particular type of card is divided
into 80 vertical columns and 12 horizontal rows. Each column is used to
represent one character. By convention, the top row is called the 12-row; the
next one is called the 11-row; and the next is called the 0-row. Then come the
1-row, the 2-row, and so on, to the last row, which is the 9-row.

Each column represents a character. In figure 2-12, the character 0 (zero)
is punched in column 36. By convention, this is done by punching a hole in
the 0-row and not punching any other holes in the column. A 1 is signified by
punching a hole in the 1-row only, a 2 by a punch in the 2-row only, and so
forth. Letters and special characters are represented by two (or more) punches
in a column. Thus the letter A is represented by punches in both the 12- and
1-rows. Other characters are shown in figure 2-12. This scheme is commonly
called *Hollerith code*, after Herman Hollerith, the inventor of punched-card
data processing.

Now, if you think of a hole as a 1 and the absence of a hole as a 0, then
each one of these columns can be visualized as a bit pattern. Starting from the
top, the bit pattern for the character 0 (zero) is 001000000000, because there
is a 0 in the 12-row, a 0 in the 11-row, a 1 in the 0-row, and 0 in all the other
rows. The pattern for the character 1 (one) is 000100000000, and that for an
A is 100100000000.

Hollerith code is just one example of a way to represent characters. There
are punched cards with 96 characters, and they use a different convention.

Extended Binary Coded Decimal Interchange Code

One of the most common ways of representing data is the *Extended Binary
Coded Decimal Interchange Code,* or EBCDIC (pronounced ib-sa-dick). EBCDIC
is used to represent data on magnetic tape, on disk, and in main memory.

F I G U R E 2 - 1 2

80-column punched card

Another popular way to represent data is the *American Standard Code for Information Interchange,* or ASCII (pronounced as-key).

Either code uses eight bits to represent characters. Figure 2-13 shows a portion of EBCDIC. There is no particular magic about the bit patterns. The fact that the pattern 1100 0001 represents an A and the pattern 1000 0001 represents an a has nothing to do with the name of the letters. The assignment of patterns to letters is arbitrary, and the designers of EBCDIC happened to choose these.

Notice that numbers are also represented in EBCDIC. When put in this coded form, numbers are considered to be textual in nature. When a number is represented in EBCDIC, no arithmetic can be done with it. Instead, the number can be read, stored, or printed. The numbers in an address, such as 95th Street, would be put into this coded form.

Computers can store numbers in a form that permits arithmetic to be done as well. In fact, several such forms are available. Numbers can be stored as decimals, as binary integers (whole numbers), or as binary numbers with fractions. These formats are described in module B of part 4.

Before describing data further, we must define more terminology. As stated, a *character* is a single letter or digit. For example, a character might be a Q or a 6. Another term, *byte*, is often used synonymously with *character*. A byte is the collection of bits needed to represent a single character. Thus, in EBCDIC, a byte is a group of eight bits. For other codes, a byte may have six or seven bits.

Characters, Fields, Records, and Files

33

```
            Character              EBCDIC Bit Pattern
               $                      0101 1011
               *                      0101 1100
               )                      0101 1101

               .
               .
               .

               a                      1000 0001
               b                      1000 0010
               c                      1000 0011
               d                      1000 0100
               .
               .
               .

               A                      1100 0001
               B                      1100 0010
               C                      1100 0100
               D                      1100 0100
```

FIGURE 2-13

Portions of the EBCDIC convention

Although *character* and *byte* are synonymous, the terms are usually used in different contexts. *Character* is usually used when referring to the logic or application of data. For example, a customer name could be 25 characters long. The term *byte* is usually used when referring to the physical size of hardware. For example, people might say that a main memory has 1 million bytes or that a disk file capacity is 10 million bytes.

A group of characters (or bytes) is called a *field*. Fields usually have logical meanings; they represent some item of data. Thus the five characters in a postal zip code are the zip code field. The nine characters in a social security number are the social security number field.

A collection of fields is called a *record*. A collection of fields about a student, for example, is called the *student record*. Figure 2-14 depicts a student status record. The numbers across the top of the record refer to character positions or columns. These numbers do not exist on the magnetic media; they are shown here just for reference. If this record were printed, the student number would appear in positions 1 through 9, the name would appear in positions 10 through 29, and so forth.

Note the use of abbreviations and special codes. Rather than write out lengthy grade levels like *sophomore*, abbreviations are used. Furthermore, the status code field contains numbers that are assigned meanings, as shown in figure 2-14. These codes are set up as *conventions* when the system is designed. Thus an 11 in the *code* field is understood to mean the student is an honor student. When codes like these are used, they must be explained in procedures for users; otherwise, people will not know how to interpret results.

A collection of records is called a *file*. All the student status records together are referred to as the *student status file*. The class enrollment file contains all the class enrollment records. Figure 2-15 summarizes this terminology: *characters* are grouped into *fields*; fields are grouped into *records*; records are collected into a *file*.

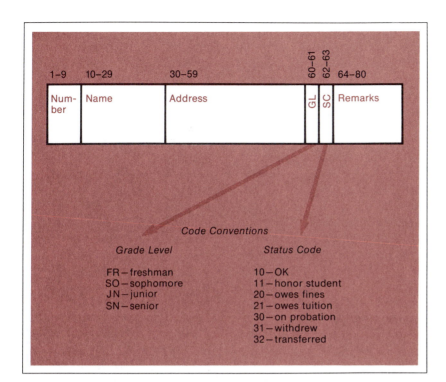

FIGURE 2-14

Fields in the student status record

FIGURE 2-15

Relationship of characters, fields, records, and files

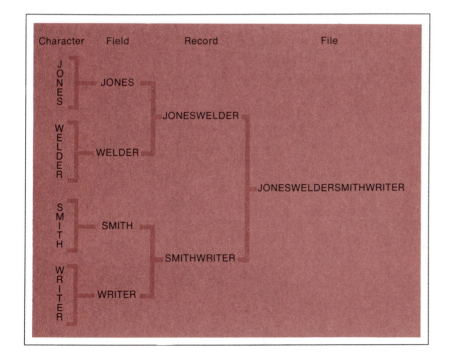

Figure 2-16 summarizes the data involved in class enrollment. The output data shows what the system is to produce; there are three types of output. Student/class enrollment data *shows which students are enrolled in which classes. This data will be stored on tape to be used by other business computer systems that do add/drop, billing, grading, and so forth. The other two types of output are both printed reports.* Student schedules *will be given to students. The* summary report *will be used by administrators when they decide whether to add or drop class sections.*

There are also three types of input for the class enrollment system. Student class request data *will provide the name, ID number, and desired classes for each student. The* student status data *is stored data listing the ID, name, address, status (honors, probation, and so on) of all students enrolled at the university. Finally, the* class enrollment data *describes the classes to be offered, their times, and their locations.*

Figure 2-17b presents a system flowchart. *This diagram summarizes the interaction of the data and the class-enrollment program. The strange shapes are not accidental; they are standard computing symbols. The standard symbols and their meanings are shown in figure 2-17a. The* ▱ *represents a*

document; *in figure 2-17b it indicates that* mark-sense *forms (the ones that require a number-2 pencil; see figure 2-8) will be read and input to the class enrollment program. Notice that the arrowhead goes in just one direction. This indicates that data is being sent to the program.*

The ◯ *represents stored data on* magnetic tape. *We can see from the figure that three tapes are required—two for input and one for output. There are two more* ▢ *. These represent reports that will be prepared as documents. Figure 2-17b shows that two separate reports, the summary data and student schedules, will be printed. Finally, the* ▢ *, which is called a* process symbol, *represents a program that will create the outputs from the inputs. In this case, the flowchart indicates that a program called* Class Enrollment *will perform this function.*

There are six files in figure 2-17b. Both the student status file and the initial class enrollment file are on magnetic tape. For the time being, we will not be concerned with how the data got there. (This topic will be discussed in chapter 5.) The format of the student status records was shown in figure 2-14.

The format of the class enrollment records appears in figure 2-18. All the field contents are self-explanatory except perhaps Days

FIGURE 2-16

Summary of data needed by the class
enrollment system

Output Data	Input Data
Student/Class Enrollment Data	Student Class Requests
Student Schedules	Student Status Data
Summary Report	Class Enrollment Data

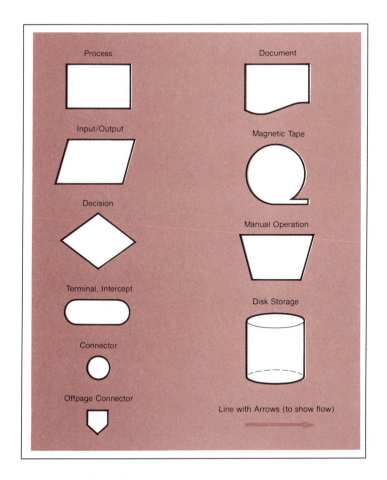

Flowcharting symbols

Class enrollment system flowchart

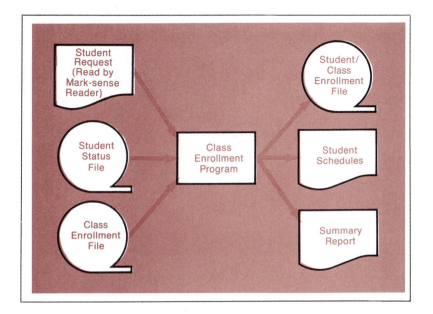

Record Position	Field Contents
1–3	Class Number
4–30	Class Name
31	Section Number
32–35	Hours Meeting
36–40	Days Meeting (MTWRF)
41–43	Maximum Number of Students
44–46	Number of Students Enrolled
47–49	Number of Students Turned Away

FIGURE 2-18

Class enrollment record format

Meeting. *This field will have letters representing the days of the week that the class meets. A Monday-Wednesday-Friday class will have MWF. A Tuesday-Thursday class will have TR. Also, the number of students enrolled and the number turned away will initially be zero.*

The remaining input file in figure 2-17b *is the student request file. Students indicate their class requests by filling out mark-sense forms like the one in figure 2-19. These forms are read by a mark-sense reader (see figure 2-8). Data that is extracted from the forms is displayed on the CRT screen. The format of this file is*

FIGURE 2-19

Student class request form

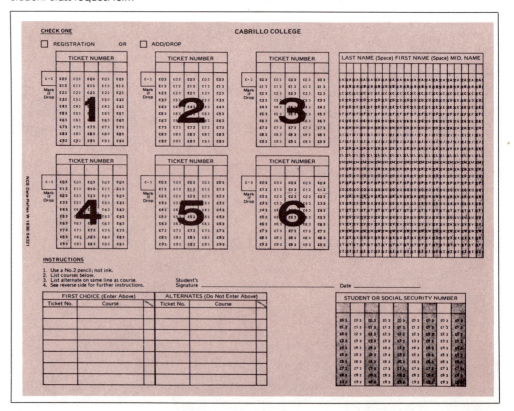

Character Position	Content
1–9	Student Number
10–29	Student Name
30	Number of Classes Requested (must be fewer than eight)
31–33	Class Number
346	Class Name
61	Section Number

Note: The last three fields repeat up to seven times.

FIGURE 2-20

Format of student request file

shown in figure 2-20. Once the operator sends this record to the computer one of two actions will occur. Either the computer will begin processing the student request immediately (to be discussed in chapter 6), or it will add the request to a file and process the entire file later as group, or batch (to be discussed in chapter 5). For now, assume the requests are collected and processed as a batch.

The remaining three files in figure 2-17b are output files. The student/class enrollment file lists classes and shows which students are in each class. We will not be concerned with its format here. The other two files are reports.

QUESTIONS

2.17 What is a bit? Why are bits used to represent computer data?

2.18 Describe the way characters are represented on punched cards.

2.19 What is EBCDIC? What is its purpose?

2.20 Define the following terms: *character, byte, field, record, file*. How do these terms relate to one another?

2.21 Give an example of each of the terms in question 2.20.

2.22 What is a system flowchart?

2.23 Explain the meaning of $\bigcirc$, $\square$, and $\square$ in a system flowchart.

2.24 Explain the conventions for status codes in the student status record.

HARDWARE

It is convenient to classify hardware according to its function in relation to data. Thus, basic categories of hardware are input, storage, output, and processing. In this section, we will discuss these categories and illustrate important hardware devices. A more comprehensive catalog of hardware can be found in the hardware photo essay.

Input Hardware

Although there are literally dozens of kinds of input devices, only a few are commonly seen.

CRTs

Probably the most common input device in use today is the *cathode-ray tube* (CRT). When this device is connected with the computer, data flows from the

Key-to-Disk and Key-to-Tape Equipment

Special Input Devices

Punched Cards

CRT screen into the processing computer's main memory. From there it can then be processed, or it can be stored on some type of storage hardware.

Other types of input hardware are *key-to-disk* and *key-to-tape*. These devices also have a CRT, but the CRT is not connected to the processing computer. Instead, data that is keyed is copied onto magnetic media such as disks or tapes (these are discussed in the next section). Later the disk or tape can be read into the processing computer. (See figure 2-21.)

Additional input hardware include *mark-sense devices* (see figure 2-8); *optical character recognition devices*, which read the characters produced by credit cards; *magnetic ink character recognition devices*, which read the ink on checks; and *uniform price code reading devices*, which are used in grocery stores. These devices are illustrated in the Hardware photo essay.

For many years, the punched card was the workhorse for data input. Cards were either punched by humans using card-punch machines or prepared by computer card punches (a computer output device). They were then sensed by card readers. Card input is bulky, slow, and cumbersome; and, although you

FIGURE 2-21

Key-to-disk equipment

HARDWARE

More and More for Less and Less

Today's fastest printers use laser technology to print over a hundred *pages* a minute.

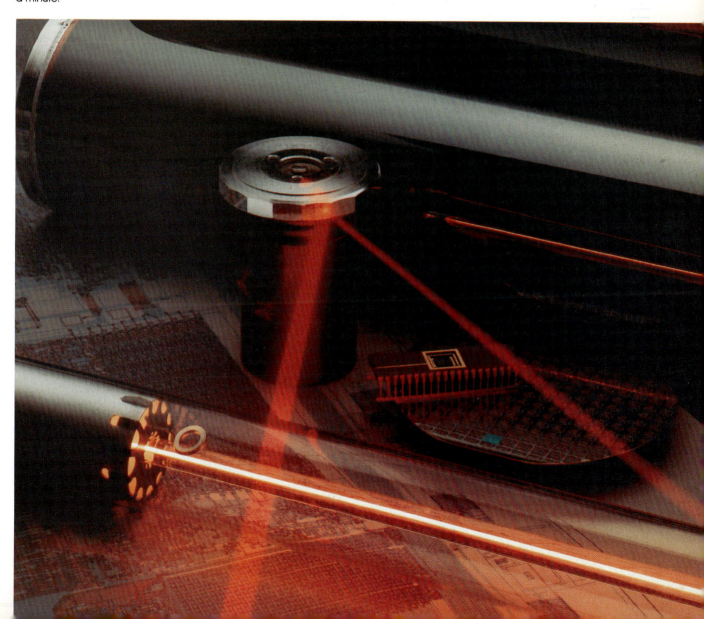

THE INPUT-PROCESS-OUTPUT/STORE CYCLE

For most systems, the processing of data involves four fundamental functions. Data is *input* to the computer, it is *processed*, results are *output*, and data is *stored* in computer-sensible form. Computer hardware can be classified according to these four primary functions.

Input hardware transforms data from a physical (often human-readable) form into a magnetic or electronic form. *Processing hardware* transforms data into desired results. *Output hardware* transforms results from an electronic form into human-readable form. Finally, *storage hardware* saves data, in magnetic form, for subsequent processing. Do not confuse storage hardware with input and output hardware. Although storage hardware performs both input and output functions, it does not transform the data into a physical, human-readable form. Rather, it saves the data in *magnetic* form.

As the following pages illustrate, there is an incredible variety of hardware, much of which serves the same function. Why? Hardware varies in speed, capacity, quality, and cost. When selecting hardware, the purchaser needs to know the system's requirements in order to buy sufficient (but not excessive) speed, capacity, and quality. See chapter 4 and the Micros Photo Essay for more information about purchasing hardware.

Data **Input** using a terminal and modem.

Processing by a popular Hewlett-Packard minicomputer.

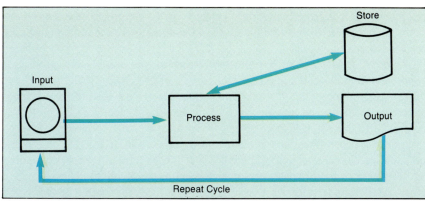

The Input, process, output/store cycle.

Storage in multiple disk units can accommodate large amounts of data.

Output in several forms is viewed by a user as he enters data.

KEYBOARD INPUT

Keyboard input hardware requires a person to key the data. Generally, the keyboard is similar to that of a typewriter. A cathode-ray tube (CRT) is usually used for displaying data.

Keyboard hardware can be online or offline. If it is *online*, the keyboard is connected directly to a computer. Data flows from the key device straight to the processing computer. If it is *offline*, the keyboard device produces a magnetic tape or disk. The tape or disk is later read by a tape or disk unit that is connected to the processing computer.

Some keyboard terminals contain a microprocessor. If so, they are called *smart* or *intelligent* terminals. There is a wide range in intelligence, depending on the power of the microprocessor contained in the terminal. The advantage of an intelligent terminal is that it lessens the communication between the terminal and the processing computer, as well as reducing the computer's workload. The disadvantage is that smart terminals are more expensive.

There are two types of keyboard operators. A *production data entry operator* works full time keying data. Such operators enter data for many different applications. Generally, data to be input arrives in large batches according to a schedule. Production data entry operators work in the data entry department, which is usually part of computer operations.

This "intelligent" terminal displays a graph of an acoustical signal.

Today's banks utilize online data entry for accurate and current information.

The second type of keyboard operator is the *end-user* operator. An end user generally does not work full time keying data. Rather, keying data is only part of the end user's job. A bank teller using an online terminal is an example of an end-user operator. Although end users employ computer equipment in their jobs, they are not assigned to the data processing department. Rather, end users work for another part of the organization. Bank tellers report to the head teller, not to the manager of data processing.

Many organizations prefer end-user data entry. The end users feel that they have greater control when they do their own data entry. They also must live with their own mistakes, and, consequently, some companies find that the accuracy of data is higher when it is entered by end users.

Data entry using keyboards is very error prone. A production data entry operator may key hundreds of documents in a single day. Unfortunately, correct computer processing requires accurate input data: "garbage in, garbage out." Therefore, procedures to verify the accuracy of data input are crucial. Such procedures might involve, for example, manually counting the number of documents processed and comparing this count with a computer-calculated count, or adding, by hand, the amounts of all orders and comparing this sum to a computer-produced sum.

Key-to-disk data entry.

An end user inputs data from his desk.

Production data entry clerks are employed by companies with continuous data entry needs.

NON-KEY INPUT

Keyboard input devices are too slow for some applications. A variety of other, special-purpose devices has been developed.

Terminals have a *cursor* that shows the user's position on the screen. The cursor might be a blinking underscore, a highlighted square, or some other, similar character. Moving the cursor around the screen takes time. Most terminals have special keys for up/down, left/right movement, but, even with these keys, cursor movement can be slow and cumbersome. A *mouse* is a handheld device for moving the cursor more quickly. The user moves the mouse around on a level surface, and the cursor moves correspondingly. Moving the mouse left causes the cursor to move left, moving it back (away from the user) causes the cursor to move up the screen, and so forth.

A *light pen* is another device that reduces cursor movement and keystrokes. Using a light pen, the user simply points the pen to the desired spot on a screen and pushes a button. The terminal senses where the light pen is located and responds accordingly. Light pens are often used to select options from a menu on a screen. The user points the pen to the menu item desired. With some terminals, the user can actually draw on the screen using the light pen.

Data entry using a light pen.

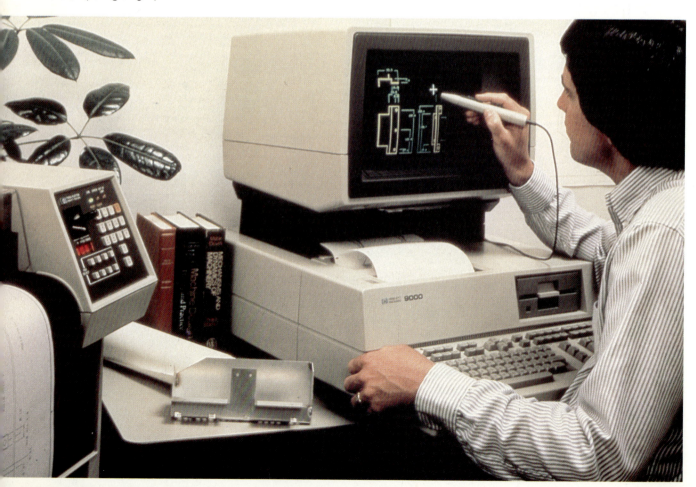

UPC (uniform product code) *bar codes* are used on grocery products. The pattern of bars corresponds to an item number. The sensing device sends the number to a computer for processing. UPC codes save time not only for the clerk, but also for the people who would otherwise mark prices on the items. Further, the grocery store can change prices with minimal effort.

Digitizers sense marks on a document and convert those marks to digital data (whole numbers). Digitizers are used in the medical profession for storing X-ray pictures magnetically.

Other, similar devices are *mark-sense form readers*, which read the exams that you mark with a number 2 pencil, and *MICR* (magnetic-ink character recognition) *devices*. MICR characters are printed with magnetic ink. The magnetism is sensed by the MICR equipment when the document is read. MICR documents are used primarily in the banking industry.

The "mouse" in the lower corner controls the movement of a cursor on the screen.

A scanner uses a low-grade laser to sense UPC bar codes in this grocery store.

A digitizer transforms graphic input into a digital format.

PROCESSISNG, HARDWARE, AND ENVIRONMENTS

Processing equipment includes the central processing unit (CPU) and main memory. There are three common types of CPUs: microcomputers, minicomputers, and mainframes. The characteristics of the three types of processors are summarized in the chart at the end of this essay.

Main memory consists of thousands of on/off devices. Each on/off device represents one *binary digit* or *bit*. A *byte* is a group of bits that represents a single character, such as *A* or *7*. Most computers have 8 bits per byte, although a few have 6 bits per byte. The size of main memory is usually stated in bytes—for example, 64K bytes. Although people often say that 64K equals 64,000, in actuality, the letter *K* represents 1024. Thus, a 64K-byte memory actually has 65,536 bytes. Common memory sizes are 64K, 128K, 256K, 512K, 1024K, and multiples of 1024K.

In recent years, the distinction among the physical characteristics of micros, minis, and mainframes has become blurred. In fact, the mini category may disappear. Smaller minis have become indistinguishable from micros, and larger minis have become indistinguishable from mainframes. Even though the differences in physical characteristics of CPU types are disappearing, major differences remain in applications and environments.

Processing in a microcomputer is occurring within one small hardware unit.

Microcomputers tend to be used for two purposes. As personal assistants, micros are used for word processing, electronic spreadsheets, personal databases, simple graphics, and education. As communications devices, micros are used to connect users to a data source, such as a company's mainframe computer, or to a data utility (a company providing data, such as stock prices, for a fee). A majority of micro programs are acquired off-the-shelf. Most micros are single-user systems.

Minicomputers are used for online, interactive applications. They perform general business functions, such as order entry, general ledger, and the like. Minis are also used in the science and engineering fields for applications like the control and monitoring of scientific equipment and computer-assisted design and manufacturing (CAD/CAM). Minicomputers are also used in specialized applications, such as circuit switching in the telephone system.

A microcomputer environment—this Apple computer sits on a desk top.

A minicomputer environment—this Wang mini resides in secretarial office space.

Mainframe computers generally process large, massive jobs. They do batch processing for large companies, such as billing for credit cards and policy processing for insurance companies. Mainframes also handle large-scale online applications, such as airline reservations, where there may be thousands of terminals active at the same time. In science and engineering, mainframes are used to process computer jobs requiring very large amounts of memory or exceedingly fast computing. Weather forecasting is an example of a science application requiring mainframes.

Micros, minis, and mainframes also differ in the environment in which they reside. Micros are desk-top computers; they can sit on the desk of the end user. The operation and control of micros is informal. Micros are generally single-user systems.

Minicomputers are used in many different environments. Minis used for business applications usually reside in small computer rooms with controlled access. The terminals connected to the mini are usually in the same building, in close proximity to the CPU. When used for science, engineering, architectural, and similar applications, minis are located in the user's work area. They reside in a back room or other out-of-the way space. When used for special-purpose applications, such as circuit switching, the minicomputer may be packaged with other electronic equipment in a common cabinet.

Mainframes are showcase computers, although for security reasons they have disappeared from ground-floor window locations. Mainframes are locked into special-purpose rooms that have extra air conditioning and even water supplies for water-cooled CPUs. Terminals for mainframes may reside thousands of miles away from the computer.

Another minicomputer environment—this mini is within an engineering office environment.

A well-organized and highly trained operations staff runs a mainframe computer and related equipment. The workload of the computer is controlled by a preauthorized schedule. Mainframes are characterized by a formal and controlled operating environment.

The Digital Equipment VAX—a minicomputer with mainframe power—blurring the definition of processor types.

An Amdahl Computer in a mainframe environment—tended by professional operators in a locked room.

IBM's System 370 in a mainframe environment.

OUTPUT

Output equipment transforms results from electronic to physical form. One common output device is the CRT screen discussed under input devices. CRTs are used both to display data being input and to display results.

Printers are a common output device. *Line printers* print a line at a time. *Serial printers* print only a single character at a time. *Full-character printers* print a complete letter the way a typewriter does. *Dot-matrix printers* print letters composed of small dots. *Impact printers* press the character to be printed onto a ribbon and then onto the paper. *Nonimpact printers* do not touch the paper; ink is sprayed onto the paper or printed using a process like that of a copy machine.

How should a company choose among all of these alternatives? The answer depends on requirements. Each of these types of printers has advantages and disadvantages. Line printers are faster than serial printers, but the quality of print is usually not as good. The characters produced by a line printer are often uneven across the bottom. Full-character printers (sometimes called *letter-quality printers*) produce very attractive output, but they are expensive. Dot-matrix printers produce less attractive output, but they are cheaper. Nonimpact printers are quiet and very fast; they are also expensive. Impact printers are noisy, but they are cheaper than nonimpact printers. Impact printers can also produce carbon copies, whereas nonimpact printers cannot.

Line printers produce output at a very high speed.

This graphics plotter displays building floor plans.

Computer paper is bulky and expensive. As an alternative, some companies produce reports on microfilm and microfiche. Generally, this procedure is done *offline*. In this mode, the computer program produces a magnetic tape containing the desired report. The tape is removed from the processing computer and mounted on a special-purpose machine. This machine reads the tape and photographs the report onto microfilm or microfiche. The special-purpose machine is expensive, and some companies use a service bureau for microphotography. They send the magnetic tape to the service bureau and receive the microfilm or microfiche back.

Voice output is emerging as a form of computer output. In its simplest form, a prerecorded message is selected and played. Examples are automobiles that instruct drivers to turn off the lights or inform them that the fuel level is low.

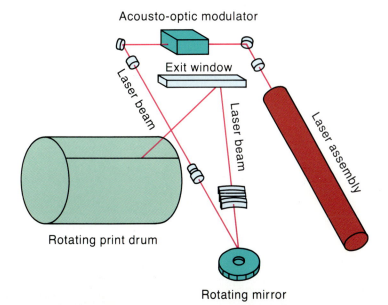

Microfiche imaging displays microfilm data, making it easier and less costly to store and retrieve.

A laser printer. Software turns the laser beam on and off and provides "bit maps"—dot-by-dot instructions for the laser, telling it to create a dark spot or leave it blank. The rotating 18-sided mirror spins at thousands of revolutions per minute and reflects the beam onto a rotating print drum.

Laser beams scan across a print drum to create text and graphics at speeds up to 20,000 lines per minute.

STORAGE

Some data must be stored because it is needed more than once. For example, for a payroll system, employee name, address, pay rate, and other data are needed every pay period. Such data cannot be left in the computer's main memory for several reasons. First, main memory is very expensive and, for the largest computers, is limited to 32 million bytes (which may sound large, but even small companies need more than that). Further, main memory is volatile. When the power is shut off, the contents of main memory are lost. Thus, computers need *secondary storage* that is less expensive and larger than main memory, as well as nonvolatile.

There are two fundamental types of secondary storage equipment. Sequential devices allow only sequential access to the data. To access the 50th record in a file, the first 49 records must first be read. Furthermore, additions can only be made to the end of a sequential file.

Magnetic tape is the most common sequential storage device. A variety of tape devices is available. The most common device uses tape that is similar to stereo tape but is ½ inch wide. Some microcomputer systems do use stereo tape, however. Tape is inexpensive; a 2400-foot reel of ½-inch tape can be purchased for $15. Because tape is cheap, it is often used for backup storage. Data that resides on other types of secondary storage is off-loaded onto tape until it is needed.

Multiple disk storage at a large computer center.

Magnetic tapes provide an inexpensive method of storing data.

The second type of secondary storage is direct-access storage. Direct-access data can be accessed in any order. The 50th record can be obtained directly, without reading the first 49 records.

There are two common types of direct-access devices. Hard, or conventional, disks consist of several circular recording surfaces mounted on a spindle. The surfaces rotate under read/write heads. Data is recorded in concentric circles called *tracks*. Floppy disks, or diskettes, are single, flexible recording surfaces. Data is written in similar tracks on either one or both sides of the floppy.

A mass storage system is a combination of direct-access and sequential storage. Data is stored on rolls of magnetic tape. When the data is needed, it is staged to direct-access devices for processing. Later the data is destaged to the rolls of magnetic tape.

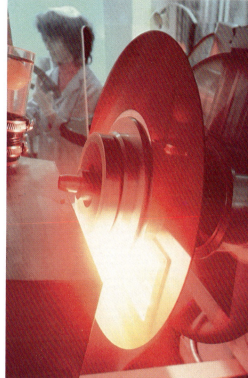

The manufacturing of a disk surface.

Mass storage can resemble a honeycomb.

A cleaning disk is inserted into a disk drive.

COMPARISON OF MICRO, MINI, AND MAINFRAME COMPUTERS

	Microcomputer	Minicomputer	Mainframe Computer
Main Memory (1000 bytes)	32–1000	2000–8000	8000–32,000
Instruction Speed (millions per second)	0.25	1–4	8–16
Disk Storage (bytes)	5–20 million	up to 1 billion	up to 20 billion
Cost	$1000–$10,000	$50,000–$250,000	$500,000–$10 million +
Notes	Usually single-user Minimum vendor support	Single-or Multi-user Often sold by OEMs	Multi-user Sold by vendor Extensive support

QUESTIONS

1. Name and describe the four fundamental functions of processing data.
2. Describe the difference between online and offline data entry.
3. Describe the difference between production data entry and end-user data entry.
4. What steps can be taken to compensate for the error-prone nature of data entry?
5. Explain the use of *cursor*, *mouse*, and *light pen*.
6. Describe two keyboard data entry devices.
7. Describe two nonkey data entry devices.
8. Distinguish among the hardware characteristics of micros, minis, and mainframes.
9. Distinguish among the processing environments of micros, minis, and mainframes.
10. Explain the difference between:
    a. Line and serial printers
    b. Full-character and dot-matrix printers
    c. Impact and nonimpact printers
11. Describe the two fundamental types of storage hardware.
12. What is a mass storage system?

may occasionally see punched cards, they have by and large gone the way of real workhorses.

Two types of storage hardware are commonly used: magnetic tape and magnetic disk.

Magnetic tape devices read and write magnetic tape similar to the tape in your stereo (see figure 2-22). Instead of recording a continuous signal, however, they record digital data in the form of 1's and 0's. We will discuss magnetic tapes further in chapter 5.

   Computer magnetic tape has the same disadvantages as the tape you have at home. First, you can read the data only in sequence. If you want to read the 112th customer record on the tape, you must first read the 111 records that precede it. Second, if you want to add a new record, or delete an old one, you must rewrite the entire tape. For these reasons, magnetic tape cannot be used for every application.

A second type of storage hardware is *magnetic disks*. Such disks store data in concentric circles, called *tracks* (see figure 2-23b). The 1's and 0's are recorded

Storage Hardware

Magnetic Tape

Magnetic Disks

FIGURE 2-22

Magnetic tape drive

41

serially around the circle. Two types of disks are common. *Floppy diskettes* are similar to stereo records, but with two exceptions. First, the disk is flexible, like a cheap demo record. Second, the grooves in a stereo record are continuous, whereas the tracks on a floppy diskette are concentric (circles inside each other).

The second type of disk device is the *conventional* or *hard disk* (see figure 2-24). Such disks are constructed of a stack of 1 to 20 hard recording surfaces mounted on a central spindle. The spindle revolves so that the data can be read or written by the heads mounted on the ends of access arms.

Both types of disk device are capable of direct access. This means that any spot on the disk can be accessed without accessing all of the preceding data. Thus, record 112 can be accessed by reading the track on which record 112 resides. We need not access the first 111 records, as we must for magnetic tape. With disk, it is unnecessary to read more than a single track of data to access a record. We will consider disk devices in greater detail in chapter 6.

Output Hardware

Although there are many types of output hardware, two devices are most common.

CRTs

We have already discussed the CRT as an input device, but it can be used as an output device as well. Responses to requests, messages, and reports can be displayed on the CRT screen. More sophisticated CRTs can also display intricate graphics.

Printers

A second common type of output device is the printer. Although there are hundreds of different brands and models of printers, they can be classified in three ways, according to their mode of operation.

Serial vs Line Printers First, there are *serial* and *line printers*. Serial printers print one character at a time. They are similar to typewriters (see figure 2-25);

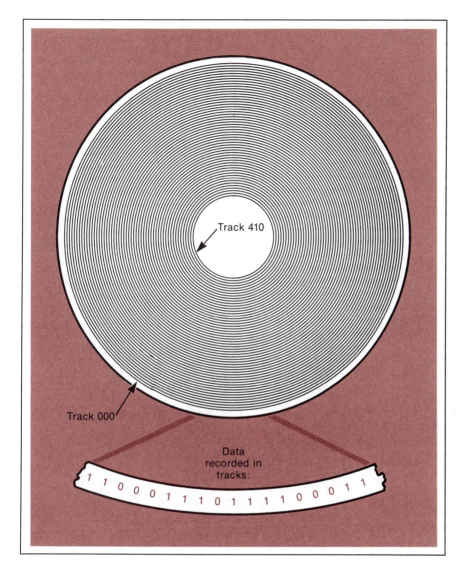

Track 410

Track 000

Data
recorded in
tracks:

1 1 0 0 0 1 1 1 0 1 1 1 1 1 0 0 0 1 1

FIGURE 2-23b

Disk surface

in fact, the balls, or elements, that are used in IBM Selectric® typewriters are used in some serial printers. Serial printers operate at speeds of 15 to 60 characters per second. Some serial printers can print in both directions so that time is not wasted on carriage returns.

Line printers print a full line at a time. Figure 2-26 shows a sketch of a line printer that uses a print drum with 136 print positions. At each position there is a band containing a complete set of characters. When a line is to be printed, the bands rotate to expose the correct character. The characters are then struck from behind by hammers, causing the line to be printed. A printer like this operates at 300 to 2000 lines per minute.

Impact vs Nonimpact Printers A second way in which printers are characterized is *impact* or *nonimpact*. For impact printers, the characters strike the paper through a ribbon. Both the serial and line printers in figures 2-25 and

FIGURE 2-24

Conventional or hard disks

FIGURE 2-25

Examples of serial printers

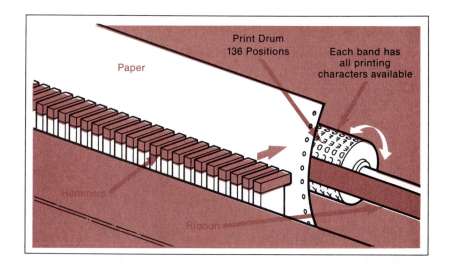

FIGURE 2-26

Print drum of line printer

2-26 are impact printers. Some nonimpact printers write on specially coated or sensitized paper. Other types of nonimpact printers spray the ink on the paper or use the same technique as Xerox® machines. Figure 2-27 shows a laser printer that uses a xerographic process.

FIGURE 2-27

IBM 3800® laser printer

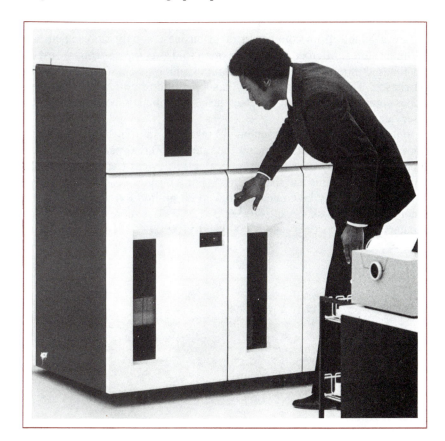

Impact printers can make several copies at a time, but they are noisy. Nonimpact printers are quiet, and some are much faster than impact printers. Speeds as high as 45,000 lines per minute are possible with ink-jet printers. Nonimpact printers cannot make more than one copy at a time, but their faster speed can compensate for this. It is likely that nonimpact printers will be used more and more in the future.

Dot-Matrix vs Full-Character Printers A third categorization of printers is *full-character* vs *dot matrix*. Full-character printers print a whole character the way a typewriter does. Dot-matrix printers print an array of dots (see figure 2-28). Dot-matrix printers do not produce as high-quality print as do full-character printers. However, they are cheaper and faster.

Figure 2-29 summarizes the categories of printers used in computer systems.

Processing Hardware

The central processing unit (CPU) executes program instructions that cause data to be read, stored, written, or otherwise processed. CPUs have three parts: a *control unit* that coordinates the timing of activities; an *arithmetic and logic unit* (ALU) that executes instructions, such as add or compare; and a *main memory* that holds program instructions and data during processing. CPUs are generally grouped into three classes.

Microcomputers

Microcomputers are the cheapest and smallest computers (see figure 2-30). They are available from computer stores, business supply stores, and large department stores. Microcomputers are often sold as computer appliances; they are purchased in much the same way that a washing machine or a refrigerator is purchased. The consumer typically has a list of desired features, and he or she does comparison shopping to select the best combination of features, price, and service.

A typical microcomputer contains 32,000 to 1 million bytes in its main memory and executes instructions at the rate of 250,000 per second. Microcomputers are usually connected to disk storage devices (tapes are more frequently used with minis and mainframes). For a business computer system, a micro would typically be connected to 5 to 20 million bytes of disk storage. For home use, less disk storage (160,000–720,000) is more common. Microcomputers usually cost between $1,000 and $10,000.

FIGURE 2-28

Dot-matrix characters

2.00	4.00	50.00	210.00	0	25
0.20	0.40	50.00	55.00	0	175
1.50	4.00	62.00	375.00	0	300
2.00	6.00	66.00	298.00	0	75
0.63	1.25	49.00	51.03	0	40
1.50	3.00	50.00	604.50	0	200
0.63	1.25	49.00	44.10	0	40
0.30	0.70	57.00	243.00	0	300
1.88	3.75	49.00	535.80	0	20

Printer	Characteristics
Serial	Prints one character at a time.
Line	Prints a line at a time.
Impact	Can make multiple copies, but is noisy.
Nonimpact	Can make only a single copy, but is very fast and quiet.
Full Character	Prints characters like a typewriter, with possible high quality.
Dot Matrix	Prints characters using dots.

FIGURE 2-29

Characterizations of printers

CPUs are often classified according to the number of bits that make up a single instruction. Generally, the greater the number of bits in an instruction, the more powerful the CPU. Microcomputers have either 8- or 16-bit instructions. Sixteen-bit micros are more powerful.

(It is difficult to explain this concept further without discussing the details of CPU design. Consider an analogy using telephone numbers. A seven-digit

FIGURE 2-30

Apple LISA microcomputer

number, such as xxx-xxxx, has the power to connect you to all the telephones within a given area code. A ten-digit number with area code, like (xxx) xxx-xxxx, has the capability to connect you to any of the telephones in North America. The larger number of digits gives you a greater range. In a loose way, the larger instruction size gives the computer more power per instruction.)

Microcomputers are most often single-user systems. Normally, only one person can use the micro at a time. Thus, microcomputers would be suitable for the analysis application at Blake Records and Tapes but would be unsuitable for the order entry application at TYCON Construction.

Minicomputers

Minicomputers are the next group of computers in terms of size, speed, and expense (see figure 2-31). Minicomputers were first developed in the 1960s as small, special-purpose computers. However, as time went on, minicomputers became more and more powerful. In the late 1960s, general-purpose minicomputers became available. Today, minicomputers have grown in capability so much that they overlap with the mainframe category of computers. The term *minicomputer* is prevalent, however, and you should know it.

Minicomputers are purchased from vendors rather than computer or department stores. They may be purchased directly from the manufacturer, or they

FIGURE 2-31

Digital Equipment Corporation VAX 780 minicomputer

may be purchased from original equipment manufacturers (OEMs). An OEM is a company that buys hardware from the manufacturer; repackages it by adding special-purpose hardware, programs, or some other feature or service; and sells the new package. The term *OEM* is confusing. It implies that OEMs make hardware, but they do not: they repackage hardware.

Minicomputer vendors (manufacturers or OEMs) provide more comprehensive support than do microcomputer stores. Such vendors can make greater expertise available in the selection and acquisition of their products; they provide more comprehensive service; and they usually stay close to their customers.

A typical minicomputer has ½ to 8 million bytes of data in main memory and executes instructions at the rate of 1 to 4 million per second. The maximum amount of disk storage supported is about 1 billion bytes. Minicomputers have either 16- or 32-bit instructions. A typical minicomputer costs between $25,000 and $250,000 for the CPU and an average amount of peripheral equipment.

Minicomputers are usually multiple-user systems. An average-sized minicomputer would be able to support 30 or 40 CRTs. Thus, a minicomputer would be suitable for TYCON's order entry system.

Minicomputers are generally located in a separate room, possibly with its own power supply and air conditioning. Physical access to the room is usually controlled for security reasons.

In the next few years, the minicomputer class of computers may well disappear. Large minis are becoming indistinguishable from mainframes, and small minis are becoming indistinguishable from micros. We may soon be left with just two categories: micros and mainframes.

The largest, fastest, and most expensive computers are called mainframes (see figure 2-32). These computers are nearly always purchased from manufacturers. Because of their size and sophistication, mainframe computers are sold with a great deal of support from the vendor. The vendor may well spend

Mainframes

FIGURE 2-32

Mainframe computer

	Microcomputer	Minicomputer	Mainframe Computer
Main Memory (1000 bytes)	32–1000	500–8000	8000–32,000
Instruction Speed (millions per second)	0.25	1–4	8–16
Disk Storage (bytes)	5–20 million	up to 1 billion	up to 20 billion
Cost	$1000–$10,000	$25,000–$250,000	$500,000–$10 million +
Notes	Usually single-user Minimum vendor support	Multi-user Often sold by OEMs	Multi-user Sold by vendor Extensive support

FIGURE 2-33

Comparison of micro, mini, and mainframe computers

considerable time and money helping the customer to select and install the hardware. Once the mainframe is installed, the vendor will be readily available to help resolve problems, to service the mainframe and related equipment, and to make repairs when necessary. Maintenance is available on a 24-hour, quick-response basis.

A mainframe computer typically has 8 to 32 million bytes of main memory, and it executes instructions at the rate of 8 to 16 million per second. Disk (or similar) storage capacities may be as great as 10 to 20 billion characters. (Twenty billion is difficult to comprehend. Consider that a storage of 20 billion characters is large enough to hold 80 characters of data for every person living in the United States.) Mainframes typically have 32-bit instructions, although some very powerful mainframes have 60-bit instructions. Mainframes cost between $500,000 and $10 million or more.

Mainframes are multiple-user systems and can support 400 or 500 CRTs while processing additional workload in the background. They require considerable power and air-conditioning facilities and so are always located in computer rooms. Access to such rooms should always be controlled for security reasons.

Characteristics of each of the three categories of CPU are summarized in figure 2-33.

HARDWARE FOR CLASS ENROLLMENT

The hardware requirements for the class enrollment system can be determined from the system flowchart shown in figure 2-17b. The system requires at least one mark-sense form reader, a printer, and three tape drives. Only one printer is required because the reports can be produced serially.

Realistically, a single CRT would

be unable to process the workload of a typical college. Probably 10 to perhaps 100 terminals would be needed. Therefore, a minicomputer or mainframe would most likely be necessary. Considering the amount of money that would be involved, CPU and other hardware selection for such a system would require careful analysis. We will consider such analyses further in chapter 4.

2.25 Describe two types of input hardware.

2.26 Describe two types of storage hardware.

2.27 Describe two types of output hardware.

2.28 Explain the difference between serial and line printers.

2.29 Explain the difference between impact and nonimpact printers.

2.30 Explain the difference between dot-matrix and full-character printers.

2.31 List three distinguishing characteristics of a microcomputer.

2.32 List three distinguishing characteristics of a minicomputer.

2.33 List three distinguishing characteristics of a mainframe computer.

Questions 2.34 through 2.36 pertain to the following flowchart:

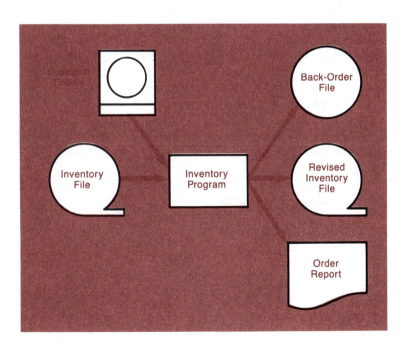

2.34 What computer hardware will be needed to run this program?

2.35 Is the order data input to the program or output from the program?

2.36 What data will be printed? What data will be stored?

PROGRAMS

We will not discuss the details of programming and program languages in this section—that is done in part 5. However, you need to know more about programs than has been described so far. Consequently, in this section, we will discuss a logic pattern that occurs in many programs, and we will introduce two tools used by programmers.

Input/Process/Output Cycle

Think for a moment about how you would solve the class enrollment problem manually. You would probably schedule the classes one student at a time. You would gather the data you need for the first student and the classes he or she requested. Then you would check for conflicts, closed classes, and so forth, and produce a valid schedule. Finally you would write the student's schedule. You would then proceed with the next student. When all of the student requests have been processed, you would be finished.

Think about this process for a moment. Can you see that it has three basic phases? There is a data-gathering phase, a processing phase, and a result-writing phase. These three phases are common to many business problems. In fact, this pattern occurs so frequently that systems developers have given it a special name. It is called the *input/process/output cycle*.

In one way or another, every computer program conforms to this pattern. Data is read into the computer, it is processed, and results are written. The cycle is repeated until all the data is processed.

This input/process/output cycle is an exceedingly powerful construct. If you ever find yourself floundering with a computer programming problem (in a test, as an assignment, or at work), think about this cycle. Consider what activity is needed for input, what is needed for processing, and what is needed for output. This pattern is very convenient for organizing your thoughts. Try it!

Figure 2-34 shows how the input/process/output pattern can be used to schedule classes. For input, *data about the student's request is read into main memory (part of the CPU), along with the student's status record and the relevent class enrollment records. For* processing, *the student's status is checked, and, if it is acceptable, classes are scheduled. For* output, *either the class enrollment or a message describing the unacceptable status is printed. Also, the class enrollment data is written to the student/class enrollment file. When all student requests have been processed in this manner, the summary report is printed.*

Developing Program Algorithms

In many ways, writing computer programs is similar to writing English (or other languages). Programs vary in length and complexity just as written documents do. Some programs are simple, like short memos. Some programs are longer, like term papers. Some programs are as long as books or even encyclopedias.

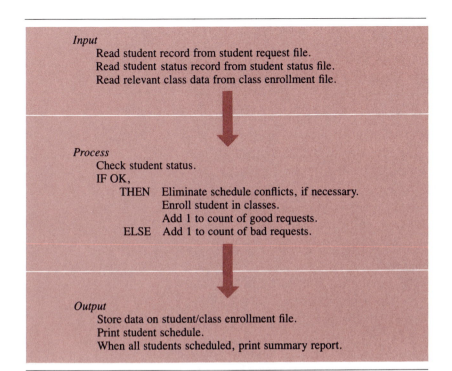

Input
  Read student record from student request file.
  Read student status record from student status file.
  Read relevant class data from class enrollment file.

Process
  Check student status.
  IF OK,
       THEN   Eliminate schedule conflicts, if necessary.
              Enroll student in classes.
              Add 1 to count of good requests.
       ELSE   Add 1 to count of bad requests.

Output
  Store data on student/class enrollment file.
  Print student schedule.
  When all students scheduled, print summary report.

FIGURE 2-34

Summary of input/process/output activity
for the class enrollment program

It is difficult to write a long paper or a book without spending some time organizing thoughts. Often people make outlines, develop chapter descriptions, and so forth. Similarly, when writing all but the simplest computer programs, people need to organize their thoughts. This is sometimes called *developing the algorithm*. An *algorithm* is a set of specific actions to take in order to solve a problem in a finite number of steps. Computer professionals have developed a host of tools for this purpose.

The computer industry is new, and professionals disagree about many topics. Currently, one of the most heated debates concerns what the best tools are for developing and organizing program logic. In this section, we will consider two tools that will be used throughout this book. They are *pseudocode* and *program flowcharts*.

Pseudocode (*pseudo* means false; thus, false code) is an informal English equivalent of program logic. To write it, the programmer or analyst just explains in words what the program is to do. For an example, refer to figure 2-35, which shows part of the class enrollment program.

The pseudocode is divided into two sections, called *paragraphs*. A paragraph is just a group of instructions that has a name and is performed as a unit. Program processing starts at the MAIN-PARAGRAPH. The first statement says DOUNTIL . . . , which means that a group of instructions is to be repeated until a condition is met. In this example, the statements that follow, down to

Pseudocode

```
BEGIN MAIN PARAGRAPH
    DOUNTIL NO DATA REMAINS
        READ STUDENT REQUEST FROM STUDENT REQUEST FILE
        READ STUDENT STATUS FROM STUDENT STATUS FILE
        READ RELEVANT CLASS DATA FROM CLASS ENROLLMENT FILE
        DO PROCESS-PARAGRAPH
        STORE DATA ON STUDENT/CLASS ENROLLMENT FILE
        PRINT ERROR MESSAGE OR STUDENT SCHEDULE AS
        APPROPRIATE
    END-DO
    PRINT SUMMARY REPORT
END MAIN-PARAGRAPH
BEGIN PROCESS-PARAGRAPH
    IF STUDENT STATUS CODE FROM STUDENT STATUS FILE IS < 20
        THEN ADD 1 TO BAD-REQUEST-COUNT
        ELSE ADD 1 TO GOOD-REQUEST-COUNT
            /Now go through class schedule steps
                    .
                    .
                    .
    END-IF
END PROCESS-PARAGRAPH
```

Pseudocode for part of the class enrollment program

the END-DO, are to be performed repeatedly until all the student requests have been processed.

A group of statements that are performed repeatedly is called a *loop*, because the logic repeats, or loops back. In figure 2-35, the first group of statements in the loop causes data to be read. Next, another procedure, called PROCESS-PARAGRAPH, is to be performed.

PROCESS-PARAGRAPH checks the student status and schedules classes if appropriate. The pseudocode to perform this function does not have to be in a separate paragraph. It could be placed in the middle of the loop. However, doing so would make MAIN-PARAGRAPH long and complex, and the author of this pseudocode elected to write it separately. Placement is purely a matter of personal creativity, taste, and clarity.

Part of PROCESS-PARAGRAPH is shown in figure 2-35. Note the IF statement. Checking conditions is very common in computer programs; in fact, this capability gives programs much of their power. In figure 2-35 the IF statement is used to check student status in accordance with the conventions shown in figure 2-14.

After PROCESS-PARAGRAPH is performed, the program logic returns to MAIN-PARAGRAPH. Here the output phase is performed, and either an error message or the student schedule is printed. (How would you like the schedule in figure 2-36?) After all requests have been processed, the summary report is written. Observe that MAIN-PARAGRAPH has the input/process/output pattern.

Do not be misled by the simplicity of these statements. Remember that figure 2-35 is *pseudo*code, not actual code. When the actual program is written in a programming language, many more details and more precise instructions must be specified. Pseudocode is a programmer's shorthand for organizing and developing program logic.

Flowcharts are a second way of organizing and presenting program logic. We have already seen one type of flowchart, called a *system flowchart,* in figure 2-17. This flowchart showed how programs and files are related. Another type of flowchart is called a *program,* or *detailed, flowchart.* These flowcharts depict program logic. Figure 2-37 presents a program flowchart for part of the class enrollment program. This flowchart portrays the same logic shown in the pseudocode in figure 2-35.

Flowcharts

You probably recognize most of the symbols from figure 2-17. However, two new symbols are shown in figure 2-37. The parallelogram ⟋⟋ represents a *read or write operation.* The data to be read or written and the file name are put inside the symbol. The diamond ◇ represents a *condition or decision.* The condition is written inside the diamond, and the arrows outside are labeled with answers to the question. Thus, if the student status is greater than 20, the schedule will not be produced.

The computer industry is currently debating whether pseudocode or program flowcharts are better. Flowcharts are older and have an established position in the industry. Pseudocode is newer, but many experts think it is easier to produce and read than flowcharts. They also say that pseudocode is easier to keep

FIGURE 2-36

Sample student class enrollment report

```
NAME:    SALLY J. PARKS

STUDENT NUMBER:  500004128                GRADE LEVEL:  SOPHOMORE


CLASS                   HOUR        DAYS

ACCOUNTING              8           MTWF
COMPOSITION II          4           MWF
HUMAN SEXUALITY         CLASS FULL
STATISTICS              2-4         TR
AMERICAN HISTORY II     UNABLE TO SCHEDULE DUE TO CONFLICTS
```

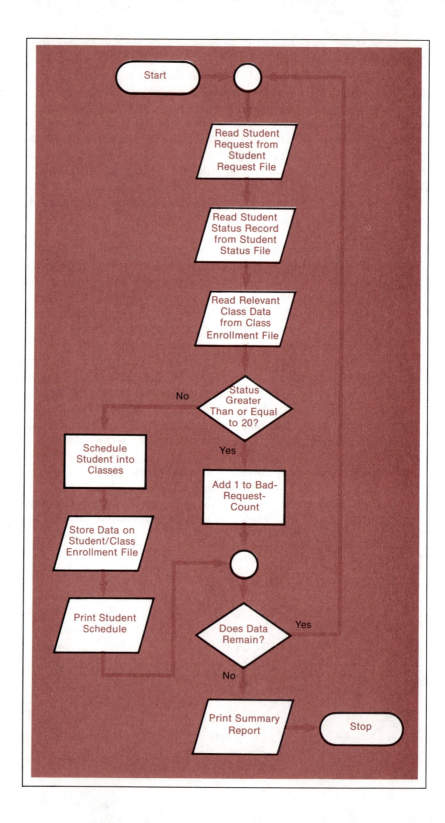

FIGURE 2-37

Flowchart for part of the class enrollment program

current because it can be maintained on word processing systems (see module E of part 4). Others think that neither should be used and that some other technique is best. Both are used in industry, and you should be familiar with them.

We have described pseudocode and flowcharts as though their only use is to develop program logic, but in fact they have another important application. Both techniques can be used to document the logic of a program. Documentation is important when programs need to be changed or when errors are discovered and programs must be fixed. Often the person who wrote the program is unavailable to make the change or fix the error. Even if that person is available, good documentation will make it easier to modify the program.

2.37 Explain the input/process/output cycle.

2.38 Describe input, process, and output activities for the preparation of paychecks.

2.39 Describe input, process, and output activities for balancing your checkbook.

2.40 Why are pseudocode and flowcharts necessary? Do professional programmers ever use them?

2.41 Explain the meaning of the following pseudocode:

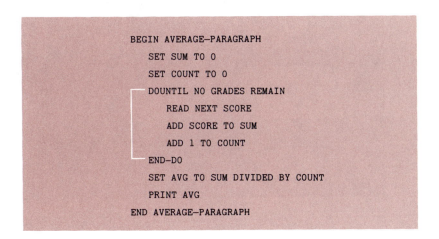

```
BEGIN AVERAGE—PARAGRAPH
    SET SUM TO 0
    SET COUNT TO 0
    DOUNTIL NO GRADES REMAIN
        READ NEXT SCORE
        ADD SCORE TO SUM
        ADD 1 TO COUNT
    END—DO
    SET AVG TO SUM DIVIDED BY COUNT
    PRINT AVG
END AVERAGE—PARAGRAPH
```

2.42 Convert the pseudocode in question 2.41 to a flowchart.

2.43 Explain the meaning of the following flowchart:

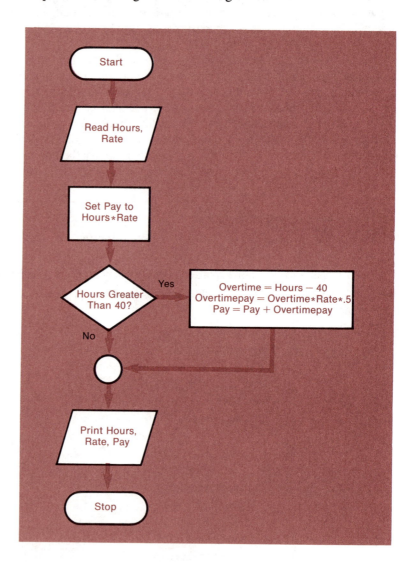

2.44 Convert the flowchart in question 2.43 to pseudocode.

PROCEDURES

Superficially, it might appear that hardware, programs, and data are the major components of a computer system. In fact, many systems have been designed on the basis of this misconception. Unfortunately, as many businesses have painfully (and expensively) learned, two additional components are required. In this section we will discuss one of them, *system procedures*.

George Shelton tried to enroll in classes at a college that used a class enrollment system similar to the one discussed in this chapter. When George examined his class schedule, he found that the college thought he owed money. George went to Scheduling to protest, but they sent him to Finance. Finance agreed with George; he owed no money. They didn't know what to do,

however, so they sent him to the computer center. The computer center sent him back to Scheduling. In desperation, George went to his adviser, who was sympathetic but didn't know what to do either. George went back to his room at the dorm, put his head in his hands, and wondered if college was for him after all.

The Need for Procedures

Why is George Shelton having this problem? Obviously an error has been made, but why can't it be corrected? Is the hardware incapable of correcting it? No. Can programs be written to correct it? Certainly.

George has a problem because of the lack of procedures. No one knows what to do.

In the early days of data processing, procedures were an afterthought, something users and the data processing staff worked out during systems implementation. Today, that is changed. Competent data processing personnel design procedures as part of the system.

Procedures are needed by systems users, operators, and developers (see figure 2-38). The users need to know how to input data and how to interpret results. They must understand their duties and responsibilities. For example, in the class enrollment system, the users (scheduling clerks) have the responsibility for correcting or returning incorrect class requests. Procedures need to

Used by	Procedure
Users	How to prepare inputs How to interpret outputs User duties and responsibilities How to correct errors
Operators	Who is authorized to provide inputs What format inputs should have When to run jobs What to do with outputs How to run jobs–tapes to use, forms to mount, etc.
Developers	How to determine requirements Standards for systems design How to write and test programs How to implement new systems

FIGURE 2-38

Examples of procedures for users, operators, and developers

be written to tell them how to do this. Additionally, users need to know how to correct errors that occur.

Procedures for operators explain how to run the system. The operators need to know who is authorized to provide inputs, what inputs to expect, how often to run the jobs, where the outputs go, and so forth. Additionally, operators need to know the mechanics of running the job, such as which tapes will be read, what sort of paper to put into the computer printer, and how many tapes will be written.

Finally, systems developers need procedures that specify a standard way of building business computer systems. These procedures explain how to determine requirements, how to develop systems designs, how to write and test programs, and how to implement new systems. We will study these activities in greater detail in part 2. The lack of systems development procedures was a major factor in the difficulties that TYCON Construction Products encountered.

Procedures are ineffective if they are lost or forgotten, and consequently they must be documented. *Documentation* means that they must be written, evaluated by concerned personnel, and approved by management. Documentation is extremely important, not only as a way to preserve the procedures, but also as a way of ensuring that the procedures are complete and understood. Most computer systems have three volumes of documentation for each system—one for users, one for developers, and one for operators.

Procedure documentation serves several important functions. First, personnel training can be more efficient and effective if new people read documentation before, during, and after training sessions. Second, written documentation helps to standardize processing and thus improve the quality of service. Without documentation, someone like George may happen to find a knowledgeable clerk and receive good service. Another person may find a substitute clerk and receive poor service, which can lead to ill will among the system clientele. Finally, documentation serves as a system memory. If the system is seldom used, people will forget the procedures. Documentation can also be used to recover from personnel loss, if critical personnel quit or become otherwise unavailable.

USER PROCEDURES FOR CLASS ENROLLMENT

Figure 2-39 presents the table of contents for the user's volume of procedure documentation for the class enrollment system. The first section summarizes the system. The next three sections are concerned with input, processing, and output. The input section describes required input data and presents data formats and input procedures. Note the portion on how to verify data completeness and format.

The processing procedures for this system are minimal because the system is run entirely by computer operations. For some systems, however, the users have more responsibility, and the procedures would be documented in this section. Section IV, Output Procedures, summarizes the outputs generated by the system. It also defines the meaning of each output data item. Definitions are essential when output data items have several possible interpretations.

```
                CLASS-ENROLLMENT SYSTEM
                User's Procedure Documentation

                     Table of Contents


  I. System Overview
     A. System Functions
     B. System Flowchart
     C. Summary of User's Procedures

 II. Input Procedures
     A. Summary of Input Data Needed
     B. Student Class Request Data
     C. Student Status Data
     D. Class Enrollment Data
     E. Data Verification Procedures

III. Processing Procedures
     A. Summary of Operation
     B. User Responsibilities

 IV. Output Procedures
     A. Summary of Output
     B. Student Schedules
     C. Summary Report
     D. Student/Class Enrollment File

  V. Error Correction Procedures
     A. Bad Input Data
     B. Incorrect Results
     C. Explanation of Error Messages

 VI. Critical Personnel
     (List of people and phone numbers for use in
     emergencies)
```

FIGURE 2-39

Example of user's procedure
documentation

Section V, Error Correction Procedures, *is crucial. This section explains what users should do when errors are discovered in computer input or on reports. This documentation either was unused or did not exist at the college where George Shelton attempted to enroll.*

Finally, there is a section listing names and phone numbers of critical personnel to be called in emergencies. This list can be invaluable when a problem occurs at a critical time (such as during class registration).

TRAINED PERSONNEL

The last of the five components of a computer system is *trained personnel*. As mentioned previously, there are four types of people involved: systems development personnel (systems analysts, programmers, and programmer/analysts), operations personnel, system users, and system clientele.

Systems analysts are people who know both the application and computing. When a system is being developed, systems analysts interview future users and determine what the requirements for the new system will be. They also design the computer systems to satisfy these requirements.

In the case of the class enrollment system, the systems analysts interviewed department heads, faculty members, scheduling personnel, college administrators, students, and computer center operators. From these interviews, they determined the requirements or the needs to be satisfied by the class enrollment system. Next, the systems analysts developed a design by creating specifications for each of the five components. The program component was then given to a programmer to build and test. Finally, the systems analysts developed a plan to implement the system and supervised this process.

Good systems analysts possess a rare combination of skills. They must be good at communicating with people; they must understand at least one business specialty; and they must know computing technology. Currently, systems analysts are in very short supply. If you would like to develop the needed skills, systems analysis would be an excellent career choice.

Programmers are computer specialists who write programs. In contrast to systems analysts, these people need not be as good in dealing with people nor do they need to know business as well. However, they must know more about computer technology. Specifically, they must know one programming language very well. Most programmers know two or three languages. Programmers also understand the technical details of computing better than systems analysts do. Sometimes systems analysis and programming are combined into one job, called *programmer/analyst*. This job requires all of the skills mentioned above. A good programmer/analyst is a rare and valuable commodity.

Once a system is designed, developed, and implemented, development personnel should no longer be involved in it. Responsibility for using systems should lie only with users and operations personnel. Most systems that last more than a few months, however, must at some point be changed. When this time comes, the systems development personnel are called in to design and implement necessary changes in the system. Such modification is called *system maintenance*. These changes are not just changes in programs; they can be changes in hardware, data, procedures, or personnel as well.

To do their job properly, systems development personnel need to know the latest in computer technology. Training is thus a recurring need (see figure 2-40). One month out of every year is not an unusual amount of training time.

Operations personnel run the computer. They need to know how to start the computer, how to stop it, and how to run programs. They also need to know how to operate equipment like tape drives, card readers, and printers. When the computer fails, the operations personnel need to know what to do to minimize the damage, and they need to know how to restart the computer.

Personnel	Training Requirements
Systems Developers	Communication skills
	Business fundamentals and principles
	Programming languages
	Computer hardware
	Computer technology
	Project management
Operations Personnel	How to operate computer
	How to handle failures
	How to run business computer systems
	Requirements for preventive maintenance
	Operations staff supervision
Users	How to prepare inputs
	How to interpret outputs
	Duties and responsibilities
	Forthcoming changes to systems

FIGURE 2-40

Examples of training needs of systems personnel

In a well-run data processing center, the majority of the processing is done according to a schedule. In addition, everything the operators need to know about running a system is documented. Therefore, neither systems development personnel nor users need be in the computer room. To enforce this measure, access to the computer room is often controlled by locks; only operations personnel are allowed in.

Operations personnel need to know how to run computer systems. They do not need in-depth knowledge of computing technology nor even of how the computer works. Consequently, operations personnel usually have less technical knowledge than systems development personnel. A typical operator has three to six months of formal training followed by about the same amount of on-the-job training.

The third category of personnel are *system users*. These people generally have no formal training in computing (that's why you'll have an advantage). They do, however, have expertise in their business specialty. Users are typically trained by the systems development personnel. This training can be *initial training*, in which the users are introduced to the system, shown its basic capabilities, and taught how to accomplish their jobs. *Recurring training* is given periodically to remind users of how they should (or can) be using the system and to inform them of any new features that have been developed. If safety or public health is involved, users can also be given proficiency examinations during the recurring training sessions.

The last group of personnel is the *system clientele*. These are the people for whom the system is designed. You are a member of the clientele of a class enrollment system, of a grade-posting system, and of many other systems as well.

The clientele of a system are usually not available or even willing to be formally trained. Thus, systems are designed so that the knowledge needed by the clientele is negligible. The input and output forms for the class enrollment system, for example, are simple and self-explanatory. The same is true for billing, grade posting, and other systems.

When the system is complex, the clientele are often guided by the system users. A good example occurs when you make an airline reservation. The reservation clerk obtains needed data by a sequence of questions and inputs the data. These questions, by the way, are often *prompted* by the computer.

The first three lines of figure 2-41 show an example of prompting. The computer typed ORIGIN: and the clerk filled in *New York*. Next, the computer typed DESTINATION: and the clerk filled in *Los Angeles*. The third line was done similarly. Then the computer responded with possible flights.

The need for trained personnel is so obvious that it is often overlooked. When users are not given formal training, system implementation is delayed until operators and users learn by experience, a slow and costly process. Furthermore, when personnel are not properly trained, they often use the system ineffectively or inefficiently. They may take one or two hours to accomplish a task that would take a few minutes if done properly. Untrained users are not able to service the clientele, either. This situation occurred in George Shelton's case.

FIGURE 2-41

Example of computer prompting

Trained personnel are an important part of a computer system. Users have a right to be trained by the development personnel. As a future business person, you should insist on proper training. You should plan time and expense for training purposes.

2.45 What are the three categories of system procedures? Explain the need satisfied by each type.

2.46 What does the term *documentation* mean? Why is documentation important?

2.47 What is likely to happen when no procedures are defined?

2.48 Describe the job requirements of a systems analyst.

2.49 Describe what a programmer does.

2.50 Compare and contrast systems analysts' jobs with programmers' jobs.

2.51 Explain what training is required for:
- **a.** Systems analysts
- **b.** Programmers
- **c.** Operators
- **d.** System users
- **e.** System clientele

If you have learned the material in this chapter, you understand more about data processing than most people. If you know that a computer system consists of hardware, programs, data, procedures, and trained personnel, then you will never be duped into thinking that if you buy a computer your problems will be over. You will know that many of your problems will have just begun. Even if you obtain a small computer with programs that can be run like a simple office machine, you realize that you will still need to convert data, develop procedures, and train personnel.

Which of these components is the most important? We might as well ask which is the most important link in a chain. Without hardware, there is no *computer* system. Without programs, the computer won't solve a specific problem, for it is a general-purpose machine. Without correct data, the system can't accurately or meaningfully solve the problem. Finally, without procedures or trained personnel, the system can't be used. Each of these five components is required. Without any one, there is no *system*. There are only four expensive components waiting to be integrated.

Many terms are introduced in this chapter. Terms that you should be sure you understand are listed here in the order in which they appear in the text.

System
Computer system
Five components of a computer
    system

Computer hardware
Input, processing, output, and
    storage hardware
Central processing unit (CPU)

Computer program
Computer programming language
BASIC
COBOL
Systems programs
Application programs
Garbage in, garbage out
Input data
Processing data
Output data
Stored data
Storage medium
Data vs information
Procedures
Crashes
Systems development personnel
Systems analyst
Programmer
Programmer/analyst
Operations personnel
Computer operator
Data entry personnel
Data control personnel
System users
System clientele
System maintenance
Bit
Characters
Extended Binary Coded Decimal
    Interchange Code (EBCDIC)
American Standard Code for Infor-
    mation Interchange (ASCII)
Byte
Field
Record
File
Coding convention
System flowchart
Mark-sense form
Document or report flowchart
    symbol

Tape flowchart symbol
Processing flowchart symbol
CRT
Key-to-disk
Key-to-tape
Punched cards
Magnetic tape
Magnetic disks
Floppy diskette
Conventional or hard disk
Serial printer
Line printer
Impact printer
Nonimpact printer
Dot-matrix printer
Full-character printer
Control unit
Arithmetic and logic unit (ALU)
Main memory
Microcomputer
Minicomputer
Original Equipment Manufacturer
    (OEM)
Mainframe computer
Input/process/output cycle
Algorithm
Pseudocode
DO statement in pseudocode
Loop
IF statement in pseudocode
Program, or detailed, flowchart
Read or write flowchart symbol
Condition or decision flowchart
    symbol
System procedures
Documentation
Initial training
Recurring training
Computer prompting

QUESTIONS TO CHALLENGE YOUR THINKING

A. Suppose a computer salesperson tells you the total cost of a computer system is $65,000 for the computer plus $410 per month for maintenance. How do you respond? What other costs might there be?

B. Computer hardware is available in a tremendous variety of speeds and capacities. In general, how can a business decide which computer to acquire?

C. Develop a system flowchart for an hourly payroll computer system. Assume that hours worked are recorded on time sheets and that there is an employee master file that contains pay rates, year-to-date totals, and so on.

D. Suppose you manage the clerks in a payroll office.
  1. Develop an outline of documentation for hourly payroll computer system procedures.
  2. Describe how the payroll clerks should be trained.

E. Describe what you believe is the appropriate amount of education for systems analysts, programmers, and operators.

F. What do you think will happen if a system is designed with:
  1. The wrong hardware?
  2. Program errors?
  3. Improperly designed data?
  4. No procedures?
  5. Poor personnel training?

CHAPTER 3

Survey of Computer Systems Applications

In this chapter, we will survey the application of computing systems. As you read, you should gain a general sense of how computers can be used. You will also realize that computing is important in every field.

NEED FOR COMPUTER SYSTEMS

Imagine yourself as president of a large, billion-dollar-a-year business, say, General Motors, IBM, or some similar company. You sit in a plush office with 16 able assistants and secretaries outside your door. As a manager, your job is to *plan, organize*, and *control* business activity. To do this, you need *information*. You need information about the company's performance, about competitors' performances, about new products, about costs, about inventories, about economic changes, about social changes, and on and on.

Why do you need this information? Your job is to make decisions and to start activity on projects that you approve. To make good decisions and to start effective projects, you need reliable and accurate information.

As president, when you need information, you ask for it. You use one or more of your company's *information systems*. Every company has information systems whether they know it or not. The secretary outside your door who has last year's profit-and-loss statement is part of an information system, as are the contents of your file drawers, the annual report, and hundreds of other information sources.

An information system does not necessarily include a computer. An information system can be composed entirely of data, procedures, and personnel. Computer hardware and programs need not be involved. There have been information systems for centuries—long before the computer was invented.

The focus of this book, however, is on *computer* systems, a subset of information systems. As you proceed through this book, you will study many different kinds of computer systems and much computer technology. Do not lose sight of the forest for the trees. Remember that you are studying an information system, and the eventual goal of all the technology and complexity is to provide better information.

The proportion of computer-based information systems to manual information systems varies from company to company. Some companies do not have computers at all. Some companies have a few personal computers. Some companies buy computer service from other companies. Some have small computers that have just one purpose, like inventory accounting or billing. At the other extreme, some companies have joined their computer systems with their typing, copying, and communications systems, so that the entire collection of information systems is computer based. There are millions (yes, millions) of companies in between these extremes (see figure 3-1).

Computer Applications Vary among Employees

Use of computers varies widely. One reason for this variance is that the needs of employees differ. You, as the president of a billion-dollar company, have different needs than I, the tape librarian. You manage the company, and I manage tapes. You don't care about the expiration date of tape number 07Q56T, and I don't care about the profitability of the Saskatoon plant. (Unless of course

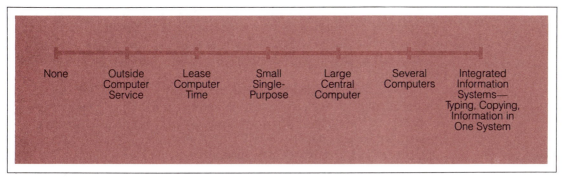

FIGURE 3-1

Range of computer use in information
systems

the profitability of the Saskatoon plant is on tape number 07Q56T!) Our
requirements for a computer system are therefore different.

In general, *the higher the level of the employee, the more summarized information needs tend to be.* At each level of management, consolidations, averages, and so forth are passed up to the next level. At the top, the information
consists of consolidations of consolidations.

A second reason computer use varies is that employees need different types
of service. Sometimes computer systems produce *status information.* The
information may be *historical,* like accounting systems that produce year-end
reports; it may be *current,* like inventory systems that maintain item counts;
or it may be *future,* like market forecasting systems that predict the size of the
market next year. (See figure 3-2).

Not all applications exist to provide status information. Some systems exist
for the production of *information-bearing documents.* A payroll system produces checks that inform banks to move money. Another such system creates
insurance policies, and a third produces wills.

Finally, some employees delegate *control* to computer systems. For example, an inventory system is designed to compare stock levels to projected sales

Service Type	Example
Status Information	
Historical	Year-End Report
Current	Inventory Stock Levels
Future	Future Market Size Estimates
Information-Bearing Documents	Checks
	Insurance Policies
Automated Control	Automatic Ordering
	Operations Scheduling

FIGURE 3-2

Types of service provided by computer
systems

and automatically generate orders when appropriate. Such control applications are actually combinations of status and production systems. The computer system evaluates status (stock level) and produces official documents (orders). However, the judgment normally provided by the manager is programmed into the computer.

Suppose someone asks you, as the president of a billion-dollar concern, to describe how your company uses computers. As you think, you realize that there are probably thousands of ways. At every level of employee, and in every specialty, there are computer-based information systems. One way you might organize such a description is by area. That is what we will do in the next sections of this chapter. We will examine systems in accounting, finance, engineering, education, medicine, law, humanities, and manufacturing. After that examination, we will then characterize systems by the type of service they provide. As you will see, there are transaction processing systems, management information systems, and decision support systems.

ACCOUNTING

Of the areas mentioned above, accounting has been the most successful at using computers, and computer-based accounting systems have had great acceptance. There are two major reasons for this success. First, the accounting profession has had many years' experience with computers. In fact, data processing grew out of the accounting machines prevalent in the 1940s and 1950s. (See module A in part 4 for a history of computing.)

Second, computers are excellent record keepers. Given accurate data and correct programs, they can work many, many hours without error. Since computers never become bored and never complain, accountants have assigned them the most tedious, time-consuming aspects of accounting.

Basically, *the purpose of an accounting computer system is to maintain data that accurately represents the financial state of the company*. For the system to achieve this goal, accurate data must be initially collected, and it must be accurately modified whenever events of accounting significance occur.

Recall the five components of a computer system from chapter 2. To maintain accurate data, an accounting system needs (1) computer hardware of sufficient capacity, capability, and speed; (2) programs that correctly instruct the computer to modify data and to produce reports; (3) accurate data to start with and accurate data about transactions (events of accounting significance); (4) procedures to enable people to operate and correct the data; and (5) trained personnel.

Characteristics of Accounting Computer Systems

Several unique properties of accounting pose special requirements for the programs and procedures. First, accounting systems usually deal with transactions expressed in terms of money. Consequently, errors can have a severe impact. Also, there is sometimes an incentive for computer crime: people can gain financially by making unauthorized changes to programs or data. This point is especially true for systems that produce negotiable outputs like checks.

Second, accounting systems usually have considerable input data. This data must be converted into some computer-sensible form, usually by keying. Unfortunately, such data conversion is error prone.

Consider these two points together. Do you see the dilemma facing the designer of an accounting system? The system involves money, and the impact of errors can be severe. At the same time, there is a considerable amount of data to be input by error-prone techniques. The consequence of this dilemma is that much of the processing in an accounting system is done to identify and correct errors. Considerable processing is also done to provide *checks and balances* between the users and the data processing department and thereby reduce the potential of unauthorized activity.

A final characteristic important to the design of accounting systems is the need to generate and save considerable data for the annual audit. This data is also needed for income tax reporting.

During the audit, the auditors often want to trace a transaction (an order, for example) from its beginning to its final resting place. If the order is processed by a computer system, the auditors may want to examine computer records. Thus, accounting systems must be designed to save data of potential interest to auditors.

Given these general comments, let's examine a familiar accounting system, *hourly payroll*. The requirements of this system are listed in figure 3-3.

The first two requirements are self-explanatory. The third requirement refers to the *general ledger* or company accounts. The system needs to generate entries for accounting. These entries will reduce cash by the amount of the payroll, accrue taxes and FICA, and make other necessary bookkeeping adjustments.

Accounting for sick leave and vacation time requires the system to add time each pay period and deduct it as time is taken. Reports must also be printed for the personnel department to use when authorizing vacations and sick-leave payments.

The requirement to print W-2 tax forms at year-end means that the system must keep track of total pay-to-date, total taxes-to-date, total FICA, and the total of any other taxable income. This data must be kept even for employees who terminate.

The next two requirements refer to changes that will be made to the employee master file. (*Master file* will be defined in chapter 5. For now, think of it as a

Payroll

1. Compute pay, taxes, deductions
2. Print paychecks
3. Produce entries for general ledger
4. Account for sick leave and vacation time
5. Print W-2 tax forms at year end
6. Accommodate new employees and changes to employee data
7. Account for ex-employees until year end
8. Minimize risk of error or unauthorized activity

FIGURE 3-3

Requirements for hourly payroll system

Payroll System Flowchart

file of permanent records.) As employees are hired, data for them must be added to the master file. Also, since pay rate is in the master file, changes must be made when employees receive pay increases. When an employee leaves the company, his or her record must be marked so that no new checks will be issued. The record cannot be deleted, however, until the W-2 form is printed at year-end. Finally, all of these requirements are to be met in a way that minimizes the risk of error or unauthorized activity.

Figure 3-4 shows a system flowchart for the payroll system. It is broken into three *phases* to provide checks and balances between the payroll department and the data processing department. During phase 1, the changes to the master file are keyed (to tape, here) and then edited by a computer program. *Editing* means the program will check the input to be sure it has the correct format, is plausible, and so forth. Note that no changes are actually made to the master file during phase 1. (The new symbol ▽ represents a *manual operation*.)

The report produced is called an *edit report*. The users must check this report, and, if they are satisfied with the changes, another run will be made to change the master file. At that time, a second report, called the *master file change report*, will be produced that shows changes actually made.

The edit report, shown in figure 3-5, is reviewed by the payroll department. If it is correct, data processing is instructed to proceed with phase 2. If not, then corrections are made and phase 1 is repeated. This sequence allows payroll personnel to ensure that only correct and authorized changes will be made.

In figure 3-5, the first two master file changes appear to be correct. However, the edit program detected an error in the third entry. This company had established a convention that all employee numbers start with a 1. This number does not, so it is flagged as an error. The new employee data for Joy Johnson must be verified by payroll. The pay change for employee 17281 also appears to have an error; probably the pay change should be 9.87, not 98.70. The program has not detected an error, so the responsibility lies with the payroll department to accept or reject this change.

These discrepancies point out the need for good procedures and trained personnel. Without them, an error may go undetected. Perhaps, too, you can see why *all* people need some knowledge about computers.

During phase 2, the edited changes are actually applied to the employee master file. The master file change report is produced; the payroll department can check the edit report against this change report to ensure correctness. If the phase 2 change report is correct, payroll authorizes data processing to perform phase 3. Otherwise, corrections are made and phases 1 and 2 are repeated.

In phase 3, a file of employee hours is input to the payroll program along with the updated employee master file. The hourly data has gone through an edit similar to that shown in phase 1. It is not shown here for the sake of brevity. The program computes pay, taxes, and deductions; accounts for time off; and produces a new employee master file containing the new year-to-date totals. It also produces three reports. The payroll register contains the entries to be made to the general ledger and a list of every check written. Payroll uses this list to verify the amounts before signing the paychecks. The second report

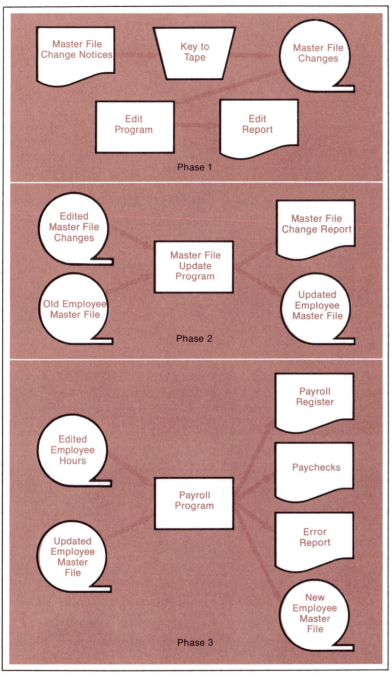

FIGURE 3-4

System flowchart for hourly payroll system

```
EMPLOYEE
NUMBER                          EMPLOYEE NAME              TYPE OF CHANGE

12481                           FRED PARKS                 PAY CHANGE TO 8.73
14618                           SALLY BATTS                PAY CHANGE TO 7.50
*** ERROR IN NEXT CHANGE--INCORRECT EMPLOYEE NUMBER  ***
02800                           JOY JOHNSON                NEW EMPLOYEE
                                ADDRESS                    1418 S. TAMARACK
                                                           ALEXANDRIA, VA 01042
                                DATE OF BIRTH              DECEMBER 11, 1944
                                TITLE                      PRODUCTION ASSISTANT
                                PAY RATE                   7.52
                                DEPENDENTS                 3
                                SOCIAL SECURITY NUMBER     522-00-1841
17281                           ELMER NILSON               PAY CHANGE TO 98.70
16415                           DOROTHY SUHM               PAY CHANGE TO 21.50
```

FIGURE 3-5

Payroll master file edit report

consists of the paychecks (see figure 3-6). The last report details any errors that have been detected—for example, a report of hourly work by a nonexistent or terminated employee.

This discussion demonstrates a typical accounting system. Can you see the need for user involvement to provide checks and balances over data processing? Note, too, that the master files keep data about payments that can be used for audit and tax purposes. The payroll registers are another permanent record.

FIGURE 3-6

Printed payroll check

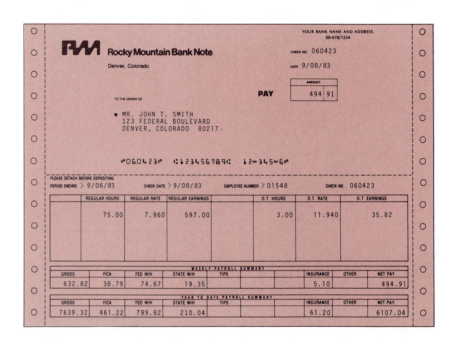

Payroll
Billing
Accounts Receivable
Accounts Payable
General Ledger
Inventory Accounting

FIGURE 3-7

Common accounting computer systems

Other Examples of Accounting Computer Systems

Figure 3-7 lists common accounting systems. We will briefly summarize them here; several of these will be discussed further in subsequent chapters.

Billing systems generate bills or statements to customers. Figure 3-8 shows a typical billing statement. *Accounts receivable* systems keep track of debts owed to the company. Reports of this system are used for collection purposes, for checking credit on new orders, and for monitoring potential bad debts. Figure 3-9 shows a sample accounts receivable report.

Accounts payable systems produce checks to pay company bills. Since accounts payable systems generate checks, they usually have the same controls and phased processing we observed in the payroll system. A common accounts payable problem concerns discounts. Suppliers often offer price reductions if payment is made within a certain time period. The company may or may not want to take the discount depending on cash available, the amounts of the debt and discount, and other factors. Some accounts payable systems use these factors to determine the best time to pay debts.

General ledger systems maintain company accounts. They perform the bookkeeping function for the company. Balance sheets and income statements are usually produced, as well as other reports. (See figure 3-10.)

Inventory accounting systems maintain records of additions and depletions from stock of finished or unfinished goods. Computer systems are often advantageous for inventory accounting, because some accounting techniques (last in, first out, or LIFO, for example) have sizable tax advantages but are com-

FIGURE 3-8

Billing statement

CONSOLIDATED INDUSTRIES

STATEMENT OF ACCOUNT WITH

TAYLOR CONSTRUCTION PRODUCTS   DECEMBER 1, 1984

INVOICE	SHIPMENT DATE	DESCRIPTION	COST
11046	10/20/83	ALUMINUM SIDING	$1148.12
11982	11/04/83	FASTENERS	37.15
12257	11/20/83	ROOFING MATERIALS	3894.84
TOTAL DUE			$5080.11

CONSOLIDATED INDUSTRIES

AGED ACCOUNTS RECEIVABLE   DECEMBER 1, 1984

CUSTOMER NUMBER	CUSTOMER NAME	CURRENT BALANCE	BALANCE OVER 30 DAYS LATE	BALANCE OVER 60 DAYS LATE	TOTAL BALANCE
37842	TAYLOR CONST.	$5080.11	$ 0.00	$ 0.00	$5080.11
39148	ABC SUPPLIES	0.00	438.10	300.14	738.24
40418	SHAKEWELL INC	127.13	541.27	1384.17	2052.57
41183	ZAVASKY INC	2312.47	0.00	0.00	2312.47
44817	ABLE ENTERPRISE	1497.12	348.97	0.00	1846.09

FIGURE 3-9

Accounts receivable report

FRONTIER IRONWORKS

BALANCE STATEMENT   DECEMBER 31, 1984
(THOUSANDS OF DOLLARS)

ASSETS		LIABILITIES	
CASH	$ 127	ACCOUNTS PAYABLE	$ 197
ACCOUNTS RECEIVABLE	583	ACCRUED EXPENSES	
INVENTORY	317	EMPLOYEE BENEFITS	349
PREPAID EXPENSES	53	OTHER	23
MACHINERY	1,483	PREFERRED STOCK	987
FURNITURE AND FIXTURES	275	COMMON STOCK	2,384
LAND AND BUILDINGS	1,788	RETAINED EARNINGS	686
TOTAL ASSETS	$4,626	TOTAL LIABILITIES	$4,626

FIGURE 3-10

Computer-generated balance statement

plex. Without the computer, many companies cannot cope with the computational requirements of the more sophisticated techniques.

There are many accounting computer systems besides those described here, but we have discussed the major ones. Other systems are similar and have the same objective of maintaining data that accurately reflect the financial state of the company.

QUESTIONS

3.1 What are the functions of management?

3.2 What is an information system? Which companies have an information system? Does an information system require a computer?

3.3 Characterize the difference between the information needs of the president and those of the production supervisor.

3.4 What are the three types of information service described in this section?

3.5 What is the purpose of an accounting computer system?

3.6 Why is much of the processing in an accounting system oriented toward error detection and correction?

3.7 Explain the purpose of the edit and the change reports. Why are both reports needed?

3.8 Briefly describe three accounting computer systems other than payroll.

FINANCE

Finance is the specialty of managing money. People who work in the finance department assess the company's need for money, determine ways to raise capital when it is needed, and evaluate proposals to spend it when appropriate.

Finance personnel use the computer primarily for three reasons. First, the calculation of interest rates, rates of return, and other such financial measures is crucial to managing money. These calculations can become very complex for large expenditures or for expenditures on complicated projects. Computers can save employee time, and they work very accurately when calculating these rates.

Second, much financial work is repetitive. Financial planning involves answering many "what if" questions. For example, a financial analyst may estimate earnings of $10,000 on a $100,000 investment for a new machine. He or she may then be asked, "What if sales go up 20 percent or down 5 percent?"

These kinds of questions can be answered easily by computer systems. The analyst may need to change only one or two input values and submit a request for another computer run to obtain the required answer. Hand-calculating a solution to the new problem might take nearly as long as determining the original solution.

A third reason for using computer systems in finance is that the alternatives to be evaluated often involve complex interactions that can be processed better by computers than by humans. In the previous example, if sales go up by 20 percent, the machine will be used more. If the machine is used more, maintenance will increase, expenses will go up, and available time will decrease. If available time decreases, a backlog will develop, orders may be lost, and so forth. Many of these interactions can be processed by financial computer systems more easily and accurately than by manual calculations.

Characteristics of Financial Computer Systems

Financial systems have a totally different character than accounting systems do. Figure 3-11 shows a typical financial system flowchart. The symbol ▢ represents a *CRT*. Because most financial work involves planning only, there is much less incentive for unauthorized activity or crime. In addition, the volume of input data is far less, so the chances of input errors are lower. However, financial plans can have a major impact on corporate strategy and

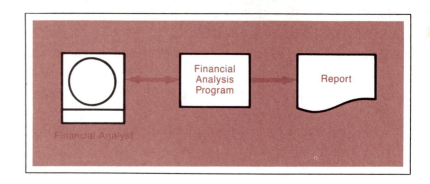

long-run corporate health. Thus, for example, the cost of an error in a financial plan can be much greater than the cost of an error in a customer bill.

Reports from a financial system are usually fewer and less voluminous than those from an accounting system. The clientele of a financial report are usually inside the firm, so the report format can be simpler and less elegant. Errors are less embarrassing and it is less time consuming to correct them. Finally, financial data is often less precise than accounting data. Growth rates, interest rates, market shares, and so forth, are usually estimates. Consequently, several estimates may be used and the results compared.

A major difference between financial and accounting systems exists in the procedures and personnel required. Accounting systems have many reports, many users, and a large clientele. Formal, written procedures are needed to integrate these people and ensure good control. Financial systems have several reports, a few users, and a small clientele. Consequently, procedures are often simple and informal. Finally, financial system users are often highly skilled, highly educated people. They require less training in computer use than the clerks and data entry personnel, who often use accounting-oriented systems. There are usually fewer of them and less turnover, so the need for recurring training is less.

Examples of Financial Computer Systems

Figure 3-12 lists common financial systems. *Capital expenditure analysis* is done to determine whether large and complex investments are worthwhile. Examples are analyzing costs and benefits for building a new manufacturing plant, introducing a new line of products, or adding a new division to a corporation.

Financial planning is another type of financial computer system. The purpose of financial planning is to project revenues and expenses over several years of operation. *Cash planning* is another important financial system. Usu-

Capital Expenditure Analysis
Financial Planning
Cash Planning
Merger Analysis
Credit Analysis
Electronic Spreadsheets

ally, money must be spent on a project for some time before money is made. This practice can lead to a cash crisis or shortage: the long-run financial picture is good, but bills can't be paid in the short run. Cash planning systems identify these situations before they occur and allow management to find supplementary sources of cash to cover the short period.

Some financial systems do *merger analysis*. Here, data about two or more companies are input to a financial analysis program, and a balance sheet and income statement are prepared assuming the companies have merged. This procedure allows management to learn the result of various merger strategies before the merger occurs.

A final type of financial system performs *credit analysis*. Banks, insurance companies, and other lenders use such systems to evaluate financial statements and determine the credit worthiness of potential borrowers. Similar systems are used by companies that buy stock or otherwise invest in other companies.

In recent years, financial personnel have begun to make extensive use of microcomputers. Quite often, financial systems involve only a single user who employs the computer to make a series of slightly different financial analyses. Micros are ideal for this application.

Electronic spreadsheets, such as VISICALC® and similar products, are microcomputer programs that greatly facilitate financial analyses. Figure 3–13a shows a typical electronic spreadsheet. It contains a student budget based on the following assumptions:

a. Income is $400 per month; housing is $160 per month

b. Food is 35 percent of income

FIGURE 3-13

Example of electronic spreadsheet outputs

	INCOME	HOUSING	FOOD	ENTERTAINMENT	SAVINGS
SEPT	400.00	160.00	140.00	50.00	50.00
OCT	400.00	160.00	140.00	50.00	100.00
NOV	400.00	160.00	140.00	50.00	150.00
DEC	400.00	160.00	140.00	50.00	0.00
JAN	400.00	160.00	140.00	50.00	50.00
FEB	400.00	160.00	140.00	50.00	100.00
MAR	400.00	160.00	140.00	50.00	150.00

a. Student budget assuming $400 income per month

	INCOME	HOUSING	FOOD	ENTERTAINMENT	SAVINGS
SEPT	600.00	160.00	210.00	75.00	155.00
OCT	600.00	160.00	210.00	75.00	310.00
NOV	600.00	160.00	210.00	75.00	465.00
DEC	600.00	160.00	210.00	75.00	0.00
JAN	600.00	160.00	210.00	75.00	155.00
FEB	600.00	160.00	210.00	75.00	310.00
MAR	600.00	160.00	210.00	75.00	465.00

b. Student budget assuming $600 income per month

c. Entertainment is 12.5 percent of income

d. Savings is income minus housing, food, and entertainment expenses

e. All accumulated savings are spent in December

Figure 3-13*b* shows a student budget with the same assumptions except that student income is assumed to be $600 per month. This second report was prepared by changing only the number for income. The electronic spreadsheet made all other calculations. If you have not used such a spreadsheet, do so at your first opportunity. They are exceedingly useful.

Computers have an important role in finance. In fact, they have changed the nature of financial planning. Because of the computer, more alternatives can be evaluated than in the past. The analysis that is done is more complete and precise than was possible previously.

Because of high interest rates, many companies have found a need to manage their financial resources very carefully. Computer systems have greatly facilitated this management; in the future, we are likely to see even greater application of computers in finance.

QUESTIONS

3.9 What are the responsibilities of people who specialize in finance?

3.10 What are the three reasons financial personnel use business computer systems?

3.11 Compare and contrast a financial computer system with an accounting system.

3.12 Explain what each of the following financial systems does:
a. Capital expenditure analysis
b. Financial planning
c. Cash planning
d. Merger analysis
e. Credit analysis

SALES AND MARKETING

Sales and *marketing* are two closely related fields that involve the selling of goods and services. People who work in these departments have many widely varying responsibilities. They analyze potential sales markets, generate ideas for products, and develop plans for selling existing products. They present products to customers through advertisements, telephone, and direct contact. They provide a point of contact for customers' questions and concerns. When sales are made, they handle paperwork like contracts and order entry documents. Sales personnel follow up to ensure delivery. When necessary, they investigate customer complaints and make corrections.

Sales personnel often work on a commission basis; that is, their earnings are dependent on the amount they sell. An important sales management task is to devise proper incentive plans. Defining territories and product responsibilities and setting quotas are other typical sales management tasks.

Sales and marketing systems fall into two broad categories. The first comprises systems used in direct support of sales and marketing *operations*, like order entry or the production of form letters. These systems are similar to accounting systems. They often have many files and reports, and they interface directly with customers. Since they deal with money and products, there can be a need for control over inputs, processing, and outputs.

Other systems do *analysis* of sales and marketing data. These systems are similar to financial systems in that they are used for determining strategies and plans, and they relate to business operations only indirectly. For example, *customer profiles* are reports of customer buying habits. They can be used to plan marketing strategies, but they cannot be used to help produce or deliver goods directly.

Analysis-oriented systems are usually simpler than operational systems. Since their clientele is within the firm, they can be less elegant, and their errors are easier to correct. Analysis systems also have less need for controls.

Examples of Sales and Marketing Computer Systems

The most common operational systems concern *order entry*. These systems receive order requests, check inventory levels, prepare invoices, and so forth. Another common operational sales system does *mail-order processing*. Orders are received by mail and processed, and customer statements are prepared. Requests for back orders can also be printed.

Computer systems are also used to check *order status*. Some systems are designed to allow order entry clerks access to computer files using CRTs. Thus an order can be monitored from order entry through production, packaging, and shipping. The customer can be informed of its progress. This capability is especially desirable for companies that manufacture goods to order that take a long time to produce.

A final type of operational sales and marketing system provides *assistance to advertising*. Mailing labels, form letters, and customized advertisements are produced. Many companies have large files of customers' or potential buyers' names and addresses. Mailing labels can be produced easily from these files. Mailing lists on magnetic tape can also be purchased. Form letters and other types of personalized advertising are commonly produced as well.

Sales and marketing also use *analysis* systems. Sales people use *customer profile reports* when making sales calls. Such reports are easily produced if order records are already stored on a computer-sensible medium. *Product penetration reports* show the sales of various products in different geographic markets. Using such a report, a marketing manager might decide to increase advertising or to assign additional personnel to underdeveloped markets.

A *sales agent effectiveness report* shows the sales of products by sales agents. These reports are helpful to salespeople in analyzing their effectiveness with different products. Such reports also show commissions and bonuses earned. Sometimes these reports compare current sales effectiveness to prior years' performances.

Market analysis systems are used to estimate the total sizes of markets, a company's share of each of them, or the distribution of markets across geographic areas, age groups, or demographic groups. For example, market analysis personnel may compare company sales over a period of time against the sales of its major competitors. This comparison may reveal that, although company sales are increasing, they are not increasing as fast as those of competitors. Obviously, the company's share of the market is falling.

This type of analysis often involves sophisticated algorithms and lengthy calculations. Computer systems ease the job of the market analyst and allow many more estimates to be prepared. Furthermore, the computer-generated estimates are apt to be more accurate than manually prepared ones.

In summary, sales and marketing systems can be divided into two groups. The *operational* systems directly support company sales. They are similar to accounting systems. *Analysis* systems are used for evaluating past performance and making plans. These systems are similar to those used in finance. In a later section, we will discuss computers used in manufacturing—systems of an entirely different type.

ENGINEERING

Engineering, which includes such areas as electrical, mechanical, industrial, aeronautical, and civil engineering, is the science of applying knowledge to practical problems. Computers aid in the design of new products. The development time of the product can be reduced by using computers as a tool in the design process. For example, in the construction of new aircraft, reshaping the fuselage, wing shape, or other exterior features can first be tested on a CRT. If the preliminary results are good, then further work can be done, such as building a model or prototype.

Electronic circuits are developed on computers to create newer, smaller, faster, and more powerful computers. These circuits are so complex that a human cannot remember and synthesize enough of the detail to design them efficiently. Programs exist that can design an integrated circuit, locate several circuits together on a circuit board, and show how the circuit boards will be used together. Computer advances could not have taken place so rapidly if these tools had not been available.

If roads or bridges are going to be constructed, computer programs exist that determine if the proposed design will meet some known sets of structural integrity. In fact, several designs can be generated in a matter of days as opposed to the months of calculations formerly necessary.

The design of new mechanical parts, gears, or power transfer assemblies can be done with calculations provided by computer programs written for that purpose. Many times the needed part may exist in a different size, and a larger or smaller piece is needed. Some programs have been written to modify an existing part by using the calculations that were done to create the original part, and then to produce a scaled-up or -down version almost immediately.

Engineers are also interested in simulating real-life problems with computers. For example, the effects of natural disasters played an important part in the design of many nuclear reactor containment structures. The structural strength needed to withstand natural phenomena was calculated, and design proceeded with that knowledge in mind. Hopefully, an atomic reactor disaster will only be simulated by computers.

The discussion of process control in the last section of this chapter is a very important use of computers in engineering and in the production of finished goods. Industrial engineers use computers regularly in their jobs of planning, scheduling, and controlling production on assembly lines.

MEDICINE

The way in which people are treated for illnesses by physicians has already changed, and the outlook for more change is sure. With the standard accounting and billing functions handled efficiently by machines, doctors are looking for new ways to use the power of computers.

Some of the uses that already exist include computer-assisted diagnosis, medical record keeping, drug studies and drug conflicts, computer monitoring of heart functions, and control of laboratory equipment.

The computer is able to serve as an extension of the health field specialist. With the decreasing cost of microcomputers, even the smallest office will have the ability to buy programs that will provide services never before available. For example, in remote areas or sparsely populated areas, communications capabilities (see chapter 8) make it possible to use larger facilities' information about hard-to-diagnose diseases. In the past, the patient was limited by his doctor's ability to analyze the symptoms of a disease and to select the correct diagnosis and treatment.

Many pharmacists use software packages that allow a patient to have a complete history of prescriptions, including any drug allergies. Billing information may be kept for a year for tax purposes. Current prescriptions can be analyzed to see if two drugs should not be given with each other. The effects of a particular drug can be reported to the pharmacist or patient.

EDUCATION

Computers can be used by well-informed educators to improve the quality of their instruction. Some of the ways computers are currently being used in education include class scheduling, curriculum planning, *computer-managed instruction (CMI),* and *computer-assisted instruction (CAI).*

Class scheduling is still a pain, but it is much less painful than it was a few years ago. Many schools can now determine which classes are full, which need additional sections, or which should be dropped from their schedules through their computerized class scheduling. Some schools have even used statistical analysis of their enrolled student body to determine which classes need to be offered before enrollment begins.

Other uses of computers by educators include computer-managed instruction (CMI). CMI is used to manage the activities a student must perform to master a particular field of study. CMI provides the tools to test a student's mastery of the subject material. If a student has a problem with a particular area of study, additional work can be selected and assigned. CMI allows the selection of a course of study for a student based on that student's needs.

Computer-assisted instruction (CAI) is the use of the computer to teach material to a student. This teaching often takes the form of drills. The function of the computer in this environment includes the presentation of material to the student through instructions and questions. The student has the opportunity to study the material, to answer questions, and occasionally to ask some questions. The computer then checks the answers provided by the student and gives immediate feedback to the student. Many CAI systems maintain records of the student's performance. Very well-written software is available on many different topics.

LAW

Computers have found their way into our legal system and provide many useful services. Lawyers are finding that the records kept by computers are accurate and easy to use. They have also found that their job is made easier by the ability to use computers for case searches and by using word processing capabilities to prepare legal documents.

Police departments have always kept records on criminal activity, descriptions, and stolen property. This information is often used to apprehend criminals arrested for other reasons. Many departments have access to the information kept in the *National Crime Information Center (NCIC)* files. This information is shared and added to by all law enforcement agencies. This sharing makes it easier to track a criminal nationwide based on his modus operandi. Just because he leaves a particular city or state does not mean that he has left his record behind him. Many law enforcement agencies even provide this information to the officer on the beat via patrol car terminals.

The judicial system is using computers to select qualified jurors. Once a qualified juror has been selected, computers can be used to summon the potential juror for a court appearance. This method of selection saves people time by avoiding some needless calls, and it saves taxpayers money by not having to pay totally unqualified jurors.

HUMANITIES

The humanities field is one area where computers have just begun to make inroads. Computers are being used for text analysis, word processing, creation of new art or music, and cataloging research or collections.

Many studies have been conducted on past literary works to determine authenticity or original authorship. These studies are performed by analyzing a known work by the supposed author, determining the statistical patterns of style, and then judging an unknown work based on those patterns. The cost of this type of activity is virtually prohibitive if noncomputing methods are used. Computer manipulation of text is exciting and is covered in Module E. This text was written with a word processor in less than half the time it would have taken with a typewriter.

As new software packages have become available, the artist and the musician have started to use the computer as an expressive tool. It is possible to create a piece of art or a new musical composition based on an idea and a few simple commands. The possibilities are only limited by the imagination.

Many museums and collections have been organized by computing facilities. The Smithsonian Institution has just recently completed a multiyear project that cataloged every artifact. The reduction of duplicate items and the ability to display more items in rotation are just two of the benefits.

QUESTIONS

3.13 Explain how an engineer (you choose the type) could use a computer on the job.

3.14 Why is a computer helpful in making a diagnosis?

3.15 Explain why computer-assisted instruction is practiced.

3.16 How does the use of computers in law help reduce crime?

3.17 Have you ever used a computer cataloging system (perhaps in your library)? Describe how the system worked.

3.18 Describe an application of computers that you would like to see.

MANUFACTURING

A company's *manufacturing* department is responsible for transforming raw materials into finished products. This transformation can be a complex task requiring four different activities. First, manufacturing personnel must order sufficient raw materials to produce the desired quantity of finished goods. This task may seem simple, but consider the great variety and vast number of components needed to produce a TV, an automobile, or an airplane! Often the lead time for ordering raw materials is six months or more. Manufacturing must determine its needs at least that far in advance so that the raw materials will be available when needed.

Second, manufacturing personnel want to schedule the use of their facilities so as to maximize productivity. For example, if a company has only two lathes, production should be scheduled to balance the use of these machines. Extra costs and time delays will occur if the machines are overloaded at one point in time and idle at another. The order of production needs to be arranged to allow uniform utilization of the equipment.

Another scheduling consideration is *machine setup time*. Suppose it takes 10 minutes to set up a saw to cut table legs and 15 minutes to set up the saw to cut table tops. If five tables are to be produced, it makes sense to cut all the legs and then all the tops. Otherwise, if the saw cuts first the legs for one table, then the top, then the legs for the next table, then the top, and so forth, much time will be wasted changing the saw setup. Many firms have increased production 20 or 30 percent simply by scheduling machines and people more effectively.

A third manufacturing activity is making components and assembling them into finished products. This task includes production labor, labor to make tools and machines, and labor for inspections and other *quality assurance* procedures.

The fourth activity is engineering. The design of new parts or new machines is an engineering responsibility, as is the incorporation of new materials or new technology into existing products.

Computer systems are used to support all four of these manufacturing activities. Some of these systems, particularly those supporting scheduling and engineering, are similar to the analysis systems discussed in the sections on finance and marketing. These systems have relatively few inputs but do considerable computing. Output reports are few, and the clientele is within the firm.

Examples of Manufacturing Computer Systems

Figure 3-14 lists computer systems commonly used in manufacturing. Systems in the first category, *materials management,* support the planning of raw materials purchasing and the control of raw materials and finished goods inventories. They also enable tracking of materials through the production process. Figure 3-15 shows a *bill of materials* for a simple backpack. If a company wanted to make 1000 of these, manufacturing personnel would need to compute the amount of raw materials needed. If, in addition, the company wanted to make tents, sleeping bags, and other products, they would need to compute the total materials required. *Materials requirements planning* (MRP) systems eliminate the manual effort required to make these computations.

Inventory control systems maintain the right quantity of parts in inventory. Inventory personnel must maintain a delicate balance. They do not want to run out of parts, but, on the other hand, they do not want to have too many parts. Excess parts must be paid for and the cost of carrying inventory can be very high. Consequently, computer systems are used to keep track of the quantity of parts in inventory, the rate at which they are used, and the time it takes to receive a delivery once an order is made. These factors, together with the costs

FIGURE 3-14

Manufacturing computer systems

Materials Management
    Materials Requirements Planning
    Inventory Control
    Materials Tracking

Facility Scheduling
    Machine Balancing
    Production Scheduling
    Operations Research

Process Control
    Manufacturing Machines
    Environment Control
    Security Systems
    Robots

Engineering
    Computer-Assisted Design
    Stress Analysis
    Spatial Conflict Detection
    Electronic Circuit Evaluation
    Aerodynamics

```
                    BILL OF MATERIALS FOR

                    HIKER BACKPACK

                    PRODUCT NUMBER 14356


MATERIAL                QUANTITY              DIMENSIONS (INCHES)

CLOTH TOP                  1                      20X12
CLOTH SIDES                4                      8X22
LEATHER BOTTOM             1                      8X14
VELCRO HOOK TAPE           1                      6X1/2
LEATHER TIEDOWN            3                      3X2
WEB STRAPS                 2                      2X35
PADDED BELT                1                      3X40
THREAD                     1                      400(FEET)
```

F I G U R E   3 - 1 5

Bill of materials example

of the parts, are used to calculate the optimum reorder point and quantity for each part.

Tracking of materials and finished goods is also accomplished using computer systems. Companies do not want to lose finished goods through accident or pilferage, nor do they want to lose material in the production line. Keeping track of materials can be a major task for a large manufacturer. Computer systems are used to process the large volume of data needed.

Facility scheduling systems are another category of computer applications in manufacturing. Systems are used to help balance machines and to minimize the amount of time wasted by machine setup or schedule conflicts. Since a typical manufacturer may have 50 machines and 500 products, production scheduling is not a trivial problem. A specialty known as *operations research* uses mathematics to solve these problems. These techniques require extensive calculations. Computer systems are heavily used for this purpose.

The next category of applications, *process control*, uses computer technology to control and operate machines. In addition to controlling manufacturing machines, these computers control air conditioning and heating, security systems, typewriters and copying equipment, and even timing equipment at sporting events.

Perhaps the most exciting application of computer technology in manufacturing is robotics. A *robot* is a programmable manipulator designed to move materials, parts, tools, or specialized devices through a series of programmed activities [9]. (See figure 3-16 and also the Computers and Society Photo Essay.) Robots are especially useful for performing boring and repetitive work and for working in uncomfortable or dangerous environments.

The social implications of robotics are enormous. Robots could drastically reduce the need for manual labor in manufacturing companies in the next

FIGURE 3-16

Robot

decade. They will certainly cause major changes in the skill level of workers. A new, technical job will likely evolve that will require a person who has knowledge of computing, machinery, and manufacturing technology. Present-day blue-collar workers will need considerable retraining to be able to fill these new jobs.

The final category of manufacturing computer systems involves *engineering*. Systems are used to assist design in a variety of ways. Designs can be displayed on CRTs, and engineers can use the computer to make modifications. Once a design is approved, *computer-assisted design* systems translate design drawings into instructions for manufacturing machinery. In the coming years, robots will even be used.

Computer systems are also used for *stress analysis* of load-bearing structures and to check for *spatial conflicts* in drawings of large buildings. Other applications are to evaluate *electronic circuits* and to investigate *aerodynamic properties* of cars, boats, airplanes, and rockets.

QUESTIONS

3.19 Describe the four activities involved in manufacturing.

3.20 Define *process control system*.

3.21 Give an example of a process control system.

3.22 Briefly explain how computers are used to support manufacturing.

THREE FUNDAMENTAL TYPES OF COMPUTER SYSTEMS

In the last section, we grouped computer systems by functional area. Another way to characterize computer systems is by the type of service they provide. Three types of service are common: transaction processing systems, manage-

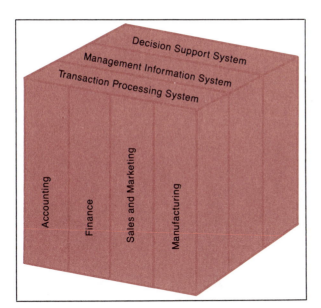

FIGURE 3-17

Relationship of three types of computer system service to functional area

ment information systems, and decision support systems. Figure 3-17 shows the relationship of functional area to type of service.

Transaction Processing Systems

A *transaction processing* system is a computer system that receives changes to the status of the company, records these changes in the company's data, and produces appropriate documents. Examples of transaction processing systems are order entry systems, airline reservation systems, and payroll systems.

The records that a company keeps about itself comprise a model of the company. Just as a model airplane represents an actual airplane, so, too, corporate data represents an actual company. The data is an extraction from reality. Transaction processing systems perform the function of keeping the corporate data model current. When an event occurs to or in the company, a transaction processing system receives a record of the event and makes appropriate changes in the data model. A transaction processing system may also produce what's termed a *real output*. Real outputs are statements or negotiable instruments (like checks). The term *real* is used to emphasize the fact that the output is sent to the business world and is not simply a change to the data model. Figure 3-18 depicts a typical transaction processing system.

A transaction processing system may have hundreds of users, as in the case of airline reservation clerks, for example. Performance and reliability are critical. If a transaction processing system is slow or fails, the impact on the using organization can be severe. Backup and recovery are therefore exceedingly important.

Management Information Systems

A *management information* system (MIS) is a system that provides past, present, and projected information about a company and its environment [16]. An

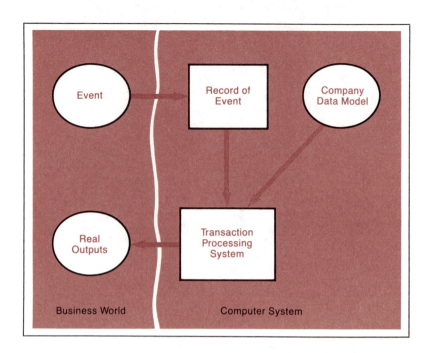

FIGURE 3-18

Transaction processing system

MIS does not necessarily require a computer, but, today, most do employ computers.

An MIS usually takes its input from the data model generated by one or more transaction processing systems. (See figure 3-19.) From these models, it generates reports used to facilitate management decision making. Such reports are predefined and are produced on a regular, recurring schedule. For example, an airline may have an MIS that produces weekly summaries of flight load data. Management may review these reports to determine the amount of food and the number of cabin attendants to schedule on that flight for some future period.

As stated at the beginning of this chapter, information needs vary among employees. In general, the higher the employee resides in the organization chart, the more aggregated are information needs. The president of a company must have aggregations of aggregations. Figure 3-20 portrays the information needs of management graphically.

Management information systems do not have the same needs for performance and reliability that transaction processing systems do. As long as a manager receives a report when it is expected, he or she does not care whether it took 30 seconds or 30 minutes to produce it. Similarly, as long as the report arrives on time and is accurate, the manager does not care that the computer failed three times while preparing it. (This is true with one exception: the manager cares how much the report costs. Poor performance and reliability cost more.)

Management information systems must, however, produce *timely* and *accurate* reports. A manager who must make a scheduling decision every Monday afternoon needs the weekly flight load data report promptly on Monday morning. If the report arrives Tuesday, the manager will be in dire straights.

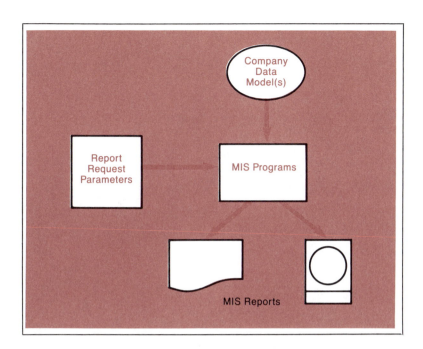

FIGURE 3-19

Typical management information system

Management decisions may have broad consequences and considerable impact on the firm. Therefore, MIS reports must also be accurate. A mistake on a $300 transaction may cost $300. A mistake on a report of the sales history of the western region may cost thousands or millions of dollars. Accuracy in MIS reports is therefore critical.

Decision support systems (DSS) are computer systems that facilitate decision making by providing tools for ad hoc data manipulation and reporting. A DSS is similar to an MIS except that MIS reports are regular and recurring, whereas DSS reports are irregularly produced and may or may not recur.

Decision Support Systems

FIGURE 3-20

Need for consolidation increases with level of management

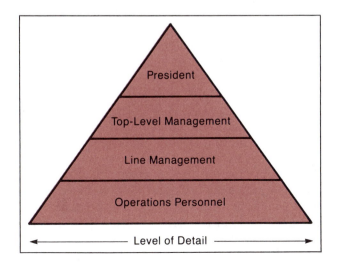

FIGURE 3-21

Information center

A DSS provides programs to retrieve, process, and report data in many different ways. Suppose, for example, that a large manufacturer is considering merging the sales forces of two regions. If this is to be done, management must develop new sales territories that provide for a fair allocation of customers to salespeople.

To develop this allocation, management may need reports about sales over a several-year period, broken down by salesperson and customer. Then, management will want to try various sales territory alternatives and see how past sales would have been distributed across the alternatives. To make this evaluation, management will require that information be retrieved and processed in many different ways. Flexibility will be essential. Also, management will want to do this evaluation rapidly, perhaps within a week or so. When the evaluation is finished, there will be no recurring need for the reports to be generated.

Thus, the keystones of a DSS are *flexibility* and *quickness*. Until recently, these attributes have been very difficult for computer systems to provide. Historically, systems development has been inflexible and slow. However, the rise of the new technology of relational database management (discussed in chapter 7) and high-level, nonprocedural languages (discussed in module K, part 5) have made flexible, quick decision support systems possible.

Along with this technology, a new data processing concept, called the *information center,* has been developed (see figure 3-21). The information center is similar to a library but, instead of books, it contains extractions from the company's operational data. An information center has all five components of a business computer system. There will be hardware (either the company's main computer or perhaps one or more supplemental computers); programs that provide powerful and flexible access to data; the extracted data; procedures; and people.

A new job is evolving in conjunction with the development of information centers. These centers are staffed by people who have expertise in the information center's data and programs and who help users to employ these facilities to get the data they need. This new job is something like that of a librarian. The information center librarian helps users but does not do their work. The users must obtain their own data and do their own research. The librarians are present to explain and to teach.

QUESTIONS

3.23 Explain the statement that a company's records comprise a model of the company.

3.24 What is a transaction processing system? Describe two important characteristics of a transaction processing system.

3.25 What is a management information system? Describe two important characteristics of an MIS.

3.26 What is a decision support system? Describe two important characteristics of a DSS.

3.27 How does an MIS differ from a DSS?

3.28 Describe an information center. What is the new job that is evolving with this center?

SUMMARY

Are you satisfied with this application survey? Probably not. There are far too many applications to summarize them all in one chapter. We didn't discuss how computers are used for preparing budgets or for analyzing expenses. We didn't discuss how they are used for controlling the timing of people and deliveries on major projects like building construction. We didn't discuss computerized typewriters called *word processors* (but see module E of part 4). We could identify dozens of applications we didn't discuss.

However, did you gain an insight into the importance of computing? Can you see that knowledge of computer systems is important to you, regardless of whether you want to be a manager, an accountant, a salesperson, or a production supervisor? It's true. In fact, knowledge of computer systems will give you the competitive edge in any position.

We began this chapter with a discussion of the information system. Some information systems involve a computer, and they will be the focus of this book. We surveyed computer systems in accounting and observed the need for control in accounting systems. Financial computer systems tend to be analytical and involve fewer people than accounting systems. We then looked at how computers are used in many different fields. Additional discussions can be found in module D. Finally, manufacturing systems emphasize control over processes.

Next, we examined computer systems from a different perspective by discussing three types of commonly provided service. Transaction processing systems keep the company's data model current and produce real outputs. Management information systems provide standardized, recurring reports to facilitate management decisions. Finally, decision support systems provide flexible, ad hoc access to company data. The information center is evolving into a data library.

WORD LIST
(in order of appearance in text)

Status information
Information-bearing documents
Control systems
Checks and balances
Hourly payroll system
General ledger
Phased processing
Editing
Manual operations flowchart symbol
Edit report
Master file change report
Billing system
Accounts receivable system
Accounts payable system
General ledger system
Inventory accounting system
Finance
CRT flowchart symbol
Capital expenditure analysis
Financial planning
Cash planning
Merger analysis
Credit analysis
Electronic spreadsheet
Sales and marketing
Operational sales and marketing systems
Analysis sales and marketing systems
Order entry systems
Mail-order processing systems
Order status systems
Advertising systems

Customer profile reports
Product penetration reports
Sales agent effectiveness reports
Market analysis
Structural stress analysis
Computer-managed instruction (CMI)
Computer-assisted instruction (CAI)
National Crime Information Center (NCIC)
Text analysis
Manufacturing
Machine setup time
Quality assurance
Materials management
Bill of materials
Materials requirements planning (MRP)
Inventory control systems
Facility scheduling systems
Operations research
Process control systems
Robot
Engineering
Computer-assisted design systems
Stress analysis
Transaction processing systems
Management information systems (MIS)
Decision support systems (DSS)
Information center

A. If you are interested in management:
  1. What is PERT? How does it work, and are computers necessary for PERT applications? What is CPM? GERT?
  2. Suppose you managed the production of a newspaper. How might you use the computer to reduce your operational costs? To provide better reader services?
  3. Interview one of your management professors. Find out other ways the computer is used to assist manufacturing personnel.
  4. What role does a top level manager have in the development of computer systems? What is the steering committee and how can it be used to control computer projects?

B. If you are interested in accounting:
  1. What are the potential dangers of using computers for accounting purposes? What steps can be taken to reduce these dangers?
  2. Interview one of your accounting professors and ask how computers have changed accounting. How do CPAs treat computer systems during an audit? Find out what SAS-3 is and why it is important to both data processing and accounting.

C. If you are interested in finance:
  1. Find out if your computer has a package of financial programs. If so, determine the interest rate on a loan with a principal of $73,000 to be paid off in 72 payments of $1450 per month.
  2. Ask one of your finance professors about financial planning. Determine how it has changed since the advent of the computer.

D. If you are interested in sales and marketing:
  1. How are computers used to support marketing? Find out about a system that produces mailing labels. How can the system detect whether or not it has a duplicate label on the list?

E. If you are interested in engineering:
  1. How are electronic circuits manufactured? You may want to reference periodicals like *National Geographic* (October, 1982) or *Scientific American* (July, 1983) to find additional information.
  2. What type of architectural processes are often computerized? Is there a firm in your locale that uses computer-aided design?

F. If you are interested in medicine:
  1. What "expert systems" (systems that aid professionals in completing their tasks) are currently functioning in medicine?
  2. Why should you use pharmaceutical systems that provide drug conflict information?
  3. Investigate how new computer-aided technology works. For example, what does a CAT scan actually do?

G. If you are interested in education:
  1. How are computers being used in the classroom today? Is there a better approach to using computer power?
  2. Attempt to use different CAI or CMI systems. Evaluate the results and compare the techniques.

H. If you are interested in law:
1. Contact your local law enforcement agency, and investigate how they use computers.
2. Investigate how computers are used in your local court system.

I. If you are interested in the humanities:
1. Locate a system that is being used to produce images, and try to arrange a demonstration of the system.
2. Investigate one of the many packages used to create and play music. Create your own musical composition.

J. If you are interested in manufacturing:
1. What is MRP? Do MRP systems always use the computer? Why or why not? What do you suppose is the major computer problem in using an MRP system?
2. Bill of materials processors are very common manufacturing systems. What, specifically, do they do? Could this activity be done without the computer?
3. Investigate the application of robots to manufacturing. How many robots exist? Which industries are using them? What types of work are they performing? Who are the major vendors? What posture have the unions taken with regard to robotics?

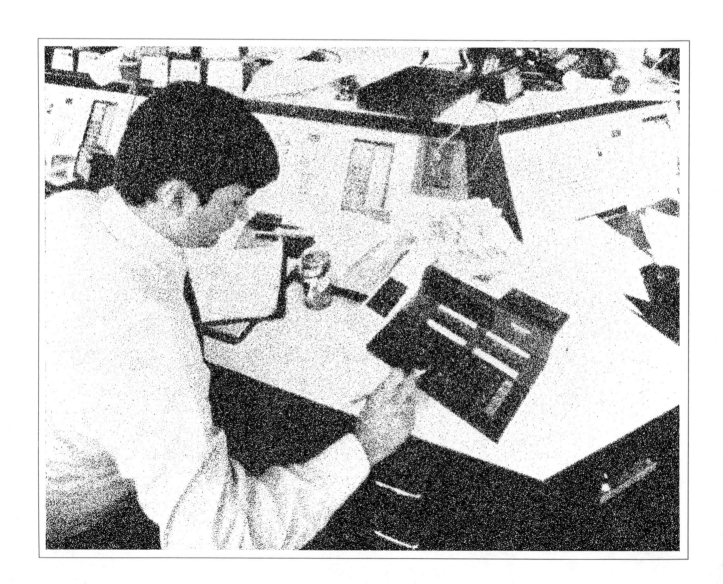

PART TWO

Fundamental Computer Systems

Part 2 of this text discusses fundamental computer systems. First, we discuss how they are developed, and then we describe the characteristics of fundamental system types. The first part of chapter 4 outlines a general process for developing systems. That process is then illustrated with a case adapted from the experience of an actual business.

The remaining chapters of this part discuss three system types. Chapter 5 discusses sequential file processing systems, chapter 6 discusses direct access file processing systems, and chapter 7 discusses database systems. All computer systems are based on one of these three types.

Observe that the fundamental types are characterized by the way in which they organize and process data. When we discuss the five components of a system, data is the middle component. On one side of data, we have hardware executing programs; on the other side of data, we have people following procedures. Since data is the interface between machines and people, it makes sense that we use data organization to characterize systems.

CHAPTER 4

The Systems Development Process

In this chapter, we will discuss the ways in which computer systems are developed. This information will be important to your career whether or not you become a computer professional. For example, if you become a business manager, you will need to know this process to ensure that your employees develop systems correctly. If you become a computer user, say, a supervisor of payroll, you will need this information to protect yourself. You will need to know what is happening, what your role should be, what you can fairly expect from the experts, and so forth. Finally, if you make the computer profession your career, you will need to know how to proceed when developing a system. This chapter will be your introduction. To become a qualified systems developer, however, you will need several courses in systems development and computer technology as well as a year or more of experience.

This chapter concerns a process. The word *process* is a strange one. It is so vague that it is easy to ignore. In this book, the word *process* means *behaviors* or *actions*. When we talk about the systems development process, we will mean the *actions* people take to build a system.

WARNING TO STUDENTS

Learning behaviors is hard. It's much easier to learn a fact. You can easily learn that two and two make four, and, what's more, you know when you've learned it. When you learn a behavior, you do not necessarily even know when you know it. We can (and will) put labels on the steps of the behavior, but those steps will be much more vague than two and two make four. Do not underestimate the importance of learning this process, however, for that reason. In fact, for your future career, this is probably the most important chapter in this book.

We will take two approaches to learning systems development. First, we will divide the process into steps and put labels on each of those steps. If this seems boring, read and learn it anyway because it is important.

Second, we will illustrate the application of these steps in a case. The case will probably be more interesting, but it will seem vague. Plan on learning in different ways from these two approaches. To prepare for an exam, study the first part of the chapter and memorize the steps of the systems development process. To prepare to develop a system, read and understand the case.

THE SYSTEMS DEVELOPMENT PROCESS

A computer system is a group of five components that interact to satisfy a need. To develop a system, we must select, install, and establish the interaction among these five components. We will need to select and install hardware (unless a suitable computer is already available). We will need to obtain programs. We will need to design data and build the initial files. We will need to design procedures for people to follow, and we will need to train the people who will be involved. Building such a system can be a complex job. The process described in the next section breaks this complex job down into simpler pieces.

Figure 4-1 lists the four stages of a systems development process. This sequence of stages has evolved over a period of time. It has been forged out of the mistakes and disasters of many systems development projects. Today, most business computer professionals agree that these activities, in the order listed, are the best way to ensure that an effective system is developed. (Professionals may disagree on the names of the stages and on the packaging of activities into each of the steps, but there is a general agreement on the basic behaviors in figure 4-1.)

The first step in a systems development project is to determine what the system is supposed to do. As shown in figure 4-2, several actions must be taken to make this determination. The first is to form a project team. This team should include both users and computer professionals. The users are primarily responsible for developing requirements and ensuring that the system will meet the intended need. The computer professionals build the components of the business computer system to satisfy those user requirements. Sometimes, the best results occur if the project team is led by a user, rather than by someone from the data processing department.

The skills needed by members of the project team will change over time. In the early stages, users have a major role. The need for technical personnel such as programmers is limited in these stages. During design and implementation, however, this situation will reverse. Technical personnel will have major responsibilities, and users will have less to do, at least until the final stages of implementation. Thus, personnel may be assigned to the project intermittently. Generally, however, the project manager should remain constant throughout the project.

The first task of the project team is problem definition. What needs to be done? The project team must clearly understand its responsibilities. Much time can be wasted if different members of the team have different perceptions of the job to be done.

Requirements Stage

Define the Problem

Determine Requirements
Evaluate Alternatives
Design
Implement

FIGURE 4-1

Four stages of systems development

Form Project Team
Define Problem
Determine Specific Requirements
Assess Feasibility (Can be done after problem definition as well)
Obtain Management Approval

FIGURE 4-2

Tasks to determine requirements

A problem is a perceived difference between *what is* and *what ought to be*. Therefore, to define the problem, the team must clearly define the present situation and then describe the desired situation. A problem is a *perceived* difference. In some lucky situations, the team will discover that the problem is only a perception, that the problem does not truly exist. In this case, the team will have saved considerable time and expense by focusing, early, on problem definition. More than one company has developed an elegant solution to a nonexistent problem, or even to the wrong problem. As carpenters say, measure twice and cut once.

Determine Specific Requirements

The next task within the requirements stage is to determine the specific requirements of the new system. Whereas the problem definitions in the prior step are broad in scope, the requirement definitions in this step are narrow and focused. At this point, *specific* needs of the users are to be determined and documented. An example of a specific requirement is the following: the CRT screen for order entry must show customer number, name, address, and credit limit.

It is vital that future system users be involved in determining specific requirements. Studies have shown that the number one cause of failure in a computer system is a lack of user involvement during requirements definition. If users are not involved, the requirements are often not realistic. In addition, if users are not involved, they have no psychological stake in the new system. In fact, they may be motivated to cause the system to fail. But, if users have participated in the development of requirements, they feel a part of the process and are as anxious as anyone to see the system succeed.

The user requirements should be documented in a journal or other written record. This journal must specifically state what the new system is to do. It becomes a storehouse of the team's knowledge about the new system. Further, documenting the requirements forces the team members to understand them clearly. Finally, this documentation is useful during testing. Does the system accomplish what it is supposed to?

Evaluate Feasibility

At some point (or perhaps at several points) during systems development, the feasibility of the project is evaluated. This *feasibility evaluation* may occur after the problem is defined, after the requirements are determined, or at both times.

The team considers three dimensions when evaluating feasibility. The first dimension is *technical feasibility*. For this portion of the evaluation, someone with computer expertise determines whether or not the problem to be solved is amenable to a computer solution. Has such a problem ever been solved by computer? Or, if not, is it likely that this problem can be solved by computer? For example, producing customer invoices can feasibly be done by computer. Deciding whether or not to change personnel policies cannot.

Once the technical feasibility is verified, then *cost feasibility* is examined by developing rough cost estimates. The approximate size and capacity of the computer required are determined. This information can be used to get a rough estimate of the cost of the computer itself. However, other costs are also involved. Programs must be purchased or developed; data must be converted; procedures must be developed; and personnel must be trained. These are all initial costs. Added to these are the operational costs incurred as the system is used. Power, maintenance, and salaries of operations personnel are examples of these operational costs.

Again, rough cost estimates are used. The purpose of the cost feasibility step is to determine whether the cost of a computer system solution is in the right range. For example, if the cost of the system is $100,000, and the estimated worth of the solution is $10,000, then a computer solution to the problem is *cost infeasible*.

The third dimension of feasibility evaluation is *schedule feasibility*. If the computer system requires a year to develop, and if a solution must be found in six months, then the proposed system is infeasible. For example, if a system is needed to compute taxes that are due on April 15, and if the system cannot be completed until July 4, then the proposed system is schedule infeasible. Another solution must be found.

Again, feasibility evaluation can be done at any point in the systems development process. In the first stage, it is most frequently done after the problem has been defined or after the specific requirements have been determined.

Once the problem has been defined, the specific requirements have been determined, and the technical, cost, and schedule feasibility have been evaluated, the results are documented. Then, a report of findings is presented to management. If management believes that the problem has been well defined; if they believe that the requirements are complete; and if they agree that the project is feasible, then a go-ahead decision is issued. Otherwise, management may direct that a part of the work be redone, or they may cancel the project.

Such *management approval* is mandatory. Management must have an opportunity to influence the flow and direction of the systems development project. As you will see, management approval is required at the end of all four stages of systems development.

After the requirements have been determined, alternatives for each component of the business computer system are developed and evaluated. Each alternative specifies hardware, programs, data, procedures, and personnel required to solve the business problem. See figure 4-3.

The objective when specifying alternatives is to find three or four feasible alternatives that will fulfill the user's requirements. To do this, each of the five components of a computer system is considered in the light of the requirements.

Identify Alternatives
    (Hardware, programs, data, procedures, people)
Evaluate Alternatives
    Cost/benefit
    Subjective evaluation
Obtain Management Approval

Obtain Management Approval

Alternative Evaluation Stage

Identify Alternatives

FIGURE 4-3

Tasks to evaluate alternatives

Then, an alternative is created by specifying the hardware, programs, data, procedures, and personnel needed to meet the requirements.

Sometimes, one of the system components is the same for all alternatives. For example, if a company already has a computer, then the hardware may be the same for each alternative. In some cases, the data needed may be the same, or the procedures to be used may be equivalent. When this correspondence occurs, the component that stays the same does not form part of the alternative.

Developing an alternative is an iterative (repeated) process. The five components are interdependent. A decision on one may change the others. This may necessitate going back and reassessing other components. For example, one type of computer hardware might seem feasible until the personnel component is discussed and the team discovers that a systems engineering specialist would be required to put the computer together and keep it running. Such an alternative would probably be deleted.

Further, the choice of one component can impact choices of other components. For example, if a company decides to write its own computer programs, in-house programming expertise will be required. For a purchased program, programming staff would be unnecessary.

Select an Alternative

Once the alternatives have been identified, the next step is to evaluate them and select one. Then, the best alternative is compared to the value of the problem solution, and a decision on whether or not to continue is made. If the decision is to continue, the design stage will begin.

Basically, alternatives should be evaluated by comparing the dollar values of benefits to costs. One way to do this is to form ratios of benefits to costs. The alternative with the highest ratio is selected. You will learn more about the process of *cost/benefit analysis* if you take a course in systems development or business finance.

In some cases, a formal evaluation of costs and benefits is not performed. Instead, the project team, together with management, meets to assess the alternatives. A decision regarding alternatives is then made on a subjective basis. Other possibilities exist [25], [30], and [31].

Obtain Management Approval

At the conclusion of this stage, the selected alternative is presented to management. Management may have concerns that were not addressed by the project team. If so, these issues may need to be studied. Otherwise, management will budget the necessary funds and approve the start of the next stage.

Design Stage

The third stage of the systems development process is to design the system. As shown in figure 4-4, by *systems* design we mean that each of the five components of a computer system is designed. Insofar as hardware is concerned, the term *design* is used loosely. Very rarely is computer equipment built; usually it is purchased or leased. Here, *design* means to determine the detailed specifications of the equipment needed and then to order it from a vendor.

Hardware Specifications
Program
    Specifications (if purchased)
    Design (if written)
Data
    File formats
    Screen formats
    Report formats
Procedures
    User procedures
    Normal processing
    Failure recovery
    Operations procedures
    Normal processing
    Failure recovery
People
    Job descriptions
    Organizational structure
    Training needs
Obtain Management Approval

FIGURE 4-4

Tasks for systems design

Sometimes programs are purchased, and sometimes they are written by the project team. If they are purchased, the detailed specifications are developed and the programs are ordered at this step. If they are written as part of the systems development, the detailed design of the programs is produced. This is often the most time-consuming part of program development. If the design is done properly, the actual coding or programming may be done quite rapidly. More will be said about program development in the next section.

The other three components of the system must also be designed. Decisions are made about data formats, including input forms, storage file structures, and layouts of outputs, such as reports. Procedures that describe how users will employ the system, as well as how the operations personnel will run the system, must be designed. Finally, job descriptions are prepared, the organizational arrangement of users and operations personnel is designed, and training programs are developed.

Obtain Management Approval

The design stage is also approved by management. At this phase, however, management may not have the expertise to assess the adequacy of the work that has been done. Therefore, they may hire independent expertise to assist in the *design review*. Even without such expertise, it is important for management to review the design and stay involved in the project. Quite often, good managers will detect a fly in the ointment, even if they do not understand the technical details. In addition, if the systems design necessitates organizational changes (which often occurs), then management's approval will be required.

If work is proceeding satisfactorily, approval will be granted for implementation.

Construct
    Install hardware
    Install (or write) programs
    Build files
    Document procedures
    Hire and train personnel
Test
    Test each component individually
    Test system
Install
    Plunge (never)
    Parallel
    Pilot
    Phased
Obtain Management Approval (of Completion)

FIGURE 4-5

Tasks in systems implementation

Implementation Stage

Construction

System Test

Installation

The last step in systems development is implementation. As shown in figure 4-5, this step has three primary tasks: construction, testing, and installation.

At this point, hardware and programs that have been ordered are installed and tested for correct operation. (Actually, this step varies according to the project. We have assumed that hardware and programs are ordered during design. If the lead time is short enough, however, orders may not be placed until implementation.)

If programs are being written instead of purchased, they are coded and tested at this step. Test data files are built. The conversion of the actual data to computer format is begun. Procedures are documented and tested by operations personnel and by users. Needed personnel are hired, and necessary organizational changes are made. Training materials are prepared and initial training is completed.

System testing usually has two different phases. First, as the hardware and programs become available, they are tested as separate *components*. Hardware is tested using test plans and procedures provided by the vendor. Programs are tested according to vendor procedures or by the programming staff. Once these components have been tested, then a *system test* of all five components is made. During this test, the critical users and operations personnel follow defined procedures. An evaluation is made to determine whether or not the system is ready for installation. If so, installation proceeds. Otherwise, the system is corrected and retested.

System testing varies widely depending on the complexity of the system, the number of personnel involved, and the degree to which the programs have already been used. A program that has just been constructed obviously will require more testing than a program that is currently used at 200 sites.

Proper installation of a business computer system is vital. If installation is done poorly, users will develop doubts and hostilities toward the system even if it is an excellent one.

There are four major *installation* strategies. The first one is to *plunge*. The new system is started and any existing manual systems are stopped. This strategy is *very dangerous*. If the new system has some errors or other difficulties, there is no backup. This strategy should be used rarely, if ever.

A second strategy is to run the new system in *parallel* with the old manual system. If any problems develop, there is a backup. This approach is expensive because two systems must be supported for some period of time. Still, many companies view this expense as a form of insurance.

When a *pilot* strategy is followed, the new system is implemented on a small part of the clientele. For example, a company might install a system on part of their customer base, say, on the customers in the state of Minnesota. Once the system is working correctly, it can be used for all customers. The pilot strategy isolates the damages in case the new system works incorrectly.

Finally, *phased* system installation means implementing it in parts. For example, for an integrated order entry/inventory system, a company could install just the inventory part of the system and verify it before implementing the order entry portion.

QUESTIONS

4.1 Name the four stages of systems development.

4.2 Describe tasks to be accomplished to determine requirements.

4.3 Describe tasks to be accomplished to evaluate alternatives.

4.4 Describe tasks to be accomplished for systems design.

4.5 Describe tasks to be accomplished for systems implementation.

VARIETIES OF SYSTEMS DEVELOPMENT

The sequence of steps described in the previous section is a tried and true way of developing a computer system. Unfortunately, however, needs vary widely; therefore, for this process to be practically useful, it must vary as well. Hence, you will find many differences in the way that systems are actually developed. In particular, the activities performed at each step depend heavily on how the *programs* are acquired. Therefore, we will now consider the three common ways of obtaining computer programs and then discuss how the systems development process changes for each of these methods.

Acquiring Programs

Once we know what we want, we can acquire computer programs in three different ways. These methods are similar to the methods we use to purchase clothing.

Off-the-Shelf Programs

We can buy clothes off-the-shelf. We go to a store, try something on, and buy it if (a) it fits, (b) we like it, (c) we think it's worth the price, and (d) we can afford it. We can wear those clothes that same day, if we want. There is little risk in this approach, but we may not get a perfect fit. Also, we may not be able to find what we want, especially if our requirements are unique. If we are

Unique requirements

six feet tall, weigh 87 pounds, and want a puce silk shirt with a hissing rattlesnake on the back (see figure 4-6), we may not find something suitable.

Similar comments apply to programs. We can go to computer stores or other vendors (as the Blake personnel did in chapter 1), and try a program on. We can buy it if (a) it fits the need, (b) we like it, (c) we think it's worth the price, and (d) we can afford it. We can use that program the same day, if we want. There is little risk, but we may not get a perfect fit. Also, we may not find exactly what we want.

The comparison with clothes breaks down in one way, however. A single person wears an item of clothing, but many people may use a computer program. It's as if we have to buy a single set of clothes for many people in the company. For that reason, we sometimes have to compromise. Some users may have to accept characteristics they do not want, and others may have to forego characteristics they do want.

Altered Programs

A second way of buying clothes is to find something that nearly fits and have it altered. With this method we are more likely to obtain a better fit, but more risk and more time are involved. We will have to buy the clothes before the alteration; afterward, the clothes still may not fit. Further, it may take a week or two for the alteration to be done.

A similar approach can be taken with programs. We find programs that nearly fit the need and then have them *altered*. As with clothes, we can employ someone else to make the alterations or, if we have the necessary expertise, we can alter them ourselves. The alteration may or may not be successful. In addition, the alteration will take time, quite often measured in months rather than days.

Custom-Tailored Programs

A third way of obtaining clothes is to have them designed and manufactured specifically for our needs. We go to a designer or tailor and he or she constructs a garment just for us. If the designer/tailor is good, we are likely to obtain precisely what we need. This may, in fact, be the only way we can obtain the puce silk shirt.

There is, however, considerable risk in this approach. The designer may go over time and budget (or may not be able to give us reliable time and cost estimates). The designer may not understand our needs. Our needs may change while the garment is being made. The designer may make what he or she wants to make instead of what we need. The designer may be anxious to force us into the latest in fabrics or fashions when a conservative wool garment would be adequate. Further, conversations and fittings will take a considerable amount of time, both ours and the designer's.

Programs can also be *custom tailored*. To do this, the users meet with computer professionals and describe what they want. The computer professionals may be in-house employees, or they may work for a different firm that specializes in custom programming.

Since a typical system has many users who have different, sometimes conflicting, needs, these meetings may take a considerable amount of time. Furthermore, all of the risks in buying custom clothing exist for building custom programs as well. The cost of programming may exceed time and budget. The designers and programmers may never understand the need. The computer personnel may be anxious to force users into the latest in technology—whether or not such technology is required.

On the other hand, custom programming may be the only way to obtain what we need. We cannot buy programs that do not exist. If the need is great enough, custom programming may well be worth the time and expense. It depends on how important the programs are to the company. Sources of programs are summarized in figure 4-7.

Off-the-Shelf
     Buy and use programs as they are
Alteration
     Buy programs and alter them (or have them altered)
Custom Design
     Design and write programs to order

FIGURE 4-7

Sources of programs

Consider the steps in figure 4-1 again. During the requirements stage, most people will decide which of the three styles of program development they wish to pursue. For example, if they perceive that their needs are common enough that an off-the-shelf program is likely to be found, they will decide to take that approach. If their needs are unique, they will probably decide that custom programs will be necessary.

In some cases, the project team will not know if a program is available or not. In this case, they will likely begin by assuming that programs are available and search for them. In the event that programs cannot be found, either programs with alterations or custom programs may be necessary. If so, part of the requirements stage will need to be repeated to gain the additional information needed for program alteration or custom development.

Requirements Stage

Activities in the requirements determination step depend heavily on the program development approach to be taken. For an off-the-shelf program, the project team need only make a list of *functional specifications*. They need to know the basic capabilities the program must have. To acquire a program for alteration, the team must have functional specifications as well as specific requirement statements regarding the alteration. The team must describe outputs, inputs, storage requirements, format of reports and screens, and so forth, for the alteration.

Finally, for custom programs, the team must do an extensive and laborious investigation into requirements. The users must be contacted and interviewed and the requirements must be documented. Users must agree that the documentation is an accurate representation of their needs. Again, developing custom programs is a time-consuming and risky task. Companies should take this option only as a last resort. Adjustments to the requirements stage are summarized in figure 4-8.

Prototyping is a new approach toward requirements definition for custom programs that has been gaining popularity. Here, the systems development personnel build a prototype system that has all of the essential features of the real system. Users try the prototype and react to it. Once agreement has been reached that the prototype is acceptable, then the actual system is developed. In many ways, a prototype is similar to an architect's scale model.

Alternative Evaluation Stage

Alternative evaluation is easier for off-the-shelf programs than it is for programs that are to be altered. Cost and schedules for off-the-shelf programs are set by a fixed, reliable bid. Furthermore, since the programs exist and will not be changed, hardware requirements are easy to determine. There is much less risk that additional hardware will be unexpectedly needed.

Usually the procedures for using an off-the-shelf program are well defined. Good documentation exists (or the team can reject programs that do not have good documentation). The number of people needed to operate and use an off-the-shelf program can readily be determined.

Programs that will be altered are harder to evaluate. How much alteration will actually be required? It often appears to be easier to add a new feature than it turns out to be. For this reason, reliable cost and schedule estimates are

Off-the-shelf programs
    Define functional specifications
Altered programs
    Define functional specifications
    Determine detailed requirements for portion to be altered
Custom programs
    Define functional specifications
    Determine detailed requirements for entire system

FIGURE 4-8

Differences in determining specific requirements by source of program

harder to make. Procedures will be unknown to some extent, and difficulties may develop.

Clearly, custom programs are the hardest to evaluate. Cost and schedule estimates may be so far off that a project that appears to be cost justifiable may, in fact, turn out to be a very poor investment. The project may even become cost or schedule infeasible. In this case, the company will be in a very difficult position. It may be too late to switch to another alternative, but the chosen alternative becomes infeasible. This was the case for TYCON Construction in Chapter 1. Adjustments to this stage for various types of programs are summarized in figure 4-9.

Design Stage

There is considerable variability in design tasks for the different sources of programs.

Systems with Off-the-Shelf Programs

When a system is developed with off-the-shelf programs, the tasks of specifying hardware, programs, and data are concrete and easy. The hardware requirements will be readily available from the vendor; program design has been done (by the vendor); and data formats will, for the most part, be determined.

If the programs do provide for adjustable screen formats, there will be a need for these formats to be designed. If the programs can produce reports in variable forms, these, too, will need to be designed.

Procedures and organizational changes must be designed, even for off-the-shelf programs. Most likely the program vendor will provide both operations and user procedures, but changes or additions to them will need to be designed.

FIGURE 4-9

Considerations for evaluation by source of program

Off-the-shelf programs
    Cost and schedule established by fixed (and reliable) bid
Altered programs
    Greater risk due to uncertainty of scope of alteration
    Reliable bids more difficult to make
Custom programs
    Cost and schedules very difficult to determine
    May be wide variance between predictions and actuality
    System that appears feasible may in fact be infeasible (TYCON)

115

The procedures must be made to conform to the company's operational practices and management style.

Systems with Altered Programs

The design tasks for systems using off-the-shelf programs will also need to be done for systems with altered programs. In addition, the design for changes to the programs will need to be developed. This process will involve designing outputs such as screens and reports. Inputs will need to be defined and the program processing activities specified. Specifications for the additional hardware that may be required for the alteration will also have to be developed.

Systems with Custom Programs

Systems in which the programs are developed from scratch require extensive design. In addition to the design tasks described for off-the-shelf programs, reports, screens, files, and program structures must all be designed. The specifications for hardware will need to be developed.

The design stage is critical for custom programs. For this reason, companies often choose to hold design reviews, during which technical personnel evaluate each others' work. The hope of such reviews is that errors or omissions will be detected before the construction begins. Such mistakes are much cheaper to correct during design than during or after construction. Reference [118] provides an excellent discussion of program design tasks. Differences in design activity by type of program are summarized in figure 4-10.

Implementation Stage

Activities in the implementation stage change dramatically depending on the type of program. Whereas implementation can be brief for off-the-shelf programs, it can take months or years for custom programs.

Systems with Off-the-Shelf Programs

Implementing systems that use off-the-shelf programs can be quite easy. There is little construction to be done. Company data must be obtained and initial files constructed; procedures need to be documented and users trained.

Testing for such a system involves verifying that the programs and hardware operate as advertised. Assuming that the programs are not new and have been used extensively by others, there should be few surprises. New programs, however, may not operate as advertised. Using the clothing comparison, pants that are not supposed to shrink may in fact shrink. The project team should detect such a situation before the system is installed.

Installing a system with off-the-shelf programs is a matter of training and coordinating the users. There may be surprises, such as those that occurred at Blake, but there should be few major problems. As the users employ the system, they may wish to make adjustments to screen or report formats.

Systems with Altered Programs

Implementation of systems with altered programs is somewhat more difficult than implementation of systems with off-the-shelf programs. The same tasks must be accomplished, but the alterations must also be constructed and tested. Then installation proceeds.

There is more risk with these systems; a serious error may be found. Consequently, the project team should allow more time for rework and correction.

Off-the-shelf programs
    Obtain hardware specifications
    Obtain program specifications
    Adjust file, screen, report formats (if necessary and possible)
    Design procedures
    Develop job descriptions and organizational structure
Altered programs
    Same as for off-the-shelf, plus:
        Adjust hardware specifications for changed programs (if
        necessary)
        Design program changes
        Design changes to data (files, screens, reports)
Custom programs
    Determine hardware requirements
    Design program structures
    Design data structures
    Design procedures
    Develop job descriptions, organizational structure, training needs

F I G U R E 4 - 1 0

Tasks for systems design by source of program

Systems with Custom Programs

Systems with custom programs require an extensive implementation period. Programs must be written and tested. Hardware must be installed, and there may be a need for more hardware than originally planned. Data files need to be constructed. There is a possibility that data design errors may have been made. If so, corrections will be required.

Testing of systems with custom programs must be extensive. Since the system has never been used, many errors are likely. It is exceedingly difficult to write programs with few errors. Furthermore, the needs of the users may have been misunderstood, and, when the users see the system, they may conclude that it needs major changes, just as custom clothes may have features that the users never wanted. (It may also be that the users did not identify these needs. When they see the system, however, they may say something like, "But that's obvious!")

Assuming the system has been carefully tested, installation need not be more difficult than with other types of systems. In fact, it may be easier to resolve installation problems, because the builders of the system are available.

The greater risk involved in custom programming, however, means that there is a significant chance of a major problem. None of the system has been used before. The company is essentially in the research and development mode, but some aspect of the company's needs is being placed on the line. Hence, implementation of such a system is always a nerve-wracking experience. Stress can be very intense.

If requirements have been carefully stated and understood; if an appropriate alternative has been selected; if design has been accurately done; if quality construction has been accomplished in accordance with the design; and if testing has been thorough, then a successful installation can result. That sentence is a long one, however, with many *ifs*. In short, it's a gamble.

Differences in the implementation stage by type of program are summarized in figure 4-11.

117

Off-the-shelf programs
    Coordinate user activities
    Implementation can be easy
Altered programs
    Construct alterations
    Test alterations carefully
    Allow extra time for corrections
Custom programs
    Construction may be difficult
    Extensive testing required
    Plan for problems and delays during installation

F I G U R E   4 - 1 1

Adjustments to tasks for implementation
by source of program

QUESTIONS

4.6 Explain the meaning of the terms *off-the-shelf programs, altered programs,* and *custom programs.*

4.7 How do activities in the requirements stage differ for development of systems using the three kinds of programs named in question 4.6?

4.8 How do activities in the evaluation stage differ for development of systems using the three kinds of programs named in question 4.6?

4.9 How do activities in the design stage differ for development of systems using the three kinds of programs named in question 4.6?

4.10 How do activities in the implementation stage differ for development of systems using the three kinds of programs named in question 4.6?

HORIZON ARTIST SUPPLY

So far, this chapter has described the systems development process in abstract terms. To help you relate this process to reality, the remaining portion of this chapter will describe the experience of one company that implemented a new system.

The Company

Horizon Artist Supply is a mail-order company that sells materials for artists and craftspeople. Horizon provides a discount to its customers by issuing a portion of its profits as dividends at year-end. Each dividend, or refund, is a percent of the total amount purchased by a customer during the year. For example, assume that profits are 10 percent of sales. If a customer orders $250 worth of merchandise during the year, his or her refund will be $25.

In 1979, Horizon experienced severe growing pains. Their customer base of about 250,000 was growing at the rate of about 30,000 per year. Sales were $3.5 million—up nearly 300 percent from $1.2 million in just three years. There were 6000 items in inventory. All orders were processed manually. The backlog of orders was growing. It sometimes took a month to add a new customer to the customer files.

FIGURE 4-12

Horizon Artist Supply order form

To place an order, a customer filled out an order form like the one shown in figure 4-12. The customer wrote his or her name, address, and customer number. Then he or she listed the quantity and items ordered. All goods had to be prepaid, so the customer calculated the amount of the bill and sent in a check with the order.

When Horizon received the order, a clerk checked the item numbers and prices and recalculated the total cost. He or she also checked the customer number and recorded a new address if appropriate. If the order was correct, or at least nearly correct, it went to the warehouse, where the goods were picked from inventory. All the items in stock were shipped to the customer. Items that were out of stock were back-ordered by Horizon, and the customer's order

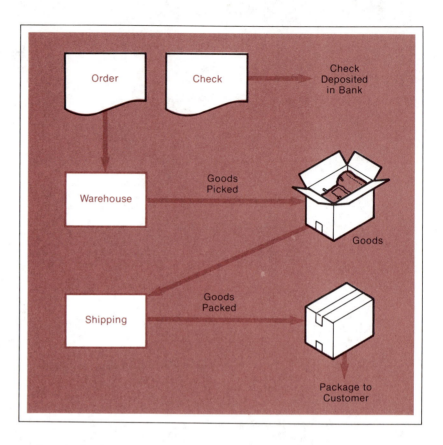

FIGURE 4-13

Processing of an order at Horizon Artist
Supply

went into the back-order file. When the back-ordered goods arrived, they were shipped to the customer (see figure 4-13).

As you might imagine, all sorts of errors and problems developed. Customers often made mistakes when ordering. Sometimes the customer number was in error; sometimes the item numbers were wrong. Very often customers made errors in arithmetic when they calculated their bills and sent checks made out for the wrong amount. If the check amount was too high, the customer received a credit; if it was too low, the customer was billed for the difference.

Horizon's back-order file had grown so much that buyers did not know what quantities to order. They often ordered 100 units of an item only to discover that 150 units were back-ordered and orders were still coming in. To prevent this situation from occurring, some buyers ordered very large quantities. Then warehouse space became a problem. The cost of carrying the large inventory reduced company profits. Customers complained about smaller dividends.

To be fair, this manual system was designed when Horizon had fewer than 50,000 customers and did about $500,000 in annual sales with 1000 products. It worked fine then, but it was no longer suitable. However, management had to spend so much time coping with the day-to-day problems that they had not found time to devise a new and better system.

In addition to these problems, Horizon was having trouble with their mailing list. They had hired a company that provided computer services (called a *computer service bureau*) to produce the mailing labels for the annual catalog and to compute and print the annual dividend checks. Once a week, Horizon sent data about new customers and address changes for existing customers to the computer service bureau. This data was supposed to be incorporated into the mailing list. Horizon also sent a list of customer orders to the service bureau once a week. The service bureau was supposed to use this data to keep the year-to-date sales total for each customer. At year-end, this figure was used to compute and produce the dividend checks.

In 1979, Horizon had a 32 percent return on their annual catalog! Nearly one-third of the addresses were incorrect. Furthermore, 17 percent of the dividend checks were either incorrect or sent to the wrong address. Horizon had repeatedly discussed this problem with the service bureau in previous years. The bureau was either unwilling or unable to improve the accuracy of the output.

In early 1980, Horizon's board of directors decided to investigate the possibility of acquiring their own computer. They hoped to be able to improve the accuracy of the mailing list. They also hoped that the computer could be used to find better ways of controlling inventory and processing orders. A committee consisting of an accountant, a buyer, and an inventory supervisor was formed.

The Computer Committee

The first meeting of the computer committee occurred in early April, 1980. Within a few minutes, the members realized that none of them knew anything about computers, nor did they know anyone at Horizon who did. Consequently, the committee decided that the first order of business was to hire someone who did. They placed the ad shown in figure 4-14 in two local newspapers. One of the committee members said, "Let's place it under *P* for *programmer*," so they did.

They had four applicants. The first two were unsuitable. One wanted part-time work, and the other was inexperienced. The third had been a programmer for several years. He talked very impressively about the job he had done building an "online bill of materials processor" for a large manufacturing company. Unfortunately, none of the committee members knew what that meant. (You will, before you finish this course.) They weren't especially impressed because they didn't want to do any manufacturing, anyway. This programmer told them that he had experienced great success with a Hewlett-Packard 3000® computer and that that was what they should acquire. With the HP 3000, he would be able to develop the programs they needed.

WANTED

A programmer to select a computer and write programs for a mail order retail company. Salary negotiable depending on experience. Send resume to P.O. Box Z, care of this newspaper. An equal opportunity employer.

FIGURE 4-14

Ad for a programmer placed by Horizon Artist Supply

The fourth person, John Abrams, did not actually apply for the job. He was an independent, free-lance consultant. He wanted to sell them his services to develop the data processing department and systems. John had an impressive record of accomplishments in a variety of businesses, but the committee wasn't looking for a consultant. They nearly decided not to invite him for an interview. However, since they had had only three other respondents, they didn't have much to lose. He was invited.

The interview with John Abrams went as follows:

Committee Chairperson: *John, we're not actually looking for a consultant. As I said on the phone, we've talked with a good many applicants. We think we've found two or three possibilities out of a dozen applicants. However, since you're so interested, we decided to spend an hour with you. What can you do for us?*

(John didn't believe a word of this. He could tell from their ad that they didn't know much about computer systems. He also knew that programmers were in short supply. He doubted that they had had a dozen applicants, if that many. He judged these opening comments to be the bravado of someone who didn't know what he was doing but was coping as best he could.)

John: *Look, let me come right to the point. It's obvious that you have a good business. The outlook for your company is very bright. You committee members are probably very good at your business specialties. But it's equally obvious that you don't know very much about data processing.*

You ran an ad for a programmer to select a computer and develop programs for a mail-order business. First of all, programmers don't usually select computers. Someone called a data processing manager does that, with the assistance of people called systems analysts. So what you really want is a data processing manager and possibly other data processing personnel.

Second, you say you want to develop programs. What you really want to do is develop something called a computer system. Programs are only one of five components of such a system. The other components are hardware, data, procedures, and trained people. Are you going to have a programmer develop those?

Finally, how do you know you want a computer? Have you done a feasibility study to see if a computer can solve your problems? Do you know how much a computer costs? Do you know how big a computer you want? Do you know how long it will take you to develop the business computer systems?

Chairperson: *Well, John, it's true we aren't experts at data processing. You may have a valid point or two. We were thinking that a Hewlett-Packard 3000 computer might be what we need.*

John: *The HP 3000 is a good machine. However, there is a great deal of computer hardware to choose from. It's difficult to make a good choice until you know specifically what you want the computer to do. There might be better computers for you.*

Finding programs may well turn out to be more important than finding the hardware. *Do you know if there are suitable programs that you can buy off-the-shelf? Can you tailor existing programs to your needs? Or do you have to develop your own programs from scratch?*

This conversation continued for an hour or so. Finally, John brought it to a close with this statement:

John: *Let me summarize my position. I'll help you decide if a computer system is for you. If it is, I'll lead you through the process of acquiring the staff and equipment. I'll help you develop the computer system you need. It will likely take a year or more to get this done. My bill for this service will depend on the amount of time it takes me. The more you do, the less my services will cost. Based on my past experience, I'd say it will probably cost between $10,000 and $25,000.*

If we come to an agreement, I will agree to structure it so that you can terminate my services during the management review at the end of any stage of work in case you're dissatisfied. Before we sign anything, why don't I give you a two-day course on how to develop a business computer system? I'll charge you $1000, which is less than my usual fee, for two days of instruction. You can listen to me and hear my philosophy before you make any larger commitment.

After John left, the committee discussed his proposal for some time. They liked what he said. He seemed to know what he was doing, but $25,000 seemed a lot to pay for nothing more than advice. Finally, they decided to hire John to teach the two-day course and then they would think about what to do after that.

"Well," said the accountant with a chuckle, *"we could always run an ad under* D *for* Data Processing Manager, *or maybe under* M *for* Manager, Data Processing.*"

SYSTEMS DEVELOPMENT AT HORIZON

The next week, John Abrams presented the two-day seminar at Horizon. In addition to the computer committee, all the vice-presidents and department managers were invited.

The course had two parts. In the first part, the components of a computer system were summarized. This discussion was very similar to the material presented in chapter 2 of this book. In the second part of the course, the process of developing a computer system was considered. This part of the course was similar to the first part of this chapter.

At the conclusion of the course, John suggested that, if Horizon did proceed with a systems development project, they should form a steering committee. This committee would be composed of senior-level managers who would set the general strategy for computer systems development and use and who would approve work at the end of each stage of the systems project. John suggested that Horizon form this committee if the results of the feasibility study were positive.

At the end of the two-day course, the project committee felt that they had a much better idea of what developing computer systems involved. Because of their new knowledge, however, they also felt more vulnerable.

The committee considered their options. They were convinced they needed some outside expertise to help them. They didn't know whether to hire a data processing manager, hire John as a consultant, or hire another consultant. They wanted to hire a data processing manager, but they didn't know what kind of person to look for. If they hired the wrong person, it might take a long time to discover and then correct their error. Considerable money might be wasted.

They finally decided to hire John, but they hedged. They hired him just to help them with the first step, determining requirements. After that, they would decide whether or not to hire him for more assistance. John agreed to these terms and the next week the requirements stage began.

The Horizon Requirements Stage

The first task was to form a project team. John suggested that the team be composed of the computer committee (accountant, buyer, and inventory supervisor) and himself. The board of directors approved this suggestion, and the three people were released from their normal duties to participate in the computer project.

Neither John nor the Horizon personnel knew whether off-the-shelf programs were available to solve Horizon's problems. They decided to examine requirements down to a level of detail that would enable them to determine whether suitable off-the-shelf programs were available. If they were not available, then portions of the requirements study would need to be repeated to gain additional details.

For five days, John and the computer committee visited Horizon personnel in the departments that seemed to be having the greatest problems. They wanted to gain an understanding of these problems and define them. They also wanted to gain a general sense of where computer systems might be useful. At the end of this period, they wrote a report documenting their findings. It had seven major points:

1. There was a need to keep an accurate file of customer names, addresses, and year-to-date purchases. This file was needed for the catalog and other mailings as well as for dividend computation. This file needed to be updated accurately whenever a customer moved or a new customer ordered. The committee learned that the service bureau had not been able to keep an accurate file because their own staff made too many keying errors when inputting changes or posting sales to the file.

   Accurate customer numbers were crucial. If a customer misstated his or her number on an order, or if it was incorrectly keyed, sales would be posted to the wrong customer. A more accurate way to input customers numbers had to be found.

2. All of the problems regarding dividends related to inaccuracies in the customer file. If this file were accurate, producing dividend checks at year-end would be simple.

3. Purchasing and inventory personnel needed a list of items in inventory. This list should show item name, item number, name of the buyer responsible for purchasing the item, name of the vendor who supplied it, and

other data. Such a list was necessary because Horizon was adding about 100 items and deleting about 10 items a month. Several typewritten lists of items existed. Unfortunately, they often disagreed with one another. Consequently, orders were being taken for items no longer carried in stock and the purchasing department was buying items no longer listed in the catalog.

4. The most time-consuming part of processing an order was verifying prices and checking the computation of the amount due. Orders could be processed much faster if a computer system computed the amount due. Order processing personnel wanted to give the computer the customer number, the item number, and the quantity for each item on the order, and then have the computer calculate the amount due.

5. The manual records of the items in inventory were a mess. At the last physical check of inventory, nearly 70 percent of the counts were in error. Shipments had arrived but had never been entered in the inventory records. Goods had been shipped and billed but were never taken out of the records. A computer system to keep track of inventory would be very helpful. John remarked, however, that a computer system would be useless unless the inventory-management procedures in the warehouse were improved.

6. Orders were currently being filled in a chaotic manner. A picker took the customer's copy of the order and walked through the warehouse filling a basket with the items ordered. Whenever the picker couldn't find an item, it was marked for back order. Sometimes this was an error. The goods were actually in the inventory, but the picker didn't know where to find them. In this case, the item was back-ordered even though it was available.

Much of this chaos could be eliminated if a computer system processed the orders and generated picking slips. The system could keep an inventory file and determine whether or not each item was available. If an item was not available, it would be marked "back-ordered" on the picking slip. The picker would not waste time looking for it. The computer could also generate back-order recommendations for buyers and reduce the number of unnecessary back-orders.

7. The computer could probably be used for other business functions, such as payroll, accounts payable, and general ledger accounting. However, there were currently no major problems in those areas. Such applications could easily be deferred until the immediate problems were solved.

After the problems were defined and documented, the computer committee and John considered the feasibility of developing business computer systems to solve any or all of these problems. John stated that, from a technical standpoint, all of the problems could be solved by computer. He knew of several companies that were using computer systems to perform similar functions. Consequently, the technical feasibility was considered certain.

From cost and schedule standpoints, however, feasibility was not so easy to determine. The costs and dates for developing systems depended on how many of the problems were to be solved. After considerable discussion, the

Feasibility Study

Phase	Systems to Be Developed
1	**Customer Master File System** including: Master file maintenance Purchase updates Dividends Mailing labels
2	**Inventory Master File System** **Inventory Accounting System** **Order Pricing System**
3	**Prepicking Order Processing System** including: Picking slip generation Back order management Order recommendations

FIGURE 4-15

Three phases for Horizon's systems development

committee decided to break the development into three phases, as shown in figure 4-15.

During phase 1, the customer master file and dividend systems would be developed. During phase 2, the inventory and pricing systems would be developed. The purposes of the inventory system would be to keep a master list of the items in inventory and to maintain a count of the items in stock, on back order, and so forth. The pricing system, given the item numbers and quantities, would then calculate the total amount due for each order. Phase 1 had to be completed prior to phase 2 because the pricing system needed accurate customer numbers for preparing invoices.

A prepicking order processing system would be developed during phase 3. The system would accept the customer number, the item number, and the quantity of each item ordered. From these inputs, it would produce a picking slip, show items on back order, and generate order recommendations for buyers. Phase 3 could be completed only after phases 1 and 2 were finished.

The cost and schedule of the phases depended very much on whether suitable programs could be found off-the-shelf, whether programs would need to be altered, or whether they would be custom developed. John suggested that the team be conservative when planning. "Let's assume," he said, "that all programs must be custom developed. If the project is feasible for this worst case, it will be feasible if we find programs to use or adapt."

Figure 4-16 shows cost estimates developed by the project team, assuming custom programming. The initial expense category includes the costs of hardware installation, program development, data conversion, procedure development, and training. It does not include the cost of hardware. Since the team assumed the hardware would be leased, cost of leasing was included as an operating expense.

Operating expenses shown in the figure include the costs of the leased hardware; program and data maintenance; operating personnel salaries; train-

Phase	Initial Expense	Annual Operating Expense
1	$100,000	$200,000
2	$275,000	$400,000
3	$600,000	$650,000

Assumptions:
1. Computer hardware is leased.
2. Growth in customers and sales is 10 percent per year.

FIGURE 4-16

Estimated costs of Horizon's computer systems

ing; and an allocation for overhead (a share of the expenses for lights, heating, buildings, taxes, and so forth). John explained that, if Horizon decided to buy computer hardware, the initial expenses would increase but the operating expenses would decrease.

As the team examined the costs, it became apparent that phase 1 by itself would not be cost justified. The cost was too great for the service; finding another service bureau would be a better solution. However, it appeared that both phases 2 and 3 would be cost justified if implemented in addition to phase 1.

Considering schedule, John said there was no realistic way that Horizon could hope to accomplish all three phases in the immediate future. Far too many tasks needed to be accomplished. Data processing personnel needed to be hired; the equipment needed to be selected and installed; and the other components of the systems needed to be developed. John predicted a disaster if all the problems were addressed at the onset.

After two days of thinking and discussing, the committee estimated that phase 1 would take about one year; phase 2 would take about 14 months; and phase 3 would take about two years. This estimate of phase 3 assumed that inventory personnel would make changes to their procedures on schedule. Thus, if Horizon started the project in May 1980, the earliest that all three phases could be finished would be July 1984 (see figure 4-17).

Management Approval

To summarize, the computer committee found that all three phases were feasible from a *technical* standpoint. However, phase 1 by itself could not be cost justified. Phase 1 followed by phase 2, or phase 1 followed by phases 2 and 3, could be cost justified. Finally, the phases were *schedule* feasible if Horizon

FIGURE 4-17

Timing of Horizon's systems development phases

could wait one year for phase 1, slightly over two years for phase 2, and about four years for phase 3.

The findings, phases, and results of the feasibility study were documented in a 15-page report. The report was sent to the board of directors, the president, and the vice-presidents. The board requested a meeting of top management and the project team. Basically, the board was pleased with the quality of the analysis and the work that had been done. They were disappointed that four years would be required for the company to have complete capability, but they observed that they had no choice. As one director said, "We have to proceed; let's just hope that not all of the programs must be developed from scratch."

Some managers tried to get the computer committee to reduce the estimates of time required for custom programming. However, John had forewarned the committee about such attempts, and they adamantly refused to give in. As John had said, "Nine women can't make a baby in one month, no matter how badly someone wants them to."

In the report to management, the computer committee did recommend formation of a steering committee. The board of directors thought this was an excellent idea. They suggested that the president and all the vice-presidents be involved initially. They also recommended that John Abrams be retained for the next phase of work and that the project team continue with its present members. With this preliminary work accomplished, the president instructed the team to proceed with development for phases 1 and 2. Phase 3 would be deferred until these phases were completed. The project team was instructed to report to the steering committee at the conclusion of the evaluation stage.

Detailed Requirements

According to figure 4-2, after the problem is defined, the next task is to determine specific requirements. If custom programs had to be developed, the requirements statements would need to be very detailed. In spite of their earlier assumption, however, the team hoped that suitable off-the-shelf or altered programs could be found. The team did not want to perform a detailed requirements study unless they had to. Consequently, at this point, the team changed course to assume that off-the-shelf or altered programs could be found.

Specifically, the team decided to determine the functions and features that they would need for both customer and inventory systems. They would not attempt to determine details such as screen formats, report layouts, and the like. John reminded the team, however, that if suitable programs could not be found off-the-shelf, then this work would need to be done later.

A sample of the functions and features required for the customer master file and dividend systems is shown in figure 4-18. These statements describe the general nature of the work to be done, but they do not provide the details that would be necessary to make alterations or develop custom programs.

When the abbreviated requirements were developed and documented, the team met with Horizon management and key users. Management wanted the users to attend so as to reduce the likelihood that a key function or feature would be omitted. The general conclusion of the meeting was that the requirements were fundamentally complete, and that the team should proceed to identify and evaluate alternatives. Management understood that requirements would have to be determined in greater detail if programs needed to be altered or custom developed.

1. Maintain records of every customer's name, number, address, phone, date of last order, date of last file change, amount of last dividend check, and total purchases to date for the current calendar year.
2. Add new customers to this file on a daily basis. Provide an edit report prior to master file update. Provide a change report. Print.
3. Modify customer's name, address, or phone number as required. Provide both edit and change reports.
4. Add amount of each order to year-to-date purchases. Correct this amount if returns are made.
5. Produce dividend checks on an annual basis. Provide both edit and change reports showing amount paid each customer and total amount paid.
6. Insert amount of dividend check into each customer's master file record.
7. Develop a method for ensuring that all changes to the customer file and all changes to amount purchased are made to the correct account.

FIGURE 4-18

Phase 1 and 2 requirements for customer
master file and dividend systems

QUESTIONS

4.11 Summarize the reasons that made Horizon decide they needed a computer system.

4.12 How should Horizon's ad have read to receive the help they actually needed?

4.13 What is the role of the steering committee?

4.14 Why did the team assume that custom programs would be needed when preparing the cost and schedule estimates?

4.15 When the project team determined the detailed requirements, they assumed that off-the-shelf programs could be found, yet when they were preparing cost and schedule estimates, they assumed that custom programs would be needed. Why did they make this switch?

The Horizon Alternative Evaluation Stage

Reminding the team of the five components in a computer system, John recommended that they begin their investigation with programs. Hardware is easier to find, he pointed out, but what good would it do to have the hardware picked out, if the necessary programs would not run on that equipment? Therefore, the team began to look for programs for both customer and inventory systems.

Programs

The project team members began by calling companies that had similar needs. They called other mail-order companies, as well as retailing companies with similar inventories. In addition, John brought in several catalogs of programs for the team to study. See reference [32].

One of the team members talked with Horizon's president who suggested that they call several companies belonging to their trade organization. These companies provided other leads. Finally, John contacted two hardware vendors and asked their sales representatives for assistance. The hardware salespeople were willing to cooperate because they knew that there would eventually be a hardware sale.

The team found that, although there were several programs available for keeping customer data, none of these programs would produce dividend checks at year-end. That particular requirement seemed to be unique to Horizon. In addition, only one of the available programs would be able to provide the potential for growth in number of customers that Horizon expected. This program was called CUSTOMER.

There were many more choices available for inventory processing. Two of them would provide all the capability that Horizon currently needed, and, with some alteration, might even be able to support the phase 3 requirements. These two programs were called ORD-INVENTORY and MAILORDER.

Hardware

The CUSTOMER program would run only on hardware supplied by vendor X. This vendor had a large number of computer systems, which were arranged in families. For example, one *family of computers* was the System 25, with Models I, II, and III. John explained that it usually is not hard to convert from one computer to another in the same family. Since Horizon planned to expand its data processing activity during phase 3 and beyond, John recommended that they pick a computer that met their current needs and that was in the low end of a family. Then, as their needs expanded, they could switch to the Model II or III. If they picked the top model of a less powerful family, they would have to switch to another family or even to another vendor's computer as their needs expanded. This approach would likely be time consuming and expensive.

The ORD-INVENTORY program would run on hardware available from either vendor X or vendor Y. Vendor Y had only one family of computers, but it appeared that Horizon's needs could be met by one of the computers in the low end of the family. Thus, computer equipment from either vendor X or Y seemed feasible.

The alternative inventory program, MAILORDER, would operate only on hardware from vendor Y. No version of MAILORDER existed for vendor X hardware. The vendor said that a version could be developed for vendor X computers, but there would be an additional cost. John recommended that the team not consider this possibility as a realistic alternative. "Let's not be their guinea pig," he said. Figure 4-19 summarizes the program and hardware alternatives.

Data and Procedures

As the project team discussed the data and procedures for the new systems, they discovered that data and procedures were nearly the same for all of the hardware and program alternatives. Data requirements did not change from one computer to another. Consequently, they decided not to include data and procedures as part of the alternatives to be presented to management. They would be designed and developed later.

Personnel

The last of the five components of a computer system is trained people. The team decided that three groups of personnel would be necessary: systems development personnel, operations personnel, and data entry personnel.

System	Program	Hardware
Customer	CUSTOMER plus alteration	Vendor X
Inventory	ORD-INVENTORY	Vendor X or Y
Inventory	MAILORDER	Vendor Y

FIGURE 4-19

Horizon's alternative programs and hardware

Two alternatives were possible for the systems development personnel. Either they could be permanent or the systems development expertise could be obtained via temporary or contract personnel. Horizon could hire temporary help themselves, or they could contract for development with an independent company (sometimes called a *software house*).

In addition to systems developers, data entry personnel needed to be hired, and both they and the users needed to be trained. (Data entry personnel would do the bulk data entry; users would do some, less voluminous, data entry and would also process orders and make queries of the data.) The team thought that four data entry employees would be required for both systems. Eight to ten users in customer service, order processing, the warehouse, and shipping would need to be trained.

Finally, operators would be required to run the new computer. The team decided that, initially, Horizon would need only eight hours per day of operation. John recommended that two operators be hired. A third, backup, operator could be obtained by training one of the data entry clerks to run the computer.

Horizon's Organizational Alternatives

The team proposed two alternative organizations, as shown in figure 4-20. In the organization shown in figure 4-20*a*, the data processing manager supervises three groups: systems development, computer operations, and data entry. The systems development staff would be permanent Horizon employees. In the second alternative (figure 4-20*b*), only the operations and data entry groups have permanent employees. The second organizational alternative assumes that systems development personnel are hired on a temporary or contract basis.

The Complete Alternatives

Considering these facts together with the organizational charts shown in figure 4-20, the project team developed four basic alternatives, listed in figure 4-21.

Alternative 1 assumes that Horizon buys CUSTOMER and ORD-INVENTORY program products. CUSTOMER would need to be altered to include the capability to produce dividend checks. Hardware would be purchased from vendor X, and either of the organizations shown in figure 4-20 could be used.

Alternative 2 assumes that ORD-INVENTORY is purchased and that hardware from vendor Y is acquired. Since CUSTOMER does not operate on vendor Y hardware, Horizon would need to develop their own programs for

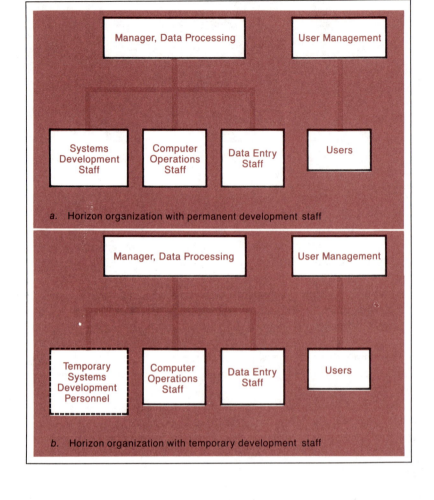

a. Horizon organization with permanent development staff

b. Horizon organization with temporary development staff

FIGURE 4-20

Two alternative organizations proposed for Horizon

customer processing. Alternative 3 is the same as alternative 2, except MAILORDER is purchased instead of ORD-INVENTORY. Both of these alternatives could use either of the organizational structures in figure 4-20.

Alternative 4 assumes that Horizon custom-writes programs for both the customer and inventory applications. Hardware could be acquired from either vendor, but only the organization in Figure 4-20a would be feasible. The team believed that, with so much custom programming, permanent staff would be necessary.

This discussion of alternatives has abbreviated some actions that would need to be taken. Realistically, more details would be addressed. Figure 4-22 lists some of the other factors that the Horizon project team considered.

Evaluation of Alternatives

The Horizon project team decided to perform an informal cost/benefit analysis. They decided to develop estimates of costs for each of the alternatives and then to compare those costs to benefits. The accounting department had already developed estimates of the amount of money that was being wasted because of

	Programs	Hardware	Organization
1	CUSTOMER (with alteration) ORD-INVENTORY	Vendor X	*a* or *b*
2	Custom Customer ORD-INVENTORY	Vendor Y	*a* or *b*
3	Custom Customer MAILORDER	Vendor Y	*a* or *b*
4	Custom Customer Custom Inventory	Vendor X or Y	*a* only

F I G U R E   4 - 2 1

Horizon alternatives

F I G U R E   4 - 2 2

Considerations when developing systems
alternatives

System Component	Issues Considered
Hardware	Type of CPU Amount of main memory Type and amount of tape, direct access, and other storage equipment Type and number of terminals Type and number of data entry devices
Programs	Number and type needed Off-the-shelf, alteration, or custom Language choice Expandability
Data	Number of files and rough format Type of data organization Data input media Report formats

Procedures	Users
	    Input activities
	    Use of outputs
	    Data editing and control responsibilities
	Operations
	    How to use equipment
	    How to operate systems
	    Backup and recovery
	    Control responsibilities

ineffective inventory control (duplicate items, sales lost due to out-of-stock conditions, wasted labor hours, and so forth). These estimates could be used as a rough guide for the value of the new system. In addition to these tangible benefits, there would be intangible benefits, such as better customer service, more satisfied customers, and better information for management decisions. The team decided not to attempt to place dollar values on these benefits, but just to list them.

Thus, the team decided to present to management the cost estimates of the alternatives, the accounting department's assessment of the value of improving inventory control, and a summary of intangible benefits. Management could use this data for a subjective decision, or they could request further evaluation using present value and other financial management techniques as described in reference [31].

The results of the cost study are presented in figure 4-23. The annual operational costs are the same for all four alternatives. The development cost of alternative 3 is the lowest at $175,000 and that of alternative 4 is the highest at $230,000. Observe that the CUSTOMER program with alterations would cost $40,000, whereas, according to the team estimate, only $50,000 would be needed for custom development.

The accounting department had estimated that over $600,000 could be saved in one year alone from better inventory management. This figure did not include the benefit of more accurate customer data, but clearly some benefit would accrue. Thus, any of the alternatives would appear to be a desirable investment.

Management Review

The team documented their findings and presented the results to management. Management was pleased with both the quality and the direction of the work. During the meeting, costs were discussed, but management also wanted to know about risks and schedule. The team stated that alternative 1 would definitely have the lowest risk because it involved the least amount of new development. Considering schedule, alternative 1 would be quickest; roughly eight months would be needed to develop the customer and inventory systems. Alternatives 2 and 3 would both take about a year, and alternative 4 would require slightly more than two years.

One manager wondered why these estimates varied so much from the initial estimates (see figure 4-16). The team explained the initial estimates had been made conservatively, assuming that programs would have to be custom developed. With off-the-shelf and altered programs, however, the team believed the new estimates to be realistic.

Management had no trouble deciding how to proceed. Given the lower risk and quicker schedule, alternative 1 was chosen even though it was more expensive than alternatives 2 or 3. As one manager remarked, the $15,000 difference between alternatives 1 and 3 was insignificant in light of the savings achieved by having the system in place four months earlier.

Considering organizational alternatives, the Horizon management wanted to proceed slowly. Their attitude was, "Let's find a qualified manager of data processing, and hire the needed operations and data entry personnel, but wait to acquire permanent systems development personnel. We may need to do it later, but let's try development with a software house first."

Alternative	Development Costs		Annual Operational Costs
1	ORD-INVENTORY	$ 30,000	
	CUSTOMER	30,000	
	Alterations	10,000	
	Computer X	120,000	
	Total	$190,000	$ 490,000
2	ORD-INVENTORY	$ 30,000	
	Custom Customer	50,000	
	Computer Y	100,000	
	Total	$180,000	$490,000
3	MAILORDER	$ 25,000	
	Custom Customer	50,000	
	Computer Y	100,000	
	Total	$175,000	$490,000
4	Custom Customer	$ 80,000	
	Custom Inventory	50,000	
	Computer Y	100,000	
	Total	$230,000	$490,000

FIGURE 4-23

Summary of costs for Horizon alternatives

QUESTIONS

4.16 Why did the team begin with programs when investigating alternatives?

4.17 What is a family of computers? How is the selection of a computer influenced by computer families?

4.18 Why didn't John want to hire the MAILORDER vendor to convert MAILORDER for use on hardware from vendor X? Would such a decision ever make sense?

4.19 Describe the two different organizational possibilities for Horizon.

4.20 Comment on the recommendation of alternative 1. Do you agree? Under what circumstances would one of the other alternatives make sense?

The Horizon Design Stage

During the design stage, specifications for each of the five system components are developed. For components that must be purchased, the procurement process is started. Starting the purchasing process during design is especially important for long lead-time components such as hardware.

We will consider design for each of the five components of the Horizon customer and inventory systems. First, however, the team had more requirements work to do.

The CUSTOMER package of programs that Horizon was going to purchase met all their requirements except for one: it would not produce dividend checks. Consequently, programs to provide this service needed to be written. Before that could be done, however, requirements for dividend check processing had to be determined.

The project team visited both the customer service and the accounting departments to obtain requirements for dividend check processing. They identified the outputs that were needed, the inputs that had to be provided to produce those outputs, and the special controls that were required because checks were to be produced. The team also visited with the vendor of CUSTOMER to ensure that the necessary alterations could be feasibly done.

Once the requirements were identified and approved by the users, the team proceeded with the design stage.

People

The project team decided to focus initially on finding critical personnel. They knew it might take some time, and they wanted to start personnel searches before proceeding with other design tasks. The Horizon project plan is summarized in figure 4-24.

As it turned out, finding the data processing manager was easier than expected. Horizon interviewed five different people for the job and eventually selected one of their own employees, Anne Franklin. Anne had worked both as a computer operator and as a data entry person in a previous job. She had come to Horizon as a supervisor in the customer service department. Consequently, she had the right background, she was known to be a reliable and efficient worker, and she was immediately available.

Anne was able to switch from her job in customer service to the project team within two weeks. After that, she was gradually given more responsibility and, within several more weeks, she became leader of the project team. John worked with Anne to develop job descriptions for the computer operations and data entry personnel. Once these job descriptions were finished, a personnel firm was engaged to locate potential employees. The lead operator and the supervisor of data entry needed to be hired first. Other personnel could be hired later, as the project entered the implementation phase.

Within a few weeks, Paul Brooks was hired as lead operator. He was scheduled to begin work for Horizon four weeks before the equipment was to arrive. This schedule gave him time to become familiar with Horizon's needs and to obtain vendor training. Anne worked with Paul to hire the second operator.

Next, Anne hired the supervisor of data entry. Other data entry personnel were hired by Anne, working with the new supervisor.

Hardware

To order hardware, the project team needed to develop specifications, negotiate with vendors, and sign an order. Using current and expected workloads, the project team consulted with the vendors of the CUSTOMER and ORD-INVENTORY programs to determine specifications. The specifications included the model of CPU, the amount of main memory, the amount of disk storage, the number of terminals, and other similar characteristics.

Given the specifications, Horizon began negotiations. They hired an attorney who specialized in computer law to finalize negotiations and write adjustments

MICROS

Selecting Your Own Computer

Confusion. So many choices. How can you decide among all of the alternatives? The **systems development process** will help you, just as it has helped other users make better decisions when buying larger computer systems.

Which microcomputer should I buy?

How important is the vendor's name?

Should I buy color capability?

What printer do I need?

What if I want graphics?

What do I need a diskette for?

Should I do word processing?

What should I do when I get the computer home?

What programs do I need?

Where should I buy the computer?

Do I need to be a programmer?

How much should I pay?

What's an electronic spreadsheet? What can I do with one?

SOME FIRST-TIME USER QUESTIONS

A familiar retail computer store—the starting point for most personal microcomputer users.

People buy microcomputers for many reasons. Some want to manage personal records, some want to forecast stock prices, some want to educate their children, some want to manage farm records, and on and on. Experience has shown that, regardless of the eventual application, there is a common process for

developing the system. This process has four basic stages: *defining requirements*, *evaluating alternatives*, *designing components*, and *implementing the system*. This photo essay reviews the process and shows how it applies to the development of a word processing system.

Jennifer Anderson thinks a word processing system may help her in her schoolwork. First, she should determine her **requirements**.

Once Jennifer knows what she needs, she should **evaluate alternatives**, starting with software.

To use her new system effectively, she must **design** procedures. She takes a class to learn what procedures are necessary.

Implementation—Jennifer is able to use the system to improve her schoolwork and even to simplify her life.

DEFINING REQUIREMENTS

The needs the system must meet are determined during requirements definition. All five components of the system need to be considered: hardware, programs, data, procedures, and people. For example, the *hardware* may need to weigh less than 50 pounds, or *programs* may be needed that will print a special report. There may also be requirements for *data*, such as that the system have sufficient storage for a month's worth of orders. An example of a requirement involving *procedures* is the need to process every order within 24 hours. A requirement involving *people* might be that the use of the system be within the abilities of the personnel currently in the organization.

Defining requirements is important regardless of the application. For example, if the system is to keep records of farm production, how will it be used? What specifically is needed? If the system is to be used for education, for what level of education is it intended? For how many children? Is color necessary? If the system is to be used to manage business records, which records? General ledger? Inventory? Fixed assets? Cash flow? Within each of these categories there are many questions to answer.

Word Processing for Jennifer Anderson Jennifer Anderson is a college student majoring in English literature. Jennifer writes many papers for her classes, and she thinks a word processing system would be useful to her.

This farmer wants to keep records of differences in cattle growth for different types of feed.

These children can learn arithmetic and other subjects using computer-assisted instruction (CAI) on a microcomputer.

Someone here needs help in managing
business records.

Jennifer obviously has requirements for
word processing.

Jennifer talked with her parents about it, and they said they would provide up
to $1000 to buy one.

Jennifer's friend Terry Carlson majors in computer information systems.
Jennifer asked Terry to help her find a system, and he agreed. "First," Terry
said, "make a list of the features you want."

Jennifer thought about it and produced the following list of characteristics:

1. It should be easy to use.
2. The display screen should be easy to read.
3. It should be able to produce papers up to 50 pages long.
4. It should generate dark, legible print.
5. It should cost less than $2500.

When Jennifer showed this list to Terry, he asked her if she wanted to do
anything besides word processing. Did she want to program the computer?
(No, not really.) Did she need graphics capability? (Not if it costs extra.) Did
she want an electronic spreadsheet? (Didn't know what that is. Maybe.) Did
she want to do any business processing, such as accounting or budgeting? (Not
really.) With this list of answers, Terry said, "Let's go see what's available.
We'll visit several stores, but, remember, don't buy the first thing you see."

EVALUATING ALTERNATIVES

During evaluation, alternatives are identified and one of the alternatives is selected. In most cases, alternatives for hardware and programs are considered. Sometimes, too, there can be alternative data organizations, procedures, or types of personnel who will use the system. All feasible alternatives should be considered and evaluated.

Programs can be acquired in three ways. These ways are similar to the ways that clothes can be purchased. First, programs can be acquired off-the-shelf. The user visits computer stores and tries various packages. If one is found that meets the need, it is purchased. As with off-the-shelf clothes, off-the-shelf programs can be used the same day they are purchased.

A second way of acquiring programs is to buy a package and alter it. This method is similar to buying a suit or dress and having it altered. As with clothes, program alteration takes time and involves some risk. After the alteration, the program may still not fit the need.

The third way of acquiring programs is to have them custom designed and constructed, just as one might buy tailored clothes. This alternative takes the most time and involves considerable risk. The programs may be more expensive than anticipated, and they may not meet the need. Further, custom programs usually have errors, because it is nearly impossible to produce error-free programs. Still, for very unique applications, custom development may be the only way that suitable programs can be acquired.

Off-the-shelf clothes are least expensive and can be worn the same day they are purchased.

Alteration of clothes takes time but produces a better fit.

Programs can also be bought and altered.

. . . and off-the-shelf software can also be used the same day.

Custom-tailored clothes may fit, but they certainly cost more.

Professional software development teams can produce custom-designed programs.

Computer magazines provide sources of software alternatives.

Some software alternatives—note the combining, or "bundling," of training materials with software.

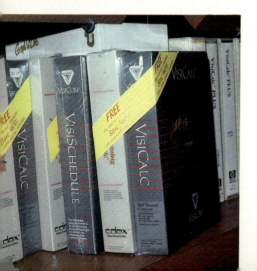

Most often, off-the-shelf programs are used in microcomputer systems. For tasks like word processing, electronic spreadsheets, database management, and business graphics, there are dozens of alternative programs available off-the-shelf.

When alternatives are being evaluated, the best strategy is to start with the most limiting component. For micros, there is more hardware available than there are suitable programs. Therefore, program alternatives should be considered before hardware alternatives. Once suitable programs are found, then hardware to run those programs can be located.

For micros, the evaluation of alternatives usually comes down to identifying the cheapest alternative that meets requirements. Sometimes intangibles, such as vendor reputation or proximity of service, are also considered.

Jennifer Anderson's Evaluation   During their visits to stores, Jennifer tried six or eight different systems. Terry told Jennifer to bring one of her papers with her and to plan on typing part of it using each system. Jennifer was glad she did this. She was surprised to find wide differences in capability. Apparently, the vendors meant many different things by the term *word processing*.

Terry explained to Jennifer that she needed to buy both hardware and programs. She should look for word processing programs that she liked first. Once she found a suitable word processing package, she could select hardware.

Jennifer followed Terry's advice and tried several word processing programs. She found the following packages acceptable: WORDSTAR, WORD/80, and SELECT.

Next, she looked for microcomputers that could run those packages. Terry explained that she would need the microcomputer, a floppy disk drive, a monitor (which is like a TV screen), a keyboard, a printer, and cables. Jennifer found that hardware was packaged differently. For some micros, the disk was included with the CPU; for others, it was separate. For some systems, the keyboard and monitor were one unit; for others, they were sold separately.

There was a wide choice in printers. Although Jennifer liked the full-character daisy wheel printers the best, she thought that a dot-matrix printer would provide acceptable quality. Generally, dot-matrix printers were cheaper, and she was told that they could also produce simple graphics if she ever wanted them.

The systems Jennifer tried are summarized in the chart on the next page. The cheapest systems were not adequate for her needs. The Commodore 64 would not allow 80 columns to be displayed on a screen. Jennifer found this unacceptable. Further, the monitor screen of the Osborne was too small. Jennifer had difficulty reading it.

Jennifer liked the remaining three systems. Although she thought WORD-STAR, WORD/80, and SELECT were acceptable packages, she liked WORD/80 and SELECT the best.

Cost was a problem for Jennifer. She had $1500 of her own to spend, and her parents had agreed to provide another $1000. That left her $800 short for the cheapest of the systems that she liked. She talked with Terry about this problem. He said that unless she could find the money to buy the system she wanted, she should wait.

Hardware	Program	Cost	Comments
Commodore 64		$1200	No 80-character screen
Osborne	WORDSTAR	$2000	Screen too small
Hewlett-Packard 86B	WORDSTAR WORD/80	$3475	Electronic spreadsheet and file manager included Large library of other programs
Digital Equipment	WORDSTAR SELECT	$4365	Color capability "soon" Excellent TEACH module in SELECT
IBM Personal Computer	WORDSTAR SELECT	$5150	Very large library of programs Color included in this price

Some typical micro hardware alternatives.

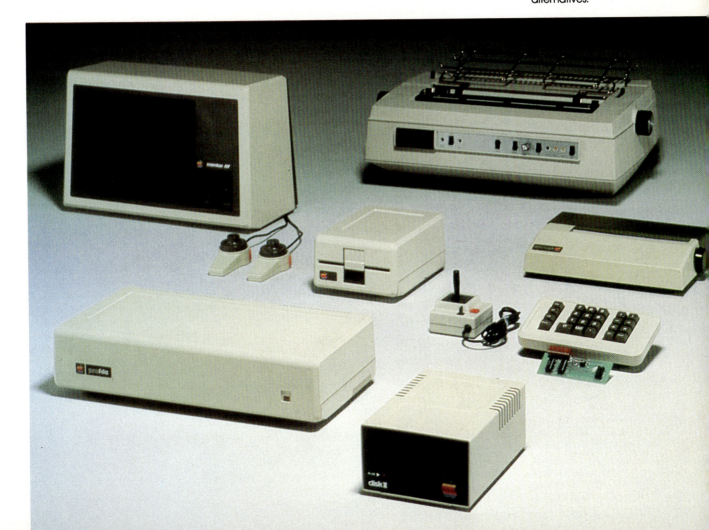

"If you buy a system you don't like," he said, "you won't use it. It would be a waste of money. Don't buy anything right now. Prices will probably come down, and you may be able to afford a system you do like in a year or two."

Jennifer didn't want to wait. She went back to the computer store manager and explained her dilemma. The manager agreed to reduce the price by another $250, but that was the rock-bottom price.

"Can I earn the difference?" Jennifer asked.

Eventually, Jennifer and the store manager made a deal. Jennifer could buy the system she wanted for $2500 plus 60 hours of labor. As it turned out, Jennifer was a good speaker and made many presentations to fellow liberal arts students on the benefits of word processing.

Jennifer met again with Terry. She told Terry that she wanted to buy one of the $3000 systems and that she liked WORD/80 better than WORDSTAR. What did he think about her buying the HP 86B with WORD/80? Terry said that sounded like a good decision. He told her that Hewlett-Packard had a very high reputation for quality, and, furthermore, if a problem did occur, Jennifer could have the system repaired at a nearby Hewlett-Packard facility. Terry also told Jennifer that, even though she didn't think she would use the computer for other applications, she might change her mind. In that case, the large library of programs available for the HP 86B would be an advantage.

Jennifer bought the system.

Hardware with software alternatives.

This Hewlett-Packard 86B, which is also popular with professionals for their word processing needs, was selected by Jennifer.

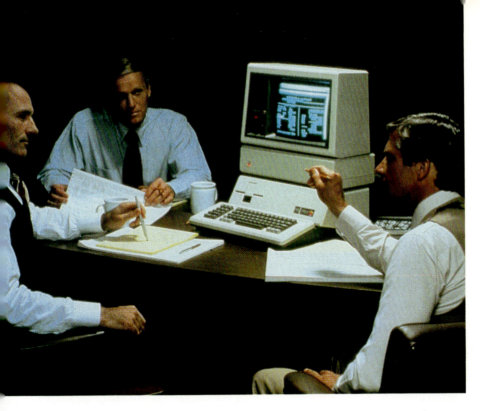

Systems analysts designing user procedures for personal microcomputers.

The design stage is often short for micro-based systems—especially if off-the-shelf programs will be used. Usually all of the specifications for hardware are known, and there is little design to be done for programs and data. Procedures, however, often require design work. For example, there need to be procedures to start the system, procedures to backup data, and procedures to restore lost data when necessary. Considering the personnel component, job descriptions may need to be developed, and quite often training programs are designed.

Design for Jennifer   Because Jennifer bought her word processing program off the shelf, only limited design work needed to be done. Of the five components of a system, Jennifer only needed to design *procedures*. She did not need to design *programs*, *data formats*, or *hardware specifications*. This work had been done by the vendor of the programs.

Further, because Jennifer was the only user of the system, she didn't need to develop job descriptions, organizational structures, or training programs. These tasks would be necessary for a larger, commercial system.

Jennifer enrolled in a class that was included in the price of the micro (eventually, Jennifer taught this class). In the class she learned the importance of backup. As the instructor said, "Be certain that, if you make a mistake, you don't lose an important document, or, even worse, lose your copy of WORD/80 or other programs."

Working with Terry, Jennifer designed procedures to keep backup copies of all her programs, as well as important documents.

"That way, if there's a fire, or if someone steals your computer and your disks, you won't have lost everything. By the way, Jennifer, be certain that your insurance covers your computer. Lock it up, and don't brag about it to your friends."

DESIGNING THE
SYSTEM

IMPLEMENTATION

The three major tasks of implementation are construction, test, and installation. During construction, hardware is received and assembled, programs are written and unit tested, data is assembled and converted to computer-sensible form, procedures are documented, and people are trained. During test, the system is used, and results are checked for validity. Finally, the system is installed and its productive life begins.

For a single-user microcomputer system with off-the-shelf programs, these tasks are simple and straightforward. They are much more complex for systems involving multiple users and custom programming or program alteration.

Jennifer Anderson's Implementation   Jennifer picked up her microcomputer from the computer store. She read the system's documentation and then assembled the components by following the manufacturer's instructions. The system was running within 90 minutes.

Next, Jennifer read the documentation about WORD/80. She found features in that product that she had not noticed during the trials at the computer stores. "Glad I read the documentation," she thought. Before Jennifer used the word processing package, she made backup copies, according to her procedures.

Next, to test the system, Jennifer typed part of one of her old papers. She had no difficulty generating the document and storing it. Unfortunately, however, she couldn't get the printer to work. For some reason, nothing happened when she tried to print her paper. She read the documentation about WORD/80 but didn't learn anything. Next, she reread the section about connecting the printer to the microcomputer. She noticed that the connector on her cable did not look like the connector in the picture in the instructions. She called the computer store, gave them the cable number, and found out that she had received the wrong cable. Jennifer went back to the store, obtained the correct cable, and installed it. This time, she had no difficulty printing her paper.

Micros in offices can assist with record keeping and perform word processing.

New music synthesizers play musical compositions that have been written, programmed, and stored on a micro.

Computer camps have become a popular method of introducing kids to microcomputers.

Micros are used at home by writers for personal word processing.

IMPLEMENTATION
(continued)

An effective computer system makes life easier, whether for bicycle sales, auto repair, architectural drawing, or other activities. It reduces menial labor, increases information, and helps people do more with less effort. The wrong computer system makes life harder. People will ignore or work around an ineffective computer system. After a while, the microcomputer will be gathering dust in a corner—the 1980s version of the hula hoop.

The key to developing an effective system is to follow the four-stage process. First, determine what the system is to do. Then, evaluate alternatives, with as much hands-on experience as possible. Next, design procedures and other components as necessary. Finally, assemble, test, and use the system. This process works whether the microcomputer system will be used by kids for education, by families managing the farm, by business people managing a business, or by students writing term papers. Try it.

Keeping an inventory of parts is not a difficult task for a small business with a micro system.

Microcomputers are being used more and more by small retail businesses.

A Nebraska farm family monitors and controls the diet of its dairy cows with a home micro system.

Professional engineers and architects may have graphics requirements for their micros.

TIPS ON BUYING A PERSONAL COMPUTER

COMPUTER SHOPPING CHECKLIST—TIPS ON BUYING A PERSONAL COMPUTER

Below is a summary of what you need to know when you shop for a personal home computer:

- Have a good idea of what computer applications you want: word processing, data management, entertainment, education, budgeting, and so forth.
- Know the functions of the basic computer hardware.
- Check with friends or colleagues who have recently purchased a computer for information and recommendations.
- Shop several different stores, different models, and different manufacturers. Call the Better Business Bureau for a reliability report on a specific company.
- Be sure to test the demonstration model and programs the retailer has available. Are the instructions easy to use and understand?
- Get firm prices on the computer equipment and software. Ask about the costs of expansion. Are both hardware and software readily available?
- Get the terms of the warranty and service arrangements.
- Ask about computer training and clubs.
- Check the refunds and exchange policy before buying.
- If the computer will be used in a home office or professional arrangement, find out if its use will be tax-deductible.

SOURCE: Better Business Bureau, *Tips on Buying a Home Computer*, 1983.

QUESTIONS

1. Describe the four stages of systems development.
2. Why did Terry caution Jennifer not to buy the first system she saw?
3. Does Jennifer's list of desired features seem complete? What other factors might you consider when buying a word processing system?
4. Do you think it was important for Jennifer to take one of her papers and actually use potential systems? Why? What should Jennifer have done if one of the salespeople would not let her try the system?
5. If Terry's expertise had not been available to Jennifer, where else could she have obtained advice and assistance for buying the microcomputer?
6. Name and describe the three ways that computer programs can be acquired.
7. Why does it make more sense to search for acceptable programs before searching for hardware?
8. Do you see why it was important for Jennifer to test her system? What would have occurred if Jennifer had waited until the night before her next paper was due to use her system? What might have happened if Jennifer had waited a month or two before complaining to the computer store about the incorrect cable?

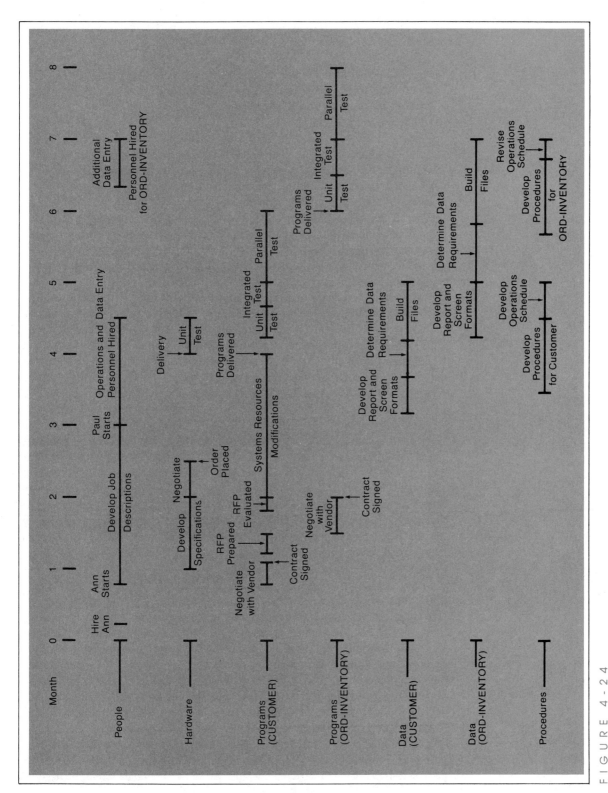

FIGURE 4-24

Horizon project plan

Programs

to the contract proposed by the computer vendor. Hardware was placed on order for delivery in six weeks.

The team needed to negotiate with vendors and order both the CUSTOMER and the ORD-INVENTORY packages of programs. They also needed to find a software house to make the alterations to CUSTOMER programs necessary to produce dividend checks.

Anne, John, and the attorney met with both vendors, negotiated acceptable terms, and signed contracts. The vendors provided documentation and scheduled training for Horizon personnel. Not only were the operators and data entry personnel trained, but the users in the customer service, order processing, warehouse, and shipping departments were trained as well.

The vendor of CUSTOMER did not want to make the alterations necessary to produce dividend checks but did recommend two companies that were qualified to perform such work. John and Anne prepared a *request for proposal* (or RFP), which is a written statement of the work to be performed, and a request for cost and schedule commitments. They sent the RFP to both companies and then met with them in person. Responses to the RFP were received in 10 days, and John and Anne selected one of the vendors, Systems Resources, to make the modifications. According to the terms of the contract, the Horizon's CUSTOMER programs were to be delivered to Systems Resources. Systems Resources would then make the alterations necessary to produce dividend checks and deliver the complete package within six weeks. (Without telling Systems Resources, John and Anne allowed eight weeks in developing the schedule in figure 4-24.)

Data

Horizon had three major design tasks to complete for the data component. First, they needed to determine the specific formats they wanted for screens and reports. When Horizon personnel were trained on the use of CUSTOMER and ORD-INVENTORY products, they were taught how to tailor screen and report formats. For example, the ORD-INVENTORY product had three different screen formats from which to choose. The Horizon users needed to decide which format they wanted. Later, during implementation, the project team would provide parameters (inputs) to ORD-INVENTORY to cause those formats to be generated.

The second data design task was to determine the data needed to establish initial files. For example, for the customer system, they would need to build a starting customer file. It would include customer name, address, and other fields of data. At this point, the team needed to determine exactly what those other fields would be. The team made this determination by reviewing the requirements statements, discussing needs further with users, and reviewing the documentation of the CUSTOMER and ORD-INVENTORY products.

They also needed to learn where the initial data was located in the company and design a procedure for obtaining that data. Once the programs had been installed, the data would be keyed and the initial file constructed.

The third design task concerned recurring data. What data would be gathered during business operations? To a large extent, the design of the CUSTOMER and ORD-INVENTORY programs would determine what data would be needed.

The project team needed to understand these requirements and ensure that the necessary data would be available. In several cases, the project team found that new forms needed to be designed. For example, the form that Horizon was using for order returns did not specify all the data that needed to be keyed for the new system.

Procedures

The final design task was to develop procedures for computer operations, data entry personnel, and users. Procedures were needed for both normal and failure recovery operations.

Both the CUSTOMER and ORD-INVENTORY packages included operations and user documentation. The project team reviewed this documentation and modified it where necessary to conform with Horizon's standard operational practices. Also, several of the order processing users complained that the documentation was unclear, so the project team wrote supplements that were more easily understood.

According to the contract with Systems Resources (the software house making the modifications to CUSTOMER), user and operations documentation for the changes and additions to the CUSTOMER product were to be delivered. John and Anne provided Systems Resources with an outline of the documentation they thought would be appropriate.

Anne and Paul worked together to develop the initial computer operations schedule. This schedule documented when programs were to be started, when reports were to be produced, where the reports were to be sent, when to perform file backup, and so forth. Anne stipulated that inputs and requests for computer runs were to be received by data entry personnel, processed by the computer operators, and returned to the data entry personnel. This scheme provided control over the activities of the operations department (see module C).

Once procedures had been designed and documented, the team moved on to implementation.

The Horizon Implementation Stage

Recall from figure 4-5 that implementation includes three phases: construct, test, and install. Horizon was actually developing two systems: customer and inventory. Therefore, they had to construct, test, and install tasks for each system. The scheduling of these tasks for the two separate systems is shown in figure 4-24. Refer to this diagram as you read the next sections.

Construction

During construction, the hardware was installed. (The installation of hardware is not the same as the installation of the *system*. All five components must be installed and tested before the system can be installed.) Programs were delivered, and the vendor assisted Anne and Paul in placing them on the computer hardware. At this point, optional program features were selected and the formats of screens and reports were specified.

Once the programs were available, the initial data files could be built. Data entry and user personnel followed the procedures developed during design to build the files. Edit reports were closely examined to ensure that only correct data was stored. John continually reminded the team that the first uses of the systems had to be successful to obtain the users' confidence. Failures would occur if bad data were stored in the initial files. Garbage in, garbage out.

Test

As these construction activities were taking place, users and operations and data entry personnel were trained. Some of the training was provided by the vendors and other training was done by Anne or Paul.

Each of the five components was tested individually, and then an integrated dress rehearsal was conducted. Hardware was tested by the vendor as soon as it was installed. Paul and the other operator then conducted their own tests to ensure that the hardware was operating. They found a problem in the way that one of the disk units had been connected to main memory. The vendor was easily able to fix the error.

Programs were tested using test data supplied by the vendors. (Systems Resources supplied data for their modifications.) Then, John and Anne ran their own tests to verify program operation. They found that two reports were not formatted correctly. The formats were easily corrected with changes to program inputs. One of the control reports produced by the Systems Resources programs also had an error in it. Anne called it to their attention, and the report was fixed within a week.

Data was tested by examining printouts of the initial files. It was a time-consuming task. Incorrect data that had been identified during construction was examined again to ensure that it had been changed.

Anne and Paul discussed procedures with the users and operations and data entry personnel, and they answered questions. By this time, the team thought the personnel were well prepared.

After each of the components had been tested separately, an integrated test was conducted using sample data. Operations started jobs in accordance with the schedule, the users and data entry personnel input data, sample reports were produced, and so forth. Several problems were identified that resulted in adjustments to the procedures.

Installation

The project team had decided to use a parallel installation strategy. The new systems would be run while the old systems continued operation. As shown in figure 4-24, the team planned to implement the customer system first and the inventory system two months later.

The customer system was installed and use began. At the end of each week, the reports of the new system were compared to reports from the service bureau. Nearly all of the differences between them were the result of errors that the service bureau had made. At the end of the month, the dividend system was run just as it would be run at year-end. (It was not year-end, but John and Anne wanted to see if the dividends could be produced correctly before paying the Systems Resources bill.) No significant errors were identified.

At the end of the month, the team recommended to management that the service bureau activity be stopped. With termination of that service, the customer system was up and running.

Next, the team turned its attention to the inventory system. (Actually, the installation and unit testing of ORD-INVENTORY had been accomplished while the parallel test of CUSTOMER was in progress. See figure 4-24.) ORD-INVENTORY installation was more difficult because more people were involved. Order processing, warehouse, and shipping personnel all had a role. As with the customer system, a parallel strategy was used. Orders were processed by the old manual system as well as by the new computer-based system. This duplicative work caused considerable extra work for the employees, and there was considerable grumbling. Management held firm to the plan for a parallel installation, however, and an entire month's orders were processed both ways.

There was one problem with the interface between the inventory and the customer systems, but, by and large, the implementation went smoothly. Several users were dissatisfied with their report formats (even though they had seen and approved samples). "I didn't understand what this would really look like," was one of the comments. Basically, however, both systems were operational, and the projects were complete eight months after management had approved the alternatives. Since this was right on schedule, management was exceedingly pleased.

4.21 Why did the project team return to requirements work after the evaluation stage? What requirements work did they do?

4.22 Using figure 4-24 as a guide, explain the actions taken by the project team to design and implement the customer and inventory systems.

4.23 In figure 4-24, what would have happened if the hardware had arrived late? What would have happened if Systems Resources had delivered the altered programs late? What would have happened if the customer system had been a failure?

4.24 Describe what you think are the major reasons that the Horizon systems development was successful.

SUMMARY

There are four fundamental stages in systems development. The first stage is determination of requirements. During this stage, a project team is formed, the problem is defined, detailed requirements are documented, and the feasibility of the system is examined. During the second stage, evaluation, various system alternatives are proposed and evaluated in terms of the dollar value of costs and benefits.

The third stage is design. The characteristics of each of the five components of a computer system are determined at this stage. For purchased components, specifications are determined. For components to be developed during the project, the designs are proposed and evaluated. The final stage of systems development is implementation. During this stage, components are constructed, the components and the system are tested, and the system is installed.

The characteristics of this process change dramatically depending on how the programs are obtained. Systems development is considerably simpler when programs are obtained off-the-shelf. Development is more difficult when programs are purchased and altered, and it is most difficult and complex when programs are custom written.

Systems development process
Requirements stage
Problem definition
Feasibility evaluation
Technical feasibility
Alternative Evaluation stage
Design stage
Implementation stage
Cost feasibility
Schedule feasibility
Management approval
Cost/benefit analysis
Design review
Construction
System test

Installation
Plunge installation
Parallel installation
Pilot installation
Phased installation
Off-the-shelf programs
Altered programs
Custom-tailored programs
Functional specifications
Prototype
Computer service bureau
Software house
Request for proposal (RFP)
Family of computers

QUESTIONS TO CHALLENGE YOUR THINKING

A. Locate a company that has recently developed a system using off-the-shelf programs. Interview the systems development personnel, the operations personnel, and the users. Did the company follow a process similar to the one described in this chapter? If not, how was their process different? Has the system been successful? What would any of the personnel involved do differently if they were to develop the system again?

B. Locate a company that has recently developed a system using altered programs. Conduct an interview as described in question A.

C. Locate a company that has recently developed a system using custom programs. Conduct an interview as described in question A.

CHAPTER 5

Sequential File Processing Systems

Data is the interface between people and computers. In many ways, data is the skeleton of the information system. The way that data is organized and processed determines the character or personality of the system. Therefore, one useful way to understand different types of computer systems is to examine the different ways that data is organized and processed. We will follow that approach in this and the next two chapters. In this chapter we will discuss *sequential file processing;* chapter 6 discusses direct access file processing; and chapter 7 discusses database processing. Any of these three alternatives could be used by Horizon Artist Supply (chapter 4), and we will refer to that company for examples.

In this chapter we will first describe the general characteristics of a sequential file system. Then we will examine the five components of a sequential-file-oriented computer system.

WHAT ARE SEQUENTIAL FILE SYSTEMS?

Sequential file systems are computer systems that have a special property: the records in files are processed in sequence. Think of your stereo tape player. You listen to songs in sequence. When you have a tape with a song that you like in the middle, you must listen to the songs before it first. Sequential file systems are similar. To find a record in the middle of the file, all the records preceding it must be read first.

Figure 5-1 shows a system flowchart for the Horizon customer master file system. This is a sequential file system. Data about customer changes, like new customers or address changes for existing customers, is keyed onto magnetic tape using a key-to-tape device. The resulting file is called the change transaction file. This file and the old customer master file are read, and a new customer master file is created. Now consider a problem: suppose there are 100 changes to be made to a file that has 100,000 customers on it. How are the correct master file records to be found? If the first transaction says to change the address of customer number 10, how is customer 10's master file record to be found?

Think about your tape player. Suppose you have a tape of nursery rhymes and you want to play "Lucy Locket." If you don't know where "Lucy Locket" is located on the tape, you will have to search the tape from the beginning until you find it. You might do this by using fast forward to advance the tape 10 feet and then listening. If you do not hear "Lucy Locket," you would advance 10 feet again, listen again, and so forth. If there are 50 nursery rhymes on the tape, you can expect, on the average, to search over 25 nursery rhymes to find the one you want.

Now suppose you want to listen to three nursery rhymes: "Ding, Dong, Bell," "Lucy Locket," and "Rub-a-dub-dub, Three Men in a Tub," in that order. If you don't know where these are located, you will have to search the tape three times. You may have to search over 75 (3 × 25) nursery rhymes before you find all three.

You can improve this process if you put the nursery rhymes on the tape in some order, say, alphabetical order. Then, assuming you want to listen to the three rhymes in alphabetical order, you can search first for "Ding, Dong, Bell" and play it. Then you can search for "Lucy Locket" and play it. Then you can find and play "Rub-a-dub-dub." At worst, you will have to search through the tape only once.

You can also catch mistakes more easily. Suppose you are searching for "Ding, Dong, Bell," but you find "Deedle, Deedle, Dumpling" followed by "Jack Sprat." What does this mean? It means "Ding, Dong, Bell" is not on the tape. If it were, it would be between "Deedle, Deedle, Dumpling" and "Jack Sprat." Thus, by having the rhymes in order, you eliminate having to search the whole tape to find that "Ding, Dong, Bell" isn't there.

Now consider Horizon's customer master file of 100,000 records. If the customers' records are in no particular order on the file, then, on the average, we will have to search 50,000 records to find the one we want. Therefore, to find master file records for 10 customers, 500,000 (10 × 50,000) records will have to be searched.

On the other hand, if the customer master file is sorted by number, and if we also sort the required changes by number, then we can find all the records in one pass of the file. Invalid numbers can also be identified quickly.

The essence of sequential file processing is that the records are sorted into some order. They are processed one after another in that order. *A sequential file system is a computer system in which the files are sorted and processed in*

Data for Sequential Systems

some predefined order. This sorting saves considerable searching, and processing can be extremely fast.

Sequential systems data has several identifying characteristics. First, there are two types of files. *Master files* keep data about continuing relationships. Examples are master files of employees, of customers, and of suppliers. Master files are usually relatively stable. In Horizon's case, a few (as a percentage) new customers may order, and some customers may be deleted, but, by and large, the same customers are processed month after month.

Transaction files contain records about events. When these records are processed, changes are made to master files or other outputs are produced. Transaction files (also called *detail files*) are erratic. For example, changes to the customer master file for one month will likely be completely different from changes for the next month. In figure 5-1 the customer modifications are an example of a transaction file.

A second characteristic of a sequential file system is that a master file is completely rewritten whenever any records in the file are changed. This is because the records must be kept in some sequential order. If a new record is to be *inserted*, the file must be rewritten to make room for the record. (Similarly, to add a new nursery rhyme, the stereo tape needs to be rerecorded.) If a record is to be *deleted*, the master file has to be rewritten to eliminate the unneeded record.

If a record is to be *modified*, the file has to be rewritten because the modified record may be larger or smaller than the existing one. Even if the record length does not change, the file is rewritten because of the difficulty of inserting the modified record in just the right place.

Have you ever tried to record a song in the middle of a group of songs? It's easy to wipe out the end of the prior song or the beginning of the next song. It's also easy to create a tape with a blank spot. These problems exist on magnetic tape, too, which is one reason that records on sequential files are not modified in place.

A third characteristic of a sequential file system is that transactions are usually processed in *batches*. The master file will be completely rewritten whether 1 percent or 100 percent of the records in the file are changed. Therefore, the more changes that can be made in one run, the better. Figure 5-2 shows a graph of the average time (time per updated record) plotted against size of the transaction file. The bigger the batch, the shorter the average time to process a transaction. Since transactions are processed in batches, sequential file processing is sometimes called *batch processing*.

Magnetic Tape Data Representation

Recall from chapter 2 that the basic building block for representing computer data is called a *bit*. A bit is a *binary digit*. Bits are grouped together to form *bytes*, or characters. Characters are represented in columns across magnetic tape.

Figure 5-3 shows a section of *magnetic tape*. Bits are represented on magnetic tape by magnetized spots. If the spot is magnetized in one direction, it is considered to be a 0. If it is magnetized in another direction, it is considered to be a 1.

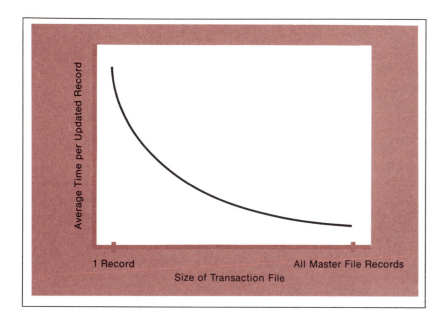

FIGURE 5-2

Average time to update a sequential file

If you turn a section of tape on its side, its format is like a punched card. However, instead of having a fixed number of characters (the card in chapter 2 had 80), it can have as many characters as the tape is long. The section of tape shown in figure 5-3 has 8 characters. Instead of having 12 rows as the punched card did, the tape has 9. These are called *tracks*. Each character is represented by a column across the nine tracks.

For nine-track tapes, characters are represented using *EBCDIC* (Extended Binary Coded Decimal Interchange Code). With this code, 8 bits are needed to represent each character (see figure 2-13). For example, the character A is represented as 1100 0001, the character B as 1100 0010, the number 1 as 1111 0001, and the number 2 as 1111 0010.

Characters are stored on tape by writing their codes in the lower eight tracks. Thus, to store the character 1, a 1 is written in the bottom track, 0's are written in the next three tracks, and 1's are written in the four tracks after that (see figure 5-3). To store the character A, a 1 is written in the bottom track, 0's are written in the next five tracks, and 1's are written in the next two tracks.

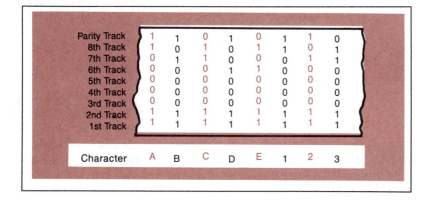

FIGURE 5-3

Character representation on nine-track magnetic tape

If you're following this discussion, you have a burning question. What about the ninth track? Why have a nine-track tape to hold an 8-bit code?

The ninth track is called the *parity track*. It is used to help detect errors. Before the tape is written, a convention is established that the tape will be written in either *even* or *odd parity*. If even, each column of the tape is to have an even number of 1's. If odd, each column is to have an odd number of 1's. The parity track is used to make each column obey the convention.

Suppose the convention is even parity. To represent the character 1 in EBCDIC, a 1 is written in the first track, then three 0's, and then four 1's. A total of five 1's are in the column. However, since each column is supposed to have an even number of 1's, a 1 will also be written in the parity track. After this is done, the column has six 1's, making it even, as it is supposed to be.

To represent the character 3, 1's are written in the bottom two tracks, then two 0's, and then four 1's. A total of six 1's are in the column. Since this column has an even number of 1's, a 0 is written in the parity track. Examine figure 5-3 and you will see how the parity track is used to give every column an even number of 1's.

How does this process help with errors? Given an even-parity convention, if the tape unit misreads one of the tracks (reads a 0 as a 1, or a 1 as a 0), it will sense an odd number of 1's. Since the convention is even, the unit has made an error and will reread the character or stop. Furthermore, if the tape has been damaged by mishandling, the tape unit will detect *parity errors*.

If you work around computer systems, you will undoubtedly hear someone say. "That tape is full of parity errors." This statement simply means that either the tape is damaged or the equipment is malfunctioning.

The code in figure 5-3 is not the only way data is represented by computers. There is another popular code that uses just 6 bits. Tape units that commonly process this code have only seven tracks.

QUESTIONS

5.1 Define *sequential processing*.

5.2 Why are records sorted on sequential files?

5.3 Explain the difference between master files and transaction files.

5.4 Why are transaction records usually batched in sequential file processing?

5.5 Why do master files need to be completely rewritten when they are changed?

5.6 What is a bit? Why are bits used to represent computer data?

5.7 Describe the way characters are represented on magnetic tape.

5.8 Define *parity* and explain how it is used for error checking.

HORIZON'S CUSTOMER MASTER FILE SYSTEM

Figure 5-4 shows a version of Horizon's customer master file system. The change transaction file is keyed using a key-to-tape device, and the old and new customer master files are stored on tape. A printer is used to output the reports. Transactions are keyed directly to

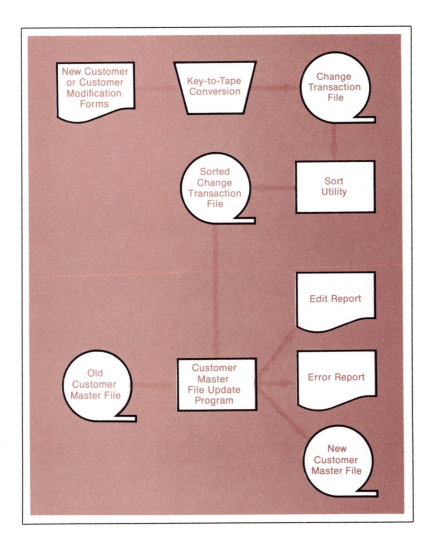

FIGURE 5-4

Tape-oriented customer master file system

tape, but they are keyed in no particular order. Consequently, they must be sorted into customer number order. After they are sorted, the order of the transaction records will match the order of the master file records.

For the system depicted in figure 5-4, Horizon clerks initiate a change to the customer master file by filling out a change request form. This form goes to data entry where it is keyed onto magnetic tape. A machine and operator performing key-to-tape data entry

are shown in figure 5-5. The tape that is generated can be a cassette tape like those used for home stereos, or it can be a reel of 1/2-inch tape commonly used for computers.

The record format for the change transaction file is shown in figure 5-6 on page 151. The data entry personnel fill in this data on the CRT screens, and a tape is created that has one record for each change.

The record code field tells the update program what function to

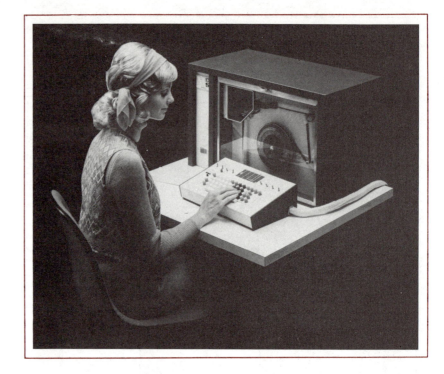

FIGURE 5-5

Operator using key-to-tape equipment

perform. A 1 in this field means to add a new customer; a 2 means to delete a customer; a 3 means to change customer data; and a 4 means to print the customer's record. This last action is taken to determine what data is on the customer's master record.

The contents of the other fields in the change record vary, depending on the value in the record code field. For codes 2 and 4, only the customer number need be specified. For code 1, all the data must be specified. For code 3, only the customer number and the data to be changed must be specified. Figure 5-7 shows some examples of change records.

HARDWARE FOR SEQUENTIAL SYSTEMS

Two types of media are commonly used for the storage of sequential data: magnetic tape and magnetic disk. Of the two, tape has been more prominently used, especially in mainframe environments. Magnetic disk, which is capable of both sequential and other types of processing, has recently become popular for sequential processing on smaller systems, such as micros and smaller minicomputers. In this chapter, we will discuss only magnetic tape. Magnetic disk will be considered in chapter 6.

Characteristics of Magnetic Tape Files

For the Horizon application, both old and new customer master files are stored on tape. Figure 5-8 shows a typical magnetic tape format. The tape has a *header* section that contains the tape serial number, identity of the owner, and

Column	Contents
1	Record Code
5–10	Customer Number
11–30	Customer Name
31–70	Customer Address
71–80	Customer Phone

FIGURE 5-6

Change transaction file record format

```
1    201143FRED J.PARKS         316 E. TAMARACK, LOS ANGELES      CA94123 2135551201
1    201144MARY ABERNATHY        934 S. LARCH, ALEXANDRIA         VA 02034 2033812347
2    101234
1    201145PETE WANDOLOWSKI       1123 17TH STREET, APT 6, MIAMI   FL 11234 6053457769
3    001214 MARY HOPKINS
2    000109
4    000044
4    109877
3    154347REX BAKER
```

FIGURE 5-7

Change transaction data

so forth. Then for each file on the tape, there is a file header that names the file and gives its date of creation and other identifying data. (More than one file can be on a tape, although in Horizon's application there would be just one.)

The records in the file are stored after the file header. Following all the records, a file trailer repeats the file header data. It indicates the end of the file. If there is another file, this grouping of file header/data/file trailer is repeated for as many files as are on the tape. Finally, the tape has a *trailer* that repeats the tape header data and signifies the end of recorded data on the tape. The headers and trailers are sometimes referred to as *labels*. A tape that has them is called a *labeled tape*.

This description generally applies to all labeled tapes. Slight variations exist among manufacturers, but the format is essentially the same. It is possible to

FIGURE 5-8

Magnetic tape format

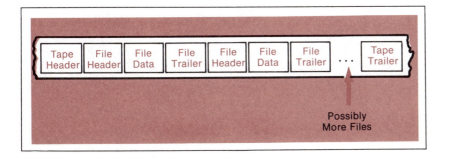

force equipment to write tapes without the labels, but it is bad practice. Without labels, the computer cannot verify that the correct tape has been mounted. If the wrong tape is mounted, valuable data may be lost. When tapes are labeled, the computer hardware will ensure that a tape that is mounted is the one that is called for.

Figure 5-9 shows a reel of tape with a *write-protect ring*. This ring must be in place before the tape can be written. Because the operator must insert the ring, this action is protection against someone's inadvertently writing on a tape that was supposed to be read. The equipment simply won't write unless the ring is in place.

Figure 5-10 shows a simple schematic of a tape read/write unit. As the tape passes under the read/write heads, the magnetic spots are either sensed (read) or created (written). Typically, a tape unit will read or write one record and then stop; read or write another record and stop; and so forth. Consequently, the tape moves forward in jerks: a quick move followed by a stop, a quick move followed by a stop. To give the equipment time to stop, there is a gap between the records on the tape, called the *interrecord* (or *interblock*)*gap*. This gap may be a ½ inch or more in size.

You may have seen pictures of magnetic tape drives in movies or on TV. Typically, the tape reels are shown whirling at great speed and not moving in jerks at all. That's because they're being rewound. Hollywood likes action and a tape drive actually reading or writing is apparently not dramatic enough.

Magnetic tape can be recorded in various *densities*. These are measured in *bytes per inch*, or *bpi*. Typical values are 800 bpi, 1600 bpi, and 6250 bpi.

Consider Horizon's master file. According to figure 5-11, there are 120 characters per master record. If a tape is recorded at 1600 bpi, then it will take 0.075 inch to hold one customer record. Do you see a problem? Most of the tape will be used for interrecord gaps! If the gaps are 0.5 inch, there will be 0.075 inch of data followed by 0.5 inch of gap, then 0.075 inch of data, followed by 0.5 inch of gap, and so forth. (See figure 5-12.)

Tape volume on write-protect ring

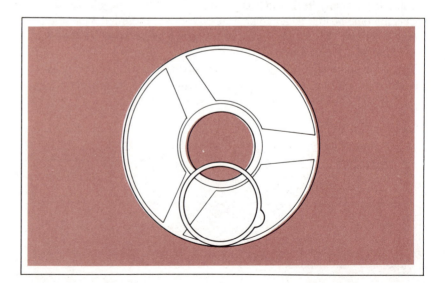

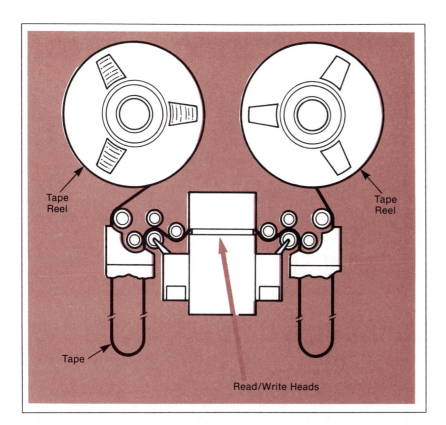

Tape
Reel

Tape
Reel

Tape

Read/Write Heads

FIGURE 5-10

Schematic of tape drive

Record Blocking

To prevent this situation, records can be blocked. This means a group of records can be written or read together as a unit, or *block*. Figure 5-13 depicts a tape with a *blocking factor* of eight records per block. In this case, a block will take 0.6 inch (8 × 0.075) of tape and be followed by 0.5 inch of gap.

How much tape will be required to hold Horizon's customer master file? There are 200,000 records. If they are blocked at 8 records per block, then 25,000 blocks will be needed. Each block and its adjacent interblock gap take

FIGURE 5-11

Customer master file record format

Position	Contents
1–6	Customer Number
7–26	Customer Name
27–66	Customer Address
67–76	Customer Phone
77–83	Year-to-Date Purchases (xxxx.xx)
84–89	Date of Last Purchase (YYMMDD)
90–95	Date of Last Master File Update (YYMMDD)
96–101	Amount of Last Dividend Check
102–108	Amount of Last Year's Purchases (xxxx.xx)
109–114	Date of 1st Order (YYMMDD)
115–120	Date of largest purchase

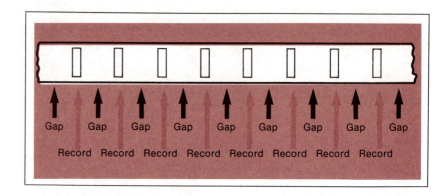

FIGURE 5-12

Horizon's customer master file record
format on tape

1.1 inches. Consequently, 27,500 inches, or 2292 feet, of tape are required. Reels of magnetic tape are available in lengths of 800, 1200, and 2400 feet, so the master file will fit on one 2400-foot reel. There will be 108 feet left over for headers and trailers. (Isn't it amazing how textbook examples always work out!) Would the data fit if the blocking factor were 4? If it were 15?

You might be wondering why there are any gaps at all. Why not compress the data into one long record? The reason is that a block must be read into main memory in its entirety. A portion of main memory, called a *buffer*, must be set aside to receive the record as it comes in from the tape. If Horizon's master file were one long record, then 200,000 times 120 bytes, or 24 million bytes, of main storage would have to be set aside for the buffer. Only the very largest computers have that much memory, and there are better uses for it. Consequently, records are usually blocked into units of more manageable size like 1000 or 2000 bytes.

Magnetic Tape Speeds

How long will it take to read or write Horizon's customer master file? The time to process a tape has two components: the time actually to move the data and the time to start and stop the tape between blocks. The time to move the data depends on the speed of the tape and the recording density. A typical speed (called the tape *transport speed*) is 200 inches per second. Thus, at 1600 bpi, a total of 320,000 bytes can be transferred per second. The Horizon master file has 24 million characters, so 75 seconds (24 million divided by 320,000) will be needed to read or write the tape.

FIGURE 5-13

Schematic of tape with blocking
factor of 8

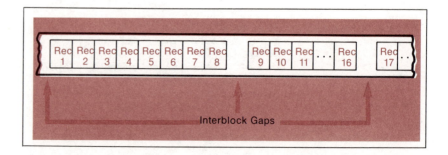

In addition, time is required to start and stop the tape between blocks. A typical time interval to stop and start a tape is 0.003 second. Assuming Horizon has 200,000 customer records blocked 8 per block, then 25,000 blocks will be needed. At 0.003 second for stop and start, a total of 75 seconds will be needed. Thus, the total time to read or write the entire Horizon master file is 150 seconds.

This figure is somewhat misleading. The computer will not devote all of its time to reading or writing this tape. There will be interference from other activity. Still, about five minutes is a realistic estimate.

QUESTIONS

5.9 Why does figure 5-4 call for change transactions to be sorted?

5.10 What is the purpose of the record code field in figure 5-6?

5.11 What are the two types of media most frequently used for the storage of sequentially organized data?

5.12 What is a labeled tape? Should most companies use labeled or unlabeled tapes?

5.13 Explain what file headers and trailers are.

5.14 Sketch the layout of a labeled tape that has three files.

5.15 What does *bpi* stand for? What are typical values of bpi for magnetic tapes?

5.16 What is the purpose of the write-protect ring?

5.17 What is the purpose of the interrecord gap? What is its disadvantage?

5.18 What does it mean to block records? Why is blocking done?

5.19 How much tape would be required to hold the Horizon customer master file if the blocking factor were 4? If it were 15?

5.20 How long would it take to read the Horizon customer master file if the blocking factor were 4? If it were 15?

5.21 How long will it take to read 7500 200-byte records recorded at 1600 bpi?

5.22 How long will it take to write 7500 200-byte records recorded at 6250 bpi?

PROGRAMS FOR SEQUENTIAL FILE PROCESSING

A Sequential File Record-Matching Algorithm

Figure 5-14 shows a system flowchart for another Horizon system, the purchase update system. This system adds the total amount of a customer's order to the year-to-date purchase total in the master record. This is a typical sequential file system.

In figure 5-14, the transaction records are sorted into the same order as the master file records. Then they are read by an update program. The update program matches a transaction record with the corresponding master file record; makes adjustments to the master data (here, by adding the order amount to the year-to-date total); and writes out the new master record.

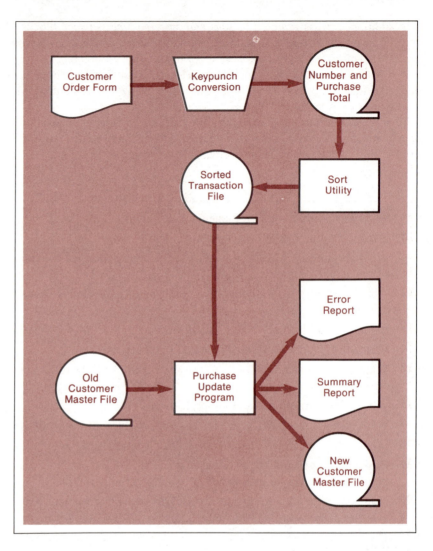

FIGURE 5-14

Horizon purchase update system

Records will be matched by customer number. The master file will be kept in order of customer number, and the transaction file will be sorted by customer number. Fields that are used the way customer number is used in this example are called *control fields* or, sometimes, *keys*.

If the update program finds any transaction records that do not have a matching master record, then the unmatched records are written to an error file. It is also quite possible that there will be master records with no matching transactions, which means some customers made no purchases. In this case, the program will copy the master record from the old master file to the new one without making any changes.

Figure 5-15 lists data that could be input to a program like the purchase update program in figure 5-14. Each transaction record contains a customer number and the amount of a recent sale. Each master record has a customer number and other data that is not shown. If we examine this data, we see that customer 100010 is on both the transaction file and the master file. The 7.95

Transaction File		Master File	
Customer Number	Amount of Sale	Customer Number	Other Master Data
100010	007.95	100010	
100020	124.85	100020	
100040	382.17	100030	.
100045	081.29	100040	.
100050	176.76	100050	.
EOF		100060	
		100070	
		EOF	

F I G U·R E   5 - 1 5

Data for purchase update program

will be added to his or her master record. Similarly, customer 100020 is on both files; 124.85 will be added.

However, the next pair of customer numbers in figure 5-15 do not match. Customer 100040 on the transaction file does not match customer 100030 on the master file. This means customer 100030 did not make any purchases; he or she had no transactions. In this case, the program copies customer 100030's data to the new file with no change.

After copying 100030's data, the program must read another master record to see if it matches transaction 100040. Note that the program reads only the master file in this case. If it read both the master and the transaction files, transaction record 100040 would be lost before it was processed.

The program reads master record 100040. Sure enough, this record matches the current transaction record. Consequently, 382.17 is added to 100040's year-to-date total. The program now reads the next two records and finds a dis-agreement: 100045 from the transaction does not match 100050 from the master.

What does this mean? Both the transaction file and the master file are sorted by customer number. The transaction number 100045 is *less than* the master number 100050. Consequently, we have detected a missing master record. 100045 is not on the master file. If it were, it would come before 100050, because the records are ordered. In this case, the program prints 100045 on the error file. Then it reads the next transaction record. It is 100050, which matches 100050 on the master file. The 176.76 is added to the master record, and it is written on the new master file.

When the program tries to read the next records from the transaction and master files, it finds EOF on the transaction file. EOF stands for *end of file*. Here, it simply means that there are no more file records to be read. All systems have ways of notifying a program that the records in a file have all been read. However, the way this is done depends on the type of computer and the language of the program. Your instructor can show you how your computer does it.

When the program encounters EOF on the transaction file, it copies all the remaining records from the old master to the new master. If it did not do this,

```
BEGIN MAIN-PARAGRAPH
    DO INITIALIZE
    DO PROCESS-BOTH-FILES
    DO FLUSH-NONEMPTY-FILE
    DO WRAPUP
    STOP
END MAIN-PARAGRAPH


BEGIN INITIALIZE
    SET EOF-MASTER TO 0
    SET EOF-TRANS TO 0
    READ OLD-MASTER-FILE IF END SET EOF-MASTER TO 1
    READ TRANS-FILE IF END SET EOF-TRANS TO 1
END INITIALIZE


BEGIN PROCESS-BOTH-FILES
    DOWHILE EOF-MASTER AND EOF-TRANS = 0
        IF CUSTOMER-NUMBER (MASTER-FILE) = CUSTOMER-NUMBER (TRANS-FILE)
            THEN /Add amount to year-to-date total in master record./
                    WRITE MASTER-RECORD TO NEW-MASTER-FILE
                    READ OLD-MASTER-FILE IF END SET EOF-MASTER TO 1
                    READ TRANS-FILE IF END SET EOF-TRANS TO 1
            ELSE IF CUSTOMER-NUMBER (MASTER-FILE) < CUSTOMER-NUMBER (TRANS-FILE)
                    THEN /This means there is no activity on the customer
                         record./
                         WRITE MASTER-RECORD TO NEW-MASTER-FILE
                         READ OLD-MASTER-FILE IF END SET EOF-MASTER TO 1
                    ELSE /This means there is a trans record with no
                         corresponding master./
                         WRITE TRANS-RECORD TO ERROR-FILE
                         READ TRANS-FILE IF END SET EOF-TRANS TO 1
                    END-IF
        END-IF
    END-DO
END PROCESS-BOTH-FILES
```

FIGURE 5-16

Pseudocode for purchase update
program (continued on next page)

```
BEGIN FLUSH-NONEMPTY-FILE
   IF EOF-MASTER = 1
      THEN /This means the master file is empty; send any remaining
           trans records to the error file./
           DOWHILE EOF-TRANS = 0
               WRITE TRANS-RECORD TO ERROR-FILE
               READ TRANS-FILE IF END SET EOF-TRANS TO 1
           END-DO
      ELSE /This means the transaction file is empty; copy any
           remaining master records to the new master file./
           DOWHILE EOF-MASTER = 0
               WRITE MASTER-RECORD TO NEW-MASTER-FILE
               READ MASTER-FILE IF END SET EOF-MASTER TO 1
           END-DO
   END-IF
END FLUSH-NONEMPTY FILE

BEGIN WRAPUP
   /Here program writes summary reports and takes other termination
       action./
END WRAPUP
```

then all the remaining records on the master file would be lost. In this case, customer records 100060 and 100070 are copied unchanged to the new master file.

It could happen that the master file runs out of data before the transaction file does. If it did, then all remaining records on the transaction file would be erroneous. They would have no matching records on the master file. In this case, they would be copied on the error report.

Figure 5-16 shows *pseudocode* for the purchase update program. This pseudocode has five paragraphs. The first one, MAIN-PARAGRAPH, simply calls the other four paragraphs in the proper order. The second paragraph is an initialization routine that sets two variables, EOF-MASTER and EOF-TRANS. Then it reads the first master record and the first transaction record.

The two variables need explanation. EOF-MASTER is used to tell the program when EOF is detected on the master file. Initially, EOF-MASTER is set to 0, meaning EOF has not been reached. When the program detects the end of the master file, EOF-MASTER will be set to 1. The same is done for EOF-TRANS. Variables used in this way are sometimes called *flags*; if the flag is up (1), the end has been reached.

Pseudocode for Record Matching

The third paragraph is PROCESS-BOTH-FILES. This paragraph is active as long as both files have data. It matches the records and does the processing. After one of the files runs out of data, the fourth paragraph is called. This paragraph, named FLUSH-NONEMPTY-FILE, does just that. If the nonempty file is the transaction file, then all the remaining transaction records are sent to the error report. If the nonempty file is the master file, then all the remaining master records are copied to the new master file.

After this process is complete, the last paragraph, WRAPUP, is called. This paragraph prints the summary report and performs any other needed termination work.

Examine paragraph PROCESS-BOTH-FILES. The first statement is a DOWHILE statement. This statement means DO the following statements WHILE the condition is true. When the condition is not true, go to the next statement after the END-DO. If the condition is not true for the first time, do not perform the *loop* at all. For this example, the condition stated is that neither the master file nor the transaction file is out of data. If they are, control is returned to the MAIN-PARAGRAPH.

The first statement inside the loop is an IF statement that checks to see whether the customer numbers match. If so, the amount is added to the customer's year-to-date purchase total. Then the new master record is written. The next records are read from both the master and the transaction files.

Note that, if the READ statement detects end of file, the EOF flag will be set to 1. If this happens, the condition in the DO statement will not be true. Activity in PROCESS-BOTH-FILES will cease.

The pseudocode in figure 5-16 corresponds to the algorithm previously described. You should read through this figure to be sure you understand the algorithm and pseudocode statements. This algorithm is typical of sequential processing logic. Understanding this algorithm will help you learn the essential characteristics of sequentially organized data. Spend the time to understand it.

The need to match transaction and master records is universal to sequential processing. Consequently, this algorithm, with a few modifications, could be used for a large class of sequential processing programs. For example, consider the master file maintenance problem summarized in figure 5-4. Additions, deletions, and modifications are to be made to the customer master file. The algorithm shown in figure 5-16 could be used to solve this problem. The only difference is in the action to be taken once two matching records are found.

Sorting

So far in this chapter, we have skipped lightly over *sorting*. This treatment is unfair, because sorting is an important activity. The sort depicted in figure 5-14 would actually be done by a computer program. However, this program would most likely be a *system utility*—that is, a program provided by the computer vendor to perform a common activity. Examples of other utilities are programs to copy data, to dump files (print their contents), merge files, and so forth.

The *sort utility* would have been written and tested by the vendor. Horizon personnel would simply run it. They would input the name of the file to be sorted, the fields to sort on, and the order (ascending or descending) in which to sort them. The utility would then sort the records and put them on an output file. If the data to be sorted is too large to fit into main memory at one time, tape or other storage equipment would be required.

Program Editing

Thus far we have assumed that programs always receive good data. Unfortunately, that is unrealistic. *Experienced programmers plan on bad data.* For example, we know that Horizon's service bureau had produced many errors because they could not input the customer number correctly. Their data entry operators made too many errors.

A good computer program always *edits* or checks the input data. If the data is known to have been produced by keyed-entry or other error-prone method, the checking should be extensive. If the input comes from a master file on, say, tape, then less checking need be done. However, this policy assumes that the data was heavily edited as it was added to the master file.

There are seemingly an infinite number of errors that could be made. Clearly, the program cannot check for all of them. However, certain types of checking are commonly done. A *reasonableness check* verifies that the input data items have reasonable values. For example, the update program in figure 5-14 might check customer number to make sure it is all numeric, that it has six digits, and that it is positive.

Another type of check is a *range check*. Here, the input data item is checked to be sure it falls in the correct range of values. Horizon may have a rule that no order can exceed $750. If so, then the purchase update program should edit the transaction record purchase amount to ensure that it is greater than 0 and less than or equal to 750.00. A program that reads ages might check to be sure they are greater than 0 but less than, say, 100 (depending on the users' optimism).

Value checks can be made if the number of values that a data item can have is small. For example, the value for sex should be M or F or perhaps blank. No other characters are acceptable. If a company has 10 plants numbered 1 through 10, the only values acceptable for plant number are the numbers 1-10. The records in figure 5-6 had a code field in the first column. Its value was supposed to be 1, 2, 3, or 4. A value check could and should be made on this field.

Value checks can be made on a portion of a field as well. For example, a company may establish the convention that all part numbers are to start with 1. If so, programs can edit part numbers for a 1 in the first position.

Check digits are another type of program edit. Here, a digit is added to a field to verify the correctness of the rest of the field. For example, consider Horizon's customer numbers. They have six digits. Suppose we sum the digits individually. For the number 100040, the sum is 5. For the number 123456, the sum is 21. To create a check digit, we take the number in the ones column of the sum and append it to the customer number. This forms a seven-digit number. Thus, 100040 becomes 1000405 and 123456 becomes 1234561.

Now suppose a data entry operator is to input customer 1000405, but mis-keys the customer number as 1000505. The program will sum the first six digits of the number and get 6. Since the 6 does not agree with the last digit (the check digit), an error will be detected. If 1234561 is miskeyed as 2234561, the check digit of 1 will not agree with the computed digit of 2 (the sum of 2, 2, 3, 4, 5, and 6 is 22).

This is an example of a type of *self-checking number*. Note that this scheme will not catch all errors. If 1234561 is miskeyed as 2134561, the check digit will not catch the error. The sum of the first six digits is still 21 even though the first two digits have been interchanged. Another type of check is required to detect this error.

What kind of a check can be used on the value of the purchase amount of the transaction file of the purchase update program? Range and reasonableness checks can be made, but they are not conclusive. If 555.00 were keyed for 055.00, neither of these checks would detect the error. Unfortunately, the program by itself cannot improve the checking of these amounts. Instead, this checking must be supplemented by manual checks performed by users and operations personnel. We will discuss this type of checking in the next section.

QUESTIONS

5.23 What is a control field? How is it used for sequential file processing?

5.24 What does it mean when:
   a. There is a record on Horizon's customer master file that does not match a record on the transaction file?
   b. There is a record on Horizon's transaction file that does not match a record on the customer master file?

5.25 Why does the matching algorithm copy the last few customer records to the new customer master file?

5.26 What is EOF? What role does EOF detection play in the matching algorithm?

5.27 Explain what the DOWHILE statement means.

5.28 What is a sort utility? Is this utility a machine or a program?

5.29 Define the following edits and give one example of each:
   a. Reasonableness
   b. Range
   c. Value
   d. Value (portion of a field)
   e. Check digit

5.30 Why are edits not conclusive?

5.31 Modify the pseudocode shown in this chapter to perform master file maintenance. Assume the records have the structure illustrated in figure 5-11.

PROCEDURES FOR SEQUENTIAL FILE PROCESSING

We described the general nature of systems procedures in chapter 2. We will not repeat that discussion here. However, sequential file systems do impose some special requirements on systems procedures. Those special needs will be discussed in this section.

Correct data is important in all computer processing, but it is given special emphasis in sequential systems. Because transactions are processed in batches, it is very easy for an erroneous update to slip through. It is very hard for humans to check every item correctly in a 1500-item list, for example. Furthermore, once an erroneous update is made to a record in a sequential system master file, it is particularly hard to fix. The entire file must be rewritten just to change one record.

Two types of procedures are employed to reduce the likelihood of errors. First, updates to master files are often made in two phases. During the first phase, a dry run (dress rehearsal) is made; all of the processing is done but the master file is not updated. A report of changes to be made is generated, and this report is examined by users. Any erroneous changes are fixed and resubmitted or removed for other corrective action. This type of processing was described previously in the Accounting section of chapter 3.

Figure 5-17 on page 164 shows a two-phased approach for the Horizon purchase update system. The edit program checks the transaction customer master number and purchase amount fields. Both reasonableness and range checks can be made on these fields. Also, a form of value check can be made on the customer number. To do this, the program checks the customer number value by searching the master file for a matching number. If found, the number is assumed good.

If the master file is large, this procedure for verifying customer number may be too expensive. In Horizon's case, reading the 200,000-record customer master file may take more machine time than is judged practical. If so, then the transaction data will be edited, but the check on the customer number will not be made until the actual update is done.

Unfortunately, even the check against the master file is inconclusive. If a valid member number is found on the master file, it is not a guarantee that *the* correct number was input. It is just a guarantee that *a* valid number was read. A check digit can be used as well, although, as explained in the last section, this technique is also inconclusive. In truth, no check is conclusive. A variety of checks are made in the hope that at least one of them will catch the errors.

The edit report is sent to the users by the data processing department. Here it is checked. Errors are sent to data entry for correction or submitted to some other corrective process. Then the edit run is repeated. When all detected errors have been eliminated, the second phase is run. The master file is actually updated.

Another procedure often used with batch systems is to make manual calculations and to compare them to the computer program's results. For example, the number of transaction records can be counted by the users before they submit them to data processing. Later, when the edit report is available, the users compare this *transaction count* to a count calculated by the transaction processing program. In this way, users will detect when transactions have been duplicated or are lost. It is important for the users to check this number on both the edit and the final update reports.

An extension of these transaction counts is known as a *batch total*. Here, the users manually compute the total amount of all purchases in the batch. They

Batch Totals

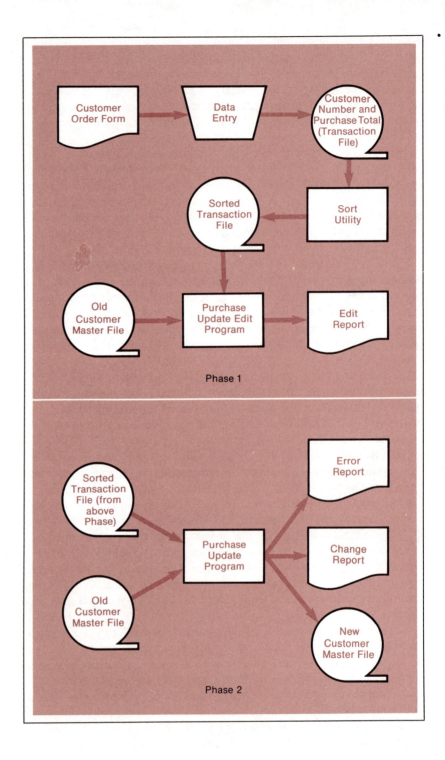

FIGURE 5-17

Two-phased purchase update system

then submit the orders to data entry. Later, when the edit report comes back, users compare the total determined by the program to the total computed manually. If the two disagree, then the difference can be traced to its cause. There may have been a manual addition error, a keying error, a missing record, or even an error in the program. If the batch is very large, it may be divided into subbatches to ease the burden of identifying errors. In this case, the program must be coded to print the subbatch totals for comparison.

Thus, users and data processing personnel maintain checks and balances on one another. Simple counts or totals are produced by the two groups using different methods. If they agree, processing is continued. If not, the error is found and corrected. This system works only when both groups are aware of their responsibilities and perform their tasks correctly. Perhaps you can see why both the users and the data processing staff are considered parts of the system.

Backup and Recovery Procedures

In addition to procedures on use, error detection, and error correction, a well-designed system also has procedures on *backup and recovery*. What happens if the computer malfunctions or crashes in the middle of a master file update run? What happens if the tape drive breaks and ruins the master file tape? What happens if an operator spills a Coke on the transaction file tape?

Here we see one of the great advantages of sequential file systems. Whenever a master file is changed, a completely new copy of the file is produced. If the old copy is kept, along with the transaction records, then the new copy can always be reproduced.

For example, the master file for the first week in January is used to produce the one for the second week. In turn, the second week's master file is used to produce the one for the third week, and so forth. If, for some reason, the master file for the third week is lost, it can be re-created from the second week's file. The transaction records for week 3 are just processed again.

A sequential system that is run weekly will generate 52 master files in one year. How many of these should be kept? Although the answer varies from application to application, a general rule is that three generations of master files and their associated transactions should be kept. Thus, when the master file for the fourth week of January is produced, the first week's file and transactions can be released (see figure 5-18 on page 166). This procedure is sometimes called *three-generation backup*.

Backup and recovery procedures are very important. There are countless horror stories of companies that have been "dead in the water" because a critical system could not be recovered. Luckily, backup and recovery is easily done for sequential systems. For other types of systems, it becomes much more difficult and expensive. (We will see this situation in chapter 6.) It becomes no less important, however.

To review, procedures for sequential file systems have three unique characteristics. First, a two-phased approach is often employed: an edit run is made, then an actual update. Second, control mechanisms, like transaction counts and batch totals, are often employed by users and data processing personnel as checks and balances. Finally, backup and recovery is accomplished by keeping at least three generations of master files and associated transactions.

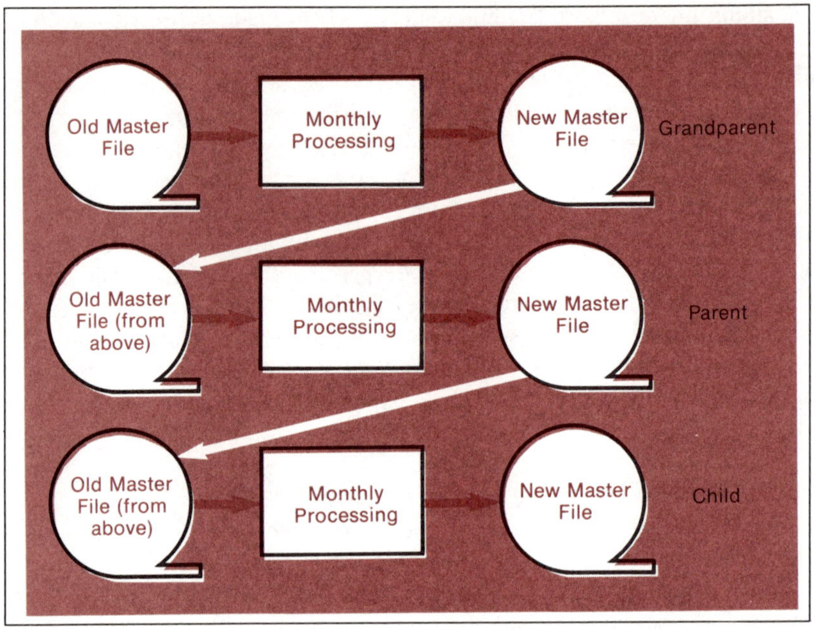

FIGURE 5-18

Three-generation backup example

PERSONNEL FOR SEQUENTIAL FILE PROCESSING

Users and operations personnel are the two groups involved with the utilization of a sequential file system.

Users

The users have two major responsibilities for which they need to be trained. First, users need to know what the control procedures are and what they are supposed to do. If transaction counts are to be made or batch totals produced, the users need to know what to do, how to do it, and what to do with the results. The design of effective control procedures is worthless if the procedures are not performed. Sometimes users take their control responsibilities lightly. They incorrectly assume that computer systems are infallible. Sometimes the users simply do not understand how the system works.

Second, the users need to know how to correct bad data. If an error is discovered during an edit run, it is easily corrected. If, however, an error gets through the edit and is applied to a master file, it may not be so easy to correct.

For example, suppose the price of an item in inventory is incorrectly stated in a master file. If orders for the item are processed with the incorrect price, it may be very difficult to correct the erroneous orders. Furthermore, once the correction is made, strange results can occur. A customer can order the part under one price and return it under another. If the first price is less than the second one, the customer may make a profit! Consequently, error correction procedures need to be designed carefully, and the users need to be trained in how to use them.

Operations

Operations personnel need to be trained in three major areas when processing sequential systems. First, they need to know about the two-phased activity;

they must not initiate master file updates until the transaction data has been inspected and approved by users. Second, operations personnel need to know the backup and recovery procedures. They must be able to perform them without assistance from the users or the data processing staff. A call at 3:00 A.M. to find out what to do because the system crashed should be a rare event.

Finally, operations personnel must follow defined procedures for handling sequential files—especially master files. In addition to obtaining user approval before updating master files, the operations personnel must release old versions of master files at the appropriate time. This requirement may sound simple, but when a tape library has thousands of tapes and when many sequential systems are in use, it is easy to mount the wrong tape. File-handling procedures need to be carefully designed and well documented. Operations personnel need to be trained to use them.

In many organizations, a *data control clerk* has a role in controlling sequential processing. This clerk, who normally resides just outside the computer room, receives job requests for processing and job outputs, such as reports, after processing. The responsibility of the data control clerk is to ensure that the inputs are complete before processing. The clerk also ensures that jobs are processed when (and only when) they are supposed to be processed and that all outputs are produced and delivered to the appropriate users. The data control clerk is thus a liaison between the users and the operations staff.

QUESTIONS

5.32 Why are errors easy to make with sequential file processing systems? Why are they hard to fix?

5.33 Explain the two-phased change process described for Horizon's purchase update system.

5.34 What is a batch total and how is it used?

5.35 Describe backup and recovery procedures for sequential file systems.

5.36 Explain the three-generation backup procedure.

5.37 Describe two user responsibilities for sequential systems.

5.38 Describe three operations personnel responsibilities for sequential systems.

SUMMARY

This chapter surveyed the first of three basic methods of organizing and processing data: sequential file organization. We began by discussing the general nature of sequential systems. These systems usually have two types of files: master and transaction. We found that, when master files are changed, a new copy of the file is created. Changes are not made in the middle of a sequential master file. Sequential systems are designed to process transactions in batches. Although transactions could be processed one at a time or a few at a time, such processing would be expensive because all of the master file must be copied.

We discussed the data and hardware used for sequential processing. Data is represented by bit patterns. A common code of patterns is EBCDIC. Data is recorded in tracks, or columns, across the tape.

In addition to data and hardware, we discussed sequential-file-oriented programs. A common problem is matching transaction records with master file records. Pseudocode of a record-matching algorithm was illustrated. The importance of program editing was emphasized, and several types of edit checks were described.

Finally, procedures and personnel requirements for sequential systems were discussed. The need for control procedures providing checks and balances between users and data processing was described. Backup and recovery procedures for sequential file systems were defined. Again, we stressed that the best-designed procedures are worthless if they are not followed. Consequently, training for both users and operations personnel is crucial.

Sequential file systems are very common. They have advantages over other kinds of systems. They are relatively simple, they are fast, and they can be easily backed up and recovered. Unfortunately, they suffer one severe limitation: direct access to a record is impossible. To read record 1000, the first 999 records must be read or at least passed over. In the next chapter, we will describe a type of file processing that does not have this disadvantage.

WORD LIST
(in order of appearance in text)

Sequential file processing	Block
Master file	Blocking factor
Transaction file	Buffer
Insert operation	Transport speed
Delete operation	Control field
Modify operation	Key
Batch processing	End of file (EOF)
Bit	Pseudocode
Binary digit	EOF flag
Byte	Loop
Magnetic tape	Sorting
Tracks	System utility
EBCDIC	Sort utility
Parity Track	Edit
Parity Errors	Reasonableness check
Even or odd parity	Range check
Key-to-tape equipment	Value check
Tape headers and trailers	Check digits
Tape labels	Self-checking number
Write-protect ring	Transaction count
Interrecord gap	Batch total
Recording density	Backup and recovery
Interblock gap	Three-generation backup
Bytes per inch (bpi)	Data Control Clerk
Record blocking	

A. A county government maintains records about the ownership of parcels of land. They keep the legal description of the property, the name and address of the owner, and the date and price of purchase. They want to design a sequential file system to maintain this data.

1. How should they sort this file?

2. If the length of the record is 150 bytes, how long would it take to read or write 45,000 of these records if they are stored on a magnetic tape file?

3. Draw a system flowchart of a tape-oriented system to maintain this file.

4. Write pseudocode to insert, delete, and change the owner in these records.

B. A music production company keeps records about concerts they produce. They keep the name of the group, the date, the place, and the gross revenue of each concert. They want to keep this data on a computer file and periodically compute the average revenue of each group as well as the average revenue at each place. Assume that they handle 50 groups and produce concerts in 200 places. The total number of concerts given so far is 3500, and they give 500 a year.

1. Design a system to keep needed records.

2. Draw a system flowchart of your recommendation.

3. Develop pseudocode for a program to add concerts to this file.

4. Develop pseudocode for a program to compute the averages.

C. Describe in detail a good application of a tape-oriented sequential file system.

D. Describe an ineffective application of sequential file processing.

CHAPTER 6

Direct Access File Processing Systems

There are three fundamental ways of organizing and processing data. One of them, sequential file processing, was presented in chapter 5. In this chapter, we will discuss the second type, *direct access* file processing. In chapter 7, we will discuss the third, database processing. None of these techniques is uniformly superior to the others. Each has its own advantages and disadvantages. The choice among these three types depends on the requirements to be satisfied.

THE NATURE OF DIRECT ACCESS PROCESSING

The distinguishing characteristic of a direct access system is that records can be accessed (read or written) from a file in any order. In contrast to sequential processing, there is no need to read all preceding records to get to a particular record. Further, there is no need to rewrite all of the file when a record is changed, inserted, or deleted.

We compared sequential systems to a stereo tape recorder. In a loose way, we can compare a direct access system to a stereo record player. You can play the third song without having to play the first or second. However, direct access computer systems can write records, whereas your record player cannot record music. Before considering how these systems operate, let's examine the need for such a capability.

The Need for Direct Access Processing

Suppose you want to withdraw money from your bank account using a cash machine on a local street corner. You insert your card and then key in how much money you want to withdraw. If the bank keeps the balance of your account on a sequential file, you will have to wait while the file is searched to find your account. If there are a large number of depositors at your bank, this search may take five minutes or more. Clearly you're going to become impatient. Perhaps you will find another bank. The bank needs to be able to access your account balance directly—without sequentially searching through the depositors' records until yours is found.

Suppose you decide to buy a new stereo. You want to pay for it using your Mastercard, Visa, or other similar bank card. A stereo is an expensive purchase, so the salesperson must call for a credit authorization before he or she can sell it to you. If the bank card processing center keeps all of its credit information on a sequential file, you and the salesperson will have to wait for the credit file to be searched. All of the records preceding yours in the file must be read. The search could take several minutes or more. To provide better service, the bank card processing center needs direct access to accounts.

Suppose you call a parts distributor for an auto part or similar product. You want to know whether they have the part in stock before you drive across town. If the distributor keeps the inventory records on a sequential file, and if there are many records in this file, you may have to wait some time for the inventory file to be sequentially searched. Again, the distributor needs direct access to the inventory file records.

In general, a direct access capability is called for when the batching and sorting of transaction records is infeasible. The bank cannot ask you to find 50 other people who want to withdraw money and then require all of you to line up in ascending order according to your account numbers to obtain money (see

FIGURE 6-1

Here's what could happen without direct
access capability

figure 6-1). The bank must be able to take the transactions (withdrawal requests)
one at a time and in random order.

Because a direct access system can process transactions in any order, it can
always substitute for a sequential system. If transactions happen to arrive in
batches in presorted order, it won't matter to the direct access system. The
system will process them as if they were random. You may wonder, then, why
sequential systems are used at all. Why not use direct access systems for all
applications? The answer is cost. Direct access systems cost more to design,
to implement, and to operate than sequential systems do. Therefore, they are
used only when the benefit is worth the cost.

When John Abrams discussed direct access systems at Horizon, he described
two possible applications. Figure 6-2 shows a flowchart for a direct access
customer master file system. Requests for changes to the customer master file
are submitted to the data entry clerks at CRTs. These clerks input the changes
to the master file program via the CRTs. Each change is made immediately to
the customer master file. Note the symbol ▢ . It represents *direct access*

**Possible Direct Access
Systems at Horizon**

173

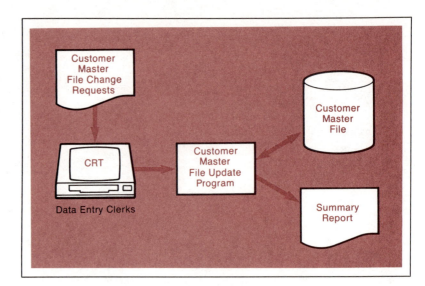

F I G U R E   6 - 2

Direct access customer master file
maintenance

Order Pricing Application

devices, which we shall discuss in the next section. These devices serve the same storage function as tape drives, but they have direct access capability.

The advantage of this system over a sequential system is that the clerks have immediate access to customer records. If they need to know what the contents of a record are, they can bring the record up on the CRT screen and examine it. Also, changes can be made immediately. The clerks do not need to wait for data entry operators to prepare input files.

Does Horizon need a direct access capability for this application? That is a good question, one that will be hard for Horizon to answer. As John explained in his presentation, either a sequential or a direct access system is feasible. The direct access system will allow immediate access to the customer data, but it will also cost more to develop and operate. Horizon will have to decide whether the benefits are worth the costs.

The second example John described concerned the pricing of orders. In this example, items are picked and packed and then moved to a shipping area. Here, a clerk extracts a copy of the picking slip from each order and sends it to data entry. The data entry personnel prepare a tape file of input data like the one used for the class enrollment system.

This file is read by the order pricing system shown in figure 6-3. For each order, the order pricing program obtains the price of each item, multiplies the price by the quantity of the item shipped (a process called *price extension*), and computes the total cost of the order. The outputs are priced invoices that are shipped with the orders and a magnetic tape file of customer numbers and order amounts. This file is input to the accounts receivable computer system (not shown).

To be able to price each order separately, the prices must be on a direct access file. If they were not, then the entire price file would have to be sequentially searched for each order. Extensive searching would be required just to find the prices of a few items on each order. Such searching would be a very time consuming process. Instead, the program shown in figure 6-3 reads the item number for each item on the order and uses this number to obtain the price of the item directly from the product price file. Then the price extension is done, and the process continues.

Although the systems shown in figures 6-2 and 6-3 are both direct access systems, they have an important difference. In the system in figure 6-2, the clerks can communicate directly with the computer via CRTs. In the system in figure 6-3, there is no such direct communication. Inputs are made via key-to-tape equipment.

A system in which the user is in direct communication with the computer is called an *online system*. This term means that the user is online or has a communication link with the computer. The master file maintenance system in figure 6-2 is an online system. The user of the pricing system in figure 6-3 has no direct communication with the computer, and so the system is an *offline system*.

Online systems can be very complex, and the technology involved is complicated. Consequently, we will defer discussing online processing until chapter 8. For now, you should simply realize that direct access systems can be either online or offline systems. In fact, most direct access systems are online, but not all of them are. Do not make the mistake of assuming that direct access systems are *always* online systems.

Given this introduction, we will now consider each of the five components of a direct access computer system. Hardware and data will be considered first, followed by programs, procedures, and personnel.

Online and Offline Systems

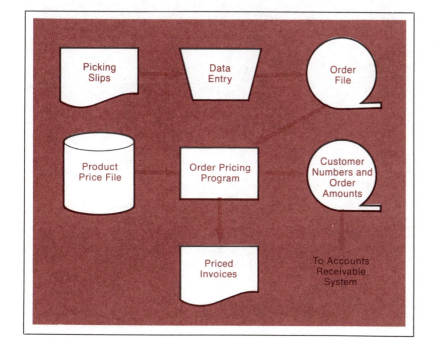

FIGURE 6-3

Order pricing system

6.1 How does direct access processing differ from sequential file processing?

6.2 Is a bank card processing company for Mastercard or Visa apt to keep credit information on a direct access file or a sequential file? Why?

6.3 Since a direct access system can always substitute for a sequential system, why have sequential systems at all?

6.4 Why is the Horizon customer master file system shown in figure 6-2 called an *online system*?

6.5 Are all direct access systems online systems?

HARDWARE FOR DIRECT ACCESS PROCESSING

The most common type of direct access device is a *disk storage unit* (figure 6-4). It has two basic components. A *disk pack* is a collection of disks with *recording surfaces*. It looks much like a stack of phonograph records mounted on a spindle (see figure 6-5). The disk pack is mounted on the disk storage unit. It revolves at high speeds. (Speeds of 50 to 75 revolutions per *second* are typical.)

The surfaces of the disks are coated with an easily magnetized substance. Data is recorded on each disk in concentric circles, as shown in figure 6-6. These circles are called *tracks*. Our comparison with a phonograph record is not perfect; the tracks on a disk surface are not continuous like the groove in a phonograph record is.

FIGURE 6-4

Disk storage unit

F I G U R E   6 - 5

Disk pack

Figure 6-7 presents a schematic of a disk storage unit and its associated read/write heads. These heads are used to read data from or write data to the tracks. In most disk units, the heads are attached to access arms that move together to position the heads at any track on the surfaces of the disks. Suppose a disk pack has 10 recording surfaces. When the access arms are fixed in a position, 10 tracks can be read—one on each surface. When the arms are moved to another position, another 10 tracks can be read. The collection of tracks that can be read when the access arms are stationed in a position is called a *cylinder*.

Not all disk storage units have *movable read/write heads*. Some units, such as the IBM 2305® have fixed heads. *Fixed-head* units have one read/write head per cylinder. Consequently, they are more expensive than movable-head units. They may be faster, however, because no time is spent moving the read/write heads to the correct cylinder.

Some disk storage units permit the disk pack to be removed. Thus, packs containing different files can be mounted in the same unit. For other systems, the disk pack must be fixed. Figure 6-8 shows one type of removable disk pack called a *Winchester disk* or *data module*. The disk pack and the access arm and heads are encased in a plastic housing, and the entire package is removed. Data modules are more expensive than disk packs like the one shown in figure 6-5, but they have higher reliability and can store more data. Some data modules are so well protected that they require no preventive maintenance. Figure 6-9 summarizes the types of disk storage units.

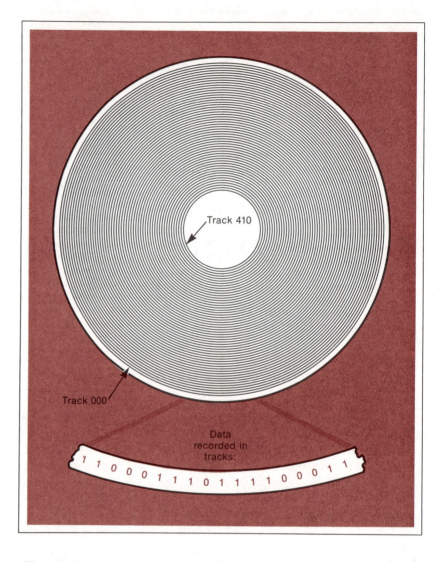

Track 410

Track 000

Data recorded in tracks:

1 1 0 0 0 1 1 1 0 1 1 1 1 1 0 0 0 1 1

FIGURE 6-6

Disk surface

You may be surprised to learn that the same amount of data is recorded on a small inner track as is recorded on a large outer track. The data is just recorded more densely on the inner track than on the outer one, thus keeping the data transfer rate constant. Because it takes the same amount of time for an inner track to make one revolution as it takes for an outer track, the same amount of data must be recorded. Otherwise data would have to be transferred faster from the large tracks than from the small ones.

Data Layout on Disks

Figure 6-10 shows a general layout of data on a disk track. Each track has a starting point that is permanently marked on the track, followed by a track header, and then blocks of data. The track header contains the name of the track and other system data. As with tape, the application data is recorded in blocks that are collections of one or more logical records. (A block can include several Horizon customer master file records, for example.) However, with

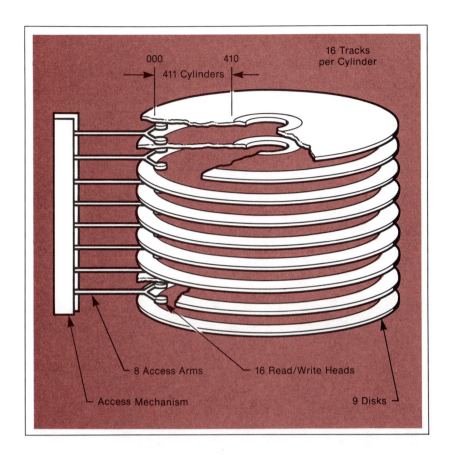

000 410
← 411 Cylinders →

16 Tracks
per Cylinder

8 Access Arms — 16 Read/Write Heads

Access Mechanism

9 Disks

FIGURE 6-7

Schematic of disk storage unit and its
read/write heads

FIGURE 6-8

Winchester disk or data module

Types of Disk Storage Units	Characteristics
Fixed or Movable Heads	Fixed heads have one head per track. Variable heads have movable access arms.
Fixed or Removable Packs	Fixed packs stay in the unit. Removable packs can be interchanged. (Packs with disk and access arms removed are called *data modules*.)

FIGURE 6-9

Summary of disk characteristics

FIGURE 6-10

Layout of data on a disk track

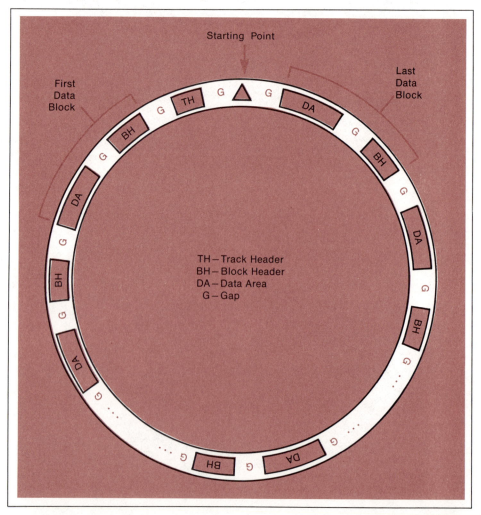

disks, each block is preceded by a block header that identifies the block, gives its length, and may indicate the contents of the block. Each computer system has its own layout peculiarities, but the general structure is similar to that shown in figure 6-10.

The capacity of a disk pack depends on the type of unit and its manufacturer. Capacities vary from several million characters to 350 million or more. For example, the Hewlett-Packard 7920® disk storage unit has 815 cylinders per pack; each cylinder has five tracks; and each track can contain up to 12,000 characters, or bytes. The total capacity is just over 50 million bytes. The IBM 3350® disk storage unit has 555 cylinders per pack; each cylinder has 30 tracks; and each track can contain up to 19,000 bytes. Total capacity for the IBM 3350 is 317.5 million bytes.

Not all of the stated capacity of a disk pack can be used for application data. Some of the space will be used for system data, like addresses, block lengths, and so forth. Some will be used for interblock gaps. Depending on block sizes and other factors, somewhere between 75 and 95 percent of the available space can be used for application data.

Recall from chapter 5 that the Horizon customer master file has 200,000 records, each 120 bytes in length. This is a total of 24 million bytes. The file would easily fit on either of the two devices just discussed. It would fit on many other devices from other manufacturers as well.

The time required to transfer data to or from a disk has three major components. *Access motion time* is the time required to position the read/write heads over the correct cylinder. The amount of time depends on how far the access mechanism must move. On the average, the HP 7920 and the IBM 3350 both take 25 milliseconds to move from one cylinder to another.

The second component of time is *rotational delay*, or the time it takes for the required data to revolve under the read/write head. At best, it is zero (when the head is over the required data); at worst, it is the time required for one complete revolution of the disk surface. The average of the two is often used for timing purposes. For the HP 7920, this time is 8.3 milliseconds, and for the IBM 3350, it is 8.4 milliseconds.

The final component of transfer time is the *data movement time*. This is the time taken to move data from the disk to main memory (for a read) or from main memory to the disk (for a write). The HP 7920 takes 0.00106 milliseconds per byte; the IBM 3350 takes 0.00083 milliseconds per byte. These specifications are summarized in figure 6-11.

Data Transfer Time on Disks

Device Type	Average Access Motion Time	Rotational Delay Time	Data Transfer Time
HP 7920	25 msec	8.3 msec	0.00106 msec per byte
IBM 3350	25 msec	8.4 msec	0.00083 msec per byte

Processing Times for Horizon's Customer Master File

Reading the File Sequentially

From the above transfer-time figures, we can estimate how long it will take to read or write all of the Horizon customer master file data. Assume the data will be stored on an HP 7920 device. First, suppose the data is read sequentially.

Horizon has 200,000 120-byte records in the master file. Let's assume eight records are blocked together. Therefore, there are 25,000 blocks of data. Considering the HP 7920, we can assume that 12 of these blocks will fit on each track. Consequently, 25,000 divided by 12, or 2084, tracks will be required. Since there are five tracks per cylinder on the HP 7920, a total of 417 cylinders will be required to hold the data.

Now, consider each of the components of transfer time. For access motion time, it will take an average of 25 milliseconds to find each cylinder. Therefore, 417 times 0.025, or 10.42, seconds will be required for access motion. For rotational delay, it will take an average of 8.3 milliseconds to find each block, so 25,000 times 0.0083, or 207.5, seconds will be required. Finally, a total of 24 million bytes of data must be transferred. Thus, 24 million times 0.00106 milliseconds, or 25.44, seconds will be required to transfer the data. Consequently, the total time to read or write the Horizon customer master file is 243.4 seconds, or about four minutes.

The time required to read or write the data for the IBM 3350 is not vastly different and will be left as an exercise.

Randomly Reading the File

How long will it take to read one of these records randomly? Unless we are lucky, we will have to move the access arm to a new cylinder to find the block. On the average, this movement will take 25 milliseconds for the HP 7920. The unit will also have to wait for the record to come under the read/write head. On the average, this will take 8.3 milliseconds. Thus, 33.3 milliseconds will be required to find the record.

Once found, the entire block (not just the record wanted) must be read, because the unit is designed to read only whole blocks (not parts of them). There are 960 bytes per block, so, at 0.00106 milliseconds per byte, a total of 1.02 milliseconds will be required to read the block. In total, then, 34.32 milliseconds will be required to read the record. Since there are 200,000 records in the file, a total of about 6864 seconds, or about two hours, will be required to read the file in random order.

Compare this to the answer we obtained for reading the file sequentially. To read a record randomly, 34.3 milliseconds are needed. To read the same record in sequential order, only about 1.2 milliseconds are required.

Why is there such a big difference in the times required to read the file? There are two reasons. First, for direct access processing, the access arms must move back and forth across the disk pack, which takes about 5000 extra seconds. Seconds, for sequential processing, when a block is read, all eight records in the block are processed. For direct access processing, when a block is read, although only one of the contained records is needed, all eight records in the block must be read. Therefore each block is read eight times instead of just once. This fact accounts for the balance of the extra time.

F I G U R E 6 - 1 2

Floppy disk

In addition to disk storage units, three other types of direct access media are in common use. One is called a *floppy disk, diskette* or, sometimes, just a *floppy*. This medium is similar to a *conventional* or *hard disk* storage unit, but there is always only one disk (like a phonograph record) instead of a stack of disks. Further, this disk is flexible, hence the term *floppy*.

The arrangement of data on a floppy is very similar to that on the disks previously described. One difference is that floppies, because of their design, contain less data. A typical floppy has two surfaces with 70 tracks per surface and 7680 bytes per track. The total capacity is just over 1 million bytes. Also, the time for access motion, rotational delay, and data transfer are considerably longer for floppies. Figure 6-12 shows a floppy disk.

Another type of common direct access medium is called a *drum*. A drum is a cylinder that can have data recorded on its outer surface. The tracks on a drum are circles around this surface, as shown in figure 6-13. Each track has its own read/write head, so there is no access motion and hence no delay for moving the access arms. Drums were more prevalent in the past than they are today. Newer, faster disks with greater capacity have replaced many of them.

A final type of direct access device is actually a hybrid or combination of tape and disk technology. Figure 6-14 shows a *mass storage device*. Data is stored on small rolls of magnetic tape and then moved or staged to direct access devices when needed. After the data is processed, it is moved from disk back to the small rolls of tape. The capacity of this unit, and of similar units manufactured by other companies, is typically in the range of 400 billion bytes. Thus, they provide very large capacity, direct access capability.

Other Direct Access Hardware

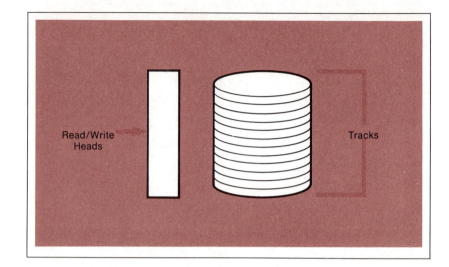

F I G U R E   6 - 1 3

Drum schematic

F I G U R E   6 - 1 4

IBM 3850 mass storage subsystem

The cost per byte of stored data is less for a mass storage unit than for the several pure direct access devices required to yield the same capacity. The disadvantage is that the data must be staged from tape to disk and back. This staging, however, is automatic; it requires no human intervention. These units, by the way, are amazing to watch. If you have the opportunity to see one, don't pass it up.

QUESTIONS

6.6 Define the terms *disk storage unit, disk pack, disk, track* and *cylinder.*

6.7 The XYZ 2000 disk pack has 10 surfaces, 200 tracks per surface, and 10,000 bytes per track. What is the total capacity of the XYZ disk pack?

6.8 What is the difference between a record and a block?

6.9 What is access motion time? Rotational delay? Data movement time?

6.10 Average access motion time for the XYZ 2000 is 50 milliseconds to move from one cylinder to the next. What is the access time to read a file of five cylinders sequentially?

6.11 Rotational delay for the XYZ 2000 is 10 milliseconds. What will be the total rotational delay to read 500 records?

6.12 The XYZ 2000 transfers data at the rate of 0.001 millisecond per byte. How long will it take to read 500 records if they are 200 bytes long?

6.13 What is the total time for the XYZ 2000 to read sequentially a file of 500 records, 200 bytes long, that occupies five cylinders? The records are not blocked.

6.14 Why does it take so much longer to process a file randomly than it does to process it sequentially?

6.15 What is a floppy?

DATA FOR DIRECT
ACCESS PROCESSING

To do direct access processing, each record in the file must have an identifier, or *key*. The key is usually one of the fields of the record. For example, the customer number could be the key for Horizon's customer master file. A part number could be the key for a file of parts in inventory. Usually, keys must be unique; only one record in the file is allowed to have a given key value. Consequently, names are not very often chosen as keys.

Now, the fundamental problem for direct access processing is to relate a particular key value to the location of the record on a direct access device. There are two primary techniques or file organizations for doing this. One is called *random*, or *direct, file organization*, and the other is called *indexed sequential file organization*.

Unfortunately, the terminology as used in industry is confusing in this area. To review, there are two types of file processing: sequential and direct access. Under the category of direct access file processing, there are two file organizations: random, or direct, and indexed sequential. Thus the term *direct* is used in two ways, as the name of a type of file processing and as the name of a type of direct access file organization. To make matters worse, the term *random* is used in the same two ways.

In this book, we will use the term *direct* to refer only to a type of file *processing* (in contrast to sequential file processing) and the term *random* to refer only to a type of file *organization* (in contrast to indexed sequential file organization). This is awkward, but it can't be helped. Industry uses the terms this way and you should be aware of its terminology.

Random File Organization

There is a variety of ways to allocate records to a random file organization. We will describe one common technique that is called a *hashing algorithm*. Basically, the value of the key is arithmetically manipulated to determine the record's location on the file.

For example, suppose Horizon has an inventory file of less than 1000 items. One way of determining record locations would be to take the last three digits of the part number as the address of the record. Thus part number 12345 would be assigned record location 345 on the file. Part number 14592 would be at location 592.

As you can see, there is a problem if two different parts have the same last three digits. Both part 12345 and part 32345 are assigned location 345. One way to solve this problem is to put one of these records in location 345 and to put the other in the next available location. Thus, the calculated address is the place to start looking for the record. Other ways are used but are not important for your understanding of computer systems (at least in this course). This addressing scheme is summarized in figure 6-15.

When this file is first created, the direct access device is formatted with 1000 empty records. These records can be thought of as empty buckets or placeholders. Then the file is loaded with the inventory data by assigning the records to file locations according to their last three digits.

Can you see the problem that could occur if the file were completely full? Suppose that when the 1000th record is loaded, the only remaining empty record is record 999. Further, suppose that the part number of the last item is 12000. Its assigned location is zero, but the next available location is 999! For this reason, randomly organized files should be only 60 to 70 percent full. Even at that, similar problems can occur.

Now, how does the system find a record? Given part number 12345, it will first find the record at location 345. If record 12345 is in location 345, the system will stop because the desired record has been found. If not, it will read the next record and so on until record 12345 is found. To modify a record, the system will first read it into main memory as just described, then modify the record contents, and then write it back out to the location in which it was found. To delete a record, the system will first find it and then replace it with an empty record, or indicate that the record is deleted by putting a special mark on it (a question mark in the first position, for example).

This discussion has assumed that the records are unblocked. If there are several inventory records per physical block, then the algorithm for computing addresses must be a little more sophisticated. Otherwise, the process is nearly the same.

Random file organization is the fastest direct access file organization. Unfortunately, it suffers from several disadvantages. First, the records are allocated

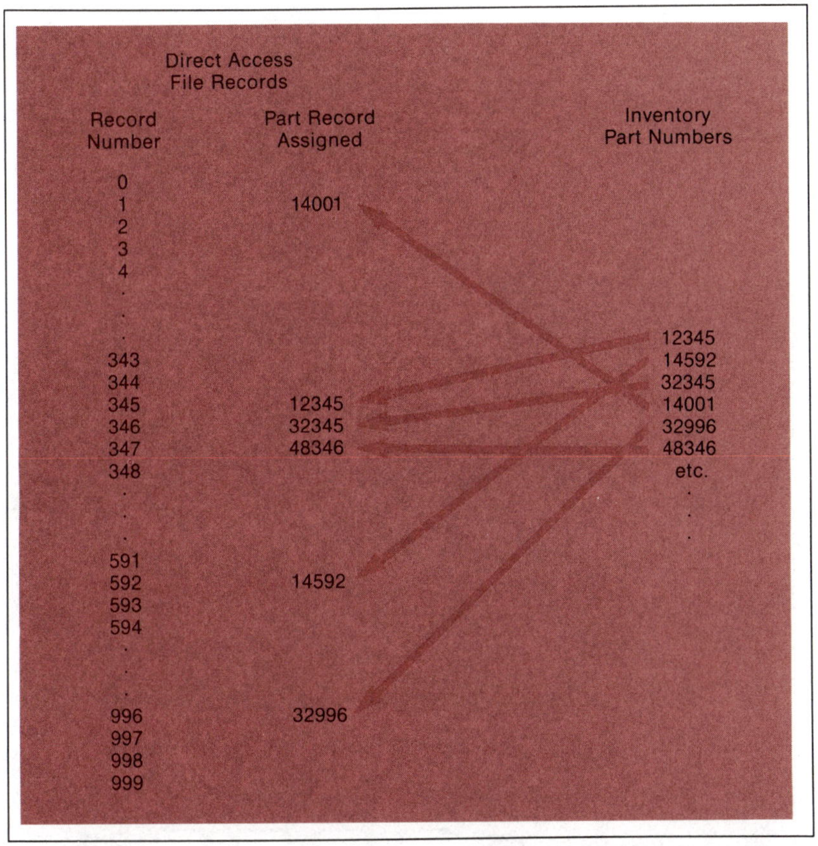

FIGURE 6-15

Allocating records to random file using last three digits

to the file in a seemingly haphazard fashion. If the records are read in the order in which they are stored on the direct access device, they are not in any logical sequence. Second, it is hard to expand a randomly organized file. If Horizon wants to have 2000 items in inventory, the file and some of the programs must be altered. Third, efficient processing often requires sorting the records in order. Finally, as mentioned, randomly organized files should never be full. Consequently, 20 or 30 percent of the file space is wasted. However, in spite of this, if the application calls for very fast retrieval, random organization can be effective.

Indexed Sequential File Organization

The second type of direct access file organization is called *indexed sequential*. This organization allows both sequential and direct access processing by storing the records in the sequential order of the key. Indexes (similar to the index of a book) are constructed for direct processing. Thus, to do sequential processing, the records are processed in the physical order of the file. To do direct processing, the indexes are used to locate a desired record, and it is then read from the file.

Since records are to be kept in the sequential order of the key, inserts pose a problem. Rather than rewrite the entire file as is done with sequential processing, indexed sequential organization puts the new records in their correct places on a track and moves the last record on the track to a special place called an

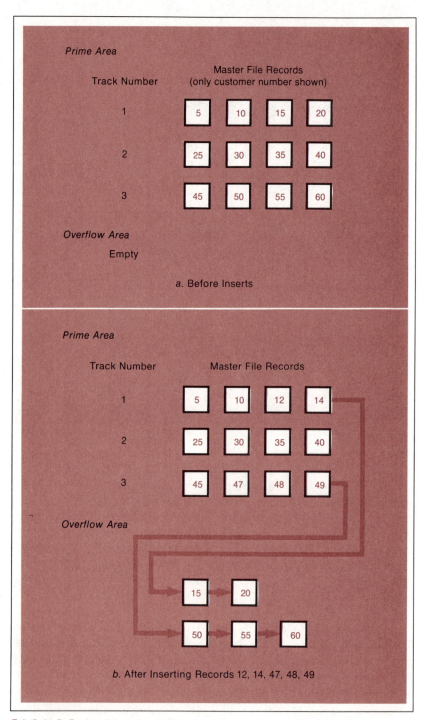

FIGURE 6-16

Inserts in an indexed sequential file

overflow area. Thus, in figure 6-16, when record 12 was inserted, record 20 was moved to the overflow area; when record 14 was inserted, record 15 was also moved into the overflow area.

When the file in figure 6-16*b* is processed sequentially, the system will read records 5, 10, 12, and 14 from track 1. It will then find records 15 and 20 in the overflow area. Then it will process the records on track 2. Thus, all of the records will be retrieved in the correct sequential order.

Indexed sequential organization is an excellent compromise between straight sequential and pure random file organizations. It is most useful in applications that call for both sequential and direct processing. A good example is credit card authorizations. At the end of the month, the credit file is processed sequentially to produce the customer bills. However, throughout the month, it is processed directly for credit authorizations.

Unfortunately, like all compromises, indexed sequential organization has disadvantages. Sequential processing is faster for a sequential file than for an indexed sequential file. Direct processing is faster for a random file than for an indexed sequential file. Also, the overflow areas take up extra file space. Finally, after many inserts, record retrieval becomes slow. Figure 6-17 summarizes advantages and disadvantages of sequential, random, and indexed sequential file organizations.

QUESTIONS

6.16 What is a key?

6.17 What are the two possible meanings for the term *direct processing*?

6.18 What are the two possible meanings for the term *random processing*?

6.19 Which of the two meanings of *direct processing* will we use in this book? Which will we use for *random processing*?

6.20 For the random file organization shown in figure 6-15, to what location will part number 45897 be assigned? Where will part number 22345 be assigned? Where will part number 22345 actually be stored?

FIGURE 6-17

Comparison of file organizations

File Organization	Advantages/Disadvantages
Sequential	Is simple to use. Is fast and efficient for large batches. Cannot update in middle of file.
Indexed Sequential	Can update in middle of file. Both sequential and direct processing are possible. Processing may be slow.
Random	Can update in middle of file. Processing is very fast. Has wasted file space.

6.21 Why should a randomly organized file never be completely full?

6.22 Name three disadvantages of random file organization.

6.23 Does an indexed sequential file allow direct access or sequential processing?

6.24 How are inserts made to an indexed sequential file?

6.25 Describe a good application for random file organization.

6.26 Describe a good application for indexed sequential file organization.

PROGRAMS FOR DIRECT ACCESS PROCESSING

Before you can get a clear picture of how direct access programs operate, we need to define three types of computer programs. Only the barest essentials are defined here. See module I for more details.

Types of Programs

Application programs direct the computer to solve specific problems. The Horizon customer file update program is one example of an application program. Application programs do not usually come with the computer; the using organization has to develop them or buy them from some program vendor.

System service programs are the second type of program. The sort utility described in chapter 5 is one example of a system service program. Other examples are the language translators, or compilers. If you have written programs, you have used the COBOL, BASIC, or some other language compiler. System service programs usually come with the computer. They are written and tested by the computer manufacturer. Data processing personnel simply have to learn how to use them.

The third category of programs is referred to as the *operating system*. These programs manage the computer's resources. They start and stop application programs; allocate tape, disk, and other types of equipment; and manage the computer's memories. Also (and this is the reason for introducing this topic here), the operating system programs provide *data management services*. In most instances, the computer manufacturer provides operating systems. See module I for more details regarding system service programs and operating systems.

When an application programmer wants to read or write a record, he or she simply codes a command like READ CUSTOMER-FILE or WRITE INVEN-TORY-RECORD. The application programmer does not need to be concerned with such activities as blocking or deblocking the record or filling and emptying buffers. Instead, all of these activities are performed by the data management portion of the operating system.

When the command READ CUSTOMER-FILE is translated by the compiler, computer instructions are inserted into the application program. These instructions ask the operating system to control the *input/output* (I/O). It controls the I/O by executing a very complex set of instructions that cause the data to be read or written.

Because of this operating system service, the job of the application programmer is greatly simplified. He or she need not be concerned with the details of how to do input and output. The programmer can spend more time solving applications problems instead of computer system problems.

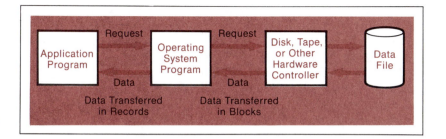

FIGURE 6-18

Application and operating system
program roles in file read records

Figure 6-18 illustrates the read process. The application program issues requests to read data, one record at a time. Each request goes to an operating system program where it is executed. A block of data is brought in from the file, deblocked, and sent to the application program.

HORIZON CUSTOMER MASTER FILE UPDATE

To illustrate a direct access application program, we will consider the Horizon customer master file update program shown in figure 6-2. Again, a clerk at a CRT inputs requests to the update program. The program then accesses the direct access customer master file. For this example, we will assume that this file has indexed sequential organization and that the key is the customer number.

Four basic actions can be taken in maintaining a master file. Records can be inserted, deleted, modified, and read. Corresponding to each of these actions is a command that the application programmer may use. Thus, when he or she codes the INSERT command, the operating system will cause a new record to be added to the file. Now, since this is a direct access application, the operating system needs to know what to call the new record—that is, what the key of the new record will be. Usually this key value is specified in a command like INSERT 123456 INTO CUSTOMER MASTER FILE. This command means to

insert a new record whose key is 123456 into the customer master file. The data for the new record will also be supplied by the application program, but the way that this is done depends on the language used. (Ask your instructor to explain how it is done in the language you use.)

Examples of other indexed sequential commands are

DELETE 123456 FROM
  CUSTOMER MASTER FILE
REPLACE 123456 IN
  CUSTOMER MASTER FILE
READ 123456 FROM
  CUSTOMER MASTER FILE

Recall that the commands for processing a sequential file named only an operation (like READ) and the name of a file. The identity or key of the record was not needed. The next record in sequential order was assumed to be the one to be processed.

A Direct Access Program for Horizon's Customer Master File

Figure 6-19 shows the pseudocode for the customer master file update

191

program. This pseudocode references three files. CUSTOMER MASTER FILE is the indexed sequential file having the customer data. SUMMARY REPORT is a printed report of the actions taken by the clerk at the CRT. This report documents changes that have been made for later reference if errors are discovered. The third file is called TERMINAL and corresponds to the CRT employed by the user.

At first, it may seem surprising to consider a user at a terminal as a file. However, because the user supplies data to the program, and because the program outputs data to the user, the CRT is like a storage file. Therefore, terminals are often processed as files in application programs.

The customer master file update program has six paragraphs, as shown in figure 6-19. This program obtains a request code from the user that indicates the activity to be performed. A 0 means stop, a 1 means insert, a 2 means delete, a 3 means modify, and a 4 means read a record. To start the process, MAIN-PARAGRAPH opens the files. (This means that the operating system will take whatever action is necessary to prepare to use the files.) Then it asks the user for the first request code. Next, PROCESS-PARAGRAPH is called. PROCESS-PARAGRAPH will stay in control until the user types the request code 0, at which time MAIN-PARAGRAPH will regain control. It will close the files and stop.

Activity in PROCESS-PARAGRAPH is controlled by a DOWHILE statement. As long as the value of REQUEST-CODE is

nonzero, PROCESS-PARAGRAPH will be executed. The first statement in the DO loop is a new pseudocode statement: the case statement. It sends control to a location, depending on the value of REQUEST-CODE. (See the comment in figure 6-19.) If the value of REQUEST-CODE is 1, 2, 3, or 4, then one of the four processing modules will be called. However, if the value is greater than 4, an error message will be written.

What happens if the user accidentally types in a negative number? There is no telling. As this pseudocode stands, an error of some unknown form will occur. You will be asked to fix this defect in question 6.31.

The four paragraphs called by PROCESS-PARAGRAPH are similar. We will discuss only one of them. The first statement in the INSERT-PARAGRAPH obtains the customer number and data for the new customer record. Then, it checks the validity of this number by attempting to read a record using it as a key. If the customer number is a valid new number, this read should be unsuccessful. If the read is successful, the customer number provided by the clerk is erroneous because it is already in use.

If the customer number is valid, the program inserts the new master record. It writes messages to SUMMARY REPORT and to the user at the CRT terminal. Then, control is returned to PROCESS-PARAGRAPH where the user is asked for the next REQUEST-CODE. If nonzero, another transaction is processed against the master file. Otherwise the program terminates.

```
BEGIN MAIN-PARAGRAPH
    OPEN CUSTOMER MASTER FILE, SUMMARY REPORT FILE, TERMINAL FILE
    INPUT REQUEST-CODE FROM TERMINAL
    DO PROCESS-PARAGRAPH
    CLOSE CUSTOMER MASTER FILE, SUMMARY REPORT FILE, TERMINAL FILE
    STOP
END MAIN-PARAGRAPH


BEGIN PROCESS-PARAGRAPH
  DOWHILE REQUEST-CODE ≠ 0
      GO TO                        (This is called a case statement. If the value of RE-
          INSERT-SECTION           QUEST-CODE is 1, control will go to INSERT-SECTION.
          DELETE-SECTION           If 2, control will go to DELETE-SECTION. IF 3, to MODI-
          MODIFY-SECTION           FY-SECTION, etc. If 5 or greater, control will go to
          READ-SECTION             ERROR-SECTION.)
          ERROR-SECTION
              DEPENDING ON REQUEST-CODE
      INSERT-SECTION
          DO INSERT-PARAGRAPH
          GO TO EXIT
      DELETE-SECTION
          DO DELETE-PARAGRAPH
          GO TO EXIT
      MODIFY-SECTION
          DO MODIFY-PARAGRAPH
          GO TO EXIT
      READ-SECTION
          DO READ-PARAGRAPH
          GO TO EXIT
      ERROR-SECTION
          PRINT "ERROR. INVALID REQUEST CODE. TRY AGAIN." ON TERMINAL
          GO TO EXIT
      EXIT
          INPUT REQUEST-CODE FROM TERMINAL
  END-DO
END PROCESS-PARAGRAPH
```

FIGURE 6-19

Pseudocode for customer master file
update program (part 1 of 3)

```
BEGIN INSERT-PARAGRAPH
   INPUT CUSTOMER DATA FROM TERMINAL
   GENERATE NEW CUSTOMER-NUMBER
   INSERT NEW RECORD ON CUSTOMER MASTER FILE
   PRINT "NEW CUSTOMER ADDED.CUSTOMER NUMBER
         IS", CUSTOMER NUMBER ON
         TERMINAL AND SUMMARY REPORT
   END INSERT PARAGRAPH

BEGIN DELETE-PARAGRAPH
   INPUT CUSTOMER-NUMBER TO BE DELETED FROM TERMINAL
   DELETE RECORD CUSTOMER-NUMBER FROM CUSTOMER MASTER FILE
   IF DELETION SUCCESSFUL
      THEN PRINT "CUSTOMER DELETED. CUSTOMER NUMBER IS", CUSTOMER-NUMBER
              ON SUMMARY REPORT
           PRINT "DELETION SUCCESSFUL." ON TERMINAL
      ELSE PRINT CUSTOMER-NUMBER AND MESSAGE "AN INVALID
              CUSTOMER NUMBER. CUSTOMER NOT DELETED." ON TERMINAL

   END-IF
END DELETE-PARAGRAPH
```

FIGURE 6-19

Pseudocode for customer master file
update program (part 2 of 3)

Characteristics of Direct Access Programs

If you compare the pseudocode shown in figure 6-19 to the pseudocode for making updates to the sequential file shown in figure 5-16, you will find that the direct access pseudocode is simpler. It is simpler because there is no need to match records against one another, as there is in sequential processing. In actuality, direct access processing is a good deal more complex than sequential processing. Most of the extra work, however, is taken care of by the operating system so the application programmer does not see it.

Because the customer master file is an indexed sequential file, it could also be processed sequentially. Therefore, the pseudocode in figure 5-16 could be used to update the customer master file with sales data. In fact, Horizon's customer system could very well use indexed sequential processing. Horizon could construct the customer master file as an indexed sequential file and use sequential processing to update the customer records with sales data. They could use direct access processing to maintain current customer data and add new customers. At year-end, they could also use sequential processing to generate the customers' dividend checks.

```
BEGIN MODIFY-PARAGRAPH
    INPUT CUSTOMER-NUMBER TO BE MODIFIED AND MODIFYING DATA FROM TERMINAL
    READ RECORD CUSTOMER-NUMBER FROM CUSTOMER MASTER FILE
    IF READ SUCCESSFUL
        THEN MAKE CHANGES TO RECORD JUST READ
                REPLACE RECORD CUSTOMER-NUMBER ON CUSTOMER MASTER FILE
                PRINT "RECORD MODIFIED. CUSTOMER NUMBER IS", CUSTOMER-NUMBER ON
                    SUMMARY REPORT
                PRINT "MODIFICATION SUCCESSFUL." ON TERMINAL
            ELSE PRINT CUSTOMER-NUMBER AND MESSAGE "THIS IS AN INVALID
                    CUSTOMER NUMBER. CUSTOMER NOT MODIFIED." ON TERMINAL

    END-IF
END MODIFY-PARAGRAPH

BEGIN READ-PARAGRAPH
    INPUT CUSTOMER-NUMBER TO BE READ FROM TERMINAL
    READ RECORD CUSTOMER-NUMBER FROM CUSTOMER MASTER FILE
    IF READ SUCCESSFUL
        THEN PRINT "READ SUCCESSFUL. CUSTOMER DATA FOLLOWS.", CUSTOMER
                    MASTER FILE DATA ON TERMINAL
            ELSE PRINT CUSTOMER-NUMBER AND MESSAGE "THIS IS AN INVALID
                    CUSTOMER NUMBER. CUSTOMER NOT FOUND." ON TERMINAL

    END-IF
END READ-PARAGRAPH
```

Pseudocode for customer master file
update program (part 3 of 3)

Random organization of direct access files places more burden on the application programmer than indexed sequential organization does. To explain it well, we would need to consider more detail than is probably necessary for your career. Consequently, we will not present pseudocode for a randomly organized file. See [27] and [56] for discussions if you are interested. For now, it will be sufficient to remember that random organization exists and that it is one of two major types of direct access file organization.

Direct access file organizations are not standardized across makes and models of computers. The syntax of commands, as well as the details of the file organizations, vary from one computer to another. The commands described in this section are generalized. They do not correspond to any particular manufacturer's language. Furthermore, some operating systems provide a larger variety of direct access organizations. These organizations are variations and extensions of the two basic types described here. If you understand these two organizations and their capabilities and limitations, you should be able to understand other variations that you encounter.

QUESTIONS

6.27 What are the three categories of computer programs?

6.28 Which of the three categories of programs requests I/O operations? Which actually processes the I/O requests?

6.29 When performing direct access I/O, the application program must specify an extra parameter. What is it?

6.30 Why consider a user at a terminal as a file?

6.31 How can the customer master file pseudocode be changed to trap any negative REQUEST-CODE and print an error message?

6.32 Explain what the case statement means.

PROCEDURES FOR DIRECT ACCESS PROCESSING

"Let's suppose," said John Abrams, "that Horizon has the customer master file on an indexed sequential file and that clerks make changes to this file directly using a customer update program. Could a clerk accidentally delete the wrong customer? Would this be hard to do? Also, could a clerk change his or her own sales amounts and thereby get an extra-large dividend at year-end?"

These questions started a loud and active conversation during which the project team discovered an important fact: Although direct access systems have great advantages and are easy to use, they are also very hard to control. *Errors are easily made and the data is vulnerable to unauthorized activity. As the discussion progressed, John explained how systems procedures can be used to provide control over direct access systems. He described two categories of procedures: those used for normal operations and those used when there is a system failure. We will consider the procedures for normal operation first.*

User Procedures for Normal Operation

Procedures need to be defined for each operation on the file. For example, there should be an insert procedure that describes the steps a clerk takes to add a new customer. There should also be procedures for deletion, for modification, and even for reading.

The insert procedure is summarized in figure 6-20. When the clerk receives a customer order, he or she first determines if the customer has ordered before. If so, then no insert is needed. If not, the clerk verifies that the name, address,

```
CHECK FOR PREVIOUS ORDER
IF NO PREVIOUS ORDER
     THEN CHECK DATA FOR COMPLETENESS
           IF INCOMPLETE
                 THEN CONTACT CUSTOMER FOR MORE DATA
           END-IF
           CHECK FILE ON BAD RISKS
           IF NOT ON BAD-RISK FILE
                 THEN ADD CUSTOMER TO CUSTOMER FILE
                 ELSE SEND ORDER TO CUSTOMER CREDIT FOR PROCESSING
           END-IF
  END-IF
```

FIGURE 6-20

User procedure for adding customer to
customer file

and phone number are complete. If more data is needed, the clerk contacts the customer to obtain the necessary items. Then, a search is made of the bad-risk file to determine the customer's credit worthiness. If no entry is found on the bad-risk file, the customer record is added using the update program. If an entry is found, the order is sent to customer credit for processing there. Customer numbers are assigned by the update program and will be printed and returned to the customer when the order is processed.

Why is this procedure necessary? Without it, as John explained, clerks will input new customers with incomplete data, or they won't know what to do if some data is missing, or they will add customers who have been problems in the past. Each clerk will take a different action and the results will be unpredictable. Worst of all, some requests with insufficient data will not be inserted, nor will they be returned to the customer. Thus, the situation occurs in which someone submits an order to Horizon and then never hears from them again. Finally, without procedures, there will be no means for reporting errors and for correcting them when they occur.

The Need for Procedures

Think for a moment about the "computer errors" publicized in the news. Frequently, these are not errors of the computer at all, but errors in procedures or errors in following procedures. Suppose that Horizon implemented this system with poorly defined procedures and, as a result, two customers' records were intermixed; say, one customer was assigned another customer's address. If that happened, one person could receive another person's order, and someone else could receive a bill for goods that he or she never received. These errors might incorrectly be blamed on the computer.

The problems that can be caused by incorrect modifications and deletions are even worse. If a clerk modifies the wrong customer record, say, when changing a customer name, then two errors are generated: the desired name change is not made, and another customer's name becomes incorrect. If the wrong record is deleted, a customer will inexplicably disappear from the file, while a customer that was to have been deleted stays on.

Because of these potential difficulties, modification and deletion procedures usually call for some type of verification before the action is taken. For example, the clerk may first read a customer record and verify that the name on the file is the name that is on the change request form. If not, the change is not made.

The verification step can be coded in the program. Thus, when the clerk types in the number of a customer to be deleted, the program will display a message like, "THIS IS THE RECORD OF JOHN PARKS IN OMAHA, NEB. IS THIS THE RECORD YOU WISH TO DELETE?" If the clerk then types YES, the deletion is made. Otherwise, the deletion is not made, and the clerk must find the correct number or return the deletion request to get the correct data.

Error-Correction Procedures

If the procedures are well designed, if they are documented, and if the clerks are trained in their use, many errors will be detected before the customer master file is incorrectly modified. In spite of this, however, some erroneous changes will be made. When errors occur, procedures are needed to correct the errors.

For example, suppose a customer writes to Horizon complaining that his address has not been changed even though he requested a change several weeks previously. To determine the source of the error, a supervisor or other employee could check past records. He or she could examine past change request forms to find out whether Horizon had received the request. If it had been received, the supervisor could find out whether it had been processed, and, if so, when and by whom it was processed. Then the supervisor could examine the summary report for that date to determine what happened. If a change was made to the wrong record, the supervisor could initiate action to correct both of the records involved.

Observe that the supervisor cannot just correct the record for the customer who complained. The other customer's record would remain in error. Also, note the need for data about past processing. Both the old change request forms and the summary report were required to find the error. Error-correction procedures need to be carefully designed ahead of time so that necessary data is kept and employees are properly trained.

Control Procedures

A third type of procedure concerns controls. The data entry clerks can willfully make erroneous changes for their own gain or for the gain of their associates. The only certain control is to maintain accurate records of the transactions processed and to compare them with the source documents.

For example, periodically a supervisor should compare the activities recorded on the summary report with the customer change request forms. Every change made to the master file should correspond to an authorized change request form. If there are changes made to the master file that do not have matching request forms, the supervisor should investigate them to be certain that they are authorized. This investigation can be a long and exhausting process if there are many changes. In some cases, it suffices to check summary data. Thus, the summary report may print the total number of insertions, the total number of deletion documents, and so forth. If the counts do not agree, then a more detailed investigation can be conducted.

In summary, the normal-use procedures for the users of a direct access system have three primary purposes. First, they must specify how the users are to employ the system to obtain correct results. This procedure includes actions to be performed when special situations occur. Second, the procedures must detail what actions are to be taken to correct errors when they are discovered. The procedures should include steps for ensuring that all the data needed to correct an error are saved for a reasonable period of time. Finally, procedures are designed to provide checks and balances against unauthorized and possibly criminal activity. Procedures are especially important for direct access systems because the users have a much greater impact and work more independently than with other types of systems. (See figure 6-21).

Operators' Procedures for Normal Operation

The computer system operators also need to follow system procedures. The operations staff need to know how to start programs, what files to mount in the direct access equipment, and how to stop programs. Additionally, security procedures need to be defined so that computer operators know who has authorized access to the programs and data, and when.

Unlike tape files, direct access files are not always dismounted. If the data resides on a disk pack that is not removable, or if a removable pack is left resident for some reason, then the data can be readily accessed. Whereas an operator is required to mount a tape volume, no action at all is required to access an available direct access file.

This fact is both an advantage and a disadvantage. Not mounting files is less work for the operations staff, but, on the other hand, it results in less control. The operators do not necessarily know what users and programs are accessing the data.

Several controls can be developed to counteract this disadvantage. First, users can be assigned *account numbers* and *passwords*. These are special numbers or code words. If the user cannot provide the correct number or code word, then the computer will not allow access to certain programs. Users in the shipping department will be restricted from the programs in the customer service department if they do not know the customer service account numbers and passwords. Further, files themselves can have passwords. A user may have to specify a password to use a program and another password to access a critical file. Additionally, passwords can be restricted as to specific functions. One

---

Users need procedures that explain:

1. How to use the system to accomplish their job.
2. How to correct errors.
3. How to ensure that only authorized activity occurs.

FIGURE 6 - 21

User procedures for normal system operation

password may permit read-only access. Another may allow both reading and inserting. A third may allow reading, inserting, deleting, and modifying.

The operations staff may be involved in setting up passwords. If so, they need procedures. Further, they need to know the importance of passwords and of not circumventing them for the users' convenience.

Another procedural responsibility of operations is to run computer jobs only in accordance with established schedules. These schedules are set up to ensure that all the computer workload can be accomplished in a timely manner; they also serve as a control measure. Because the user of a direct access system can have nearly unlimited ability to modify the contents of a file, such systems are often restricted for use during normal business hours only. The hope is that the activity will be adequately supervised during this time.

Thus, procedures need to be defined that describe what programs are to be run at what times. The operations staff also needs to have a procedure for making exceptions to the schedule. This procedure may merely be the name of someone to call to authorize the changes in schedule.

A final procedure for the operation of a direct access system is periodically to obtain *backup copies* of the direct access files. This need can be met by copying or dumping the direct access data to a tape file. New generations of master files are not created as a by-product of processing, as they are in sequential systems. Updates are made in place. When they are made, the old data is lost. If the file is damaged in some way, the data can be restored only from a backup copy.

Backup Procedures

Procedures need to be defined that tell the operations personnel when and how to backup the direct access files. Procedures should also be defined for the operations supervisors to check periodically on backup activity to ensure that it is being properly performed. This step is crucial. Many companies have learned through great agony and expense how important appropriate backup is for direct access systems.

The procedures for normal use for operations personnel are summarized in figure 6-22. We will now discuss procedures used when there is a failure in some part of the system.

User Procedures During Systems Failure/Recovery

When there is a failure in a direct access system, both the users and computer operators need procedures describing action they should take. The users need to know what to do while the computer is out of operation. Later, they need to know what to do when the computer first becomes operational. If the system is online and the users rely on it for the performance of their jobs, they need to know what to do while the system is down. For example, if bank tellers use an online direct access system to post deposits and withdrawals to banking accounts, the tellers need to know what to do when the system fails. Do they continue to accept deposits? If so, what data do they gather for entry to the system when it is again running? Can the tellers allow withdrawals? If so, how do they verify account balances?

The problem for Horizon is not as severe as it might be for a bank. If the customer master file update program won't work, the data entry clerks can simply wait until the system is operational: they have no customers waiting in

Operators need procedures that explain:
1. How to start and stop programs. 2. Which files to mount on devices. 3. How to assign account numbers and passwords. 4. How to maintain integrity of the security program. 5. How to run jobs in accordance with the established schedule. 6. How to handle exceptions. 7. How to back up direct access files.

FIGURE 6-22

Operators' procedures for normal system operation

line. If Horizon uses direct access processing to price orders, failure might be more disruptive. The shipping area may fill up with orders that have been filled but not priced. The picking of new orders may have to be deferred until the shipping area is cleared. In this case, procedures have to be developed describing what to do until the system is again functioning.

Once the system is repaired, users need procedures describing their recovery activity. Usually, some work must be redone. The amount of rework depends on the severity of the error, the adequacy of the backup and recovery techniques, and luck. Users need procedures for determining how much work must be redone. For example, the users of the Horizon customer update program could check to see if the last five changes they made to the file were recovered. If not, then the users might go back 25 changes to see if they were recovered. Continuing in this way, the users could discover how much work needed to be redone. Sometimes the operations personnel can help; they may know that the files were recovered accurately as of 8:00 in the morning and that all subsequent changes must be redone.

Operators' Procedures During Systems Failure/Recovery

Considering computer operations, recovery of a direct access system is a three-step process. First, the operators must have a procedure for determining the general source of the problem. It might be a direct access device malfunction, a CPU or memory failure, a program error, or some other problem. Operations personnel need to know which of these sources of error is at fault so that they can notify the appropriate personnel.

This notification is the second step of recovery. Since operations personnel generally are not trained or experienced in fixing problems, they call in appropriate experts to make repairs. Consequently, they need a list of names and phone numbers for repair purposes, as well as special instructions for the large variety of errors that can occur.

Once the repairs are in progress, operations personnel can begin preparing for the final step of recovery: recovering files and restarting programs. Whenever there is an unscheduled stop of a direct access computer system, there is always a chance that some data is lost. If the computer fails in the middle of an update, for example, part of the record can be changed and part not changed.

To recover from this failure, it is necessary to restore the file to its condition before the failure and to restart the programs where they were when interrupted. This is easy to say but difficult to do. The file can be restored from its most recent backup copy, but then all of the changes since the backup was made must be reapplied. The computer can take this action if all of the changes have been recorded. Otherwise, the users will have to repeat all of the activity since the backup copy was made.

Since these backup and recovery activities are so complex, operations personnel need detailed procedures to follow. Procedures for recovery from system failure are summarized in figure 6-23.

To review, direct access systems can be much easier to use than sequential systems. However, this ease of use means that errors can be made more easily and that unauthorized activity is harder to control or prevent. Further, direct access systems are considerably more difficult to backup and recover than sequential systems. This difference is caused by the fact that updates are made in place and no backup files are generated as a by-product of processing, as they are with sequential systems.

These disadvantages can be counteracted only by people following well-designed and well-documented procedures. It is impossible to counter these disadvantages with more hardware, a faster CPU, or other types of equipment. Thus, the careful design of procedures for both users and operations personnel is crucial to the successful implementation and use of direct access systems.

PERSONNEL FOR DIRECT ACCESS PROCESSING

The final component of a direct access computer system is trained personnel. Again, there are two groups to be trained: users and operations personnel. Both groups need training in using the equipment and following established procedures.

User Training

Users need to be trained in how to prepare inputs and how to use outputs. If the direct access system is offline, then this training is similar to that for users of sequential systems. If the system is online, then users need to be trained in the use of CRTs or other devices.

Generally, users will be more comfortable if they are given some minimal introduction to computer processing during this training. Also, they need to be assured that they cannot ruin millions of dollars of computing equipment from their CRT. (They may, however, be able to ruin data files, so they should be

FIGURE 6-23

Procedures for recovery from system failure

Personnel	Procedures
Users	What to do while the computer system is inoperative What to do when the computer system first becomes operational
Operators	How to detect the general cause of the failure Whom to contact to have the problem fixed How to restore files and restart programs

trained in how *not* to do that.) After these preliminaries, users should be shown how to use the CRT.

When they have learned how to use the equipment, users need to be trained in the use of procedures. They should be given documentation that they will have on the job and shown how to accomplish their job using the computer system and the documentation. Even the best procedures are worthless if users do not understand or believe in them. Therefore, users should be given procedure rationale. Some activities may seem silly or inconsequential when considered just from the user's viewpoint. When this is the case, the users will often stop following the established procedures. To prevent this situation from occurring, users should be given insight into the need for all procedures.

Operator Training

Training for operations personnel is similar. The operators need to be taught how to use the direct access equipment and how to perform any special maintenance or testing activity. They should be shown how to handle removable disk packs and the like so as to minimize the chance of damage. Finally, operations personnel need training in the established procedures. As indicated previously, backup and recovery is especially important for direct access processing, and operations personnel should be trained and rehearsed in the backup and recovery procedures. Periodic inspections should be made to ensure that the procedures are known, remembered, and followed.

QUESTIONS

6.33 What are the two categories of procedures needed for direct access systems?

6.34 Describe three types of procedures for users of a direct access system?

6.35 What procedures do operators of an online system need?

6.36 What user procedures are needed when a direct access system fails?

6.37 What operations procedures are needed when a direct access system fails?

6.38 Describe training needed by users of direct access systems.

6.39 Describe training needed by operators of direct access systems.

SUMMARY

This chapter has presented an introduction to direct access file processing systems. We began with a discussion of the need for direct access processing. In those situations in which sorting and batching are infeasible, direct access capability is required. We then described the characteristics of each of the five components of a direct access computer system. Direct access hardware includes disks, floppy disks, drums, and mass storage equipment. Direct access data can be organized in either of two basic forms. Indexed sequential file organization permits both direct access and sequential processing. Random organization can be very last, but it permits only direct access processing.

We described the pseudocode for a direct access program to maintain the Horizon customer master file. The program itself is actually simpler than a sequential program because many functions are taken care of by the operating system. We then described procedures for direct access processing. The importance of these procedures cannot be overemphasized. Direct access systems are easy to use; this ease of use means errors can easily be made. The only effective controls over these errors are well-designed and well-implemented procedures. Finally, we briefly summarized the training requirements for direct access system users and operations personnel.

In the next chapter we will consider the third way of organizing and processing data: database systems. When you finish that chapter, you will understand the three fundamental types of file processing on computer systems.

WORD LIST

(in order of appearance in text)

Direct access
Direct access device flowchart symbol
Price extension
Online system
Offline system
Disk storage unit
Disk pack
Disk recording surface
Track
Cylinder
Movable read/write head disk storage device
Fixed-head disk storage device
Winchester disk
Data module
Access motion time
Rotational delay
Data movement time
Floppy disk
Diskette
Conventional or hard disk
Drum

Mass storage device
Key
Random file organization
Indexed sequential file organization
Hashing algorithm
Overflow area
Application programs
System service programs
Operating system programs
Data management services
Case statement
User procedures for normal operations
Operators' procedures for normal operations
Account numbers
Passwords
File backup copies
User procedures during systems failure/recovery
Operators' procedures during systems failure/recovery

QUESTIONS TO CHALLENGE YOUR THINKING

A. Estimate the amount of time required for an IBM 3350 to read the Horizon customer master file both sequentially and randomly. Use the same file data as used for the HP 7920 estimates. The IBM 3350 performance characteristics are summarized in figure 6-11.

B. Although random and indexed sequential file organizations are standard, many computer systems have special varieties of them. Find out what variations your computer has and compare them to random and indexed sequential as described in this chapter.

C. Find out whether your college or university has business computer systems using direct access technology. If so, investigate the five components of the direct access system. In particular, determine whether or not you believe the procedures in use are sufficient. Are they well documented?

CHAPTER 7

Database Systems

"This darn bank," thought Jeremy Williams. "They still don't have my address right. I've told them to change it twice already, but they still have it wrong!"

"Look at this, John," said Tricia Lucero. "We get three separate mailings from the bank. One is for our checking account; another is for our savings; and the third is for the car loan. It's confusing. Every week we get another piece of paper from them. Why don't they put it on one statement? It would sure save on their mailing costs and be less confusing for me."

"Fred, FRED, FRED! Where is that data I wanted on the Parks's loan application? I asked for it a week ago. We need to take some action on this request. Get it for me!"

"I'm sorry, Ms. Baker, I can't find it in all these computer printouts. I asked data processing to give me the data last week. They said it would take a month to write the programs. I told them you had to have it right away. The next morning these three boxes of computer printouts were on my desk. I guess the data's here somewhere."

These people are all expressing frustration at the information system used by a bank to process customer accounts. These systems are all batch-oriented file processing systems. They are shown in figure 7-1.

Batch-Oriented File Processing Systems

Figure 7-1a depicts the system used to process checking accounts. Every evening, deposit slips and canceled checks are input to the check processing program, along with the check master file. The deposits are made to the accounts. Checks are canceled as long as the balance is large enough. The program produces a new check master file and a file of bank transfers as output. Further, a summary of account balances is printed for use by the tellers the next day. At the end of the month, the master file is used to print customer statements.

The customer savings system is shown in figure 7-1b. This system is similar to the check processing system except that no file of bank transfers is produced. Finally, figure 7-1c shows the system used to account for customer loans. Payments are posted to the accounts as they arrive. Once every two weeks, a report is printed showing the status of the various loan accounts.

These three systems are typical batch-oriented file processing systems. They are effective insofar as they account for financial transactions accurately and allow the bank to conduct business in an orderly manner. However, as we have seen, they have disadvantages.

Disadvantages of File Processing Systems

First, file processing systems like these have *duplicated data*. The customer's name, address, and other data may be recorded several times. If a customer has both checking and savings accounts, his or her personal data will be recorded twice: once in the check master file and once in the savings master file. People who have checking, savings, and loans will have their data recorded three times. If a customer has multiple checking or savings accounts, his or her data will be recorded even more times.

Why is this a problem? Consider what happens when a customer moves, changes name, or changes other personal data. All files containing the data must be updated. The new address, for example, must be inserted in the check-

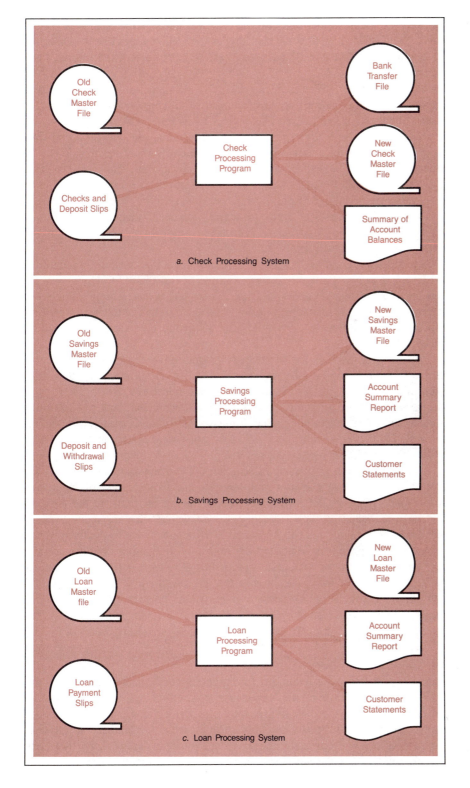

a. Check Processing System

b. Savings Processing System

c. Loan Processing System

FIGURE 7 - 1

Batch-oriented file processing systems

207

ing, savings, and loan master files if the customer has all three types of accounts. This correction isn't hard to make as long as the bank realizes that the customer has all three account types, and as long as the bank can readily find all three account numbers.

In practice, most such modifications are made successfully, and customers are satisfied. On occasion, however, someone slips up and some of the necessary changes are not made. This happened in Jeremy Williams's case. He had three separate checking accounts: one for personal use, one for a part-time business, and one for a local chess club of which he was treasurer. When he moved, the bank changed the address in only one account. He kept complaining, and eventually the addresses in all three accounts were changed.

Another disadvantage of duplicated data is wasted file space, which can be a problem when files are large. Typically, however, adequate file space is available and not very expensive. Therefore, the problem of data integrity is a more important disadvantage.

A second disadvantage of file processing systems like those shown in figure 7-1 is that data is not integrated. For example, it is difficult to obtain all of the data for one customer. People like Tricia Lucero like to have a single, integrated statement. This is a reasonable request. And she's right that the bank's mailing expenses would decrease substantially if they produced a single statement for each customer.

However, as the files are structured, producing an integrated statement is difficult. A program would have to be written to obtain customer data from each of the master files and to print it on a single form. Since the account numbers are different for the three types of accounts, the bank would need a file that showed all account numbers for every customer. Even then, producing integrated statements from the files would not be easy. (If you wonder why, write pseudocode to produce the report.)

A third disadvantage of systems structured like those shown in figure 7-1 is that new requests and one-of-a-kind requests are difficult to implement. Ms. Baker knew that Mr. Parks had had trouble paying his loans in the past and that he had written several bad checks. She wanted her assistant, Fred, to determine how many such checks had been written and what his loan repayment situation was. Fred was frustrated because data processing couldn't seem to give him that data. In fact, data processing personnel were also frustrated because they couldn't provide the data that Fred wanted.

In this chapter, we will discuss a style of data processing that overcomes these disadvantages. Called *database processing*, it represents data in an integrated manner.

WHAT IS DATABASE PROCESSING?

Database processing is a technique for organizing and manipulating *integrated data*. Relationships among the records are represented, and these relationships are used to process the data. For example, suppose a company keeps records about company departments and about employees. In a database application, these two types of records are integrated into a single database. Furthermore, the relationship between department and employee records is represented. Thus, it is possible to retrieve all the employees who work in department 123 or to determine the name of the department in which employee Jones works.

Figure 7-2 shows how programs relate to the database. Contrast it with figure 7-1. In figure 7-1, the programs perform I/O on the files directly. In figure 7-2, the programs call upon an intermediary, called a *database management system (DBMS)*, to do the I/O. Programs in a database application do not issue READs and WRITEs for data. Instead, they call the DBMS and ask it to retrieve or enter needed data.

In a sense, the DBMS operates like a data librarian. Programs pass data to it for storage. Later, they recall it and perhaps change the data and store it

FIGURE 7-2

Bank processing using database technology

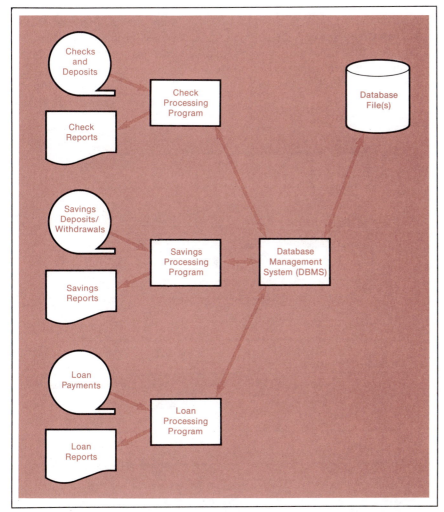

again. The programs might also ask the DBMS to delete the data. To do this, the program needs to identify the data by key. The DBMS uses the key value to find the data in the database. Users or application programs share the data just as books are shared in a library.

Advantages of Database Processing

To see the advantages of database processing, consider the processing needs of the bank discussed previously. Figure 7-3 shows four types of records. The first record contains data about a customer, such as name, address, and other data. The second record is a checking account record. It has account number, account type, balance, and so forth. The remaining two record types have data about savings accounts and loans.

Figure 7-4 shows some examples or instances of these record types. The lines represent *record relationships*. Thus, customer Jones has checking account number 1000 and savings account number 5050. Jones does not have a loan with the bank. Customer Parks, the second example, has all three types of accounts.

In a database application, all of this data, including the relationships, is sent to the DBMS for storage. Later, when an application program asks for data about Jones, the DBMS retrieves the Jones record shown in figure 7-4. If the application program wants to process Jones's checking account, it then asks for the Jones checking record. In this case, the DBMS retrieves the record for

F I G U R E   7 - 3

Four record types in bank database

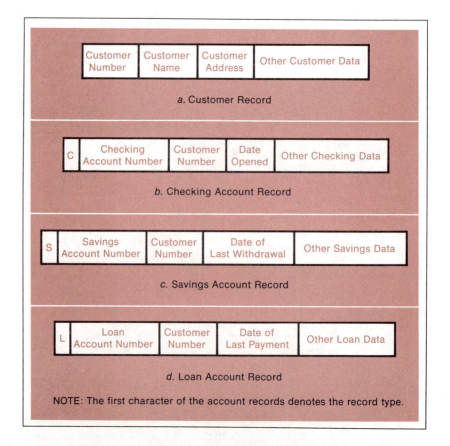

a. Customer Record

| Customer Number | Customer Name | Customer Address | Other Customer Data |

b. Checking Account Record

C | Checking Account Number | Customer Number | Date Opened | Other Checking Data |

c. Savings Account Record

S | Savings Account Number | Customer Number | Date of Last Withdrawal | Other Savings Data |

d. Loan Account Record

L | Loan Account Number | Customer Number | Date of Last Payment | Other Loan Data |

NOTE: The first character of the account records denotes the record type.

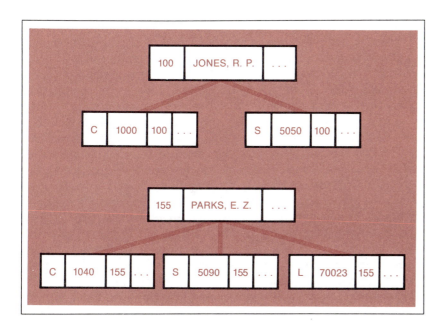

FIGURE 7-4

Two examples of bank records

checking account number 1000 and sends it to the application program. The retrieval was done by *relationship*—not by key value or sequential position.

Using database technology, the bank has three programs to do its account processing. The checking program refers to customer and checking data to cancel checks. The savings program refers to customer and savings data to post deposits and withdrawals. The loan program refers to customer and loan data to post payments against loans.

All three of these programs refer to the same copy of the customer data. Thus, the duplicated data that we noticed for file processing in figure 7-1 has been eliminated. When Jeremy Williams changes his address, it will need to be changed only once for all three of his checking accounts.

Additionally, integrated processing of customer accounts is possible. To produce a consolidated statement, an application program simply retrieves a customer record from the database along with all of that customer's accounts. The consolidated statement can be produced from this data.

Finally, database applications provide more general ways of accessing data. As just illustrated, records can be accessed by *relationship*. Additionally, records can be accessed by any of several keys. In chapter 6, we defined *key* as a field that is used for identification purposes. Database systems generalize on this concept. *Multiple keys* are allowed. Thus, customer records can be accessed by customer bank number, or by customer social security number, or by some other key. Additionally, database systems support *nonunique keys*. Such keys identify groups of records. A key on zip code, for example, identifies all the customers living in a particular area.

Thus, a DBMS is a general-purpose program that provides multiple ways of accessing data. New requests and one-of-a-kind requests are more easily satisfied by database applications.

In addition to these multiple access paths, most DBMS vendors supply a special utility called a *query/update utility* to complement the DBMS. Such a utility provides an English-language-like capability to access or update data in the database. Using multiple keys and the query/update utility, someone like Fred can obtain data such as that required by Ms. Baker. See module K for a more detailed discussion of query/update and related processing.

Database processing can provide one more advantage as compared to file processing systems. Some database systems create *program/data independence*; that is, the programs are independent of the format of the data on the files. To understand this concept, examine figure 7-2. The application programs do not process the files directly; rather, they ask the DBMS for the data. Therefore, when a file format is changed, only the DBMS is impacted. Although DBMS processing must be changed, the application programs can be left alone.

The database processing environment differs drastically from the file processing environment. For file processing, when a file is changed, all of the programs that process the file must be changed. In a large system, 50 programs or more could be involved. In fact, in a file processing environment, sometimes desired changes to the files are not made because of the amount of work necessary to modify the affected application programs.

The advantages of database processing are summarized in figure 7-5.

Disadvantages of Database Processing

Unfortunately, nothing is all good in the data processing environment, and so it is with database systems. Database processing has several major disadvantages. First, it can be expensive. For mainframe computers, the DBMS itself may be costly, usually $100,000 or more. Although the cost of the DBMS is less for minis and micros (about $10,000 and $1,000, respectively), other costs are still high.

For example, database processing usually requires considerable hardware. All database files must reside on direct access devices, and the storage requirements can be large. In fact, an integrated database usually requires more storage space than the sum of the files it contains. For example, if file A takes 10 cylinders and file B takes 20 cylinders, a database containing files A and B might take 40 or 50 cylinders. The additional space is used to keep data representing the relationships among records, as well as data to enable processing by multiple keys.

Furthermore, the DBMS is an additional program. The CPU must execute application programs, the DBMS, the operating system, and other programs. That is a lot of processing. A large, powerful CPU is often required for database processing.

Development costs are another factor adding to expense. Because database structures can be complex, the systems development process can be lengthy. Highly paid and well-trained personnel may be required, so both labor and training costs can be high.

In addition to expense, risk is higher for database systems development. The initial design of the database can be difficult. The database structure must be developed and defined to the DBMS. The database structure must support the needs of the users on the one hand, and it must deal with the peculiarities and limitations of the DBMS product on the other hand. Because of this duality, awkward compromises are sometimes necessary.

The definition of *database structure* that is input to the DBMS is sometimes called a *schema*. An example of a schema for the bank database is shown in

Advantages	Disadvantages
Elimination or reduction of duplicated data	Expensive
	DBMS
Integrated processing	More hardware
Generalized access to data	Development costs high
Program/data independence	Higher risk
	Difficult initial development
	Vulnerability to crash

FIGURE 7-5

Database processing advantages and disadvantages

figure 7-6. The schema describes data items, record contents, and record relationships.

After the schema is defined, the data must be loaded into the database. Special utilities (usually supplied by the DBMS vendor) are used for this purpose. Furthermore, application programmers must learn to use special commands to process the database. This learning takes time. Finally, since a database will be shared among many users, procedures that describe who can do

FIGURE 7-6

Example of schema for bank database

```
RECORD DEFINITION: NAME IS CUST-RECORD,
    FIELD IS CUSTOMER-NUMBER, INTEGER (10),
    FIELD IS CUSTOMER-NAME, ALPHA (20),
    FIELD IS CUSTOMER-ADDRESS, ALPHA (30),
    . . . other customer fields here
RECORD DEFINITION: NAME IS CHECKING-RECORD,
    FIELD IS TYPE, ALPHA (1) VALUE IS 'C',
    FIELD IS CHECK-NUMBER, INTEGER (8),
    . . . other customer fields here
RECORD DEFINITION: NAME IS SAVINGS-RECORD,
    FIELD IS TYPE, ALPHA (1), VALUE IS 'S',
    . . . other savings fields here
RECORD DEFINITION: NAME IS LOAN-RECORD,
    FIELD IS TYPE, ALPHA (1), VALUE IS 'L',
    . . . other loan fields here
RELATIONSHIP DEFINITION: NAME IS CUST-CHECK,
    PARENT IS CUST-RECORD,
    CHILD IS CHECKING-RECORD.
RELATIONSHIP DEFINITION: NAME IS CUST-SAVINGS,
    PARENT IS CUST-RECORD,
    CHILD IS SAVINGS-RECORD.
RELATIONSHIP DEFINITION: NAME IS CUST-LOAN,
    PARENT IS CUST-RECORD,
    CHILD IS LOAN-RECORD.
```

what to which data must be negotiated and documented. All of these activities mean that substantial initial work is required; this work may or may not be successful.

A third disadvantage of database processing is *vulnerability*. If the check master file in figure 7-1*a* is damaged, checks cannot be processed, but savings and loan applications continue to run. In the database environment, however, when something happens to the database files, none of the applications can operate. The bank is incapacitated until the database file is fixed. These disadvantages also are summarized in figure 7-5.

In summary, database processing trades machine resources for human resources. It uses the computer less efficiently, but, once the database is defined, it enables people to work more efficiently. They can get the data they need in less time. Since people have become increasingly expensive, and computers have become drastically cheaper, trade-offs of this kind are often smart business decisions. For this reason, database processing is likely to be used more and more. In fact, some people believe that eventually all computer processing will be database processing.

Database Definition and Types

The term *database* is used by many people in many different contexts. Sometimes people use the term generically, meaning a base of data. Other times they use the term more specifically, to refer to the type of integrated processing discussed in this chapter. To distinguish between these two uses, we will spell the term as two words, *data base*, when referring to a generic base of data, and as one word, *database*, when referring to this specialized, integrated process.

Database Definition

A database is a self-describing collection of integrated records. *Self-describing* means that the format of the database is recorded within the database. Therefore, everything the DBMS needs to know about the structure of the database is within it. Using a library as an analogy, the card catalog listing all the material in the library is kept inside the library itself.

The phrase *integrated records* means that relationships among records are represented. For example, the fact that customer Jones has checking account number 1000 is known. Such relationships may be stored in the data, or they may be derived from the data when needed. Either way, integrated record processing is possible.

Types of Databases

There are three varieties, or species, of database. The *integrated company database* evolved in the early 1970s, when database processing originated. At that time, many companies planned to build a single, integrated database of all their organizational data. This approach was sometimes successful, but, for the most part, it was too ambitious. The data needs of companies varied widely across divisions or other boundaries, and the human effort needed to administer such a database was too great.

A second species of database is the *regional database*, which has data about a group of related systems. Common examples of regional databases are a production database, a human resources database, and a marketing database. Such databases support many different computer systems, but they do not contain all of the corporate data.

| Integrated Company Database |
| Single repository of computer-sensible corporate data |
| Regional Database |
| Repository of data for a group of related systems |
| Personal Database |
| Electronic filing cabinet |

FIGURE 7-7

Three types of database

The *personal database* is the third species. Personal databases are usually stored on personal computers and are like electronic filing cabinets. For example, a salesperson might have a personal database with records of clients, sales calls, and orders. The relationship among these records would be stored in the database. A personal database is a self-describing collection of integrated records, but only for one individual. The three species of database are summarized in figure 7-7.

In the first part of this chapter, we have presented a brief introduction to database processing. Now we will discuss each of the five components of a database-oriented business computer system. Data is the component most drastically impacted by the database approach, so we will discuss it first.

QUESTIONS

7.1 Why didn't the bank correctly change Jeremy Williams's address?

7.2 Why did the bank send three separate mailings to Tricia Lucero?

7.3 Why didn't data processing give Ms. Baker the data she wanted?

7.4 What is database processing?

7.5 What is the function of a DBMS?

7.6 How does a DBMS eliminate data duplication?

7.7 How does a DBMS allow integrated processing?

7.8 How does a DBMS generalize on the concept of a *key*?

7.9 What is program/data independence?

7.10 Name four advantages of database processing.

7.11 Name four disadvantages of database processing.

7.12 Why do some people think database processing will be used more and more frequently in the future?

7.13 Distinguish between data base and database.

7.14 Describe and give an example of corporate, regional, and personal databases.

DATABASE DATA

To understand the data component of a database application, you need to understand three concepts. First, there are three fundamental ways in which records can be related. Second, in a database system, there will be a variety of *forms*,

Fundamental Record Relationships

Hierarchical Record Relationships

or *views*, of the same data. Third, to represent record relationships and allow processing by more than one key to be done, database systems create systems data, sometimes called *overhead data*. We will consider each of these in turn.

A database is a self-describing collection of integrated records. Another way of saying this is that a database is a self-describing collection of files and *relationships among records* in those files.

The phrase *relationships among records* is critical. If a database were only a group of files, then those files would not be integrated. The employee records in the employee file, for example, would have no correspondence with the department records. In a database, a facility must be provided to relate records to one another.

What are record relationships? Database experts have determined three basic ways in which records can be related.

The first relationship type is *hierarchical*, or *tree*. A tree is a collection of records in which all of the relationships between record types are one-to-many. Figure 7-8a shows an example of a tree relating department records to employee records. For each department, there are many employees. However, each

FIGURE 7-8

Example of a tree relating departments to employees

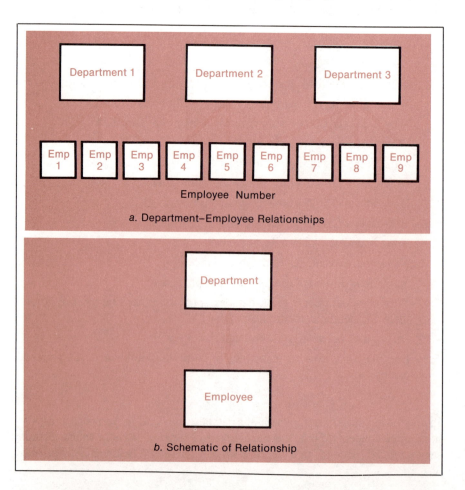

a. Department–Employee Relationships

b. Schematic of Relationship

employee works in only one department. This *one-to-many relationship* is symbolized by the single/double-arrow notation in figure 7-8*b*.

Figure 7-9 shows a tree of records for a checking application. Three record types are involved. The first is the customer record; the second is a checking record; and the third is a transaction record (canceled checks). Again, notice the one-to-many relationships. Each customer can have many checking accounts, but an account corresponds to only one customer (joint accounts are considered to be one customer with two names). Each account can have many transactions (checks), but a transaction corresponds to only one account.

These record structures are similar to family trees. In fact, the terminology *parent* and *child* is sometimes used. In figure 7-8, the department records are parents and the employee records are children. In figure 7-9, customer records are parents and transaction records are children. Account records are both

FIGURE 7-9

Example of a tree relating customers and accounts

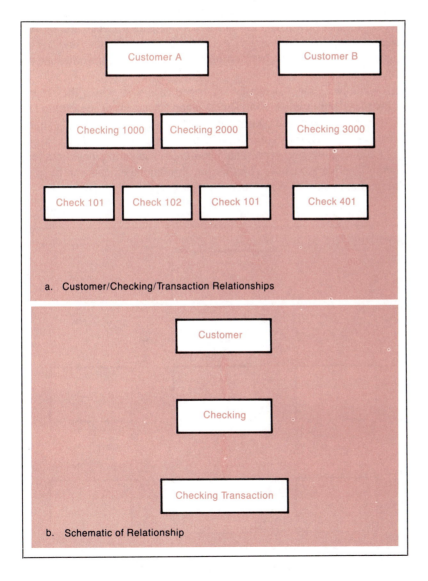

a. Customer/Checking/Transaction Relationships

b. Schematic of Relationship

children (to customer) and parents (to transactions). In a tree structure, each child has, at most, one parent.

Trees can involve many record types and have several levels. Figure 7-10 shows a tree used for processing at the bank introduced at the start of this chapter. There are seven record types, six one-to-many relationships, and three levels. Trees frequently occur in database applications.

Network Record Relationships

The other two kinds of record relationships are called *networks*. They allow a record to have more than one parent. Figure 7-11 shows a *simple network*. Here, an order record has two parents: a customer record and a salesperson record. The network is called simple because the parents of the order record are of different types. Put another way, in a simple network, all relationships are one-to-many, even though some records may have more than one parent.

The third record relationship is called a *complex network*. In this type of structure, a record can have multiple parents, and the parents can be of the same type. Figure 7-12 (page 220) shows a complex network among student and class records. One student is enrolled in many classes, and a class is composed of many students. In a complex network, the relationships are many-to-many.

Database management systems vary in the ease with which they represent these structures. For example, IMS (Information Management System), a DBMS supplied by IBM, represents hierarchies well, but it does not easily represent complex networks. IDMS (Integrated Data Management System), a DBMS sold by Cullinet Software, represents hierarchies and simple networks readily, but complex networks require redefinition. Similar statements can be made of all other commercial DBMS products.

FIGURE 7-10

Schematic of bank relationships

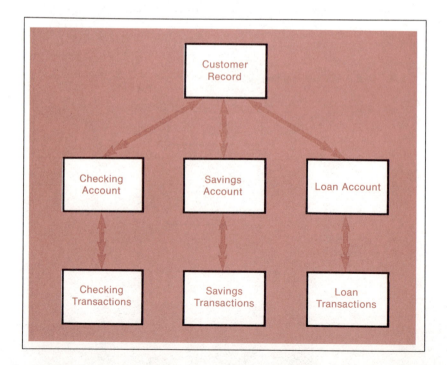

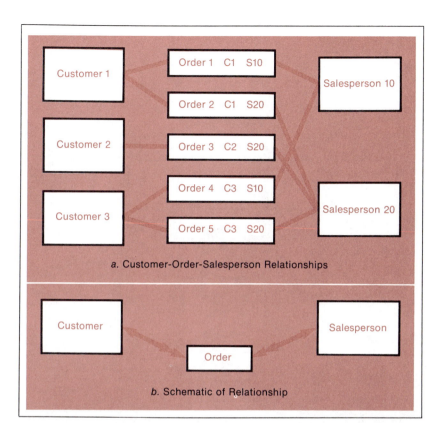

a. Customer-Order-Salesperson Relationships

b. Schematic of Relationship

FIGURE 7-11

Illustration of simple network

You may be wondering why these relationship types are important to you. For some systems, when the database is created, all of the record relationships have to be defined. To define them, the data processing personnel will make a sketch similar to those shown in figures 7-8b through 7-12b. You may be asked to specify what kind of a relationship exists between records in your area of business. Knowledge of the three types of relationship will then be helpful to you. In any case, this knowledge will enable you to communicate better with data processing personnel.

To review, a database is a self-describing collection of files and record relationships. Three types of record relationship can exist: tree, or hierarchy, simple network, and complex network. These relationships are defined in the database schema. Now we will turn to the second concept essential to an understanding of database data.

Three Views of Database Data

In a database system, a variety of forms, or views, of the data is defined. One such view is called the *schema*, or *conceptual view*. It is the complete logical view of the data. The term *logical* means the data as it is perceived by a human. In fact, the data may be stored on the files in a form completely different from what humans see.

A second view of the data is called the *subschema*, or *external view*. This view is a subset or, in some cases, a transformation of the conceptual view. Consider the schema illustrated in figure 7-9. The check processing program

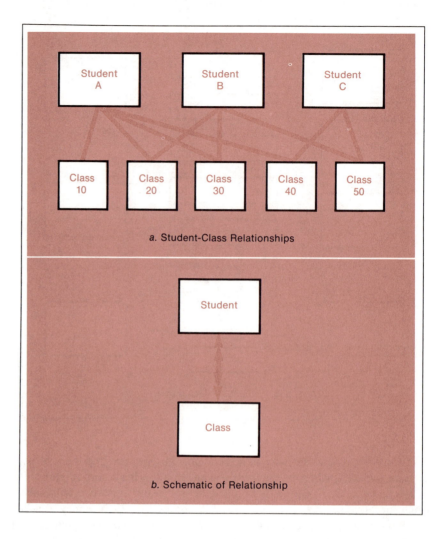

a. Student-Class Relationships

b. Schematic of Relationship

FIGURE 7-12

Illustration of complex network

does not use the savings or loan records. From a security and control standpoint, it is desirable that these records not be seen by the check processing program.

To provide such security, a subschema, or external view, that includes only the customer and checking records is defined. The checking program then processes the database through this view. It appears to the program that no other records exist. Other types of transformations are possible, such as re-naming fields, rearranging fields in the record, and even modifying relationships.

A third view of the data is called the *internal*, or *physical view*. This is the form of the data as it appears to a particular processing computer. It describes how data is physically arranged and how it is allocated to files.

Each of these views must be defined before the database can be processed. Usually the database administrator (see Personnel section that follows) writes the conceptual and external views. Often the internal view is created automat-ically by the DBMS when the database is defined.

The ability to have multiple views of the data is very convenient. It means that external views can be tailored to the needs of the application. Even though

Type of View	Description
Schema (Conceptual)	Complete logical view of the data
Subschema (External)	Subset or transformation of schema
Physical (Internal)	Appearance of data to computer

FIGURE 7-13

Three views of data supported by database processing

the data is centralized and shared, it can appear to each user in a format that is familiar and useful to him or her.

Figure 7-13 summarizes the three views of data. Again, the essential concept for you to understand is that, in database processing, there is a variety of views of the same data. You, as a user of an external view, may be seeing only a portion of the database. Seemingly unimportant rules or restrictions on your processing may be very important when considering the other views of the database.

Database Overhead Data

The third concept essential to an understanding of data in database systems is that systems data, sometimes called *overhead data*, is created to allow processing by more than one key and to represent record relationships. Because of this overhead data, the size of a database may be 200 or 300 percent greater than that of the original data. The exact amount depends on how many keys and record relationships are represented as well as the particular DBMS in use.

There is a hot debate among database experts regarding what is the best way to structure and process overhead data. Rather than get involved in that debate, we will show two examples that are typical of the structures used.

Consider first the problem of having more than one key. Suppose that we have a group of customer records on a direct access file. Suppose also that the primary key for these records is customer number. A hashing algorithm is used to allocate a customer record to a relative record number in the file. (In case you've forgotten, this sentence means that the customer number will be input to a formula that will produce an address on the file for this record. See chapter 6, figure 6-15, for more detail.) The data might appear as in figure 7-14.

Now, suppose that, in addition to accessing the records by account number, the users want to access them by zip code. One way to do this is to read the entire file, looking for all the records with the desired zip code. However, this search is time consuming if there are many records in the file and wasteful if few of them have the desired zip code.

Indexes

To make this process more efficient, some database systems build a file of overhead data called an *index* (or, sometimes, an *inverted file* or an *inverted list*). This index is similar to an index for a book. It shows which records have which zip code values. Figure 7-15 pictures such an inverted file.

If a user or application program wants to know all of the customers with zip code 22042, the DBMS will search for 22042 in the index. It will find 22042 as the second entry. Then the DBMS will use the indicated record

Record Number	Customer Number	Zip Code	Other Data
1	1000	22042	
2	1010	22042	
3	2030	98040	
4	4030	22042	
5	1050	01418	
6	2055	98040	
7	4070	01418	
8	3070	01418	
9	3090	53520	
10	4090	53520	
11	1095	22042	

FIGURE 7-14

Customer records on direct access file

numbers to find customer records desired. Thus record locations 1, 2, 4, and 11 contain customer records with zip code 22042.

Whenever customer records are added, changed, or deleted, the DBMS will modify the index. If there are several indexes (there will be one for each key in use), the modifications of them will become burdensome. That is a price of having the additional access capability.

Linked List Structure

Record relationships can be represented by indexes, but, for variety, we will study another approach. Suppose that we want to represent the one-to-many relationship between departments and employees. Assume that both types of records are loaded on a direct access file, as illustrated in figure 7-16. Locations 1, 3, and 5 hold department records. The other locations hold employee records.

FIGURE 7-15

Example of inverted file for figure 7-14

Zip Code Value	Customer Records Having Corresponding Value
01418	5, 7, 8
22042	1, 2, 4, 11
53520	9, 10
98040	3, 6

To represent the relationships, we will add a *link field* to each record. This field has a record location, or address, of another record. In a department record, this link field points to the first employee record for that department. In an employee record, the link field points to the next employee in the same department. The last employee record in a department has a zero in the link field.

Examining figure 7-16, we see that department 100's link field points to record position 2, or employee 20's data. Thus we know that employee 20 is in department 100. Employee 20's link field points to record position 7, which contains employee 80. Finally, employee 80's link field points to position 10, which contains employee 15's data. The link field for employee 15 is 0, indicating that there are no more employees in the department. Thus, employees 20, 80, and 15 work in department 100.

If you follow the links in the other records, you will discover that employees 25 and 70 work in department 200 and that employees 30 and 40 work in department 300.

Data structures like this one are called *linked lists,* because link fields (sometimes called chains) are used to maintain relationships as lists of data items. Linked lists can also be used to represent multiple keys.

A new and simplified method of representing database data is becoming popular. This data representation technique, called the *relational model*, has been known for many years but has only recently become practical from a performance standpoint.

The Relational Model

Record Number	Link	Record Type	Contents
1	2	D	Department 100 data
2	7	E	Employee 20 data
3	4	D	Department 200 data
4	8	E	Employee 25 data
5	9	D	Department 300 data
6	0	E	Employee 40 data
7	10	E	Employee 80 data
8	0	E	Employee 70 data
9	6	E	Employee 30 data
10	0	E	Employee 15 data

FIGURE 7-16

Linked lists used to represent record relationships

The relational model portrays data in the form of tables. For example, in figure 7-17, the customer, checking, and savings files are each depicted as tables. The rows of the tables contain records, and the columns of the table contain fields. So far, there is nothing special about this method. The uniqueness of the relational model lies in the representation of relationships.

In figure 7-17, where is the relationship between customer and checking records? There is no apparent linked list structure and there is no apparent index. How do we know which checking records correspond to which customer records? The answer is that a relationship is defined in the data. A customer and a checking record are related if the customer numbers in each record are the same.

You may be asking, "What's so special about that? Isn't that a natural human way of expressing relationships?" The answer is yes. The specialness of the relational model is that it allows humans to view data and relationships in a way that is natural for them. They need not be aware of such structures as linked lists.

FIGURE 7-17

Customer, checking, and savings data recorded as relations

CUSTOMER (NAME, NUMBER, STREET, CITY, STATE)

JONES	1234	1505	SCENIC DRIVE	SEATTLE	WA
PARKS	2345	727	88TH AVE	TACOMA	WA
FRANKLIN	3456	3344	14TH ST	BELLEVUE	WA

CHECKING (CUST_NUMBER, CACCT_NUMBER, BAL)

1234	885566	1284.19
1234	899042	17.14
3456	877127	4456.88

SAVINGS (CUST_NUMBER, SACCT_NUMBER, BAL, TYPE)

1234	777234	44345.81	10
2345	773388	8790.31	10
2345	776845	812.34	20
2345	799833	1345.99	10

When data is represented in relational form, it becomes possible to develop powerful and easy-to-use query languages. One such language is *Structured Query Language,* or *SQL*. We will show two examples. To print the names of customers in Seattle, we would say,

```
SELECT CUSTOMER_NAME

FROM CUSTOMER

WHERE ZIP_CODE 98040
```

To print the names of customers who have a checking balance greater than $1,000, we would say.

```
SELECT CUSTOMER_NAME

FROM CUSTOMER, CHECKING
WHERE CUSTOMER_NUMBER CHECKING_CUST_NUMBER

AND BALANCE GREATER THAN 1,000
```

Observe that this last example requires the DBMS to recognize that a relationship exists—that is, customer numbers are equal—between rows in the CUSTOMER and CHECKING tables. For more information, see module K and references [124] and [133].

QUESTIONS

7.15 What is another way of saying a database is a collection of integrated files?

7.16 Describe a hierarchical, or tree, record relationship other than those shown in this book.

7.17 For your answer to question 7.16, which records are parents and which are children?

7.18 What is a simple network relationship? Give an example.

7.19 What is a complex network relationship? Give an example.

7.20 Name and describe the three views of a database.

7.21 Why is the external view or subschema necessary?

7.22 Why is the internal view necessary?

7.23 Suppose a company has a database that includes a file of sales data. One of the fields of records in this file is month of sale. If there is an inverted file on this field, how many entries will it have?

7.24 Sketch an example for the situation described in question 7.23. Use the format shown in figures 7-14 and 7-15.

7.25 Consider the example shown in figure 7-16. Suppose a department that has employees 72, 82, and 92 is added. Also suppose employee 20 is moved to the new department. Sketch the appearance of the file after these changes are made. Use the format in figure 7-16.

7.26 How is data represented using the relational model? How are relationships represented?

7.27 Give an example of two relational tables for student and enrollment data. Show how the relationship between students and enrollments is represented in the data.

DATABASE HARDWARE

Database applications seldom require special hardware. They may, however, require *more* hardware. Because database files must be direct access files, a company may need to increase the amount of direct access space. Furthermore, database processing places a greater burden on the CPU because of the processing required. Thus, a larger, more powerful CPU may be needed.

In some specialized applications, companies have found it advantageous to use *database machines*. Such machines are special-purpose computers whose sole function is to manage the database. The database machine is connected to a second CPU that does applications processing. The database machine stores and retrieves data on behalf of the application processing computer. To date, database machines have had limited acceptance.

PROGRAMS FOR DATABASE PROCESSING

Figure 7-18 shows the relationships of programs involved in database processing. Messages arrive at the CPU and are accepted by the operating system. The operating system is a program that manages the computer's resources and controls the flow of processing. The operating system sends messages to the appropriate application program. For example, a deposit transaction (message) would be delivered to the deposit processing application program. To process the transaction, this program may need to retrieve data from the database or store data within the database. When these functions are needed, the application program calls on the database management system for service. The DBMS obtains or stores the data as instructed. When the application program has completed the transaction, it sends a response, via the operating system, back to the user. See module I for more information about operating systems and chapter 8 for information about the receipt and delivery of messages.

Functions of a Database Management System

The primary functions of the DBMS are listed in Figure 7-19. First, the DBMS must store, retrieve, and update data. These operations must be performed in such a way as to preserve and update user and overhead data. Second, the DBMS should provide a *data dictionary* or user-accessible catalog of data descriptions. The users should be able to access the dictionary to determine the contents of the database.

Additionally, the DBMS should provide facilities to control concurrent (occurring at the same time) processing. A database is a shared resource. Many different applications programs and many different users can access it concurrently. When two users try to modify the same record at the same time, errors can be generated.

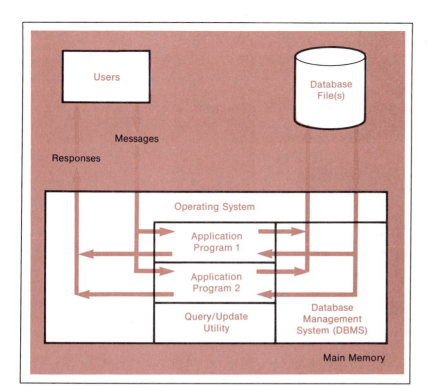

FIGURE 7-18

Program relationships in the database environment

To prevent these problems from occurring, DBMS products must supply special commands to lock records that might be modified or deleted. When the application program issues one of these commands, the DBMS will not allow other users to access the record until the first user is finished. Chapter 8 discusses the concurrent update problem in greater detail.

The fourth major function of a DBMS is to recover from failure. Computers fail; processing can stop unexpectedly. Disk heads crash and ruin data. When events such as these occur, the DBMS must have facilities to support recovery. For example, it must be possible to restore the database from a previous save and to reapply transactions.

Another function of the DBMS is to provide security facilities. The database is a valued resource. With powerful query languages, data can be readily accessed, both by authorized and unauthorized users. Therefore, the DBMS must provide passwords and other protective measures. Observe that the DBMS

FIGURE 7-19

Major functions of a DBMS

1. Store, retrieve, and update data
2. Provide a data dictionary
3. Control concurrent processing
4. Recover from failure
5. Provide security facilities
6. Provide utility services

cannot provide security. The DBMS can provide only facilities for people to use so that *they* can provide security.

The final function of the DBMS as listed in figure 7-19 is to provide utility services. The structure of the database may change; when such a change occurs, the database may need to be unloaded, altered, and reloaded. If so, programs to perform these services are needed. Rather than force each organization using a DBMS to write its own programs, the vendors of the DBMS provide generalized utilities that perform these services. Other utilities clean up files by consolidating unused space; improve the efficiency of the overhead data; and backup the database.

The cleanup programs require explanation. As the database is processed, both user data and overhead data are changed. Sometimes data is moved. After thousands of such changes, processing sometimes slows down. Data that was initially consolidated is now spread over many cylinders or even many disk packs. To improve efficiency, the data can be rearranged on the files. Utility programs are sometimes provided by the DBMS vendor to do this.

There are other, more sophisticated functions of a DBMS, but they are beyond the scope of this text. See [48] and [56] for more information. Figure 7-20 lists several popular DBMS products and the companies that sell or lease them.

Using the DBMS

Users can interface with the DBMS in one of two ways. First, they can use application programs that call the DBMS for service. In terms of figure 7-18, the user sends a message or transaction to the applicable application program. In the course of processing the transaction, the program calls the DBMS.

The second mode of access to a database is through a *query/update utility*. This utility is a program or a portion of the DBMS that provides generalized access to the database. Query/update programs are not application programs in that they do not solve problems like order entry or inventory. Instead, they are used to access records and perhaps to modify them. The user names a file and gives the key or keys for records desired. The query/update program responds with qualifying records. Commands are available to insert and delete records as well. The SQL examples in the previous section are typical query commands.

FIGURE 7-20

Examples of database management systems (DBMS)

Database Management System	Supplier
ADABAS	Software AG of North America
IDMS	Cullinet Software
IDS	Honeywell Corp.
IMS, SQL/DS, DB2	IBM Corp.
IMAGE	Hewlett-Packard Corp.
TOTAL	CINCOM Corp.
SYSTEM 2000	Intel Corp.
MODEL 204	Computer Corp. of America
RBASE 4000	Micro RIM Corp.
dBASE II	Ashton-Tate Corp.

For the system shown in figure 7-18, a query/update command is entered like any other command. The operating system routes it to the query/update utility instead of to an application program.

Application programs are different in a database processing environment than in the file processing environment. The ability to process records by many keys and by record relationships is a characteristic unique to database processing. Common programming languages do not have commands or statements for such processing. For example, the BASIC language has INPUT and PRINT statements, and the COBOL language has READ and WRITE statements, but these are inadequate to initiate the powerful actions a DBMS can perform.

In response to this problem, some DBMS vendors have defined *special DBMS commands* for the application programmer to use. These commands augment the standard language statements. Because these statements are not part of the standard language, the language translators (or compilers) cannot process them. Therefore, the application program with special database commands is first translated by a program supplied by the DBMS vendor. This program is called a *precompiler*. The precompiler translates the special database commands into standard language commands. Thus a FIND command that is not part of COBOL will be translated into a legitimate COBOL command.

This procedure is illustrated in figure 7-21. The application program INVOKES a named subschema and thereby identifies which database it will process. The INVOKE is not a standard command. Therefore, the precompiler must translate it. The precompiler finds the named subschema in the schema library. It uses this data to substitute the correct code in the COBOL program's data division. The particulars of this translation are not important to you at this stage. Rather, you should strive to understand the precompilation process.

The dictionary shown in figure 7-21 is a special file or database maintained by the DBMS for its own use. It is the data dictionary referred to in figure 7-19. It contains names of programs, fields, records, files, and procedures, as well as the relationships of all of these. In figure 7-21, the precompiler is inserting data about the program it is compiling, such as program name, subschema used, processing type (read vs modify), and so forth.

Of course, it would be possible to have a DBMS without a precompiler. In that case, the application programmer would have to insert the necessary data statements and calls to appropriate DBMS routines. In fact, some primitive database management systems have no precompiler and therefore require this step. It is a disadvantage, however, because it is much easier for the application programmer to use the special commands.

7.28 Do database systems require any special hardware? Do they require any more hardware?

7.29 Explain the roles performed by the operating system, the application program, and the DBMS during the processing of a message.

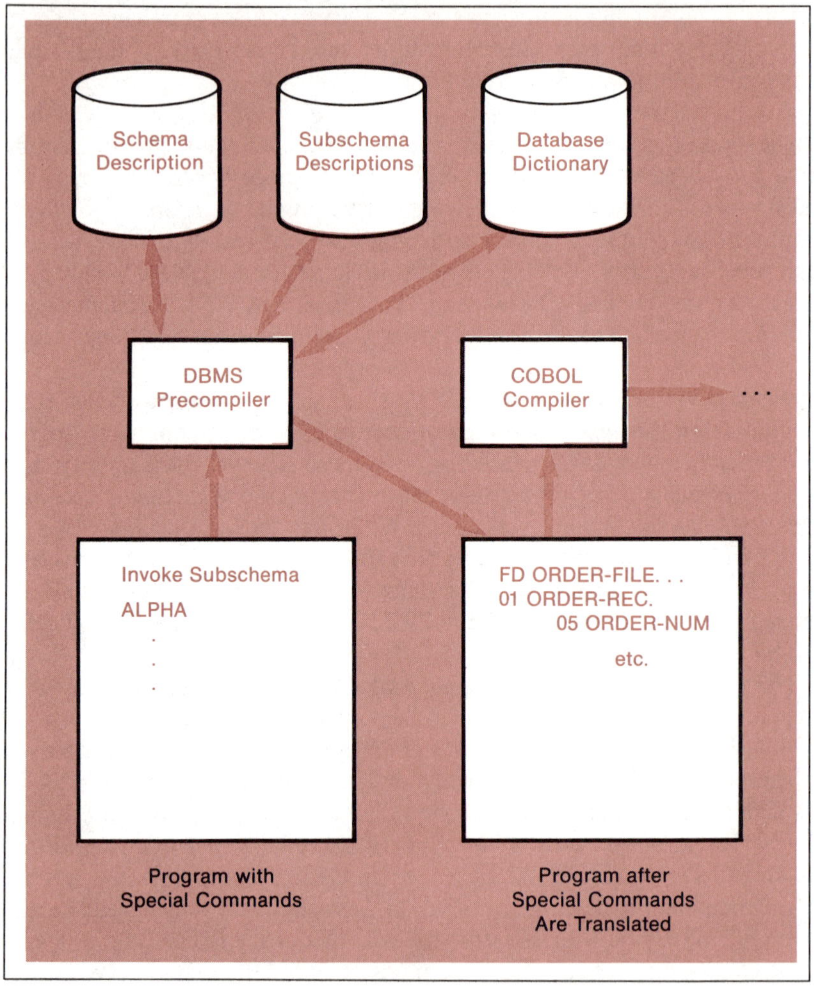

FIGURE 7-21

Use of DBMS precompiler

7.30 Describe the six major functions of a DBMS.

7.31 Explain the difference between an application program and a query/ update utility.

7.32 Why do application programs contain special commands to process a database?

7.33 What is the function of a DBMS precompiler?

7.34 What are the contents of the data dictionary? How is it used?

PROCEDURES FOR DATABASE PROCESSING

The procedures necessary for database-oriented computer systems are extensions of those required for more basic types of processing. Like other systems, database systems must have user procedures explaining how to use the system under normal and abnormal operating conditions. Procedures must also be developed that utilize the DBMS security features to ensure that only authorized personnel can perform authorized activity.

Since database applications are often online, the procedures for control, error correction, and recovery described for direct access processing in chapter 6 pertain to database processing as well. To implement these procedures, programmers need to be taught how to use DBMS facilities. Controls need to be developed to ensure that programmers follow these procedures. Additionally, users need to be instructed to follow procedures, and, periodically, managers should verify that procedures are being followed.

Regarding backup and recovery, users must have procedures describing what they should do when the system is unavailable due to failure. They should know how best to carry on their responsibilities, what data to keep, and what to do first when the system becomes operational.

In addition to these procedures for programmers and users, procedures must be developed and documented for operations personnel. These procedures should explain how to run the system, how to perform backup and recovery operations, and how to control the system to ensure that only authorized activity occurs.

Procedures for Sharing the Database

In addition to the procedures necessary for online processing (to be discussed in chapter 8), special procedures must be developed because the database is a shared, integrated resource. Without careful management, users can interfere with one another. For example, consider the database depicted in figure 7-10; this schema could be used by the bank discussed at the beginning of this chapter.

Suppose that a customer who has a checking account and a bank loan decides to move to another city. In the process of moving, the customer closes his or her checking account. If the clerk in the checking department deletes both the customer's checking account and the customer's record, then information about the customer's loan may be lost. This is because, when the customer record is deleted, the loan record will not have a parent. Depending on the DBMS in use, records without parents may be deleted automatically.

A simple solution to this problem is to have the checking department clerk examine the database to determine whether the customer has accounts in other departments. However, the clerk may be processing a subschema that does not include the loan or savings records. If so, he or she will be unable to determine whether the customer has other accounts.

This example illustrates the problems that can occur in database processing. These problems occur not only because the data is shared, but also because the data is integrated—there is only one customer record for all checking, savings, and loan processing.

Processing Rights and Responsibilities

To prevent users from interfering with one another, the company must determine the *processing rights and responsibilities* for all users. For each record (or even each field), the company must decide which users can read, insert, modify, or delete data. Furthermore, each of these users must have a procedure to follow when performing the activity.

Figure 7-22 shows the processing rights negotiated at the bank. All departments can access customer records, but only the new accounts department is allowed to add, modify, or delete such records. (Further, when deleting records, they must follow the procedure shown in figure 7-23.)

Command	Customer Records	Checking and Transaction Records	Savings and Transaction Records	Loan and Transaction Records
Read	New Accounts Checking Savings Loan	Checking Savings	Savings Checking	Loan
Insert	New Accounts	Checking	Savings	Loan
Modify	New Accounts	Checking	Savings	Loan
Delete	New Accounts	Checking	Savings	Loan

FIGURE 7-22

Department processing rights for the bank
database

Authorities for the other record types are shown in the remainder of figure 7-22. Note the checking and savings departments are allowed to read each other's records. They can thus check to make sure that transfers from savings to checking (or checking to savings) are successfully made.

Figure 7-23 shows the procedure that new accounts personnel must follow when a customer record is to be deleted. First, the checking, savings, and loan departments must all certify that the customer's accounts are successfully closed.

FIGURE 7-23

Bank procedure for deleting customer
records

```
SEND REQUEST FOR CUSTOMER DELETION TO CHECKING, SAVINGS, AND
    LOAN DEPARTMENTS
IF ALL THREE DEPARTMENTS APPROVE DELETION REQUEST
    THEN IF CUSTOMER HAD NO SAVINGS OR LOAN ACCOUNTS
            THEN DELETE CUSTOMER RECORD
            ELSE CHANGE CUSTOMER STATUS TO INACTIVE
                CHANGE ADDRESS IF APPROPRIATE
        END-IF
    ELSE DEFER OR DESTROY DELETION REQUEST IN ACCORDANCE WITH
            DEPARTMENT INSTRUCTIONS
END-IF

AT YEAR END, SEND TAX FORMS FOR SAVINGS AND LOAN ACCOUNTS
    DELETE ALL INACTIVE CUSTOMERS
```

If all three concur, and if the customer had no savings or loan accounts, the record is deleted.

If the customer had savings or loan accounts, the record is marked inactive. It will not be deleted until the close of the calendar year, because year-end statements must be sent to the savings and loan customers for tax purposes. If the customer's record were deleted, the bank would have no address to send the statements to.

This discussion has illustrated the decisions the bank must make about processing rights in order to ensure that users' activities do not interfere with one another. A similar community-oriented view must be taken when considering changes to the database schema.

For example, suppose that the checking department wants to add a code letter to the customer number in the customer record. Making such a change will impact the savings and loan departments. Most likely they will have to change their application programs as well as their forms and documents. Clearly, the code letter change cannot be made without agreement from these departments.

Suppose that they are opposed to it. Negotiations will then have to be conducted to determine the best solution for all concerned. If the code letter change is so important that it justifies the additional expense and effort to the savings and loan departments, then it will be done. Otherwise, another way must be found to satisfy the needs of the checking department.

The point of this example is that changes to the database can be made only after the needs of all users have been considered. To consider them effectively, procedures for change must be developed. The procedures describe how changes can be suggested, how the input of all using departments is received, and how the change decisions will be made. Such procedures bring order to the change process and ensure that all proposals receive fair and adequate consideration. They also ensure that all departments have a chance to express opinions.

DATABASE PERSONNEL

Database environments have users, operations personnel, and systems development people just as all other computer systems do. In addition, however, one or more individuals are concerned with managing and protecting the database resource. This individual (or group) is called the *database administrator* (or *office of database administration*). Both the individual and the office are abbreviated as *DBA*.

Databases are shared, and, since the beginning of the human race, whenever people have had to share something, conflict develops. In a broad sense, the job of the DBA is to anticipate conflict, provide an environment for the peaceful resolution of conflict, and protect the database so that it can be used effectively. The DBA has three separate functions, as summarized in figure 7-24.

Managing Data Activity

First, the DBA manages data activity. Note the wording here. The DBA does not perform data activity (inserting accounts, canceling checks, etc.); users do that. The DBA manages this activity.

As discussed in the last section, it is necessary for the processing rights of all users to be carefully determined. The DBA is the focal point for negotiating these rights. The DBA meets with the users to determine who wants to do what

DBA Tasks and Subtasks

1. Manage data activity
   a. Processing rights
      (1) Provide focal point for negotiating
      (2) Document
      (3) Enforce
   b. Concurrent update and backup and recovery problems
      (1) Define problems
      (2) Develop solutions and standards
      (3) Ensure that adequate training is done
      (4) Evaluate problems

2. Manage database structure
   a. Manage schema and subschema designs
   b. Determine data standards
   c. Document database structure
   d. Manage changes to structure

3. Evaluate DBMS performance
   a. Resolve performance problems
   b. Determine need for new features

FIGURE 7-24

Job responsibilities of the database administrator (DBA)

to which data. The DBA is (or should be) an unbiased arbitrator for resolving any conflicts. As time goes by, the business will change and user needs will change. The DBA serves as a focal point for changing the user processing rights as necessary.

Once the processing rights have been determined, they need to be documented. The DBA is responsible for developing this documentation. The DBA is also responsible for enforcing the processing rights. If a department or individual violates the agreed-on policy, complaints are given to the DBA. The offender is informed of the need to follow the policy. More stringent measures are taken if necessary.

Since the DBA is charged with the responsibility for protecting the database, the problems of concurrent update and of backup and recovery are important to him or her. First, the DBA must determine what the potential problems are and how serious they can be. These problems vary from one DBMS to another, as well as from one application to another. Once the problems are known, the DBA meets with users, operations personnel, and the systems development staff to develop solutions.

As mentioned previously, part of the concurrent update solution may be to develop standard ways of processing the database. Application programs may need to lock records (gain individual access) before they are updated, for example. In addition, standard procedures must be developed for backing up the database. Procedures for recovery are also important.

The DBA is responsible for ensuring that adequate means are found to solve concurrent update and backup and recovery problems. Further, these means must be documented. All involved personnel from the user and operations departments must be trained. Although the DBA may not do all of this documenting and training, he or she must make sure that it gets done.

Finally, the DBA is charged with the responsibility for investigating problems that occur and for finding solutions to prevent reoccurrence. The DBA may meet with involved personnel to change standards, procedures, processing rights, or other activity.

Managing Database Structure

In addition to managing data activity, the DBA must also manage the database structure. If the DBA has been appointed at design time, he or she leads the tasks of defining the schema and subschemas—that is, identifying the fields, records, and relationships that will exist in the database. Subschemas must also be defined that allow users or application programs to accomplish their assigned tasks and that support the negotiated processing rights. Subschemas should not contain unnecessary data.

Defining the schema is the same as developing data standards for the company. Users must agree on how many characters will be in the customer account number, for example, or on which fields will be in the customer record. Further, the relationships that can exist among records must be standardized. Again, whenever more than one person develops a standard, conflict will develop. The DBA has the responsibility for resolving this conflict.

Once the schema and subschemas and related standards have been determined, the DBA ensures that the decisions are documented. The DBA must also ensure that the database is developed in accordance with these decisions.

Business is a dynamic activity. No schema, however well developed, will last without change. Users will want to add new capability or to change existing procedures. The operations staff will want to add new equipment or to change computers. The systems development staff will find a better way to do things.

The DBA is charged with the responsibility of managing change to the database structure. As discussed in the Procedures section, such changes must be made carefully. If not, a change made for the benefit of one user will cause problems for others.

To manage change, the DBA must receive requests for changes and periodically present these requests to a group representing all using organizations, computer operations, and systems development. Potential changes should be discussed with the representatives. In a subsequent meeting, the changes should be discussed again and potential problems identified. If there are no conflicts, or if ways of eliminating the conflicts can be found, the changes can be made. This change process is managed by the DBA.

Evaluating the DBMS Performance

A third area of DBA responsibility concerns DBMS performance. Because the DBA is the focal point for conflict resolution, when users complain that the system performs too slowly or that it costs too much to run certain jobs, the DBA will be involved. He or she will serve as an interface between the users and the operations and systems development staffs.

Sometimes the performance problem can be resolved by *tuning*, which means changing DBMS parameters set at installation time. The amount of main memory allocated to the DBMS is an example of such a parameter. Other performance problems can be fixed by cleaning up the database using utility programs supplied by the vendor. In some cases, a high-performance feature of the database can be acquired. At worst, a more powerful CPU can be obtained.

Vendors of DBMS products periodically announce new features at extra cost. When such announcements are made, the DBA must determine whether the new features are needed. The DBA considers each feature in light of user requirements. Again, the DBA will meet with users, operations personnel, and systems development personnel to make this determination.

DBA Organizational Placement

Figure 7-25 shows two acceptable alternatives for organizational placement of the DBA in the company. Both of these organizations have worked well. Experience has shown that a lower placement gives the DBA too little power and exposure to be effective. A higher placement removes the DBA from the day-to-day problems.

A close look at either of these organizations reveals a problem for the DBA. The DBA has responsibility for all aspects of database processing, but he or she has direct line control over few of the personnel involved. In fact, the DBA works closest with users, yet the DBA and the users are not even shown on the same organization chart!

Consequently, the DBA must be a diplomat. He or she must be able to convince people to conform to the database standards primarily on the basis of rational argument. Good communication skills and a thorough knowledge of organizational politics are needed for this position. The DBA must have good rapport with senior managers in the using departments, as well as with those in data processing.

If worst comes to worst, the DBA is not without weapons. He or she can control the priority of user jobs and thus determine how much service a user gets. People who do not cooperate will find it harder and harder to use the computer. In fact, frequent violators of established procedures may find the computer won't process their jobs at all.

Who should fill the DBA position? Database experts generally agree that it should be a nontechnical person who has been in the company for some time. Although the DBA has responsibility for some technical matters, the expertise to perform these duties can be borrowed when needed. It is more important for the DBA to be a diplomat than a technical expert. The DBA needs to know personnel well, so he or she should have worked in the company for some time.

QUESTIONS

7.35 What procedures do users need for operation of a database system? What do they need for backup and recovery?

7.36 What procedures do operators need for operation of a database system? What do they need for backup and recovery?

7.37 Explain why the activities of one user must be coordinated with the activities of another.

7.38 What does the term *processing rights and responsibilities* mean?

7.39 What procedures are needed to ensure orderly change to database structure?

7.40 What does *DBA* mean?

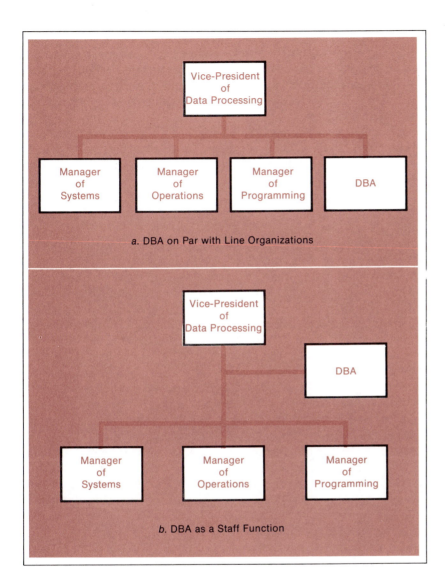

a. DBA on Par with Line Organizations

b. DBA as a Staff Function

FIGURE 7-25

Two acceptable alternatives for DBA placement

7.41 In a broad sense, what is the job of the DBA?

7.42 What are the three major functions performed by the DBA?

7.43 Does the DBA perform data activity? If not, who does?

7.44 What role does the DBA have in defining processing rights and responsibilities?

7.45 What is the DBA's responsibility with regard to concurrent update and backup and recovery problems?

7.46 What does the DBA do with regard to developing database structure?

7.47 What is the major management problem of the DBA?

7.48 What qualities and characteristics should the DBA have?

SUMMARY

Database processing is a technique for organizing and manipulating data files in an integrated manner. Relationships are represented, and these relationships are used to process the data. To provide this capability, a large, complex computer program is required. This program is called a database management system, or DBMS. The DBMS is an intermediary between the application programs and the database.

The advantages of database processing are (1) the elimination or reduction of duplicated data; (2) integrated processing; (3) easier implementation of new requests and one-of-a-kind requests; and (4) the creation of program/data independence.

The disadvantages of database processing are (1) expense; (2) difficult initial development; (3) vulnerability to data problems; and (4) the need for much hardware.

Three concepts are crucial to understanding database data. First, a database contains a collection of integrated files. Second, in a database, there exists a variety of forms, or views, of the same data. Third, to represent record relationships and enable processing by more than one key, database systems create overhead data.

Recently, companies have been able to organize and process databases using the relational model. Data in such databases is represented as tables. Relationships are contained within the data.

A DBMS has six major functions: store, retrieve, and update data; provide a user-accessible catalog of data descriptions; control concurrent processing; recover from failure; provide security facilities; and provide utility services. There are two modes of accessing database data. One is through an application program, and the other is through the use of a query/update facility.

Because a database is a shared resource, procedures must be developed to control conflicts that arise. Users must process the database in ways that will not adversely impact other users. Further, the rights and responsibilities of all users must be well known and documented. The backup and recovery process is crucial.

Finally, the database administrator or office of database administration is required for successful operation of a database system. The job of the DBA is to anticipate conflict, provide an environment for the peaceful resolution of conflict, and protect the database so that it can be effectively used. Specific areas of responsibility are to manage data activity, to manage database structure, and to evaluate the DBMS performance.

WORD LIST

(in order of appearance in text)

Duplicated data	Multiple keys
Integrated data	Nonunique key
Database processing	Query/update utility
Database management system (DBMS)	Program/data independence
	Database structure
Record relationship	Schema
Key	Vulnerability

Integrated company database
Regional database
Personal database
Database form, or view
Overhead data
Hierarchical, or tree, relationship
One-to-many relationship
Parent
Child
Simple network
Complex network
Schema, or conceptual view
Subschema, or external view
Internal, or physical, view
Index
Inverted file

Link field
Linked list
Relational model
Structured Query Language (SQL)
Database machine
Data dictionary
Special DBMS commands
DBMS precompiler
Processing rights and
  responsibilities
Database administrator (DBA)
Database administration (DBA)
Manage data activity
Manage database structure
Evaluate DBMS performance
Tuning

A. Suppose you work for Horizon Artist Supply. The Director of Data Processing asks you whether Horizon needs a database capability. How do you respond? What would be the advantages to Horizon? The disadvantages? How should Horizon determine whether or not a database is appropriate?

B. Sketch a schema for an academic database. Follow the form in figure 7-10. Your schema should include data about students, classes, faculty, departments, colleges, advisers, and grades. Show all the appropriate record relationships and label them with their type (hierarchical vs simple network, for example). Define a subschema, or external view, that would be used by a grade processing program. Define another subschema that would be used by a class enrollment program.

C. Show how indexes could be used to represent all three types of record relationships.

D. Show how linked lists could be used to represent nonunique keys.

E. Extend the structure in figure 7-16 to represent simple networks. Extend it to represent complex networks.

F. Locate a nearby organization that is using a DBMS. Interview a responsible person to find out the name of the DBMS, its cost, and how satisfied the organization is. How long did the conversion to the database take? Were there any special problems that other organizations should avoid? How has the support from the vendor been?

G. For the organization you interviewed for question F, determine whether any special procedures have been instituted since the database was installed. How does the organization handle concurrent update problems? Have processing rights and responsibilities been negotiated and documented? Have there been conflicts among users? Has the company appointed a DBA? If so, what are the DBA's responsibilities? What organizational or management problems have developed since the database was implemented?

QUESTIONS TO CHALLENGE
YOUR THINKING

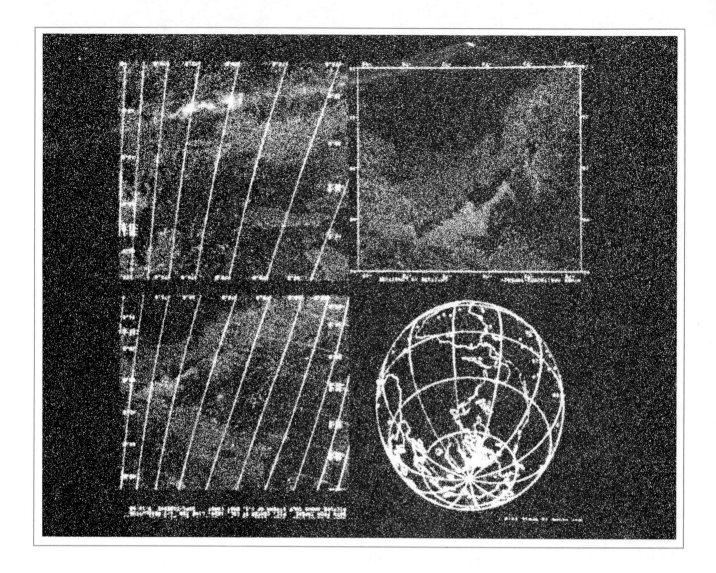

PART THREE

Teleprocessing and Distributed Systems

In part 2 of this book, we considered systems development and three fundamental ways in which computer systems organize and process data. Although categorizing systems according to data management technique is useful, other groupings are possible. In this part, we will consider systems categorized according to a different dimension: communications.

In chapter 8, we will examine teleprocessing systems. The prefix *tele* means "distance." In these systems, the processing is done at some distance from the user or the originator of the request for processing. In chapter 9, we will discuss distributed computer systems. These systems are similar to teleprocessing systems, except that the processing is not done in one centralized location. Instead, data storage, update, and control are distributed among several geographically separated computers.

These two chapters have a common format. First we will discuss the essential character of each advanced computer system. Then we will examine the five components of the systems and show how they differ from the components of the more fundamental systems presented in part 2.

If you want only a summary of these topics, you can read the first 10 pages or so of each chapter. To obtain a greater understanding, you should read the descriptions of the five components as well.

CHAPTER 8

Teleprocessing Systems

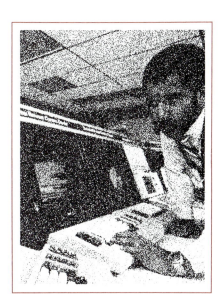

Wagner Pleasure Boats manufactures motor and sailing boats for recreational use. Their smallest boat is a 14-foot runabout. Their largest is a 35-foot sailboat. Wagner is located in Los Angeles, California.

Seven months ago, Wagner bought another company, Sabre Marine Hardware, located in Tampa, Florida. The cost of parts for boat construction had skyrocketed. They hoped to be able to reduce these costs by producing parts themselves.

Within a few months, it became apparent that Sabre was an unhealthy company. Their inventory was mismanaged; the costs of manufacturing were far too high; and employee morale was low. Consequently, Wagner Pleasure Boats decided to send their chief hotshot problem solver to Florida to clean house. The problem solver was to fire inept managers and replace them with well-qualified personnel. Further, inventory costs were to be reduced and the manufacturing process made more efficient.

Suppose that you are Wagner's chief hotshot problem solver. After you arrive at Sabre, one of your first observations is that there is little, if any, reliable information available on the company's operation. The accounting system is in a shambles. The few computer reports that are produced are nearly worthless. The inventory system is so full of errors that no one pays attention to it—and so on.

This situation is particularly shocking to you because you are accustomed to the high-quality data processing service you have received at Wagner. There, reports are accurate and delivered on time. The manufacturing computer system is the backbone of the company's operation. You decide to eliminate Sabre's ineffective computer systems and to convert to the systems used at Wagner.

The question is, how? Sabre's current computer is too old and too limited to handle the Wagner programs and data. One possibility is to acquire another computer at Sabre and to install the programs from Wagner's data processing department. However, you took data processing in college, so you realize that a computer system is more than just hardware and programs. In addition, you will need data, procedures, and trained personnel.

It's this last component that concerns you. Sabre has been so mismanaged for so long that you doubt that you can find enough high-quality personnel to make the Wagner system operate. You could start a training program and build a data processing staff. You have enough other problems, however, and don't want to take the time to do that.

Another possibility occurs to you. Is there a way that you can access the Wagner computer in Los Angeles from the Sabre facility in Tampa? Could you somehow send the input data to Los Angeles for processing and have the results returned to Tampa? Even better, is there a way that people in Tampa can use CRTs that are connected to the computer in Los Angeles?

Until the mid-1960s, most data processing was done on centralized, batch-oriented computers. However, for many applications (like Wagner's), it was undesirable or infeasible for the data to be brought to the computer center for processing. The movement and delivery of the data on punched cards, magnetic tape, printed reports, and so on, took too long and was too expensive.

People began to wonder whether telephones or other communications facilities could be used to transfer data. Today, a wide range of capabilities for such data transfer has been developed.

Simply stated, *teleprocessing* is data processing at a distance. The term is derived from a combination of the terms *telecommunications* and *data processing*. You know by now what data processing is, so only the term *telecommunications* needs to be defined.

Telecommunications is communicating at a distance, usually using some form of electromagnetic signal similar to that used for radios and TVs. The subject of telecommunications is a broad one that includes the transmission of voice, messages such as telegrams, facsimile (pictures), and data. The latter, called *data telecommunications* or *data communications*, is concerned with moving data from point to point, from terminal to computer, and even from computer to computer.

Now we can be more specific. A teleprocessing system is a computer system in which one or more of the five components are physically (geographically) distributed and the components are connected into a system using telecommunications facilities. All forms of telecommunications can be used. Data communication is used to transfer data from one site to another, voice communication is used to integrate distributed personnel, and message communications is used to implement distributed procedures.

The system used at Horizon Artist Supply represents the simplest form of teleprocessing system. Data entry clerks use CRTs to process the direct access files for the customer master file and inventory systems (see figure 8-1). This system is considered a teleprocessing system because the clerks and the CRTs are physically removed from the computer.

This system is a simple one. Most clerks are in the same building as the computer and the others are not more than 100 meters (about 300 feet) away from it. As is frequently the case, all of the hardware is supplied and maintained by the same vendor, a situation that eliminates compatibility problems. Both the CPU and the operating system are designed to support just this type of teleprocessing. Only a modest amount of work is required to install the hardware. (The other four components may require extensive work, however.) Consequently, Horizon does not need a staff specialist for communications processing.

Figure 8-2 shows the teleprocessing equipment configuration for a medium-sized bank that has three branches and operates a bank card authorization center. In addition to the CRTs and CRT-like terminals, there are cash machines and a *remote job entry (RJE) station*. The RJE station has a card reader, a printer, and a CRT for the operator to use. This equipment is used to submit batch jobs from the remote card processing center.

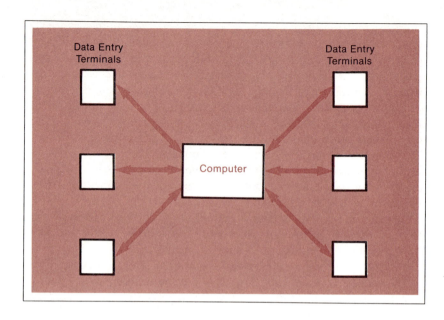

FIGURE 8-1

Teleprocessing system used by Horizon
Artist Supply

FIGURE 8-2

Teleprocessing equipment configuration
for medium-sized bank

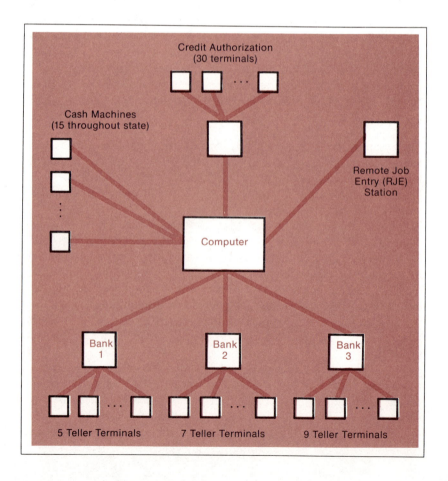

The bank's teleprocessing system is considerably more complicated than Horizon's. The communication lines are much longer and involve the telephone company and other organizations. The hardware is supplied by several vendors. Getting it to work together is not easy. Maintenance and problem fixing are sticky when one vendor blames the problem on another. Further, the operating system was designed to be general purpose. Someone must tailor it to the bank's environment. The bank needs at least one communications and operating system specialist on staff to install and maintain the hardware and programs.

The bank has less control over the terminal environment than does Horizon. The equipment may be misused, abused, or even fraudulently used. Since the applications are financial in nature, efforts must be taken to provide security. Finally, *response time* (the time it takes the computer to respond to a request or statement) is important to the bank. If response is too slow, customers will be kept waiting in line. Customer service will suffer. This differs from the Horizon case, in which clerks, not customers, must wait.

The third teleprocessing configuration, for Worldwide Shipping Company, is depicted in figure 8-3 on page 248. Clearly this third configuration is the most complex of the three examples. Here, computer users in Alaska, Hawaii, and Europe communicate with the company's headquarters in New York. Not only are multiple vendors involved, but multiple communications media are used as well. Phone, microwave, satellite, and other types of communications equipment are used. All of the equipment must work together in spite of different speeds, conventions, and vendors.

Additional problems occur because of the international link. Europe, Canada, and the United States have different laws and customs. Furthermore, the equipment is designed to operate to different standards. Because this system is a large and complex configuration, multiple CPUs are involved. Some computers will be used to handle communications resources and traffic but not to process data. This company may use several hundred CRTs. To build this system and maintain all the equipment requires a large staff of communications specialists.

Rationale for Teleprocessing Systems

Businesses develop teleprocessing systems for two major reasons. First, because the business is geographically distributed, the data originates, is processed, and is used at different places. In the example of the bank, customers transact business at a local bank, but the data is processed at a central facility. Outputs like the bank's financial statements then go to the bank's headquarters at still another location.

The second reason that teleprocessing systems are developed is economy. A central facility is established so that every bank does not need separate data processing facilities. The banks are connected to the central facility via telecommunication links. This system allows the business to gain *economies of scale*, or cost reductions, by having one large computer instead of several smaller ones.

Unfortunately, these economies of scale do not extend indefinitely; as more systems are added to the central computer with teleprocessing, the facility becomes hard to manage and expensive to operate. Figure 8-4 shows the average cost of data processing as it relates to the size of the computing facility.

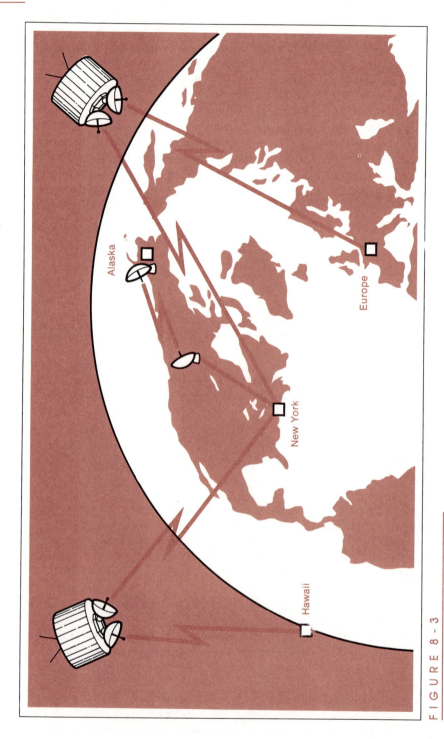

FIGURE 8-3

Teleprocessing configuration for
Worldwide Shipping Company

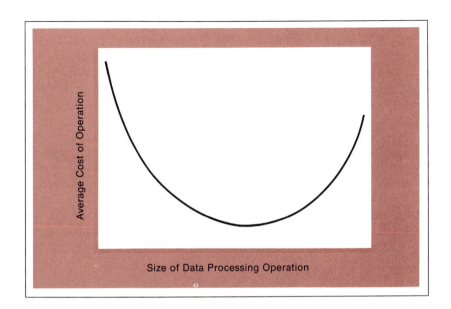

FIGURE 8-4

Average cost of data processing vs size

At first, the average cost decreases as the size increases, but, at some point, the computer becomes hard to manage and the average costs go up.

When a single, central computer becomes too large to manage effectively, another will be acquired and some applications transferred to it. At this point, the company will have two (or more) teleprocessing systems (see figure 8-5). Usually, these systems need to communicate in order to share data or facilities. Consequently, they are connected via telecommunications. The result is one large teleprocessing network with applications processing occurring at two separate sites. This setup is called *distributed processing*, because the processing of application data is distributed on two or more computers in the teleprocessing network. (See chapter 9.)

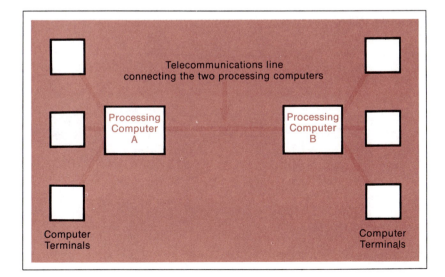

FIGURE 8-5

Example of distributed processing using two computers

To review, there are three major configurations of data processing systems. In the first, called *centralized processing*, processing is centralized on a single computer. Applications are batch oriented; inputs arrive at, and outputs depart from, the computer center on physical media like cards or printed reports.

In the second major configuration, the components of the computer system are geographically separated but united into a system by telecommunications equipment. Processing of the data is still done on a single computer, however. Finally, in the third configuration, the system components are geographically separated, and applications processing is done on more than one computer.

In the past, data processing services have evolved from centralized to teleprocessing to distributed configurations. Recently, however, some businesses have started with minicomputer systems that support teleprocessing and thereby skipped the centralized stage. Horizon Artist Supply is a case in point.

We will consider teleprocessing systems in this chapter. Centralized systems were considered in part 2; distributed systems will be discussed in the next chapter.

Teleprocessing Applications

Teleprocessing applications can be divided into two broad categories: offline and online. For *offline* applications, the data is transmitted from a remote location to the processing computer and stored. When a batch of data is complete, the computer processes it and then returns the output to the remote location as a batch.

Remote job entry (RJE) is a good example of offline teleprocessing. A computer run is input via RJE equipment like that shown in figure 8-6. The run is transmitted to the processing computer and stored on its files. After some

FIGURE 8-6

Remote job entry (RJE) station

period of time, the run is processed and the results stored on files at the central computer. Later still, the outputs are sent to the RJE station for printing.

Batched data transmission is another example of offline processing. Here, groups of data are sent to the central computer in batches. For example, a day's worth of sales data may be sent. The batch of data is then processed by one or more application programs at the central computer. The results are then returned to the remote terminal and printed as a batch.

For *online* teleprocessing applications, the remote terminal is directly connected to the processing computer. Data is not sent in batches. Rather, a single record or message is sent; it is acted on by the processing computer; and the results are returned. Then another message is sent, and so forth.

Query and response systems are online applications. Here the user sends a request for information like, "How many seats are available on Flight 102?" The processing computer determines the answer and returns it to the terminal. Such questions are acted on one at a time, not in batches.

Transaction processing is another online application. The user sends a transaction like, "Add $1000 to Account Number 123123," and the processing computer takes the indicated action. A message is then returned indicating whether the operation was successfully executed or not.

Online program development is a third example. Users write programs at terminals by sending one line of code at a time to the processing computer. The computer then either translates the code and stores it, if correct, or stores the code for later translation. Either way, the user sends one line at a time. Unlike RJE, the program is not sent as a batch. Figure 8-7 summarizes these classifications of teleprocessing applications.

This discussion completes a general introduction to teleprocessing systems. We will now consider each of the five components of a teleprocessing system and show how they differ from components of a centralized computer system.

FIGURE 8-7

Types of teleprocessing systems

Application	Teleprocessing System
Offline	Remote Job Entry Data Transmission
Online	Query and Response Transaction Processing Online Program Development

QUESTIONS

8.1 Why did Wagner's problem solver want to access the Los Angeles computer from Tampa?

8.2 From what two terms is the word *teleprocessing* derived?

8.3 What is telecommunications?

8.4 Define a teleprocessing system.

8.5 Why is a medium-sized bank's teleprocessing system more complicated than Horizon's?

8.6 What are the two major reasons for developing a teleprocessing system?

8.7 How does centralized processing differ from teleprocessing?

8.8 How does teleprocessing differ from distributed processing?

8.9 Describe an offline teleprocessing application.

8.10 Describe an online teleprocessing application.

TELEPROCESSING HARDWARE

If you examine the teleprocessing systems depicted in figures 8-1, 8-2, and 8-3, you will see that there are three basic types of hardware involved in each: terminals, transmission media (lines), and central computers. Let's consider the transmission media first.

Transmission Media

A wide variety of media can be used to transmit signals. The simplest and easiest is a pair of wires that connect the terminal to the computer. The most sophisticated is a satellite. In between these extremes are telephone lines, radio, cable-TV lines, and so forth. These media are classified according to their *speed, mode*, and *type*.

Line Speed

The speed of a communication line is measured in *bits per second* (bps). Transmission media fall into three groups, based on speed. The slowest group is called *narrowband* and permits communication at the rate of 45 to 150 bps. A simple pair of wires will allow narrowband communication. The second group is called *voice grade* and permits maximum transmission rates of 1800 to 9600 bps. These lines are called voice grade because their speeds are typical of those that can be obtained over a voice-oriented telephone line.

Regular telephone lines like those in your apartment or home can be used for data transmission. However, such lines allow a maximum of only 1800 bps processing. To obtain higher speeds, a line must be leased from the telephone company and given special *conditioning*. Only then is the maximum speed of 9600 bps possible.

The third category of communication lines is called *wideband*; these lines permit very high speed communication at the rate of 500,000 bps or more. Communication via satellite is a good example of wideband service. Figure 8-8 summarizes these three categories.

Communication line speeds are sometimes given in another unit, called *baud*. This term refers to the number of times per second that a line signal can

FIGURE 8-8

Speed of communication lines

Line Speed	Transmission Rate
Narrowband (telegraph)	45 to 150 bps
Voice grade (telephone)	1800 to 9600 bps
Wideband (microwave or satellite)	500,000 bps or more

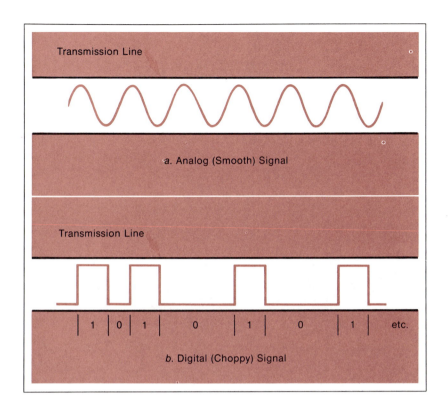

FIGURE 8-9

Modes of communication lines

change its status. It is not the same as bps; the speed in terms of baud is less than the speed in terms of bps. For data processing purposes, the term *bits per second* is always more informative than baud, and you should use it.

Line Mode

In addition to speed, communication lines are classified according to mode. Two modes are possible: analog and digital. *Analog lines* carry signals that are continuous waves. The sounds of a siren and of a smooth melody can be thought of as analog signals. Voice telephone lines are analog lines (see figure 8-9a).

    Digital lines carry signals that have sharp peaks and valleys. The sounds of a barking dog and of a dripping faucet are similar to digital signals. The graph in figure 8-9b illustrates a digital signal.

    When a terminal sends a message to the central computer, it will do so by sending a series of bits. Thus, it might send the sequence 1, 1, 0, 1, 0, 1. As you might guess, such a message is more easily carried by a digital line than by an analog one. The peaks of the digital line can be used to represent 1's and the valleys can represent 0's (see figure 8-9b).

    Sending a series of bits on an analog line is not as simple. Somehow the continuous signal must be transformed to carry the bits. This transformation is called *modulation* and *demodulation*.

    Figure 8-10 on page 254 shows a common type of modulation called *frequency modulation*. This type works by causing the signal to oscillate faster to represent a 1 and to oscillate slower for a 0. *Amplitude modulation* works by making the signal larger (louder) for a 1 and smaller for a 0.

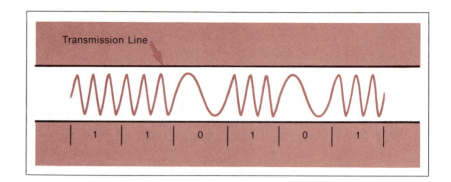

FIGURE 8-10

Analog signal representing 1, 1, 0, 1, 0, 1 using frequency modulation

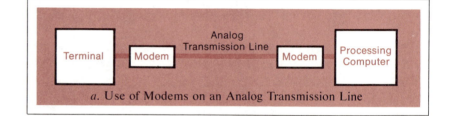

FIGURE 8-11

Use of modems

a. Use of Modems on an Analog Transmission Line

b. Modem

To transmit digital signals over an analog line requires a special device called a *modem*, or *mo*dulator-*dem*odulator. As shown in figure 8-11*a*, when the terminal sends a message to the central computer, it sends its digital message to the modem. The modem encodes the message into an analog signal and sends it over the analog communication line. At the other end, another modem receives the analog signal and converts it to digital (binary) form.

Although modems, or *data sets* as they are sometimes called, are innocuous looking (see figure 8-ll*b*), they can be expensive. It is not unusual for a commercial-grade modem to cost $3000 to $6000. Smaller modems can be purchased for $300 to $500.

The third classification of communication lines is by type. A communication line can be simplex, half-duplex, or full-duplex. A *simplex line* is designed for one-way transmission; that is, a signal can go from the terminal to the central computer, but not back. Simplex lines are cheap, but they are not very useful for teleprocessing.

Half-duplex lines can carry a signal in either direction, but only one way at a time. Thus, the terminal can send a message to the computer, but the computer must wait until the terminal is finished before it sends a message back. Half-duplex lines are like a road that is wide enough for only one car.

Full-duplex lines can carry messages in both directions simultaneously. Thus, while the terminal is sending a message to the computer, the computer can be sending a message to the terminal. A good application for a full-duplex line is an RJE station. While the terminal is sending the computer a job, the computer can be sending the terminal the results from a previous job for printing.

The characteristics of communication lines are summarized in figure 8-12.

Line Type

When a company decides to implement a teleprocessing system, it must determine not only the characteristics described above, but also the sources from which the communication lines will be obtained. One obvious choice is for the company to *build its own communications system*. For several reasons, however, this option is seldom chosen. First, the distances involved must be small enough that wires or coaxial cable can be used. Second, considerable expertise is required, and such experts may be unavailable or too expensive. Third, communications technology is rapidly changing; most companies do not want

Sources of Communication Lines

Line Classification	Characteristics
Speed	Narrowband (45 to 150 bps maximum) Voice grade (1800 to 9600 bps maximum) Wideband (500,000 plus bps maximum)
Mode	Analog (modems required) Digital
Type	Simplex (one-way transmission) Half-duplex (one way at a time) Full-duplex (both ways simultaneously)

FIGURE 8-12

Summary of characteristics of transmission lines

to become locked into a system using present technology. This situation would occur if the company built an expensive communications capability.

A second source for communication lines is *common carriers*. In the United States, many (but not all) common carriers belong to the Bell System. Common carriers provide two types of lines: switched and private. *Switched lines* are like those in your apartment or home; they are called switched because you can dial any other phone and the connection will be made by switching various phone circuits together.

If the communication line is to cover a long distance, companies have choices of programs. Using *direct distance dialing*, the company pays for each minute of the call just as you do when you dial long distance. This practice is expensive if there is much traffic.

Another option for switched lines is to obtain WATS (*Wide Area Telephone Service*) capability. Here, the company pays a fixed amount for a large number of long distance calls. The fixed amount is considerable (in the range of $1500 per month), but it will be cheaper than direct distance dialing if there is heavy use. Other choices are becoming available as communications processing becomes more prevalent.

Private lines (or, sometimes, *leased lines*) are a second type of service that can be obtained. Private lines are leased from the common carrier and provide a fixed path from one point to another, or from one point to several others. Since the path is fixed, special improvements, or *conditioning*, can be made so that the maximum transmission rate can be as high as 9600 bps. Figure 8-13 compares the advantages and disadvantages of switched and private lines.

In the United States, analog lines can be obtained on either a switched or a private basis. However, digital lines are available only on a private basis. In Canada and other countries, digital capability can be obtained on both switched and private lines.

A third source for communication lines is the *satellite carriers,* such as RCA AMERICOM. These companies either have their own satellites or pay to use those of other organizations. They provide both wideband and voice grade lines. The satellites are used as reflectors; they receive signals and transmit them back to an earth station (see figure 8-14). In this way, large amounts of data can be transmitted long distances. Unfortunately, there is a lengthy delay in the transmission because of the distances involved.

FIGURE 8-13

Advantages and disadvantages of switched and private lines

Type of Line	Advantages	Disadvantages
Switched	Destination points not fixed Costs based on use	Slower speed May possibly get busy signal Noise problems
Private (Leased)	Line never busy Fast speed Fixed cost Line conditioning possible	Fixed destination High cost for low volume

Videoconferencing Attracts Growing Interest Despite High Costs

MIAMI BEACH, Fla.—Twenty million meetings held in the U.S. every day could be affected by videoconferencing, according to Dennis Conroy, manager of consulting services for Coopers & Lybrand. . . .

Conroy pointed out a number of factors that contribute to the current interest in videoconferencing, the process whereby people in different locations hold meetings through the use of video images transmitted over communications lines. The emphasis on white-collar productivity and the growing complexity of the business environment are important factors, as are the stress and cost of travel, he noted.

The advent of new, less expensive technology makes the idea of staying in the home office to conduct meetings even more attractive, Conroy said.

Although videoconferencing has been widely praised as a means to cut travel costs significantly, Conroy said that travel costs are actually only cut by 15% to 20%. Other benefits, however, make videoconferencing a means for more effective meetings, he claimed. These include greater participation in meetings, since more people can be involved, and the improvement of communications within a company when, for instance, a new product is announced. In this case, it is easier to inform more people, especially those away from the home office, Conroy said.

Training can also be improved when classes are held via electronic meetings, Conroy explained.

By JIM BARTIMO, CW Staff
Computerworld, April 4, 1983

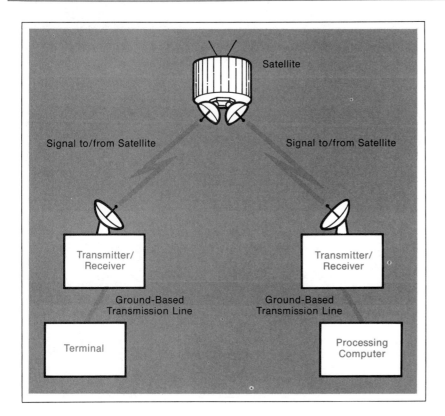

FIGURE 8-14

Example of satellite communications

Line Management

A final source of communication lines is the *value-added carriers,* such as TYMNET. These companies lease communication lines from the common and satellite carriers, add additional services, and sell the improved capability to other companies. In this way, they act as distributors of communication lines. The term *value added* is used because these companies add better error detection and recovery, as well as faster response. Value-added carriers also have more flexible lease plans. Companies can pay for just the service they use, and lease periods are shorter. Figure 8-15 summarizes the sources of communication lines.

A common problem in telecommunications processing is that the terminals are not active enough to keep the lines busy. In this situation, several terminals can be connected to the same line, as shown in figure 8-16. This is called a *multidrop* configuration, because the terminals are "dropped off" the line.

When several terminals share the same line, a potential problem is created. If two or more of them use the line simultaneously, their messages will become garbled. To prevent this problem from occurring, two line management methods are used.

In the *polling* method, the central computer asks each terminal if it has a message to send. If so, the terminal is directed to send it. The central computer then asks the next terminal, and so forth, in round-robin fashion. In figure 8-16, the terminals are polled in the order 5, 4, 3, 6, 2, 1, 5, 4, 3, 6, 2, 1, and so forth. If a terminal needs to be serviced more often, it can be included in several places in the polling order.

Polling works well, but it can waste CPU time. If none of the terminals has a message to send, the CPU is asking a lot of questions for nothing. A second technique, called *contention*, overcomes this disadvantage.

FIGURE 8-15

Summary of communication line sources

Source
1. Company-Built
2. Common Carriers
3. Satellite Carriers
4. Value-Added Carriers

FIGURE 8-16

Multidrop transmission line

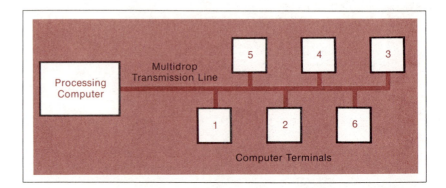

When a line is managed by contention, each terminal listens to the line before sending a message. If the line is busy, it waits a period of time and listens again. Eventually, when the line is not busy, the terminal sends its message. When two terminals start to send messages at the same time, they notice the contention and stop. They then wait different lengths of time and try to send their messages again.

Contention is similar to a human discussion without a leader. It works well as long as no one speaks too frequently and as long as no one speaks very long at a time. Using this comparison, if a terminal sends messages too frequently, or if it sends a single message that is too long, then other terminals will incur long delays in sending messages. Additionally, to work well, the line must have considerable excess capacity. Otherwise, terminals will get too many busy signals.

Like so many data processing alternatives, neither polling nor contention is better in every situation. Polling allows the line to be busier but requires CPU time; contention requires idle time on the line but does not involve the CPU. It becomes a question of which is cheaper—CPU time or line capacity.

Communication lines provide the vital link needed to integrate terminals with the processing computer in a teleprocessing system. However, to be effective, additional hardware is required at both the terminal and the computer ends of this link. We will consider terminal-oriented communications hardware next.

QUESTIONS

8.11 What are the three types of teleprocessing hardware?

8.12 All communications media can be classified according to speed, ___, and ___.

8.13 Narrowband communication lines transmit at the rate of ___ to ___ bps.

8.14 What are two other speeds of communication lines (besides narrowband)?

8.15 What are the two communication line modes?

8.16 Which mode is closer to the format of computer data?

8.17 What is the function of a modem?

8.18 Name the three communication line types.

8.19 Why do most companies not build their own communications system?

8.20 What is a common carrier?

8.21 Explain the difference between switched and private lines.

8.22 What is a value-added carrier?

8.23 Explain the difference between polling and contention.

Communication Terminals

Three kinds of terminal equipment are primarily used in teleprocessing systems. The first type are the CRT devices. *Teleprinters* are the second type. This equipment has a keyboard with a printer enclosed or attached. Figure 8-17 pictures a typical teleprinter. The third type of equipment is used for remote job entry. Typically, RJE stations have a card reader, a printer, and a CRT or

Pillar of the Information Society

Videotex brings the much-touted electronic information society to our doorstep. There are over 30,000 videotex terminals spread throughout more than 20 countries; by the end of the decade, say many forecasts, videotex will be present in up to 10 percent of North American homes and offices. It will be as accepted as the telephone and television.

Dozens of field trials, and now an increasing number of commercial services, illustrate the value of videotex. For example Grassroots, a commercial videotex service in Manitoba, has proved very successful with its initial subscriber roster of 500 farmers. . . . In addition to agricultural information, Grassroots offers an electronic catalog for teleshopping, computer games, and graphics-enhanced bedtime stories for the kids. Grassroots subscribers pay only for the terminal (which can be purchased or leased) and for the usage of telephone lines; the information is provided free by the sponsors and advertisers through Infomart, an electronic publishing house. Grassroots will soon spread into other parts of Canada. The service has also inspired plans for at least 17 projects in the U.S.

Another videotex success story is Teleguide. This service provides terminals in public locations throughout Toronto, such as hotel lobbies, shopping malls, train and bus stations, museums, and popular tourist sites. Anyone can walk up to a terminal and get information about transportation schedules, maps of tourist attractions, calendars of local events, lists of entertainment attractions, restaurants, and so on. Users access an average of 1000 pages per terminal each day. Here again, the advertisers and information providers pay, not the users. Teleguide terminals now number 500; within a year there will be over 1200.

Simplicity and extreme "user-friendliness" should help videotex capture a much larger audience than on-line data bases, which require some computer experience. Videotex's color graphics appeal both to users and to information providers—and particularly to advertisers who like visual aids to jazz up their product pitches. Business services offering financial information, travel schedules, and tourism information have been well-received around the world. On the consumer front, teleshopping, home banking, and electronic messaging are becoming more popular.

The surprisingly rapid development of videotex standards will promote information interchange among various data bases. Two protocols have been established, one in North America based on the Canadian Telidon format, the other in Europe based on the format of Britain's Prestel. Present efforts to harmonize the two standards should further stimulate videotex.

Videotex will prosper from its strong synergy with personal computers, office work stations, and on-line text terminals. In North America alone there are now over two million personal computers, and a growing number of office workstations; all can serve as videotex terminals. Personal computer makers such as Apple already offer Telidon interface modules, and independent software houses sell videotex packages for other computers. In addition, many new office communication systems integrate telephone, on-line data bases, and videotex functions.

Properly designed and packaged, videotex will entice not only farmers and tourists but also executives and salespeople, students and homemakers. Cost is not a problem; as long as there's an audience, there will be advertisers and information providers willing to pay to capture it. So hold off on the obituaries; videotex is here to stay.

By KEITH Y. CHANG
High Technology, May, 1983
Keith Y. Chang is director of the Telidon field trails for the Canadian Department of Communications (Ottawa).

teleprinter. Some RJE stations also have disk storage to accumulate input before sending it or to receive output before printing.

In the past few years, terminals have changed drastically. At first, terminals were slow and difficult to use; they functioned as slaves of centralized computers. They were essentially human-oriented input/output devices. Recently, however, inexpensive microprocessors have been integrated into the terminal equipment. The result is called an *intelligent* (sometimes *smart*) *terminal*.

Because these terminals have microprocessors, they can be programmed to perform any number of tasks. They can have sophisticated screen formats like the one shown in figure 8-18. They can have special keystrokes that allow data to be scrolled up or down when there is more data than can fit on the CRT screen at one time. Other special functions include inserting or deleting text; moving data items, lines, or other groups of characters on the screen; and so forth.

Additionally, intelligent terminals can be programmed to perform data editing. Input data can be checked for type limits (character vs numeric) and completeness, and check digits can even be calculated and checked during input.

Finally, if a terminal has storage equipment like a floppy, it can be used to store data for batch transmission. As the operator keys in data, it is edited and

FIGURE 8-18

Example of sophisticated screen format

stored. After some period of time, say, an hour, the data is then transferred from the floppy to the central computer in a batch. Processing in this mode can reduce communications costs. Instead of the communication line's being in use for an hour, it is used only for the time required to send a batch. The line is not active while the operator pauses, corrects errors, and so forth.

Some terminals can be extended with intelligence and storage to the point that they are computers themselves. They can do batch processing or even handle queries and transactions. However, this expansion makes the system a distributed one, and we will consider this possibility in the next chapter.

Multiplexors and Concentrators

Typically, a communication link operates at much faster speeds than a terminal. A medium-speed line transmits data at the rate of 9600 bps, whereas a human reads at about 50 bps and types at about 15 bps. Further, there are human delays for thinking time. To reduce this imbalance, two types of communications equipment are used: multiplexors and concentrators.

A *multiplexor* receives several slow-speed transmission lines and combines them into one high-speed line. One method, shown in figure 8-19, is called *time-division multiplexing*. Here, five 300-bps lines are combined into one 1500-bps line. Each slow line is allocated one out of every five character positions on the fast line. If it has nothing to send, a blank character (shown as b in the illustration) is sent in its position.

Note that, on the receiving end, the signal must be demultiplexed into its components; in this case, there would be five outputs. Demultiplexing is similar to a line at the post office. People (messages) enter in one line and are distrib-

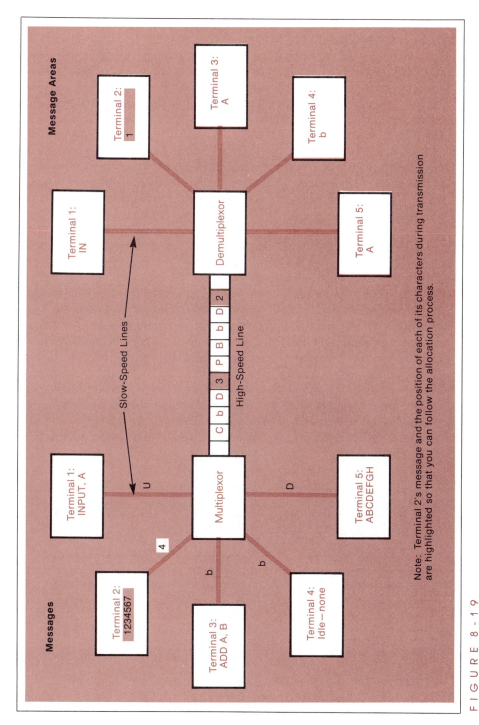

Note: Terminal 2's message and the position of each of its characters during transmission are highlighted so that you can follow the allocation process.

FIGURE 8-19

Operation of multiplexor

263

uted to windows (terminals). Unlike the post office, however, a message must go to a specific terminal.

A *concentrator* is an intelligent multiplexor. It combines several slow-speed lines into a single fast line, but it does it more efficiently and performs other services as well. Concentrators allocate time on the fast line in accordance with need. For example, instead of allocating every fifth character to a terminal, it allocates many characters to busy terminals and no characters at all to idle ones. Blanks are not sent.

Additionally, concentrators can compress data by removing repeated characters and by more sophisticated techniques. The compressed data is sent over the transmission line and then decompressed into its original format. Concentrators provide error detection and correction capabilities not found in multiplexors.

Also, some terminal equipment operates on a different character code than others. (Remember EBCDIC in chapter 2?) One terminal may represent characters with a 7-bit code, while another uses 9 bits. A concentrator can convert all of these codes to a single convention.

Finally, concentrators can help the central computer to manage communications equipment. For example, a multidrop line might be connected to a concentrator. If so, the concentrator can poll the terminals and send their messages down the fast line to the central computer. This relieves the CPU of the responsibility of polling and also reduces traffic on the fast line. Figure 8-20 shows such an application.

Do not confuse polling and contention with multiplexing and concentration. The objective of polling and contention is to allow multiple terminals to share the same line but with no change in line speed. The message leaves the terminal and is received at the central computer at the same speed. On the other hand,

FIGURE 8-20

Example of remote concentrator application

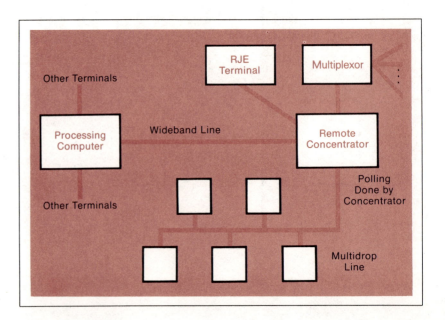

THE CHIP

The Heart of the Computer

At the heart of the computer is the tiny silicon chip, still shrinking in size. It has reduced the cost of computers as well as their size and placed the technology in everyone's hand. How is it done?

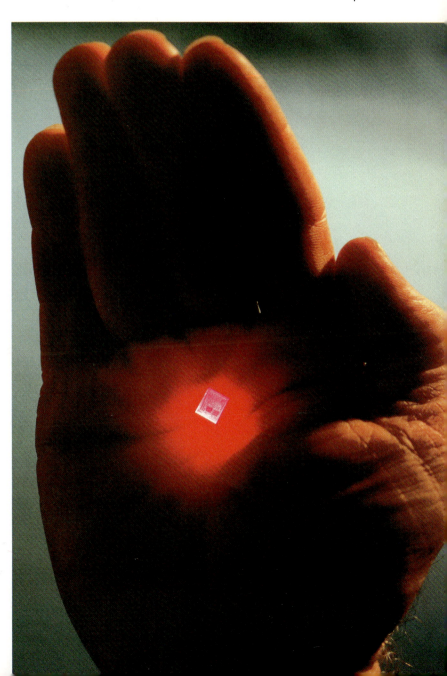

THE CHIP: FROM THE BEGINNING

These rocks are melted into nearly pure silicon.

The silicon comes from rocks in the southeastern United States, not from sand as is popularly believed.

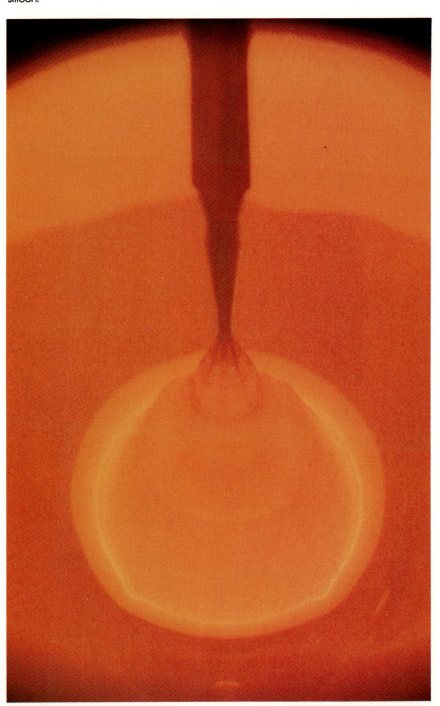

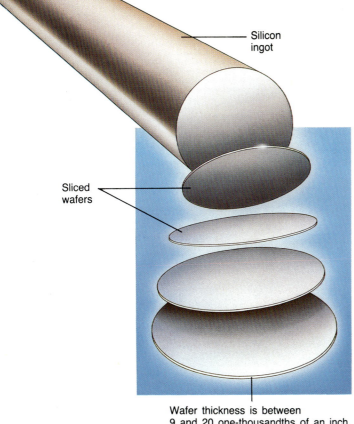

Silicon ingot

Sliced wafers

Wafer thickness is between 9 and 20 one-thousandths of an inch.

Wafers are sliced from the ingot and polished.

Ingots, or long silicon crystals, are grown from the melt.

Enlarged circuit designs are used to determine the circuitry to be reduced onto the chip.

THE CHIP:
SILICON WAFER

The design is reduced to a "mask" size that will put a million circuit components on a chip.

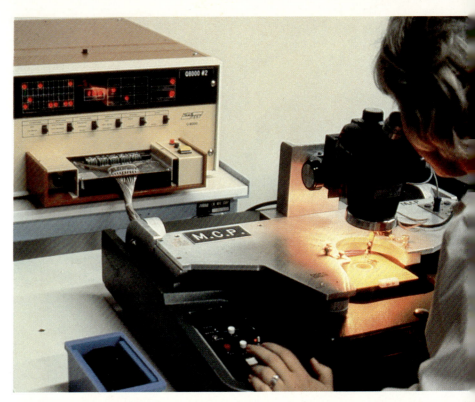

Masking plate with circuit design

Photoresist
Oxide layer
Silicon wafer

Wafer thickness is between 9 and 20 one-thousandths of an inch.

A masking plate is placed on top of the wafer.

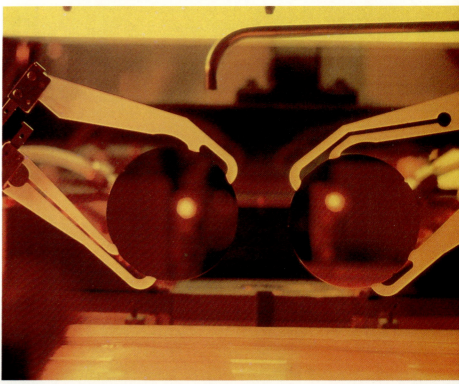

A light-sensitive plastic, called *photoresist*, is applied to the wafer.

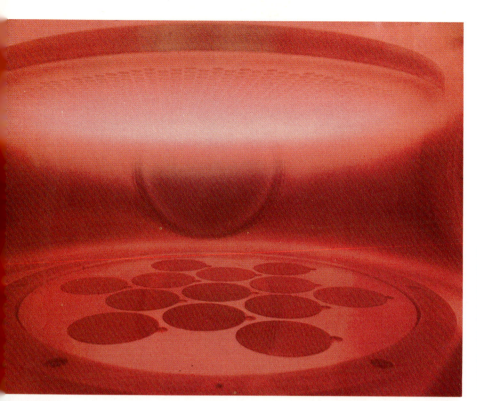

The wafer is flooded with ultraviolet light, which "prints" the mask pattern on the exposed photoresist.

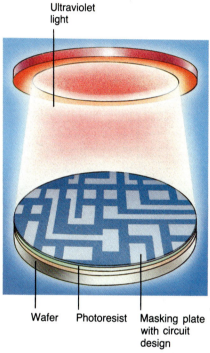

Ultraviolet light

Wafer   Photoresist   Masking plate with circuit design

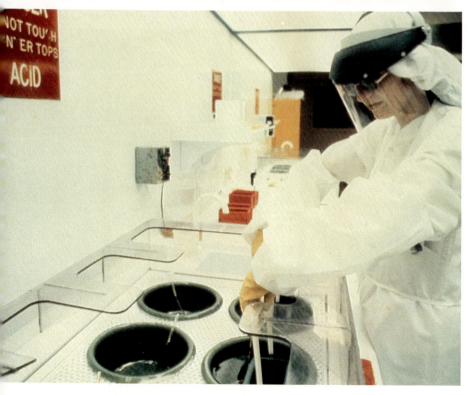

The wafer is then washed in chemicals that remove the resist from the exposed areas, leaving the pattern, or blueprint, for the circuitry.

THE WAFER BECOMES A MICROPROCESSOR

To create the necessary negative and positive zones, chemicals called doplants are embedded on the circuitry.

Mask blueprint imprints on photoresist

Chemical doplants are embedded to create positive and negative zones

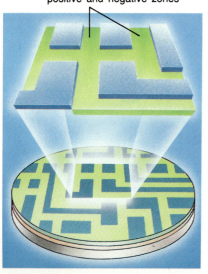

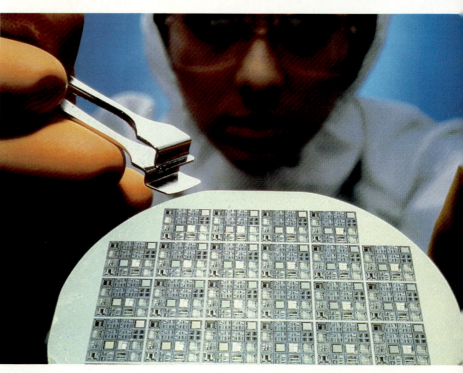

Each wafer is cleaned and carefully inspected.

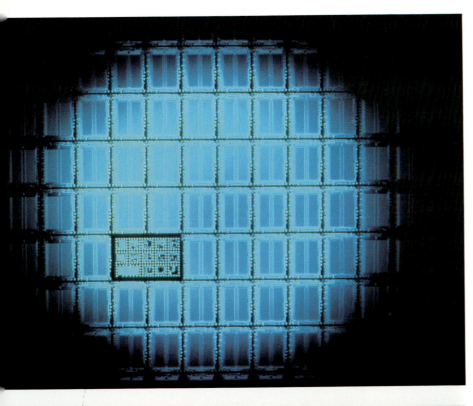

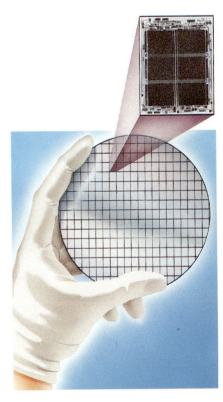

A single wafer thus contains many individual chips, each now a microprocessor.

THE CHIP:
ITS BLUEPRINTS

Each chip is then diced, or cut from the wafer with a diamond saw.

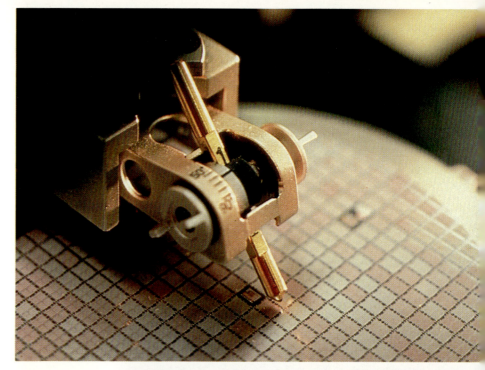

Reflected light can produce a colorful mosaic of the wafer's chips and individual circuitry.

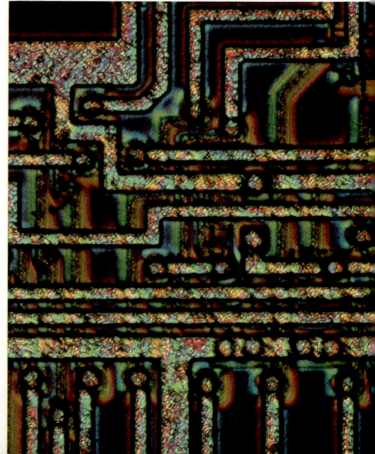

ANATOMY OF INTEL'S 80186

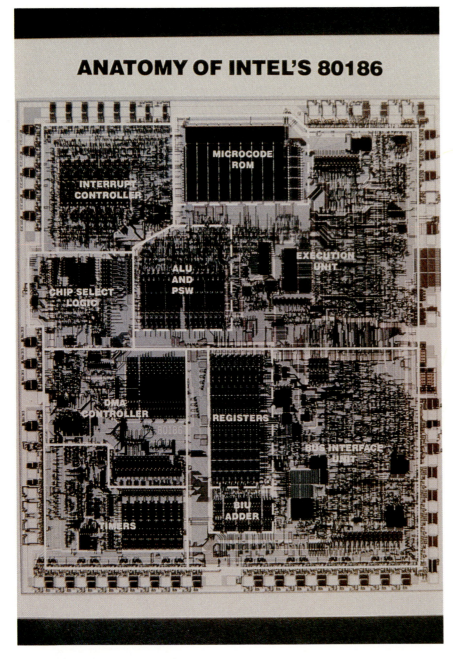

The components of a popular Intel chip design are labeled.

Chips are then bonded, or attached to a lead frame, and sealed.

THE CHIP BECOMES A "BOARD"

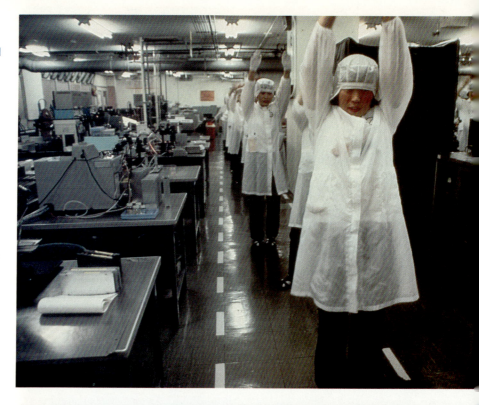

Japan is a leader in chip fabrication, and the Japanese approach to teamwork sometimes includes a "seventh-inning stretch."

The lead package of chips is assembled into a board.

A board with its microprocessor
packages is loaded into a computer.

Intel board components are labeled.

8049

SBC 80/05 8085

THE CHIP: COMMON APPLICATIONS

This microwave oven is controlled with a microprocessor.

Vehicle microprocessor systems in the 1980s.

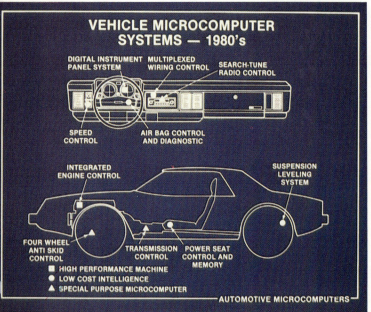

Microprocessor control of a gas pump.

Microprocessors in a typical kitchen and service area.

An Apple microcomputer *system*, with microprocessors inside and a chip at its heart.

Today's football scoreboard, courtesy of microprocessors.

THE CHIP: FUTURE APPLICATIONS

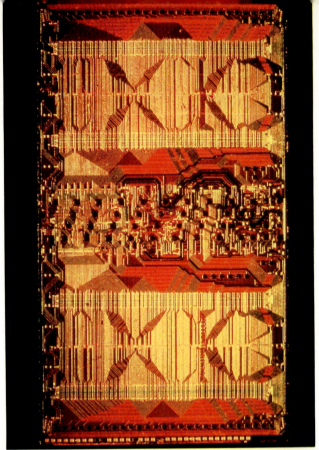

This IBM "super chip" continues to provide more memory on less space: 288,000 bits of data are stored on this ⅜-inch chip.

New technology: the bubble chip.

BUBBLES
- Mass Storage—Up to one million bits per chip

- Nonvolatile

- Replacement for mechanical, rotating disk memories

- Excellent for harsh environments (military applications)

- Applications range from small portable data-gathering equipment to crash recorders in aircraft.

- Naturally radiation resistant

New technology: ion beam etching of silicon chips may someday replace the masking process.

Ion beam etching directed by computer.

Japan serves a challenge to the United States for future growth in the chip industry.

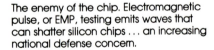

The enemy of the chip. Electromagnetic pulse, or EMP, testing emits waves that can shatter silicon chips . . . an increasing national defense concern.

QUESTIONS

1. Why are computer memories that are embedded on chips smaller and cheaper than first-generation computer vacuum tubes?
2. Why are "clean rooms" used in chip manufacturing?
3. List ten common applications of microprocessors.
4. What damage to a country's defense could be effected by EMP?
5. Distinguish between a microprocessor and a microcomputer.
6. Name a possible new application for cheaper and more powerful chips.

multiplexing and concentration allow the line to be shared by combining several slow-speed lines into one fast line.

So far, we have discussed communication lines and communications equipment at the terminal end. The third component of a teleprocessing system is the central computer.

At the computer end, there are four basic tasks to be performed. First, the incoming transmission on analog lines must be demodulated. As discussed, demodulation will be done by a modem at the central site. Second, if the incoming signal was produced by a multiplexor or concentrator, the original messages must be reassembled. In the case of multiplexing, each character must be added to the correct message. For our previous example, every fifth character is part of the same message. If the signal was produced by a concentrator, then the reassembling of the messages will be more complex. In simple terms, whatever was done to create the signal from the concentrator must be undone to reproduce the original messages.

The third task is called *code conversion*. A terminal may represent characters differently than the CPU and other terminals do. If so, the CPU will have to convert the characters to a common code. If a concentrator is in use, some of this work will have been done by it.

After the messages have been reassembled and converted to the correct code, the final task of the CPU is to pass them to the application program. This job is done by the operating system when the application program executes an instruction like "INPUT A, B."

Once the messages have been processed by the application programs, outputs may have to be returned to the terminals. All the steps just described are completed in reverse order. Also, if some terminals expect to be polled, the CPU must do that unless a remote concentrator has the responsibility. Figure 8-21 summarizes these tasks.

Now, these tasks represent a lot of work for the CPU. When you consider that the CPU is also supposed to execute the application programs, as well as run the rest of the operating system to manage file input/output and other tasks, you may wonder if it will have enough time to accomplish all of its tasks. In fact, for some systems, it is a problem. The CPU has too many things to do and can't keep up with the workload.

Teleprocessing at the Central Computer

Tasks
1. Demodulate analog signals
2. Demultiplex multiplexed signals (includes undoing concentrator's work, if applicable)
3. Convert character codes
4. Pass data to correct application program or other destination (file, for example)
Note: Repeat tasks in reverse order to send output to terminals.

FIGURE 8-21

Teleprocessing tasks at the central computer

In these situations, two solutions exist. One is to acquire a larger, more powerful CPU, which, unfortunately, can be expensive. A second solution is to acquire another, smaller CPU to handle just the communications tasks. Such computers are called *front-end processors* or *communications controllers*.

A front-end computer acts in many ways as a concentrator does, but it resides in close physical proximity to the central computer. It accepts inputs from terminals, multiplexors, and remote concentrators and merges them together for the CPU. It performs code conversion, does error checking and correction, and polls the terminals if necessary.

WAGNER PLEASURE BOATS (Continued)

As you may have guessed, Wagner's chief hotshot problem solver wasn't really you. Instead it was Joan Adams. She did investigate the possibility of processing remotely from Tampa to Los Angeles, and, within two months, Sabre had a remote job entry terminal that was connected to the computer in L.A. Two ambitious data processing employees were sent to Tampa for six months to convert the most important applications over to the Wagner systems.

As it turned out, those two people stayed in Tampa. As fast as they could convert a system, Joan and some of her new managers were requesting that other systems be converted. Soon, the Tampa operation outgrew the single RJE terminal; users in manufacturing, engineering, and purchasing were processing from CRTs that were connected to the computer in Los Angeles.

Figure 8-22 shows the communications hardware configuration two years after Sabre had been acquired by Wagner Pleasure Boats. The CRTs and the RJE station in Tampa were connected to a concentrator. It sent all of the traffic to Los Angeles over a wideband, digital leased line. Some of the terminals in Tampa

were connected to the concentrator over a multidrop line. The terminals in manufacturing were polled by the concentrator. The terminals in purchasing were managed by contention. The engineering terminals were not active more than two weeks out of four. When they were active, however, they required very high transmission rates. They were displaying engineering drawings on the CRT screens, and these drawings had a lot of detail that had to be transmitted. Because these terminals needed high speeds, they were connected directly to the concentrator.

As you might imagine, all of this activity had quite an impact on data processing operations in Los Angeles. Wagner upgraded their CPU to a faster and larger model. After a year, even that wasn't enough. Consequently, they acquired a small computer to act as a communications front-end. This computer received input from Tampa and dispersed outputs. Additionally, it managed local CRTs on multidrop lines, as shown. Figure 8-22 shows messages coming to the front-end labeled IN-WATS. These messages are sent by salespeople in the field who carry small teleprinters with them. The salespeople call the IN-WATS number (an 800 number) and

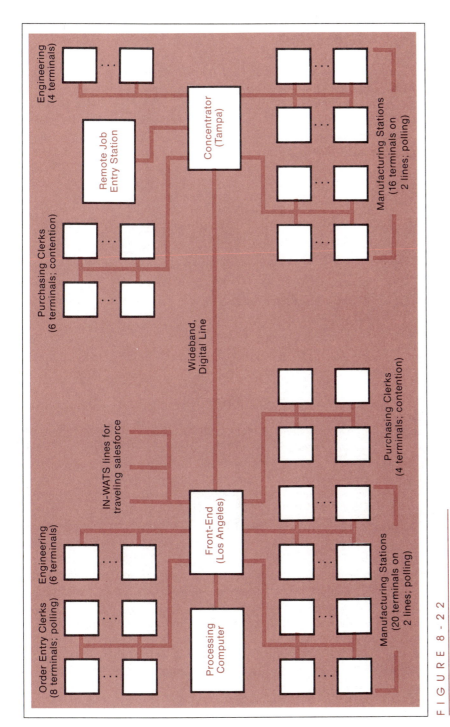

F I G U R E 8 - 2 2

Communications equipment used by
Wagner

267

are connected to the computer. From their hotel rooms, phone booths, or wherever they are, they can then key in orders and receive information back from the computer.

The terminals in figure 8-22 generate a chaotic situation. All of them can be sending or receiving messages simultaneously. The

concentrator and the front-end work together to bring order to this chaos. The result of their efforts is an organized stream of input from the front-end to the processing CPU. To understand what happens next, we need to discuss the second component of a teleprocessing system: programs.

QUESTIONS

8.24 What is an intelligent terminal?

8.25 Explain the difference between a multiplexor and a concentrator.

8.26 How is polling different from multiplexing?

8.27 Describe communications processing that must be done by a CPU or front-end.

8.28 Why do companies use front-ends?

8.29 Examine figure 8.22. Explain the function of each piece of equipment illustrated.

PROGRAMS FOR TELEPROCESSING SYSTEMS

Three types of programs are used in the teleprocessing environment: the *operating system, communications control programs*, and *application programs*. The operating system controls the processing computer's resources (not including communications equipment), and the application programs process the users' data to produce information. See module I for more about operating systems.

Communications control programs (CCP) control the flow of messages across the communications equipment. In figure 8-22, there are three places where programs are used to control the flow of messages. Both the concentrator and the front-end have programs to perform polling, multiplexing, code conversion, and so forth. In addition, the processing computer has a program to control the flow of messages inside its own memory.

Programs for the concentrator and the front-end can be purchased from the vendors of this equipment and tailored to the specific environment, or they can be developed by the using organization. The details of these programs are beyond the scope of this book. You should be aware that the programs exist, however, and that they must be acquired.

(As an aside, some of the earlier concentrators and front-ends were not programmable. They were easier to install but not nearly as flexible as later ones. With the advent of inexpensive microprocessors, nearly all concentrators and front-ends are programmable.)

Figure 8-23 shows a schematic of the contents of main memory of the processing computer. The *operating system* is shown at the top of memory; it

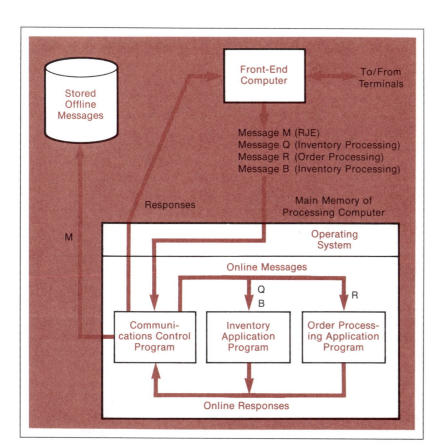

Message M (RJE)
Message Q (Inventory Processing)
Message R (Order Processing)
Message B (Inventory Processing)

F I G U R E 8 - 2 3

Programs involved in communications processing

is the set of programs that control the computer's resources, allocate and de-allocate files, execute I/O, and so forth. As messages are delivered to the processing computer, they are received by the operating system and delivered to another program, the communications control program. This program determines whether the message is to be acted upon immediately (online applications), or whether it is to be stored on a file for later processing (offline). If the message is an online type, the communications control program routes it to the correct application program. If databases were in use, a database management system would also appear in figure 8-23. Its position and function would be similar to that shown in figure 7-18.

Two *application programs* are shown in figure 8-23. One performs inventory processing. The other is used to process customer orders. In reality, there could be many more application programs. Messages are delivered to these programs and processed. When results are available, they are sent back to the communications control program and routed to the terminal that is waiting for a reply.

In figure 8-23, four messages are being transferred to the processing computer by the front-end. The first will be sent to the inventory application program; the next will be sent to the order processing program; the third will be sent to the inventory application program; and the fourth will be stored on the file for later processing.

Teleprocessing Application Programs

You should recognize an important detail. Although there may be many order entry clerks, there will be only one order processing program. As transactions arrive for order processing, they will have to wait in line just as humans do at the grocery store. When the order processing program is finished with an order, it will take the next one in line, and so forth. If orders arrive faster than the order processing program can handle them, a wait will develop.

Teleprocessing systems are amazing when you think of the work involved. In the Wagner Pleasure Boats case, a message originates on a terminal in Tampa, is sent 3000 miles to a front-end in Los Angeles, then is transferred to a processing computer, and eventually finds its way into the correct program residing in a main memory of perhaps 10 million bytes! It is then processed and a return message retraces all of these steps. The entire operation may take five seconds or less.

Protocols

In order for the message to be routed through this maze of processors, it must be packaged. When you want to send a package through the mail, you wrap it and put *to* and *from* addresses on the outside. A similar technique is used to package messages. As shown in figure 8-24*a*, header and trailer data are added to a message for routing and error-control purposes. The header shows where the message is to be delivered and where it is from. The trailer contains parity bits for error checking. In fact, in some systems, the trailer has enough data so that the error can be detected and corrected without retransmission.

There is a difference between the way post office packages and teleprocessing messages are wrapped, however. In teleprocessing applications, a message may be wrapped several times. The process can be compared to putting a package inside a bigger box, then rewrapping and readdressing it, and so on, several times.

Consider an order entry transaction that originates in Tampa. It is wrapped as shown in figure 8-24*a* and sent to the concentrator. Now, the message is marked for delivery to the order processing program. The concentrator does not know just where that is. So, the concentrator wraps the message again,

FIGURE 8-24

Message packaging techniques

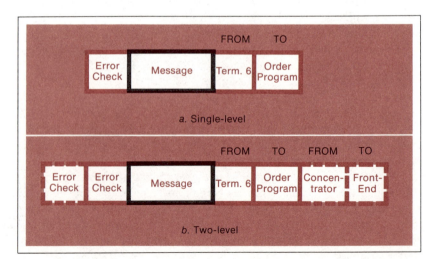

a. Single-level

b. Two-level

specifying the front-end as the *to* address and the concentrator as the *from* address. This procedure is shown in figure 8-24b.

When the message is received at the front-end, the outer layer of packaging is removed. Another one may be added. This time, the *to* address is the processing computer and the *from* address is the front-end.

The number of layers of packaging depends on the complexity of the communications facilities. In one important international standard, the International Standards Organization Open Systems Architecture [66], up to seven levels of packaging have been defined.

The term *protocol* is used in the communications business to refer to the way that a message is packaged and handled between two communicating programs. Because the equipment on a communications system is likely supplied by different vendors, it is important that national and international standards on protocol be used. If two computers, say, a concentrator and a front-end, conform to the same standard, they can interface successfully with each other. However, if they operate on different protocols, then they cannot be used together. Consequently, one of the important considerations during the design of a communications facility is that all components operate on the same protocol.

If you ever buy communications equipment, you may hear the terms *asynchronous* and *synchronous protocol*. Asynchronous protocols send packages containing only one character. Synchronous protocols send packages containing many characters. Asynchronous protocols result in slower processing, but, because only a single character is sent, coordination is simple. Synchronous protocols are faster, but coordination is more difficult.

Coordinating Processing

A question you may be asking is, What happens if a computer sends a message and it is never received on the other end? For example, suppose that the concentrator sends a message to the front-end, but a lightning bolt strikes the phone line, and the message is never received. Without some type of control, the concentrator will wait and wait for a response, but none will ever come, because the front-end never knew it was supposed to do something.

To prevent this situation from occurring, the programs in the concentrator and the front-end are structured so that, whenever one of them receives a message, it sends a *message acknowledgment* to the other. Consequently, if a processor sends a message, but does not receive an acknowledgment in an agreed-upon time, it will retransmit the message. Further, these programs are written to ensure that the messages are received in the correct order and that there are no errors in transmission.

Figure 8-25 on pages 272 and 273 shows two algorithms used to control message transmission in this way. One of these is for the processor that is sending the message, and the other is for the receiver. These algorithms are simpler than those actually used, but they illustrate the programming that must be done.

The essential idea in these algorithms is that the sender receives an acknowledgment for every message it transmits. Furthermore, the sender will not transmit the next message until acknowledgment is received for the current one.

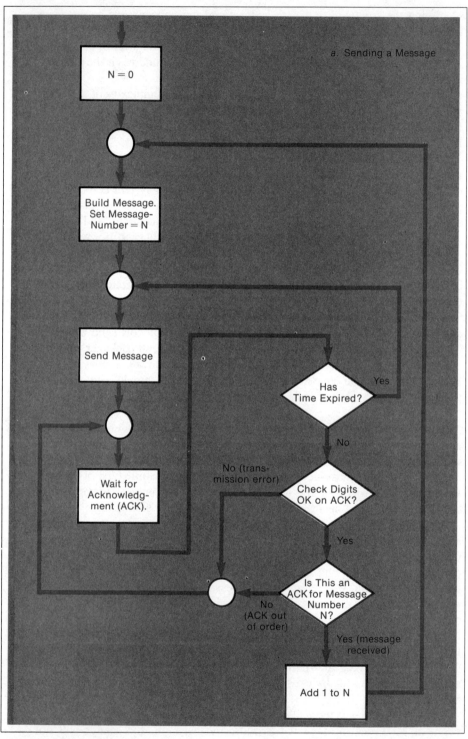

FIGURE 8-25

Simple algorithms for controlling
transmission [part 1 of 2]

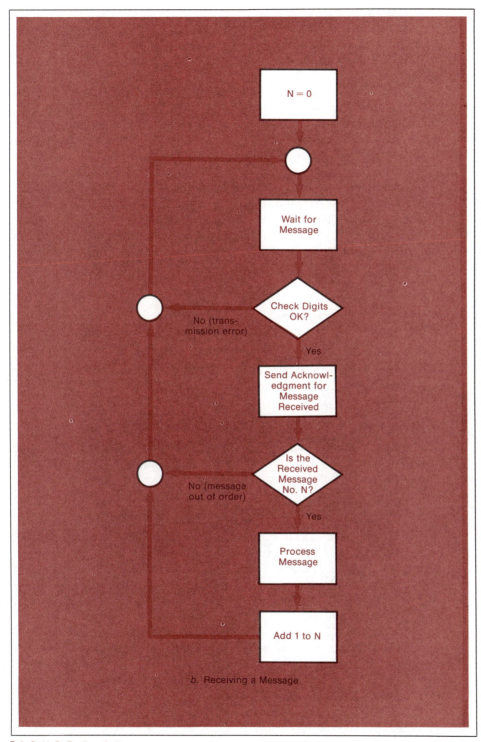

b. Receiving a Message

FIGURE 8-25

Simple algorithms for controlling
transmission [part 2 of 2]

In figure 8-25, part 1, the sender builds the message, transmits it, and waits for acknowledgment. If no acknowledgment is received in a given period of time, the message is retransmitted. Additionally, if a bad acknowledgment is received, or if the acknowledgment is for the wrong message, the sender will still wait and retransmit if necessary.

There are two reasons that an acknowledgment may not be received. First, the receiver may not have received the message (because of a lightning bolt, for example). In this case, it is appropriate for the sender to retransmit. Second, the receiver may have received the message, but the acknowledgment may have been destroyed on its way back to the sender. In this case, the sender will retransmit even though the receiver got the message. Therefore, when the duplicate message is received, the receiver must send another acknowledgment; otherwise, the message will be sent again and again and again.

The easiest way to understand how these algorithms work is to try them. Ask someone to play the part of the receiver and send a few messages to him or her. See what happens if either the message or the acknowledgment is lost.

QUESTIONS

8.30 What types of programs are used in the teleprocessing environment?

8.31 What are the functions of the communications control programs?

8.32 If there are 10 order entry clerks, all performing the same function, must there be 10 order entry programs? Why or why not?

8.33 What is a *protocol*?

8.34 Illustrate the packaging of a message with a three-level protocol.

8.35 What happens if a message is lost between a terminal and a computer? What keeps the terminal from waiting indefinitely for a response to a message the computer never received?

TELEPROCESSING DATA

The third component of a computer system is data. In the teleprocessing environment, data is subject to three special considerations. First, it must reside on direct access files; sequential processing takes far too long. Imagine your reaction if, when you wanted to withdraw money from your bank, you had to wait while the bank's entire depositor file was sequentially processed. It might take 20 minutes or more.

In the case of Wagner Pleasure Boats, the purchasing, order entry, and manufacturing personnel want their data to be available immediately. The data must therefore reside on direct access files. Further, the files must be mounted on the devices. Thus, if the files are stored on removable volumes, the operators must be sure that the volumes are mounted.

The second special consideration for teleprocessing data concerns its vulnerability. Efforts must be made to preserve the accuracy (sometimes referred to as the *integrity*) of the data. Because the data is *online*, and because there can be multiple users of the same data, it is easy for the files to be changed incorrectly. Furthermore, because the files are shared, when problems develop, it is difficult to determine who or what is responsible.

Consider the case of Wagner Pleasure Boats. Suppose that an order entry clerk confuses two part numbers. He uses the part number for bolts whenever he orders diesel engines, and he uses the part number for diesel engines whenever he orders bolts. Chances are that, after two or three days, the order entry files will be a mess. There will be a great backlog on diesel engines. Furthermore, other order entry clerks will be misinformed. If one of them tries to input an order for a diesel engine, he or she will be told that there is a great backlog. The company may lose an important order.

As another example, suppose that Wagner has two order files—one for customer orders and one for in-plant orders for items used in production. If the order entry clerk accesses the wrong file (which is possible, because both files are online), havoc will result on the production line. This, by the way, will all be blamed on the computer, even though the order entry clerk is at fault.

Because data is online, and because data integrity can be a problem, adequate *security* must be provided for the files. At a minimum, all online files should be protected by account numbers and passwords. Only users with certain account numbers should be able to access the file. Additionally, these users must be assigned *passwords* that restrict the actions they can take. For example, read-only passwords might be used.

The account number restriction will prohibit users in purchasing, say, from accessing order entry files. The passwords will keep order entry clerks from making unauthorized changes to order entry files. These features are needed not just to keep computer criminals out. They are needed to bring control and order to everyday activity.

In addition to these precautions, some businesses use *encryption* to protect their data. Encryption is the coding of data so that it is unintelligible. Substituting one character for another is a simple encryption scheme. More sophisticated techniques are needed for real applications. Data can be encrypted when it is sent over communication lines and when it is stored on the files. Encryption is *not* effective unless the programs that do the encrypting and that use the data are protected from would-be infiltrators as well.

IN-WATS capability like that shown in figure 8-22 is particularly susceptible to unauthorized access. Some companies have automatic answering. A caller is connected to the computer with no human intervention. This facility is convenient but not secure. A much better approach is to have the caller identify him- or herself to an operator, who then transfers the call to the computer. Some computer terminals initiate conversations by broadcasting their identities. The front-end or processing computer can be programmed to check this identifier against a list of authorized terminals before proceeding.

To review, there are three special considerations for data in the teleprocessing environment. The data must be online, and, consequently, data integrity must be carefully managed. Finally, because online data is vulnerable, security is vitally important.

PROCEDURES FOR TELEPROCESSING SYSTEMS

The procedures needed to operate a teleprocessing system successfully are an extension to the procedures that we have discussed previously. For users, there must be procedures describing how to use the system under normal conditions. These include how to start and stop the system, as well as how to use it. Additionally, there must be procedures describing user activity during abnormal operation. These include how to tell if the system is operating incorrectly, what to do if it is, and so forth. There must also be procedures for users to follow when the computer system has failed. These procedures describe what data must be gathered for restoration and what activities the users can allow before the system is operational. For example, bank tellers may allow deposits to accounts but not withdrawals.

For operations, there need to be similar procedures both for normal operation and for operation during failure. The operations staff needs specific instructions about how to identify failures, what to do or whom to call, and how to recover files and restart programs.

In addition to these standard system procedures, teleprocessing systems require two other types of procedures. To illustrate the first, consider what happened at Wagner.

About six weeks after a new teleprocessing order entry system had been implemented, Wagner's customer service department got a few complaints from customers who had been promised goods that had never arrived. Customer service personnel checked the order entry procedures. They seemed all right. The order entry clerks had checked to ensure that the items were in inventory; they were; an order had been generated.

Furthermore, shipping reported that they had received orders for goods that were not in inventory. At this point, data processing personnel were brought in to examine the situation.

Eventually, the source of the error was discovered; it involved the interaction of two clerks attempting to order the same part simultaneously. Figure 8-26 summarizes the action.

Concurrent Update Procedures

Because the processing computer has only one CPU, it cannot process two orders that are truly simultaneous. Instead, it will do some processing on one, then some processing on another, and so forth, until both are completed. However, the computer works so fast that it appears to the users that their orders are processed simultaneously. In computer terminology, the orders are processed *concurrently*.

What happened in the example in figure 8-26 is that the computer read an inventory record for clerk A, and then read the same record for clerk B. Next, clerk A took the last item from inventory and updated the inventory record. Subsequently, clerk B took what he or she thought was the last item from inventory and updated the record. At this point, the inventory showed 0 items for that part, but the last part had been issued twice!

Clerk A's Activity	Clerk B's Activity
Read inventory record for item X.	Read inventory record for item X.
Take last item X from inventory.	Take last item X from inventory.
Set item count to 0.	(Clerk B's copy of the record does not show that clerk A just took the last one.)
	Set item count to 0.
Replace item X inventory record.	Replace item X inventory record.

FIGURE 8-26

Example of concurrent update problem

This is called the *concurrent update problem*. It can occur in any system in which more than one user is allowed to update the same file. To get around the problem, programs have to be written to place *record locks* before updates are made. The record is locked by giving exclusive control of it to one user. Other users cannot obtain the record until the first person is through with it.

In Wagner's case, this portion of the order processing program had been written by a new programmer who did not understand the need for locking and unlocking. Once the problem was fixed, Wagner's data processing department developed new procedures for the coding of programs to ensure that this situation would not recur.

Additionally, Wagner developed new procedures for users to prevent concurrent update problems. Basically, the users were given two new commands. One was a READ command for information purposes only. The other was a READ command for update purposes. Thus, if a clerk wanted to know only the number of items in inventory, he or she would use the first read. However, if the clerk wanted to determine if there were a sufficient number of items in inventory, and, if so, to order them, then he or she would use the second read command. Programs were written so that, if the user tried to update after using the first command, an error message was generated.

To summarize, teleprocessing systems are multiple-user systems. As such, they are susceptible to the concurrent update problem. Obviously, procedures must be developed for both programmers and users to ensure that such problems do not occur.

Backup and Recovery Procedures

Teleprocessing *backup and recovery* also requires extensions to the standard procedures. Examine figure 8-23. Imagine what happens if the computer fails after all four messages have been input to the processing computer's main memory. Parts of order transactions and parts of inventory transactions may have been completed. Then again, they may not have been. When a computer fails, there is no sure way to tell what has occurred.

Since the status of the machine is unknown, the status of the files is also unknown. Suppose that, during recovery, the first inventory message is processed again. It may have been processed successfully before the failure as well. In this case, it will be processed twice. On the other hand, there is the danger that it was not processed before the failure. In this case, it will be skipped if it is not processed during recovery.

One solution to this problem is to restart from a backup file and reapply all the transactions processed since the backup was made. However, this procedure can be very time consuming. The users will be impatient if they are waiting for the system to return so that they can resume their jobs.

Another problem when reprocessing is that it is difficult to repeat the exact sequence. If two transactions are recovered in a different order than that in which they were originally processed, strange results can occur. For example, if, during the original run, customer A got the last part 123, but, during recovery, customer B gets the last part 123, then the order documents produced during the original run will disagree with the recovered files. This type of activity can create great havoc in a company.

Another interesting possibility to consider is what may happen if the front-end in figure 8-22 fails. Assume that it just quits. Then none of the terminals can talk to the processing computer, and the processing computer cannot talk to the terminals. This stand-off is material for the nightmares of the systems staff.

The subject of backup and recovery for teleprocessing systems is a difficult one. We cannot solve Wagner's problem here. You should be aware of the need for backup and recovery, however, and know that procedures must be written to cover all possibilities.

TELEPROCESSING PERSONNEL

The personnel required to operate a teleprocessing system are also an extension to those required for batch systems. As with any computer system, both the users and the operations staff must be trained in procedures. Further, the systems development staff must know how to build and maintain programs for online processing. Programming in this mode is different from batch programming. Some additional training may be required.

In addition to these standard personnel requirements, several specialists may be needed. *Hardware communications specialists* know how to maintain and repair communications-oriented hardware. They also are important members of a communications design team. These people maintain an inventory of diagnostic equipment. They are called upon whenever there is a communications hardware failure.

These personnel are expensive and hard to find. Therefore, only companies having large communications systems have such specialists on staff. Other companies contract with vendors or with independent communications consulting companies to supply these personnel when needed. For simple telecommunications systems like that described for Horizon, the vendor provides communications support under the maintenance contract for the computer. Independent expertise is needed when several vendors are involved.

Software communications specialists know how to build and maintain the programs on communications processors like concentrators and front-ends. They also specialize in products like the communications control program shown in figure 8-23. The level of expertise required to maintain these programs is much the same as the level of expertise needed to maintain the operating system. Some companies have one or more people who maintain all of these programs. This group is sometimes referred to as the *systems shop*, because they maintain the systems programs.

In addition to these experts, there is a person who is woefully neglected in most companies. He or she is vital to the success of a large teleprocessing system. That person is the *buyer* or *purchaser* of this equipment. Buying or negotiating leases for communications equipment is a tricky business. The equipment is complex; there are many pitfalls; and there are more than a few fly-by-night companies. Companies that intend to build large communications systems are well advised to use trained buyers when contracts are to be negotiated and signed.

A final person who is especially important in teleprocessing systems is called the *data administrator*. This person is the custodian of the shared data in the teleprocessing system. He or she is responsible for resolving conflicts between users, for ensuring that procedures are followed, and, in general, for protecting the data. This job is similar to that described for the database administrator in chapter 7. The job is simpler, however, because there is less data sharing.

QUESTIONS

8.36 The three special conditions for data in teleprocessing systems are ___ data, careful management of data ___, and a vital need for data ___.

8.37 Why are passwords needed for online teleprocessing files?

8.38 What is encryption?

8.39 Describe the concurrent update problem. How can it be prevented?

8.40 Why are teleprocessing systems difficult to backup and recover?

8.41 What two types of specialized personnel are needed to support a teleprocessing system?

SUMMARY

This chapter has introduced the major concepts of teleprocessing systems. We defined the terms *teleprocessing* and *telecommunications* and described three examples. Businesses develop teleprocessing systems because the business enterprise is geographically distributed, as well as for economic reasons. Because of economies of scale, it can be cheaper to have one central computer with communications capability than to have many disconnected, distributed computers.

We identified three stages in the growth of computer capability: *centralized*, in which all computing is done in batch mode on a single computer; *teleprocessing*, in which all applications processing is done on a single computer, but the users are connected via telecommunications equipment; and *distributed*, in which applications processing is done on distributed computers.

In the remainder of the chapter, we discussed the five components of a teleprocessing system. Considering hardware, communication lines were discussed in some depth. Lines can be classified according to speed (narrowband, voice grade, and wideband), mode (analog and digital), and type (simplex, half-duplex, and full-duplex). We also discussed sources of communication lines.

Other hardware components discussed included teleprinters, remote job entry terminals, and CRTs. Finally, multiplexors, concentrators, and front-end computers were described.

Three types of programs are needed in the teleprocessing environment. The operating system is needed to control the computer's resources. Communications control programs are written to transmit messages from a terminal to the relevant application program and then back again. Such programs are used on concentrators, on front-ends, and as the communications control programs inside the processing computer's main memory. Finally, application programs perform tasks like inventory, order entry, and other user-related functions.

In the teleprocessing environment, data is used by more than one person. The integrity of the data can easily be lost. Therefore, the data must be subjected to rigorous security controls. Furthermore, because problems can occur as a result of concurrent updates, special procedures for users and programmers must be devised. Special backup and recovery procedures are also needed because of the complexity of teleprocessing systems.

Finally, we discussed the personnel needed for teleprocessing systems. In addition to the usual people, communications specialists for both hardware and software are needed. A specially trained buyer is also important. Finally, because the data may be shared among many users, there is a need for a data administrator.

WORD LIST

(in order of appearance in text)

Teleprocessing
Telecommunications
Data communications
Remote job entry (RJE) station
Response time
Economies of scale
Distributed processing
Centralized processing
Offline processing
Batched data transmission
Online processing
Query and response systems
Transaction processing
Online program development
Communication line speed
Communication line mode
Communication line type
Bits per second (bps)
Narrowband
Voice grade
Line conditioning
Wideband

Baud
Analog lines
Digital lines
Frequency modulation
Amplitude modulation
Modulation
Demodulation
Modem
Data set
Simplex lines
Half-duplex lines
Full-duplex lines
Common carrier
Switched lines
Direct distance dialing
Wide Area Telephone Service (WATS)
Private (leased) lines
Satellite carrier
Value-added carrier
Multidrop line
Polling

Contention
Teleprinter
Intelligent terminal
Multiplexor
Time-division multiplexing
Concentrator
Code conversion
Front-end
Operating system
Communications control program
Application program
Protocol
Asynchronous protocols
Synchronous protocols

Message acknowledgment
Data integrity
Online data
Data security
Passwords
Encryption
Concurrent update problem
Record locks
Backup and recovery procedures
Hardware communications
   specialists
Software communications specialists
Systems shop
Data administrator

QUESTIONS TO CHALLENGE YOUR THINKING

A. Suppose again that you are Wagner's problem solver. How would you decide whether to expand your own local data processing facility or to communicate with the facility in Los Angeles? What costs would you consider? What benefits would you measure? How would you proceed?

B. Suppose Wagner did not acquire a concentrator in Florida. How would the system configuration shown in figure 8-22 change? How many lines would be needed between Tampa and Los Angeles? What additional equipment might be needed?

C. Suppose the users of the teleprocessing system shown in figure 8-22 complained that response time was too slow. What could be done to improve it?

D. Find an organization that has a teleprocessing system. Interview the director of data processing or other responsible individual to find out how they do backup and recovery. What backup files are kept? How often are they obtained? How are transactions saved? How is the recovery performed? What procedures are there for users and for operations personnel? Are there any special programming restrictions?

E. In the past few years, several notorious computer crimes have been committed using teleprocessing systems. Pick any one of them and find what you believe was the cause or causes of the crime. Was the problem in hardware, programs, data, procedures, or personnel? What can be done to prevent the recurrence of the crime in the future?

CHAPTER 9

Distributed Computer Systems

In this chapter, we will discuss *distributed data processing systems*. The term *distributed* is used because applications are processed on computers that are distributed throughout the company. Distributed processing systems are computer systems in which multiple computers are used to run *application programs*.

THREE EXAMPLES OF DISTRIBUTED PROCESSING SYSTEMS

Distributed data processing is not the same as teleprocessing. Figure 9-1 shows a teleprocessing system. In this figure, users and terminals are distributed. There are also multiple computers: the concentrator, the front-end, and the applications processing computer. However, only one of the computers is used to process application programs. *Applications* processing is *not* distributed.

ERD Pharmaceutical

Figure 9-2 shows a distributed processing network used by a pharmaceutical company. This system has three computers: the central applications processing computer, the front-end, and the marketing applications processing computer. This system is different from a teleprocessing system because there are two computers doing *applications* processing. A microcomputer does marketing analysis, and a mainframe does other applications processing.

Therefore, the distinguishing characteristic of a distributed system is not that users or terminals are distributed. It is not that there is more than one computer in use. The distinguishing characteristic of distributed processing is that more than one computer processes application programs.

Distributed processing allows the applications processing to be done in the best place for the application—not in the place where a large, centralized computer happens to be. This arrangement has two advantages. First, it can be cheaper. When applications processing is moved toward the user, there is less traffic on the communication lines. There is no need for the data to be sent to a centralized location for processing and for the results then to be returned. Thus, communications costs go down.

Second, distributed processing gives the users greater control over the data and its processing. Often the users operate distributed computers. They can determine the data to be processed, the order of processing, and the quality of service. Also, users in one department are not inconvenienced by users in another department if each group of users has its own computer.

If you view data processing as a method of producing information from raw data, then data processing is a type of manufacturing. In these terms, distributed data processing is similar to distributed manufacturing. The computer (plant) is moved close to the location where the product is needed.

An *applications node* is a computer in a distributed network that does applications processing. Each applications node has a computer, programs, data, procedures, and users. Thus, each node has all of the components of a computer system. However, within this definition, there is a wide range of capability because there can be variation in how much these components are distributed.

Examine the pharmaceutical company's distributed network in figure 9-2 again. Once a day, all of the sales data is sent from the mainframe computer to the microcomputer over the communication line. This data is saved on a

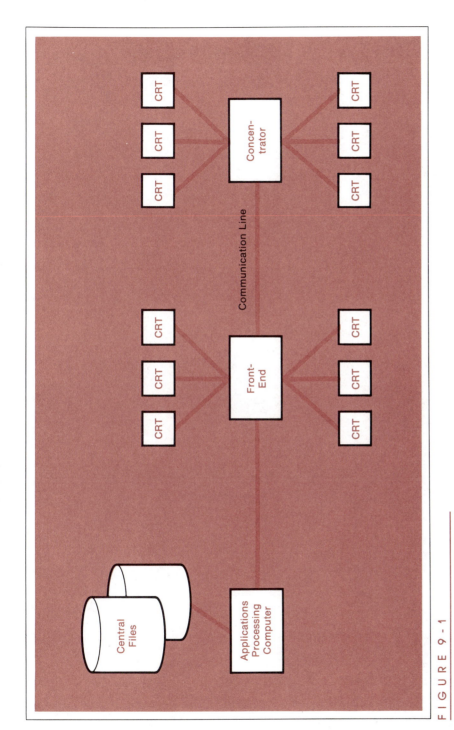

F I G U R E   9 - 1

Teleprocessing example

F I G U R E   9 - 2

ERD distributed processing system

local microcomputer file. The marketing analysis department later scans this data and copies parts of it to several other files. These files are then used by analysis programs to produce marketing reports. The marketing analysts also examine the data in these files using a query utility.

This is a simple distributed system. There is only one distributed computer, and it processes only marketing-related data. The flow of data is one way; the marketing department does not send any data back to the mainframe. Thus, marketing analysis does not change any files used by any other department. If they make a mistake, only the marketing department will suffer the consequences.

In this system, the mainframe is a *master* and the microcomputer is a *slave*. The mainframe decides when to send the data, and it decides what data to send. There is no interaction between the two computers to determine what to do. Further, the mainframe never receives data from the micro. No interactions are initiated by the micro. Finally, since the mainframe keeps a copy of everything it sends to the microcomputer, the mainframe is not dependent on the micro for any data.

Figure 9-3 shows a distributed data processing system that is more complex than the pharmaceutical company's. FRAMCO Distributing has seven locations throughout the United States and Canada that operate as autonomous profit centers. Each location is considered to be an independent company. Each location manager shares in the profits made by his or her company.

FRAMCO Distributing

Each location has its own computer and does its own data processing. However, for reasons of compatibility and maintenance, the programs are the same and the files have a common format. The programs are used for order processing, inventory, and accounting. There are files of customer, price, inventory, order, and general ledger data.

Additionally, FRAMCO headquarters has a computer of its own. It receives data from the other seven computers and produces consolidated financial statements. It also extracts marketing and other data that is used by centralized purchasing and planning departments. Consequently, each location computer must be able to communicate with the headquarters computer. Furthermore, the applications nodes must be able to communicate with each other.

According to FRAMCO policy, if one location is out of a part, it must try to locate the part at another location. Before the distributed system was developed, order clerks did this manually over the telephone. This procedure was too slow to be effective. Consequently, FRAMCO built the distributed system so that all seven location computers could communicate with one another. Now, when the local inventory does not have a part in stock, the local computer determines if another FRAMCO location has it. If so, the part is ordered from the other location. This processing is done by the computers. The order entry clerks need not call or take other direct, human action.

Figure 9-3 shows a processor labeled *message switcher*. It is a computer much like a front-end processor. It receives messages and sends them to the correct location. It is used to reduce the number of communication lines necessary to connect all of the computers to one another. To illustrate, we will calculate the

Computer Communication

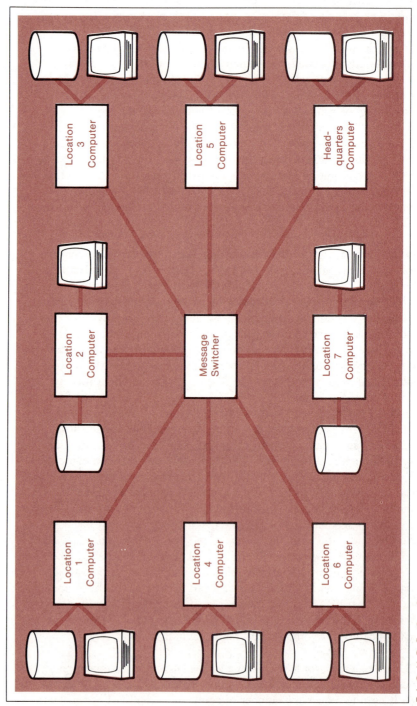

F I G U R E   9 - 3

Computer network for FRAMCO
Distributing

288

number of lines needed to connect all of the computers without a message switcher.

First, seven lines will be needed to connect the headquarters computer to all seven locations (see figure 9-4). Then six more lines will be needed to connect location 1 to locations 2 through 7 (location 1 is already connected to the headquarters computer). Next, five more lines will be needed to connect location 2 to locations 3 through 7 (location 2 is already connected to headquarters and to location 1). Four lines are needed to connect location 3 to locations 4 through 7, and so on. In total, $7 + 6 + 5 + 4 + 3 + 2 + 1$, or 28, lines will be needed if there is no message switcher.

Examine figure 9-3. Observe that, with the message switcher, only eight lines are needed. Thus, the message switcher greatly reduces the number of lines needed and hence reduces the communications costs.

The distributed network shown in figure 9-3 is considerably more complex than the one in figure 9-2. First, there are eight computers instead of just two. FRAMCO must operate all of these, ensure that they are properly maintained, and have them repaired when necessary. Also, programs must be maintained for each computer. Because they are all the same, this task is not as difficult as it could be. However, maintaining seven uniform copies of a program is difficult. Whenever changes are made to one program, great care must be exercised to ensure that the same changes are made to all copies of it. If not, over a period of time, the programs will diverge. Processing will not be identical at each location.

Another complexity of the FRAMCO system is that there is no clear master/slave relationship. The eight computers operate as *colleagues*. As with humans,

FIGURE 9-4

Computer network without message switcher

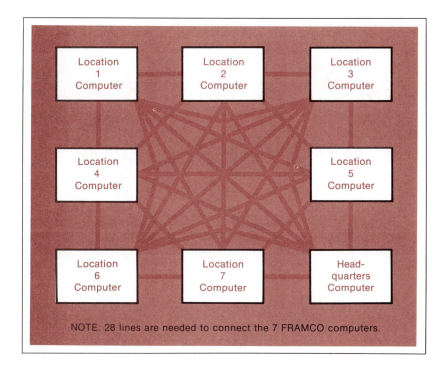

NOTE: 28 lines are needed to connect the 7 FRAMCO computers.

equality requires more frequent and more sophisticated communication. The computers can request services from one another, but they must be prepared for rejection. Another computer may be too busy, or it may be inoperative. Furthermore, while a computer is requesting a service from one computer, it may be receiving a request from a different computer. All of these actions must be coordinated, and the processing must be done systematically without error.

Finally, unlike the ERD system, FRAMCO's computers are very *dependent on one another for data*. No computer in the network possesses all of the FRAMCO data. Backup and recovery must be carefully performed at each node so that no data is lost. This demands close coordination of activity and careful data management.

Super-Burger Restaurant Franchises

A third example of a distributed processing network is shown in figure 9-5. Super-Burger Restaurant Franchises has 20 restaurants in each of four regions throughout the United States. Each restaurant has a microcomputer that controls the operations of the cash registers (which also have micros). The restaurant computer keeps track of raw goods received, goods produced, foods sold, cash receipts, and so forth.

The restaurant microcomputers are connected to regional minicomputers via communication lines. The regional computers obtain data from the restaurant computers twice a day. This data is used to maintain a raw-goods inventory for each restaurant, and to order and schedule deliveries of raw goods three times per week. The regional computers also produce bimonthly financial statements for each restaurant and for the region as a whole.

Finally, the four regional computers are connected to a headquarters com-

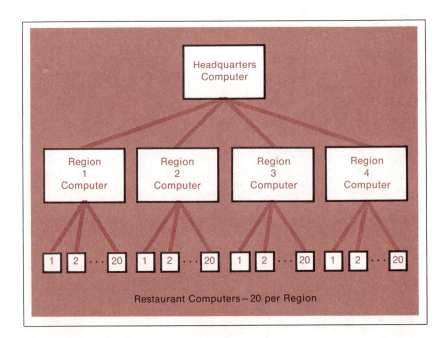

puter. They send financial statements as well as other marketing and inventory data to headquarters. This computer, also a mini, produces consolidated financial statements, ranks the profitability of the 80 franchises, develops marketing forecasts, and schedules procurement of major supplies. Furthermore, this computer is used to assess the market potential of future franchises and to predict the best locations for new restaurants.

Super-Burger considered obtaining a mainframe computer for their headquarters. When they evaluated alternatives, however, they found that a mini would do the job. This alternative was possible because so much processing was done in the regions. From this example, you can see that mainframes are not always needed to manage minicomputers.

The computer network shown in figure 9-5 is an extension of the simple network used by ERD. Super-Burger has a two-level *hierarchy of computers* connected in multiple master/slave relationships. The headquarters computer is a master over the regional computers. The regional computers are masters over the restaurant computers. Thus, the regional computers operate as both masters and slaves.

Distributing Programs

In order for the headquarters computer to produce useful summaries, the data that it receives from the regional computers must be consistent. To ensure this consistency, all of the programs used by the regional and restaurant computers must be the same. This uniformity is difficult to manage because, whenever a restaurant computer program is changed, programs at all 80 restaurants must be updated.

There are two ways to accomplish this task. First, Super-Burger could send computer professionals to each of the restaurants with a new copy of the program and have them install it. This approach would be expensive. It would involve many people and a lot of travel. It would also be wasteful because the task to be performed is very simple.

A better approach, and the one that Super-Burger uses, is to have the regional computers *downline load the new programs*. In other words, regional computers install new versions of the programs remotely over the communication lines. This approach not only saves money but enables the entire process to be completed in a few hours. Consequently, changes to the restaurant programs can be made more frequently.

The data in the Super-Burger Restaurant system is duplicated just as ERD's data is. The restaurant computers send copies of their data to the regional computers. The regional computers in turn send copies of their data to the headquarters computer. The restaurant computers keep one week's worth of data for their own processing and for backup of the regional computers' data. The regional computers keep data on an annual basis. The headquarters computer keeps financial data indefinitely.

Distributing Personnel

There are no data processing personnel at the restaurants. The microcomputers receive input from the cash registers and requests from the regional computers. There is no need for computer operators. Many of the restaurant employees do not even know the computer is there. A restaurant manager can get some data

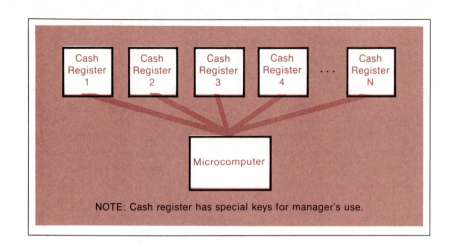

NOTE: Cash register has special keys for manager's use.

FIGURE 9-6

Super-Burger Restaurant microcomputers

by using special keys on one of the cash registers. He or she also gets reports from the regional computer. (See figure 9-6.)

At a regional facility, there are no systems development personnel, but there are three computer operators. These operators run programs and disperse outputs. The users at the regional locations are purchasing agents and managers.

The headquarters has a full complement of data processing personnel. There are systems development personnel (application programmers, systems analysts, communications specialists, and systems programming experts). The headquarters computer is supported by a staff of three operators. There are also marketing, purchasing, and management users.

Because of the large number of computer locations without on-site systems development personnel, there is a great need for well-documented, standardized procedures. Each restaurant manager has clear instructions on how to start and stop the computer and what to do in the event of a failure or an emergency. The names and phone numbers of critical personnel are also available. The data processing department is proud of the fact that these names have seldom been used. The microcomputers have been very reliable.

CHARACTERISTICS OF DISTRIBUTED SYSTEMS

As with teleprocessing systems, the components of a computer system in a distributed environment are physically distributed. In the Super-Burger example, the consolidated financial statements are produced by hardware and programs at headquarters. The personnel, including users, of this system are also at headquarters. However, the data and the procedures for obtaining the data are distributed throughout the company.

In contrast to a teleprocessing system, however, a distributed system has at least one complete computer system resident at each applications node. The node has processing hardware, programs, data, procedures, and users for at least one system. This fact is one way to discriminate between teleprocessing and distributed systems.

As you can imagine, distributed systems are complex to develop. In fact, almost no company starts out to build a distributed computer system. Instead, a company usually moves to a distributed system in one of two ways. The first way is that a company with a very large central computer may decide to *offload* some of their processing to a distributed computer. This usually happens when the central computer processing load is so big that it is hard to manage. There may be so many systems to run that the operations staff has trouble scheduling them. The quality of service may be poor because it becomes impersonal. Also, cost considerations may indicate that expanding the existing computer is more expensive than acquiring an additional, smaller one. (Refer back to figure 8-4.)

Another common reason for offloading a central computer is that the systems development staff is far behind in development effort. In some companies, it takes 18 months or more before work starts on a new project. In these companies, the users sometimes become so frustrated that they acquire systems with off-the-shelf programs to install and run themselves. (Recall Blake Records and Tapes in chapter 1.) The systems development staff may be happy to be relieved of another request. This situation can lead to problems, however, if the system is not properly integrated into the rest of the company's data processing operations.

A second way a company can move to a distributed system is to *build up to it*. Here, the company may have one applications processing computer that is too small for the current workload. Instead of upgrading the computer, however, they decide to buy more small computers.

Usually a company takes this second course of action if local control of the data processing resources is important. In FRAMCO's case, for example, each location is considered to be an independent company. FRAMCO therefore decided to let each location have its own data processing center under its own operational control. It would have been feasible for FRAMCO to develop a centralized teleprocessing system, but they decided not to do this for organizational and political reasons.

Captain Grace Hopper, USN, one of the pioneers of the data processing profession, has presented an interesting analogy about distributed systems. She says we should think about the pioneers as they struggled across the Great Plains. When they wanted to move a rock, they would hitch an ox to the rock. If the rock was so big that the ox couldn't move it, they didn't attempt to grow a bigger ox. Instead, they used two oxen for the job.

A company with a distributed system uses the same technique. Instead of trying to build a bigger computer, it uses two or more computers to accomplish its work.

Distributed processing systems have several advantages. First, they can be less expensive. It is often cheaper to use minicomputers and microcomputers to perform a task than to use a larger mainframe. If the data processing organization operates on the right-hand portion of the graph in figure 8-4, it will be cheaper to obtain additional, smaller computers. Distributed systems can also reduce data communications costs because data is processed close to the source rather than being sent away for processing.

293

Firms Seen Gearing Up for Networked Micros

Now that personal computers are a fact of life in major corporations, firms are gearing up for the next step—the networking of microcomputers in distributed processing schemes.

Microcomputers will represent a major thrust in the distributed processing of many companies, possibly at the expense of more traditional distributed processing mechanisms such as minicomputers, according to industry observers. There may be significant differences between the new breed of local networks and previous distributed processing methods, they said.

"Networked personal computers are definitely replacing minicomputers in applications formerly served by minicomputers," said Harold Kinne, senior vice president of Future Computing Inc.,

a Richardson, Texas, consulting firm. "It has gotten to the point where people who would have bought multi-user systems are now buying personal computers," he added.

Although this is true of stand-alone microcomputers, rapidly emerging personal computer networking capabilities are heightening the trend. "Every personal computer sold in the future must have a networking capability and the advent of local-area networks has been one of the most impressive developments," Kinne said.

Many managers agree with Kinne's assessment, and one result of the new thrust is that information system (IS) managers will have to be more vigilant in assuring the integrity and currency of data. "It is

so easy to create a copy of a file, and then fail to have it updated," Kinne said.

Dave Moore, vice president of systems and programming for Mellon Bank in Pittsburgh, agreed: "There is a danger beyond the security issue. Networking microcomputers presents tremendous synchronization problems in terms of the data the user is accessing and its currency."

In a recent survey of computer users, Data Decisions Inc. noticed a slight decline in the number of companies currently involved with distributed data processing projects, a finding that surprised the Cherry Hill, N.J., market research firm. Although users were not asked why these projects were on hold, the firm suggested that the recession and a trend toward microcomputers

Second, distributed systems give the users greater control over the processing of their data. Often, users operate the computer themselves. They can determine the quality and the scheduling of the services they receive. Additionally, distributed systems can be useful in companies in which the systems development staff is behind in their development schedules. Off-the-shelf programs may be available that will successfully accomplish the users' jobs.

Finally, distributed systems can be tailored to the company's organizational structure. For example, FRAMCO has seven autonomous locations that are connected on a more or less equal basis. This decentralized configuration matches the company's decentralized philosophy. On the other hand, Super-Burger has a computer configuration that matches a traditional organizational hierarchy. The regional computers are supervisors of the restaurant computers. The headquarters computer supervises the regional ones. Each of these systems meets the needs of the organizational structure of the company that owns it.

The advantages of distributed processing systems are summarized in figure 9-7.

taking over applications that were previously the domain of minicomputer-based distributed systems were to blame. . . .

"Distributed processing is to the early 1980s what MIS was in the early 1970s," said Moore. "There is a lot of talk, but. . . ."

However, IBM surely has some interesting capabilities up its sleeve for its Personal Computer line that may well involve SNA and other network offerings. But there may be an important difference between them and recently announced microcomputer networking schemes.

Users were very intrigued when IBM announced its intent to provide 3270 compatibility for its Personal Computer, but interest in networking microcomputers has been heightened further by recent personal computer announcements by Texas Instruments Inc. and NCR Corp. Both of the new units join several other microcomputer offerings in that they can operate in conjunction with the Omninet local network of Corvus Systems Inc., San Jose, Calif. Many different microcomputers can thus operate on the same local network, Kinne said.

Recent announcements of mainframe-to-microcomputer software by such vendors as Management Science America (MSA) Inc., Atlanta, have also piqued the interest of users and managers in networked microcomputers.

It may be at best hard and at worst meaningless to attempt a precise definition of distributed data processing, Kinne observed. But a potential definition of distributed data processing in the traditional sense, he said, is where a powerful mainframe computer is connected to less powerful minicomputers or terminals. But with microcomputers connected with local-area networks, all nodes are typically treated as the same.

"The personal computer is a very intelligent terminal, and if one of the nodes on a local-area network is a mainframe computer, that's fine," Kinne said.

"The way the industry is going, the executive workstation you hear everything about will be the personal computer," he said.

By WILLIAM P. MARTORELLI
Info Systems News, March, 1983

Distributed processing systems also have several disadvantages. First, they are complex to set up. Communications facilities must be obtained. The computers must be connected to one another. Furthermore, the programs must be made to interact with one another. Close coordination is required throughout the

Disadvantages of Distributed Systems

Advantages	Disadvantages
Can be less expensive	More complex to build
Greater control to users	Close coordination required for data compatibility
Quicker development if off-the-shelf programs can be used	Greater need for standards and documentation
Tailored to organizational structure	Problems of multivendors

FIGURE 9-7

Summary of distributed processing systems

distributed system to ensure that all data is compatible. Confusion will result if one division of the company reports sales data from the previous month, while another reports sales data from the current month.

Additionally, distributed systems are often run without the guidance of data processing professionals. This policy is risky unless the personnel are well trained and have complete, well-written documentation of all necessary procedures. Finally, distributed systems are often a mixture of equipment. The computers may be supplied by a variety of vendors; the communication lines, by other vendors; and the programs, by still other vendors. In this environment, compatibility can be a problem. It may be difficult to make the equipment operate together. Also, recovery may be difficult if one vendor inaccurately claims that a problem is due to another vendor's equipment. Figure 9-7 also summarizes the disadvantages of distributed processing.

Given this overview of distributed processing, we will now describe the five components of a distributed system in greater detail.

QUESTIONS

9.1 What is the difference between teleprocessing and distributed processing?

9.2 Why may distributed processing be cheaper than teleprocessing? Refer to figure 8-4 for your answer.

9.3 How does distributed processing give the users greater control?

9.4 What is an applications node?

9.5 Describe two reasons that the pharmaceutical company's distributed system is simpler than FRAMCO's system.

9.6 What is a message switcher? Why is it useful?

9.7 If FRAMCO had 10 computers instead of 8, and if there were no message switcher, how many communication lines would be needed?

9.8 What does the term *downline loading* mean?

9.9 Why does Super-Burger need well-documented, standardized procedures?

9.10 Why may a company decide to offload its centralized or teleprocessing computer system?

9.11 Why may a company decide to install new computers even though its existing computer could be expanded to meet its needs?

9.12 Explain the statement, "A distributed system can be tailored to a company's organizational structure."

DISTRIBUTED HARDWARE

The basic hardware components of a distributed computing system are computers and high-speed communication lines. The computers at each applications node of the network can be micros, minis, or mainframes—all types are used. These computers are employed for both applications processing and communications control. In some systems, a single computer is used for both functions. In others, one computer is dedicated to applications processing and another is dedicated to communications control. Front-ends and concentrators are examples of this last type of application.

There are three basic configurations of computers in networks: *star, ring*, and *hybrid*.

Figure 9-8 shows a *star* configuration. A central computer is connected to other computers on the periphery of the star via communication lines. In a star configuration, the central computer is usually a master. It controls the operation of the computers at the points of the star. Furthermore, the master can serve as a message switcher to enable communication to exist between one peripheral computer and another. Note, however, that the master computer has control. It can shut off such communication if it so chooses.

Star Configuration

An extension to the star configuration is called a *hierarchical star*. Here, the central computer is connected in star fashion to computers that are themselves the centers of other stars. Figure 9-9 shows an example. If you examine this configuration carefully, you will see that it is the arrangement of computers used by Super-Burger Restaurant Franchises in figure 9-5.

Figure 9-10 illustrates computers connected in a *ring*. Each computer is connected to some or all of its neighbors in basically an equal relationship. In a ring configuration, usually no one computer has central control over all the others. Each computer operates autonomously. The computers function as cooperating partners or *colleagues*.

Ring Configuration

In figure 9-10, not all computers are connected directly to all the other computers. This arrangement is acceptable. More than likely, computer A seldom needs to communicate with computer C. When it does need to, it can send its message to computer B and ask B to forward the message to C. If A

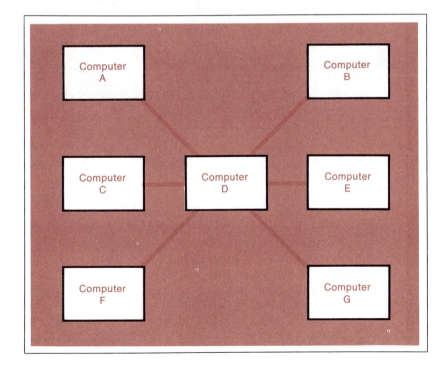

F I G U R E 9 - 8

Star network configuration

297

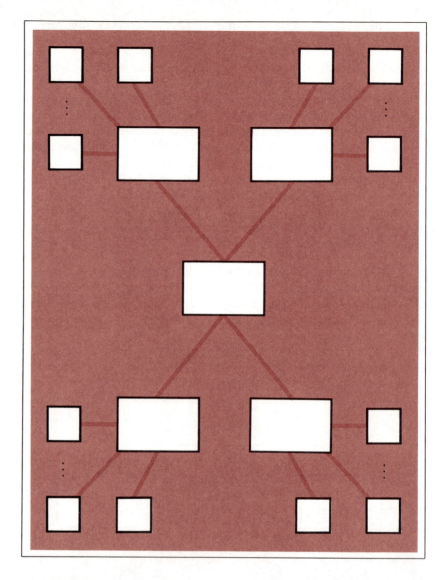

FIGURE 9-9

Hierarchical star network configuration

needs to communicate with a more distant neighbor, it can send the message to B, B can send it to C, C to D, and so forth. Thus, each computer needs programs to forward messages to its neighbors.

FRAMCO Distributing elected to connect its computers in what is basically a star configuration, as shown in figure 9-3. However, the central node of the star is not really a master computer. Rather, it is just a message switcher that reduces the communications costs of connecting all of the computers. FRAMCO could have connected its computers in a ring like the one shown in figure 9-10. In this case, if computer A needed to communicate with computer D, computers B and C would have to forward the message.

Hybrid Configuration

The third type of distributed hardware configuration is called a *hybrid*. It is a combination of a ring and a star. As shown in figure 9-11, the hybrid consists

The Accelerating Boom in Local Area Networks

Consider the problem of Sam Jones, owner of an auto parts store.

He has three microcomputers to expedite billing and record keeping, but he still runs up and down the stairs between the office and the store to check on files and to give the bookkeeper updated information.

But if Jones were able to hook his computers together so that they could talk to each other, sales data developed downstairs could immediately be keyed into the system and received by the bookkeepers in the office above.

The answer to Jones' problem is the local area network, which a recent report published by the International Data Corporation says is one of the fastest-growing segments of the computer industry.

Local area networks allow computerized equipment, including personal computers, word processors, centralized data storage devices and electronic printers, to transfer information within a limited area—as on the premises of Jones' store or between a company's office and its factory.

Besides the electronic devices linked together, the network consists of the wire or cable used to carry data and special circuitry that allows the data to be transmitted and received.

IDC estimates that at the end of 1981 there were 8,160 local area networks installed worldwide and that there will be 37,000 by 1986.

According to IDC, there was only a handful of vendors of local area networks as of year ago. But the

firm says there are about 45 now, and the number is growing rapidly.

Vendors fall into one of these categories:

• **The computer systems firm** that provides local area network technology designed to connect the equipment it sells.

• **The component supplier** who provides the pieces needed to allow the user to construct his own local area network.

• **The local area network system vendor** who provides the means to allow interconnection of equipment from several vendors.

Nation's Business, February, 1983

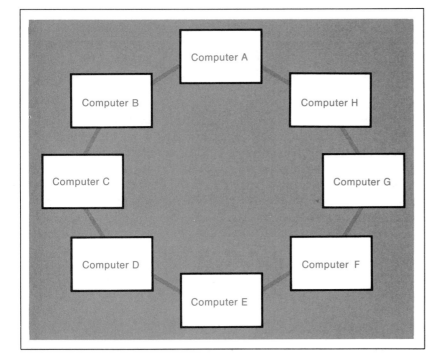

FIGURE 9 - 10

Ring network configuration

of a ring of computers, each of which is the center of a star. The hybrid configuration is used for very large networks of computers.

For one important application of the hybrid configuration, the nodes of the ring form what is called a *communication subnetwork*. The nodes are sophisticated message switchers that do no applications processing. Instead, they communicate with one another on the ring and with the computers on their star. Their sole purpose is to route messages.

Local Area Networks

You may hear the term *local area network* used to refer to a type of distributed system. A local area network (LAN) is not a special hardware configuration. Rather, it is a distributed system, of any of the types discussed in this chapter, that is restricted to a limited geographical area (1 to 20 kilometers). A local area network might be constructed in a single building, or in a factory, or on a college campus. Because the distance is restricted, communications alternatives become feasible that would be infeasible for longer distances. For example, one type of LAN uses digital communication lines without repeating stations. The repeating stations are not needed because of the short distance; eliminating them enables the speed of the line to be greater. See [53] and [55] for more information.

Comparison of Star and Ring Configurations

Suppose you work for FRAMCO and you are trying to decide whether the star configuration in figure 9-5 or the ring structure in figure 9-10 is more appropriate for your company. To make this decision, you might examine the *cost*, *performance*, and *reliability* of these configurations.

Cost

Considering costs, which of these two configurations is cheaper? If the costs of the communication lines are proportional to distance, you might favor the alternative that has the minimum distance. (Communications costs are sometimes proportional to distance and sometimes not. Other cost factors are the speed and type of the line, the vendor, the timing and amount of service, and the equipment needed to utilize the line. We will ignore these issues in this evaluation. See [62] and [66] for more realistic assumptions.)

For this comparison, assume that communications costs are proportional to distance and that the computers are arranged in a circle. In the star configuration, there is one communication line for each computer on the periphery of the circle. If the length of the radius of the circle is r, then the total length of the communication lines will be $N \times r$, where N is the number of computers on the periphery.

For the ring configuration, the length of the communication lines is the same as the circumference of the circle. From high school geometry, you may remember that this is $2\pi r$, where, again, r is the radius of the circle. Since π is about 3.14, the length of the ring communication lines is about $6.28 \times r$.

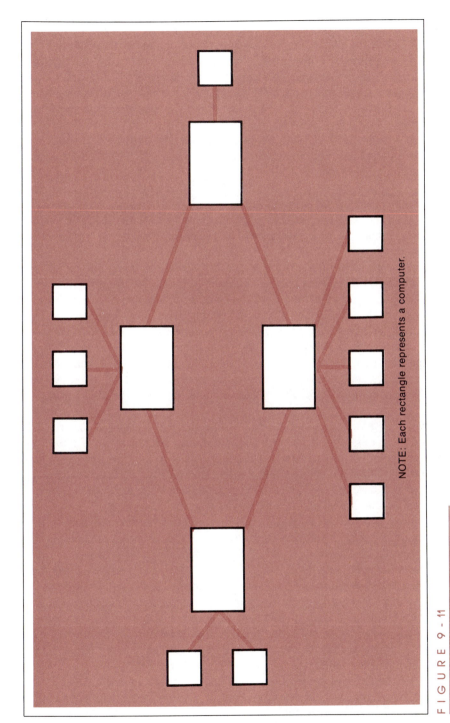

NOTE: Each rectangle represents a computer.

F I G U R E   9 - 11

Hybrid network configuration

Therefore, the length of lines for the star is $N \times r$, and the length of lines for the ring is $6.28 \times r$. Thus, if N is less than or equal to 6, the star has shorter lines. However, if N is 7 or greater, the ring has shorter lines. In FRAMCO's case, N is 8, so the ring has shorter communication lines.

However, there are other costs. The computers on the ring must be programmed to pass messages. This program may be expensive. Also, the computers on the ring may have to be large to handle the message-switching workload. On the other hand, the ring does not need a message switcher like the star does.

If you worked for FRAMCO, you could compute these costs. Most likely, you would find the ring configuration to be cheaper. But what about performance and reliability?

Performance

The performance of the network depends on how performance is defined, as well as on the workload to be processed. Suppose that FRAMCO considers the time it takes to process transactions as the only important performance consideration.

If the computers seldom need to communicate with computers other than immediate neighbors, then the ring configuration may give better performance. Messages do not need to be sent to the switcher before arriving at their destinations. On the other hand, if some computers frequently communicate with nonneighbors, the star structure may give better performance. Another factor to be considered is the speed of the message switcher vs the speed of the computers. If the message switcher is fast, it will speed communications in the star. If the computers pass messages quickly, the ring will be faster. Assume that you do an analysis for FRAMCO and determine that the star is faster.

Reliability

So far, you have found that the ring is cheaper and the star is faster. Now, consider the reliability of the two configurations. What happens if one of the communication lines between two computers fails in the ring structure? Suppose the link between nodes A and B fails. Then, if B wants to send a message to A, B will have to send it in a roundabout fashion. The message will be sent backwards—across all computers. B will send the message to C, then C will send it to D, and so on, until H sends it to A. This sequence will be very time consuming, but the message will get through. Now suppose that another link fails, say the link between E and F. At this point, the ring is broken into two *noncommunicating sections*: B-C-D-E and F-G-H-A. Messages cannot get between nodes on these two sections (see figure 9-12).

Consider the same case for the star structure. Assume that two links fail: one between node A and the message switcher, and another between node E and the message switcher. In this case, neither A nor E will receive any messages at all, but the rest of the network will be unimpaired (see figure 9-13).

Which of these situations is better? We could argue either way. The ring is better because at least some of the nodes can communicate with A and E. The star is better because the network is never divided into noncommunicating sections. There is another important factor, however.

What happens if the message switcher fails for the star configuration? In this case, all of the nodes are out of communication with one another. No messages can be sent at all. The star is very dependent on the message switcher.

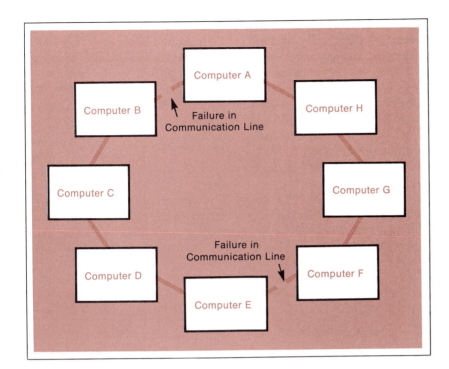

FIGURE 9 - 12

Broken ring caused by two line failures

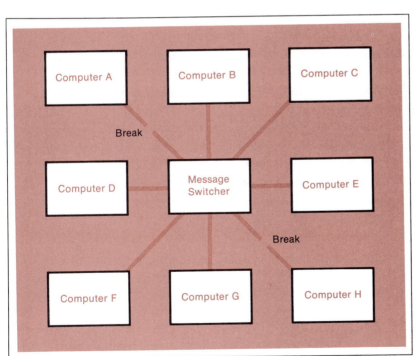

FIGURE 9 - 13

Star network with two line failures

Consequently, it should be high-quality, very reliable hardware. When it does fail, FRAMCO must know how to get it fixed quickly. They might even go so far as to buy a second message switcher for backup purposes.

303

To determine the answer to the reliability issue, you need more data about the reliability of the computers and the lines, as well as about the workload to be processed. You could build a statistical model of the network and perform an analysis. You might find either configuration to be more reliable.

Assume that you find the ring to be more reliable. If so, you have determined that the ring is cheaper and more reliable, but the star is faster. Which do you choose? You would do a cost/benefit study as discussed in chapter 4 to determine the best system for FRAMCO. The point here is that you should realize that neither star structures nor ring structures are the best for all circumstances. Both can work well. Both can lead to disaster. The appropriate choice depends on the application.

We have discussed the characteristics of communication lines in detail in chapter 8, so we will not repeat that discussion here. However, you should realize that computers operate at very high speeds, millions of times faster than a person at a terminal. Consequently, the communication lines must be very high speed. Wideband satellite communications are often used in large computer networks.

QUESTIONS

9.13 What are the three basic computer configurations in distributed networks?

9.14 Under what conditions does a star configuration have shorter communication lines than a ring? Under what conditions does a ring have shorter communication lines than a star?

9.15 Which costs less, a ring or a star configuration?

9.16 Which has better performance, a ring or a star configuration? What factors must be considered to answer this question?

9.17 Which has greater reliability, a ring or a star configuration?

9.18 What happens to a ring structure if one of the communication lines fails? What happens if two communication lines fail?

9.19 What happens to a star structure if one of the communication lines fails? What happens if two communication lines fail?

9.20 What happens to a star configuration if the message switcher fails?

9.21 Should the communication lines in a distributed network be narrowband, voice grade, or wideband? Why?

PROGRAMS FOR DISTRIBUTED PROCESSING

The programs used at the applications nodes of a distributed network are the same types as those used by teleprocessing computers, as discussed in chapter 8 (at least at the level of detail we are concerned with in this book). Each node must have an operating system that controls the system's resources, a communications control program (CCP) that controls the message transfers, and application programs. The node may also have a database management system (DBMS) if databases are being processed. However, additional functions must be added to these programs.

Types of Distributed Programs

The operating system (excluding the CCP) will be different in the distributed environment. The differences are primarily in the data management or I/O processing. The operating system must be written to recognize that application programs may attempt to access files that reside on a computer at a different location. When this situation occurs, the operating system must generate a message to the other computer to obtain the data. Also, a computer may receive a transaction that must be processed on a different computer. In this case, the operating system must route the transaction to the correct computer.

Similar considerations apply to the DBMS. Local application programs may try to extract data from a database that resides on another computer. Again, when this occurs, the DBMS must recognize the situation and obtain the data from the correct source by generating the appropriate message request.

The CCP also has additional duties in the distributed environment. It must be able to receive messages from any of the computers connected to its node, translate them if necessary, send them to the appropriate application program or to the DBMS, or take other action. The translation may be required because the computer that generated the message may be an entirely different type from the local computer. The character code, number of bits per word, and so forth, may be different.

The CCP will also be required to receive messages from local application programs or the DBMS, format them, and transmit them to the correct nodes for processing. Such messages may be responses to requests from these other nodes, or they may be requests for other nodes to perform some actions.

In addition to all of this, the node may have its own terminals with which to communicate. Thus, the CCP must not only talk with other computers, but also control the terminals, as is done in a teleprocessing environment. Clearly, the CCP will be a large, complex program.

Application Programs

Because it is impractical to rewrite application programs every time they are moved from one node to another, these programs must be written to minimize their dependence on local computer systems. Therefore, systems developers go to great pains to make distributed system applications independent of their environment. Thus, an application program is designed to access a file without knowing where that file is. Similarly, an application program may converse with a user at a terminal without knowing whether that user is connected to the local computer or to another computer in the distributed network.

This independence actually makes the job of the application programmer easier. He or she need not learn the details of every computer system in the network. Instead, the programmer learns a generalized way of performing I/O or accessing terminals. The burden is on the operating system and the CCP to execute these generalized commands.

Problems with Distributed Programs

Developing and maintaining the types of programs just discussed is difficult in distributed systems. First, the computers on a distributed network are often smaller and more limited than centralized mainframes. Main memory is smaller. The programs will not have as much storage space in which to operate as they have on a mainframe. Constraints on main memory, CPU processing speed, and online file space can cause systems developers to limit the capability of the programs more than they would like to.

Another complicating factor is that the nodes of a distributed network are often operated by the users without the assistance of experienced data process-

System/Program	Function
Operating System or DBMS	Locate input/output files on another computer Generate messages for remote I/O Access and update directory of data
Communications Control Program	Receive messages from other nodes Send messages to other nodes Translate computer codes
Application Programs	Issue location-independent requests for I/O

FIGURE 9-14

Special tasks for distributed programs

ing personnel. Therefore, the application programs have to be *self-instructional*, or written so that minimal formal training is needed. Further, the computer itself must be easy to run. Users cannot be expected to perform all of the functions that a well-trained operator can perform. This fact places constraints on the operating system as well as on the CCP, the DBMS, and the application programs.

As discussed in the Super-Burger example, programs must sometimes be *downline loaded*. That is, a program can be changed or installed remotely using another computer. In some systems, all types of software must be downline loaded—not just application programs. The need for this capability is especially great when there are many nodes in the network, when the nodes are separated by great geographical distances, or when they are located in hazardous working areas. Figure 9-14 summarizes considerations for distributed programs.

QUESTIONS

9.22 Are application programs on a distributed system different from those on other types of systems? Why or why not?

9.23 Is the operating system on a distributed system different from that on other types of systems? If so, how?

9.24 Is the DBMS (if used) on a distributed system different from that on other types of systems? If so, how?

9.25 Is the communications control program on a distributed system different from that on other types of systems? If so, how?

9.26 Name two reasons why programming can be difficult on distributed computers.

DISTRIBUTED DATA

The characteristics of data in the distributed environment can best be examined by considering two questions that the designer of a distributed computer system must answer. First, where is the data to be located? Second, how will it be updated? We will consider each of these in turn.

In a distributed system, data can be broken down into two broad categories: local and global. *Local data* is needed only at the local node. Local data is processed solely by the application programs that run on the local computer. One node never requests another node's local data. For example, consider FRAMCO Distributing. At a given location, the number and amount of a given sales invoice is local data. Only the local order processing or accounts receivable programs need the data. The data is of no use to any other computer in the FRAMCO system.

Global data is needed by a program or programs that run on at least two computers in the distributed system. For example, the total sales figures at a given FRAMCO location are needed by the local general ledger programs and also by the headquarters general ledger programs.

The percentage of local vs global data varies from company to company and from application to application. One rule of thumb in data processing is that 80 percent of the data at a node tends to be local and 20 percent tends to be global. These percentages are not based on any scientific study, but they are a rough guideline.

Turning now to the question of where to locate the data, one basic principle is that *local data stays local*. It almost never makes sense to move local data from the node on which it is used. The communications costs are too high.

Unfortunately, it is not so easy to decide where to put global data. The first consideration is whether it should be centralized or partitioned. If it is *centralized*, one of the computers in the distributed network stores all of the global data. Then, whenever a node needs some global data, it sends a message for it to the global data computer. In the FRAMCO example in figure 9-3, one of the computers, perhaps the headquarters computer, could store all of the global data.

If the global data is *partitioned*, then it is spread on several computers throughout the network. Whenever a node needs some global data, it must first determine where the global data it needs is located. Then it can access the data on that computer.

One advantage of centralized data is simplicity. Every node knows where the data is located. The concurrent update problem can be handled by one processor. A disadvantage of centralized global data is that the global data computer can be a performance bottleneck. All computers are dependent on the global data computer for data. If it is slow, processing on all other computers will also be slow.

A second disadvantage concerns reliability. If the global data computer fails, then all of the nodes in the network will be unable to continue any processing requiring global data.

Partitioning global data eliminates the performance bottleneck and the reliability problems. Unfortunately, updates of partitioned data are much harder to control.

The systems development personnel must decide not only whether to centralize or partition global data, but also whether the data is to be *replicated* or *nonreplicated*. If it is to be replicated, several copies of the data are stored

307

Category	Number of Copies	
	Nonreplicated	Replicated
Centralized	All global data is located on a single node.	Complete copies of all the global data exist on several nodes.
Partitioned	Global data is broken into pieces. Only one copy of each piece exists, but the pieces reside on different nodes.	Global data is broken into pieces. Several copies of some pieces exist or copies of all pieces exist.

F I G U R E 9 - 15

Allocation of global data in distributed networks

around the network. Either centralized or partitioned data can be replicated, as illustrated in figure 9-15.

To replicate centralized global data, the entire collection of global data is stored at several locations in the network. Then, the nodes need only keep lists of the computers having the replicated data. They do not need directories that show the locations of particular kinds of data; all of the data is located at each of the nodes. Replicating global data eliminates the bottleneck and reliability

DATA FOR SUPER-BURGER RESTAURANTS

Super-Burger Franchises might decide to have replicated, centralized global data. If so, they might store all of the global data on each of the regional computers. (See figure 9-5.) Then, when any of the restaurant computers needs global data, it simply accesses its regional computer.

Super-Burger would decide to take this course only if the restaurant and regional computers frequently needed all of the global data. If these computers needed only part of the global data, Super-Burger might decide to have replicated, partitioned global data. In this case, multiple copies of the partitioned global data would be stored.

Suppose, for example, that each restaurant needs access to the summarized sales data for the region in which it resides. Further, suppose the regional computers need summarized sales data for all four regions. In this case, Super-Burger would divide the global data into five parts: the summarized data for region 1, the summarized data for region 2, the summarized data for region 3, the summarized data for region 4, and the summarized data for all four regions.

Now, the summarized data for region 1 would be replicated at each of the 20 restaurant computers in region 1, that for region 2 would be replicated at the 20 restaurants in region 2, and so forth. Further, the summarized data for all four regions would be replicated at each of the four regional computers. This scheme is illustrated in figure 9-16.

Global Data Partitioned into Five Parts	Global Data Replicated on Nodes
Summarized sales data for region 1	All restaurant computers in region 1
Summarized sales data for region 2	All restaurant computers in region 2
Summarized sales data for region 3	All restaurant computers in region 3
Summarized sales data for region 4	All restaurant computers in region 4
Summarized sales data for entire company	All four regional computers

FIGURE 9-16

Example of replicated, partitioned data
for Super-Burger Restaurants

problems discussed above, but it introduces the problem of concurrent update control.

Data Directory

When data is partitioned or replicated, each node must have access to a *dictionary*, or *directory*, that gives the location or locations of each type of data. This dictionary is used by the operating system or the DBMS whenever a user or application program attempts to access global data.

The dictionary itself is global data, so an interesting question is, Should it be partitioned or replicated? If so, then a dictionary of dictionaries is necessary. This situation becomes complex and is beyond the scope of this text, but you might enjoy puzzling over this question.

Replicated, partitioned data allows for the greatest flexibility in storing data across the distributed network. Unfortunately, it is also the most complex and the hardest to control.

At the start of this section, two questions were mentioned. One was, Where is the data to be located? As shown in figure 9-15, there are four possibilities for allocating data in the network. The second question was, How is the data to be updated? This second question poses some very difficult problems for the designers of distributed systems.

Updating Distributed Data

What happens when two users or application programs want to update the same record concurrently? As we saw in chapter 8, it is possible for one of the updates to be lost. This predicament occurs when user A reads a record, user B reads the same record, user A updates the record, and then user B updates the record. In this case, user A's update is lost.

To prevent this situation from occurring, users or application programs are supposed to lock records before they update them. This policy is reasonably straightforward for centralized, nonreplicated data. The lock involves only the computer that has the global data. However, what happens if the data is replicated? Then the lock must be in place on two computers. That doesn't sound too difficult until you consider what happens if the locks are applied *simultaneously* (as they could be). Then one user has the record locked on one computer, and another user has the record locked on a different computer. Both locks are in place, but neither user has absolute control over the record. One of the locks will have to be released and control of the record given to the other user. This is difficult to coordinate and is very time consuming.

Even nonreplicated, partitioned data is susceptible to these problems. An application program may need to update several records with the same transaction. For example, to record a sale, an application program may need to insert a new order record, modify the contents of a customer record, and modify a salesperson record. These last two records should be locked throughout the update process. However, if they are located on different computers, then we again have the problem of invoking locks on separate machines, as well as the potential for two users locking each other out.

So, of the four styles of allocating data to a distributed network, three of them pose significant problems regarding the concurrent update problem. It is beyond the scope of this book to solve these problems; in fact, some of them have not yet been solved. You should be aware of them, however.

DISTRIBUTED PERSONNEL

It is easier to distribute hardware, programs, and data than to distribute personnel. First, hardware, programs, and data are cheaper than personnel. With the advent of microprocessors and other cost-saving electronic technology, hardware is becoming cheaper and cheaper. Meanwhile, because of inflation and other factors, personnel are becoming more and more expensive.

(Because people write computer programs, and because the cost of people is rising, you might think that the cost of distributing programs is also increasing. However, once a program is written and tested, the cost of producing a second copy is negligible. Therefore, if a program that already exists can be installed and used on a distributed node, its cost is minimal.)

People are hard to distribute not only because they are expensive, but also because they are harder to obtain and train. More computers can be manufactured, and additional copies of a program can be inexpensively made by a computer. But training a systems analyst or a programmer takes a long time. Therefore, there is currently a critical shortage of knowledgeable people. Companies cannot easily locate another 20 programmers or operators to staff a distributed system.

In addition to these problems, people are hard to distribute because they need support organizations. An operator needs a boss. He or she needs someone to report to, someone to learn from, someone to provide positive feedback or correction when required. A single operator is apt to feel out of place and isolated from the mainstream of the company's data processing activity.

Alternatives to Distributed Personnel

Because of these problems, data processing personnel are often not distributed with the hardware, programs, and data. Instead, distributed systems are designed to be operated by the users who are already present in the distributed locations. These people are already hired; they are already trained in their jobs; and they already have a support organization.

Clearly, a user cannot be expected to perform the same tasks as a well-trained operator or programmer. This fact is considered in the design of distributed systems. The programs are written to be easily used. Operations procedures must be simple, well documented, and as self-explanatory as possible.

For example, to start the computer, the user should only have to turn it on. Messages that prompt the user's next action should be displayed on the CRT screen. These messages must be easy to understand. The required action must be such that a person with only a week or two of training can accomplish it. Additionally, it is absolutely essential that standardized procedures be well documented and that users be trained in following them.

To reduce the burden of training, some organizations have chosen to have two or three users at each site designated as *key user personnel*. These key people are given special training. They are called upon when the equipment fails, when a user has difficulty accomplishing a task, or when special actions such as file backup must be performed. In this way, these people become paraoperators at the distributed location.

There are some tasks that are too difficult for even key user personnel to perform, such as installing new programs or initially operating new equipment. These tasks can be performed by data processing personnel who travel on a temporary basis to the distributed location, or they can be performed *downline* from a remote computer, as discussed previously.

Operations personnel are sometimes distributed when the workload is too heavy or complex for users to perform. Further, in some cases, tasks arise that are too difficult for users and that cannot be done by data processing personnel on a temporary basis. An example is running a daily system having a complex sequence of jobs, each requiring tape and disk files. In such cases, some operations personnel have to be distributed. This distribution usually occurs only in the larger, more sophisticated computer installations.

How operators are distributed depends on the configuration of equipment and the data processing needs. For example, consider Super-Burger Restaurant Franchises. Super-Burger has no computer operators at any of its 80 restaurant locations. However, even though it would like not to have operators at the regional centers, the users cannot perform all of the tasks required. Consequently, Super-Burger has three operators at each regional location. These distributed personnel are in addition to a full staff of operators at the headquarters computer center.

Systems Development Personnel

In addition to users and operators, systems development personnel are required to develop and support distributed computer systems. Programmers, systems analysts, and specialists are needed. The specialists include communications experts, hardware experts, and probably personnel for maintaining the operating systems, communications control programs, and database management systems. If there are several types of computer hardware in the network, a company may need experts for each type.

In most instances, the systems development personnel will be consolidated in one location. Super-Burger, for example, has its entire systems development staff at the headquarters facility. There is really no need for the development staff at distributed sites. In fact, Super-Burger wants to maintain tight control over developmental projects and refuses to authorize the development of any systems in the field. They believe that this is the only way they can ensure strict standardization of their programs.

Why Personnel Are Not Distributed	Ways to Avoid Distribution
Too expensive Hard to obtain and train Difficult to support and control	Training users to run systems Designing systems for ease of use Training key personnel Loading downline Providing temporary data processing personnel Centralizing development

FIGURE 9-17

Personnel considerations for a distributed system

Figure 9-17 summarizes the considerations for distributed personnel. Generally, as few data processing personnel as possible should be distributed. People cost too much, are hard to find, and require support organizations. Consequently, users take on as much of the operations function as they can.

Systems development personnel are required for distributed systems, and considerable expertise may be needed to maintain the distributed network. These personnel are generally not distributed, for control as well as economic reasons.

PROCEDURES FOR DISTRIBUTED PROCESSING

The procedures needed to operate a distributed system successfully are generally the same as those for other data processing systems. However, because the computers may be operated by inexperienced personnel, the procedures must be better documented and easier to understand than procedures for other systems. The procedures must also be complete and unambiguous. The computers will be operated by personnel who are miles apart and in fact may never meet. If the processing is to be uniform from one computer to the next, the procedures must be clear and complete.

Because the distributed computers are intended to communicate with one another, there must be procedures explaining how to make such a connection, as well as what to do if the connection does not work. Further, users (or operators) must know what their responsibilities to other computers are when their computer fails. They must also know what to do when another computer in the network fails.

This knowledge is particularly important for networks having partitioned data. If a computer that has critical global data fails, the personnel involved with other computers must know what to do. Procedures are required to explain how to get needed data, or how to get along without it until the failed computer has been repaired.

Users of a distributed system need the usual procedures on how to interact with the computer systems they use. However, with a distributed system, they may also need procedures on how to run the computer, including backup and recovery and other special tasks.

Procedures and standards for program development are particularly important in distributed systems. Programmers must know how to lock data before updating it, what conventions must be followed to obtain data, special techniques to be used (or avoided) in order to communicate with other programs, and so forth. Programs used in the distributed environment should be very well tested and able to handle erroneous conditions without failing themselves. This requirement is necessary because these programs will be run by inexperienced personnel in locations remote from the systems development staff.

QUESTIONS

9.27 What are two broad categories of data?

9.28 Where should local data be stored in a distributed environment?

9.29 Global data can be either centralized or _____ .

9.30 Into how many pieces is centralized global data broken?

9.31 What is the maximum number of pieces that partitioned data can be broken into?

9.32 What is an advantage of centralized data?

9.33 What is an advantage of partitioned data?

9.34 Explain the difference between replicated centralized data and nonreplicated centralized data.

9.35 Explain the difference between replicated partitioned data and nonreplicated partitioned data.

9.36 What is the purpose of a distributed system dictionary, or directory?

9.37 Explain why problems occur when locks must be invoked on two separate computers.

9.38 Of the four methods of allocating data to distributed computers, which one does not pose significant problems regarding concurrent update? Why is it not used in all cases?

9.39 Why is it easier to distribute hardware, programs, and data than personnel?

9.40 What is meant by the statement that people need support organizations?

9.41 Since data processing personnel are hard to distribute, how do companies staff their distributed computers?

9.42 What is the function of distributed key personnel?

9.43 Under what conditions are computer operators distributed?

9.44 Are systems development personnel likely to be centralized or distributed? Why?

9.45 What are the differences between procedures used in distributed systems and procedures used in other types of systems?

9.46 What special procedures are needed for systems that have partitioned data?

9.47 What procedures are needed for program development in a distributed system?

SUMMARY

In a distributed data processing system, application programs are run on more than one computer. These computers are connected to one another via communication lines. Distributed systems are like teleprocessing systems in that the terminals and users are distributed, and there can be more than one computer. However, distributed systems differ from teleprocessing systems in that application programs are run on more than one computer. In a teleprocessing system, the application programs are run on a centralized computer.

There is a wide variety of distributed data processing configurations. Computers can be connected in master/slave relationships, or they can be connected as partners or colleagues. The nodes of the distributed networks can be simple microprocessors or large mainframes. Distributed computers can be totally interconnected, or there can be few connections. Distributed computers can be autonomous and independent, or they can be interconnected and very dependent.

Distributed processing has several advantages. It may be cheaper than teleprocessing because communications costs are less. Distributed systems also allow users to have more control because the computer is located close to the need for the data processing services. Further, a distributed system can result in shorter development if off-the-shelf programs can be found that meet user requirements and that can be integrated into the distributed system. Finally, distributed networks, because of their flexibility, can be tailored to the organizational structure of the company.

Distributed processing also has several important disadvantages. First, such systems are difficult to build, and close coordination is required to maintain data compatibility. Second, there is a greater need for standards and documentation. Finally, distributed systems usually involve multiple vendors, and this requirement can lead to maintenance problems.

There are three basic configurations of distributed hardware: star, ring, and hybrid. In a star configuration, a central computer is surrounded by distributed computers. In a ring, the computers are connected in a circular manner without a central controller or computer. A hybrid configuration is a combination of these two.

None of these three configurations is superior to the other two for all circumstances. The choice depends on the requirements, the budget, and the equipment that is already in place.

Application programs in the distributed environment are not much different from application programs in the teleprocessing environment. The major difference is that application programs or users may request data that does not reside on the local node. In this case, the operating system or the DBMS, whichever controls the data, must determine where the data resides and obtain it.

The communications control program is different in the distributed environment. It must be able to communicate with other nodes; that is, it must accept messages from them and respond as well. This interaction may be difficult if the computers in the system are made by several manufacturers.

Distributed data can be local or global. Local data nearly always stays on the local node. Global data can be centralized or partitioned. Further, global data can be replicated or nonreplicated. There are significant problems regarding concurrent update for partitioned or replicated data.

It is difficult to distribute data processing personnel. Consequently, systems are designed to be as independent of operators and systems development personnel as possible. Users thereby have a greater responsibility for running computer systems, but they also gain greater control.

Finally, distributed systems must be very well documented and procedures must be very clear. Users will not be computer experts, and they must be able to remember and understand necessary procedures. Users must also coordinate their activities with one another over some distance. Thus, procedures must be standardized and uniformly documented.

Distributed data processing system
Applications node
Master/slave relationship
Message switcher
Colleague relationship
Data dependency
Hierarchy of computers
Downline loading
Offload processing
Star configuration
Hierarchical star configuration
Ring configuration
Hybrid configuration

Communication subnetwork
Local area network (LAN)
Self-instructional programs
Local data
Global data
Centralized data
Partitioned data
Replicated data
Nonreplicated data
Data directory
Simultaneous locks
Key user personnel

A. Suppose that you work for Horizon Artist Supply. Do you think distributed processing is appropriate for their environment? How would you determine whether or not it is?

B. Suppose that Horizon decided to open retail stores and to add several warehouse shipping points. Would distributed data processing be appropriate? If so, should data processing costs or other considerations play a role in determining the location of the new installations? Assume that Horizon opened stores in Los Angeles, Anchorage, Denver, Atlanta, and Boston. Assume also that warehouse/shipping points were located in Los Angeles, St. Louis, and Richmond. Describe one feasible distributed processing configuration. Show where applications nodes and equipment like concentrators, message switchers, RJE stations, and terminals could be located. Describe communication lines connecting the hardware.

C. Suppose that FRAMCO Distributing has five locations instead of eight. Further, suppose that the locations are Seattle, Los Angeles, Atlanta, Montreal, and Chicago. The headquarters is in Atlanta. All the other facts introduced about FRAMCO are the same. What sort of a distributed configuration do you think is appropriate? If you need more data, stipulate the data you need and then assume values for it that support your recommendation.

315

D. Do you think distributed processing is appropriate for your college or university? What organizations might have their own processing computers? Describe the kinds of hardware and programs you think would be appropriate for these user organizations. Is there any global data? If so, should it be centralized or partitioned? Should it be replicated or nonreplicated? What personnel and procedures will be required to operate this distributed system?

E. For some organizations, teleprocessing is more appropriate than distributed computing. For other organizations, just the opposite is true. Characterize the organizations for which teleprocessing is more appropriate and those for which distributed computing is more appropriate. How are they structured? What management philosophies are prevalent? How is senior management rewarded? What services do their customers expect? What products do they buy and which do they sell? Describe other characteristics that you think are important.

F. To answer this question, first read module C, *Computer Crime, Security, and Control*. Discuss special considerations necessary when controls for distributed systems are designed. Are distributed systems more vulnerable to computer crime? How can organizations be structured to improve control in distributed systems? Is it desirable for distributed personnel to know how to program? What should distributed personnel know?

PART FOUR

Special Computing Topics

In this part, we will present five independent sections, or modules, on a variety of computer topics. The modules provide information that may not be of interest to all students. You can read none, one, or all of these sections, in any order. It is assumed that you have read chapters 1 and 2.

MODULE A
History of Data Processing

MODULE B
Numbers Representation and Computer Arithmetic

MODULE C
Computer Crime, Security, and Control

MODULE D
Computers and Their Impact on Society

MODULE E
Word Processing Systems and Office Augmentation

MODULE A

History of Data Processing

The history of computing began thousands of years ago when people first started to count on their fingers. In fact, fingers and toes were probably (who knows for sure?) the earliest computational devices. As business and commerce developed, however, a need arose for a calculator with a capacity greater than 20.

The abacus shown in figure A-1 is an early form of such a calculator. Different versions of it were used for centuries by people of many nations and areas of the world. The abacus was used even before numbers were represented in writing. Other computational devices were constructed throughout the centuries. The numerical wheel calculator (figure A-2) was the predecessor of the adding machines and manual calculators that were commonly used before the rise of the electronic calculator. The slide rule (figure A-3) was another type of computational device.

FIGURE A-1

Abacus

FIGURE A-2

Numerical wheel calculator

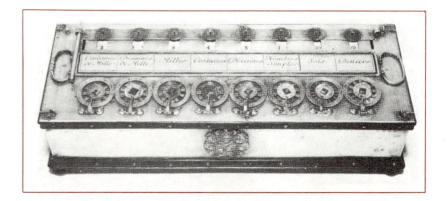

High-Tech Japanese Turn to Age-Old "Calculator"

TOKYO—Here in the land that gave the world the desk-top calculator, the pocket calculator and the wristwatch calculator, the preferred way to tally bills, balance budgets and check accounts is to use a 2,400-year-old instrument with wooden beads.

It's an abacus, and it's almost everywhere.

Step up to a ticket window of the famed *Shinkansen,* or Bullet Train, the 136 mph pride and joy of the National Railway. Appropriately, the clerk will punch your request into a large computer as modern as tomorrow, and within seconds your tickets will spew forth.

How much is that, please? He'll turn to his abacus and flick some well-worn wooden beads up and down on rows of metal rods. In even fewer seconds than it took the computer to do its job, he'll tell you the cost.

Or ask a Japanese friend to convert a dollar figure into yen, or solve some other mathematical problem. He'll gaze somewhere past the end of his nose and wave his right index finger around for a moment, presumably writing numbers in the air. But what he's really doing is flicking the beads of an imaginary abacus.

Or drop in at any of the hundreds of jam-packed, high-tech shops in Tokyo's Akihabara district, where the latest in electronics is sold at discount.

After ogling over an astounding array of semiconductors, computer parts, sound equipment—or calculators—ask the clerk for a price, less discount, and if you're a foreigner, less import duty as well.

Turning his back on the glittering technological gadgetry, he'll flick the beads around on his little wooden device. Then, especially for foreigners, he will punch the answer into a pocket calculator and display it in glowing electronic figures.

And in the Tokyo offices of one of the largest insurance companies in the country, the silence of hundreds of fingers punching calculators has been replaced by the soft clack of abacuses or, as they're known here, *sorobans.*

Why? They're more accurate and thus save time and money.

After declining sharply in use during the past few years, as pocket calculators became as inexpensive as a Big Mac and a Coke at Macu Donarudo, the abacus is staging a comeback.

Companies that live by numbers—insurance firms, banks, trading houses—were finding that clerks, their minds numbed by endlessly punching calculator buttons, were committing an appalling number of errors, most commonly misplacing decimals.

"When you punch a bunch of numbers into a calculator, it doesn't mean anything to you," said Toshihiko Fujita, public relations officer for Sumitomo Life Insurance Co. "But when you use a *soroban,* it instills the concept of figures in everyday life."

According to Fujita, the company realized about four years ago that calculator-punching clerks were committing gross mathematical errors, turning thousands into millions, millions into billions and billions into trillions. Then someone remembered that the abacus is based on calculating in increments of 10—just the thing for straightening out decimal errors.

The company swiftly imposed restrictions on calculator use and began classes to sharpen up abacus skills for those who had forgotten them over the years.

"Today," said Fujita, "almost 100 percent of our people use the *soroban* instead of a calculator. Their work is faster and more accurate."

By LEWIS M. SIMONS
San Jose Mercury, June 23, 1983

As far as we know, Charles Babbage is the father of computing. This amazing man was far ahead of his time. He developed the essential ideas of a computer over 100 years before the first computer was constructed. He was so advanced that practically none of his contemporaries appreciated him. In addition to

CHARLES BABBAGE AND HIS MACHINES

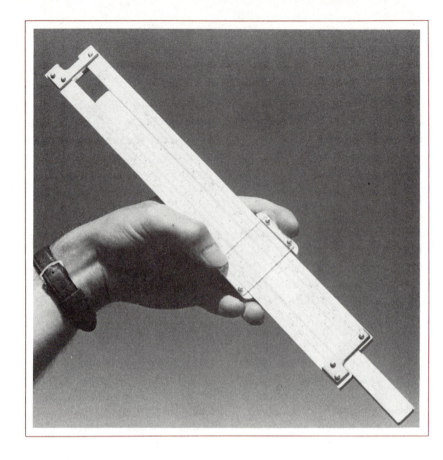

FIGURE A-3

Slide rule

computing, Babbage made contributions to mathematics, optics, underwater navigation, railroads, industrial engineering, mechanics, and other fields.

Many of the mistakes that Babbage made continue to be made today, and so it is worth considering his life's activities in some detail.

Babbage's Life

Babbage was born in England in 1792 (George Washington was still alive). His father was a wealthy banker who left him a sizable fortune. Babbage says that he suffered from high fevers, and so he was sent to a private tutor "with instructions to attend to my health; but, not to press too much knowledge upon me: a mission which he faithfully accomplished" [88, p. 11]. Babbage relates, "My invariable question on receiving any new toy was, 'Mamma, what is inside of it?' " Apparently, if she couldn't answer, he tore it apart.

Some time prior to 1822, Babbage and his friend John Herschel were checking data calculated for the Astronomical Society. In frustration, Babbage remarked to Herschel, "I wish to God these calculations had been executed by steam." (Steam engines were common.) In 1822, Babbage proposed the design of a *difference engine* composed of gears and wheels (see figure A-4). This engine would automatically compute functions of the form

$$y = a + ax + ax^2 + \ldots ax^6$$

In 1823 the British government granted Babbage money to build the engine. The first government-sponsored computer project was on! Like most of those to follow, the project fell behind. By 1833 the government had invested 17,000 pounds, and only part of the difference engine was completed. Meanwhile, Babbage's active mind had been extending the possibilities of automated computing. By 1834 he had developed the idea of an *analytical engine*. The analytical engine would compute *any* mathematical function. It embodied most of the concepts that early computers did.

In 1834, Babbage asked the government whether it wanted him to finish the difference engine or start on the analytical engine. After eight years of frustrating correspondence, Prime Minister Robert Peel told Babbage that the gov-

Babbage's difference engine

ernment was going to abandon the project. This case may have established a record for governmental delay!

The analytical engine had a main memory that Babbage called *the store*. It was to have room for 1000 variables of 50 digits each. It had an arithmetic and logic unit that he called *the mill*. Programs for the mill were written on punched cards. The engine would drive a typesetter. It had logical capability and could ring a bell or take other action when a variable passed zero or exceeded the capacity of one of the words. All of these operations were to have been implemented mechanically.

People had a hard time understanding the concept. Mathematicians asked him how it would use logarithms. He told them that it wouldn't need logarithms, because it could compute any function. Some people didn't believe this claim, so he showed them how it could be programmed to ask an attendant to supply a logarithm from a library of cards. Furthermore, it would check for the correct logarithm. The procedure he described in 1864 is exactly the same as the procedure used today to check tape labels. (See chapter 5.)

Ironically, Babbage got more attention from outside England than from within. He had two automated devices in his home, a clockwork lady who danced and a portion of the difference engine. He reported that his English friends would gather about the dancing lady, whereas an American and a Hollander studied the difference engine. In fact, a Swedish printer, George Scheutz, built the only complete version of the difference engine (except for the one made recently by IBM). Babbage was delighted and helped Scheutz explain it.

We know about the analytical engine largely from a paper written by an Italian, L. F. Menabrea. This paper was written in French and translated into English by Ada Augusta, the Countess of Lovelace. There is interesting social commentary here.

Ada Augusta was the only legitimate daughter of the poet Lord Byron. She was an excellent mathematician and understood Babbage's concepts perhaps better than anyone. In 1842, when she translated Menabrea's paper of 20 pages, she added 50 pages of "notes." Babbage wanted to know why she didn't write a paper of her own. "I never thought of it," she replied. In fact, she didn't sign her translation or her notes, but used the initials *A.A.L.* instead. Apparently, ladies didn't do such things.

However, ladies could go to the race track. The Countess loved racing, and it may have been inevitable that she would use the difference engine to determine horse bets. Apparently, it didn't work too well. She lost the family jewels at the track. Her mother, Lady Byron, had to buy them back.

The Countess died of cancer at the age of 36, just 10 years after reading Menabrea's description. Her death was a big loss to Babbage and perhaps to the world. A new programming language, ADA, is named after Ada Augusta Lovelace. (See module J.)

Babbage was a fascinating person. He was very social; he worked and played hard. Charles Darwin reported lively dinner parties at Babbage's home. Another person complained of barely being able to escape from him at 2:00 in the morning. Babbage once said that he would be glad to give up the rest of his life if he could live for three days 500 hundred years in the future.

Babbage once spent several months riding railroad cars around the United States. He was doing research on railway and train design. It is sad that he could not know that the very tracks he was riding on would someday carry trains controlled by computers having the design he envisioned. He would also have been interested to know that those same computers would someday be used to steal over 400 railway cars. (See module C.)

Babbage died in 1871. He never saw the analytical engine developed. And he never knew how right he was. At the time of his death, he was bitter about the lack of government support. However, his autobiography does not seem bitter, and he probably was not the frustrated and unhappy man some people report. If you're interested in Babbage, read the excellent book, *Charles Babbage and His Calculating Engines,* edited by Philip and Emily Morrison [88].

Lessons We Can Learn from Babbage

Many of the errors Babbage made have been repeated again and again in the computer industry. For one, Babbage began with vague requirements. "Let's compute numbers by steam" sounds all too much like "Let's use a computer to do billing." Much more precise statements of requirements are necessary.

Second, it appears that Babbage started implementing before design was complete. Much work had to be redone. His engineers and draftsmen often complained that they would finish a project only to be told the work was wrong or not needed because the design had been changed. The very same complaint has been made by countless programmmers since then. Another mistake Babbage made was to add more and more capability to his engines before any of them was complete. As his work progressed, he saw new possibilities, and he tried to incorporate them into his existing projects. Many data processing systems have remained uncompleted for the very same reason.

Work on the difference engine was set back considerably by a crisis over the salary of Babbage's chief engineer, Joseph Clement. Clement quit, and Babbage had little documentation to recover the loss. Further, Clement had the rights to all the tools. Who knows how many systems projects have failed because indispensable programmers quit in the middle? Working documentation is crucial for successful system implementation.

Even Lady Lovelace's losses at the track have a lesson. Systems ought not to be used for purposes for which they weren't designed. The computer industry has experienced much inefficiency because systems are applied to problems for which they weren't designed.

There was no electronics industry to support Babbage's ideas. All of the concepts had to be implemented in mechanical components, and the tolerances were so fine that they could not be manufactured within the limitations of nineteenth-century technology. Furthermore, Babbage's plans were grandiose. Building a computer with 1000 50-digit numbers was a large task. He might have been more successful if he had completed a smaller computer first, and then built credibility with his government and solidified his funding before starting on a larger one. Many government-sponsored projects fail today because of a lack of technology to support grandiose plans. The lessons we can learn from Babbage are summarized in figure A-5.

327

Babbage's Mistakes

Vague problem definition and requirements
Implementation started before design was complete
Requirements added during implementation
Working documentation not complete
Dependency on one person
System used for unintended purposes
Grandiose plans that exceeded existing technology

We do not know what impact, if any, Babbage's work had on future development. One pioneer, Howard Aiken (see below), reported that he worked for three years before discovering Babbage's contributions. We do not know about the others.

HERMAN HOLLERITH

In the late nineteenth century, the U.S. Census Bureau had a problem. The bureau was supposed to produce a census of the U.S. population every 10 years. However, the 1880 census took seven and one-half years to finish. By the time the census data was processed, much of it was no longer useful. Furthermore, at the rate that the population was growing, the Census Bureau was afraid that the 1890 census would not be finished before the 1900 census was due to begin.

In 1879, the bureau hired Herman Hollerith to help them. He worked for the Census Bureau for five years and then started his own company. Hollerith designed and managed the construction of several punched-card processing machines (see figure A-6).

In 1889, the bureau held a contest among Hollerith and two competitors to determine whose system was the fastest. Hollerith's system required only one-tenth of the time needed by his nearest competitor. Using this equipment, the first count of the 1890 census took only six weeks! However, the final, official count was not announced until December of 1890.

Hollerith's equipment was an extension of the work of the Frenchman Joseph Marie Jacquard. Jacquard designed looms in which punched cards controlled the pattern on woven material. In Jacquard's looms, needles fell through holes in the cards. The needles lifted threads in a way to produce a pattern. This technique had been used in the weaving industry since 1804.

Hollerith extended this concept by using the cards to control electric circuits. Data was punched on three-by-five-inch cards and fed into a machine that moved the cards over a group of pins. If there was a hole in a card, the pin would fall through the hole and touch a pan of mercury. This contact closed a circuit and registered on a meter. Apparently, the machine worked so well that the humans became exhausted. There is a story that occasionally someone would pour all of the mercury into a nearby spittoon. The machine would stop and everyone could rest.

COMPUTERS AND SOCIETY

More Uses, More Users, More Questions

The robots are coming! Or are they? Is this Star Wars setting a myth or reality?

ROBOT MYTHS AND REALITIES

R2D2 and C3PO are fiction. At this time, state-of-the-art robotics does not even include voice recognition and communication in one language, let alone C3PO's claim to over six million forms of communication. Today's mobile robots can do little more than avoid objects, utter a few canned phrases, and wave an arm or two around in the air. Such robots are toys.

Industrial robots, on the other hand, are very much a reality. Although they are unexciting to see, industrial robots are quite useful, performing repetitive, sometimes dangerous, tasks with a high degree of reliability. Industrial robots cut airplane parts, pack candy, drill holes, and remove parts from hot ovens. Further, such robots are cost effective. In 1981, a robot could be operated at $5.50 an hour; during that same year, the average wage and benefit expense for a comparable laborer was $18.10.

Industrial robots have the potential to eliminate drudgery and meaningless labor. They can replace humans in unpleasant environments, such as mines or hot factories. Industrial robots can also work in dangerous environments, such as the bowels of nuclear reactors or in the presence of highly contagious and dangerous diseases.

Robots at a Ford plant are tireless and uncomplaining workers, but 24 million industrial workers are worried about increasing automation.

This new-found friend is actually being controlled by a human being a few feet away.

Japan has emerged as a leader in the practical application of robotics.

Asimov's Three Laws of Robotics

1. A robot may not injure a human being, or, through inaction, allow a human being to come to harm.

2. A robot must obey the orders given it by a human being except where such orders would conflict with the First Law.

3. A robot must protect its own existence as long as such protection does not conflict with either the First or Second Law.

This "Apprentice" robot from Unimation is used for arc welding.

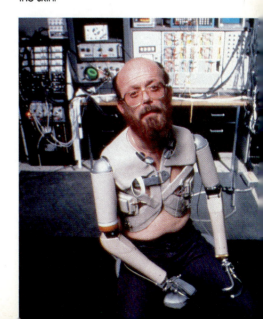

A victim of a power line accident tries out his new electronic arms, activated by motion sensors and electrical signals from the skin.

But what are the social consequences? If robots take over spot welding, what will happen to the world's spot welders? If robots take over auto painting, what will happen to the world's auto painters? Although robots will create some new jobs, the ratio of lost jobs to new jobs will not be one to one. Further, today's spot welders are unlikely to be tomorrow's robot mechanics. What will the response of the labor unions be? What *should* the response of the labor unions be?

Futhermore, the use of robots means a loss of control. Who is responsible if a robot accidentally kills someone? If robots can be programmed to produce useful work, they can also be programmed to commit crimes. Who is responsible if a robot intentionally kills someone?

Less dramatically, considering that robots follow standardized procedures, will products become so similar that our environment becomes uniform, sterile, and bland? Will craftsmanship and creativity in workmanship disappear? Does today's laborer have only three choices—to become a technologist, an artisan, or unemployed?

HEALTH AND MEDICINE

Computers prolong life and reduce pain and suffering. Computers help doctors to detect diseases; they improve diagnoses; they enable surgeons to operate more precisely; they monitor critically ill patients. Computer systems analyze the occurrence of disease and help determine causes and means of prevention.

Computer technology also helps people to compensate for or overcome handicaps. Hearing can be improved; artificial limbs can be made more useful; optical sensors can detect eye movements, thus enabling paraplegics to turn pages or cause other action to occur by moving their eyes.

All of these benefits are possible, but not without social cost. People are confronted with new ethical dilemmas. When is someone really dead? At what point should life-sustaining equipment be removed to allow a person to die? At what point is life no longer worth living? Who pays the cost of maintaining a person who cannot afford to be maintained? Such questions necessitate a new morality. Meanwhile, physicians, relatives, and friends are forced to make life-and-death decisions.

Futhermore, what are the biological consequences of introducing technology into medicine? If the evolution of the human race is governed by the law of the survival of the fittest, what happens when the unfit are maintained? Should people with certain diseases or medical conditions be prohibited from procreating?

By controlling the processes of aging and by using artificial organs, doctors may extend life expectancy to 100 years or more. When it becomes possible, should it be allowed?

Imaging systems help doctors with patient diagnosis.

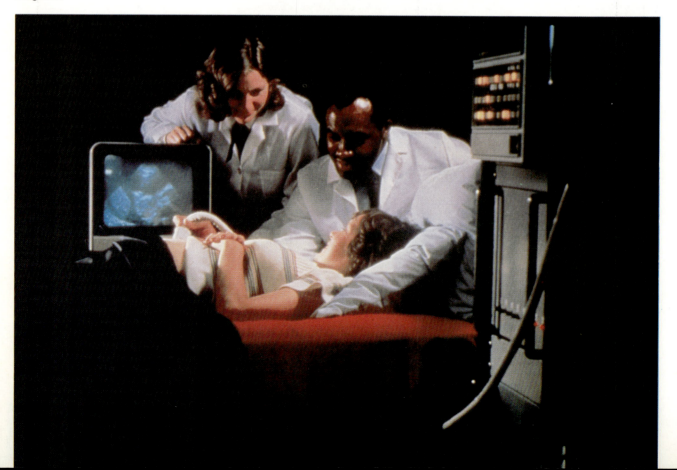

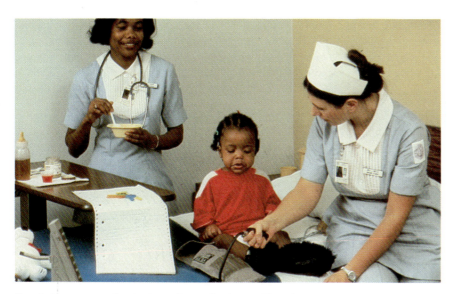

Hospitals use computers to streamline patient record keeping.

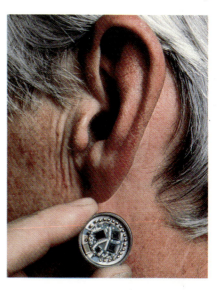

Small hearing devices continue to shrink, with medical research producing circuitry as tiny as nerves and neurons.

Understanding and duplicating human speech integrates medical research with computer technology.

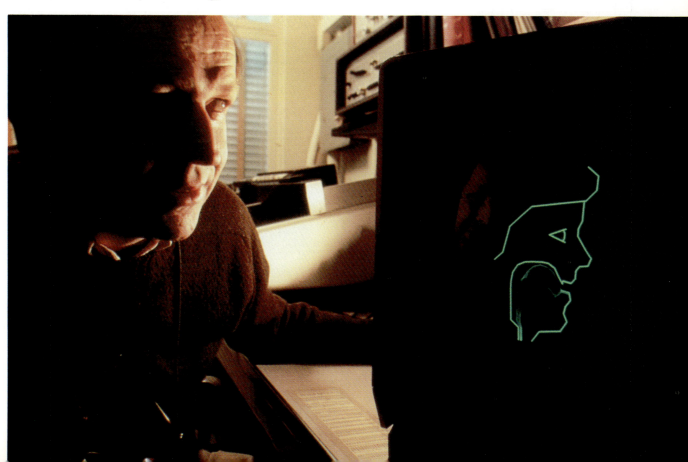

BUSINESS

The computer has revolutionized the way we do business. Credit checking, order processing, travel reservations, automated manufacturing, typing, communications—all have been changed by computers. In fact, many services we take for granted would be impossible without computer technology.

Many law firms use computers to organize, store, and retrieve information.

ATMs, or automatic teller machines, are becoming as commonplace as human tellers.

Stockbrokers and investment houses use computers to provide customers with current information.

Warehouses throughout the world use computerized inventory control.

Computers improve productivity and operating efficiency. Product quality can increase, costs can decrease, or both. Consider the telephone: because of the computer, long distance service has improved, while costs have decreased. Computer technology can substantially improve our material well-being.

At the same time, however, computers can create standardized, sterile, and inflexible environments. With computers, warm and friendly offices can become cold and hostile. Decision making can be constrained, and people can lose freedom of action. Computer systems provide new opportunities for crime. Privacy can be invaded, and sometimes the victim is unaware of the invasion.

Worst of all, computer systems contribute to the acceleration of our pace of life. With computers, we can acquire better and cheaper things more and more rapidly. But do we want better and cheaper things, more and more rapidly? Computers do not help us answer that question.

EDUCATION AND TRAINING

Educational games and drill and practice programs can improve the quality of education and increase teacher productivity. Educational software can make learning easier and more fun, and it can respond to individual differences. For example, computer-assisted instruction (CAI) can respond to each student's level of knowledge. Students who answer all questions correctly can be introduced to new and more difficult material. Students who consistently answer incorrectly can be presented with more basic material or with tutorial discussions.

Even more exciting, computers offer opportunities to teach subjects in entirely new ways. Computer graphics can be used to present mathematical principles, such as the concept of a limit. Students who are exposed to mathematical concepts from a graphical point of view appear to gain improved intuition into mathematical concepts.

Simulation provides another educational possibility. Students can perform chemistry or physics experiments on the computer. For example, students can instruct the computer to combine chemical compounds, and the computer will simulate a chemical reaction. Such simulation can reduce laboratory expenses, as well as allow students to learn from experiments that would be too dangerous to do in reality. High school geometry has been taught in the same fashion for centuries. With the computer language LOGO, however, geometry can be taught using entirely new methods.

Many teachers find that microcomputers stimulate curiosity and learning.

Languages such as LOGO take children beyond the game-playing and into programming.

Unfortunately, there are not enough computers to go around. According to one estimate, there are more than 200 students for every microcomputer. (In contrast, IBM has one computer terminal for every two employees.) The benefits of computer-based education will have little impact until this ratio is drastically reduced.

Even then, what are the social costs? Will computers take the humanness out of teaching? Will students feel more isolated and alone when using computer-based systems? A classroom may be slow and inefficient, but it is social. Will the cost of computer-assisted instruction be less well-developed social skills?

Computer-assisted instruction (CAI) provides a learning system for a wide variety of subjects.

Simulation is used for the training of both pilots and flight controllers.

COMMUNICATIONS

The world gets smaller and smaller. Reporters at remote sites write stories on word processing systems and submit their stories over communications lines to a computer at the newspaper's headquarters. The paper is composed in electronic form and sent via satellite to distributed printing plants. Finally, near the point of sale, the paper is printed.

Printing presses across the United States receive satellite-transmitted pages for printing and daily local distribution.

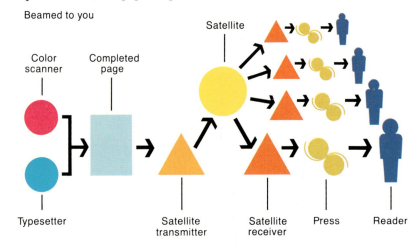

Beamed to you

Color scanner — Completed page — Typesetter — Satellite transmitter — Satellite — Satellite receiver — Press — Reader

Newspaper by satellite. Computer and satellite technology are used to allow *USA Today* to be printed overnight across the United States. Computer-set type and reproduced photographs are laid out as newspaper pages. The pages are converted to electronic impulses and beamed to the WESTAR III satellite 22,300 miles above the earth. The satellite broadcasts the signals back to receiving stations at the print sites.

The *USA Today* newsroom reporters enter their stories using computer terminals.

USA Today provides a practical example of today's computer communications technology.

Using teleconferencing, business people in different locations meet face-to-face without travel. Air traffic controllers instruct pilots whom they never meet to fly airplanes that they never see, except electronically. Airplanes are kept on the ground in Seattle because of crowded airspace in Chicago. A shopper at home in Milwaukee buys a TV from a store located in Phoenix using a credit card from a bank in Memphis. In less than five seconds, computers in Milwaukee, Phoenix, and Memphis communicate to verify credit and inventory levels, to generate the shipping invoice, and to record the sale.

It becomes easier and easier to "reach out, reach out and touch someone," whether that someone is a friend, a business associate, a business, or a computer. What are the consequences of all this reaching out? Closer communication, better understanding among people, a world view instead of a neighborhood view are some consequences. Others are a furious pace of life, confusion and complexity, and more information than we are capable of handling. According to Bell Laboratories, the weekday edition of *The New York Times* contains more information than a person in the sixteenth century received in an entire lifetime. How can we cope? Do we need a computer to say "no thanks" when someone reaches out?

Air traffic controllers "watch" planes electronically.

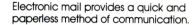

Teleconferencing is used by large companies for face-to-face communication without travel.

Electronic mail provides a quick and paperless method of communication.

CBS and AT&T combine to introduce catalogue shopping by videotext, allowing customers to browse, select, and pay using terminals.

COMMUNICATIONS AND CONTROL

Computers control processes. They run machinery, regulate the speed of production lines, monitor power plants and refineries, and control space probes. Computers instructed a robot on Mars to perform experiments—experiments that, ironically, were concerned with searching for signs of life. Computers assimilate more data than human beings, make decisions in split seconds, and work tirelessly at boring and repetitive jobs. They are ideal for industrial control.

This seventh Space Shuttle launch used computers for communications and control, orbited communication satellites for Canada and Indonesia, and employed a robotic arm to deploy and retrieve a space platform.

User-transparent communications control is effected at the Bell Telephone network center.

NASA's Deep Space Network control center communicates with and controls spacecraft traveling in and exploring deep space.

But should we trust computer control? If surgeons avoid surgery and lawyers avoid lawsuits, will computer programmers avoid automated airplanes? Who is responsible for mishaps? Computers introduce possibilities for crime, sabotage, and blackmail. Are these possibilities being examined, discussed, and controlled?

Control of electricity and water is essential to our society and impossible without the aid of computers, such as those shown here at the Bonneville Power Authority.

Military use of computers can combine computer graphics and computer communications to provide commanders with realistic representations of troop movements as they are occurring.

GOVERNMENT AND
LAW ENFORCEMENT

Computers facilitate the making, the keeping, and the breaking of the law. Computer systems control the massive flow of paperwork through the U.S. Congress. Computer systems keep congressional schedules, record ballots, send and receive electronic mail, maintain records of correspondence, and help to produce the *Congressional Record*.

Congressman Charles Rose of North Carolina uses a local communication network for status information on legislation.

Today's sheriff with today's gold: recovering $50,000 worth of computer chips.

Computers assist law enforcement by keeping records of crimes and criminals. Using computers and communications, police can check records on a suspected stolen automobile without stopping the vehicle. More information for law enforcement means greater safety for police and less disruption for law-abiding citizens. Computer systems also increase the efficiency of police operations, producing lower costs and better law enforcement.

Unfortunately, computer systems provide new opportunities for crime, necessitating new laws and new law enforcement techniques. If money in a French bank is stolen in the United States through communications with a computer located in Switzerland, which country's laws pertain? Suppose such a crime is suspected. Who investigates it? Where and how?

Suppose someone steals software by copying it. How should the investigating officer proceed? Since no object was stolen, what evidence should be gathered? Clearly, the investigation of computer crime requires special training. Who has this training?

In a police car, computers can access information on suspects immediately.

Law enforcement agencies, such as this one in Louisiana, provide network communication with other agencies throughout the world.

SUMMARY

Computer systems are tools; as such, they are instruments for accomplishing jobs or solving problems. Tools have no conscience. They can be used for good or evil, for creation or destruction, for benefit or harm. Whether a tool is beneficial, on balance, depends on the people who use it.

In the preceding pages, you have seen some of the ways computer systems benefit society. Each of these applications is, in itself, good. The tool behind these applications, however, is ethically neutral. Computers are powerful tools, and the more powerful the tool, the greater the potential danger. To avoid such danger, human beings need to gain awareness and to maintain control.

The Japanese are pioneering the development of a street map navigation display for visitors to a city.

QUESTIONS

1. Describe two benefits and two dangers of robotics. What can you, as a citizen, do to reduce the dangers?

2. Summarize the ethical problems caused by the introduction of computers into the medical field.

3. Consider the consequences to you of obtaining better and cheaper goods, more and more rapidly. At what point does the acquisition of material goods lose value to you? How can you structure your life to reflect this priority?

4. Describe two advantages and two disadvantages of computers in education. On balance, do you think the impact of computers in education will be positive?

5. Summarize the ways in which computer technology has made the world smaller and smaller. On balance, has this change been beneficial? What changes do you expect to see if the world continues to shrink?

6. Suppose a computer-controlled process explodes and kills several people. Subsequent investigation shows that the problem was caused by an error in a computer program. The vendor of the program had detected the error and sent a correction to all users. However, employees of the company in which the explosion occurred had not made the change. Who should be held responsible?

7. Suppose someone steals software by copying it. What evidence do you think is necessary to prove that the crime occurred?

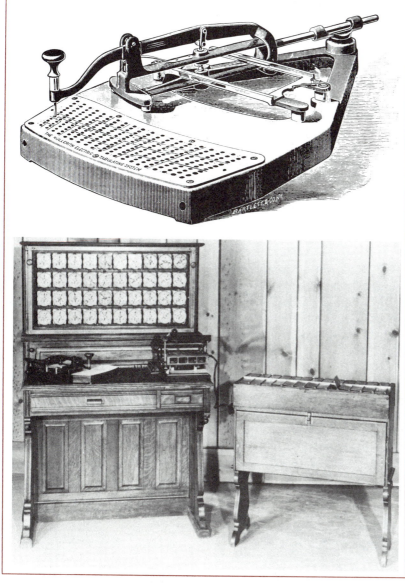

Hollerith decided he had a marketable idea. He sold his equipment to railroads and other large companies that had computational problems. This step represented the start of the punched-card industry. Hollerith built up his business and then sold it to the company that later was to become IBM (International Business Machines).

Hollerith didn't know it, but he was setting the pace for many entrepreneurs to come. Hundreds of computer people have done the same thing he did. They have taken a good idea, developed it, formed an attractive company, sold it, and enjoyed many trips to the bank. Perhaps you can do the same.

The punched-card industry was the beginning of automated data processing. The earliest computer systems were developed around punched-card technology. Companies found that to use this new technology successfully, they needed to build systems composed of hardware, programs, data, procedures, and trained personnel.

Programs? Well, sort of. As the punched-card equipment became more sophisticated, it became possible to change the wiring of the equipment to make it do different things. People who changed the wiring were doing an elementary form of programming. Programming as we know it today did not exist until stored-program computers were developed in the middle of the twentieth century. However, the concepts used in computer systems started evolving with the 1890 census. The idea of developing systematic procedures to direct machines to turn data into information was born in that year.

EARLY COMPUTERS

In 1937, Howard G. Aiken proposed the use of electromechanical devices to perform calculations. He was a graduate student at Harvard at the time, and the IBM Corporation gave him a grant to pursue his ideas. IBM was active in the punched-card industry. They may have felt that electromechanical calculators would be useful to them.

In 1944, Aiken and IBM completed an electromechanical calculator called the Mark I. This computer had mechanical counters that were manipulated by electrical devices. The Mark I could perform basic arithmetic, and it could be changed to solve different problems (see figure A-7).

At about the same time, the U.S. government signed a contract with the University of Pennsylvania to develop a computer that would aid the military effort during World War II. As a result of this contract, John W. Mauchly and

FIGURE A-7

Mark I computer

Who Invented the Computer?

Standard texts and encyclopedias generally give the credit to a pair of scientists who created a machine during World War II to calculate, among other things, the trajectories of bombs. This machine is usually thought to be the first that solved complex practical problems by the use of a simple electronic language consisting of positive and negative pulses.

But it was preceded by a machine (though a more limited one) that also performed complex calculations, invented in the 1930s by a physicist in the Midwest. Was this, as some scholars contend, the true inspiration for all computers to come? Or was it, as others argue, merely a sophisticated toy?

The physicist who invented that early machine is Dr. John V. Atanasoff, now nearly 80 years old and determined to get the credit he thinks he deserves.

"I haven't been given my due, but I might be partially to blame," Atanasoff said in a recent interview. "To get ahead in the world, you have to make a lot of noise, and maybe I didn't make enough." But now Atanasoff has written a detailed article, to appear in the Annals of the History of

Computing, that spells out his version of the invention of the computer and marks his first published reflections on the issue.

Dimming the Lights

Dr. John W. Mauchly and Dr. J. Presper Eckert, scientists who worked at the University of Pennsylvania, are the men he wishes to displace in history. They built a machine known as Eniac (for Electronic Numerical Integrator and Computer). The machine, a vast assemblage of vacuum tubes (18,000), resistors (70,000) and capacitors (10,000), weighed 30 tons and drew so much power that the lights of West Philadelphia dimmed slightly whenever it was switched on . . .

Mauchly and Eckert applied for a patent. It was granted in 1964 after much delay. By that time the rights had been purchased by Sperry Rand, which hoped to reap huge profits from royalties during the 17-year life of the patent. But Honeywell, another company that made computers, decided to search for a way to avoid payment. They attacked the validity of the patent in court.

Lawsuit Filed

Honeywell filed a lawsuit in 1971 claiming that Eckert and Mauchly had "pirated" their ideas from a visionary who had built a vacuum-tube computer at Iowa State College (now University) in the 1930s. The unsung inventor was Atanasoff . . .

Atanasoff showed his invention to anyone who displayed interest. During the 1940s Mauchly traveled to Iowa to see Atanasoff's computer, and the two men subsequently exchanged letters.

Any Objections?

"Is there any objection," Mauchly asked in one letter, "to my building some sort of computer which incorporates some of the features of your machine?"

That letter, along with other items, helped sway the judge. In 1973 the court found that "Eckert and Mauchly did not themselves first invent the automatic electronic digital computer, but instead derived the subject matter from one Dr. John Vincent Atanasoff." The patent was ruled invalid.

By WILLIAM J. BROAD
The New York Times, March 27, 1983

J. Presper Eckert developed the first all-electronic computer, called the *Electronic Numerical Integrator and Calculator*, or *ENIAC*. Unlike the Mark I, ENIAC had no mechanical counters; everything was electronic.

Although Mauchly and Eckert are often given credit for developing the first electronic computer, this is apparently not completely true. Their work was based in part on work that had been done by John V. Atanasoff. Atanasoff was a professor at Iowa State and, in 1939, he had developed many ideas for an all-electronic computer. In 1942, he and a graduate student, Clifford Berry, completed an electronic computer that could solve systems of linear equations.

ENIAC (the Mauchly/Eckert machine) was used to perform many different calculations. It had 18,000 vacuum tubes, 70,000 resistors, and 500,000 soldered joints. The ENIAC could perform 5000 additions per second. It used 150,000 watt-hours of power a day—so much that, when it was turned on, the lights in one section of Philadelphia dimmed. Unfortunately, it was inflexible. Changing its program meant rewiring and thus required considerable time and resources. Since it could be changed, it was programmable. However, it was not programmable in the sense that we understand the term today.

In the mid-1940s, the mathematician John von Neumann joined the Mauchly/Eckert team. Von Neumann proposed a design for a computer that stored programs in its memory. He also developed other concepts that were to become the foundation for computer design for thirty years. Two computers evolved from this work: the *EDVAC* (Electrical Discrete Variable Automatic Computer) and the *EDSAC* (Electronic Delay Storage Automatic Calculator). Both machines stored programs. EDSAC was completed in England in 1949, and EDVAC in the United States in 1950.

At the time, the potential of these machines was not understood. Atanasoff couldn't get support from Iowa State. The administration thought that there would be a need for only three of four of these devices throughout the United States. Furthermore, Hermann Goldstine reports that, in the late 1940s, none of the ENIAC-EDVAC staff was promoted to full professor at the Moore School of Engineering. People didn't seem to feel the work was going to be very important.

Another social commentary: The first programmers for the Mark I and the ENIAC were women. Captain Grace Hopper, USN, programmed the Mark I and Ms. Adele Goldstine programmed the ENIAC. Both of these women were talented mathematicians. Their presence undoubtedly helped to establish women's strong position in the computer industry.

John Mauchly and Presper Eckert decided to follow in Hollerith's entrepreneurial footsteps, and, in 1946, they formed the Eckert-Mauchly Corporation. This ripe young company was purchased by the Remington-Rand Corporation. Their first product was *UNIVAC I* (Universal Automatic Computer). It was the first computer built to sell. The Census Bureau took delivery of the first one in 1951, and it was used continually until 1963. It now resides in the Smithsonian Institution (see figure A-8). Sperry Rand still manufactures a line of computers under the name *UNIVAC*, although these computers are a far cry from the UNIVAC I.

Meanwhile, other companies were not idle. IBM continued development on the Mark I computer and eventually developed the Mark II through Mark IV, as well as other early computers. Burroughs, General Electric, Honeywell, and RCA were also busy with computer developments.

IBM took an early lead in the application of this new computer technology to business problems. They developed a series of business-oriented computers and sold them to their punched-card customers. Because IBM had a virtual monopoly on punched cards (they had been sued for it by the U.S. government in the 1930s), they were in a strong position to capitalize on the new technology.

UNIVAC I

Furthermore, IBM had an extremely effective marketing philosophy. They emphasized solving business problems. They developed products that were useful to businesses, and they showed business people how to use those products. IBM provided excellent customer service and good maintenance.

This philosophy paid off. Some other companies had better computers, but their computers weren't packaged to provide total solutions to business problems. IBM was the first company to understand that wise business people don't buy the best *computer*; they buy the best *solution* to their problem. Today, many vendors have adopted this philosophy. They sell solutions to business problems, not just computers. However, the fact that IBM understood it first has much to do with their strength in the computer market today.

The computers manufactured in the 1950s are often called *first-generation computers*. Their major components were vacuum tubes. Most of them used magnetic drums as their primary storage devices. Main memory as discussed in this book did not exist at that time.

Because of the number and size of the vacuum tubes, these computers were huge. Furthermore, they generated tremendous amounts of heat, were expensive to run, and experienced frequent failures. A large first-generation computer occupied a room the size of a football field. It contained row upon row of racks of tubes. A staff of a half-dozen people was required just to change the tubes that burned out.

In the late 1950s and early 1960s, vacuum tubes were replaced by transistors. This development led to *second-generation computers*. These computers were much smaller than vacuum-tube computers, and they were more powerful. A

COMPUTERS IN THE 1960s AND 1970s

new type of main storage was developed. It was called *core memory* because it used magnetized, doughnut-shaped cores. The term *core* is still used today. Some people use *core* synonymously with *main memory*. This usage is incorrect. Most main memories today do not contain magnetic core.

The first high-level programming languages were developed during this stage. First-generation computers were programmed in machine code, but second-generation computers were programmed in assembler language and English-like languages, such as FORTRAN and ALGOL. (See module J.) Further, primitive operating systems were installed on second-generation machines. Operating system programs controlled the use of the computer's resources.

Most second-generation computers could run only one program at a time. Therefore, to speed things up, certain input and output operations were done *offline*. For example, punched cards were read and their contents copied to tape without the computer's involvement. Then the tape was read into the computer and processed, and the generated output was written to tape. The tape was then dismounted and printed on a separate machine. This process was followed because tape units could read and write much faster than card readers or printers could operate. Figure A-9 shows the IBM 7094, a typical second-generation computer.

Most of the computer systems at this stage were for accounting. The computer was used to produce checks for payroll and accounts payable, and to keep track of inventories. General ledger was also computerized. However, processing was done in batches. Inputs were gathered into groups and processed, and outputs were produced. Applications that required interaction like order entry could not be done.

In the 1960s, the *third generation of computers* became available. In these computers, *integrated circuits* were used instead of transistors. An integrated circuit is a complete electrical circuit on a small chip of silicon (see fig-

FIGURE A-9

A second-generation computer—the IBM 7094

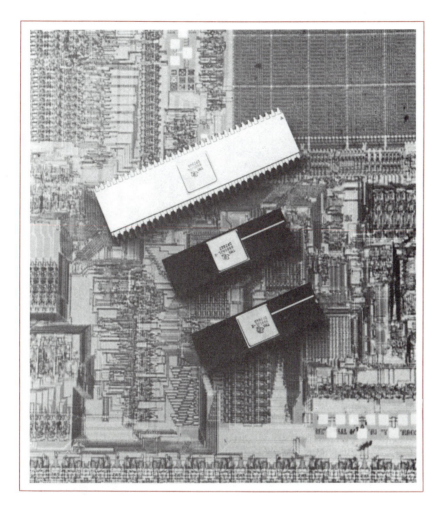

FIGURE A-10

Integrated circuit on a silicon chip

ure A-10). Because of these chips, third-generation computers are smaller and more powerful than second-generation computers. Figure A-11 compares the sizes of vacuum tubes, transistors, and integrated circuits.

Vast improvements were also made in programming during the third generation. Sophisticated operating systems were developed. These systems allowed many programs to be executed concurrently. Slow input and output operations like card reading or printing could be performed in the background. One job would be in processing while another was being read and the outputs of a third were being printed. The computers ran programs and every now and then took a little time to handle slow I/O. This arrangement eliminated the need for the offline processing typical of second-generation computers. Figure A-12 shows a typical third-generation computer.

Third-generation computers also supported online, interactive processing. Users could interact with the computer to perform functions like online order entry or online airline reservations. Although some online processing had been done by earlier, military systems, these applications were very specialized and

335

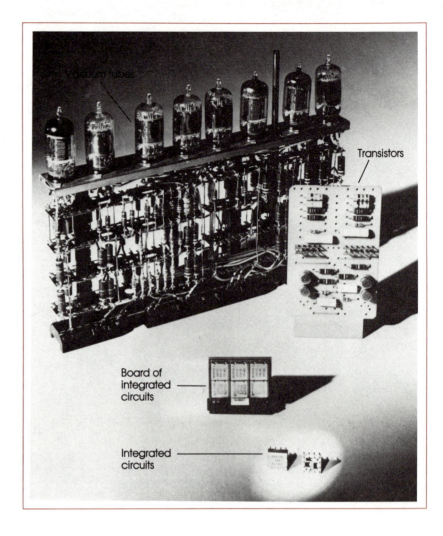

Vacuum tubes

Transistors

Board of
integrated
circuits

Integrated
circuits

Three generations of hardware
components

not economical. The third generation of computers made it possible for online processing to be a standard product.

Minicomputers appeared in the mid-1960s. Initially, minis were small, special-purpose machines designed for military and space applications. Gradually, however, the capability of these machines has increased to the point that the more powerful minicomputers and the less powerful mainframes have overlapped. Figure A-13 shows a Digital Equipment VAX minicomputer, a very powerful machine that exceeds the capability of many so-called mainframes. Thus, it is hard to distinguish between the two categories of computers. (See chapter 2 for more discussion of this topic.)

THE FOURTH GENERATION

The fourth generation of computers is characterized by *very large scale integration (VLSI)*. With VLSI, thousands of transistors and other components can be placed on a single quarter-inch silicon chip. In fact, an entire CPU can

A third-generation computer—the
Honeywell 6000

reside on a single chip. The computer that may have occupied a football field in 1952 today is less than half the size of a penny.

VLSI chips can be mass-produced, which means that they can be manufactured and sold in quantities of thousands. Because so many are sold, the costs of research, development, and tooling are spread over many items. Thus, VLSI chips are extremely cheap. A circuit that may have cost $50,000 10 years ago can now be purchased in quantity for $10 or less. Thus, VLSI technology has caused a tremendous decrease in the price/performance ratio of new computers.

A computer on a chip is called a *microprocessor*. When the chip is installed with electronics to perform input and output, as well as other functions, it is called a *microcomputer*.

Microprocessors were not designed with forethought. They just happened. The companies that manufacture silicon chips found ways to put more and more circuitry on the chip. They were increasing the circuitry to support other products. For example, the Intel 8008, a microprocessor, was originally intended to be the controller for a CRT terminal. For a variety of reasons, the chip was not used for this purpose.

Because Intel had developed the product, however, they put it in their catalog. To their surprise, apparently, it sold very well. The company saw the demand, put a design team together, and a year later introduced the Intel 8080 microprocessor, shown in figure A-14. This product has become one of the most popular microprocessors. Other manufacturers quickly followed suit. Today there are dozens of microprocessor products to choose from.

F I G U R E A - 1 3

The DEC VAX minicomputer

F I G U R E A - 1 4

The Intel 8080 microprocessor

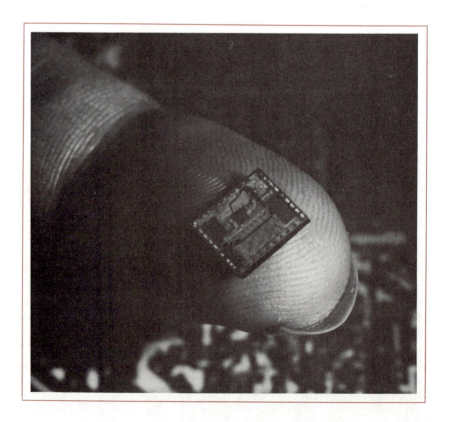

All of this development means that computers have become cheaper and cheaper. Some experts believe that the cost of computer CPUs will soon be essentially zero. At least, the cost will be negligible compared to that of other components of a computer system.

These inexpensive microprocessors may well lead to entirely new computer architectures. Since microprocessors are so cheap, it becomes feasible to develop and market *supercomputers*, or computers that are banks of many microprocessors. For example, a supercomputer could be a 100×100 array of microprocessors. It boggles the mind to consider the power of such a machine.

COMPUTERS IN THE 1980s

The advent of the microcomputer started a revolution in the computer industry. Early micros, such as the TRS-80 and the Apple II, were priced under $2000; at this price, they were affordable to millions of people and businesses. Consequently, Apple, a company that did not exist in 1975, had sales in excess of $1 billion in 1983.

Although the cost of hardware dramatically decreased in the fourth generation, the cost of developing programs increased. Programming is a highly labor-intensive activity, and the cost of programming labor has been rising substantially. Cost decreases in hardware were often offset by cost increases in program development. Additionally, program complexity increased, and developing programs became more and more risky.

For these reasons, in the 1980s, businesses have been seeking cheaper ways of acquiring programs. One way has been to utilize off-the-shelf programs as much as possible. Another way has been to increase the productivity of programmers with higher level languages. We will consider each of these alternatives in turn.

Off-the-Shelf Programs

When the microcomputer hit Main Street, ways were found to use computers in nearly all industries. Not everyone, however, wanted to learn about computer technology and programming. In response to this need, the microcomputer became a consumer product. Whereas most of the buyers of computers prior to 1980 were computer-knowledgeable professionals, most of the buyers of micros after 1980 were not. To be successful in the new marketplace, microcomputers had to be designed for users who do not have, and who are unwilling to acquire, much knowledge about computer technology. Most people want to solve their problems rather than learn how to program.

Thus, packaged programs became very important. People wanted to buy programs off-the-shelf. Because of this demand, products like VISICALC (an electronic spreadsheet) were incredibly successful. In the early 1980s, a new industry was born: microcomputer software. Many companies began to construct general-purpose micro software, and this software became a commodity. Traditional retailers, such as Sears, began to carry computer software in their line. Advertising also reflected this change: "Buy two, get one free" was one slogan.

Because micro software is priced inexpensively (less than $500 in most cases), the traditional vendor's sales call became cost prohibitive. Having a salesperson call can easily cost more than the price of the product. This imbalance led to the need for new software distribution channels, and another entirely new industry was born. Companies like Softsell were formed to obtain micro software from vendors and place it with retailers. Such companies provide training and sales assistance to the retailers as well.

Packaged programs have also become important in the mini and mainframe markets. Many large businesses have found that they can buy programs for common applications such as general ledger. These programs can be purchased and installed much more quickly, less expensively, and with far less risk than custom programs can be developed. Packaged programs are likely to become more popular in the future.

Unfortunately, not every problem can have a packaged solution. Some problems require custom programs. Here the industry got a boost from an unexpected quarter.

Relational Database Management

In the early 1970s, companies began to demand more from the data they had stored. Data had been collected for specific, isolated purposes. Management wanted to bring this isolated data together to obtain more integrated information. This need led to the rise of database technology (discussed in chapter 7).

In the 1980s, a new branch of database technology, called the *relational model,* became important. Relational technology had been known for some time, but it has been too difficult to implement with acceptable performance. As the price/performance ratio of CPUs fell, however, this situation changed. Relational database processing became feasible for many (but not all) needs. Furthermore, relational database management systems became available for micros as well as for minis and mainframes. Products such as RBASE 4000 were developed and marketed especially for microcomputers.

A key element of the relational model is that data is represented as tables. Relationships among different tables are carried in the data. Because tables are familiar, relational processing seems more natural to users and programmers.

Additionally, high-level, nonprocedural languages (see module K), such as Structured Query Language (SQL), have been developed for processing relational databases. Such languages are much easier to learn than traditional programming languages. Some companies have found that programmer productivity has improved by several orders of magnitude when relational processing was used instead of more traditional methods. Not only are professional programmers more productive, but, for some applications, especially those involving simple queries, many users are able to do their own programming. In some cases, the need for programmers to implement new query requests has been eliminated.

Communications among Computers

The 1980s have also been characterized by increased use of data communications. Computers are linked to one another via very high speed data lines. Satellites are used to communicate around the world. Figure A-15 shows part of the configuration of a network of large computers called the ARPA (Advanced Research Project Agency) network. (See chapter 8 for more details on communications processing).

Many people believe that there will soon be data utilities. Such utilities will supply computer processing and data banks to subscribers much like other

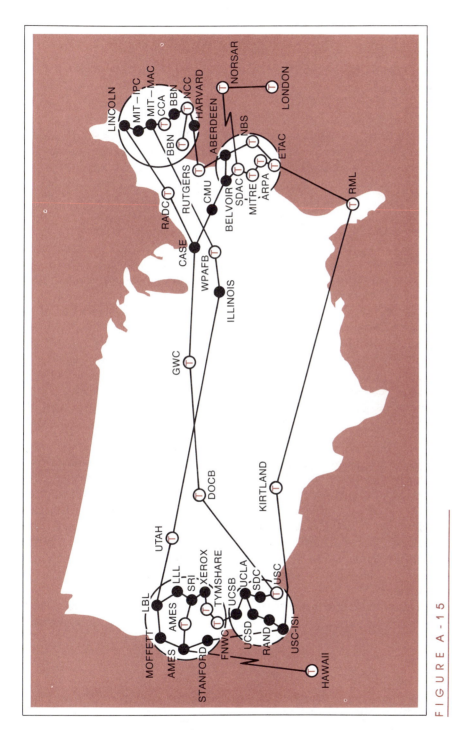

F I G U R E   A - 1 5

A portion of the ARPA network of computers

341

The Fifth Generation

The American computer industry has been innovative, vital, and successful. Today we dominate the world's ideas and markets in this most important of modern technologies. But what about tomorrow?

Japanese planners view the computer industry as vital to their nation's economic future and have audaciously made it a national goal to become number one in this industry by the latter half of the 1990s. They aim not only to dominate the traditional forms of the computer industry, but to establish a "knowledge industry" in which knowledge itself will be a salable commodity like food and oil.

To implement this vision the Japanese have both strategy and tactics. Their strategy is simple and wise: to avoid a head-on confrontation in the marketplace with the currently dominant American firms; instead to look out into the 1990s to find an arena of great economic potential that is currently being overlooked by the more short-sighted and perhaps complacent American firms; to move rapidly now to build major strength in that arena. The tactics are set forth in a major and impressive national plan of the Ministry of International Trade and Industry (MITI) called Fifth Generation Computer Systems.

The Japanese plan is bold and dramatically forward-looking. It is unlikely to be completely successful in the ten-year period. But to view it therefore as "a lot of smoke," as some American industry leaders have done, is a serious mistake. Even partially realized concepts that are superbly engineered can have great economic value, preempt the market, and give the Japanese the dominant position they seek.

If we focus our efforts, we should have little trouble dominating the second computer age as we dominated the first. We have a two- or three-year lead; that's large in the world of high technology. But we are squandering our lead at the rate of one day per day.

America needs a national plan of action, a kind of Space Shuttle program for the knowledge systems of the future. The stakes are high. In the trade wars, this may be the crucial challenge.

High Technology, June, 1983

utilities supply electricity. Initially, the subscribers will be businesses, but eventually individuals could be members. With this capability, people could obtain news, magazines, business statistics, even books or other literature at home. This communication could take place over cable TV lines. Individuals could use the data utility to order goods and services as well as to receive information. Some of these activities are currently being done.

Another significant development has been the rise of *distributed data processing*. This aspect of data processing is discussed in detail in chapter 9. As explained in that chapter, the availability of cheap computers has allowed applications to be distributed away from a centralized data processing center. This development has given business users much greater control over their data.

QUESTIONS

A.1 Explain what people can learn today from the experiences of Charles Babbage.

A.2 What role did the U.S. Census Bureau play in the development of computers?

A.3 Explain the contribution to the development of computers made by each of the following individuals:
   a. Charles Babbage
   b. Herman Hollerith
   c. Howard Aiken
   d. John Mauchly
   e. J. Presper Eckert
   f. John V. Atanasoff
   g. John von Neumann
   h. Captain Grace Hopper

A.4 How did Herman Hollerith set the pace for computer entrepreneurs?

A.5 What was the IBM marketing philosophy in the early days of computing? How did it help them?

A.6 Characterize the machines and programs of each of the four generations of computers.

A.7 Explain why computers are becoming inexpensive.

A.8 Why has the cost of developing computer programs not decreased as the cost of hardware has?

A.9 Name and describe two ways to decrease the cost of acquiring programs.

SUMMARY

Although the history of computation began thousands of years ago, the development of computers is a recent phenomenon. In the early 1800s, Charles Babbage developed many of the design concepts used in today's computers. However, these concepts were not implemented at that time. Many of the mistakes that Babbage made are still being made today.

In the late 1800s, the U.S. Census Bureau had a problem. They hired Herman Hollerith to develop automated ways of computing census data. This led to the development of punched-card equipment and the beginning of the punched-card industry.

Computers were not actually developed until the mid-1940s. Early computers were produced through the cooperation of universities, government, and industry. There have been four generations of computers so far. First-generation computers had vacuum tubes, and main storage was a magnetic drum. These computers were huge and very hard to maintain. Programs were written in machine code.

Computers in the second generation used transistors and had main memory made of magnetic core. They were smaller and still very expensive. High-level languages were developed for programming, and rudimentary operating systems were invented.

The third-generation computers have integrated circuits on silicon chips. These chips are used both for the arithmetic and logic unit and for main memory. Third-generation computers are much smaller and cheaper than first- or second-generation computers.

343

Today we are in the fourth generation. Computers have become significantly cheaper and more powerful. In the near future, the cost of a CPU will be essentially zero. We may see the development of supercomputers that are banks of microprocessors.

Unfortunately, the costs of developing programs has increased during this same time period. To compensate for these increases, businesses have sought more and more packaged programs. Additionally, relational database processing has provided a dramatic increase in professional programmer productivity; it has also enabled some users to do some of their own programming. We can expect to see more communication among computers and more distributed processing as the 1980s unfold.

WORD LIST
(in order of appearance in text)

Abacus	Machine code
Charles Babbage	Transistors
Difference engine	Core memory
Analytical engine	High-level languages
Ada Augusta Lovelace	Offline input/output
Herman Hollerith	Third-generation computers
Howard G. Aiken	Integrated circuits
Mark I	Online processing
John W. Mauchly	Minicomputers
J. Presper Eckert	Fourth-generation computers
ENIAC	Very large scale integrated circuits
John V. Atanasoff	(VLSI)
John von Neumann	Microprocessor
EDVAC	Microcomputer
EDSAC	Supercomputer
Captain Grace Hopper	Off-the-shelf programs
Ms. Adele Goldstine	Relational database processing
UNIVAC I	Structured Query Language
First-generation computers	Data communications
Second-generation computers	Distributed data processing

QUESTIONS TO CHALLENGE YOUR THINKING

A. The rate of computer technology development has been astronomical in the last thirty years. What impact do you think this growth has had on industry? How do you think a company can best cope with this type of growth if it continues in the future?

B. What impact do you think the rapid change in technology has had on education? How do you think education will change as computers become less and less expensive?

C. Judging from the past, what do you think is going to happen in computing? What impact will computers of the future have on business? How will the business of the year 2000 use computer technology?

MODULE B

Numbers Representation and Computer Arithmetic

DECIMAL AND BINARY NUMBERS
Binary Arithmetic

OCTAL AND HEXADECIMAL NUMBER SYSTEMS

CONVERSIONS BETWEEN NUMBER SYSTEMS

FLOATING-POINT NUMBERS
Fractions and Round-off Error

DECIMAL NUMBERS

In this module, we will discuss how computers represent numbers and do arithmetic. This information supplements material in chapter 2. Make sure you have read chapter 2 before continuing with this section.

Computers represent two basic types of data: *numeric* and *alphanumeric*. Numeric data is numbers that can be processed arithmetically. Alphanumeric data is numbers, letters, and special symbols like #, $, and %. Alphanumeric data is not processed arithmetically. Even if alphanumeric data consists entirely of numbers, the computer represents it such that it is impossible to perform arithmetic on it.

Alphanumeric data is represented by character codes like EBCDIC. This type of representation was discussed in chapter 2, and we will not repeat that discussion here. Instead, we will discuss the format and processing of numeric data.

DECIMAL AND BINARY NUMBERS

To understand how numbers are represented in the computer, try to recall your second-grade math. Remember Mrs. Gazernenplatz (your second-grade teacher)? When she wrote a number on the board like 5437, she said that the 7 is in the ones place, the 3 is in the tens place, the 4 is in the hundreds place, and the 5 is in the thousands place. The meaning of the symbols is 5 times 1000, plus 4 times 100, plus 3 times 10, plus 7 times 1.

Later, in algebra, you learned that another way to write 1000 is 10^3 ($10 \times 10 \times 10$), another way to write 100 is 10^2, to write 10 is 10^1, and to write 1 is 10^0. Thus, each place is a power of 10. The power starts with 0 and increases by 1 for each place to the left of the decimal point. (See figure B-1.)

In the computer, numeric data is often represented in binary form. The binary number system has only two digits (or symbols), 0 and 1. Each binary place has a *bit*, or binary digit. Examples of binary numbers are 110110, 01110, 11111, and 00000. The number 0121 is not a binary number. The symbol 2 is not defined in binary. As explained in chapter 2, binary is used because the symbols 0 and 1 are easy to represent electronically.

Binary numbers are constructed the same way as decimal numbers, but, instead of powers of 10 in the places, powers of 2 are used. Thus, there is the ones place 2^0, the twos place 2^1, the fours place 2^2, the eights place 2^3, and so forth, as shown in figure B-2. The binary number 1010 is interpreted as 1 times 8, plus 0 times 4, plus 1 times 2, plus 0 times 1, or 10 in decimal. Figure B-3 shows the first 16 binary numbers.

FIGURE B-1

Decimal place notation

5437 Decimal Is:		
5 × 1000		5 × 10^3 (thousands place)
+ 4 × 100	or	+ 4 × 10^2 (hundreds place)
+ 3 × 10		+ 3 × 10^1 (tens place)
+ 7 × 1		+ 7 × 10^0 (ones place)

1010 Binary Is 10 in Decimal Form:		
1×8		1×2^3 (eights place)
$+ 0 \times 4$	or	$+ 0 \times 2^2$ (fours place)
$+ 1 \times 2$		$+ 1 \times 2^1$ (twos place)
$+ 0 \times 1$		$+ 0 \times 2^0$ (ones place)

Humans like to work with decimal numbers, but computers are more efficient when working with binary numbers. Therefore, when many calculations are to be performed, the computer converts decimal numbers to binary form. Calculations are made in binary. Results are then reconverted to decimal before they are printed. We will discuss how to perform these conversions after we discuss binary arithmetic.

Binary numbers can be added much the way decimal numbers are added. You add one column at a time and carry when necessary. In binary,

Binary Arithmetic

$$0 + 0 = 0$$
$$0 + 1 = 1$$
$$1 + 0 = 1$$
$$1 + 1 = 10$$

Thus, when two 1's are added, a 1 is carried into the next place. The following are examples of binary addition:

```
                      1 ◄──(carries)──► 1111
    0010            1010                 1111
  + 0101          + 0010               + 0001
  ──────          ──────               ──────
    0111            1100                10000
```

Although subtraction can be done in binary just as it is done in decimal, computers usually do not do this. In fact (here's an amazing thing), *most*

Binary	*Decimal*	*Binary*	*Decimal*
0000	0	1000	8
0001	1	1001	9
0010	2	1010	10
0011	3	1011	11
0100	4	1100	12
0101	5	1101	13
0110	6	1110	14
0111	7	1111	15

computers cannot subtract! Instead, they find the result of a subtraction by adding in a special way. This technique is called *complement addition*.

Suppose that you want to compute 8 minus 3 in decimal. To do this subtraction using complements, you add 8 to the tens complement of 3 and throw away the carry. The tens complement of a number is the value you add to the number to get 10. Thus, the tens complement of 3 is 7 because 3 plus 7 is 10. The tens complement of 6 is 4 ($6 + 4 = 10$) and the tens complement of 2 is 8 ($2 + 8 = 10$).

Now, to compute 8 minus 3, you add 8 to the tens complement of 3 and throw away the carry. Thus, 8 plus 7 (the tens complement of 3) is 15. Throwing away the carry, you get 5. This equals 8 minus 3, as shown in figure B-4. Like magic, isn't it? Try it! Compute 9 minus 2. The tens complement of 2 is 8. Add 9 and 8 to get 17. Throw away the 1 and you have 7, which is 9 minus 2!

Try it again. Compute 9 minus 5. The tens complement of 5 is 5 ($5 + 5 = 10$). Adding 9 and 5, you get 14. Throw away the carry to get 4, which is 9 minus 5.

What happens if you get a negative number? Suppose that you compute 3 minus 6? The answer should be -3. Using complements, we add 3 to the tens complement of 6. Thus, we add 3 to 4 and get 7, which is not -3.

What happened? There is an additional rule. If there is no carry to throw away, the answer is negative. In this case, take the tens complement of the answer and add a minus sign.

Thus, 3 minus 6 is computed by adding 3 to 4 (the tens complement of 6) to get 7. However, there is no carry, so the answer is negative. We take the tens complement of 7 and add a minus sign. The answer is -3, as it should be (see figure B-5).

Try 7 minus 9. The answer should be -2. Take the tens complement of 9, which is 1. Add 7 and 1 to get 8. There is no carry, so the answer is negative. Take the tens complement of 8 and add a minus sign. The answer is -2. It works! You probably think it's done with mirrors.

Computers do the same thing in binary. To form the twos complement of a binary number, the computer just turns all the 1's to 0's and all the 0's to 1's. Then it adds 1. Thus, the twos complement of 0110 is 1001 plus 1, or 1010.

F I G U R E   B - 4

Subtraction using complement addition

To compute $8 - 3$,
  a. Find the tens complement of 3, which is 7.
  b. Add 8 to the complement of 3 to obtain 15.
  c. Throw away the carry to obtain 5, the difference of 8 and 3.

To compute $9 - 5$,
  a. Find the tens complement of 5, which is 5.
  b. Add 9 to the complement of 5 to obtain 14.
  c. Throw away the carry to obtain 4, the answer.

To compute 3 − 6,

 a. Find the tens complement of 6, which is 4.
 b. Add 3 to the complement of 6 to obtain 7.
 c. There is no carry, therefore the answer is negative. Take the tens complement of 7, which is 3, and add a minus sign. The answer is −3.

To compute 7 − 9,

 a. Find the tens complement of 9, which is 1.
 b. Add 7 to the complement of 9 to obtain 8.
 c. There is no carry, therefore the answer is negative. Take the tens complement of 8, which is 2, and add a minus sign. The answer is −2.

FIGURE B-5

Subtraction using complement addition—
negative answers

$$
\begin{array}{r}
(\text{carry}) \longrightarrow 111 \\
1111 \\
+\ 1010 \\
\hline
11001
\end{array}
$$

Suppose that we want to compute 1111 minus 0110. The answer should be 1001. To compute this subtraction, we add 1111 and the twos complement of 0110. Using the complement from above, we add 1111 to 1010.

Now, we throw away the carry and the answer is 1001, as it should be. If there is no carry, the number is negative. Complement the answer by switching 1's and 0's and adding 1.

Thus, computers do not know how to subtract. Instead, they add complements, and they do it very fast. Forming twos complements is quick and easy. Adding is also easy.

Computers multiply by successive additions. Thus to multiply 7 times 8, the computer adds eight 7's together. To multiply 1234 times 438, it adds 438 1234's together. Division can be done by successive subtractions.

OCTAL AND HEXADECIMAL NUMBER SYSTEMS

Working with binary numbers is easy and convenient for computers, but it is a hassle for people. Adding the binary number 11010101110100 to the binary number 1101001000011111010011011101 is a chore. It's also very easy to drop a bit and get the wrong answer. To make errors less likely, people have found a way to shorten binary numbers.

One way is to group the binary symbols into threesomes and to represent the threesomes by a number. The table in figure B-6 shows how to represent

Binary numbers and their abbreviations
(octal equivalents)

Binary Number	Octal Equivalent		Binary Number	Octal Equivalent
000	0		100	4
001	1		101	5
010	2		110	6
011	3		111	7

three binary digits with a single digit. The first column has all the possible three-place binary numbers, and the second column has the symbols used to represent them.

Now, let's use this table to shorten some binary numbers. Group the binary symbols into threes and substitute the corresponding single digit from figure B-6.

$$111011 \quad \text{becomes} \quad 111 \ 011 \quad \text{or} \quad 73$$
$$011010 \quad \text{becomes} \quad 011 \ 010 \quad \text{or} \quad 32$$
$$111000 \quad \text{becomes} \quad 111 \ 000 \quad \text{or} \quad 70$$
$$111111 \quad \text{becomes} \quad 111 \ 111 \quad \text{or} \quad 77$$

Notice that the symbols 8 and 9 are not used in this abbreviation scheme. 7 is the largest symbol. We have created a number system that has only eight symbols: 0, 1, 2, 3, 4, 5, 6, and 7. This number system is called *octal* because it has eight symbols.

Figure B-7 shows the decimal equivalents of some octal numbers. In the decimal system, we have the ones place, the tens place, the hundreds place, and so forth. In binary, we have the ones place, the twos place, the fours place, the eights place, and so forth. In octal, we have places for the ones, the eights, the sixty-fours, and other powers of eight. The octal number 3456 is equal to 3 times 512 ($8 \times 8 \times 8$), plus 4 times 64, plus 5 times 8, plus 6 times 1, or 1838 in decimal.

As mentioned, octal is used primarily as a shorthand for binary. It is very easy to convert from octal to binary. We just replace each octal symbol with the three binary symbols that it represents. Thus, 234 octal in binary equals 010 011 100.

Several manufacturers produce computers that abbreviate binary with octal. Control Data Corporation makes computers that have 60 bits per word (address-

Octal numbers and their decimal
equivalents

Octal Number	Decimal Form	
47	$4 \times 8 + 7 \times 1$	or 39
312	$3 \times 64 + 1 \times 8 + 2 \times 1$	or 202
4057	$3 \times 512 + 0 \times 64 + 5 \times 8 + 7 \times 1$	or 1583

able unit of storage). When the binary value of a word is printed by their machines, it is usually shown in octal. Thus, instead of printing 60 binary symbols like

111111111111111111111111111111111111111111111111111111111111

they print the octal number 7777777777. Such a number is much easier for humans to understand and manipulate.

Sometimes computers print a *dump* at the end of a run that terminated abnormally. This dump shows the values in certain critical areas of main memory. The values in these critical areas will be in binary, but the computer will print them in octal so that they will be easier for humans to understand.

Some computers, such as IBM machines, have 32 bits per word. In this case, the octal number system cannot readily be used to abbreviate the stored values, because 32 bits cannot be broken into groups of three. Instead, the word is divided into eight groups of 4 bits. This division presents a problem, however.

Four bits can represent the decimal values 0 through 15. To abbreviate 4 bits using one character we need 16 symbols. We can use the symbols 0 through 9 to represent the first 10 numbers, but we need other symbols to represent the last 6. Figure B-8 shows how this representation is done. We have chosen other symbols (letters) that have an implied order.

The binary values 0 through 1001 are represented by the decimal characters 0 through 9. The binary value 1010 equals decimal 10. However, we need a single symbol to represent 1010. Hence we use the letter A. Letter B represents 1011, C represents 1100, and so forth.

This scheme creates a number system with 16 symbols: 0 through 9 and A through F. It is called the *hexadecimal* number system. The places in this system are powers of 16. There is the ones place, the sixteens place, the 256's place, the 4096's place, and so forth, increasing by powers of 16. As shown in figure B-9, the hexadecimal number A14E represents 10 times 4096, plus 1 times 256, plus 4 times 16, plus 14, or 41,294 in decimal.

On computers that have 16- or 32-bit words, the dumps and other binary printouts are produced in hexadecimal. To convert from hexadecimal to binary,

Binary Number	Hexadecimal Equivalent	Binary Number	Hexadecimal Equivalent
0000	0	1000	8
0001	1	1001	9
0010	2	1010	A
0011	3	1011	B
0100	4	1100	C
0101	5	1101	D
0110	6	1110	E
0111	7	1111	F

Binary numbers and their hexadecimal equivalents

Hexadecimal Number	Decimal Form		
79	$7 \times 16 + 9 \times 1$	or	121
E4	$14 \times 16 + 4 \times 1$	or	228
A1C	$10 \times 256 + 1 \times 16 + 12 \times 1$	or	2588
A14E	$10 \times 4096 + 1 \times 256 + 4 \times 16 + 14 \times 1$	or	41,294
1F7C8	$1 \times 65,536 + 15 \times 4096 + 7 \times 256 + 12 \times 16 + 8 \times 1$	or	128,968

FIGURE B-9

Hexadecimal numbers and their decimal
equivalents

just substitute the bit pattern for each character from figure B-8. Thus, A14E in hexadecimal represents 1010000101001110 in binary.

So far, we have discussed four number systems. Decimal numbers are traditionally used by people. Binary numbers are used by computers, mostly because the binary symbols 0 and 1 are easy to represent electronically. However, it is hard for people to work with binary numbers. Therefore, binary numbers are sometimes abbreviated using either octal or hexadecimal numbers.

CONVERSIONS BETWEEN NUMBER SYSTEMS

Sometimes people and computers need to convert a number from one system to another. For example, we may need to know what the hexadecimal number A1A equals in decimal. We may also need to know what the decimal number 789 equals in octal, and so forth.

It is easy to convert from binary, octal, or hexadecimal to decimal. In fact, we have already seen how. Just multiply each symbol by its place value. In binary the place values are powers of 2, in octal they are powers of 8, and in hexadecimal they are powers of 16.

It is also easy to convert from binary to octal or from binary to hexadecimal. Just use the table in figure B-6 or in figure B-8. To convert from decimal to binary, to octal, or to hexadecimal is not so easy, however.

Such conversions can be done by the *division/remainder method*. This method uses successive divisions by the base number. For example, to convert decimal to binary, the decimal number is successively divided by 2. To convert from decimal to octal, the decimal number is successively divided by 8. As the divisions are done, the remainders are saved; they become the transformed number.

Examine figure B-10. Three conversions are shown. In the first, the decimal number 37 is converted to binary. 37 is repeatedly divided by 2 until the quotient is 0. As the division is done, the remainders are written on the right-hand side. The equivalent binary number is read from these remainders, from the bottom up. Thus, 37 in decimal equals 100101 in binary.

In the second example, the decimal number 92 is converted to octal. 92 is repeatedly divided by 8 until no whole division is possible. Then the number

Division *Remainder*

2 | 37
          1

2 | 18
          0

2 | 9
          1

2 | 4
          0

2 | 2
          0

2 | 1
          1

Answer: 100101 binary

a. Decimal 37 Converted to Binary

Division *Remainder*

8 | 92
          4

8 | 11
          3

8 | 1
          1

Answer: 134 octal

b. Decimal 92 Converted to Octal

Division *Remainder*

16 | 489
          9

16 | 30
          E

16 | 1
          1

Answer: 1E9 hexadecimal

c. Decimal 489 Converted to Hexadecimal

FIGURE B-10

Decimal to binary, octal, and
hexadecimal conversions

is read from the remainders. 92 decimal equals 134 octal. Finally, 489 is converted to hexadecimal. Again, 489 is repeatedly divided by 16 until no whole division is possible. The remainders are kept on the right-hand side. Note that the remainder of 14 is represented by the hexadecimal symbol E and not by 14. 489 in decimal equals 1E9 in hexadecimal. In practice, such conversions are done by special hand calculators.

FLOATING-POINT NUMBERS

The binary format just described is only one of the ways that computers represent arithmetic numbers. Another format is called *floating point*. This term is used because the decimal point of the number is allowed to move, or float. The same form can represent 0.45 or 4500. The advantage of this form is its flexibility. It can represent very large and very small numbers, as well as fractions.

Floating-point numbers are represented in *exponential* or *scientific form*. The decimal number 1257 is represented in exponential form as 0.1257 times 10^4. This notation means that 1257 equals 0.1257 times 10,000 ($0.1257 \times 10 \times 10 \times 10 \times 10$). Numbers from other number systems can be represented similarly. Thus, the binary number 1011 equals 0.1011 times 2^4 ($0.1011 \times 2 \times 2 \times 2 \times 2$). Similarly, the octal number 765 equals 0.765 times 512 ($0.765 \times 8 \times 8 \times 8$).

In each of these cases, the fractional number is called the *mantissa* and the power of the base is called the *exponent*. The mantissa of 0.1257 times 10^4 is 0.1257 and the exponent is 4.

Scientific notation can represent fractions as well as whole numbers. The decimal number 0.0123 is 0.123 times 10^{-1}. The number 0.000345 is 0.345 times 10^{-3}. In this latter case, the mantissa is 0.345 and the exponent is -3.

Floating-point numbers use exponential notation. Each computer word has two sections. One section holds the exponent, and the other holds the mantissa. On IBM computers, for example, the first 8 bits of a word hold the exponent (a power of 16), and the remaining 24 bits hold the mantissa (see figure B-11).

On Control Data computers (CDC), the first 12 bits hold the exponent (a power of 8), and the remaining 48 bits hold the mantissa. Because more bits are used to represent the mantissa on CDC computers than on IBM computers, greater precision is possible. The mantissa can have a larger number of characters.

Both the mantissa and the exponent have a sign. The sign of the mantissa indicates whether the number is positive or negative. The sign of the exponent indicates whether the number is greater or less than 1.

The particular method of representing floating-point numbers is beyond the scope of this book. You should know that they exist and that they are represented in a special way in the computer. You should also be aware that, because of the special format, extra instructions (and time) are required to process floating-point numbers.

Some small computers have only one type of number. Some microcomputers have only integer numbers and integer instructions. Others have only floating-point numbers and instructions. If you purchase one of these computers, you should make sure that it has floating-point capability if you need it. Otherwise, you will have to program your own floating-point capability, and that is a chore.

Fractions and Round-off Error

Fractions can be represented in two ways. The first is floating-point format, as just described. The second way is *fixed-point binary format*. For this format, numbers are represented in binary, but a binary point is assumed to exist. For example, a binary point could be defined as being to the left of the third bit in a word. Then the binary number 110111 would be interpreted as 110.111. See

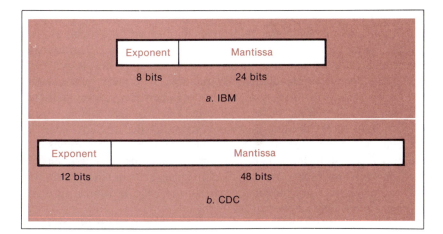

figure B-12 for other examples. When using this format, the program defines where it wants the point to be, and all operations are based on that definition. Note that in this case the binary point cannot float; every number has the same number of places to the right of the point.

There is a curious fact about fractions. A fraction that can be represented exactly in one number system may not be representable exactly in another. For example, the decimal fraction 0.1 cannot be evenly represented in hexadecimal (or binary). It is slightly more than hexadecimal 0.199.

The fact that 0.1 cannot be evenly represented in binary is very important in business. The dollar value $12.10 does not have an even representation. More important, the value $1.1 trillion does not have an even representation either!

Assume that you ask the computer to sum the value $0.01 one hundred times. If 0.01 is represented in binary, you may not get $1.00. Instead you may get $0.99999999999999. This problem, called *round-off error*, can be inconvenient and embarrassing to computer personnel. Sometimes it looks like the computer can't add.

Fixed-Point Format	Binary Number	Is Interpreted As
XXX.XX	11101	111.01
	10011	100.11
	10001	100.01
X.XXXX	11101	1.1101
	10011	1.0011
	10001	1.0001
.XXXXX	11101	.11101
	10011	.10011
	10001	.10001

Because of this problem (and for other reasons as well), some computers have the ability to perform arithmetic in decimal. In this case, the inputs are never converted to binary, and the round-off error does not occur. Unfortunately, decimal arithmetic is slower than binary arithmetic. Therefore, decimal arithmetic is only done when calculations are minimal. In business, such a situation often occurs. Many business systems need only perform simple additions or multiplications. Therefore, the decimal form of data is often used in business.

Figure B-13 shows decimal digits represented in the EBCDIC code. Two "hex" characters are used to represent each decimal. F1 represents 1, F2 represents 2, and so forth. Note how inefficient this scheme is. Two hex characters, or 8 bits, are needed for each decimal character. In binary form, these 8 bits can represent all of the numbers from 0 to 255. In decimal form, they can represent only the numbers from 0 to 9.

Using the code shown in figure B-13, the decimal number 287 is represented F2F8F7. Other examples are shown in figure B-14. This format is sometimes called *unpacked* (or *zoned*) *decimal form*.

In figure B-13, the first hex character for each of the digits is F. To reduce the storage taken by decimal numbers, all but one of the F's can be removed. This is called *packed decimal form*. Thus, in figure B-14, the decimal number 287, which has unpacked decimal notation F2F8F7, has the packed decimal notation 287F. All but one of the F's has been removed. The remaining F is put at the end of the number.

In many applications, numbers must have signs. They can be positive or negative. In packed decimal notation, the last hex position is used to denote a sign. This format is called *signed decimal form*. If there is a hex C in the last character, the number is positive. If the last character is a D, the number is negative. Thus, 287C represents + 287, and 287D represents − 287. The notation 287F is still valid. It just means the number 287 is unsigned. Figure B-14 has other examples.

QUESTIONS

B.1 Which of the following are valid binary numbers?
- **a.** 1101
- **b.** 1200
- **c.** 9812
- **d.** 0000

FIGURE B-13

EBCDIC code representation for decimal numbers

Decimal Number	EBCDIC Code (Hexadecimal)	Decimal Number	EBCDIC Code (Hexadecimal)
0	F0	5	F5
1	F1	6	F6
2	F2	7	F7
3	F3	8	F8
4	F4	9	F9

Decimal Number	Decimal Form		
	Unpacked	*Packed*	*Signed*
287	F2F8F7	287F	287C (+287)
			287D (−287)
1492	F1F4F9F2	1492F	1492C (+1492)
			1492D (−1492)
77	F7F7	77F	77C (+77)
			77D (−77)

B.2 Decimal places have values of ones, tens, hundreds, and so forth.
   a. What are the values of binary places?
   b. What are the values of octal places?
   c. What are the values of hexadecimal places?

B.3 Add the following binary numbers:
   a. 110 + 001
   b. 110001 + 001110
   c. 111111 + 0000001
   d. 11101 + 00011

B.4 How do most computers perform subtraction?

B.5 Do the following subtractions using complements:
   a. 9 − 4 (decimal numbers)
   b. 1101 − 0001 (binary numbers)
   c. 1111 − 0101 (binary)
   d. 4 − 9 (decimal)
   e. 0011 − 0100 (binary)

B.6 What are octal numbers used for?

B.7 Convert the following numbers to decimal:
   a. 1101 binary
   b. 1110101 binary
   c. 453 octal
   d. 7671 octal
   e. A21 hexadecimal
   f. ABC hexadecimal

B.8 What are hexadecimal numbers used for?

B.9 Convert the following numbers to binary
   a. 789 decimal
   b. 1234 decimal
   c. 643 octal
   d. 77777 octal
   e. CE4 hexadecimal
   f. FEBCAD hexadecimal

B.10 What causes round-off error? Why is it important in business?

B.11 How can round-off error be eliminated?

B.12 Show the unpacked and packed decimal forms of the following numbers:
  a. 12345
  b. 484930
  c. 23
  d. 1

B.13 Show the signed decimal form of the following numbers:
  a. −19
  b. 7345
  c. −78965
  d. 0

SUMMARY

Computers represent two types of data: numeric and alphanumeric. This section has described the representation and processing of numeric data. The binary number system is most often used to represent numeric data. In binary there are only two symbols, 0 and 1. In decimal the place values of a number are ones, tens, hundreds, thousands, and so forth. In binary they are ones, twos, fours, eights, sixteens, and so forth.

Binary numbers are added just like decimal numbers are. However, instead of carrying when the sum of two numbers exceeds 9, we carry when the sum exceeds 1. Subtraction is usually done by computers in complement form. The complement of the number to be subtracted is added to determine the answer.

Two other number systems are used to abbreviate binary numbers. The octal number system has eight symbols; each octal symbol represents 3 bits. The hexadecimal number system has 16 symbols; each hex symbol represents 4 bits. Octal is used when the computer's word size is a multiple of 3 bits. Hexadecimal is used when the word size is a multiple of 4 bits.

Floating-point numbers allow the decimal point to shift. They represent both very large and very small numbers. They can also represent fractions. In addition to floating-point form, fractions can be represented by fixed-point binary. Here, a fixed location of the binary point is assumed.

Decimal fractions are not necessarily represented evenly in binary. For example, 0.1 does not have an even representation in binary. This means that computers can make round-off errors. To eliminate this problem, some computers can perform decimal arithmetic. In this case, numbers are not converted to binary. Arithmetic is done in decimal form. Data is carried in packed decimal format.

WORD LIST

(in order of appearance in text)

Numeric data		Complement addition
Alphanumeric data		Tens complement
Bit		Twos complement

Octal number system
Dump
Hexadecimal number system
Division/remainder method
Floating-point number
Exponential form
Scientific form

Mantissa
Exponent
Fixed-point number
Round-off error
Unpacked decimal format
Packed decimal format
Signed decimal format

MODULE C

Computer Crime, Security, and Control

Harold Johnson applied for a systems analysis/programming job at Modern Record Distributing Company (MODREC). Harold was young, only 25, but he had an impressive background. He had major responsibility in the development of three different computer systems at his prior place of employment. His reason for leaving was that he believed the major challenges were over, and he wanted something new.

In fact, Harold was very bright and eager for new opportunities to apply his problem-solving skills. He was highly motivated and willing to spend long hours solving difficult problems. Furthermore, he was courageous and would stand up to anybody when his ideas were disputed. He was also creative and adventuresome, and he enjoyed challenges posed by people. In short, he had all the skills and traits needed to be a superior systems developer.

MODREC was a spin-off company. At one time, it was a division of a large, traditional record manufacturer. The separate company was created when MODREC's sales exceeded $5 million, and the directors of the parent company thought it made sense to form a subsidiary. MODREC specialized in distributing rock music of interest to people under 30.

MODREC's first president was the son of one of the parent company's directors. He was promoted into his position through influence and not ability. Consequently, MODREC sales began to slip, personnel morale fell, and MODREC lost many opportunities.

MODREC's small data processing department was managed by the chief accountant. The accountant meant well, but he was very uneducated about data processing. When Harold Johnson applied for the systems analysis/programming job, the chief accountant was delighted. He made Harold an excellent offer, and Harold came to work.

In his first year, Harold made many contributions to the data processing department. There was a vast improvement in the level of service. Sales people were given better information about their customers. The time it took to deliver an order was cut in half. Sales went up. Further, the accounting systems were improved, and the chief accountant had better information than ever.

Unfortunately, Harold began to feel discontented. Nobody paid attention to him. He felt that no one recognized the contributions he made. He probably would have gone to another company, but, after a year, MODREC gave him a substantial pay increase. He thought that he would have trouble earning as much money elsewhere.

As Harold worked with the accounting systems, he began to notice MODREC'S large profits. These profits were possible in spite of ineffective management, because MODREC had a very large markup. Harold concluded that MODREC was ripping off their customers.

One day, Harold mentioned this notion to Joan Everest, the manager of a neighborhood record store that ordered from MODREC (see figure C-1).

"Harold," said Joan, almost in jest, "why don't you reprogram one

FIGURE C-1

Harold and Joan plotting a computer crime

of those computers to offer special discounts to my store? Perhaps I could share the savings with you."

Harold was never quite the same. He was bored at work, and the technical challenge of programming such special discounts excited him. Additionally, he was angry with the way MODREC had treated him, and he believed that it was unfair for them to make so much profit. Joan needed the financial help, and MODREC could easily afford to lose $40,000 to $50,000 per year. In some ways he felt he was playing a game of Robin Hood—stealing from the rich and giving to the poor.

Once Harold decided to cooperate, the technical aspects were easy. In fact, Harold was disappointed at the lack of challenge. He changed the pricing program to look for Joan's customer number and to reduce her prices by 85 percent. He was the only one to see the special copy of the program. The unchanged version was kept in the program documentation library for appearances.

Harold Johnson is a typical computer criminal. In addition, he was caught. We will explain how as this module progresses.

Consultant Profiles
Typical Computer Felon

DEDHAM, Mass.—A computer felon is usually between the ages of 18 and 40, male—and a nice guy.

According to the U.S. Justice and Treasury Departments' profile of a computer felon, he is also aggressive, trusted, has no prior criminal record and usually works alone, consultant John R. Maples told a recent Northeastern University seminar on "Industrial Espionage in High Technology" here.

Maples, who is senior vice-president of operations and training for Special Security International Corp. of Roanoke, Va., spoke about computer security from the corporate security director's point of view.

Background Check
Because the computer felon often cracks the computer system out of financial need, Maples suggested that a thorough background check be performed on all data processing professionals, including a check on their credit rating.

He identified four ways in which the computer felon is likely to strike:

● Physically. "This ranges from actual vandalism and damage to equipment, to information destruction, falsified entry and fraudulent use of data." As an example, Maples pointed to a group of New York high school students who used a classroom terminal to dial into a Canadian corporate data system.

● Transactionally, by tapping into a computer system under the auspices of a legitimate user, usually to divert funds electronically.

● Via programming, by altering a computer program to gain computer time or data or to divert funds. Maples cited the recent theft of $21.3 million from the Wells Fargo bank engineered by two bank employees and a sports promoter.

● Electronically. "This ranges from illegal use of a personal computer system to access classified data of a business to wiretapping of communication lines to obtain proprietary information or divert funds."

There are times when a company should fear not only individual criminals, but competing companies. "People think that only product information is in danger, but so is marketing and personnel information," Maples explained to the attendees at the seminar.

Maples gave the example of one DP professional who printed out employees' resumes for sale to a headhunter.

Leaving software security to DP professionals, Maples suggested that hardware can be secured best by a multilevel system—posting obstacles outside the building, outside the computer room and at the equipment itself.

"Card-key security is probably the best thing going today," Maples said, pointing out that the more expensive fingerprint identification system has roughly a 6% error rate in both preventing authorized personnel from entering the computer room and allowing unauthorized personnel into that area.

By JIM BARTIMO
Computerworld, March 7, 1983

WHAT IS COMPUTER CRIME?

No one knows for sure how many computer crimes have occurred or what the total losses have been. Computer crime statistics are difficult to obtain and most sources claim their statistics are unreliable. In *Crime by Computer*, Donn Parker estimates that $300 million is lost per year through computer crime. He

Former Students Indicted for Altering Grades

JAMAICA, N.Y.—Two former Queens College students—one who had been employed at the school's DP center—were indicted last month on charges of falsifying a total of 154 grades in the computerized records of 19 different students. The alterations allegedly took place from 1974 to 1977, with some students reportedly paying hundreds of dollars for the revised grades.

James Chin, 35, and Tom Tang, 26, voluntarily surrendered to New York police on the day the indictments were announced. At their arraignment later that day, both Chin and Tang plead not guilty.

Both were freed without bail since neither had any prior arrests and since they had voluntarily surrendered. The hearing was adjourned to Jan. 15, when a trial date may be set, according to a spokeswoman for the district attorney's office.

Queens District Attorney J.

Santucci said the indictments of Chin and Tang resulted from an investigation begun last spring by his office's Rackets Bureau and his detective squad, with the assistance of the city Department of Investigation, the Board of Higher Education's Office of General Counsel and the administration of Queens College.

Chin, formerly Queens College's senior computer operator, is employed by Printronics Corp. of America in New York. He was indicted on one count of falsifying business records, first degree; one count of bribe receiving, second degree; two counts of receiving a reward for official misconduct, second degree; and one count of violating a state education law section dealing with unlawful acts in respect to examinations.

Tang, a salesman for Burroughs Corp. in Warrendale Heights, Ohio, was not employed at the college during the period of his alleged crime, but was a student. He has

been indicted on one count of falsifying business records, first degree.

The Chin indictment charges him with 131 grade falsifications on the computer records of 15 students, including himself, and with receiving approximately $300 from one student for whom he falsified 22 grades and $100 from another for whom he falsified 11 grades.

The Tang indictment charges him with arranging for the falsification of 23 grades on the computer records of four students, including himself. Tang did not accept money for his part in the falsifications, according to the spokesman for the district attorney's office, and the 23 grade changes he is charged with arranging are separate from the 131 grade changes allegedly made by Chin. If convicted, Chin could receive a sentence of up to seven years in jail and Tang could get a four-year sentence.

By MARGUERITE ZIENTARA
Computerworld

estimates the average loss per crime at $450,000. Compare this to the $10,000 that is typically lost in a full-service bank robbery, or the $19,000 that is lost in the average conventional bank embezzlement.

Figure C-2 presents computer crime data published by the Bureau of Justice Statistics [73]. From 1958, the year of the first reported computer crime, to 1979, a total of 669 cases were reported. In many of those cases, the amount of the loss was undetermined (companies are reluctant to state their losses). The average of the known losses was $1.685 million per crime.

There are many stories of computer crimes. (See the "Profiles" in this module.) Some seem downright ludicrous. It's hard to tell what's fact and what's fable. The following three cases, however, have been well documented.

Year	Total Cases	Total Known Losses	Average Known Loss
1958	1		
1959	1	$ 278	$ 278
1962	2		
1963	2	2,081	1,040
1964	6	2,600	1,300
1965	8	126	63
1966	3	28	9
1967	4	10	5
1968	12	12,454	2,075
1969	20	3,011	376
1970	38	19,353	967
1971	59	16,137	849
1972	73	14,524	518
1973	75	233,066	6,474
1974	73	8,162	247
1975	84	98,312	2,006
1976	59	52,601	1,461
1977	87	67,853	1,330
1978	42	15,207	633
1979	20	200	200
Totals	669	$546,001	$1,685

FIGURE C-2

Computer crime statistics

(Losses in thousands of dollars)
Source: *Criminal Justice Resource Manual*

Pacific Telephone

Jerry Schneider was a child prodigy who developed his own telecommunication system at the age of 10. By the time he was in high school, he had started his own electronics company. While he was a part-time college student, he found a way to steal electronic equipment from the Pacific Telephone Company. He used a terminal in his home to order parts without being charged for them. He learned the correct account numbers, passwords, and procedures by taking old computer printouts and other documentation from a telephone company trash container.

He had expensive telephone components delivered to his home and other locations. He got bored with the project and, to add more excitement, had the company deliver a $25,000 switchboard to a manhole cover at the intersection of two streets. The company delivered and he picked up the switchboard in the telephone truck that he had bought at a telephone company surplus auction.

Much of the equipment that he stole in this way he resold to Pacific Telephone. In fact, he used their own information system to determine what they were low on so he would then know what to steal.

Schneider was caught when one of his own employees informed on him. The employee wanted a pay raise, and Jerry refused. When he was apprehended, Pacific Telephone refused to believe that he had stolen as much inventory as he claimed. He said he had stolen $800,000 to $900,000 worth; they said $70,000.

Crime Expert Foresees DP-Aided Murder

SAN JOSE, Calif.—Computers have already been involved in a wide assortment of crimes including fraud, theft and espionage. Someday they might even be used to commit murder, according to computer security expert Donn B. Parker.

In fact, the first known computer-aided murder attempt may have already taken place, Parker said last week at the Hewlett-Packard Co. (HP) General Systems Users Group meeting here.

The suspected murder attempt occurred only about a month ago when the air traffic control system at New York's Kennedy International Airport suspiciously malfunctioned and nearly caused a mid-air collision involving an airliner carrying Soviet Ambassador Anatoly Dobrynin.

No one was harmed during the incident, but Parker plans to investigate the equipment failure anyway to find out whether it resulted from human tampering, as some observers have speculated.

Appearing at the HP users group meeting as keynote speaker, Parker voiced fears that the traditional traffickers in computer crime will soon be joined by much more dangerous practitioners, especially organized groups like hostile foreign powers, the Mafia and international terrorist bands. Computers are rapidly replacing bank vaults as the preferred method of "storing" money, and as the world traffic in electronic "cash" steadily grows, so does the threat that it will one day become the target of large, unscrupulous organizations with a vast capacity to cause harm.

By JEFFRY BEELER
Computerworld West Coast Bureau

Another famous computer crime concerned the Penn Central Railroad. In the early 1970s, someone modified a freight flow system to send boxcars to a small railroad company outside Chicago. There, the boxcars disappeared! Apparently, they were repainted and sold to or used by other railroads. Estimates vary, but somewhere in the vicinity of 400 boxcars disappeared. Somehow, the computer system was modified so that it would not notice that railroad cars were missing.

The Penn Central case is mysterious. Although a Philadelphia grand jury was convened to investigate the case, and although some stolen boxcars were found, Penn Central refused to acknowledge the affair. For some reason, it was in Penn Central's interest to minimize attention to the crime. No criminal action was ever taken. There were rumors that organized crime was involved.

Penn Central Railroad

A third famous case occurred in 1973. This large fraud involved the Equity Funding Corporation. Over 20 people were convicted on federal charges. Estimates of loss are as high as $2 *billion*.

Equity Funding was a conglomerate of companies that specialized in investments and insurance. Top-level management distorted the company's financial situation to lure investors. They also created artificial insurance policies.

Although the media described this crime as a modern computer fraud, there is some debate about whether it can be blamed on the computer. Most of the criminal activity did not involve the computer. All of the phony accounting was done manually.

Equity Funding Corporation

The Equity Funding case is very complex. Over 50 major lawsuits were filed. Basically, the fraud was accomplished by inflating the company's reported income. This misrepresentation was done in two ways. First, the company's officers declared income and assets that didn't exist, simply by writing them into financial statements. The firm's auditors have been severely criticized for not detecting this activity.

The second way income was inflated did involve the computer. Massive numbers of phony documents were generated by a computer system. These documents were supposed to be valid insurance policies. In fact, they were computer fabrications. The phony policies were sold to other insurance companies for cash.

In retrospect, it is amazing that these documents were accepted at face value. The system was audited, but it was designed to print only valid policies at the times audits were being done. Further, insurance industry personnel believed in computer-generated documents. It didn't occur to them that the computer could produce phony data.

Types of Computer Crime

These three short stories represent only a few of the ingenious ways that people have found to commit crimes with computer help. Most computer crimes fall into one of the five categories shown in figure C-3. Sometimes, the *input to the computer is manipulated*, as was done in the Pacific Telephone case. Other crimes are perpetrated by *changing computer programs*, as Harold Johnson did.

A third type of computer crime is to *steal data*. Such data might be the names and addresses of a company's customers. It might be proprietary designs or plans. Fourth, *computer time can be stolen*. The criminal either uses the time or sells it to others who may not be aware that the time is stolen. For example, a computer communications system may be used to transmit unauthorized data. In one case, a company's message-switching system was used daily to broadcast racing results.

Finally, *computer programs can be stolen*. Computer programs are very expensive and time consuming to produce. They can give a company a competitive edge in its marketplace. Therefore, stealing programs is a criminal act.

The theft of computer data and computer programs is very hard to detect. It can be done simply by copying the computer files having the data or programs. Since the original copy is not missing, companies have difficulty knowing a crime was even committed.

FIGURE C-3

Types of computer crime

Type of Crime
Manipulating computer input
Changing computer programs
Stealing data
Stealing computer time
Stealing computer programs

Many computer crime experts think the cases we know about are only the tip of the iceberg. Some companies have been victims of crimes and have not acknowledged it. They wanted to avoid adverse publicity. A bank that lost money by computer crime would not want its customers to know it. Further, businesses do not want to advertise their vulnerability. They may not know how to prevent similar crimes in the future, and they certainly do not want the crime advertised in the newspapers. Therefore, they do not prosecute.

For this reason, computer criminals are often not penalized. Further, when they are, they typically receive light sentences. Jerry Schneider spent only 40 days in jail and lost just $8500 in a court battle.

Figure C-4 shows 12 warning signals indicating that the potential for computer crime exists. These signals are characteristics of companies in which crimes have occurred. Let's hope that, in the course of your business career, you will not work for a company that demonstrates many of these signs. However, if you do, you should be aware of the possibility of computer crime.

Most of the characteristics listed in figure C-4 indicate poor data processing management. Except for the items concerning audits, every one of these characteristics is a violation of a principle discussed in this course. Thus, good data processing management is needed to build and use systems that are less susceptible to computer crime.

PREVENTING COMPUTER CRIME

Unfortunately, there is no such thing as a completely secure data processing installation. First, computer manufacturers do not provide completely secure computers. An ingenious programmer can find a way to modify the operating system. Once such a modification is made, computer security features like passwords and account numbers are ineffective.

Second, many, if not most, data processing departments are so busy just keeping up with their business and the changes in computer technology that

1. The computer seems to run the company; management just reacts.
2. Management expects computers to solve major existing problems.
3. Management does not (cannot) communicate with the EDP staff.
4. Users are told how their systems will be designed.
5. There are no documented standards for the development of new applications or the maintenance of existing ones.
6. Technical management is actively involved in programming and troubleshooting.
7. Programmers are uncontrolled; they can do what they want with the computer.
8. EDP staff has easy access to data and to program libraries.
9. Errors occur so frequently that adequate investigation is not possible.
10. Auditors treat the computer like a mysterious black box.
11. Management fails to implement audit recommendations.
12. No EDP audits are performed.

FIGURE C-4

Signals indicating potential for computer crime

Throwing the Book at Industrial Spies

On the morning of Saturday, Sept. 4, Martin A. Alpert drove to the Sheraton hotel at Cleveland's Hopkins International Airport. As the businessman walked into the room of William W. Erdman, he felt uncomfortable about the concealed tape recorder he was carrying. But his uneasiness apparently went unnoticed by Erdman, who introduced his two associates. The three men then explained to Alpert—as his tape recorder captured the entire meeting—how they could provide him with the secret designs of a new computer.

The episode sounds like an excerpt from a spy thriller, but it is actually reconstructed from the civil lawsuit and affidavits that International Business Machines Corp. filed on Sept. 14, claiming Erdman and his associates—all IBM employees—stole its trade secrets. In June, IBM had cooperated with the Federal Bureau of Investigation in an elaborate "sting" operation that snared 18 Japanese businessmen for allegedly stealing its trade secrets. Through

such daring undercover work, determined litigation, and uncharacteristic publicity, IBM has apparently declared open season on those employees and competitors who it believes are stealing its secrets. "We will do whatever we must to protect our company's assets," declares John R. Opel, IBM's president.

A Spate of Lawsuits

The computer giant is calling attention, in the process, to a snowballing security problem that is plaguing the entire information processing industry. "IBM has the best security in the industry," notes Robert T. Fertig, president of Enterprise Information Systems Inc., a Greenwich (Conn.) industry analyst. So, he comments, "if IBM is having a few leaks and problems, you can imagine the problems the others are having." Agrees Chester E. Martine Jr., patent counsel for Storage Technology Corp.: "There's no doubt that in the industry, these trade-secrets lawsuits are increasing." In July, STC settled a

case in which it had sued 13 former employees for misusing proprietary information when they helped form Ibis Systems Inc., a computer memory systems manufacturer in Duarte, Calif.

Having former employees arrested or charging competitors with theft of trade secrets is nothing new. But "most often, cases are settled out of court because of the huge expense of litigating them," says James H. Pooley, a California attorney and author of a recently published book, *Trade Secrets*. IBM, however, is apparently abandoning this stance. Instead of quietly firing Erdman, an IBM executive, and IBM engineers Lewis C. Eggebrecht and Peter J. Stearns for allegedly stealing secrets concerning IBM's popular Personal Computer—and offering to sell them to Alpert, president of Tecmar Inc., a Cleveland manufacturer of attachments for the IBM computer—IBM took them to court. And the company announced the lawsuits to the press in the same way it would a new product.
Business Week, October 4, 1982

they do not find the time to consider computer security adequately. Inputs to the computer are not as well controlled as they should be. Outputs are not checked for accuracy and completeness. Furthermore, security issues are often superficially considered when systems are designed or when programs are written. Most companies have the attitude that computer crime "won't happen here."

Finally, effective security can be costly. It takes time and resources to build a secure system. Additionally, the system may be more expensive to operate because of security features. If a user must spend half of each working day to verify outputs, then, in a year, half of the person's salary is spent for security. Good security on the computer will also mean that programs operate more slowly. More instructions must be processed for security functions. Thus, more computer power will be required.

Most companies must strike a balance between no security at all and as near perfect security as possible. How much security is needed depends on the potential loss and the level of threat. An accounts payable system probably needs more security than a system that produces company telephone lists.

In *Crime by Computer*, Parker reports a surprising and distressing fact. Most computer crimes are caught by accident. In some cases, the computer failed and irregularities were discovered while someone was fixing it. In other cases, people consistently spent more money than they were earning, and the source of the additional money was traced back to a computer system. The IRS has caught some of these people for not paying taxes on their criminal earnings. In other cases, the FBI caught them in illegal gambling activities.

The distressing part of this statement is that few crimes are caught as a result of controls in the computer system. Apparently, few systems provide protection against computer crime. However, this vulnerability need not exist; systems can be designed to thwart unauthorized activity. We will see how in the next section.

COMPUTER AUDITING AND CONTROLS

The American Institute of Certified Public Accountants has recognized the possibility of computer crime or other unauthorized activity. This organization has issued an official statement (called SAS-3) directing CPAs to pay special attention to computer systems. As a result of this statement, auditors are paying more and more attention to data processing departments and personnel.

Further, groups of auditors and data processing personnel have worked together to develop recommended procedures or *controls* over data processing operations. In the remainder of this module, we will discuss these controls. To show the usefulness of them, we will relate each control to the MODREC case introduced at the start of this module.

The term *EDP controls* originated with the accountants and auditors. *EDP* is an accounting term that means *electronic data processing*. EDP controls are features of any of the five components of a computer system that reduce the likelihood of unauthorized activity. Figure C-5 summarizes the basic categories of EDP controls.

Management
Organizational
Data center resource
Input/processing/output
Data administration
Systems development

FIGURE C-5

Categories of EDP controls

371

Harold Johnson was dissatisfied with the management at MODREC. He felt underappreciated. Because his boss was only the chief accountant, Harold was buried in the finance department. Consequently, neither he nor anyone else in data processing had access to top management.

Top management did not have access to Harold or data

processing, either. They knew little of what he was doing, and they had only a limited idea of how data processing operated. They spent considerable money on data processing operations, but they did not know how the money was spent. In short, there was a large gulf between top-level management and data processing.

Management Controls

Over the years, professionals have learned that management situations like the one at MODREC are an invitation to trouble. Senior management of a company should take an active part in the management of the data processing function. They do not have to be walking the machine floor, mounting tapes. However, they should recognize the importance of data processing to the company, and they should set the direction for, and be actively involved in, data processing plans.

It may seem surprising that this statement even needs to be made. However, in the past, too many managers have washed their hands of data processing. They have stayed as far away from the computer as possible. Perhaps they didn't understand computing; perhaps they were afraid of it; or perhaps the data processing personnel spoke in strange ways. In any event, data processing went its own way. In some cases (like Harold's), data processing personnel felt disassociated from the company. They felt rejected and unappreciated, and computer crime was the result.

Senior management can handle data processing in several ways. First, they can demonstrate an appreciation for and an interest in the data processing function. Occasional visits to the computer staff, recognition of them in the company newsletter, and references to data processing in the year-end report are examples of showing their interest.

Senior management can recognize data processing in another large and important way as well. They can place the data processing function high in the organizational structure. Instead of burying data processing somewhere in accounting or finance where none of the senior managers ever see or hear of it, they can make it a department on a par with other departments. Figure C-6 shows two ways that data processing can be raised from the company bilges to gain the attention it deserves.

Next, management can understand the company's vulnerability to computer crime. Once they do, they can communicate the importance of controls to the entire organization. As we will see, controls on the data processing function involve more than just the data processing department. To encourage other departments to cooperate, management needs to be very positive about the need for controls.

Another responsibility for management is to form a steering committee. As stated in chapter 4, such a committee controls data processing development

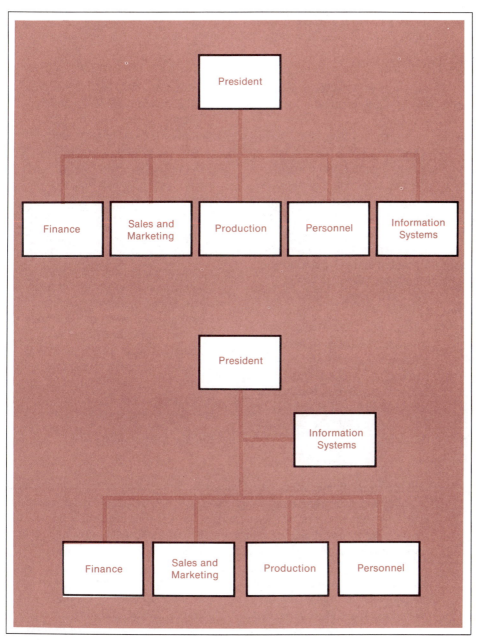

FIGURE C-6

Two organizational structures recognizing
the information systems department

efforts. Committee members receive reports about project status and provide
go/no go decisions as appropriate. Refer to chapter 4 for more information
about the steering committee.

Finally, management can take a role in data processing by requesting and
paying attention to periodic operations reports. Management should know how

373

well the computing resources are being used, how happy or unhappy the users are with the data processing function, and what the major data processing problems are. These reports increase the amount of communication between the data processing department and senior management. Management control responsibilities are summarized in figure C-7.

Harold Johnson had free access to the computer and all of its resources. When Harold needed a tape file to determine Joan's account number, he walked into the tape library and got it. When he wanted to obtain the pricing program, he instructed the computer to print a copy of it. After he made the changes, Harold put the changed program into the standard program library. No one checked Harold's authority to do these things.

Organizational Controls

Organizational controls concern the organizational structure of the company. We have already mentioned that data processing should be organizationally on a par with other functions of the company. In addition, the company should be structured so that there is separation of authorities and duties.

> 1. Data processing is placed at high organizational level.
> 2. Senior management demonstrates knowledge and good attitude toward data processing.
> 3. Data processing steering committee takes active role in DP.
> 4. Management requests and reviews periodic reports.

The MODREC case is a good example of what can happen when there is no separation. Data processing employees had unlimited access to the computer. MODREC should have at least two categories of data processing personnel: operations and development. These groups should provide checks and balances on each other. The operations group should control the equipment and the production program library. The development group should develop new programs in accordance with requirements. They should not have access to the tape library or to the production programs.

If this were the case, the authorities would be separated. Only the programmers could develop program changes, and only the operations department could change the production library. Further, making changes to the program library would require a supervisor's authorization.

Separating authorities and duties provides checks and balances in the system. In general, the more people and the more levels of management that are involved in authorizing and performing duties, the less susceptible the system is to unauthorized activity.

After Harold Johnson changed the pricing program to give Joan the special discounts, he wanted to test it. After all, he didn't want to make a mistake and give the discounts to the wrong customer. However, to test the change, he needed to mount the customer and price files on the tape drives. To avoid suspicion, Harold stayed at work after hours the next week. Since none of the managers paid any attention to data processing, they didn't ask what Harold was doing. In fact, nobody asked Harold what he was up to. Harold took his time, and after three short nights, he had fully tested his program. Not only was he sure it would work, he was also sure no one could trace the changes to him.

Data center resources must be controlled. Use of computer equipment should be restricted to authorized personnel. Processing should be controlled by schedules, and review of processing logs. Also, access to the computer must be controlled. Only authorized personnel should be allowed in the computer room. This restriction not only protects the equipment from damage, but also helps to ensure that outputs are delivered only to the right people. Furthermore, limiting access to the machine room reduces the level of chaos and helps eliminate operator errors.

Computer operations need to be controlled as well. Procedures and job schedules should be documented and followed. A supervisor should examine operations to ensure that the procedures are followed, and records of all com-

Data Center Resource Controls

DP Training Seen Leading Inmates to Computer Crime

NEW YORK—Federal agencies sometimes launch convicted felons on careers in computer crime by offering prison inmates DP training as well as access to income tax and other sensitive federal data banks, according to Sen. Abraham Ribicoff (D-Conn.).

The Senate investigation of federal computer security Ribicoff directed last year found the Bureau of Prisons training and then paying prison inmates to write computer programs for the U.S. Department of Agriculture.

In the process, some convicts learned to crack Internal Revenue Service (IRS) computer codes. They filed bogus tax returns and then received large tax refunds while serving penitentiary sentences, Ribicoff said last week in his Computer Expo '79 keynote address here.

One convict received a $25,000 IRS refund while doing a stretch at Leavenworth federal penitentiary. He was caught and convicted of tax fraud, Ribicoff said. The IRS knows of many similar cases and is "deeply concerned" about the extent of tax fraud behind prison walls, he added.

Training in Wrong Area

Many of the inmate DPers are serving sentences for white-collar crimes such as counterfeiting and securities violations, the senator said. One convict-programmer has been arrested 25 times and convicted of 14 felonies; he is still in his early 30s.

"It was not my committee's intention to question the very valid principle of rehabilitation for prisoners. But a man with 25 arrests and 14 felony convictions might be better taught to be an auto mechanic or [learn about] some other worthwhile trade that would not require him to be involved in sensitive financial transactions for the federal government," Ribicoff said.

by BRAD SCHULTZ
Computerworld Staff

---

puter activity need to be kept. These records should be reviewed. It should be very difficult for operators to deviate from the established schedule and procedures.

In addition to protecting computing resources during normal operations, plans and procedures are necessary to recover from problems. All files and libraries should be backed up by copies stored in secure, off-premise locations. Further, recovery procedures need to be well documented and the staff trained in the execution of them.

There should also be a disaster recovery plan that explains what to do in case of fire, flood, earthquake, or other disaster. The company should consider having backup hardware and programs available in other locations. The procedures and data necessary to use the hardware must be available in the backup location. Resource controls are summarized in figure C-8.

Harold Johnson did not have to modify program inputs. He found a way to provide special discounts by changing the processing. This process changed the outputs. If anyone had ever examined the invoices generated by the pricing program, they would have seen that something was amiss. Luckily for Harold, MODREC did not have a policy of examining outputs.

1. Access to computer center is controlled.
2. Operating procedures are documented.
3. Program libraries are secure.
4. Backup and recovery procedures exist.
5. There is protection from natural hazards.
6. There are documented emergency procedures.

F I G U R E   C - 8

Data center resource controls

Input, Processing, and Output Controls

In general, there should be controls over inputs, processing, and outputs. First, the authorized form of input data should be documented. The operations personnel should be trained not to accept improper input data. Second, data processing personnel should be trained not to make changes to input data. Such changes should be made by the system users.

Where appropriate, control totals should be used. For example, when the users send the weekly payroll to data processing, they should calculate (independently) the sum of the hours worked or a similar total. The payroll program should be written to calculate the total number of hours worked and to print this total on a summary report. The report should be examined by the payroll department after the payroll run to ensure that the manually prepared total and the computer-generated total match.

Similar totals can be kept on changes to master files, number of accounts payable checks to be issued, and so forth. Users must be trained to compute these totals and to treat them seriously. Often, they are the most important control in the computer system.

Inputs to teleprocessing applications are harder to control. A program can be coded to accept only certain inputs from certain users or certain locations. However, it is possible to fool such a program. Therefore, the use of terminals must be limited to certain individuals and to specified times. Further, the supervisors of these individuals need to be trained to review their subordinates' terminal activities.

There must also be controls over the processing of data. As stated earlier, all operations procedures should be documented and followed. The performance of the operators should be monitored periodically. The operations department should keep records of all errors and system failures. The corrections for each of these should be documented. These records should be reviewed periodically by data processing supervisory personnel to determine whether or not the failures are related to (or covers for) unauthorized activity. The records can also be used to determine whether or not there is a need for additional training, as well as to assess employee performance.

Finally, the outputs of all data processing activities should be controlled. Procedures for disseminating outputs should be documented and followed. Outputs should be given only to authorized users, and these users should examine the outputs for completeness and accuracy. Control totals produced by programs should be reconciled against input control totals.

Outputs from online systems are hard to control. Where data is changed on line, it can be very difficult to trace the sequence of activities. For example, a price might be changed several times and no written record generated. The absence of records can make the job of the auditor impossible. Consequently, online programs are often programmed to log transactions on computer tape. These logs are saved and used for error correction or for audits. Figure C-9 summarizes input, processing, and output controls.

Other EDP Controls

Some EDP controls are not oriented toward preventing criminal activity. Instead, their purpose is to encourage effective use of EDP systems. Data administration controls are one example. Controls over systems development are another. We will not discuss these controls in this module. They are important to systems designers and auditors, and, if you make either of these professions your career, you should learn more about them.

MODREC—THE REST OF THE STORY

Harold Johnson and Joan Everest were able to continue their crime for eighteen months. During that period, they obtained $150,000 worth of records for $22,500. The crime would have gone on longer, except for a change of management at MODREC.

A new president was hired, and he expected better performance from the entire company. As part of his improvement program, he required the sales force to increase sales. When one of the new sales managers reviewed the performance of the region containing Joan's store, he detected something suspicious. It seemed that the volume of sales should have netted larger income. He examined the sales invoices for the past year and saw what had been going on. He contacted the new president, and the game was up.

Harold was actually relieved. The strain of continuing the crime had begun to wear on him. Furthermore, he was frustrated. He liked to brag about his creations, and he wanted to tell his friends about the crime. He thought it was clever and he wanted credit for it.

MODREC threatened to sue for damages, but a settlement was made out of court. Harold and Joan paid MODREC $50,000, and Joan turned over a sizable part of her record inventory. Surprisingly, Harold had saved all but a few hundred dollars of the money Joan had paid him. He really didn't participate for the money.

Criminal action was taken. Since both Harold and Joan were first-time criminals, they received light sentences. Each spent 60 days in jail and was fined $5000.

QUESTIONS

C.1 How much money is lost due to computer crimes every year?

C.2 Describe five types of computer crime.

C.3 List 12 indications that an organization is vulnerable to computer crime.

C.4 How have most computer crimes been discovered?

C.5 What are EDP controls?

C.6 List the categories of EDP controls described in this module.

Category	Type of Control
Input	Documentation of authorized input format
	Separation of duties and authorities
	Verification of control totals
	Online system input controls
Processing	Documented operating procedures
	Reviews of processing logs
	Adequate program testing
Output	Documented output procedures
	Control over disposition of output
	Users trained to examine output

FIGURE C-9

Input/processing/output controls

C.7   Describe management controls.

C.8   Describe organizational controls.

C.9   Describe data center resource controls.

C.10   Describe input/processing/output controls.

SUMMARY

Computer crime is an important issue. Millions of dollars are lost each year. There are five types of computer crime: manipulating input, changing programs, stealing data, stealing computer time, and stealing programs.

The characteristics of companies that are vulnerable to computer crime are known. Most of these characteristics reflect bad data processing management and violate the principles of effective data processing discussed in this book.

In order to prevent crime, companies need to develop better controls within their computer systems. These controls fall into several areas: management, organizational, data center resources, input/processing/output, data administration, and systems development. EDP controls will not guarantee that crime is eliminated, but they will reduce the likelihood of crime.

WORD LIST
(in order of appearance in text)

Computer crime
EDP
EDP controls
Management controls
Organizational controls

Data center resource controls
Input/processing/output controls
Data administration
Data administration controls

QUESTIONS TO CHALLENGE YOUR THINKING

A.   What organizations or industries do you believe are particularly vulnerable to computer crime? If you worked for one of these companies, what would you do to reduce the likelihood of computer crime?

B. What would you do if you believed computer crime was happening at a company for which you worked? Would you report it? If so, to whom? Suppose you didn't report it, but later someone found out that you knew about it all along? What might happen?

C. How can computer crime be detected? What role do you think accountants and auditors have in the detection of computer crime?

D. Find out more about SAS-3. (Ask an accounting professor.) What does it mean to public auditors? What does it mean to data processing professionals? How do you think you should react to an EDP auditor?

E. Are existing laws sufficient for prosecuting computer crimes? Are special laws needed? What is the Ribicoff Computer Crime Bill? What actions do you think need to be taken?

MODULE D

Computers and Their Impact on Society

THE POSITIVE IMPACTS OF COMPUTING

THE IMPACT OF THE COMPUTER ON BUSINESS
Electronic Funds Transfer

COMPUTER SYSTEMS IN THE HEALTH PROFESSIONS

COMPUTER SYSTEMS IN THE LEGAL PROFESSIONS

COMPUTER SYSTEMS IN POLITICS

ARTIFICIAL INTELLIGENCE

THE NEGATIVE ASPECTS OF COMPUTING

CONTROLLING COMPUTER IMPACT

In the 1950s, people said that we were entering the atomic age. It didn't turn out that way. We entered the computer age instead. Computers have invaded every corner of our society, changed it, and altered the lives of the people who live in it. People over 50 have a hard time visualizing machines that can think. People under 30 expect machines to think. People in between are the pioneers of the computer age.

Computer technology has been both beneficial and harmful. In this module, we survey its benefits and discuss its costs. We try to determine what people can do to increase the good and minimize the bad. In today's society, the relevant question is, How can we best use computer technology? For good or ill, computers are here to stay.

THE POSITIVE IMPACTS OF COMPUTING

Because we in North America have ready access to computing resources, we tend to take them for granted. Some people say that the major reason the Soviets never put a person on the moon was a lack of computer technology. In the 1960s, the Soviets wanted desperately to send someone to the moon for publicity purposes. They had the rocket power and technology, but they could not develop sophisticated enough control systems. Their space flights had to be controlled from the ground. The United States put computer control capability into the spaceships (see figure D-l). Few people realize the importance of computing to the space program. Even fewer realize the importance of the space program to computing. (It led to the development of microprocessor technology.)

To show the positive impact of computing, we will survey the applications of computer technology in our society. We will discuss computers in business, health, law, and politics. We will also describe some exciting developments in a field called *artificial intelligence*.

THE IMPACT OF THE COMPUTER ON BUSINESS

Computers are one of the few bright spots on the business horizon. In a time of rising prices, computers are the only resource that is getting both cheaper and better. We have discussed specific computer systems throughout this book. Therefore, we will not discuss more of them here. Instead, we will discuss the impact computing has made on the character of business.

The biggest change computers have made in business concerns the control of organizations and the allocation of resources. Their impact in this area is so subtle that it is hard to notice, but computers have gradually changed the character of business. Giant corporations like IBM, American Telephone and Telegraph, or The Boeing Company could not exist without computers. Without computers they could not account for their operations, control their personnel, or manage projects. The design of the Boeing 747 took 16 million engineering hours. This work could not have been coordinated without computing (see figure D-2).

Largeness may seem bad to you, but consider that, if these companies were smaller, there would be fewer computers, fewer telephones, and fewer airplanes. Think about it the next time you fly nonstop from Chicago to Hawaii! (From Chicago to Milwaukee?) Further, many people are employed by these

Computer technology made the moon
landings possible

companies. Without them, these people would have to be doing something
else, or perhaps they would be doing nothing.

Computers have changed more than just the size of business. They have
improved the control of resources. Consider the chair you are sitting in. The
production, distribution, and sale of that chair and others like it were most
likely controlled by computer systems. (Unless you made it yourself, in which
case think about the tools you used.)

Why did the manufacturer decide to make the chair? Most likely, a market
study was done by a computer system. Where did the raw materials come
from? The manufacturer probably used a computer system to decide what to
order and to control its raw material inventory. How was the chair routed
through the manufacturing process? A computer system may well have been
used to determine the production schedule and routing. Computer systems were
used to put the chair in inventory, to accept the order for the chair, to take the
chair out of inventory, to ship the chair to the distributor, and to route the train
or truck that carried the chair. Computer systems were used to put the chair
into the distributor's inventory, to accept the retailer's order, to take the chair
out of inventory, to transport it to the retailer, to put it into the retailer's

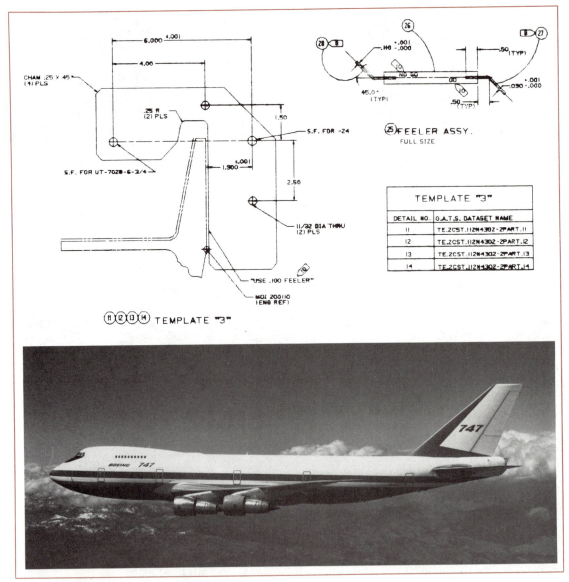

FIGURE D-2

Boeing 747 could not be produced
without computers

inventory, to price it, and to record the fact that someone bought it. The chair
has been handled by so many computer systems, it should have byte marks on
it! (See figure D-3.)

Furthermore, the process isn't over. If the chair belongs to a company or
organization, computer systems are used to keep it in the equipment inventory,
to depreciate it, to consider it for balance and income statements, to consider
its impact on taxes, and, eventually, to scrap it. Even then, the process continues. If the chair is made of metal, it may be sent to a scrap dealer who will

FIGURE D-3

Chair processed by too many computer systems—byte marks visible.

use computer systems to control the shipment of the scrap and the production of new metals. The new metal will be sold, distributed, and stored in inventories using computer systems until the day (you guessed it) it finds its way into the production of a new chair! The cycle will repeat itself. There's no escaping computer systems; they're everywhere.

Now, why is this situation good? It's good because products can be manufactured more cheaply when they are well controlled. There may be six different ways of producing, delivering, and selling a chair. Of the six, we want to use the least expensive way. Why spend more than we have to? By improving control, computers help management to produce goods for less.

Given recent inflation, it may seem that goods are terribly expensive. However, if goods were not made in large quantities (allowing economies of scale to be realized), they would be much more expensive than they are. Prices are high, but no society in history has had as many products to choose from. Some people say we live as well as kings lived in previous times.

Additionally, computers have improved the quality of work. They have eliminated many tedious chores. Accountants, for example, can spend more time on creative work, like designing accounting systems or providing better auditability and control, and less time adding columns of numbers.

Furthermore, computer technology has created a whole new industry. Thousands of jobs have been created by computers, and thousands more are yet to be created. Many of these jobs are creative, fun, and challenging. They are great improvements over the mundane jobs that have been eliminated.

Electronic Funds Transfer

A new business system, called *Electronic Funds Transfer System* (EFTS), is on the horizon. When implemented, this EFTS will have a major impact on society.

Our existing checking and banking system is expensive to operate. Consider an example. Suppose you live and bank in Los Angeles, and you attend school in New York. When you write a check to the university bookstore, the processing shown in figure D-4 occurs. Much of this processing involves physically handling your check. Humans are needed to key the input, to sort, to distribute, to mail, and so forth. Since humans are expensive, the process is expensive.

Several schemes have been proposed to reduce this expense. Some people have suggested that we have a *checkless society*. Instead of physical checks, all purchases would be made by electronic transactions. Individuals and businesses would have national account numbers. When someone makes a purchase, the merchant would input both numbers and the amount of the purchase. This amount would be deducted from the customer's account and added to the merchant's account (less a processing fee). This system is an extension to the VISA and Mastercard systems.

Individual deposits would be handled the same way. When people were paid, their employers would make electronic deposits to employee accounts. At the same time, the employer's account would be reduced.

If this system were operational, there would be no obvious need for money. We could have a *cashless society*, in which both checks and money would be eliminated. All purchasing and payments would be handled electronically.

Other forms of EFTS have been proposed. *One-way checks* are physically moved only to the bank of first deposit. In figure D-4, that is the bookstore's bank. Thus, the physical check does not go beyond step 3. The bookstore's bank creates an electronic transaction that represents the check in steps 4 through 11. Canceled checks would not be returned. Instead, people would receive a monthly printout of the transactions recorded. This setup is sometimes called *truncated check flow*.

FIGURE D-4

Existing system for processing checks

Step	Processing Action
1	You deposit money in your Los Angeles checking account for school expenses.
2	You write a check to purchase books at your university bookstore in New York.
3	The bookstore deposits your check with its New York bank.
4	The New York bank deposits the check for credit in the Federal Reserve Bank of New York.
5	The Federal Reserve Bank in New York sends the check to the Federal Reserve Bank in Los Angeles for collection.
6	The Federal Reserve Bank in Los Angeles forwards the check to your Los Angeles bank. The amount is deducted from your checking balance.
7	Your Los Angeles bank tells the Federal Reserve Bank in Los Angeles to deduct the amount of the check from its deposit account.
8	The Los Angeles Federal Reserve Bank pays the New York Federal Reserve Bank for the amount of the check.
9	The New York Federal Reserve Bank pays the bookstore's bank in New York.
10	The bookstore's bank credits the bookstore's account.
11	Your Los Angeles bank photographs the check and sends you the canceled check at the end of the month.

The one-way check system is a compromise between existing systems and the checkless society. It would save physical processing and yet be similar to the existing system. This similarity is important to bank customers. Research and experience have shown that people will not regularly make electronic debits to their accounts. People prefer to write checks that take several days to be processed.

In spite of this preference, some form of EFTS is probably inevitable. Unfortunately, EFTS creates the potential for serious social problems. These problems are listed in figure D-5. First, the *invasion of individual privacy* can occur. Currently, checks are not stored in computer-sensible form. Therefore, the systematic investigation of one account is impossible. EFTS would make such investigations possible. Second, governmental agencies could *secretly monitor* the activities of individuals. Furthermore, they could *control people's lives* by restricting the types of purchases that could be made.

A fourth disadvantage is *reduced competition* among banks. A few large superbanks or financial utilities might be created. In this case, bank service would suffer and expenses would probably increase. EFTS also opens the door to *large-scale thefts*. Billions of dollars would be vulnerable to computer criminals. Very large thefts could go undetected for years.

Increased vulnerability is another problem. The financial industry would become susceptible to credit blackouts when computers or communications failed. Furthermore, EFTS introduces the possibility of financial sabotage by terrorist groups or foreign governments.

Clearly, there are substantial problems to be overcome before EFTS becomes a reality. Congressional hearings have been held on the subject, and it is hoped that problems will be thoroughly solved before EFTS is implemented. In the meantime, keep your checkbook handy.

Both hospitals and doctors have used computers to improve service and reduce costs. First, they use computers for typical business functions—general ledger, billing, accounts receivable, inventory, and so forth. Additionally, they use computing for problems unique to health, as summarized in figure D-6.

Computer systems are used to keep *patient records*. Because of the large number of diagnoses and the technical terms used, these systems are difficult to build. A system using the steps shown in figure D-7 has been successfully implemented, however. Technical terms are often given unique codes. Once the records are input to the computer, it is easy to search on these codes. Thus, the computer can be used to determine the effectiveness of different treatments.

COMPUTER SYSTEMS IN THE HEALTH PROFESSIONS

1. Invasion of privacy
2. Secret monitoring of individuals' activities
3. Control over individuals' lives
4. Reduced bank competition
5. Large-scale theft
6. Disaster due to system outages or sabotage

FIGURE D-5

Potential problems of electronic funds transfer

Machine-Made Body Joints

Despite their high-tech elegance, bone implants are manufactured in a peculiarly old-world fashion. But before long, these prostheses may be designed and built by the most twentieth-century of craftsmen: computers.

To produce implants now, doctors first X-ray a patient's joint, allowing them to calculate the dimensions of the bone. Then they make drawings and templates of the joint and send these to a laboratory that actually constructs the prosthesis. If, while the patient is in surgery, the resulting implant does not fit precisely, the surgeon may have to reshape the bone.

All of this soon promises to change. At the Hospital for Special Surgery in New York, doctors are now working with an elaborate piece of machinery called CAD-CAM—for Computer Assisted Design and Computer Assisted Manufacture—that could streamline the production of implants while markedly lowering their cost.

Scheduled for operation at the hospital sometime this year, CAD-CAM is a two-pronged system that both blueprints and constructs. In order to make use of the machinery's design capability for implants, doctors first X-ray a patient's joint in numerous cross-sectional slices. When analyzed together, these build a three-dimensional portrait of that portion of the skeleton. Next, the X-ray is placed on a light-sensitive screen, which allows it to be read by both the doctor and the computer. Recalling designs that have been programmed into its memory, the computer then suggests a prosthesis shape, taking into consideration such variables as the patient's age and ambulatory condition. The design is then encoded onto a punch-tape that is fed into the computer's manufacturing machinery. This apparatus—essentially a set of very sophisticated lathes and milling machines—whittles a block of titanium into the proper size and shape, readying it for implantation. Notes Albert Burstein, director of the hospital's department of biomechanics, "Now we can do a computer analysis to determine things that used to be determined in the operating room."

Science Digest, July, 1983

Pharmacy systems are used to record the drugs used by patients. Such systems can even assist the doctor in planning the treatment course. Furthermore, these systems can notify the pharmacist if harmful combinations of drugs have been prescribed. (One doctor may prescribe a drug that conflicts with a drug prescribed by another doctor. The doctors won't know about each other if the patient doesn't tell them.)

Some pharmacists use computers to provide income tax records for their customers. The system records the cost of each prescription, and a receipt for the total is printed at year-end. This process saves customers record keeping.

FIGURE D-6

Computer applications in medicine

1. Administrative business functions
2. Patient records
3. Pharmacy records
4. Nursing stations
5. Radiological analysis
6. Monitoring of patient health
7. Diagnosing illnesses

1. Doctor dictates patient data into tape recorder.
2. Nurse screens tape for time-critical actions.
3. Tape transcriptionist inputs data using CRT. Codes are used for technical terms.

Pharmacists like it because the customers have an incentive to use only one pharmacist.

Computer systems are used to help nurses. The *nursing station* shown in figure D-8 prints patient drug histories and treatment plans. The nurses record patients' vital signs (pulse, blood pressure, etc.) via this station.

Computers are used in radiology to *analyze X-rays*. Patterns are identified and reported. Figure D-9 shows how a computer is used to help orthodontists plan treatments. The dentists send patient X-rays to the computer service company. These X-rays are input to the computer. The effect of different treatments is then simulated by computer. From this, the orthodontist can plan the best treatment.

Computers are used to *monitor patient health*. Seriously ill patients such as those having cardiovascular problems (heart attacks, for example) can be connected to computer monitoring systems. Sensors are taped to the patient, and the computer watches for abnormal activity. If it is detected, messages are

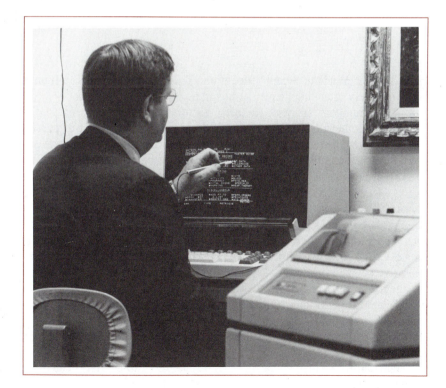

389

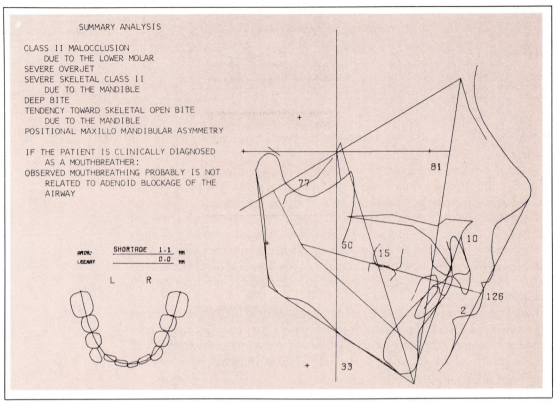

SUMMARY ANALYSIS

CLASS II MALOCCLUSION
    DUE TO THE LOWER MOLAR
SEVERE OVERJET
SEVERE SKELETAL CLASS II
    DUE TO THE MANDIBLE
DEEP BITE
TENDENCY TOWARD SKELETAL OPEN BITE
    DUE TO THE MANDIBLE
POSITIONAL MAXILLO MANDIBULAR ASYMMETRY

IF THE PATIENT IS CLINICALLY DIAGNOSED
    AS A MOUTHBREATHER:
OBSERVED MOUTHBREATHING PROBABLY IS NOT
    RELATED TO ADENOID BLOCKAGE OF THE
    AIRWAY

ARCH: SHORTAGE   1.1 MM
LEEWAY   0.0 MM

L   R

FIGURE D-9

Computer used to analyze and plan
orthodontic treatment

displayed on terminals at a central location. There are even plans to monitor patients remotely after they leave the hospital.

Further, computers are used to help doctors *diagnose illnesses*. Patient symptoms and other data are input to a computer program. A list of possible illnesses and suggested treatments is produced. Such *knowledge-based* or *expert systems* serve as computer-sensible repositories of human knowledge. They have been especially useful in diagnosing rare diseases.

COMPUTER SYSTEMS IN THE LEGAL PROFESSIONS

Computers are used in all of the legal professions (see figure D-10). In *law enforcement*, computers are used to keep criminal data. The FBI maintains the National Crime Information Center (see figure D-11). Records of criminals, stolen property, and crimes are kept on files in this system. State law enforcement agencies can query this system when they need information. They can also add data to the system. Other computer files are maintained by the FBI and the CIA as well.

Many states also use computers in law enforcement. The state of Washington keeps driver license information in computer files. When a car is pulled over by the state patrol, the driver's license can be checked immediately. The officer sends the license number to a central location by radio, and a terminal operator

Legal Element	Application
Law Enforcement	National Crime Information Center
	Other crime centers
	Online access to drivers' licenses and other data
Courts	Case histories
	Scheduling courtrooms, personnel, and cases
	Administrative tasks
Attorneys	General business applications
	Allocation of attorney time
	Trial support
	Word processing
	Legal research

FIGURE D-10

Computer applications in the legal professions

FIGURE D-11

Clerk accesses the National Crime Information Center

accesses the license files. Within minutes, the officer can obtain a complete driving history.

Courts use computer systems for a variety of purposes. Case histories are kept by computer systems. Courtrooms, personnel, and cases are scheduled by computer. Administrative tasks, like keeping track of costs, are also handled by computer systems. Computers are used to help select juries.

Attorneys are major users of computer systems. Law firms use computers for standard business applications like general ledger, billing, and accounts receivable. Computer systems are used to record expenses and to allocate attorneys' time to clients. Trial support systems keep case histories, maintain inventories of evidence and lists of witnesses, and keep schedules of activities for the trial attorneys. Word processing systems (see module E) are frequently used in the legal profession.

One of the most promising legal applications of computing involves research. Computers are used to query files of legal history (see figure D-12). Relevant past cases and legal precedents are found much faster by computer systems than by humans.

COMPUTER SYSTEMS IN POLITICS

Computer systems are frequently used by politicians (see figure D-13). *Computer voting systems* are popular. Using these systems, citizens vote by punching holes in cards or otherwise creating a computer-sensible document. Computers read these documents and tabulate votes to determine election outcomes.

FIGURE D-12

Legal librarian using computer for legal research

FIGURE D-13

Computer applications in politics

1. Election support—vote tabulation
2. Predicting election outcomes
3. Campaign letterwriting
4. Legislative administration

COMPUTER GRAPHICS

An Art, A Science, A Tool

A picture is worth a thousand words, but why? Some experts believe that there are fundamental differences between the way the human brain processes words and the way it processes pictures. Words are processed one at a time. Visual images, on the other hand, seem to be processed in parallel. Many separate brain circuits process different parts of the visual image simultaneously. Consequently, humans are able to assimilate more data graphically than they can by reading words or tables of data.

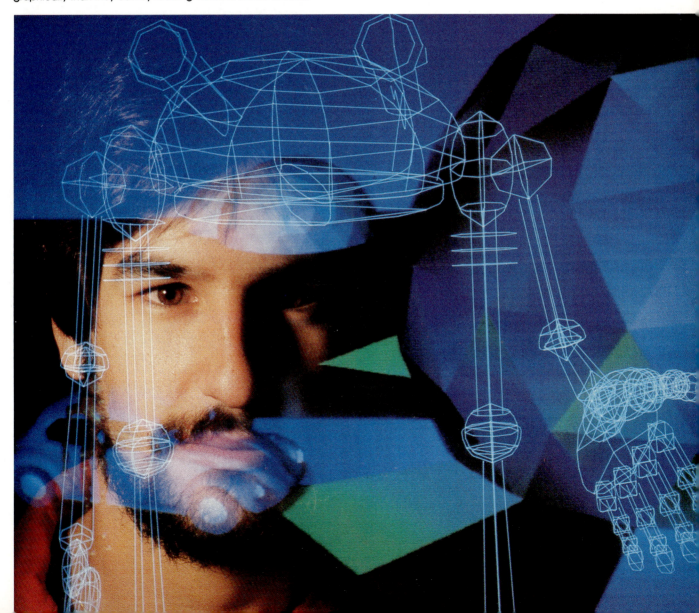

BUSINESS GRAPHICS

Business data can be complex. A table of monthly sales data for six different salespeople may be hard to interpret. When this data is converted to a graphical format, however, relationships among salesperson performance are easily seen.

Because of the advantages of graphics, businesses have used them for years. Unfortunately, until recently, graphics were both slow and expensive to produce. A human artist was often required to work for hours to produce one graph. With the advent of the computer, and especially the microcomputer, that situation has changed. Today, multicolor pie charts, bar graphs, and line plots can be displayed on a computer screen in a matter of seconds. Furthermore, little operator training is required.

Business graphics can be produced in a variety of forms. They can be displayed on a CRT or on a special graphics terminal. Simple graphics can be printed on paper using a dot-matrix printer; more complex graphics must be printed with a plotter. Because such graphic output is in electronic form, it can

An extensive display of graphics hardware by Tektronix.

be sent over communications lines and displayed in locations far removed from one another. Graphics can also be recorded on 35-millimeter film for slide presentations.

Common business graphs, such as bar graphs and pie charts, are quickly produced with business graphics hardware and software.

3-D graphics can be used to provide an interesting presentation of a business graph or chart.

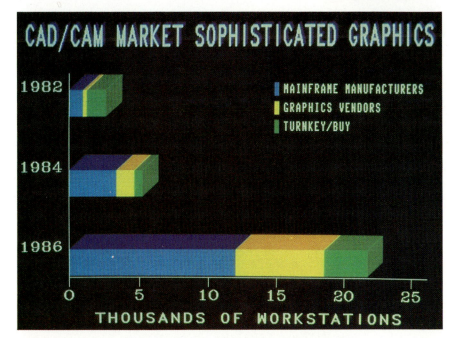

This colorful bar graph projects growth for engineering design graphics.

Graphics used in process control applications visually inform the operator of any changes in the process.

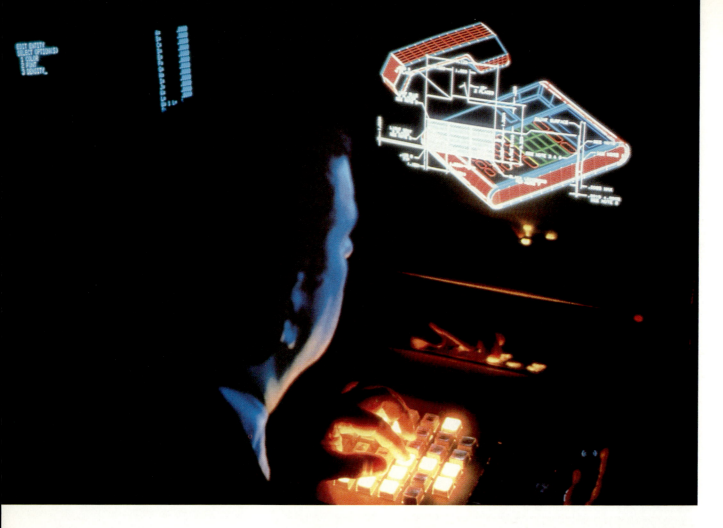

ENGINEERING GRAPHICS

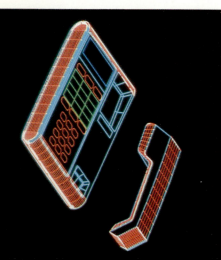

Computer-assisted design (CAD) and computer-assisted manufacturing (CAM) were two of the earliest applications of computer graphics. CAD technology is used by engineers to design products, develop plans for architectural projects, and define the flow and operation of manufacturing processes, as well as for other applications. Once a design has been drawn, the computer can enlarge it, reduce it, or rotate it to be viewed from a new angle. Details of manufacturing techniques, such as the length, location, and order of cuts, can be shown on the drawing. Such cutting sequences can be output to numerically controlled machines that cut the material according to the design specifications.

For even greater utility, drawings can be combined. Engineers can determine if two parts will fit together, and composite designs can be developed. In this way, the work of several engineers can be combined into one drawing.

Airplane design and manufacturing frequently involve CAD/CAM, or, to use a new term, computer-assisted engineering (CAE). In the design of an airplane, the surface shape is critical. Engineers make line drawings that reveal

An engineer uses CAD/CAM graphics to transform a set of specifications into a graphic model of a familiar telephone.

surface shape. More detail can be added to the drawing as the design progresses. The computer can show the entire airplane or only a particular portion, such as the left wing.

CAD/CAM has enabled engineers to design this Boeing 767.

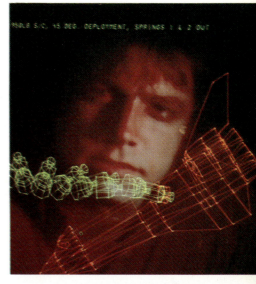

Space flight vehicles were early subjects of sophisticated design graphics.

In the future this model of the airplane will be done with a hologram.

Electronic circuits are frequently designed using CAE. Symbols for common electrical components, such as resistors, transistors, and the like, are moved about on the graphics screen and connected to form a circuit.

Solid object modeling displays objects in three dimensions. Shading and highlighting can be added to the object to create a realistic picture.

Engineers at General Motors have used graphics for auto design for years.

Graphics allow the designer to view the object from a variety of angles.

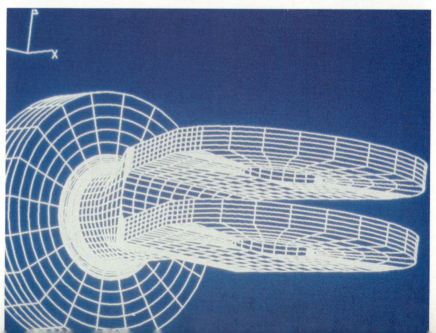

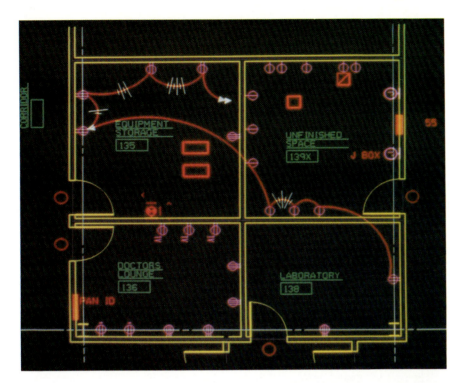

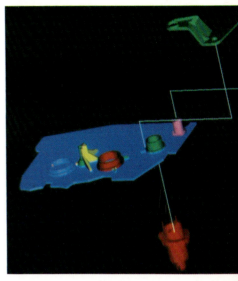

Modeling of solid objects provides a 3-D image of these mechanical parts.

An architect's building design.

The light pen is a common input device when graphics are used for electronic testing.

Graphics are produced on a screen by illuminating spots, called *pixels* (picture elements). For a black and white display, the pixel is either illuminated or not. For color displays, pixels contain cells of blue, green, and red. To produce a color, one or more of these cells is illuminated.

Characters, such as letters of the alphabet, are produced by illuminating groups of pixels, a process similar to that used in a dot-matrix printer. Illuminating pixels in a circular pattern, for example, produces a zero.

Suppose a screen consists of 80 rows and 100 columns of pixels. Any particular pixel can be identified by its row and column number. Thus, pixel (20,30) is the pixel in row 20, column 30. To draw a shape, we need only specify which pixels are to be illuminated.

A screen having only 60 rows and 80 columns of pixels would generate low-quality images. A standard TV screen has 512 pixels horizontally and 256 pixels vertically. A professional-quality graphics screen would have more. The Tektronix 4054, for example, has 3125 rows and 4096 columns of pixels. The greater the number of rows and columns, the higher the *resolution* of the image. To obtain high resolution, a special screen is required, and, because there is more data to store, larger main memories and magnetic storage are needed.

There are several ways of generating computer graphics. At the lowest level, commands to graphics programs are embedded in application programs. In BASIC on the Apple computer, for example, the sequence of commands shown at the left will cause a square to be drawn.

```
10   HLIN 30, 50 AT 20
20   HLIN 30, 50 AT 40
30   VLIN 20, 40 AT 30
40   VLIN 20, 40 AT 50
```

The first command draws a horizontal line from column 30 to column 50 at row 20. The second command draws a horizontal line from column 30 to column 50 at row 40. The third command draws a vertical line from row 20 to row 40 at column 30, and the last command draws a vertical line from row 20 to row 40 at column 50. Other systems have similar commands.

A second way of drawing graphics is to move a pen from one place to another. Commands are available to lower, raise, and to move the pen about. A line is drawn whenever the pen is moved while it is in the down position.

Drawing a Square Using Apple BASIC
Graphics Commands

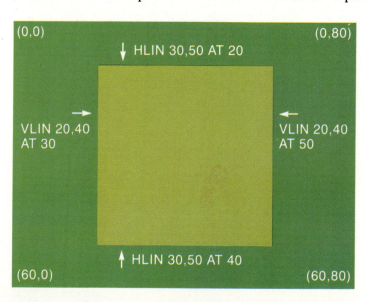

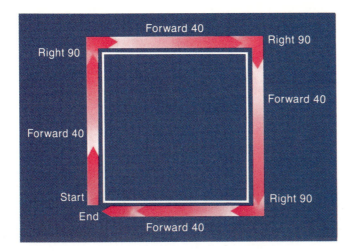

The programming language LOGO operates in this manner. The LOGO pen, however, is carried by a (simulated) turtle. The turtle can rotate and move forward and back. A line is drawn whenever the turtle moves with its pen down. The LOGO commands shown at the right will draw a square.

The first command tells the turtle to lower its pen. Then the FORWARD 40 command instructs the turtle to move forward forty units or steps. The RIGHT 90 command instructs the turtle to turn 90 degrees to the right. Commands are repeated to draw the square.

The commands embedded in Apple BASIC and the LOGO commands are both procedural. The user instructs the computer to take specific actions to produce the graph.

Some graphics packages are nonprocedural. For these, the user simply states what graphic design is desired and provides necessary data. Specific commands for generating the graphic are then issued by the graphics program. The following is typical of the interaction needed to generate a pie chart. Small letters are printed by the program; capital letters are provided by the user.

```
graphic desired: PIE
title: SALES BY SALESPERSON
number of data points: 4
data and label: 270, FRED
data and label: 817, JANE
data and label: 775, DON
data and label: 439, MARY
```

With this input, the graphics program will produce a pie chart showing percentages of sales. Each piece of the pie will be labeled with the name of the appropriate salesperson.

Graphics packages like this are available to produce bar charts and XY plots as well as to compute and plot data trends and other similar graphs. The computer graphics spectrum is broad and extends from simple graphs like bar charts, to intricate designs produced according to mathematical equations, to the sophisticated graphics involved in computer animation.

```
PENDOWN
FORWARD 40
RIGHT 90
FORWARD 40
RIGHT 90
FORWARD 40
RIGHT 90
FORWARD 40
```

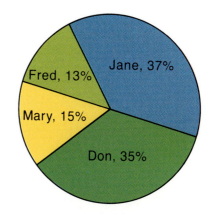

Pie Chart Produced Using Nonprocedural Graphics Program

SCIENCE AND GRAPHICS

Computer graphics are used in many scientific disciplines. For example, photos from space are produced using *image processing* techniques. Cameras sense light intensity or colors and record the sensations as digital data. This data is transmitted to earth, where it is interpreted by programs and transformed into a visual image. In some cases, images are improved by processing; programs analyze the digital data statistically and make lines more definite or add (or subtract) shadows. Image processing techniques can produce graphics from photographs and TV screens as well.

Imaging by satellite.

This color mosaic uses 42 Landsat images to depict the entire state of California.

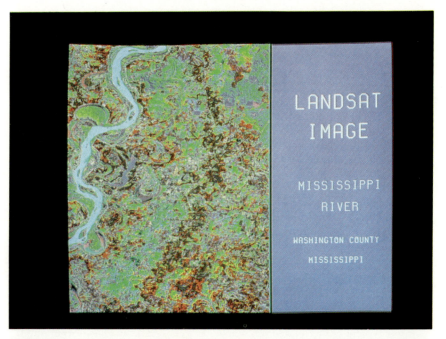

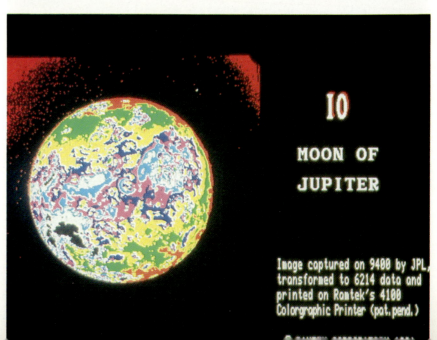

This image was captured by NASA's Deep Space Program.

Scientific disciplines produce large amounts of data. Imagine the tables of data needed to describe the location of clouds over the United States! Yet, a map with clouds drawn over it is easily understood. Complicated results of scientific studies or experiments can also be shown graphically.

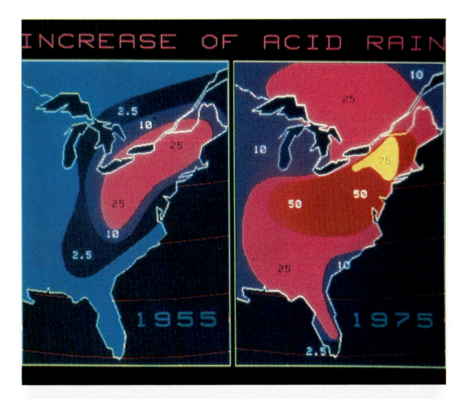

This graph presents a tremendous amount of data, yet it is quickly understood.

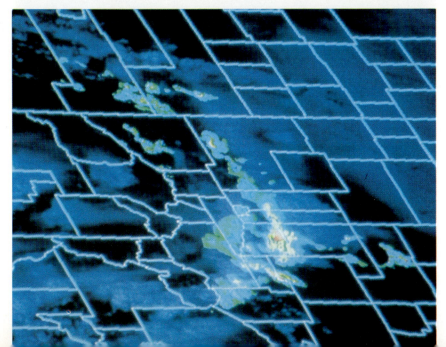

Scientists can use weather graphics displays for both study and explanation.

Astronomers, physicists, and chemists use graphics techniques to combine data and build models of the phenomena they study. In astronomy, for example, a graphical model of a constellation could be constructed from thousands of recorded observations.

In medicine, image processing is used to view the functioning of internal organs. These same techniques are used in industry to inspect objects that cannot be seen directly. Movement, growth, and change can be studied using graphical simulation. For example, in botany the growth of a plant can be simulated by producing images of the various stages in plant development. Simulation is used in other sciences as well.

Graphics can aid in visualizing and understanding a critical process within the body.

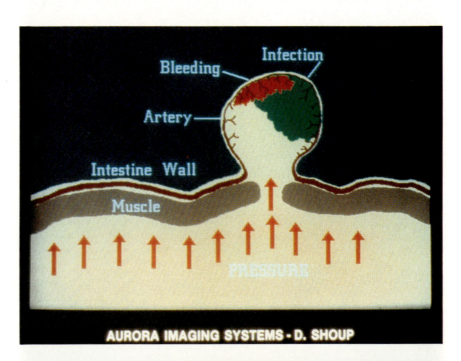

A CAT-Scanner (for computer-actualized tomography) scans the body and transmits a map of dots to provide color images of internal organs.

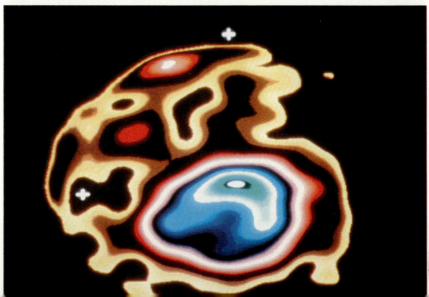

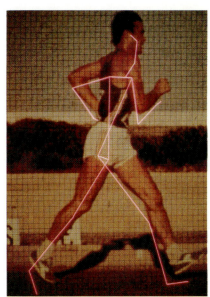

Medical researchers at the Olympic Training Center in Colorado use a digitizer to input data necessary to synthesize motion. Millions of bits are processed to produce stick figures that can then be used to analyze a runner's form and performance.

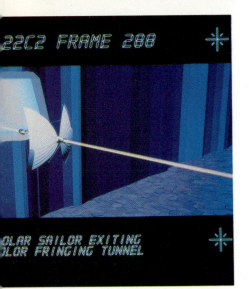

22C2 FRAME 288

OLAR SAILOR EXITING
OLOR FRINGING TUNNEL

In the movie *Tron*, new developments in computer graphics were applied to animation in a process called *computer-generated imagery*.

Animation generated by computers is used for both video games and cartoon features.

Many scenes in recent science fiction movies, like *Tron* and *Return of the Jedi*, have been produced using computer graphics and a process called *animation*. Using this process, a mathematical description of one or more objects is stored in the computer. Then, computer programs move the object from one location and orientation to another location and orientation. The movement is recorded on film.

Animation requires that equations regarding object shape, object movement, location and movement of light source, location and movement of camera, and other parameters be input to the computer program. Adjusting the shape, colors, and shadows of an object as the object, the camera, and the light source move is exceedingly complex. In fact, in *Tron*, over two hours of processing were required on a VAX computer to generate a 52-second scene.

Computer graphics are used in other forms of entertainment as well. Much of the excitement of video games, for example, is due to their high-quality graphics.

Computerized frame creation for animation.

In addition to its applications in the entertainment field, computer graphics has become an art medium in itself. Abstract and geometric designs can be constructed by plotting curves according to mathematical equations. Computer programs can even produce original designs. Random numbers can be input into equations that specify points to be drawn. Each time the program is run, a different graph is generated. Authors of the program have no idea what designs will result.

With some graphics systems, pictures can be painted by moving a cursor around the screen. The artist selects a color and then paints the screen with the cursor, just as a canvas would be painted with a paintbrush.

Computer art has been developed to the point that it is virtually impossible to distinguish it from photographs and paintings.

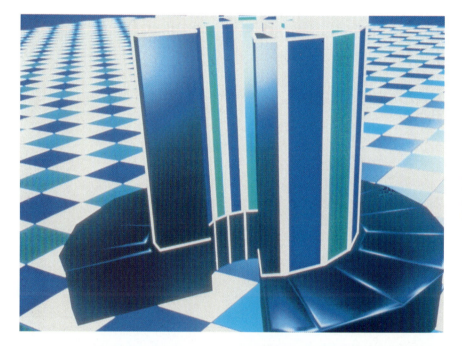

The CRAY-1 is a mainframe super computer built by Cray Research; this is a computer art rendering of the CRAY-1.

The CRAY-1's self-portrait?

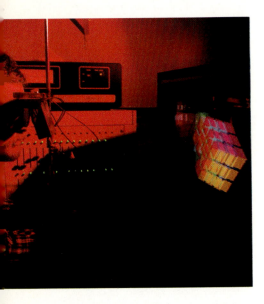

Research in 3-D graphics should make images in the future even more exciting.

Will the engineers use holograms in CAD/CAM applications in the future?

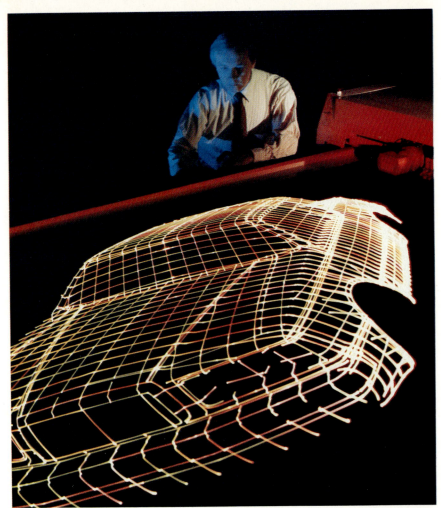

QUESTIONS

1. Describe one application of computer graphics in each of the following disciplines: **a.** Business **b.** Engineering **c.** Science **d.** Entertainment **e.** Art

2. Explain computer animation. Why is animation difficult?

3. What is a pixel? Explain how pixels produce graphics images.

4. What shape would the following LOGO program generate?

PENDOWN
FORWARD 30
RIGHT 120
FORWARD 30
RIGHT 120
FORWARD 30

In Less than Four Months
Reagan Nets $2 Million from Mail

WASHINGTON, D.C.—"Ronald Reagan is a tremendously well-known commodity and therefore a very well-received and successful letter-signer," according to the head of the Reagan for President Committee's direct mail fund-raising campaign, which has netted almost $2 million, since Nov. 13.

Roger Stone, who has been involved with direct-mail fund-raising for seven years—"a very long time when you're 27 years old"—now heads both the fund-raising and political persuasion mailing efforts as the committee's director of finance communications and deputy political director.

In direct-mail efforts, vast lists of names, addresses, political and interest group affiliations and previous donations can be stored on computer tape for eventual feeding to laser printers or word processors.

By culling from such lists the names of individuals with specific interests or donors who have given at particular monetary levels, direct mailers can aim "personalized" letters at those most likely to respond favorably.

"Our people are used to a tremendous amount of personalization," Stone noted, "and that does have a very definite effect" on the success of our appeals.

Stone has sent out an average of 250,000 letters monthly for a total of about 1.5 million letters since November. Divulging one of the secrets of the campaign's success, he said, "You should never, in my view, mail out any letter without asking for money.

"The fund-raising letter has a much stronger pitch for funds" compared with a political persuasion letter, in which the request for funds is "almost incidental," but always there.

Another criterion for success is timeliness, Stone explained. "Our mailings are based on what the current political happening is, whether it's Iowa or New Hampshire, whatever the goal is."

by MARGUERITE ZIENTARA
Computerworld, November, 1979

Computers are used to predict election outcomes. For national elections, all of the major TV networks use computers to predict results. As the early returns on the East Coast become available, they are used to predict the national outcome. This practice presents a problem. If the predictions are made before the polls close on the West Coast, some people may not vote. They may think it is not worthwhile to vote for someone who is obviously losing. Thus, the predictions may influence the election. In fact, it would be possible for someone to sway an election by manipulating these predictions.

Politicians use computers to *raise money*. Records of potential campaign contributors are kept on computer files. At intervals, these records are used to produce "customized" letters asking for money or making political statements. According to the Profile article shown on page 394, Ronald Reagan's campaign organization sent out 250,000 letters per month prior to the 1980 election.

Computers are also used by legislatures. The U.S. Congress uses computers to tally votes. Congressional personnel use the computer system to determine the status of votes, the names of members present or absent, and so forth (see figure D-14).

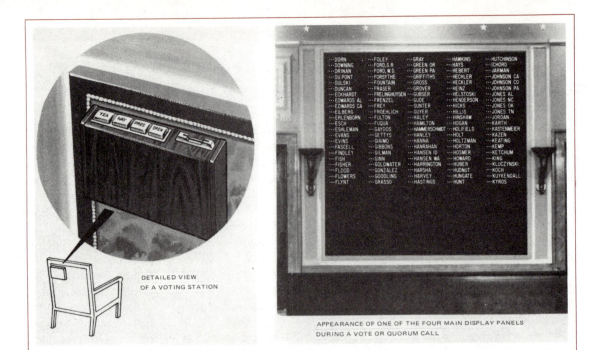

DETAILED VIEW
OF A VOTING STATION

APPEARANCE OF ONE OF THE FOUR MAIN DISPLAY PANELS
DURING A VOTE OR QUORUM CALL

APPEARANCE OF A SUMMARY DISPLAY PANEL WHILE A VOTE IS IN PROGRESS

Computer system used by the U.S.
Congress

Probably the most fascinating projects in all computing are the efforts to build machines that think. The capability of these machines goes beyond the logical and arithmetic activity normally associated with computers. In some ways, these machines appear humanlike.

"The brain," said Marvin Minsky of MIT, "happens to be a meat machine." Many scientists agree with this philosophy. And they take it one step further. If the brain is a machine, then it may be possible to build another machine that has the same capability or even greater capability. Research to build such machines is called *artificial intelligence*.

Although work began in this field in the mid-1950s, results were slow to come. There were early programs that could successfully play easy games like tic-tac-toe. There were also programs that could play reasonable games of checkers. Promises were made that there would soon be chess-playing programs, but this timing was overly optimistic. Respectable chess-playing programs have become available only in the last five years.

Language translation was also harder than expected. In the 1950s, people said that it would be only a short time before computers were able to translate. However, it was discovered that human language is very complex. Early programs simply substituted a word in one language for an equivalent word in another. With this procedure, the saying "The spirit is willing, but the flesh is weak" was translated to "The booze is good, but the meat is rotten." One scientist said that programs had to be taught that when Mary had a little lamb, she didn't have it for lunch!

Attempting to translate human language led to a greater understanding of language. The theory of transformational grammar resulted from this work. Today there are programs that can do limited forms of translation, but considerable work still needs to be done.

One subset of artificial intelligence is oriented toward simulating human dialogue. In 1963 at MIT, Dr. Joseph Weizenbaum decided to build a machine that would simulate the conversation between a psychoanalyst and his or her patient. Weizenbaum's program was called ELIZA. This program was enhanced by Kenneth Colby and renamed DOCTOR. In *Machines Who Think*, Pamela McCorduck reports the following conversation between DOCTOR and a distinguished foreign visitor [84, p. 254]:

Doctor: Good afternoon. Please type in your name.
(This visitor typed his name.)
Doctor: What brought you here to see me today?
Visitor: Oh, nothing much. I'm feeling a bit tired, that's all.
Doctor: Why do you think you're feeling a bit tired?
Visitor: Well, I've been traveling a lot, and away from home.
Doctor: Tell me about your family.

According to Ms. McCorduck, the conversation continued in an intimate manner. Even though the visitor knew he was talking with a machine, he continued to reveal his personal fears and concerns.

Scientists debate whether this program has any therapeutic value. Weizenbaum says that it does not. He wrote it only to simulate a conversation. Others think that it may provide some therapy.

Computers to Supervise Nuke Plants

Specialists are now designing intelligent computers to help nuclear power plant operators diagnose and solve sudden malfunctions. Once perfected and installed, the new systems could provide warnings of breakdowns and, almost instantaneously, suggestions for repairs.

"The typical day in the control room is dull," says Michael Bray, an engineer with the Idaho National Engineering Laboratory (INEL), a firm designing the programming for the new systems. "But when anything unusual takes place, the operator has to jump from a situation in which nothing is happening to one in which everything is happening." Not the best environment for decision making.

Swift thinking and unflappable, the new computers will circumvent such problems. These elaborate artificial intelligence systems are immeasurably more sophisticated than conventional computers. Their most significant feature is an ability to reason backward as well as forward; thus, they can both build to a conclusion from a set of facts and infer causes from a single result.

"Leak in progress," a screen might flash. "Based on current plant state, suggest emergency procedures three through five. Close valves to isolate systems."

The machines are impressive but by no means perfect. INEL researcher Theodore Hatcher stresses that the computers, though being developed since 1978, are still in such a preliminary stage that "we're not even aware of all the bugs. We're still trying to get the data into their memories." He also emphasizes that the new equipment will be only an aid. "The technician is free to choose not to use the computer's suggestion," he says.

How well the reactor computers will work thus remains to be seen; even so, officials enthusiastically tout their value. "People need everything they can come up with to make their work safer for themselves and the community," says one spokesman. "If artificial intelligence can do this, that's great."

Science Digest, July, 1983

One of the most impressive developments in artificial intelligence is *robotics*—the production of robots. The Stanford Research Institute developed a famous robot named Shakey. Shakey could propel itself and avoid objects in its path. It could also be programmed to perform simple tasks like picking up toy blocks or boxes. One of the most complex tasks it performed was the assembly of an automobile water pump from parts scattered on a table. (See figure D-15.)

Robotics has become an important industrial discipline. Robots are currently used to perform boring and repetitive jobs in automobile production. They can also be used in hostile environments where humans cannot work. Nuclear power plants are one example; outer space is another. Robots will soon be used in other types of production as well. A new and very important career field is developing that combines production expertise with knowledge of computer technology and robots.

The work in artificial intelligence continues. Many of the problems have been more difficult than anticipated, and one result has been a keener appreciation for the human mind. Still, many scientists think that it is only a matter of time before intelligent machines exist. Hermann Kahn, an analyst at the

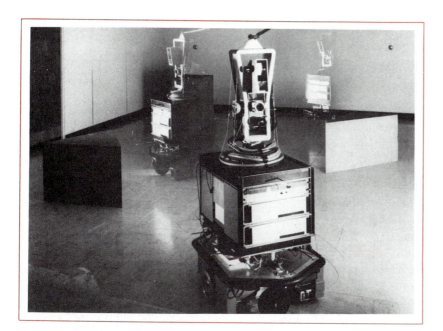

FIGURE D-15

Shakey—Stanford Research Institute's robot (it is no longer "living")

Hudson Institute, thinks machines will ultimately surpass human beings. He says:

> I find it a very unpleasant prospect. . . . The computer may write better poetry than human beings, better drama, make more perceptive judgments . . . before the end of the century. It may turn out that the only way to do this is that the computer itself will have to learn by experience [84, p. 56].

THE NEGATIVE ASPECTS OF COMPUTING

Unfortunately, the impact of computers has not been entirely positive. There have been social costs in the application of computer technology as well. These costs are summarized in figure D-16.

Some aspects of computing have served to decrease the quality of life. For one, computers have eliminated jobs. Although it is true that they have created other jobs, the new jobs have not always been available to the people whose jobs were eliminated by the computer.

For example, suppose a new order entry system is installed at a company. Several order entry jobs may be eliminated, and several data processing jobs

FIGURE D-16

Societal costs of computing

1. Elimination of jobs
2. Impersonalization of business
3. Human abuse caused by
    Improper data handling
    Poor systems design

Here Come the Robots: Home Automatons Are Rolling to Market, but Will They Sell?

By PHILIP FAFLICK

With its round head, beady eyes and red-buttoned pot belly, it looks like an armless, three-foot-high plastic snowman. Rolling across the floor on big black wheels, it embodies one of man's most enduring dreams: the personal robot, programmed to do its master's bidding. Inside its molded skull a kind of sassy intelligence seems to be at work. "What strange-looking creatures," it intones nasally in the direction of some gawking visitors at its home base, Androbot, Inc., in Sunnyvale, Calif. "Where are your wheels?"

The robot's name is BOB (Brains on Board). At present it cannot even fetch a beer from the refrigerator, but its buoyant creator, high-tech millionaire Nolan Bushnell, 40, foresees an almost boundless future for the $2,500 machine. Concerned about crime in your neighborhood? Not to worry. "Home security," says Bushnell, "is

just moments away." With the proper software, he claims, BOB could patrol a house and call the police when its heat sensor sniffs an intruder. When BOB isn't watching the house, he could be cleaning it. "As soon as we get an arm on him, vacuuming will be easy," says Bushnell. Eventually, he hopes, "BOB will be programmed to fetch things—get the paper, pick up after its master, put loose socks in the hamper and stray shoes in the closet" . . .

Despite the flurry of commercial activity, many experts remain skeptical about the near-term prospects for personal robots. Bertram Raphael, a Hewlitt-Packard engineer who in the 1960s helped build Shakey, the first artificially intelligent mobile robot, for the Stanford Research Institute, says that robots can be as exasperating and recalcitrant as small children. "When we said, 'Shakey, move forward three feet,' " he recalls,

"the only thing we could be absolutely sure of was that he would not move exactly three feet." Adds M.I.T. computer expert Marvin Minsky: "It's easy to program robots to do isolated tasks, but very difficult to write a balanced program that can switch from one function to another."

Until sophisticated programming is developed, robots like BOB . . . will probably be bought as surrogate household pets. "These robots will be perceived as companions, like dogs or cats," says the trend-watching Helmers. Still, the image of the apron-clad, broom-toting automaton is by now well established in myth, movies and popular literature. As Bushnell optimistically puts it: "Can anyone really envision the year 2000 without robots running around the home?"

Reported by Robert T. Grieves/New York and Dick Thompson/San Francisco, *Time*, March 7, 1983

may be created. But the people who were data entry clerks yesterday probably are not qualified to be systems designers or programmers today. Thus, computers can put some people out of work. (This, by the way, is all the more reason for you to learn all you can about computers.) Unfortunately, the people put out of work tend to be the least skilled; it may be hard for them to find other work.

In addition to eliminating jobs, computers have changed the environment of some business activities. Business has become more impersonal. People have been treated as if they were numbers instead of human beings.

Actually, this treatment should not be blamed on computers; it should be blamed on people. Computers themselves don't make business more imper-

Police Robot Trundles Where It's Too Perilous for Humans

PAGE, Ariz.—It was the sort of situation that gets people killed.

In a house trailer in Cottonwood, Ariz., a troubled man had been holed up for 12 hours. His wife and infant daughter had escaped, but the man inside remained silent, unreachable, armed and unpredictable.

Then this little, one-armed robot rolled up to the trailer and emphatically told the man that he ought to be more reasonable, or the police would use tear gas.

The man agreed that talking might be a good idea, so the machine deposited a mobile telephone at the front door and trundled away in an electric whir.

A half-hour later, after a telephone discussion with police negotiators, 27-year-old Frank Hauk came out, concluding a historic moment in law enforcement. Never before had anyone in America ever been brought to peaceful surrender and arrest with the help of a robot.

According to Arizona Public Safety Department Sgt. Dave Audsley, the machine's supervisor, Hauk said after his arrest that he thought the robot was "neat."

By GARY BLONSTON
Knight-Ridder News Service, May 24, 1983

sonal. Laying the blame for impersonalization on the computer is like laying the blame for murder on the weapon. Suppose a person is found standing over a gunshot victim with a smoking gun. The person explains to the investigating officer that he or she is not responsible because the gun shot the man. How far would that line of reasoning go?

Surprisingly, this line of reasoning goes far in computing. How often have you heard, "The computer won't let me do that"? Did you ever want to ask, "Who controls the computer? Who programmed the computer? Does the computer make decisions for itself?" Obviously, it doesn't. Since the computer cannot speak up to defend itself, people hide behind it to avoid responsibility.

Now, back to the coldness in business. In some cases, when computer systems were installed, businesses became inhumane. This occurred partly because people were discovering how to use computer technology; they made mistakes. It occurred partly because the people who designed and developed the computer systems tended to be machine oriented. They had little regard for the machine's impact on people. As people learn how to integrate computer technology into businesses, impersonalization will be less likely to occur. However, there is little doubt that computer processing is standardized processing. It will always be hard for computer systems to deal with exceptions as well as humans can.

In addition to these disadvantages, there has been a certain amount of computer abuse. The abuse stems from two sources: *improper data handling* and *bad systems design*.

Data is relatively easy to collect and store. Once data is in magnetic form, billions of characters can readily be sent from one computer to another—across the nation or across the world. Further, the data doesn't wear out; it doesn't fade with time as people's memories do. Under these coι ἰtions, it is hard for people to have privacy. If someone defaults on a home mᴄ ᵍage, a record of the default may be distributed across the nation. It may be ᴀ ᵃilable to credit bureaus for years.

Lenders may consider this capability an advantage, but many people do not. People change and grow. Don't most people have something in their past that they would prefer to forget? With computer technology, forgetting about the past may be a thing of the past.

The potential for abuse by totalitarian government is tremendous. It is technically possible to gather enough data to know the earning and spending habits of every person in the nation. With EFTS it is possible to prohibit certain people from making certain purchases, or from living in certain areas, or from working at certain jobs. Again, this capability may be an advantage in some ways, but it is clearly a disadvantage in others.

Thus, computer technology presents the opportunity for serious infringements on individual rights and privacy. Today, these infringements are mostly possibilities, but the potential is certainly real.

Perhaps the greatest abuse occurs when computer systems produce inaccurate information. There are many stories about people who have been refused employment or credit because their records were in error, or because they were confused with someone having the same name. The individuals who learned about such errors were the lucky ones. The unlucky ones didn't receive jobs, or credit, or whatever, and never knew why.

Just thinking about this possibility fills us with anger and disgust. Yet, should we blame computer technology for these errors? Although computer technology created the potential for these errors, they were not made until some person created a system and another person used the system to create a problem. Ultimately, the responsibility for the errors lies with people.

The second category of computer abuse occurs when systems are designed poorly. For example, the class enrollment system in chapter 2 would not enroll George Shelton in classes because it thought George owed money to the university. In fact, George did not. George's frustration occurred because the finance people recognized that George was in good standing, but the computer did not. Further, George found no one who knew how to correct the error.

In this example, the class enrollment system was poorly designed. It was too difficult to rectify an error. There have been many similar cases. One person was sent threatening letters because she refused to pay a bill for $0.00. Finally, she sent a check for $0.00. The letters stopped coming, but then her bank refused to process the check for $0.00. She had to explain the situation several times to rectify the error.

Sometimes, people are abused by computer technology because they are unable to obtain services they need and deserve. There are cases of utility companies terminating service to homes because computer systems determined incorrectly that bills were several months overdue.

Perhaps the worst situations develop when the computer is used to intimidate people. Computer-generated letters that look and sound official sometimes cause people to do things that they are not obligated to do. People who do not know their rights or how to deal with computer errors are likely victims.

All such cases of systems abuse are preventable. When they occur, they reflect poor systems design or personnel errors. The computer is nearly never at fault. The problem lies with incomplete or inaccurate procedures or with poorly trained personnel.

CONTROLLING COMPUTER IMPACT

Computers have the capacity to be a boon to mankind and to help us solve our greatest difficulties. However, they also have the capacity to be destructive, to limit personal freedom, and to eliminate personal privacy. How can we best obtain the benefits of computer technology while minimizing the dangers?

First, the greatest strength we have is knowledge. As people take courses like this one, as they learn what computer systems should be, and as they learn what the dangers of computing technology are, they will demand better treatment.

Most likely, you will not believe anyone who says, "The computer won't let me." If you hear that statement, speak to as many of the involved supervisors as you can. Let the supervisors know that you are aware that people often hide behind the computer to avoid responsibility. Encourage them to take control over their organization. Computers are not supposed to be dictators; they are supposed to be servants. Go to the president of the organization if you need to. He or she deserves to know who the apparent company leader is—the computer!

As more and more people learn how to deal with computers, they will exercise more power as consumers. They will learn to observe the quality of computer service and will choose to do business with companies that have good systems. As time passes, competition in the marketplace will eliminate companies that operate substandard computer systems.

In addition to consumer knowledge, legislation will help to eliminate computer abuse. Several laws have already been passed, and others are pending. The Fair Credit Reporting Act of 1970 established laws that give individuals the right to see credit data that is maintained about them. This act also stipulates that people can challenge the credit data and that it must be changed if it is erroneous. The Freedom of Information Act of 1970 also gave individuals access to data collected by government agencies.

Another law gives citizens rights with respect to data gathered by the government. The Privacy Act of 1974 stipulates that individuals must be able to learn what information the government collects about them. The government must also state what the data will be used for. Data gathered for one purpose cannot be used for a different purpose without the permission of the individual. Further, individuals have the right to have erroneous data changed. Finally, this act clearly lays the responsibility for maintaining correct data on the organization that keeps it. The responsibility for ensuring that data is not misused lies with the government.

Unfortunately, this act applies only to governmental agencies. Legislation that applies to private organizations and companies is yet to be adopted. Some states have passed such legislation, and others are considering it. Such legislation is not popular with businesses because the costs of compliance will be high.

Knowledge and legislation are the tools we have to control the impact of the computer on society. As citizens, we have the responsibility to make our voices heard. We can be effective by using our consumer power, by knowing our rights and insisting on fair and legal treatment from businesses, and by expressing the need for responsible computer systems and operation to our governmental representatives. If you become involved with the design or operation of computer systems, you will have an opportunity to ensure that the systems are responsibly designed and used.

QUESTIONS

D.1 How has computer technology improved the quality of life in our society?

D.2 Explain how computer technology has changed the character of business.

D.3 Explain five ways that computers are used in medicine.

D.4 Explain five ways that computers are used in the legal professions.

D.5 Explain four ways that computers are used in politics.

D.6 How has computer technology improved the quality of work?

D.7 How has computer technology worsened the quality of life in our society?

D.8 React to the statement "Computers create more jobs than they eliminate."

D.9 Explain how the philosophy "But, officer, this gun shot this man" applies to computer abuse.

D.10 Explain how you can use your knowledge of computers to control the impact of computer technology on our society.

D.11 Explain the benefits of the following laws: Fair Credit Reporting Act of 1970, Freedom of Information Act of 1970, and Privacy Act of 1974.

SUMMARY

In the future, we can expect society's problems to increase. Energy will be scarcer; natural resources will be scarcer; increasing population will place a greater burden on the environment; and competition for scarce resources will cause considerable social unrest. Improving the allocation and control of resources is essential to the solution of these problems. As we have seen, allocation and control are strengths of computer systems. Further, computers are getting cheaper. From these facts, it seems apparent that computers can and should play a major and increasing role.

The computer has brought both benefits and harm to our society. Without the computer, many of our present activities would be impossible. In business, the computer has greatly improved the control and allocation of resources. Activities on a large scale are only possible because of computing. In medicine, new techniques and treatments have become possible because of computers. Computers are used in important ways in the legal professions and in politics. Finally, the computer industry has provided many challenging jobs.

On the other hand, computers have been harmful. Jobs have been eliminated. Standardization has resulted in people being treated as numbers. Business has become colder in some cases. Further, some computer systems have abused people. Data has been in error, and people have been unfairly denied credit or jobs. Additionally, it is difficult for people to have privacy in the computer age. Finally, some systems have been poorly designed and have caused people to be mistreated.

In the future, we must hope to maximize the benefits of computer technology and minimize its harmfulness. In this effort we have two main strengths: our knowledge about how computers can be used, and legislation. Computers are not in themselves bad. They become bad only when people misuse them. We must use our strengths to avoid this misuse.

Electronic Funds Transfer System
(EFTS)
Checkless society
Cashless society
One-way checks

Truncated check flow
Artificial intelligence
Robotics

WORD LIST
(in order of appearance in text)

QUESTIONS TO CHALLENGE YOUR THINKING

A. Imagine that for some reason all of the computers in existence stopped operating. For some reason, they just quit. What would be the impact on our society?

B. Suppose that you could wind time backwards 40 years. Like Superman, you could fly around the earth and undo time. If you could, would you eliminate computers? Do you think the world would have evolved in a better way without computers?

C. Do you think a machine can think? Do you think computers can be built that will duplicate or surpass the human mind?

D. Do you think machines should think? Do you think it is morally right for people to build intelligent machines? Is it possible to build machines that will someday be smarter than we are? Could they enslave us?

MODULE E

Word Processing Systems and Office Augmentation

WHAT IS WORD PROCESSING?
Word Processing Example
Advantages of Word Processing

WORD PROCESSING HARDWARE

WORD PROCESSORS AND COMMUNICATIONS

OFFICE AUGMENTATION

In this module, we will describe word processing systems and discuss the application of computer technology to the office environment. Word processing systems are computer-driven typewriters, although, as we will see, they have much greater capability than a typewriter.

First, we will introduce word processing by describing its features, capabilities, advantages, and costs. Then, typical word processing hardware will be illustrated. Next, the possible interfaces of word processing with data processing and other office machines will be discussed. Finally, we will describe computer-based tools available to augment the office work force.

WHAT IS WORD PROCESSING?

Word processing systems use computer technology to facilitate the preparation of documents. A person uses a keyboard to compose or type a document that appears on the CRT screen. When the person makes a typographical error, he or she simply backspaces and types the correct character over the error. Additionally, a powerful set of commands is available to move words around, to insert and delete words, and to perform other editing functions.

Once a document has been prepared, it can be saved on magnetic disk. It can be printed using a computer-driven printer. Once a document has been stored on disk, it can be retrieved, edited, and printed again. Thus, word processing is particularly useful in environments where documents go through several drafts before they are finished.

Word Processing Example

This book, its accompanying workbook, and other supporting materials were written on a word processor. (See figure E-1.) To illustrate the power of such systems, we will show how the paragraph immediately above could be changed using special word processing commands.

Figure E-2 shows how that paragraph appeared on the word processor CRT screen. Now, suppose you decide to change the first sentence, beginning with the words

```
Once a document has been prepared, it can be . . .
```

to read

```
A document can be saved . . .
```

On a word processor, there is a Replace key or command. To make the above change, you simply hit the Replace key, and then show the system which words you want to replace. Word processors have a cursor, which is an underline character that moves to different places on the CRT screen. There are buttons to push to move the cursor around. To replace the words *Once a document has been prepared, it . . .* , you move the cursor to the letter *O* and hit a particular key. Then you move the cursor to the letter *t* in *it*, as shown in figure E-3. Then you hit a key labeled *Execute*. At this point, the word processor will remove these words and ask you what you want to replace them with. (See figure E-4.) You then type the words *A document* into the hole the system has created and hit the key again. The paragraph now reads as shown in figure E-5.

FIGURE E-1

Use of word processing equipment

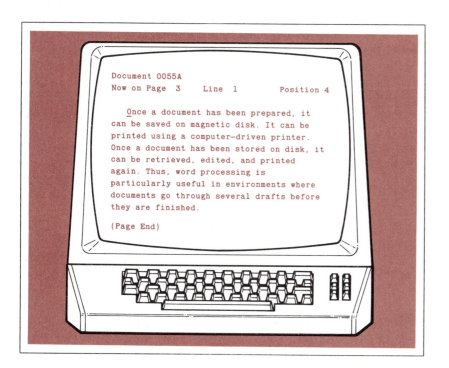

FIGURE E-2

Paragraph of this book on a word
processor

Document 0055A
Now on Page 3   Line 1   Position 4

    Once a document has been prepared, it
can be saved on magnetic disk. It can be
printed using a computer-driven printer.
Once a document has been stored on disk, it
can be retrieved, edited, and printed
again. Thus, word processing is
particularly useful in environments where
documents go through several drafts before
they are finished.

(Page End)

Document 0055A
Now on Page 3   Line 1   Position 40
Replace what?

    Once a document has been prepared, it
can be saved on magnetic disk. It can be
printed using a computer-driven printer.
Once a document has been stored on disk, it
can be retrieved, edited, and printed
again. Thus, word processing is
particularly useful in environments where
documents go through several drafts before
they are finished.
(Page End)

FIGURE E-3

Replacing a phrase on the word processor

You shortened the sentence by making this change. Therefore, the system automatically moved words to the left and adjusted the paragraph to fill the hole. The format of the whole paragraph has been automatically changed.

In addition to replacing, word processing systems can delete and insert. When a deletion is made, words and lines are adjusted to fill any gaps created. When an insertion is made, words are moved to allow space for the new characters.

Many other features are provided. Special keys are available to allow indentions, to cause one or more lines to be centered on a page, and to move or copy characters. For example, the paragraph used in figures E-2, E-3, and E-5 was typed only once. The word processor made copies for the examples.

Another feature of word processors is variable margins. Suppose you want to type the same paragraph but with wider margins. To make this adjustment, you set the new margins and hit a special key. The word processor then moves words from line to line to conform to the new margins. The same paragraph then appears as shown in figure E-6.

All of this rearranging is done simply by typing a few keys. As you can see, a word processor makes it easy to add or delete words, sentences, or paragraphs. In fact, whole pages can be added to a document, and the document will be adjusted to accommodate the changes.

There are many other useful features of word processing systems. Documents can be merged, form letters can be prepared, many "original" copies can be made, columns of numbers can be added, numbers can be aligned on decimal points, and so on.

Document 0055A
Now on Page 3   Line 1   Position 4
Replace with?

can be saved on magnetic dis*

FIGURE E-4

Word processor is ready to accept new
phrase

Advantages of Word Processing

Word processing systems have simplified secretarial activity. Before word processing systems were developed, secretaries and typists had to completely retype pages or even entire documents when changes were made. They had to be careful not to make mistakes because fixing errors took considerable time. With word processing, changes are simple to make and typographical errors are eliminated by overstriking.

Because of these advantages, secretaries with word processing systems can be much more efficient. In fact, it has been estimated that word processors reduce typing time by 50 percent. Thus, if a secretary spends half of his or her time typing (say, four hours per day), a word processor will save half of this time (two hours per day). That is 25 percent of the total time available!

While these savings are significant, word processors can be used to obtain even greater savings. Some companies have found that they do not need to employ typists to prepare documents. Because mistakes are easy to correct and editing is easy to do, many professionals have found that they can compose directly on a word processing screen. In this case, typists are not needed. For example, some lawyers can produce more work by typing on a word processing system than by writing on paper or dictating. They use the word processor not to eliminate the cost of a typist, but rather to speed up their work.

People in other professions have learned this shortcut, too. For years, programmers and systems analysts used computer text editors to prepare documentation. These text editors were the predecessors of word processing systems. Many auditors and consultants have begun to use word processors for composition as well.

```
Document 0055A
Now on Page  3      Line  1          Position 15

    A document can be saved on magnetic
disk. It can be printed using a computer-
driven printer. Once a document has been
stored on disk, it can be retrieved,
edited, and printed again. Thus, word
processing is particularly useful in
environments where documents go through
several drafts before they are finished.

(Page End)
```

FIGURE E-5

Paragraph of this book after replacement

Great cost savings are possible when professional people compose on word processors. People who can produce work in two-thirds to one-half as much time are then free to do other work. People who do their own editing also have greater control over the quality of their work.

The cost of a typical word processing system is between $5,000 and $20,000. That may seem expensive, but the annual salary of a typist is in that range. If the word processor can save the work of one typist, it pays for itself in a year.

WORD PROCESSING HARDWARE

The configuration of a typical word processing system is shown in figure E-7. It has four components: *work stations* (the CRTs used to input documents), a *CPU*, a *disk system*, and a *printer*.

The CPU of a word processing system need not be very powerful, at least not by data processing standards. Only a little intelligence is required to move text around and to keep track of it. Because typists and printers operate at slow speeds, the CPU need not be fast. Microprocessors have been very successful as word processing CPUs.

Two types of disks are used in word processors. The most common are floppy disk systems. Usually, there are master and backup drives. The master drive maintains the systems programs and the copies of documents that are currently being produced, edited, or printed. The master floppy typically holds about 100 pages of documents.

The backup drive is used to copy documents for storage. Floppies are readily mounted and dismounted on this drive. When a document is to be stored, a

Document 0055A
Now on Page 3   Line 1   Position 4
     A document can be saved on
magnetic disk. It can be printed
using a computer-driven printer.
Once a document has been stored on
disk, it can be retrieved, edited,
and printed again. Thus, word
processing is particularly useful
in environments where documents go
through several drafts before they
are finished.
(Page End)

FIGURE E-6

The same paragraph after margin
changes

floppy is mounted on the backup drive and the document is copied to it. The floppy can then be filed in a cabinet or on a bookshelf. Later, when the document is needed, the floppy is mounted on the backup drive and the document copied onto the master disk. Once there, it can be edited or printed. A backup floppy typically holds more data than the master; 120 pages is typical. (See figure E-8.)

The second type of disk is a hard disk similar to that used for direct access file processing. (See chapter 6.) These disks are much more expensive than floppies, but they have far greater capacity. They can hold 500 to 1000 pages of documents. When hard disks are available, the system programs and current documents are kept on them. Floppies are still used for backup.

The fourth component of a word processing system is a printer. It is usually important to have high-quality print for word processing applications, so the printers are generally expensive, full-character printers. Daisy wheel printers are often used. They have removable print wheels, as shown in figure E-9. A variety of print styles is available.

Word processing printers typically operate at 40 to 50 characters per second. Although this is much slower than other printers (4000 characters per second is typical for a line printer), it is much faster than manual typing. The quality of the print on a word processing printer is better than that on a typical line printer. Both upper- and lower-case letters are available.

Word processing printers are bidirectional. Instead of returning the carriage to the left margin on every line, they print in both directions. Thus, every other line is printed backwards. This is surprising to see, but is actually simple for the CPU to control.

Terminal Tedium

PLYMOUTH, Mass.—The building is in an industrial park three miles from the famous rock. And it is a factory of sorts, despite the burnt sienna carpeting and the indirect lighting.

The people who work here process health-insurance claims for Blue Shield of Massachusetts. The facility is highly automated, and the work is done with video display terminals (VDTs). Six hours a day, except for one 15-minute break, processors sit before their terminals transferring data from claims forms to a company computer system.

The computer revolution came to Plymouth a little more than a year ago, and a claims processor here offers a counterrevolutionary criticism: "The girls at work call it a sweatshop. Most of them figure they won't last more than two years."

Over the past decade, computer-based automation has reached into many an American office, changing the nature of work and making the video display terminal nearly as ubiquitous as the typewriter. Sophisticated systems have helped to increase productivity and reduce employers' labor costs. . . .

A Throwback?

More and more, however, critics are beginning to question whether the new technology is improving the lot of office workers. Could it instead be producing new forms of tedium and certain of the abuses of 19th-century factory life, namely, piecework and exploitation of labor? . . .

The term "office automation" encompasses the use of computers by all types of white-collar workers, including managers. But the labor issue seems confined to the automation of the most routine office jobs. Most controversial of all are the high-volume data-processing centers such as Blue Shield's Plymouth production center. These electronic factories make use of the most sophisticated technology and, critics say, the most questionable labor practices.

Controlled by the Machine

A recent study by the U.S. Public Health Service offers some support for the criticism. The study looked at three types of workers: professionals who occasionally used video display terminals, clerical workers who did data processing with video display terminals, and clerical workers who had comparable jobs but who did the work manually.

"The clerical workers using the VDTs reported by far the most physical and mental stress," says Barbara Cohen, a research psychologist who helped conduct the study. The terminal users had to follow rigid work procedures and didn't have any control over their work, Mrs. Cohen notes. "It was the machine that was controlling them."

The electronic factory is mostly a creature of banks, insurance companies, credit-card concerns and other companies with particularly large data-processing requirements. In appearance, these places tend to be similar: a large, quiet room with video display terminals grouped in clusters or rows. The terminals are linked to a central computer. Data processors serve as electronic-age stevedores, loading and retrieving information.

By JOHN ANDREW
Wall Street Journal, May 6, 1983

Word processing systems can become very large. It is possible to have 20 or 30 work stations and five or six printers on a single system. Systems this large are very expensive, however. A cost of $50,000 to $200,000 is typical.

WORD PROCESSORS AND COMMUNICATIONS

Many companies have found that they can increase the usefulness of their word processing systems by having them communicate with other office equipment. One common application is to connect a word processor to an *intelligent copier*

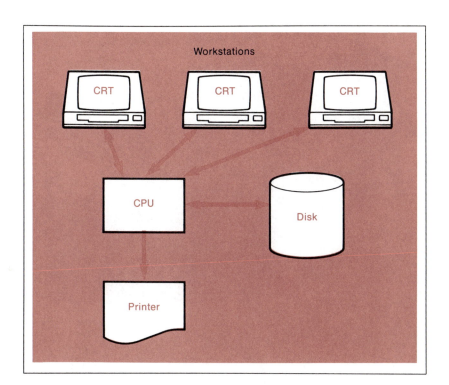

FIGURE E-7

Components of a word processing system

FIGURE E-8

Using a floppy disk system for backup

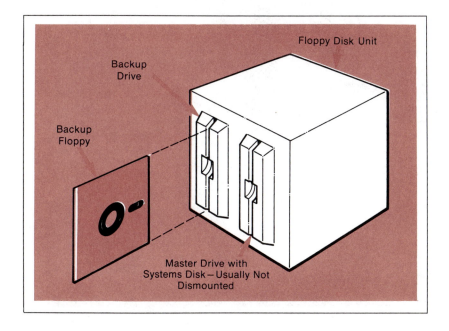

413

FIGURE E-9

Daisy wheel print mechanism

FIGURE E-10

Intelligent copier

like the one shown in figure E-10. These copiers are like Xerox machines, but they can accept both printed source documents and electronic input.

When word processors and intelligent copiers are used together, the word processor sends instructions and text to the copier. For example, a secretary at a word processing work station might issue a command to make 100 copies of a certain document. The word processor would retrieve the text of the document from storage and send it to the copier with a command to make 100 copies. Because the copier operates at much higher speeds than the word processing printer, this setup will be more efficient than printing 100 originals.

Another possibility is to connect several word processing CPUs together. This arrangement is effective for companies that have offices in several geographic locations. When word processors are connected together, documents that are prepared in one location can be printed in others. Thus, instead of sending a printed document to another location by regular mail, the electronic form is sent over communication lines.

A system of distributed word processors and intelligent copiers is shown in figure E-11. This system is used by a law firm with offices in Los Angeles, Washington, D.C., and Anchorage, Alaska. Because all three cities have word processing systems, documents prepared in any of the locations can be transmitted electronically to any of the other locations for printing. Further, because both L.A. and Washington have intelligent copiers, the text of source documents can be sent from either of these cities to the other.

Although the benefits of distributed word processing are great, the combination of word processing and data processing can be even more useful. When they are combined, the word processing CPU is connected on the data processing CPU by communications lines or by shared files. In the latter case, a fixed disk is connected to both computers. The computers leave messages for each other on the disk.

Accounts receivable is one application that can benefit from this combination. The data processing system can maintain the accounts receivable file and process order invoices and payments as they occur. Periodically, the data processing computer can send messages to the word processing computer to generate form letters to customers. For example, if a customer's bill is overdue, the data processing computer can direct the word processing computer to prepare a letter asking for payment. This action can be recorded in the data processing computer's files. Subsequent letters can be made more threatening if needed and appropriate.

One law firm has developed an even more ingenious and profitable application for a combination of word and data processing systems. This firm has several hundred standard paragraphs for wills. When a lawyer prepares a will, he or she selects all of the standard paragraphs that are appropriate. If slight modifications are needed, they are made and recorded on the word processing system. The word processor passes a file of paragraph numbers and modifications to the data processing computer, where this data is stored along with the name of the client.

Whenever a law change impacts one of these paragraphs, a data processing program searches all of the wills to determine which ones contain that paragraph. A file of names of people with affected wills is then sent to the word

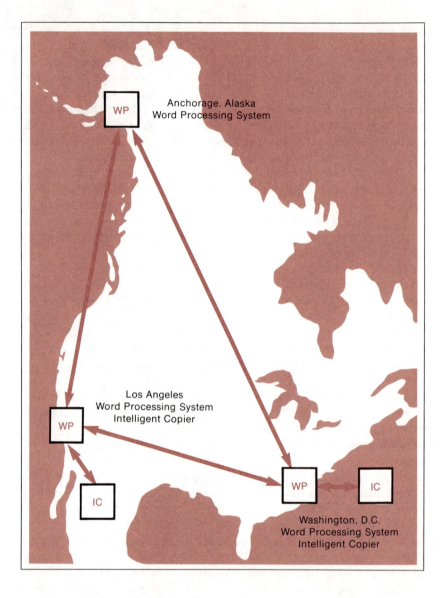

Anchorage, Alaska
Word Processing System

Los Angeles
Word Processing System
Intelligent Copier

Washington, D.C.
Word Processing System
Intelligent Copier

FIGURE E-11

Network of word processors and
intelligent copiers for a law office

processor computer. The computer prepares form letters to these people telling
them that the law has changed and asking if they want their wills updated.

Meanwhile, a firm lawyer rewrites the standard paragraph to conform to the
new law. The new standard paragraph is then added to the files of the word
processor.

When responses are received from people who want their wills updated,
this fact is input to the data processing system. This system sends the list of
paragraph numbers to the word processing system, which then generates the
new wills. The data processing computer also conveniently prepares a bill for
each client. It is typed by the word processor and sent to the client a few days
later.

Automated Work Stations: A Challenge for Professionals

During the next 10–15 years, professionals of all kinds—white collar, engineering and medical—will use multifunction work stations to access corporate, industrial, governmental, research and commercial data bases. These work stations will provide print-outs, and interface with other peripheral devices for input, output and distribution. They also will do independent processing. Local networks, PBX or public data networks will serve as communications links.

In this office of the future, the work station will tolerate user errors, and it will be user-friendly. It will be easy to use and understand. Besides typing, the system's user interfaces will incorporate touch and voice communications. Displays will be alphanumeric or pictorial, with options for either black-and-white or color.

Storage on Demand
Professionals will see one page or several, flip pages back and forth,
zoom in for detail, and retrieve information from local files or outside data bases. Storage will be available on demand, with access to it for retrieval or inquiry. Each work station will have a software package, tailored to its professional's needs, with a high-level, English-like conversational language appropriate to the user's specific functions and to the general functions of the office.

Additional software will facilitate communications between work stations and people, and from work station to work station. It will support face-to-face interactive communication and information distribution.

Because such an all-purpose work station does not yet exist, a user must choose less general equipment on the basis of specific needs. To decide on a specific work station, the professional must understand the nature of his or her office and the way work is done there.

An office can be defined broadly as people performing various functions. Thus, variable working
groups can constitute a single-office firm doing a specific type of business or a large corporation's multifunctions performed by many people who specialize in a range of activities. A number of functions can be generalized in that they are common to many types of offices. However, some functions are office-specific.

Traditional Disciplines
Traditionally, the computer industry organized office functions into the disciplines of data processing, word processing and office automation. Surrounding these disciplines are the common functions of storage, distribution and communications as shown in Fig. 1. General functions such as these are needed by many professionals.

By BETTY M. BRODIE
The Office, June, 1983

Using this system, a law firm can update a will for about $5. The standard charge to a client for updating a will is about $65. Therefore, the firm makes considerable profit on each will that it updates. Furthermore, the clients of this firm have very up-to-date wills.

Word processing, intelligent copiers, online data processing systems—computers are bringing automation to the office. In fact, some people use the term *office automation* to refer to the movement of computer technology into the office. We will avoid that term in this book because it is misleading. No amount

OFFICE AUGMENTATION

of computer equipment will *automate* the office. Instead, computer technology can be used to *augment* the capabilities of office personnel.

Figure E-12 lists common applications of computer technology in the office. Computers acting as stand-alone systems can provide a variety of services. *Word processing* systems simplify the task of preparing documents. *Graphics* programs can generate simple charts, such as bar graphs, pie charts, and XY plots. *Electronic spreadsheets* (see chapter 3) can be used for financial calculations as well as for many other purposes. Easy-to-use database management systems are available to store and retrieve *personal databases*. Programs are available to keep *calendars* and *telephone numbers* and to provide *reminders* of tasks to be accomplished.

When computers have communications capability, even more possibilities exist. *Communicating word processing* systems have already been discussed.

Electronic mail is another possibility. When this system is used, each subscriber has a mailbox. When a person wants to see what mail has been delivered, he or she simply opens the mailbox by issuing commands to the electronic mail system. That system then prints whatever (electronic) messages have been sent to that user's address. Similarly, when a subscriber wants to send a message, he or she simply types the message (possibly using a word processing system), and then provides the addresses of all mailboxes to which the message is to be sent. Many people prefer electronic mail to the telephone because the recipient of the message need not be physically present in his or her office when the message is sent.

An office computer can also serve as a *window to data sources*. Such sources may reside on a company's own large computers, or they may reside outside of the company. In either case, the office computer communicates with the computer having the data.

Given the current trend of cheaper computers and more expensive labor, we can expect the application of computer technology in the office to increase more and more. Some people think that the paperless office is possible. Others think that this expectation is unrealistic. Most likely, paper will never be replaced, but more and more documents will probably be stored in computer systems.

As communication systems are standardized, intercompany communication can also be done electronically. In the not-too-distant future, letters as we know them today may be eliminated. They will be prepared on word processing systems, shipped electronically from one company to another, and then stored

Stand-alone Computer
Word processing
Graphics
Electronic spreadsheets
Personal database management
Calendars, telephone directory, reminder systems
Computer with communications
Electronic mail
Window to data sources

in an individual's electronic mailbox. After reading such mail, the recipient can destroy it or store it in a word processing file. A letter sent this way may never be printed.

The automated office may sound futuristic, but it is probably not as far away as you think. The office you retire from will likely have undreamed of applications of computer technology. You will be a pioneer in the application of computer technology to the office.

QUESTIONS

E.1 What is a word processing system? What does it do?

E.2 Describe three word processing edit facilities.

E.3 How has word processing simplified the typist's job? According to the text, about how much time do word processors save?

E.4 How can professional people take advantage of word processing systems?

E.5 How much does a small word processing system cost? How much does a large one with 20 terminals and several printers cost?

E.6 Name the four components of a word processing system.

E.7 What is an intelligent copier? What are the advantages of coupling word processors and intelligent copiers together?

E.8 What are the advantages of coupling two or more word processing computers together?

E.9 What are the advantages of coupling word processing and data processing computers?

E.10 Describe applications of computer technology to the office.

SUMMARY

Word processing systems apply computer technology to the preparation of documents. People use CRTs to input source documents and edit them using powerful word processing commands. Documents can be stored on disk, and they can also be printed.

Word processors greatly simplify the job of the typist. However, the greatest savings occur when professionals compose documents directly on word processors. This practice not only eliminates the need for a typist, but also enables the professional to work more productively.

Word processors can be connected to other office equipment. When tied to intelligent copiers, they can produce many copies of documents. When interfaced with other word processors, they allow remote word processing to be done. When word processors are connected to data processing computers, great savings and improvements in service become possible.

Computers are bringing automation to the office. In addition to doing word processing, office computers can prepare graphics, compute and display electronic spreadsheets, maintain personal databases, keep calendars and telephone numbers, and send reminders. When office computers communicate with one another, electronic mail is possible. Finally, office computers can serve as windows to remote data sources.

WORD LIST
(in order of appearance in text)

Word processing
CRT
Replace command
Cursor
Insert command
Delete command
Variable margins
Word processing work station
CPU
Floppy disk

Hard disk
Daisy wheel printer
Intelligent copier
Office augmentation
Graphics
Electronic spreadsheets
Electronic mail
Electronic mailbox
Data sources

PART FIVE

Computer Programming

The modules in this part discuss computer programs and programming. Module F introduces the BASIC programming language. The purpose of this module is to acquaint you with computer programming and to give you confidence in writing simple programs. Module G discusses the design of computer programs and the characteristics of good programming style. The third module really consists of eight parts, which introduce more advanced BASIC statements. The discussion incorporates the design concepts presented in module G.

Module I discusses programs and defines the functions of language compilers, systems utilities, and operating systems. Module J surveys computer languages and describes the characteristics and requirements for languages in business, scientific, and systems applications. Module K describes nonprocedural programming, which is a new style of programming that promises incredible increases in productivity. Finally, module L describes some of the popular applications packages.

MODULE F
Introduction to BASIC Programming

MODULE G
Designing Simple Computer Programs

MODULE H
BASIC Programming

MODULE I
Systems Programs

MODULE J
Survey of Computer Programming Languages

MODULE K
Nonprocedural Programming

MODULE L
Popular Applications Software

MODULE F

Introduction to BASIC Programming

PROGRAMS?

HOW DO I GET STARTED?

OVERVIEW OF BASIC, WITH SIMPLE

SAMPLE PROGRAMS
PRINT Statement
Assignment Statement
INPUT Statement

A PROGRAMMING EXAMPLE

Programming is an exciting and challenging facet of the computer industry. Anyone can learn to write instructions for computer systems. Being a mathematician or an engineer is not necessary. Your early efforts may be frustrating, but remain patient and calm. In this book, numerous examples and explanations are given with each new topic that you learn. Other people will be struggling along with you as you learn to direct a computer using the language BASIC.

BASIC is an acronym. It stands for Beginners All-purpose Symbolic Instructional Code. This language was developed in the mid-1960s at Dartmouth College by John G. Kemeny and Thomas E. Kurtz. The language is widely accepted by microcomputer (personal, home, or small business computer) users. It is frequently used by educators to teach simple programming. There are standard rules for the language BASIC, much as we have grammatical rules for English. The rules (standards) for BASIC are determined by the American National Standards Institute (ANSI). This language standard must be met by a computer vendor before the vendor's implementation of BASIC is considered correct. Vendors often add extra features or extensions to the language to make certain tasks possible or easier. Each implementation of BASIC is unique, yet similar to all the others.

Learning to program on computers can be fun and helpful to your understanding of how computers work.

PROGRAMS?

What is a program? A *program* is a set of instructions written for a computer. We are going to write instructions using the language BASIC. There are hundreds of other programming languages, but BASIC has some particular features that have value to us. Some of these features include ease of program entry, immediate editing of entered program statements, and simple language rules. What can a program do? A program can direct the computer to do any job that can be defined as a logical sequence of steps. Usually, a program can be written to accomplish any job, given enough time and money.

Programs can contain two types of errors. *Syntax errors* are errors caused by not following the rules of writing a language. The command PRINT A is a valid BASIC command. If the word PRINT were misspelled as PRIT, a syntax error would occur. Computer language translators look for and report these types of errors. The other type of program error is called a run-time or *logic error.* These errors are caused by instructing the computer to do a task incorrectly. For example, if you were supposed to add two numbers, but had written the instructions to subtract the two numbers by mistake, this would be an example of a logic error. These type of mistakes are sometimes called runtime errors because they occur at the time a program is run. Language translators cannot find these kinds of mistakes because you have written valid program instructions. These types of mistakes take the most work to prevent and correct.

A BASIC statement cannot be executed directly by the computer. A translation process must take place. Figure F-1 illustrates this translation. The translation from BASIC statements (*source* code) to machine-executable (*object*) code can be done in two ways. One type of translation is done by a sophisticated

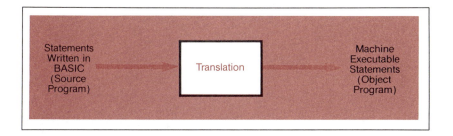

program called an *interpreter.* As each statement is entered, it is checked for syntax errors. If a BASIC statement cannot be recognized, an error message is produced. After the command to run the program is given, the interpreter looks at a BASIC statement, determines what needs to be done by the computer, and constructs the machine-executable instructions needed. Then the computer executes them. After the first set of translated machine instructions are executed, the interpreter looks at the next BASIC statement. This process continues until program execution is complete. This method of preparing and executing programs is commonly used. The translation process must take place every time the program is run.

Another method of translation is called *compiling.* Each BASIC statement is entered without having a syntax check performed. Any errors in syntax are reported by the compiler (again a sophisticated program) when it is told to translate the source program. If there are no syntax errors, the BASIC statements that a *programmer* (person who writes programs) has written are translated to produce an object code module. The object module is a collection of machine executable instructions representing the BASIC program. This object module can be executed many times without recompiling. Because the translation must be done only when changes are made to the source statements, this method of translation is efficient if the same program is to be run many times.

HOW DO I GET STARTED?

Learning how to use a new piece of equipment is often frightening. Computer equipment looks extremely complex and fragile. However, most computer hardware has been built in such a way that you can't hurt it easily. Treat your equipment with respect, don't force things, and you won't hurt anything. If you don't know how to type, I can sympathize with you. Learning to type may be the largest barrier you have to overcome. The computer keyboard works in much the same way a typewriter keyboard does.

In general, a computer system must have some sort of *input device,* a *processor,* and an *output device.* For practical use, the system must also have some sort of long-term storage for *secondary storage,* usually in the form of cassette tapes, diskettes (floppy disks), hard disks, or magnetic tapes. Figure F-2 shows this input, process, output, secondary-storage relationship. The arrows on the diagram show the flow of data through the various pieces of computer equipment. Examples of input devices are keyboards and card readers. Data that is to go into a computer system must go through an input device.

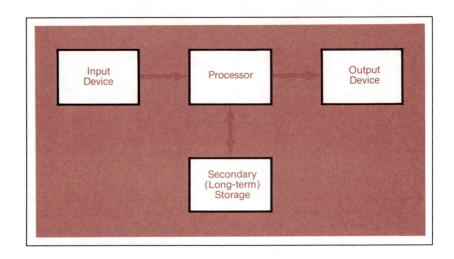

FIGURE F-2

Relationships among input and output devices, processor, and secondary storage

the program and the processing data, an arithmetic logic unit (or ALU) that actually executes the program's instructions, and a control unit that controls the timing between the memory and the ALU (see figure F-3). Any program must be in memory to execute, and all data must be in memory to be used. Memory is of limited size, and is typically measured in units of K, where K = 1024 characters. There are two primary types of memory: *random-access memory* (RAM), and *read-only memory* (ROM). RAM memory can be thought of as the computer's scratch pad. Programs and data are manipulated in RAM memory. Most RAM memory does not retain its contents if electrical power is lost. ROM memory is used to store data and programs that are needed by the computer on a permanent basis.

Examples of output equipment are cathode-ray tubes—commonly called CRTs, or video display terminals (VDTs), or monitors (perhaps simply television sets)—and printers. The keyboard unit (input) and CRT may be combined into a single unit commonly known as a terminal. If data is to be used, it must be recorded in some fashion that a person can use.

FIGURE F-3

The processor, or central processing unit (CPU)

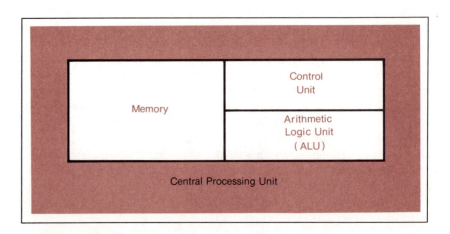

Examples of secondary-storage devices are: cassette tape drives, diskette or floppy disk drives, and hard disk drives. Data is often stored on secondary storage to be used in later processing. Programs and data can be transferred between machines on secondary-storage media. Because memory is of limited size, data usually is stored on a device with greater capacity and retention.

You will typically use a terminal to work with your computer. You will type in all of your commands to the computer through the terminal keyboard, and you will receive messages from the computer on your terminal CRT display. When you desire to have a permanent copy of your work on the computer, you will probably request that the work be printed on the printer. If you are working with a microcomputer, you will probably handle the tape cartridges or diskettes yourself. If you use a larger system (a minicomputer), trained personnel will be working behind the scenes to ensure that tapes or disks are available as you need them.

The common aspects of operation of computer systems must be understood before we look at each individual vendor's system. All machines must have some sort of electrical power supplied. The power is usually turned on by one or more switches. The computer system must then have a program that controls the functions of the hardware. This program is called an operating system. The system will ask for commands with a simple prompt. The commands will instruct the system to perform certain functions. These will be covered in the chapter on system commands.

You have probably wondered how similar various computer systems are. Rest assured that the same functions are performed, though they may be done in different ways. Just as car manufacturers think they have built the "better mousetrap" by placing an ignition keyhole in a different place, computer builders have tried different ways of doing things. Since you are a beginner, I recognize that most of what you are seeing is confusing at this point. To minimize the confusion of learning about your computer, please refer to Appendix 7 which tells how to start many types of systems. After you have learned how to turn on your system, proceed to the programming examples in this module. If your system is not listed in Appendix 7, check with your instructor to find which system is most like yours. If none of these systems are like yours, refer to the system documentation. Differences in many popular versions of BASIC are listed in the table in Appendix 3. Use the space in figure F-4 to record the specific facts about your system.

F.1 What does the acronym BASIC mean?

F.2 What is a program?

F.3 Explain the difference between source code and object code.

F.4 Programs are translated by two methods. Explain them and give the advantages of each.

F.5 List the steps needed to be able to begin programming in BASIC on your system.

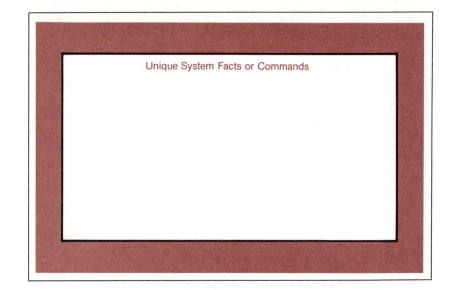

Unique System Facts or Commands

FIGURE F-4

System facts or commands for your own system

SUMMARY

BASIC is an acronym that stands for Beginner's All-purpose Symbolic Instruction Code. It was developed in the 1960s by Kemeny and Kurtz. We use the language BASIC to write instructions for computers. These instructions are called programs. Each program must be translated in one of two ways. Programs are either (1) interpreted, or (2) compiled to be translated. The program we write is called source code, and the translated program is called object code.

Computer systems are a collection of input, processing, output, and secondary-storage devices. Examples of these devices, respectively, include the keyboard, CPU, printers, and diskette drives. Each computer system is unique on the surface, but all computers function similarly internally. We looked specifically at how to start using our own computer systems.

WORD LIST

(in order of appearance in text)

BASIC	Input device
Program	Processor
Syntax error	Output device
Logic error	Secondary Storage
Source code	Central processing unit (CPU)
Object code	Memory
Interpreter	Arithmetic logic unit (ALU)
Compiling	Random-access memory (RAM)
Programmer	Read-only memory (ROM)

OVERVIEW OF BASIC, WITH SIMPLE SAMPLE PROGRAMS

So far, we have learned how to turn our computers on, and how to prepare the computer for BASIC programming. We still have much material to learn, but let's step back and take a look at some things that can be done using BASIC. Don't worry about not understanding everything that you will see in this section. All of the different BASIC statements in the following sample programs will be explained in later modules and are summarized in appendix 8. Right now we are merely attempting to look at the "big picture" and to give you an idea of where learning to program will take us. It is important that you can begin programming very early in your learning experience. The programs in this chapter can be entered on most systems as they appear. This is not an attempt to teach any of the statements contained in the chapter in depth.

Learning to use a computer terminal can be very easy. Don't get upset if something doesn't work exactly the way you heard about it or the way you read about it. The computing industry is changing extremely rapidly. Modifications in the programs that control your programming may change the wording or display of commands. Even within a single installation, terminals that look the same can act differently. The power switches may be located in different positions. The color displayed by the terminals may be different. Even the current (or active) typing location on the screen (known as a *cursor*) can be represented by different shapes (box or line), intensities, or blinking.

The characters get to the screen from the computer, not from the keyboard, after a key is depressed. The computer must recognize the key depressed, perform the function desired, and respond so the person using the computer knows that the input has been accepted. The position on the screen where the characters print is related to the current location of the cursor. In effect, the cursor is the next print position used for output operations.

The RETURN (or ENTER or ↵) key must be pressed after every line of BASIC code of any *system command*. The act of pressing the RETURN key in this chapter will be represented by <CR> which stands for "carriage return." If the computer is not responding to your last command or the cursor has not jumped down to the next line waiting for your input, perhaps you have forgotten to <CR>. The system will not always place a character or acknowledgment on the screen when you press the RETURN key, so you will need to remember whether or not you have done a <CR>.

In the following sections, we will write small programs using the PRINT, assignment, and INPUT statements. The BASIC *statements* are preceded by *line numbers*. The commands to the system don't have line numbers. The system commands needed are included in the examples. The programs will grow in size up to each NEW system command. If you should make an error in typing, an error message will probably be displayed. If you do see a typing error, try retyping that line. If you cannot figure out what is causing the problem, try starting over with the most recent NEW system command. If your computer requires a program name with the NEW command, use the name PROG1 (to stand for "program number one").

PRINT Statement

First, let's look at the PRINT statement. The PRINT statement tells the computer to display (or print) some piece of information. This allows the person using the computer (user) to see information that has been processed by the computer. To print strings of characters (words) type in

```
NEW <CR>
10 PRINT "COMPUTERS ARE FUN" <CR>
RUN <CR>

COMPUTERS ARE FUN ← Computer response to the command RUN
```

431

Note that we used the system command RUN to tell the system to run (begin to execute) our program. Note also that we had to depress the return key <CR> after typing in the system command NEW, and after the BASIC PRINT statement, as well as after the system command RUN. The first thing entered was the system command NEW. This command clears the work area and lets you start a new program. The PRINT statement caused the computer to print out the phrase COMPUTERS ARE FUN that we saw on the display. The BASIC statements we type in remain in our *work area* (a scratch pad in computer memory to hold our program) until we tell the computer to clear the work area using the NEW system command. (A warning is in order here. When the NEW command is used, any program in the work area will be erased. If you want to retrieve it, you cannot unless it has been saved. The process of saving a program will be explained in more detail later). We shall therefore continue to see line 10 each time we use the LIST system command. Remember that BASIC statements have a line number in front of them, and system commands never do. This means that system commands are never a part of the program itself.

The *arithmetic operators* in BASIC look much like the ones we know from mathematics courses. The plus (+) means addition, the minus (−) means subtraction, the asterisk (*) means multiplication, and the slash (/) means division. If we desire to print out problem solutions, we can type in the following on our terminal:

```
20 PRINT 27 / 9 <CR>
30 PRINT 3 * 6 <CR>
LIST <CR>
```

```
10 PRINT "COMPUTERS ARE FUN"        Computer response
20 PRINT 27 / 9                     to the system
30 PRINT 3 * 6                      command LIST
```

```
RUN <CR>
```

```
COMPUTERS ARE FUN
   3                                Computer response to
                                    the system command RUN
  18                                (output)
```

In this series of instructions, we additionally asked the computer system to divide 27 by 9 in line 20, and to multiply 3 times 6 in line 30, printing each result. Once we had typed in the new program lines 20 and 30, we asked the computer system to list our program, using the LIST command. The program lines were then displayed by the computer system. When the listing was taking place, note that the previous line we had keyed (line 10) was also displayed. If we choose to add lines to a program, we must use different line numbers than those that already exist. If we want to replace an existing line, we need only to type in the new statement with the same line number. If we want to delete an existing line, typing in the line number with nothing following it will delete the line. Note that we again asked for the program to be run or executed by using the system command RUN. The system command RUN starts execution at the lowest numbered line, and executes the statements in line-number sequence from there. The program execution produced the results printed below the system command. The phrase COMPUTERS ARE FUN on the first line, the result of the division on the next line, and the result of the multiplication on the third line are produced by the three PRINT statements.

We can also print out strings containing numbers, as is done by adding the following statement at line 40:

```
40 PRINT "NUMBER 1" <CR>
LIST <CR>

10 PRINT "COMPUTERS ARE FUN"
20 PRINT 27 / 9
30 PRINT 3 * 6
40 PRINT "NUMBER 1"

RUN <CR>

COMPUTERS ARE FUN
 3
 18
NUMBER 1
```

BASIC statements are inserted in programs based on line number. If we want to insert a BASIC statement between two other BASIC statements, we can choose a number between the line numbers of the two statements involved. We can leave blank lines between output by typing in a PRINT with no information requested. Both of these points are illustrated as follows (line 25):

```
25 PRINT <CR>
LIST <CR>

10 PRINT "COMPUTERS ARE FUN"
20 PRINT 27 / 9
25 PRINT
30 PRINT 3 * 6
40 PRINT "NUMBER 1"

RUN <CR>

COMPUTERS ARE FUN
 3
 18
NUMBER 1
```

Please note that we departed from the scheme of numbering the BASIC statements by 10. Because BASIC statements are listed and usually executed in statement number order, we chose to insert the blank line PRINT statement between the PRINT statements containing divide and multiply operations. The reason that we try to increment our BASIC line numbers by 10 is to give us an opportunity to come back and insert lines between existing lines as our needs change. Let's see how well you have understood the PRINT statement. From the following example, determine what the output will look like.

```
NEW <CR>
10 REM SAMPLE OF PRINT STATEMENTS <CR>
20 REM PRINT MINIMUM POINTS FOR AN "A" <CR>
30 PRINT "THIS TEST HAS" <CR>
40 PRINT "200 POINTS POSSIBLE" <CR>
50 PRINT <CR>
60 PRINT "IT TAKES A MINIMUM OF" <CR>
70 PRINT .9 * 200 <CR>
80 PRINT "POINTS TO RECEIVE THE TOP GRADE" <CR>
90 END <CR>
RUN <CR>
```

Did you figure out the output? Yes, there are a few new statements in this sample. At lines 10 and 20, another new BASIC statement, the REM (remark) statement was used. It is for the use of the programmer, and is used to help clarify what is being done with the other BASIC statements. The computer interprets this statement when the program is being RUN, but knows that no computer operation should take place. Program control is passed directly to the next BASIC statement. The REM statement is included in the LIST option. Often the REM statement is called a *comment*.

Also included in the example is a BASIC statement that lets the computer know where the physical (and usually logical) end of the program is. All BASIC programs should have an END statement as the last statement. The purpose of the END statement is to terminate program execution, and to return to the system command level. If the END statement is not included, the program's ending point is not easily found by the interpreter or the system. If a mistake is made by numbering the END statement before other executable BASIC statements, those statements following the END statement will not be executed.

The output produced is as follows:

```
THIS TEST HAS
200 POINTS POSSIBLE

IT TAKES A MINIMUM OF
 180
POINTS TO RECEIVE THE TOP GRADE
```

If you understand how this output is produced, you have a good start on understanding the PRINT statement.

Although the PRINT USING statement is a nonstandard BASIC statement, it is available on many systems. (It is not available on Apple systems.) The rules for usage of PRINT USING vary widely from system to system. The PRINT USING statement contains the format of the line image that is to be used for output of the variables. The variables used must match the definitions in the format string. Some systems allow the format string to be a separate image statement. In those cases, the <"format string"> is replaced with the line number of the image statement.

If PRINT USING is supported on your system, you can use it to improve the format of your printout. The control characters for Microsoft BASIC are defined according to the table in figure F-5. The complete set of control characters is given in section 1 of module H. The following example may help you visualize the use of PRINT USING:

```
60 PRINT USING " ### POINTS POSSIBLE"; 200 <CR>
```

If your system uses the image statement, then the following program would reflect the use of the image statements.

```
30 PRINT USING 40; 200 <CR>
40 : ### POINTS POSSIBLE <CR>
```

The printout from either run would appear as follows:

```
200 POINTS POSSIBLE
```

Notice that, because of the PRINT USING, we are able to control the locations where fields are printed. It is then possible to line up numbers on the right-hand side. People are much more comfortable when they see all of the dollar figures, names, and such, lined up on a report. PRINT USING makes the job of lining up items on reports a lot easier.

Now that we have the print lined up nicely, it would be helpful to have the printout appear on paper. Microsoft BASIC uses the command LPRINT or LPRINT USING to cause printed output to go to the printer. Other systems require that you "open" the printer for use, and "close" it when you are done. The "200 points possible" message above could be printed as follows:

```
5 OPEN "LP:" FOR OUTPUT AS #6 <CR>
60 PRINT USING " ### POINTS POSSIBLE"; 200 <CR>
70 CLOSE #6 <CR>
80 END <CR>
```

Formatted output is not standard in BASIC, so please check with your instructor or reference manual if none of these methods work for you.

Assignment Statement

The assignment statement performs operations and stores the results in a memory location in the computer. The memory locations are named by using a particular letter to represent each location. These letters are known as *variable*

Character Used	Control for	Example of Use
#	Numeric data, one symbol for each number to be printed	###
!	First character of string goes here	!
\<n spaces>\	Print 2 + n characters in string	\ \
&	Print variable-length string	&

names, because they name locations that can vary in value as the program runs. The assignment statement may optionally be preceded by the word LET. We can store numeric data as follows (lines 10 and 20):

```
NEW <CR>
10 R = 28 <CR>
20 D = 2 * R <CR>
30 PRINT R;D <CR>
RUN <CR>

 28 56
```

We can also store alphanumeric data (alphabetic, numeric, or special characters). A string is a collection of alphanumeric data. The variable names for strings end with a "$".

```
30 C$ = "I LIKE THIS" <CR>
40 PRINT R;D,C$ <CR>
LIST <CR>

10 R = 28
20 D = 2 * R
30 C$ = "I LIKE THIS"
40 PRINT R;D,C$

RUN <CR>

 28 56           I LIKE THIS
```

Since we wanted to store a string at line 30, we had to let the computer know in some way which characters we wanted. This was done by the use of quote marks (" ") around the phrase I LIKE THIS. We can place inside the quote marks any characters we want. Note that the former line 30 (PRINT R;D) was replaced by the assignment statement for C$, to show that lines can be easily changed. The PRINT statement at line 40 has the request for information about C$. A very few systems require that a DIM (dimension) statement be used whenever strings are to be used. If your system is like this, define the string using the following DIM statement:

```
5 DIM C$(30)
```

Substitute the name in the later examples (S$, N$, or R$) for C$ as needed.

Did you notice that the semicolon and comma have different effects on the output? The implementors of different versions of BASIC have agreed that certain positions should be used to line up output produced by the PRINT statements. On many systems, the columns 1, 16, 31, 46, . . . have been reserved as these positions called *print zones*. Much like a typewriter tab key, the comma tells the computer to skip to the next tab position. The semicolon says not to skip any positions before printing. (The reason that the numbers are still spaced apart is because each number is printed with a position for the sign. If the number is positive, the sign does not print. If these numbers had been negative, a minus sign would have printed in front of each number).

Let's try and determine the output of a program that contains assignment statements.

```
NEW <CR>
10 REM SAMPLE PROGRAM USING ASSIGNMENT STATEMENTS <CR>
20 S$ = "I'M GETTING BETTER AT THIS<CR>
30 W = 5 <CR>
40 L = 3 <CR>
50 A = W * L <CR>
60 PRINT S$ <CR>
70 PRINT L;" x ";W;" = ";A <CR>
80 END <CR>
RUN <CR>
```

The output looks like the following:

```
I'M GETTING BETTER AT THIS
 3 x 5 = 15
```

How can we be sure that the result of our program is correct? Just because we now have a printed display that says three times five equals fifteen, does that necessarily mean our program produced the correct result? Program testing is a very important part of the program development process. Each time that we create a new program or change an existing program, we need to check our results very carefully. The computer will do only what it is told to do and if we tell it to do the wrong operations, then it will do the wrong operations time after time. If the multiplication had been more difficult than 3×5, perhaps making the calculation by hand or on a calculator would have been an appropriate check. As our programs become more complex, our testing will need to be more thorough.

To emphasize how important it is to check computer results, suppose line 50 above had been the statement

```
50 A = W + L <CR>
```

The result (8) would have been far different than the expected 15. Even with as little as we know about programming at this point, we could program the computer to produce incorrect results. This could happen intentionally or accidentally. Do not assume that facts written by computers are true. It is easy to make the computer lie. It is your responsibility as the end user of computer programs to validate the results occasionally to prevent needless errors.

We will continue to see assignment statements used throughout this chapter, and in almost any BASIC program written.

INPUT Statement

The INPUT statement allows the computer user to enter new data each time that a program is executed. The INPUT statement can be used to enter a single value, more than one value, or words and phrases. Consider the following examples:

```
NEW <CR>
5 REM SAMPLE PROGRAM USING THE INPUT STATEMENT <CR>
10 PRINT "ENTER A NUMBER" <CR>
```

```
20 INPUT N <CR>
70 PRINT "THE NUMBER ENTERED WAS ";N <CR>
100 END <CR>
RUN <CR>


ENTER A NUMBER
? 3 <CR>
THE NUMBER ENTERED WAS 3
```

The PRINT statement at line 10 is called a *prompt*. The computer will print the phrase in the PRINT statement just before executing the INPUT statement at line 20. The INPUT statement causes the question mark to be displayed and the computer will pause, waiting for the user to key the requested information. The number 3 is entered by the user at run time. Note that the <CR>must be pressed to indicate that the user completed entering data, which allows the program execution to continue.

Now consider asking for and entering more than one value.

```
30 PRINT "ENTER 3 NUMBERS SEPARATED BY COMMAS" <CR>
40 INPUT X,Y,Z <CR>
80 PRINT "THE OTHER NUMBERS WERE ";X;Y;Z <CR>
LIST <CR>


5 REM SAMPLE PROGRAM USING THE INPUT STATEMENT
10 PRINT "ENTER A NUMBER"
20 INPUT N
30 PRINT "ENTER 3 NUMBERS SEPARATED BY COMMAS"
40 INPUT X,Y,Z
70 PRINT "THE NUMBER ENTERED WAS ";N
80 PRINT "THE OTHER NUMBERS WERE ";X;Y;Z
100 END

RUN <CR>


ENTER A NUMBER
? 3 <CR>
ENTER 3 NUMBERS SEPARATED BY COMMAS
? 70, 76, 81 <CR>
THE NUMBER ENTERED WAS 3
THE OTHER NUMBERS WERE 70 76 81
```

We also have the opportunity to enter phrases at run time as is shown in the following example.

```
50 PRINT "ENTER YOUR NAME" <CR>
60 INPUT N$ <CR>
90 PRINT "THE NAME ENTERED WAS ";N$ <CR>
LIST <CR>
```

```
5 REM SAMPLE PROGRAM USING THE INPUT STATEMENT
10 PRINT "ENTER A NUMBER"
20 INPUT N
30 PRINT "ENTER 3 NUMBERS SEPARATED BY COMMAS"
40 INPUT X,Y,Z
50 PRINT "ENTER YOUR NAME"
60 INPUT N$
70 PRINT "THE NUMBER ENTERED WAS ";N
80 PRINT "THE OTHER NUMBERS WERE ";X;Y;Z
90 PRINT "THE NAME ENTERED WAS ";N$
100 END

RUN <CR>

ENTER A NUMBER
? 3 <CR>
ENTER 3 NUMBERS SEPARATED BY COMMAS
? 70, 76, 81 <CR>
ENTER YOUR NAME
? DORIS <CR>
THE NUMBER ENTERED WAS 3
THE OTHER NUMBERS WERE 70 76 81
THE NAME ENTERED WAS DORIS
```

Let's see how well you understand the INPUT statement. Here is a program that uses the INPUT statement. Determine what the output is.

```
NEW <CR>
10 REM INPUT STATEMENT EXAMPLE <CR>
20 PRINT "NAME A ROOM IN YOUR HOUSE" <CR>
30 INPUT R$ <CR>
40 PRINT "ENTER THE LENGTH AND WIDTH," <CR>
50 PRINT "SEPARATED BY COMMAS" <CR>
60 INPUT L, W <CR>
70 PRINT "AREA OF ";R$ <CR>
80 PRINT "IS ";L * W <CR>
90 END <CR>
RUN <CR>
```

The output from this program will be determined by what is entered by the user at run time. We can tell by looking at the program that we are to name a room in our house. Next, we will be asked for the length and width of the room named. A calculation takes place that produces the area of the room. Assume "living room" is keyed as the response to NAME A ROOM and 14 × 20 are the measurements given. Running this program would then produce the following output:

```
NAME A ROOM IN YOUR HOUSE
? LIVING ROOM <CR>
```

439

```
ENTER THE LENGTH AND WIDTH,
SEPARATED BY COMMAS
? 14, 20 <CR>
AREA OF LIVING ROOM
IS 280
```

The first line of output is produced by the print statement at line 20, which is serving as the prompt for the INPUT statement at line 30. Lines 40 and 50 serve as the prompt for the INPUT statement at line 60. Because area is calculated by length times width, a message is produced stating that the area of the room described is 280.

If you have made it this far, then you are ready to start solving some simple problems. I will state a problem, and then give some possible solutions to you. As with any computerized problem, the solutions I give you are just three possible solutions. There are many other equally valid and equally correct answers.

Example Problem

You own a toy shop, and you have just received your latest shipment of puzzles. Unfortunately, your calculator is broken, so you don't have an easy way to check the invoices. You do have a small computer that you could use, and you decide to write a small program to check your cost. Each puzzle cost $3.14, and you received 150 of them.

Develop three separate solutions assuming that you have available (1) only the PRINT statement, (2) only the assignment and PRINT statements, and (3) only the INPUT, assignment, and PRINT statements.

If you had only the PRINT statement available to use, this problem could be solved as follows:

```
NEW <CR>
5 REM PROGRAM TO FIND TOTAL COST OF 150 PUZZLES <CR>
10 PRINT 3.14 * 150 <CR>
20 END <CR>
RUN <CR>


 471
```

This solution will work only for puzzles that have a cost of $3.14. To make it work for other puzzle costs, you would have to retype line 10 changing the number 3.14 to the correct cost. This program would not work for a generalized puzzle where the cost and number of puzzles may vary, unless the user also knows how to program.

If you knew about the assignment statement, you could solve the problem as follows:

```
NEW <CR>
5 REM FIND THE TOTAL COST OF 150 PUZZLES (P) <CR>
6 REM IF THE UNIT COST IS $3.14 (C) <CR>
10 C = 3.14 <CR>
20 P = 150 <CR>
30 PRINT C * P <CR>
```

```
40 END <CR>
RUN <CR>
```

```
471
```

To change this solution, we would need to change line 20 every time we were given a different number of puzzles. If the cost was different, we would need to change line 10.

If we knew about the INPUT statement, we could write the program so it would work in general for any quantity and cost. We could then solve the problem as follows:

```
10 REM THIS PROGRAM FINDS THE TOTAL COST OF ITEMS <CR>
20 REM GIVEN THE QUANTITY AND THE UNIT COST <CR>
30 PRINT "ENTER THE QUANTITY" <CR>
40 INPUT Q <CR>
50 PRINT "ENTER THE UNIT COST" <CR>
60 INPUT C <CR>
70 PRINT "THE TOTAL COST IS ";Q * C <CR>
80 END <CR>
RUN <CR>

ENTER THE QUANTITY
? 150 <CR>
ENTER THE UNIT COST
? 3.14 <CR>
THE TOTAL COST IS 471
```

All three solutions solve the problem, and all are equally correct in their use of BASIC. The solution using the INPUT statement is the most general, and can be used for different quantities of toys (or any items) at different costs with no programming change. The user does not have to be a programmer. Because of this, it is the only really useful solution.

Throughout this module, <CR> has been used to denote the action of depressing the RETURN (or ENTER) key. This notation is not used in the following modules, because by now you have probably developed the habit of typing a carriage return after every system command or BASIC statement.

A PROGRAMMING EXAMPLE

Coverage of the following problem is optional. With this problem, and others similar to it in other chapters, an attempt is made to provide a comprehensive program. Each example teaches an additional BASIC statement or additional knowledge needed to write BASIC programs.

Most programs are part of a larger system of programs. For example, if you were running a business, the accounts receivable control provided by your computer system would have many programs doing the job. There would probably be an entry program, a program that produced a list of all the transactions entered (audit list), an update program, a billing program to produce statements, and an aging program to keep track of how old the accounts became. Each one of the programs would have to be designed, developed, and tested.

We are going to write a simple payroll system. This system is simple because not all of the functions needed to do a complete payroll are going to be provided. A system that large could take another entire book to develop.

Understanding how a payroll system works is important. The steps generally include (1) the ability to create and maintain an employee record, (2) entry of hours worked, (3) calculation of the amount owed the employee, removing any needed deductions, (4) reporting the amounts calculated on a report known as a payroll register, and (5) updating the amounts to the employee's record.

Other functions performed by a payroll system could include (1) writing the checks themselves, (2) producing a list of the checks written (check register), (3) producing totals to be used on quarterly reports, (4) creating documents to show employee's earnings for the year (W-2 forms), (5) supporting lists about the employees (year-to-date earnings, master lists), (6) doing the record keeping for vacation and sick time, and (7) producing documents to make entry of data easier (time input sheets).

Each section entitled "A Programming Example" will do some portion of one of the above jobs. Some programs will be enhancements or enlargements of earlier programs, adding BASIC statements learned in that portion of the module. For the early payroll programs, only a few employees will be processed. With this background in payroll systems, let's look at a program to make input easier, a time input sheet.

The time input sheet can be printed from the employee file, listing the current employees. For now, we simply print blanks to be filled in by the user. For this payroll system, it is important to know how many hours were worked, and if there is a change in employee information. These changes could include a name change or a pay rate change. The output required is the following:

```
EMP. #  HOURS   EMPLOYEE INFORMATION CHANGES
_____  __.__   _____
_____  __.__   _____
_____  __.__   _____
_____  __.__   _____
```

The employee number is used to identify which employee the hours are to be applied to. If this input sheet was generated by the computer system, other helpful information such as the employee names and their current pay rates could be printed.

The logic needed to print this input sheet is very straightforward. Each of the lines of output is generated by a PRINT statement. The program could be created as follows:

```
NEW
10 OPEN "LP:" FOR OUTPUT AS FILE #1
15 PRINT #1 "EMP. #  HOURS   EMPLOYEE INFORMATION CHANGES"
20 PRINT #1 "_____   __.__   _____"
30 PRINT #1 "_____   __.__   _____"
```

```
40  PRINT #1 "_____    __.__  _____"
50  PRINT #1 "_____    __.__  _____"
60  CLOSE #1
70  END

RUN

EMP. #  HOURS  EMPLOYEE INFORMATION CHANGES
_____   __.__  _____
_____   __.__  _____
_____   __.__  _____
_____   __.__  _____
```

If additional lines were needed for new employees, the program would have to be changed by adding more PRINT statements or by asking the computer to repeat an operation. We will learn how to ask the computer to repeat operations in a later module. Some systems do not require line 10 or 60 if the BASIC command LPRINT is used instead of PRINT #1. However, LPRINT is nonstandard BASIC.

QUESTIONS

F.6   What is a cursor?

F.7   What does the PRINT statement do?

F.8   How can you replace a BASIC statement in your work area?

F.9   Describe one way to delete a BASIC source statement line.

F.10 What is one way to leave blank lines between output?

F.11 What type of data can be stored with the assignment statement?

F.12 How do commas affect the PRINT statement?

F.13 How do semicolons affect the PRINT statement?

F.14 Why is there a space on the left side of positive numbers in output?

F.15 What is the function of an INPUT statement?

F.16 Why are programs tested?

F.17 Explain what the commands RUN and LIST do.

F.18 Give an example of a BASIC statement to print the name MARY.

F.19 Write a program to multiply 26.2 by 497.23.

F.20 Write a program to multiply any two numbers. Use the program to find the following answers.
   a. $26.2 \times 497.23 = $ _____
   b. $57.9 \times 54.732 = $ _____
   c. $379.5 \times 327.9 = $ _____
   d. $9.978 \times 29.43 = $ _____
   e. $482.9 \times 3.747 = $ _____

F.21 Write a program to find the average of any four numbers. Use the program to find the average of the following sets of numbers.

a. 35, 67, 52, 96   Average = _____

b. 67.9, 45.6, 78.2, 98.7   Average = _____

c. 3.67, 5.48, 2.32, 8.49   Average = _____

F.22 Write a program to calculate simple interest ($I = PRT$). Find the interest for the following.

a. $P = \$100$ $R = 8\%$ $T = 1$ year $I = $ _____

b. $P = \$534.57$ $R = 7.75\%$ $T = 7$ years $I = $ _____

c. $P = \$13,317.96$ $R = 9.1\%$ $T = 3\ \frac{1}{2}$ years $I = $ _____

F.23 Write a program that prints your name in a message.

F.24 Use the computer to calculate your library fines. Have the computer ask you the fine per day, the number of days late, and how many books you have borrowed.

F.25 Write a program that calculates the final cost of an item if the sales tax rate is 3.5% when the price is entered. Print the price, tax, and cost including tax.

F.26 Write a program that prints the sum, difference, and product of any two numbers.

F.27 Write a program to input two numbers, compute their product, and print the original two numbers as well as the product. Label your output.

F.28 Write a program to input two numbers, add 7 to each number, and print the results. Label your output.

SUMMARY

The PRINT, assignment, and INPUT statements were explained by example in this module. The intent of the module is to give a sample of what the programming language BASIC can do. I recommend that you attempt to work through the examples presented within this module on your own system.

WORD LIST

(in order of appearance in text)

Cursor	REM statement
RETURN or ENTER key <CR>	Comment
System command	END statement
BASIC statement	PRINT USING statement
Line number	Assignment statement
PRINT statement	Variable name
RUN command	DIM statement
NEW command	Print zones
Work area	INPUT statement
LIST command	Prompt
Arithmetic operators	

MODULE G

Designing Simple Computer Programs

THE INPUT/PROCESSING/OUTPUT CYCLE

GENERAL STRATEGY FOR DESIGNING SIMPLE PROGRAMS

ADDING MORE LOGIC— INITIALIZATION AND TERMINATION

USING PSEUDOCODE TO SPECIFY PROGRAM LOGIC

In the previous module, we paid little attention to program design. We typed statements into the computer without any prior planning. Although this procedure is acceptable as a way of gaining familiarity with programming, it is bad strategy in general. A better practice is to design the program before typing any statements.

If you are like most students, however, you do not have a clear idea of how to develop a design. You may have a vague notion of what a program design is, but you may not know where to start. This module should help you know how to proceed.

There are two phases to the development of a simple program: (1) design, and (2) programming and testing. During design, you determine a logical sequence of steps to solve the problem. You specify an *algorithm*. During programming, you write statements conforming to this design. Then you test the program.

In this course, you will probably be tempted to omit the design phase. You may want to sit down at the microcomputer or CRT and just start typing. *This approach is a big mistake*. Sure, you can solve simple problems this way, but you will have difficulty with larger problems. Furthermore, experience has shown that the total time involved in developing a fully tested program is less if a thorough design is made. Therefore, you are strongly encouraged to design before you program.

In this module, we will first discuss a logical pattern that is common to most computer programs. Then a general strategy will be given for designing programs. Next, three examples to illustrate the technique will be shown. Finally, a few hints on how to write good flowcharts and pseudocode are presented. In the next module (module H), you will learn how to transform these designs into BASIC language programs.

THE INPUT/PROCESSING/ OUTPUT CYCLE

First of all, what is a computer program? It is a sequence of steps, or instructions, for the computer to execute in order to solve a particular problem. Most computers are general-purpose machines. They can add, subtract, and do other arithmetic. They can also make simple decisions. However, they do not know how to solve specific problems, like order entry or payroll. To solve a specific problem, they must be given detailed instructions. These instructions are the program.

Most computer programs follow a pattern. Once you understand this pattern, it will be easy to see how to develop the logic for programs. To understand the pattern, think about how you would solve a specific problem like payroll. How would you produce the payroll for 10 people?

First, you would gather the data, say, hours worked and pay rate, for one of the employees. Then, you would compute the amount you needed to pay, and, finally, you would write the check. You would perform these steps for each employee until the paychecks for all 10 had been written.

Notice the pattern in your work. You first gather data (input), then you compute the pay (process), and then you write the check (output). After you have done this procedure for one employee, you cycle back and repeat the process for another employee. You repeat these steps until all the input has been processed.

This pattern occurs so frequently in computing, it has been given a special name: the *input/process/output cycle* (see chapter 2 for more discussion of this cycle). Nearly all computer programs conform to this pattern. First they input data, then they process it, and then they produce output. After they perform these three steps, they repeat the process. If, for example, there are 150,000 employees on the payroll, then the payroll program will repeat these three steps 150,000 times.

Think about this cycle. Input, process, output, repeat; input, process, output, repeat. Whenever you start to design a computer program, look for this pattern. If you start to get confused or lost, think about this cycle. You want to input, process, output, and repeat as long as there is input data.

GENERAL STRATEGY FOR DESIGNING SIMPLE PROGRAMS

Over the years, many programmers have learned a trick. They initially approach a program design problem backwards. They start with the output! The first thing an experienced programmer does is to determine what a program is supposed to produce. For example, suppose we are given the following programming problem:

Design a program to compare the performance of pairs of students. The program should read the names of two students and the amount each has scored. Then it should print the name of the person scoring higher. If they have scored the same amount, it should print the words TIE BETWEEN and both of their names. It should repeat the process for another pair of students until all data has been processed.

Now, what is the output of this program supposed to be? It should be one of two messages:

```
THE PERSON WHO SCORED HIGHER IS _____

TIE BETWEEN _____ AND _____
```

We now know exactly what the program is to produce. The next step that professional programmers take is to identify the input. What data is available? It's like cooking. Having decided to make an apple pie, what ingredients do we need to make it?

What are the inputs in our example? There are two names and two amounts. For discussion purposes, let's call the first student N1 and the second student N2. Let's also call the amount for the first student A1 and the amount for the second, A2.

These abbreviations—N1, N2, A1, and A2—are *program variables*. They are called *variables* because their values vary. At one point, the variable N1 can have the value MARY JONES. At another point, it can have the value FRED SMITH. (Note that in our design, we need not distinguish between string and numeric variables; N1 need not be N1$ until the program is written.)

So far, we have identified two steps that are followed by professional programmers. First, they identify the outputs of the program, and then they determine the inputs. The third and final step is to determine the program logic, or how the inputs can be manipulated to produce the outputs.

Think again about cooking. The program logic is equivalent to the directions in a recipe. We know the outputs (pie) and the inputs (ingredients). We now must determine a method of producing the outputs.

There are two common ways of expressing program logic. One way is to express it in *flowcharts*, and the other is to express it in *pseudocode*. Both techniques can be effectively used. Programming professionals do not agree on which is the better technique. We will look at both.

Figure G-1 shows a flowchart for the program logic in our example. Four symbols are shown. The oval ⬭ is used for initiation and termination only. The parallelogram ▱ is used to represent either input or output processing. A rectangle ▭ is used to represent operations. Finally, a diamond ◇ is used to represent decisions or questions.

Examine figure G-1. As promised, it has the input/process/output structure. First, we input the data about the two students. The program tells the computer to read N1, A1, N2, and A2. This instruction means that the computer is to obtain these values from a user at a terminal or from some other input medium.

Assume that the computer reads the data shown in figure G-2. The value of N1 is MARY JONES and the value of A1 is 10,348. N2 is FRED SMITH and A2 is 9,345.

Now what is to be done with this data? The next operation is a decision instruction. Inside the diamond is a question. If the answer to this question is yes, the computer is to follow the arrow labeled *Yes*. If the answer to the question is no, the computer is to follow the other arrow labeled *No*.

Decisions are always represented in this way. There is a question inside the diamond, and the yes and no answers are written on the arrows leading out of the diamond. In figure G-1, if A1 equals A2, then the TIE message is written. Otherwise, another decision is executed.

This next question is whether A1 is greater than A2. If so, then name N1 is written to the report. Otherwise, name N2 is written as the person with greater sales.

Note that all of the arrows ultimately point to the bottom of the flowchart. There, the flow of control goes back to the read operation to obtain the next set of data.

Again, look for the input/process/output cycle in this flowchart. Data is read, it is processed (here the processing consists of decision making), and messages are output. The cycle is then repeated.

Have you noticed something strange about the flowchart in figure G-1? It has no end. The process never terminates. Clearly, we do not want to continue feeding data to this program until doomsday. We must determine a way to cause the computer to stop.

We want the computer to stop executing this program when we are out of data—that is, after the last two students are processed. There are several ways to do this. For one, we can input a special data item at the end of the input to signal end of data. Thus, we might put a negative amount scored in A1 to represent the end of data. However, if a student misses more questions than

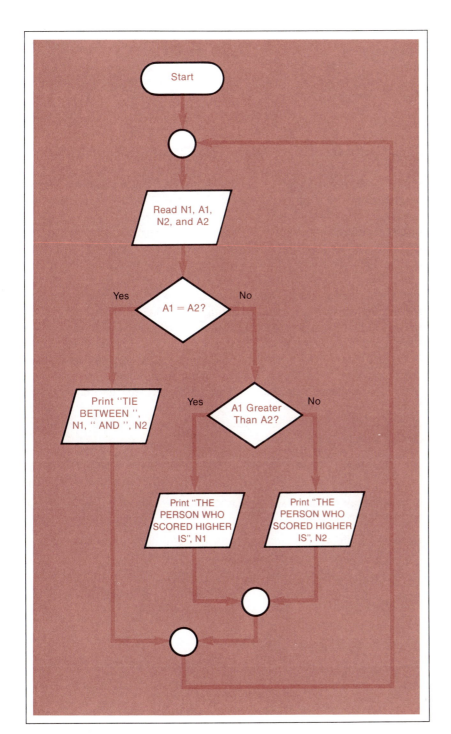

MARY JONES	94	FRED SMITH	86
ROGER CONLON	100	CAROL CONLON	89
LEROY LEE	92	HAROLD SIMPSON	99
JOE COOL	61	ZONA REEVE	73

he gets right, negative scores may be a valid data item. Therefore, this approach may not be the best one.

Another possibility is to put a special label in the N1 name position. Thus, when we read a record with name equal to END-OF-DATA, we can cause the program to terminate. This possibility is shown in figure G-3.

A different approach is to allow the computer to determine when we are out of data. Using this approach, after each read, we ask the computer's operating system if we are out of data. If not, we process. When the computer signals end of data, we stop. This approach is often used. The only difficulty is that each computer signals end of data in a different way, and we may have to change our program to make it run on another computer.

Now, let's review the general strategy. There are three steps. First, determine what the outputs of the program will be. A good technique is to write (by hand) sample lines of output. This approach will help you to be sure you understand what the program is to do. Second, determine what the inputs to the program will be. What data items will be available to produce the desired outputs? Third, specify the program logic. So far, we have shown how to perform this step using flowcharts. Before going any further, you should try out this sequence. Consider the following problem:

Design a program to read a customer name and the amounts of two purchases and then to sum the purchases together. If the sum of the purchases is equal to zero, it should print the customer name and a message stating that the customer had no orders. Otherwise, it should print the customer name and the sum of the orders. It should repeat the process for the next customer. The program should stop when END-OF-DATA is read.

Perform the three problem-solving steps for this problem before you go on.

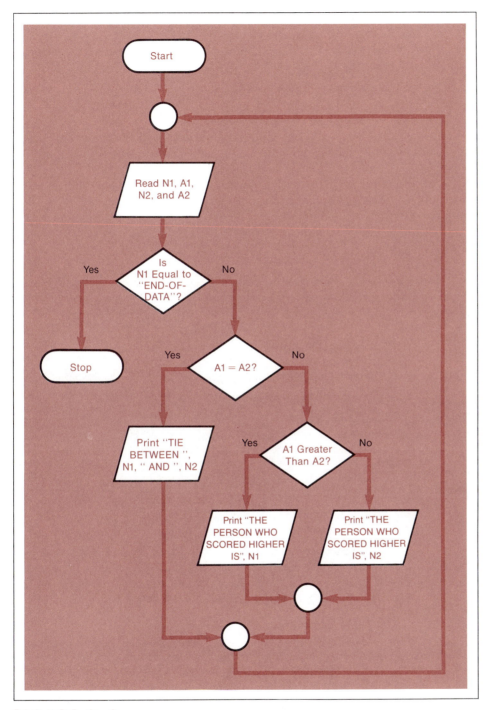

Terminating flowchart for student score
comparison problem

Are you cheating? Did you perform the three steps? Your hair will curl (or go straight) if you go on without performing the three steps.

How did you do? What are the outputs? They should be one of two messages like the following:

```
CUSTOMER _____ HAD NO ORDERS.

CUSTOMER _____ ORDERED _____ THIS MONTH.
```

What are the inputs? There are three variables. One is customer name, which we will call C, and the other two are amounts ordered, which we will call A1 and A2.

What is the program logic? Figure G-4 shows one potential solution to this problem. Note that it has the input/process/output cycle structure.

QUESTIONS

G.1 Consider the following problem:

A program reads a customer name and total purchases for one month. If the total of the purchases equals zero, it prints the customer name and a message stating that the customer had no orders. Otherwise, it prints the customer name and the amount of the orders. It repeats the process for the next customer. It stops when END-OF-DATA is read.

    a. What is the output from this program?
    b. What is the input?
    c. Develop a flowchart of the program logic.

G.2 Consider the following problem:

A program sums customer order amounts. The program reads a record containing customer name followed by three amounts. The amounts are added together. Then the name of the customer and the sum of the orders are printed. After a customer record is processed, the program repeats the process for the next customer's record. End of data is signaled by a −9999 in the first amount-ordered field.

    a. What is the output from this program?
    b. What is the input?
    c. Develop a flowchart of the program logic.

G.3 Repeat the exercise in question G.2 but satisfy the following additional requirement: If the sum of the orders is greater than 10,000, the program should print the words BIG CUSTOMER after the sum of the orders. Specify the outputs and inputs and develop a flowchart.

G.4 Consider this problem:

A program computes employee pay. It reads a record containing employee name, pay rate, and hours worked. It calculates gross pay (rate times hours). Employees are not paid extra for overtime. The program prints the name of the employee and his or her gross pay. If the number of hours worked is zero, the message DID NOT WORK is printed. The program repeats to process the next employee record. End of data is signaled by a −99 in the pay-rate field.

    a. What are the outputs?
    b. What are the inputs?
    c. Develop the program flowchart.

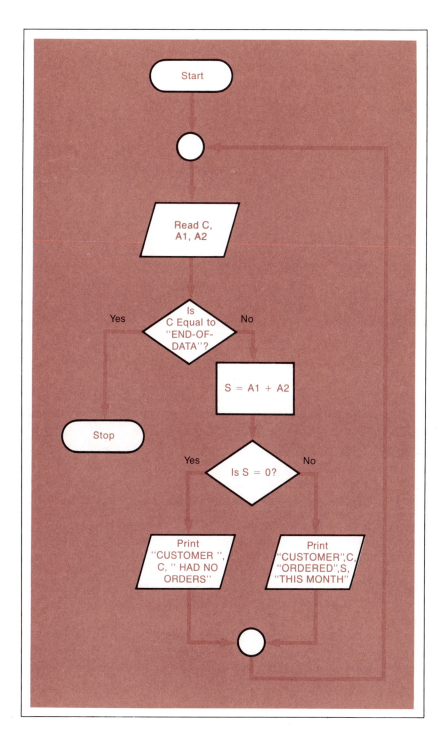

Flowchart for customer order problem

In the last section, we discussed the input/output cycle, and we showed how it is fundamental to most programs. However, some problems require an extension to this pattern. To illustrate this extension, consider the following problem:

> A company maintains a computer file of employee records containing employee number, employee name, age, pay rate, and total pay-to-date. They want to print the total pay-to-date for each employee. They also want a report that shows the total number of employees, their average age, their average pay rate, and the sum of the pay-to-date for all employees.

If you were to write a program to produce such a report, how would you proceed? You would identify the outputs, then identify the inputs, and then specify the program logic. Proceeding in this way, we have:

Outputs

The following message should be written for each employee:

```
EMPLOYEE _____ HAS BEEN PAID $XXXXXX.XX.
```

Also, at the end of the report, the following messages should be output:

```
THERE ARE XXXX EMPLOYEES IN THIS COMPANY.
THE AVERAGE AGE OF THE EMPLOYEES IS XX.X YEARS.
THE AVERAGE PAY RATE IS $XX.XX PER HOUR.
THE TOTAL PAYROLL SO FAR THIS YEAR IS $XXXXXXX.XX.
```

Inputs

The program will need to read values for the following variables from the data records:

NAME, the name of an employee
AGE, the age of an employee
PAY-RATE, the pay rate of an employee
EMP-PAY, the total pay-to-date for an employee

Now, to specify the program logic, we need to make a flowchart or write pseudocode (we will discuss pseudocode soon). However, before we do that, do we know how to get averages? To get the average of 10 numbers, we sum them and divide by 10. To get the average pay rate, we need to sum the pay rates and divide by the number of employees. This operation presents some questions: How do we know the number of employees? How do we sum the pay rates?

Suppose we create two more program variables. One we will call NEMP for the number of employees. The other we will call TPR for total pay rates. Now, every time we read an employee record, we will execute the following statements:

```
ADD 1 TO NEMP.
ADD PAY-RATE TO TPR.
```

Because we are adding to the variables every time we read an employee record, when we are finished, NEMP will have the total number of employees and

TPR will have the total pay rates. To get the average pay rate, we will divide TPR by NEMP.

Now, we have created a problem. What was the first value of NEMP? Before we read the first employee record, what was NEMP equal to? If you are like most students, you have assumed that NEMP was zero. After all, when you count something, you always start your count value at zero.

Unfortunately, the computer is not that smart. NEMP is equal to whatever happens to be in the main memory location assigned to NEMP. It might be zero, but it might be -345673822 or 1819.786540 or even the characters JUNK. Therefore, before we use the variables NEMP or TPR, we must *initialize* them to zero.

This operation is easy enough to do—we just insert statements like the following:

```
SET NEMP TO 0.
SET TPR TO 0.
```

There is a problem, however. Where do we put these statements in our program design? So far, we have said that every program has the pattern input/process/output/repeat. Now, if we put these initializing statements in the *process* part of this pattern, the variables will be reset to zero every time we repeat. We have to change our pattern.

The more complete pattern for computer programs looks like this:

INITIALIZE ACTIVITY.

INPUT, PROCESS, OUTPUT, REPEAT.

TERMINATE ACTIVITY.

Note that we have inserted a step before we begin the input/process/output cycle and that we have inserted a step after this cycle. In the initialize step, we will give starting values to all the variables that need them. In the termination step, we will perform any activity that needs to be done after all the inputs have been processed.

What termination activity do we have in this problem? We are supposed to print the number of employees, their average age, their average pay rate, and the total pay-to-date. We cannot print these items in the input/process/output cycle because we must wait until all employees have been processed. Therefore, we will do it in the termination step.

Figure G-5 shows a flowchart for this program logic. The initialize, input/process/output, and termination sections of this flowchart are boxed in the figure. The arrow on the right-hand side of the flowchart represents the repeat portion of the input/process/output cycle.

Figure G-5 illustrates how the initialization and termination portions fit in the program. The initialization portion is performed once in the beginning. The termination is performed once at the end. In between, data is input, processed, and output. This cycle is repeated over and over until the data is exhausted. This fact is detected in figure G-5 by reading the characters END-OF-DATA in the name field of a record.

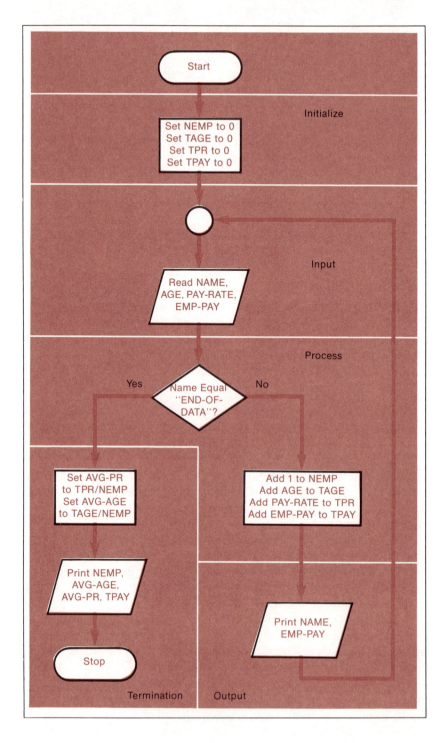

Flowchart for employee pay problem with totals

This discussion is summarized in the sequence of steps shown in figure G-6. We hope that this sequence will help you to develop program logic. You might want to try that sequence on the following problems.

G.5 Suppose that a company keeps records of employee names, numbers, hourly pay rates, and numbers of hours worked. Develop the logic of a program that will compute gross pay, assuming no special payment for overtime. Compute taxes according to the following table:

If Pay Is		
Greater Than or Equal to ($)	But Less Than ($)	Then Taxes Are
0	500	15%
500	1,000	$750 + 20% of the amount over $500
1,000 or greater		$175 + 30% of the amount over $1,000

For each employee, the program should print the employee's name, number, pay rate, hours worked, gross pay, and taxes. The company also wants to know the total number of hours worked, the total gross pay, and the total taxes for all employees. Finally, the report should show the average tax per employee. Follow the steps shown in figure G-6 and show all your work.

G.6 Assume that a company keeps computer records of sales. On each record are the customer number, customer name, salesperson number, salesperson name, and dollar amount of the sale. The records are ordered by customer number; all the records for a given customer are contiguous (next to one another). The company wants a report that lists the name of each customer and the amount of each purchase. The company also wants to know the

Step	Action
1	Identify the outputs.
2	Identify the inputs.
3	Specify the program logic:
	a. Determine whatever equations, variables, etc., are required to transform the inputs into the outputs.
	b. Develop a flowchart of the input/process/output cycle.
	c. Add necessary initialization activities prior to beginning the input/process/output cycle.
	d. Add termination activities necessary to perform after all the data is processed.

total number of sales, the number of customers, the total of all the sales, and the average sales amount. Follow the steps shown in figure G-6 and show all your work.

USING PSEUDOCODE TO SPECIFY PROGRAM LOGIC

In chapter 2 and elsewhere in this book, we have used pseudocode to specify logic. In this section, we will show how you can use it to portray program designs.

The term *pseudocode* means "false code." This name is appropriate because pseudocode looks like a programming language, but it isn't. Pseudocode statements are simpler. They are free-form English. They do not conform to the strict punctuation rules of a programming language.

As illustrated in chapter 2, to use pseudocode, you break up the program into parts, which we have called *paragraphs*. Another term for paragraph is *procedure*. We have avoided that term throughout this text because it can be confused with the fourth component of a computer system, *procedures* (for people). In this module, we will follow the more common pseudocode terminology, however, and use *procedure* to mean a group of pseudocode statements. Do not confuse pseudocode procedures with procedures for people.

Each procedure will be a major step in the program logic and will be given a name. Within a procedure there are three types of instructions. Imperative statements tell the computer to do something like ADD 1 TO NEMP. These instructions are executed in sequence.

A second type of instruction is the IF-THEN-ELSE instruction. It is used to portray a decision. The form is:

```
IF condition
    THEN group-1 statements
    ELSE group-2 statements
END-IF
```

If the condition is true, then the group-1 statements are executed. Otherwise, the group-2 statements are executed. For example:

```
IF A IS LESS THAN B
    THEN ADD 1 TO B
        SUBTRACT 2 FROM C
    ELSE ADD 1 TO A
END-IF
```

If A is less than B, then 1 is added to B and 2 is subtracted from C. If A is equal to or greater than B, then 1 is added to A.

Sometimes there is nothing to do if the condition is not met. In this case, the IF structure appears as follows:

```
IF A condition
    THEN group of statements
END-IF
```

There is no ELSE, and there are no statements to execute if the condition is not true. This is sometimes called a *null ELSE*.

The final type of pseudocode statement is the DO statement, which is used for iteration. There are two forms. The first is the DOWHILE statement.

```
DOWHILE A IS LESS THAN B
    ADD 1 TO A
    SUBTRACT 1 FROM B
    ADD 1 TO COUNT
END-DO
```

Figure G-7 shows a flowchart of the logic of this DOWHILE. In this example, the three statements in the DO loop are executed as long as A is less than B. When A becomes equal to or greater than B, the next instruction after the DO loop will be executed. If A is less than B the first time, these statements will be skipped and never executed.

The DOUNTIL structure is similar to DOWHILE except that the group of statements in the loop is always executed at least once. Consider the statements:

```
DOUNTIL A IS EQUAL TO OR GREATER THAN B
    ADD 1 TO A
    SUBTRACT 1 FROM B
    ADD 1 TO COUNT
END-DO
```

As shown in figure G-8, these statements operate the same as the DOWHILE with one exception. The three statements in the DO loop will always be executed at least once. The comparison of A and B is done after the three statements have been executed.

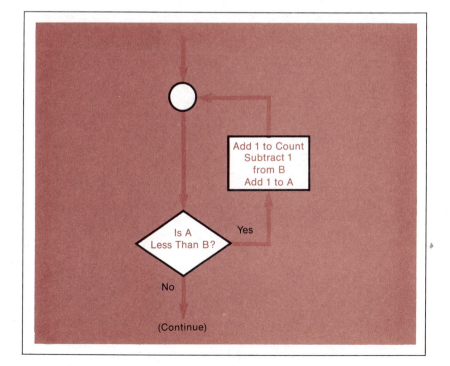

(Continue)

459

The sequence of program development steps shown in figure G-6 applies to pseudocode as well as flowcharts. The only difference is using pseudocode instead of flowcharts in the last step.

A pseudocode example is shown in figure G-9. This example portrays the same logic as the flowchart in figure G-5 and is relatively straightforward. One place that you might be confused is where the end-of-data condition occurs. The variable EOF-FLAG is initialized to zero, indicating that end of file (EOF) has not occurred. Then, the statements in PROCESS-PROCEDURE are repeated in a DO loop until EOF-FLAG becomes 1.

How does EOF-FLAG become 1? When END-OF-DATA is read in the NAME field, EOF-FLAG is set to 1. However, there is a problem. Once EOF is detected, we do not want to execute the remainder of the statements in the DO loop. Therefore, we insert an IF statement. If end of data is reached, the statements under the ELSE will be skipped. Then, before another loop is made, the condition EOF-FLAG = 1 is checked. It will now be equal to 1, and the PROCESS-PROCEDURE will terminate.

To see how this operation works, create some sample data and run through the logic. You might want to do this exercise with a friend to be sure you keep each other's logic straight.

Most data processing experts think that this way of handling EOF is clumsy. They discovered that the logic can be simplified if the first record is read in the initialize paragraph. Then, when PROCESS-PROCEDURE is executed, a valid record will already be available. The record is processed, and the next read is then done at the bottom of the process loop.

FIGURE G-8

Flowchart of DOUNTIL logic

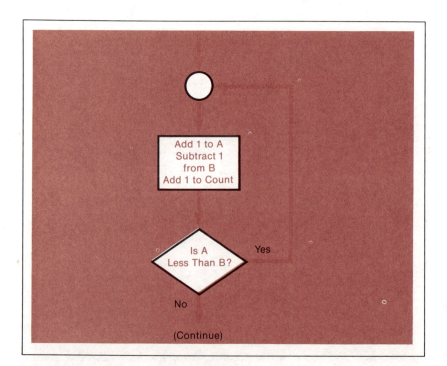

```
BEGIN EMPLOYEE—SUMMARY PROCEDURE
    DO INITIALIZE—PROCEDURE
    DO PROCESS—PROCEDURE
    DO WRAPUP—PROCEDURE
    STOP
END EMPLOYEE—SUMMARY PROCEDURE

BEGIN INITIALIZE—PROCEDURE
    SET NEMP TO 0
    SET TAGE TO 0
    SET TPR TO 0
    SET TPAY TO 0
    SET EOF—FLAG TO 0
END INITIALIZE—PROCEDURE

BEGIN PROCESS—PROCEDURE
    DOWHILE EOF—FLAG = 0
        READ NAME, AGE, PAY—RATE, EMP—PAY
        IF NAME EQUALS "END—OF—DATA"
            THEN SET EOF—FLAG TO 1
                 GO TO PROCESS—EXIT
            ELSE ADD 1 TO NEMP
                 ADD AGE TO TAGE
                 ADD PAY—RATE TO TPR
                 ADD EMP—PAY TO TPAY
                 PRINT NAME, EMP—PAY
        END—IF
    PROCESS—EXIT
    END—DO
END PROCESS—PROCEDURE

BEGIN WRAPUP—PROCEDURE
    SET AVG—PR TO TPR/NEMP
    SET AVG—AGE TO TAGE/NEMP
    PRINT NEMP, AVG—AGE, AVG—PR, TPAY
END WRAPUP—PROCEDURE
```

FIGURE G-9

Pseudocode used to express the logic in figure G-5

This method is shown in figure G-10. Note what happens if there is no data at all—that is, if the first record is END-OF-DATA. In this case, EOF-FLAG will be set to 1 by the IF statement in the initialize paragraph. The DO loop in PROCESS-PROCEDURE will never be executed because EOF-FLAG will be 1 the first time through. This IF, by the way, is an example of an IF without an ELSE clause.

Do you think figure G-10 is simpler than figure G-9? Most professionals do. The logic may seem a little backwards to you the first few times you see it, however.

The first read can also be put in the initialize section of flowcharts. Figure G-11 shows this approach for the problem first illustrated in figure G-5. Note the read at the bottom of the figure. From now on, all of our pseudocode and flowcharts will have the first read in the initialize section. In almost every case, this method will result in better designs.

Again, the best way to understand this logic is to create some sample data and run through the logic. See what happens when the read is in the initialize procedure and at the end of the process procedure.

QUESTIONS

G.7 Repeat the exercise in question G.5, but use pseudocode instead of flowcharts to represent the logic. Process EOF as shown in figure G-9.

G.8 Repeat the exercise in question G.5, but use pseudocode instead of flowcharts. Process EOF as shown in figure G-10.

G.9 Repeat the exercise in question G.6, but use pseudocode instead of flowcharts. Process EOF as shown in figure G-9.

G.10 Repeat the exercise in question G.6, but use pseudocode instead of flowcharts. Process EOF as shown in figure G-10.

SUMMARY

In this section, we have discussed ways to design or develop the logic of simple programs. We began by describing the input/process/output cycle. This cycle is common to computer programs. Next, we discussed a way to approach writing computer programs: first, specify the outputs; second, specify the inputs; and third, develop the program logic.

One technique for showing logic is flowcharting. We use graphic symbols like rectangles and boxes to represent program logic. A few reminders for writing good flowcharts are shown in figure G-12.

After we discussed the input/process/output cycle, we added another feature to program logic. In some cases, there is a need for initializing activity before the input/process/output cycle is started. There is also a need in some cases for termination activity after this cycle is finished. We showed how to represent this type of logic in flowcharts.

The last sections of this module were concerned with pseudocode. Pseudocode is an English-like language for specifying program logic. We used procedures, simple imperative statements, IF-THEN-ELSE statements, and

```
BEGIN EMPLOYEE-SUMMARY PROCEDURE
    DO INITIALIZE-PROCEDURE
    DO PROCESS-PROCEDURE
    DO WRAPUP-PROCEDURE
    STOP
END EMPLOYEE-SUMMARY PROCEDURE


BEGIN INITIALIZE-PROCEDURE
    SET NEMP TO 0
    SET TAGE TO 0
    SET TPR TO 0
    SET TPAY TO 0
    SET EOF-FLAG TO 0
    READ NAME, AGE, PAY-RATE, EMP-PAY
    IF NAME EQUALS "END-OF-DATA"
        THEN SET EOF-FLAG TO 1
END INITIALIZE-PROCEDURE


BEGIN PROCESS-PROCEDURE
    DOWHILE EOF-FLAG = 0
        PRINT NAME, EMP-PAY
        ADD 1 TO NEMP
        ADD AGE TO TAGE
        ADD PAY-RATE TO TPR
        ADD EMP-PAY TO TPAY
        READ NAME, AGE, PAY-RATE, EMP-PAY
        IF NAME EQUALS "END-OF-DATA"
            THEN SET EOF-FLAG TO 1
    END-DO
END PROCESS-PROCEDURE


BEGIN WRAPUP-PROCEDURE
    SET AVG-AGE TO TAGE/NEMP
    SET AVG-PR TO TPR/NEMP
    PRINT NEMP, AVG-AGE, AVG-PR, TPAY
END WRAPUP-PROCEDURE
```

Alternative to figure G-9 for processing
EOF

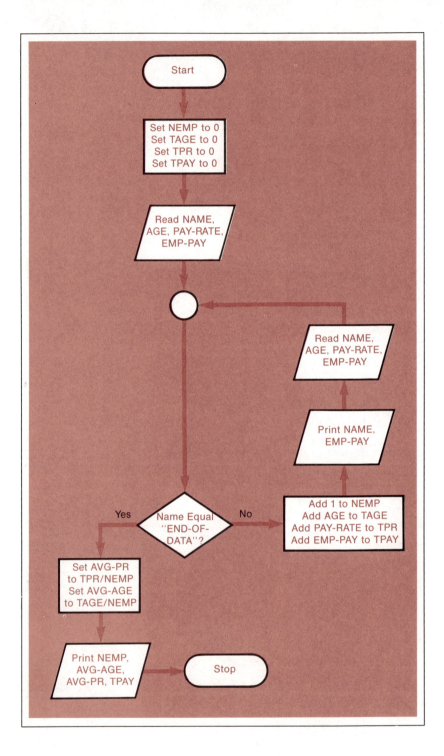

Flowchart from figure G-5 with initial read

1. Every flowchart should have one and only one START and one and only one STOP.

2. Imperative statements should be enclosed in rectangles.

3. IF statements or decisions should be enclosed in diamonds. A question is always written inside a diamond. The question must be answered by Yes or No. Answers to the question are written on the arrows leading out of the diamond. Keep the direction of the arrows consistent. If the Yes is to the left in one place, keep it to the left in all places.

4. Input/output operations are shown in parallelograms.

5. DOWHILE and DOUNTIL structures should be presented as shown in figures G-7 and G-8.

6. Every line should have an arrowhead on it; otherwise, it may be hard to follow the flow of the program logic. When lines join, use the connector, or circle, symbol.

7. In general, the logic should flow from top to bottom, and left to right.

FIGURE G-12

Hints for developing program flowcharts

FIGURE G-13

Hints for writing pseudocode

1. Break the program into small paragraphs or procedures. For the programs you write, there will usually be initialize, process, and terminate procedures. For more complex programs, the process procedure itself may be broken into smaller modules.

2. Name all procedures. Use a name that describes what the procedure does. Start each procedure with a BEGIN statement and terminate it with an END statement.

3. Specify operations in the procedures by imperative (commandlike) sentences.

4. Use IF-THEN-ELSE statements to show decisions. Indent statements under the THEN and the ELSE for clarity. Terminate the IF statement with an END-IF that is at the same margin as the IF statement.

5. Use DO statements for iteration. Remember the DOUNTIL loop is executed once before the condition is checked. A DOWHILE loop will never be executed if the condition is untrue. Indent statements in the DO loop. Use an END DO to terminate the DO loop.

6. Many times, pseudocode can be simplified if the first read statement is included in the initialize procedure. Then, A DOWHILE statement is used to control the input/process/output loop. The read statement is put at the end of the loop. Thus the pattern becomes:

    initialize (including the first read)
    process, output, input, repeat
    terminate

7. One of the chief advantages of pseudocode is its flexibility. You can do or write just about anything as long as it is logically correct and clear.

DOUNTIL and DOWHILE statements to specify program logic. Hints for using pseudocode are shown in figure G-13.

We have discussed only the essential techniques for designing program logic. These essentials will work well as long as programs are not complex. For more complex programs, more sophisticated techniques are required.

WORD LIST

(in order of appearance in text)

Input/process/output cycle	Paragraph or procedure
Program variables	IF-THEN-ELSE
Flowcharting	DOWHILE
Pseudocode	DOUNTIL

QUESTIONS TO CHALLENGE YOUR THINKING

A. You are given the task of designing an edit program. This program is to read new customer records containing customer numbers, names, credit limits, and account balances. Your program is to verify that the records conform to the following rules:

1. Customer number is all numeric.

2. Customer number is five digits.

3. Customer credit limit is one of the values 500, 1000, or 1500.

4. Customer balance is equal to zero.

Your program should list all of the records that do not conform to these rules. After all data has been processed, your program should print the number of records accepted and the number of those rejected. Specify the outputs and inputs, and prepare a flowchart of this program's logic.

B. Repeat the exercise in question A, but specify the outputs, inputs, and pseudocode of the logic.

C. You are given the task of designing an inventory program. This program is to read inventory part records containing the following fields: part number, quantity on hand, item cost, item price, and reorder quantity. The program is to compute and print the following information for each part:

1. The inventory cost of the part (quantity times item cost)

2. The potential value of the parts on hand (quantity times item price)

3. The profit contribution of each part (price minus cost)

4. The difference between the number on hand and the reorder quantity

Furthermore, your program should produce a printed listing of all parts for which the quantity on hand is less than the reorder quantity. Additionally, your program should compute and print the total number of parts numbers, the total number of parts, the total inventory cost, and the total inventory value. Specify the outputs and inputs, and prepare a flowchart of the program logic.

D. Repeat the exercise in question C, but specify the outputs, inputs, and pseudocode of the program logic.

MODULE H

BASIC Programming

In this module, we will learn some of the simple ways of getting data in and out of the computer. We will learn about variables, assignment statements, PRINT statements, INPUT statements, and READ and DATA statements. You will recognize some of these statements from your earlier work with examples.

Defining Variables

Part of the power of programming is the ability to manipulate different sets of data using the same operations. The data is placed in computer storage by the program. We must have a way of naming these storage locations so the programmer can reference the data easily. Programmers call these locations *variables*. Think of a variable as a box somewhere in primary storage (main memory) that holds the value needed. These values can either be numeric or alphabetic. The system must be told which type of data is being stored. The *default* data type is numeric—that is, the system assumes that a variable is numeric unless you indicate otherwise. Picture the value 41.0 stored in a variable we'll call A.

A

| 41.0 |

We can replace the value of A with some other value, say 21.0, and our variable now looks like this:

A

| 21.0 |

We can place in a variable any value our computer can store. Note that the former value of 41.0 is lost entirely, and that there is no evidence that it ever existed. For example, if you own a tape recorder, and record music on a tape, the music will remain on the tape until you record other music on the same spot on the tape. Then, all evidence of the earlier recording is gone. The value of 21.0 for A will remain the same until it is changed by some other BASIC statement or is lost by losing the power to our system.

Numeric variables are named by using one letter from the alphabet (A through Z) or by using one letter from the alphabet followed by a single digit (0 through 9). We therefore have 286 choices for numeric variable names. Examples of valid numeric variable names are

```
A        Z1
B2       I
```

Examples of invalid numeric variable names are

```
AA       COUNTER
1B       2
```

Your implementation of BASIC may have different naming conventions, so check the rules for naming variables on your system. These are the standard naming conventions, and they work with all BASIC dialects. If your system allows you to use longer names, doing so makes your program more readable, but makes it less portable from system to system.

Computers handle numeric data according to the type of data it represents. There are three primary types of numeric data. The first type is called *floating point,* or real. Real numbers are the numbers you are used to working with every day. These numbers include digits to the right of the decimal point. The second type of numeric data is called *integer.* Integer numbers do not include any digits to the right of the decimal point. Integers can be thought of as whole numbers. They may be positive or negative. The last data type is *exponential.* These numbers are like floating point numbers, but may be very large or very small.

Some implementations of BASIC assume that the variables named are floating point numbers, unless the starting letter of the variable name is between I and N inclusive. Variables that start with these letters are assumed to be integers. This is significant because, with integers, the fractional part of the number is lost. For example, if 29 is divided by 5, the result will be 5 using integer arithmetic. The decimal portion is chopped off (*truncated*). This characteristic of integers can be put to good use. You should be aware that this capability is available.

Many people think of computers as "number crunchers," but this is certainly not the main function of a computer, particularly in a commercial environment. Computers can handle character data as well as numeric data. What is a character? A character can be any of the following: any letter of the alphabet, the digits from 0 through 9, space or blank, and any of the special characters such as !, @, #, $, %, ^, &, *, (,), —, +, =, ?, and so on. BASIC allows us to enter characters into the computer in groups. These groups of characters are called *strings.* Variables that hold character data (strings) are named using the letters of the alphabet with the additional character $ on the end of the variable name to denote a string variable. Strings are usually enclosed in quote (") marks. Examples of valid string variable names in ANSI BASIC are

    A$ B$

Many versions of BASIC allow a letter, number, and $ (for example, C1$) as a valid string variable, but this is not part of the standard. Examples of *invalid* string variable names are:

    1A$ $A1
    $B   HEADING$

Variables are assigned values during the execution of a program. In other words, some value must be placed in the variable ("box") after you type RUN. Assignment statements, INPUT statements, and READ and DATA statements can change the value of a variable.

Statement Formats and the Assignment Statement

What makes up a complete BASIC statement? Program lines in BASIC have the following format:

    nnnnn   BASIC verb   operands

where *nnnnn* is a line number (often listed as line # in technical manuals), BASIC *verb* is any word that is allowed to begin a valid BASIC statement (such as PRINT, INPUT, or END), and *operands* are the required variables or constants for the BASIC verb. If no line number is used, the BASIC statement will be executed immediately by the system. This is known as *direct-execution mode*.

Every BASIC program line begins with a line number. Line numbers indicate the order in which program lines are stored in memory. Line numbers are also used as references when changing programs and when writing certain types of BASIC branching statements. Line numbers should be in the range 0 through 32767. Some systems allow the range 0 through 65529. I recommend using the smaller range to allow portability from one system to another.

An assignment statement should always have the name of the variable to be replaced on the left side of the = sign, and the value or expression you want assigned on the right side. The format of the assignment statement is the following (where square brackets indicate that the item is optional):

nnnnn   [LET] <variable> = <expression>

The following are examples of valid assignment statements:

```
50  A = 1.0
60  C = 99
90  D = A
170  B = 141.0
190  W$ = "PAM"
220  B$ = "SARAH"
```

The assignment statement allows us to assign a particular value to a variable. Note that the numeric assignments need not have a decimal point (.). Also note that the string data is inside quote marks. The quote marks may be optional on your system.

Let's look again at the format of a BASIC assignment statement. What is a variable, and what is an expression? A variable is a variable name, using the rules given earlier. An expression is a constant (such as 1.0 or "PAM"), another variable, or a pair of variables and/or constants connected by an operator. What is an operator? An *operator* is the symbol that represents an *operation*. For example, + represents addition. Some of the available operators are

+	addition
−	subtraction
*	multiplication
/	division
^ or **	exponentiation

An asterisk is used as the symbol for multiplication so that it won't be confused with the variable named X.

As expressions become more complex, we must worry about the order in which the expression will be evaluated. This is known as the order of operations, or *hierarchy of operations*. Parentheses override any other operator, so they are listed first in the hierarchy of operations. Some of the rules are listed in figure H-1. We will cover intrinsic or library functions (2), the relational operators (6), and the logical operators (7, 8, and 9) in later modules.

Assume for this discussion that the variables A = 15, B = 5, C = 3, D =

1. Parentheses	Evaluated first
2. Intrinsic or Library Functions	
3. ^ or **	Left to right if separated by other operators, but right to left for A ** B ** C
4. * or /	Left to right
5. + or −	Left to right
6. Relational Operators	
a. > means "is greater than"	
b. >= means "is greater than or equal to"	
c. = means "is equal to"	
d. <= means "is less than or equal to"	
e. < means "is less than"	
f. <> means "is not equal to"	
g. == means "approximately equal to"	
7. AND	
8. OR	
9. NOT	Evaluated last

FIGURE H-1

The BASIC hierarchy of operations

of operations, and note how the parentheses can make a difference in the results. The computer will follow the rules listed in figure H-1 if a decision about the order of operations must be made. Depending on what was desired, the statement

```
F = B + C * D
```

could be interpreted as

```
F = B + (C * D)     or     F = (B + C) * D
F = 95                     F = 240
```

The computer executes multiplication before addition, so it will get the answer 95 if no parentheses are used. If we were calculating an average,

```
F = A + B + C + D / 4
```

would not be correct, but

```
F = (A + B + C + D) / 4
```

is. Let's look at a complex expression.

```
F = A * B ** C - D / E
    ↑   ↑    ↑   ↑
    2   1    4   3    would be the order of operations.
```

According to the order of operations, the above statement is logically equivalent to the following sequence of statements:

```
X = B ** C
Y = A * X
```

```
Z = D / E
F = Y - Z
```

Remember that you can't assign strings to numeric variables, or assign numbers to be used for calculations to string variables.

PRINT Statement

If you have the most wonderfully executing program in the world but have no output, you still have nothing. A program has no value unless it produces some sort of output, so there are, as you may suspect, commands that tell the computer to do output. (The assignment statement does not cause the computer to do output. It only manipulates variables in memory). BASIC has only one output statement, the PRINT statement, but it may take several forms. For now, we will study the most simple form of the PRINT statement that is available. It is the form that causes output to take place in a format that people can read. The PRINT statement prints whatever descriptions and variables are named. The format of the PRINT statement is:

nnnnn   PRINT [<list of expressions>]

If the list of expressions is omitted, a blank line will be printed. If the list of expressions is included, the values of the expressions are printed at the terminal. The expressions may be numeric or string expressions. Examples are included in the following programs. Please note this program:

```
10 A = 41.0
20 B = 80.0
30 PRINT A,B
40 END
```

If you type this program into your system and type the system command RUN, you see the numbers 41.0 and 80.0 printed on your terminal. If you reverse the variables named in statement 30 as follows

```
10 A = 41.0
20 B = 80.0
30 PRINT B,A
40 END
```

you see 80.0 and 41.0 printed on your terminal. If the variables named are numeric, their values are printed on the terminal. They are printed in the order they appear in the PRINT statement. Note that we have separated the variables with a comma. We could use a semicolon (;) as the separator and get a different result. Try the following code:

```
10 A = 41.0
20 B = 80.0
30 PRINT A;B
40 END
```

Did you attempt to RUN this program? Did you notice how the distance between the two numbers changed when you used the semicolon? The BASIC language PRINT statement has tab stops to space output. These tab stops are like tabs

on a typewriter and occur in some systems at columns 1, 16, 31, 46, . . .
(every 15th column). The comma in the PRINT statement tells the system to
skip to the next tab stop before printing the next number (or the next characters,
as we'll see later). The semicolon doesn't skip at all before it prints the number
or characters. It can be regarded as a separator. The comma and semicolon are
controlling the motion of the cursor, which in turn controls the position of the
print.

If you choose to leave a comma or semicolon at the end of a PRINT statement, this "tab control" carries over to the next PRINT statement or INPUT
statement executed. Consider the following BASIC program:

```
10 A = 41.0
20 B = 80.0
30 C = 15.0
40 PRINT A,B,
50 PRINT C
60 END
```

When you RUN this program, do you notice how all three values appear on
the same line?

The numbers on the display are nice to see but, if there were a description
of the numbers, they would be easier to understand. Consider the following
code:

```
10 A = 41.0
20 B = 80.0
30 PRINT "FIRST VALUE","SECOND VALUE"
40 PRINT A, B
50 END
```

When this program is typed in and RUN, note that there are now headings
above the numbers that describe them. In our simple example this may not
seem too significant but, when the terminal screen or printed page is full of
numbers, a description certainly helps explain what the numbers mean. After
all, if you don't know what the numbers mean, what good are they?

PRINT USING Statement

As we have written various programs, we have used semicolons and commas
to control output formats. Many times we desire output that fits a very specific
format. For example, if we were going to print dollar figures on a preprinted
form (such as a statement), we would desire that the fractional numbers have
two decimal places, and that the decimal positions line up. If we wanted to list
three employees' hourly wages, the following program would print a hard-to-
read report:

```
10 W1 = 6.00
20 W2 = 10.49
30 W3 = 5.50
40 PRINT "EMPLOYEE 1 WAGE"; W1
50 PRINT "EMPLOYEE 2 WAGE"; W2
60 PRINT "EMPLOYEE 3 WAGE"; W3
70 END
```

RUN

```
EMPLOYEE 1 WAGE 6.
EMPLOYEE 2 WAGE 10.49
EMPLOYEE 3 WAGE 5.5
```

Although the PRINT USING statement is a nonstandard BASIC statement, it is available on many systems. The rules for usage of the PRINT USING vary widely from system to system. One format of the PRINT USING is

nnnnn   PRINT USING <"format string">;<list of expressions>

The PRINT USING statement contains the format of the line image that is to be used for output of the variables. The variables used must match the definitions in the format string. Some languages allow the format string to be a separate image statement. In those cases the <"format string"> is replaced with the line number of the image statement. The image statement takes on the form:

nnnnn   : format control characters

or

nnnnn   IMAGE format control characters

The image statement is normally defined with a colon at the beginning of the statement (or occasionally with the word IMAGE). If PRINT USING is supported on your system, you need to use format control characters. The format control characters for Microsoft BASIC are defined according to the table in figure H-2. For systems using the image statement, the following substitutions are often made:

Character Used	Control for	Example of Use
#	Numeric data, one symbol for each digit to be printed	####
$	Dollar sign to be printed here	$#####
$$	Floating dollar sign	$$####
+	Print plus or minus sign	+#######
−	Print minus sign only	−#######
+ or −	Trailing sign at end of number	#######−
**	Leading spaces to be filled with *	**###.##
**$	Leading * symbols followed by floating dollar sign	**$##.##
!	First character of string goes here	!
\<*n* spaces>\	Print 2 + *n* characters in string	\ \
&	Print variable-length string	&
_	Underscores precede and follow literal strings to be printed as they appear	_EQUALS_
^^^^	Print in exponential format	##.##^^^^
%	This symbol appears in output to indicate that the value to be printed was larger than the format specified	

E	Alphanumeric data (prints strings); must be preceded by apostrophe ('); prints an entire string	'E
L	Alphanumeric data, one symbol for each character, left-justified	'LLLLLLL
R	Alphanumeric data, one symbol for each character, right-justified	'RRRRRRR
C	Alphanumeric data, one symbol for each character, centered	'CCCCCCC

The following example, which prints a table of numbers along with their cubes and squares, may help you visualize the use of PRINT USING.

```
30 PRINT "NUMBER    SQUARED    CUBED"
40 FOR I = 1 TO 10
50 J = I * I
60 K = J * I
70 PRINT USING "  ##        ###        ####"; I; J; K
80 NEXT I
90 END
```

If your system uses the image statement, then the following program would reflect the use of the image statements:

```
30 PRINT USING 90
40 FOR I = 1 TO 10
50 J = I * I
60 K = J * I
70 PRINT USING 100, I, J, K
80 NEXT I
90 :NUMBER    SQUARED    CUBED
100 :  ##        ###        ####
110 END
```

The printout from either run would appear as follows:

NUMBER	SQUARED	CUBED
1	1	1
2	4	8
3	9	27
4	16	64
5	25	125
6	36	216
7	49	343
8	64	512
9	81	729
10	100	1000

Notice that, because of the PRINT USING, we are able to print a table with numbers that are lined up on the right-hand side. People are much more comfortable when they see all of the dollar figures, names, and such, lined up on a report. PRINT USING makes the job of lining up items on reports a lot easier.

Now that we have the print lined up nicely, it would be helpful to have the printout appear on paper. Most companies use printed reports extensively and, with large volumes of output, it is more efficient to work from a printed report. Microsoft BASIC uses the command LPRINT or LPRINT USING to cause printed output to go to the printer. Other systems require that you "open" the printer for use, and "close" it when you are done.

If your system requires the OPEN and CLOSE statements, you must choose a channel number from one through twelve (or fifteen) to use for output. The channel number is the way you communicate to the system where you want your output routed. The channel number is then named in the PRINT statement. The additional statements of OPEN and CLOSE have the following formats:

nnnnn   OPEN <filename> FOR <mode>AS<file or channel number>

or

nnnnn   OPEN <mode>,[#]<file or channel number>,<file name>

nnnnn   CLOSE [[#]<file number>[,[#]<file number>]...]

where *mode* is INPUT (I), OUTPUT (O), or RANDOM (R). We will use only the output mode now, and will learn to use the other modes in later sections. The file or channel number identifies the channel from one through twelve (or fifteen) that is to be used. The file name is the name of the file to be used or created. Some systems have special names for the system printer that can be used as the file name. Otherwise, a file name must be chosen, and that file printed out using a system command such as SAVE.

The employee hourly wage sample used earlier could be rewritten to include channel number output as follows:

```
5 OPEN "LP:" FOR OUTPUT AS #6
10 W1 = 6.00
20 W2 = 10.49
30 W3 = 5.50
40 PRINT #6 "EMPLOYEE 1 WAGE"; W1
50 PRINT #6 "EMPLOYEE 2 WAGE"; W2
60 PRINT #6 "EMPLOYEE 3 WAGE"; W3
70 CLOSE #6
80 END
```

Output is not standard in BASIC, so please check with your instructor or reference manual if none of these methods work for you.

INPUT Statement

The assignment statements that we have been using for the values 41.0 and 80.0 are fine but, if we want to change the program to use two different numbers, then we have to rekey the assignment statements. In effect, we have to rewrite the program. Most users will not be programmers, and they won't have the ability to rewrite the program. Even with the ability to program, I am against programming that can be avoided. Fine, you say, what do I have to do to avoid reprogramming every time I want to change those data values? BASIC provides us with the INPUT statement to do the job. The format of the INPUT statement is:

nnnnn   INPUT [;][<"prompt string">;]<list of variables>

Consider the following program:

```
10 INPUT A
20 INPUT B
30 PRINT "FIRST VALUE","SECOND VALUE"
40 PRINT A,B
50 END
```

Statements 10 and 20 allow the user to enter values for the variables A and B after the system command RUN has been typed. Because we can enter values while the program is running, we say that the values for the variables are entered at run time. When the system command RUN is typed in, the program begins execution. When the INPUT statement is executed, the user sees a question mark (?) at the terminal. The computer system is saying, "I have found an INPUT statement that you have in this program, and I need a value for the variable named in the INPUT statement. Please enter the variable value after the question mark I have printed." After responding to the first ? (giving the system the value for A), then a second question mark will appear requesting the value for B. Therefore in this example, you will receive one, then another (two total) question mark prompts. After the user responds by typing in a number following each question mark, the program will direct the computer system to print a heading and the two numbers before ending.

It probably would be helpful to have a phrase telling you what was being asked for by the INPUT statements. I recommend the following method of programming these phrases.

```
10 PRINT "ENTER THE FIRST NUMBER";
20 INPUT A
30 PRINT "ENTER THE SECOND NUMBER";
40 INPUT B
50 PRINT "FIRST VALUE", "SECOND VALUE"
60 PRINT A, B
70 END
```

The phrases preceding the INPUT statements are commonly known as prompts. Try to use meaningful, unabbreviated phrases to describe what should be entered. Use the semicolon on the prompt to force the user input to occur on the same line as the prompt. The INPUT statement gives a user the ability to change program variables while the program is running. This is known as interaction, or *interactive programming*.

INPUT commands can contain more than one variable named to be obtained as input. For example, statements 10 through 40 above could be replaced with:

```
10 PRINT "ENTER TWO NUMBERS SEPARATED BY A COMMA";
20 INPUT A,B
```

This is primarily for the convenience of the programmer, and sometimes makes the program harder to read and understand from the user's point of view. If the user enters less than the number of values required, the system will continue to ask for numbers, using only the system-generated question mark. If the order of the numbers is important and many numbers are needed, the system prompts for more numbers without an indication of what they should be.

INPUT can also be used to input string variables, such as names. For example, suppose you wanted to write a program that allowed you to type in your first name, then your last name. The desired output is last name, comma, and first name. The program and output would be as follows:

```
10 PRINT "ENTER FIRST NAME (IN QUOTES)";
20 INPUT F$
30 PRINT "ENTER LAST NAME (IN QUOTES)";
40 INPUT L$
50 PRINT L$; ", "; F$
60 END

RUN

ENTER FIRST NAME (IN QUOTES)?"JOHN"
ENTER LAST NAME (IN QUOTES)?"SMITH"
SMITH, JOHN
```

READ and DATA Statements

Another possible way of assigning values to variables is the use of the READ statement. READ reads values from another type of BASIC statement, the DATA statement. The format of the READ statement is:

nnnnn   READ <list of variables>

READ statement variables may be either numeric or string. The values read from the DATA statement must agree in type. In other words, variables named in the list of variables that are string variables must read string constants from the DATA statement, and variables that are numeric must read numbers from the DATA statement. If not, a syntax error will result when the program is run. The format of the DATA statement is

nnnnn   DATA <list of constants>

DATA statements are nonexecutable (do not cause the computer system to perform a function at run time) and may be placed anywhere in the program. A DATA statement may contain as many constants as will fit on a line. Any number of DATA statements may be used in a program. The READ statements access the DATA statements in line number order, and the DATA items may be regarded as one continuous list of data. You can think of the information contained in the DATA statements as a piggyback part of the program. DATA statements are not part of the algorithm (steps to solve the problem).

The earlier program (which printed two numbers as output) could be coded using the READ and DATA statements as follows:

```
10 READ A, B
20 DATA 21.0, 80.0
30 PRINT A, B
40 END
```

The DATA statement serves as a holding area (pool) of data values. Every time a READ is executed, one value from this pool of values is retrieved. The computer keeps track of which value is to be read next. When we talk about which value is to be read, we refer to the position as the data (pool) pointer. Each time a value is used by a READ statement, the pointer is positioned to read the next available data value in the pool. All DATA statements in the program are collected together in a single pool in the order that they appear in the program. Because of this collection process, you can code the DATA statements immediately following each READ (I like this method for simple programs), or you can group all of your DATA statements together at the beginning or end of your program. Please follow your instructor's preference.

There are two other things you should know about READ and DATA.

1. If you attempt to do a READ when your data pointer is past the end of the pool, you will get a program error. You have attempted to READ data that doesn't exist. You have read past the end of pool or end of file.

2. You can reset the position of the data pool pointer with the RESTORE or RESET statement.

Sometimes the logic of your program dictates the necessity of reusing the data pool. If we wanted a program that could easily be changed to calculate grade cut-off points for different grading scales, we would like to be able to change a minimum amount of our program. The DATA statement can be changed in the following program with ease to accommodate other grading scales. The values for the grade percentages are reset every time a new total of points possible by section is entered.

```
10 PRINT "ENTER SECTION ONE TEST POINTS POSSIBLE ";
20 INPUT P
30 READ P1, P2, P3, P4
40 DATA .90, .80, .70, .60
50 P1 = P1 * P
60 P2 = P2 * P
70 P3 = P3 * P
80 P4 = P4 * P
90 PRINT "POINTS NEEDED FOR AN A = "; P1
100 PRINT "POINTS NEEDED FOR A B = "; P2
110 PRINT "POINTS NEEDED FOR A C = "; P3
120 PRINT "POINTS NEEDED FOR A D = "; P4
130 PRINT "ENTER SECTION TWO TEST POINTS POSSIBLE ";
140 INPUT P
150 RESTORE
160 READ P1, P2, P3, P4
170 P1 = P1 * P
180 P2 = P2 * P
190 P3 = P3 * P
200 P4 = P4 * P
210 PRINT "POINTS NEEDED FOR AN A = "; P1
220 PRINT "POINTS NEEDED FOR A B = "; P2
230 PRINT "POINTS NEEDED FOR A C = "; P3
240 PRINT "POINTS NEEDED FOR A D = "; P4
    repeat statements 130 through 240 for as many sections as needed
360 END
```

479

A personal note about READ and DATA is in order. There are limited cases where READ and DATA should be used. Always ask yourself if you would be better off using assignment statements or INPUT statements before using READ and DATA. How can you decide when you are better off using an INPUT statement? If the data to be manipulated will change almost every time the program is run, then use an INPUT statement. How can you decide when you are better off using an assignment statement? If the data is of a constant nature, and is very unlikely to change, use an assignment statement. Even in those situations where the data will change because of some outside rule (tax rates, for example), a well commented assignment statement is easier to understand when you have not seen the program in some time. Most of the time, your programs will be more clear if you avoid using READ and DATA, and instead use remarks describing why you have used assignment or INPUT statements.

Remark Statement

A very important statement is the REM (remark) statement. The remark statement is a nonexecutable statement. It is for the programmer's use to clarify what is being done by the program. As the computer system executes the program and encounters a REM statement, control will be passed directly to the next statement. The format of the REM statement is

nnnnn   REM <remark>

where remark is an explanatory remark about the program. Often the contents of the REM statement are known as a comment. These comments can be used for internal documentation of the program. REMarks are entirely free format and can be used in any way by the programmer. You may find some uses for remarks that are not listed and, if that use is helpful to you, please use it.

Some typical uses of REM statements include the following.

1. A data dictionary of variables. This is where every variable used in the program is named, and the meaning of the variable is given in an English phrase. This is particularly helpful in large programs where many variables are used.

2. A short overview of what the program does in a general sense is often given in the REM statements.

3. An explanation of a section of code or of a single complex statement is common. These short comments are extremely easy to add when the program is being written, and they make life so much easier when maintenance (changes) to the program must be made. Unfortunately, we tend to forget the details of a program as time goes on, and these simple comments often trigger our memory of what was done. If the person responsible for maintenance is not the person who wrote the program, the comments are invaluable.

4. REM statements can be used to partition the code by leaving blank lines in the listing, separating sections of code. Lines of asterisks can be keyed to draw attention to the start of a new or unique section of code.

Good programmers use comments liberally. Comments explain what has happened in the program, and they often extend the life of a program because it can be readily changed to keep up with changing requirements. There is no good excuse for not using remarks in a production program. The examples in this book are explained in the surrounding text. If the programs were not explained in the text, my use of comments would have been very liberal. The best argument against using comments is that they take up disk storage space, and they do. Well-done comments are also worth every character! If a program will not fit on a disk because of too many comments, break it down into smaller programs. Don't remove the comments except as a last resort. You will not write programs large enough in this course for storage space to be a problem.

The program in figure H-3 is fully commented to show examples of each of the above uses of remarks. Lines 90 through 160 contain the data dictionary. Lines 10 through 70 contain a short overview of the function of the program. Lines 231, 232, and 241 are all examples of short explanations of what the code is supposed to do. Lines 321 through 323 show a partitioning of the code using the REM statement. Finally, other useful information is in the code at lines 160 through 191.

FIGURE H-3

A sample payroll program

```
10 REM THIS PROGRAM PRODUCES THE MINIMUM SCORES NEEDED
20 REM TO ACHIEVE A CERTAIN LETTER GRADE BASED ON THE
30 REM POINTS POSSIBLE.  EACH CLASS SECTION MAY HAVE
40 REM DIFFERENT QUANTITIES OF POINTS AVAILABLE, SO FOR
50 REM EACH SECTION TEST POINTS ARE ASKED FOR.  THE
60 REM CALCULATIONS ARE DONE USING A DATA STATEMENT
70 REM REPRESENTING THE 90, 80, 70, 60 SCALE
80 REM
90 REM VARIABLES USED:
100 REM P  THE TOTAL POINTS POSSIBLE ON EACH SECTION TEST
110 REM P1 THE PERCENTAGE NEEDED FOR AN A
120 REM P2 THE PERCENTAGE NEEDED FOR A B
130 REM P3 THE PERCENTAGE NEEDED FOR A C
140 REM P4 THE PERCENTAGE NEEDED FOR A D
150 REM
160 REM PROGRAM AUTHOR  RANDY JOHNSTON
170 REM DATE CHANGED   REASON FOR CHANGE
180 REM 11/14/82       NEW PROGRAM
190 REM 01/12/83       INCORPORATED MARILYN BOHL COMMENTS
191 REM 03/03/83       CHANGED LOGIC TO REMOVE GOTO
200 REM
210 PRINT "ENTER SECTION ONE TEST POINTS POSSIBLE";
220 INPUT P
230 READ P1, P2, P3, P4
231 REM THIS DATA STATEMENT WOULD NEED CHANGED IF THE
```

481

```
232 REM GRADING SCALE CHANGED FROM 90, 80, 70, 60
240 DATA .90, .80, .70, .60
241 REM CALCULATE POINTS NEEDED FOR THE RESPECTIVE GRADES
250 P1 = P1 * P
260 P2 = P2 * P
270 P3 = P3 * P
280 P4 = P4 * P
290 PRINT "POINTS NEEDED FOR AN A = "; P1
300 PRINT "POINTS NEEDED FOR A B = "; P2
310 PRINT "POINTS NEEDED FOR A C = "; P3
320 PRINT "POINTS NEEDED FOR A D = "; P4
321 REM
322 REM *******************************************************
323 REM SECTION TWO CODE
330 PRINT "ENTER SECTION TWO TEST POINTS POSSIBLE ";
340 INPUT P
350 RESTORE
360 READ P1, P2, P3, P4
361 REM CALCULATE THE RESPECTIVE GRADES
370 P1 = P1 * P
380 P2 = P2 * P
390 P3 = P3 * P
400 P4 = P4 * P
410 PRINT "POINTS NEEDED FOR AN A = "; P1
420 PRINT "POINTS NEEDED FOR A B = "; P2
430 PRINT "POINTS NEEDED FOR A C = "; P3
440 PRINT "POINTS NEEDED FOR A D  = "; P4
460 REM IF MORE THAN TWO SECTIONS ARE NEEDED, THE
470 REM STATEMENTS FROM 321 - 440 COULD BE DUPLICATED
560 END
```

FIGURE H-3 *(continued)*

END and STOP Statements

The END statement and the STOP statement both force the program to stop execution. The formats for these instructions are

nnnnn   END
nnnnn   STOP

The STOP instruction will produce the message BREAK IN LINE *nnnnn* or STOP IN LINE *nnnnn* and will leave open any files that are being used. The STOP can be used to help locate execution (run-time) errors by allowing the direct execution mode to be used.

The END statement should be the last statement of the program. It marks the physical and logical end of the program and releases any files being used by the program. If neither statement is used, the BASIC program does not know to stop execution, and will run forever.

The majority of processing in a commercial environment is done in steps. These steps are used to break down processing into manageable pieces. In between steps, there is a need to keep the information being processed for later use. This is accomplished by putting the records on secondary storage (disk or diskette).

Let's continue to use the hour-entry example from the previous module. The employee number and hours worked need to be saved for later processing. This gives the person working with the payroll system a chance to enter hours, review the entry done, and continue processing at a later time.

The most common method of saving files in BASIC is using sequential methods. This means that the records are written one after another. We want to save the employee number and hours worked, and the statements added to the hour-entry program in figure H-4 allow us to write this information to secondary storage for later use. We will input this information in a later program. The −1 at the end of the data serves as a trailer record to signal a later program that there are no more records in the file. These numbers can be retrieved with the INPUT statement by using the following lines in a program:

```
OPEN "HOURS" FOR INPUT AS FILE #3
INPUT #3,E;H
```

A Programming Example

FIGURE H-4

Sample program illustrating file creation

```
10 REM PAYROLL HOUR ENTRY PROGRAM
20 REM THIS PROGRAM ALLOWS ENTRY OF HOURS, AND PRINTS
30 REM A RECORD OF THE HOURS ENTERED
40 REM A GRAND TOTAL OF HOURS IS PRODUCED
41 REM THE EMPLOYEE NUMBER AND HOURS ARE SAVE FOR LATER
42 REM PROCESSING
50 REM
60 REM VARIABLES USED:
70 REM E = EMPLOYEE NUMBER
80 REM H = HOURS WORKED
90 REM T = TOTAL HOURS FOR ALL EMPLOYEES
100 REM
110 REM
120 OPEN "LP:" FOR OUTPUT AS FILE #1
121 OPEN "HOURS" FOR OUTPUT AS FILE #2
130 T = 0
```

```
140 PRINT "ENTER EMPLOYEE # (-1 TO END) ";
150 INPUT E
160 IF (E < 0) THEN 220
170 PRINT "ENTER THE HOURS WORKED (XX.XX) ";
180 INPUT H
190 T = T + H
200 PRINT #1 USING "EMP. ";"###";" HAD ";##.##;" HOURS";E;H
201 PRINT #2,E;H
210 GOTO 140
220 PRINT #1 USING "*** TOTAL HOURS *** ";"####.##";T
221 PRINT #2 -1.
230 CLOSE #1
231 CLOSE #2
240 END

RUN

ENTER EMPLOYEE # (-1 TO END) 1
ENTER THE HOURS WORKED (XX.XX) 40.00
ENTER EMPLOYEE # (-1 TO END) 2
ENTER THE HOURS WORKED (XX.XX) 45.00
ENTER EMPLOYEE # (-1 TO END) 3
ENTER THE HOURS WORKED (XX.XX) 41.00
ENTER EMPLOYEE # (-1 TO END) -1
```

Produced as printed output will be

```
EMP.  1 HAD 40.00 HOURS
EMP.  2 HAD 45.00 HOURS
EMP.  3 HAD 41.00 HOURS
*** TOTAL HOURS *** 126.00
```

Produced as output written to the secondary storage will be

```
  1.  40.
  2.  45.
  3.  41.
 -1.
```

FIGURE H-4 (continued)

H.1 What is a variable?

H.2 What are the rules for naming variables?

H.3 What does alphanumeric mean?

H.4 What is a string?

H.5 What is an operator?

H.6 List the order of operations.

H.7 What is the advantage of using the READ and DATA statements?

H.8 What is an image statement?

H.9 What is the PRINT USING statement used for?

Practice Programs

H.10 Write a program to print your name in block letters. A sample is shown.

```
XXXXXXX     XXXXX     X           X
   X          X       XX         XX
   X          X       X X       X X
   X          X       X  X     X  X
   X          X       X   X X     X
   X        XXXXX     X    X       X
```

H.11 Write a program that contains the following DATA statement, and averages the numbers contained in it:

DATA 14.3, 21.5, 4.51, 18.4

H.12 Given the following table, write a program that calculates the number of square feet of plywood sold and the amount of the sale in dollars. The price per square foot is $0.28.

Sale	Length	Width
1	8 feet	4 feet
2	4 feet	2 feet
3	6 feet	4 feet

SUMMARY

The assignment statement is fundamental to most computer languages. Assignment statements name locations in memory that are to receive new data values. These data values are variable in nature and the locations containing them are given short alphabetic names. Programmers call these locations variables. Variables can be either numeric or alphanumeric. Numeric variables are named by using one letter from the alphabet (A through Z) or by using one letter from the alphabet followed by a single digit (0 through 9). Alphanumeric (string) variables are named by using one letter from the alphabet followed by the character "$".

Assignment statements are of the form:

nnnnn   variable = expression

where expression is a constant, variable, or a variable and/or a constant connected by an operator. Operators are symbols like + (which means addition), and are evaluated in the order shown in figure H-1.

The PRINT statement directs the computer system to produce output in the form named. Numbers and strings can be printed. The position of the output is controlled by commas, semicolons, and use of the PRINT statements.

The PRINT USING statement is a nonstandard BASIC statement that provides us with a method of improving the format of our output. The PRINT USING statement prints according to an image definition that uses format control characters.

The INPUT statement allows the operator to enter values to be used by the program as it executes. The use of PRINT statements in conjunction with the INPUT statements serve to prompt the user for the correct information.

The READ and DATA statements provide another way of assigning values to variables. The values are kept in a data pool. The assignment statement and INPUT statement accomplish most of the tasks that can be provided by the READ and DATA statements.

The REM statement allows the programmer to put explanatory remarks (comments) throughout the program. REM statements can be very helpful if used properly.

The STOP and END statements halt program execution. The END statement should be the last statement of every program.

WORD LIST
(in order of appearance in text)

Variable	Operation
Default	Hierarchy of operations
Floating point numbers	Image statement
Integer numbers	CLOSE statement
Exponential numbers	OPEN statement
Truncated	Mode
Character	Interactive programming
String	READ statement
Direct-execution mode	DATA statement
Operator	RESTORE or RESET statement
	STOP statement

SECTION 2—SYSTEM COMMANDS

Now that you have had a chance to look at how some computers physically work, we must be concerned about how you use your system to run BASIC programs. We must use system commands to tell the computer what we want done. Figure H-5 shows the relationship of system commands to what is done on the hardware. Please take time to understand this diagram and the table in figure H-6, which lists the common system commands. Most of the commands work directly on the program in the work area.

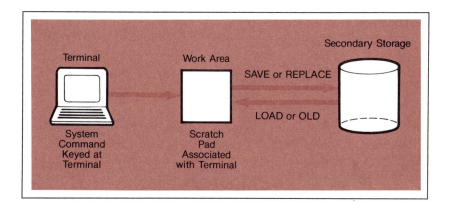

Command	Function
NEW	Create a new program work area (erasing previous contents)
LIST	List the program in the work area
RUN	Run the program in the work area
RENUM	Renumber the program lines (not available on all systems)
DELETE	Delete a specific line or lines
SAVE	Save the program in the work area by placing it on secondary storage
LOAD (or OLD)	Load a program into the work area from secondary storage
REPLACE (or RESAVE)	Replace the program of the same name in secondary storage with the program from the work area
CATALOG (or DIR)	List all the programs on the disk(ette) that is currently in the disk(ette) drive
RENAME	Rename a program on secondary storage
UNSAVE (or PURGE or ERASE or KILL)	Delete a program from secondary storage

Notice from previous sample programs that the commands NEW, LIST, and RUN are used to make the computer do certain jobs. There are other commands that make our programming easier. Let's cover them in the order of the table.

Once you have logged on to your system, there is an area reserved in main storage called the work area. The work area (scratch pad associated with your terminal) is manipulated by system commands. When the NEW command is used, the work area is cleared. This command allows you to start a new program by erasing any contents of the work area.

On a few systems, you are given the opportunity to give the new program a name at this time. Programs are generally named using the following conventions:

1. Up to 8 total characters may be used (6 on many systems.)

NEW Command

2. The first character must be an alphabetic character.

3. No spaces (imbedded blanks) are allowed within the name.

4. Try to make the program name somewhat descriptive of what the program does. For example, if a program is to print payroll checks, PAYCHK is a logical choice for the program name. HOWCAT would probably not be a wise choice for a paycheck program name.

It is also helpful if programs are named generically. *Generic naming* means that programs of similar functions have similar names. Examples of generic naming for a payroll system could be PAYCHK (payroll check), PAYREG (payroll register), and PAYW2 (payroll W-2 forms). All of the programs in the payroll system start with the letters PAY.

The whole idea behind naming a program is to specifically identify the program in a meaningful way.

LIST Command

The LIST command allows you to list at the terminal the current contents of your work area. It is often helpful to look at the BASIC statements that are currently in your source program. As your programs get larger, you may find that your terminal screen does not hold all of the lines in your work area, or that you simply want to look at just a few lines of your program. You may ask for specific lines by line numbers with the LIST option. The following format and examples show some of the available options:

LIST [<line number>[−[<line number>]]]

```
LIST
LIST 10–100
LIST 150
```

The first LIST command directs the computer to list all of the lines in the work area. The second directs the computer to list lines 10 through 100. The last LIST command directs the computer to list only line 150. The LLIST command is sometimes available to get a listing on the system printer.

RUN Command

The RUN command tells the system to do the steps necessary to execute the BASIC source statements in your work area. Each BASIC statement that we have coded is translated to tell the computer to do what is described by the BASIC source statement. Once RUN has been typed, the system starts the BASIC interpreter. The translation of the BASIC statements takes place and the CPU executes them. If a syntax error exists, it will be reported by the interpreter when an attempt is made to execute that statement. The RUN command can also be used to load a program from secondary storage in addition to the translation and execution. The format and three examples of the RUN command follow:

RUN [<line number>]　　　or　　　RUN <filename>

```
RUN
RUN 400
RUN "PAYCHK"
```

The first RUN command will run the program in the work area. It starts at the beginning of the program because no line number was given. The second RUN command will begin execution at line 400. The last RUN will load a file from secondary storage into memory and run it.

RENUM Command

As we code (write) complex programs or make additions to existing programs, there is sometimes a need to renumber the BASIC statements. Some systems offer the RENUMber command to do this job. The format and some examples follow.

```
RENUM [[<new number>][,[<old number>][,<increment>]]]
```

```
RENUM
RENUM 1000,,20
RENUM 200,100,50
```

The first RENUM statement renumbers the entire program. The first line number will be 10, and the line numbers will be incremented by 10. The second RENUM command also renumbers the entire program, but the first line will be 1000, and the line numbers will be incremented by 20. The last RENUM command renumbers the lines from 100 up so they start with line 200, and increment by 50.

In some implementations of BASIC, this function is not a system command, but is a user-written program or a utility supplied by a vendor. Be sure to check with your instructor or in the system manuals for information about the availability and format of the RENUM command.

DELETE Command

The DELETE command can be used to instruct the system to remove unwanted program lines. You should always take care when keying the line numbers that you want to delete. Adding an extra zero or two to a line number can cause unfortunate grief when using the delete command. You will undoubtedly make this mistake at some point in time (we all do), so don't worry about it. If you have made this mistake, keep calm, and try to remember whether you have a copy of your program on secondary storage. Depending on the amount of work you have done, it may be worth your time to reload the old copy and make the changes to your program again. If not, just retype the deleted lines, and learn from experience.

The format of the DELETE command and some examples follow:

```
DELETE [<line number>][-<line number>]
```

```
DELETE 70
DELETE 30-60
DELETE -50
```

The first DELETE command deletes line 70. The second DELETE command deletes lines 30 through 60, inclusive. The last DELETE command deletes all lines up to and including line 50.

There is one other way to delete lines. Simply type in the line number of the unwanted line with nothing after it, and press return. The reason this method deletes a line is because it stores an empty line. BASIC ignores empty lines. Some systems use other commands to delete lines, but DELETE is the most common system command to do the job.

SAVE Command

The SAVE command is used to direct the computer to copy a BASIC program from the work area to some form of permanent secondary storage (cassette, diskette, or disk). After investing time and effort in creating a program to do some job for you, it makes good sense to save the program for future use. Why reinvent the wheel by coding the same program over and over again?

There are other good reasons for SAVEing a program. Assume you have a limited amount of time to work on a program. Any work that can be done, no matter how short the time period, can be saved for later use. When programs become large, it is not practical (and sometimes not even possible) to enter all of the source statements at one time. As a program is being entered for the first time or being changed, it should be saved every so often for your own protection. Remember from earlier discussions of memory that, if power is lost, the contents of memory are also lost. Losing power can happen in a myriad of ways from a power switch accidentally being flipped, to a power cord being pulled from an outlet, to a loss of electricity due to a storm. The more conscientiously a correct program is saved from a work area, the less chance you have of losing the program. The format and an example of the SAVE command follow:

SAVE <filename>

```
SAVE "PAYCHK"
```

This SAVE command would save the contents of the work area on secondary storage, using the name PAYCHK.

LOAD or OLD Command

If a program has been saved on secondary storage, we can direct the system to place the program back into the work area. This gives us additional opportunity to edit (change) the program, or to run the program again. The system command that does this job is LOAD (or OLD on some systems). LOAD directs the computer to copy the source program from secondary storage to the work area. The format and two examples follow:

LOAD <filename>[,R]

```
LOAD "PAYCHK"
LOAD "PAYCHK",R
```

The first LOAD command would load the program PAYCHK from secondary storage into the work area. The second LOAD command would load the program PAYCHK from secondary storage into the work area, and the ",R" option directs the system to RUN the program also.

REPLACE or RESAVE Command

Programs commonly need to be changed while being developed or after being used for a period of time. These changes are necessary because of program errors, a change in the requirements of the program, changes in governmental regulations, or computer system changes. Program changes are often referred to as maintenance. After a program has originally been saved using the SAVE command, many systems require that all subsequent changes to the program be saved on secondary storage using the command REPLACE or RESAVE. This prevents you from accidentally wiping out a previously written program with the same name.

CATALOG or DIR Command

Over a period of time, our human memories often forget what programs we have written, how they were written, or even what their names are. The system will tell us what programs are available on the secondary storage if we use the CATALOG command. The CATALOG command will direct the system to give us the program name, and other useful information such as the size of the program. CATALOG is a function of some versions of BASIC. (The IBM PC uses the command FILES instead of CATALOG.)

If the CATALOG command is not available in your version of BASIC, the DIR (directory) command is available on microcomputers from CP/M or DOS to do this job. This command directs the system to list the programs on the secondary storage. When the DIR command is executed from the system level, the contents of the work area frequently are lost.

RENAME Command

If we have accidentally given a program a wrong name, or want to change the program name for any reason, we can have the system rename the program using the RENAME command. The name of the program on the secondary storage is changed, but none of the references to the program name in the source code itself are changed. The format and an example follow.

RENAME<filename>[AS]<filename>

```
RENAME "PAYPRG"  "PAYREG"
```

UNSAVE, PURGE, ERASE, or KILL

If you discover that you no longer want a program, you can tell the system to remove it from the secondary storage device by using the UNSAVE, PURGE, ERASE, or KILL command. This command directs the system to remove the entry that identifies the program from the directory of the secondary storage. Your system may use one or more of the commands. KILL is shown here:

KILL <filename>

```
KILL "PAYREG"
```

The KILL command shown would delete the program PAYREG from secondary storage.

Other Considerations

A note of convenience may be helpful at this point. There are special control commands that can be used while editing. These special control commands are often obtained by pushing special function keys or a combination of keys. For example, many systems will stop printing output to a terminal if the key labeled CTRL is pushed and *held while* the letter S is pushed (often shown as CTRL-S or ^S). To restart the scrolling, CTRL-Q might be used. Some systems will restart screen scrolling by depressing any key. The ability to tabulate (skip many spaces to a specific point) by using CTRL-I is common. To show an end-of-file condition, CTRL-Z or CTRL-D may be keyed. To cancel a job,

CTRL-C or CTRL-BREAK may be used. These are just a few examples of many that are available on various systems. Consult your instructor or machine manual for these computer-dependent step savers.

If your system uses diskettes, you may need to learn to initialize the diskettes for use with your system. Different systems use different format diskettes, and each system supplies a program to format new diskettes as needed. Formatting prepares the diskette for use by writing control information where it is needed on the diskette. Any previous contents of the diskette are destroyed. Because of this, you should be sure that any diskette you intend to format is no longer needed for its previous purpose or is new.

QUESTIONS

H.13 Describe the relationship between the work area and secondary storage.

H.14 What are system commands used for?

H.15 Which system commands are absolutely required to run a BASIC program?

H.16 Which commands direct the system to copy BASIC programs to and from secondary storage?

H.17 What special system commands exist on your system?

H.18 Describe what each of the following system commands does.
   a. DELETE 50–100
   b. LIST 50
   c. LIST 20–220
   d. RENUM
   e. NEW
   f. SAVE"GLENTRY"
   g. DELETE – 100
   h. RUN

H.19 Given the following program

```
10 A = 39
20 B = A / 3
30 PRINT A,B
40 A = 24
50 B = A / 3
60 PRINT A,B
70 END
```

write the system commands that instruct the computer to delete lines 10 through 30, then to renumber the statements in the altered program so that the line numbers begin at line 10, and increment by 10. Finally, list the program.

H.20 Assume that the program in problem H.19 is named THIRDS. What would be printed after the following lines have been typed?

```
40
50
60
SAVE "THIRDS"
```

```
READY
LOAD "THIRDS"
RENUM
READY
LIST
```

H.21 Write the set of commands necessary to change THIRDS to eliminate the second calculation, allow entry of any number, and save it under the name "THIRD."

SUMMARY

Every computer system has certain commands that direct the computer to do a particular function. While using the language BASIC, it is helpful to remember that all the system commands work with an area in memory called the work area. The work area is a scratch pad where BASIC source statements are written. All system commands direct the computer to execute certain functions using the BASIC source statements in the work area.

The table of commands and functions (figure H-6) should be reviewed.

WORD LIST
(in order of appearance in text)

Generic naming
RENUM command
DELETE command
SAVE command
LOAD or OLD command

REPLACE or RESAVE command
CATALOG or DIR command
RENAME command
UNSAVE, PURGE, ERASE, OR
    KILL command

SECTION 3—DECISIONS

Up to this point, we have written programs to do some simple operations on the computer. We have not yet seen one of the most powerful areas of computing. Computers can test conditions and take actions based on the results of the tests. We write IF-THEN statements to cause them to do so. We will also cover the use of the GOTO statement in this section.

IF Statement

The IF statement in any form is always attempting to test some condition. Note the following format:

nnnnn   IF <condition> THEN statement

The *condition* part of the IF statement is built by making a statement that can be answered as either true or false. We build these conditions by expressing constants, variables, or expressions in some sort of relationship. Often these conditions are enclosed in parentheses. The condition (relationship) can then be evaluated based on the current values of the variables involved. If we paid overtime of all hours worked over 40, we could state the condition as follows: are the number of hours worked greater than 40?

The relationships are expressed using the *relational operators*. Remember from the earlier discussion of order of operations that the relational operators are less than ($<$), less than or equal to ($<=$), greater than ($>$), greater than or equal to ($>=$), equal to ($=$), or not equal to ($<>$). When calculations are done in BASIC and the answers do not come out exactly evenly, we occasionally use the relational operator approximately equal to (==). Using these operators, we can test relationships between variables.

When comparisons are made on numbers or letters, we expect the letters or numbers to occur in sequence. In English, we demand that the letters appear in "alphabetical" order. The numbers must appear in numeric order. The special characters such as #, $, and, & also have an order in which they appear. Even the character that represents a blank space appears in this sequence in a particular place. The order is known as a *collating sequence*. Appendix 2 lists the collating sequence used by many systems. Any comparisons made with the relational operators will evaluate the sequence of characters based on the collating sequence.

If there are multiple conditions to test, we can use the *logical operators* to combine the tests needed. The logical operators are AND, OR, and NOT. Let's say you want to combine two conditions before you pay overtime. The employee must have worked over 40 hours AND must be an hourly employee. When writing the BASIC statement, you would join the two conditions with the operator AND. If you wanted to pay overtime when the weekly hours were greater than 40 OR the hours for any one day were greater than 8, the two conditions could be joined by the condition OR. In any case, if you want the opposite of what is stated you can use the logical operator NOT.

The logic of the IF-THEN statement is diagrammed in figure H-7. The flowcharting symbol that represents a test is the diamond-shaped symbol. The rectangular shape represents a process that must be done (in this case, a statement). Remember that flowcharts are read from top to bottom, and from left to right, unless the direction is modified by an arrow.

The conditions expressed in the IF statement can be as simple as the payroll-hour question or extremely complex.

FIGURE H-7

Logic of the IF-THEN statement

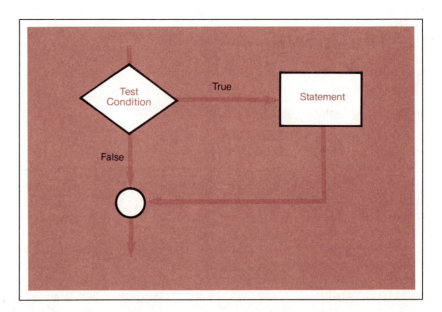

The statement portion of the IF statement can consist of several different options. One option is to transfer control of the program flow. Remember that, when we start the execution of a BASIC program, the lowest-statement-number BASIC statement is executed first, then the next lowest, and so forth until a STOP or END statement is encountered. We can change this order of execution with a few BASIC statements. The IF is one such statement. If a line number is the statement following the THEN, then the flow of program control will be transferred to that line number.

Another option for the IF statement is to have any other valid BASIC statement as the statement following the IF. ANSI Minimal BASIC allows only some types of statements, but most implementations of BASIC have been written to accept all statements. Many implementations have been extended to allow more than one statement to be included in the THEN.

The flow of control for the IF statement could look like this:

IF   (Condition)   THEN Statement
      False   True

Next BASIC Statement

Note the following examples.

```
100 IF (H * 3 > 41) THEN 40
110 IF (D <= 0.0) THEN 70
120 IF (P = T * 4 - 81 / R) THEN Z = 27.0
130 IF (S = 1.0) THEN PRINT "S HAS REACHED 1.0"
```

Please note that, in the above examples, the statement portions of the IF-THEN statements did some different things. In the first two examples, if the condition tested was true, the next statement executed would be line 40 (for H * 3 > 41) or line 70 (for D <= 0.0). This type of alteration of program execution is called a *conditional transfer,* or a conditional branch of program execution. We are telling the program to execute different program lines based on the result of a test. This is the most common usage of the IF statement and conforms to the ANSI standard. At line 120, the statement we want to have executed is an assignment statement. In the last example, we chose to print out a message if a particular condition was true. Lines 120 and 130 are not ANSI standard, and may not work on your implementation of BASIC.

When computer languages are implemented on computer systems, certain words take on particular meanings. These words are called reserved words, or *key words*. They serve as signals to the interpreter or compiler that a particular function is desired. So far, we have used the BASIC key words PRINT, INPUT, END, REM, READ, and DATA. These key words direct the computer system to print, accept input from the user, stop execution, skip to the next executable statement because a programmer's explanation follows, accept data from the data pool, or add data to the data pool respectively.

The words IF and THEN are the BASIC reserved (key) words in the IF-THEN statement. These two words let the computer know that a conditional test is going to occur (IF), and then mark the end of the condition and start of the statement to be done (THEN). Please take careful note that the THEN portion of the IF-THEN statement is executed only when the condition expressed is true.

Let's say we have a friend named Joe who knows about all the computer skills we are gaining. He knows that computers can do some pretty sophisticated things. Joe requests a simple program. Joe is working part-time to pay for his classes and has been told that, if he works over 40 hours, he will receive time-and-a-half (1.5 times his normal wage). Joe would like to know how much he should receive as gross pay if he works a certain number of hours. You would like to know for your job, too, so you decide to write the program. It asks for hourly rate, and the number of hours worked.

Remembering the design strategy you learned earlier, you decide the output should look like the following:

```
FOR _ _ _ HOURS AT _ _ _ PER HOUR
THE GROSS WAGE IS _ _ _ _ _ _ _ _
```

The input needed to calculate the gross wage is the number of hours worked and the hourly rate. These two items will also appear in the output.

Next, you attempt to determine the processing logic. Although you have not had a lot of programming experience, it seems that this job should not be too tough, and you have a pretty clear idea of how to do the whole job, except for knowing when to calculate the time-and-a-half. While thinking the problem through to design your logic, you discover that two INPUT statements, a calculation for regular time, a calculation done for overtime only if the number of hours is over 40, and two PRINT statements should do the job. Figuring out how to keep the overtime calculation from being performed every time is the tough part. Then you discover that the BASIC statement IF can test conditions. You recognize that the condition you must test for is when the number of hours worked has become greater than 40. Two statements will calculate the correct gross wage. The pseudocode could look like this:

```
BEGIN GROSS-WAGE PROCEDURE
   INPUT RATE, HOURS
   WAGE = RATE * HOURS
   SET OVERTIME TO ZERO
   IF HOURS > 40
      THEN OVERTIME = RATE * (HOURS - 40) * .5
   ENDIF
   GROSS = WAGE + OVERTIME
   PRINT RATE, HOURS, GROSS
END GROSS-WAGE PROCEDURE
```

Here's one method of solving the problem:

```
5 REM PROGRAM TO CALCULATE GROSS WAGE
6 REM R = HOURLY RATE, H = HOURS WORKED
7 REM W = GROSS WAGE, E = OVERTIME WAGE
10 PRINT "ENTER THE HOURLY RATE (KEY $3.50 AS 3.50)";
20 INPUT R
30 PRINT "ENTER NUMBER OF HOURS (40 1/2 AS 40.50)";
```

```
40 INPUT H
50 REM R HAS THE HOURLY WAGE, AND H CONTAINS THE HOURS
60 REM MULTIPLYING THE TWO TOGETHER GIVES GROSS WAGE(W)
70 W = R * H
80 REM NOW CHECK TO SEE IF THERE WAS OVERTIME
90 REM ASSUME THE OVERTIME WAGE (E) IS ZERO
100 E = 0
110 IF (H > 40.0) THEN E = R * (H - 40.0) * 0.5
120 W = W + E
130 PRINT "FOR ";H;" HOURS AT ";R;" PER HOUR"
140 PRINT "THE GROSS WAGE IS ";W
150 END
```

This solution does do the job, but it has some shortcomings. You find that, if you want to find out about more than one wage at a time, you must RUN the program a number of times. What happens if you must do more than one calculation when the number of hours is greater than 40? There are other BASIC statements that help with these problems, and we will learn about them later.

GOTO Statement

There are times in the decision making process when we need to do more than a single statement. Often when we are making a test, we want to do one or more statements if the condition is true, and to do one or more other statements if the condition is false. We will use the GOTO statement in this circumstance. We will explain other uses for the GOTO in the next section.

The GOTO statement unconditionally transfers control from the current statement to the statement named by line number in the GOTO statement. The form of the GOTO statement is as follows:

nnnnn   GOTO nnnnn

The GOTO statement will always "branch" (transfer program execution) to the line number named. Examples of the GOTO statement are:

```
50 GOTO 10
180 GOTO 350
```

Note that branches can be either forward or backward in the program. We will talk about forward branches in this section, and we will discuss backward branches in the section on loops.

Let's use the GOTO statement to build one of the three program constructs used in pseudocode, the IF-THEN-ELSE-ENDIF. The logic for IF-THEN-ELSE-ENDIF is shown in figure H-8. This program structure is very important because you can logically follow the program from the IF statement to the "ENDIF," treating the entire sequence of statements in the structure as one logical unit.

Let's go back to the payroll example, but change it to report the regular-time gross wage and the overtime gross wage separately. Examine the following program to do that job.

```
5 REM PROGRAM TO CALCULATE GROSS WAGE
10 PRINT "ENTER THE HOURLY RATE (KEY $3.50 AS 3.50)";
```

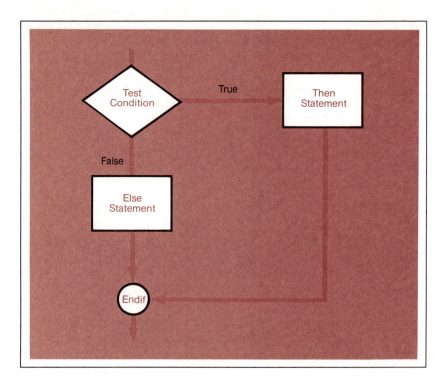

Logic of the IF-THEN-ELSE-ENDIF "statement"

```
20 INPUT R
30 PRINT "ENTER NUMBER OF HOURS (40 1/2 AS 40.50)";
40 INPUT H
50 REM R HAS THE HOURLY WAGE, AND H CONTAINS THE HOURS
60 REM MULTIPLYING THE TWO TOGETHER GIVES GROSS WAGE
70 REM DO THE WAGE CALCULATIONS BASED ON THE
80 REM NUMBER OF HOURS (FIGURE OVERTIME AS NEEDED)
90 IF (H > 40.0) THEN 150
100 REM DO THE REGULAR HOUR CALCULATIONS
105 REM ** ELSE **
110    W1 = R * H
120    W2 = 0.00
130 GOTO 180
140 REM DO THE OVERTIME HOUR CALCULATIONS
145 REM ** THEN **
150    W1 = R * 40.0
160    W2 = R * (H - 40.0) * 1.5
170 REM ** ENDIF **
180 PRINT "FOR ";H;" HOURS AT ";R;" PER HOUR"
190 PRINT "THE GROSS REGULAR WAGE IS ";W1
200 PRINT "THE GROSS OVERTIME WAGE IS ";W2
210 END
```

Note how the GOTO at line 130 branches around the program code that cal-culates the overtime. Indeed, if we had just finished calculating the regular time, there is no need to calculate overtime. Also note the special remarks at line 105, line 145, and line 170. The remarks signal the programmer that an ELSE is beginning, a THEN is beginning, and the IF statement is complete.

Another good habit to form is to indent the "then" and "else" portions of the IF statement. This makes the code easier to read and shows that your intention is to have the indented statements included as part of the IF statement. Remember that the BASIC interpreter will not know that your statements are part of the IF just because they are indented. The indentation is for the programmer's reading convenience. The indentation is allowed because BASIC is free-format and does not require that key words or operands appear in particular places.

Inside the "THEN" or the "ELSE" sequence of statements, one of the statements may be another IF. If this happens, remember to indent for the first IF as well as the second IF statement. An IF statement that is a part of another IF's "THEN" or "ELSE" statement is called a "nested IF." We say that the second IF statement is *nested* inside the first IF statement.

ON-GOTO Statement

Another type of GOTO statement alters program execution by branching to one of several specified line numbers, depending on the value returned when an expression is evaluated. This statement is the ON-GOTO statement. The word ON is important, because it specifies when this type of GOTO is supposed to be executed. The ON statement is another type of conditional transfer. It is often used to replace several IF statements. The format follows:

nnnnn　　ON <condition> GOTO <list of line numbers>

The condition is any valid BASIC expression. If the expression has the value of one up through (but not including) two, the statement at the first line number named will be given program control. If the expression has the value of two up through (but not including) three, the statement at the second line number named will be given control. We can name as many line numbers as we wish. If the value of the expression is less than or equal to zero, or is greater than the largest value accommodated by the line numbers named, an error may result. An IF statement before the ON-GOTO to eliminate these conditions is a wise move. An example of using this statement instead of IF statements follows:

```
            If X=1  X=2  X=3          Then the statement
              ↓     ↓     ↓           executed next is
  70 ON X GOTO 150, 210, 250
```

which is equivalent to

```
  70 IF (X = 1) THEN 150
  80 IF (X = 2) THEN 210
  90 IF (X = 3) THEN 250
```

On some systems, if the value being tested is not in the range of acceptable values for the ON-GOTO, the program will stop with an error message. Most systems execute the statement following the ON-GOTO statement if none of the conditions are met.

Assume that you would like to let a user of one of your programs make a choice from three items. You can use the ON-GOTO to make the coding for this quite easy. The following program shows the ON-GOTO being used this way.

```
10 REM A SIMPLE PROGRAM TO SHOW THE SELECTION OF
20 REM FIELD NUMBERS
30 REM F = FIELD NUMBER CHOSEN
40 F = 0
50 PRINT "ITEM ONE (1)"
60 PRINT "ITEM TWO (2)"
70 PRINT "ITEM THREE (3)"
80 PRINT "ENTER NUMBER OF ITEM DESIRED";
90 INPUT F
100 IF ((F <= 0) OR (F >= 4)) THEN 40
110 ON F GOTO 500, 600, 700
   .
   .
   .
```

Other statements to perform Item One, Two, or Three

Some systems allow placing a numeric value or reserved word in the "condition" position of the ON-GOTO to intercept certain program conditions. When the GOSUB statement is introduced, it may be used in place of the GOTO statement. The rules will be the same. Consult your instructor or system manuals to check this feature on your system.

Debugging Techniques

With the added power of the IF and GOTO statements, we can start to control the flow of our programs, and we can make more powerful programs. Unfortunately, we can begin to cause logic errors within our programs. If we accidentally enter the wrong line numbers in our GOTO statements or don't include everything we wanted inside an IF, an error can result.

If you are having trouble with a particular value, try adding PRINT statements to your program at those points where you would like to know the value of a variable. The print produced does not have to be fancy as long as it tells you what was causing your error.

If you would like to know if a sequence of statements is being executed, you can add PRINT statements with messages to you to show where the program flow is going.

Another tool is the use of STOP statements. You can place a STOP statement where you want the program to stop so you can use many statements in the direct execution mode. You may then PRINT any variables that you are interested in. Program execution can be restarted by the CONT (continue) statement.

Any statements that you can use to help you understand a program logic error should be used. The best way to prevent program logic errors is by careful program design and careful keying when the program is being entered.

A Programming Example

In a commercial environment, calculation of a payroll would be based on parameters set up by the government, company, and individual employee's wishes. For example, the government would dictate the tax rates, the company would pay a certain hourly rate, and the employee may wish to voluntarily have money withheld from his check for certain purposes. All of these various parameters would need to be maintainable by the person responsible for running the payroll. Retrieving the information for these parameters would require a maintenance program.

By the end of this module, you should have enough skills that you could learn to write a maintenance program. Since we are not to that point yet, assumptions must be made about how this payroll system is going to work. Throughout the next sections, we are going to write the program needed to calculate the payroll. First, we will calculate the wages using the hour records generated in the earlier sections and generate a payroll register. Then, expansion of the program will include calculating taxes, and calculating voluntary deductions. Assumptions will be used that would not be needed if the master records or parameter records were available.

This company pays the same hourly rate to all employees. They also pay overtime at the time-and-a-half rate for all hours worked greater than 40. The program listed in figure H-9 calculates the wages for the employees we have on file.

H.22 Why is the IF-THEN statement important?

H.23 Diagram the logic of the IF-THEN statement.

H.24 What is the GOTO statement used for?

FIGURE H-9

Modified payroll program

```
10 REM THIS PROGRAM CALCULATES THE PAYROLL FOR A COMPANY
20 REM TO DO THIS JOB, THE FOLLOWING STEPS ARE DONE:
30 REM  1) WAGES ARE CALCULATED
40 REM  2) TAXES ARE CALCULATED
60 REM  4) A PAYROLL REGISTER IS PRINTED
70 REM
80 REM FILES USED:
90 REM  HOURS IS A FILE CONTAINING THE EMPLOYEE
100 REM NUMBER AND THE HOURS WORKED
110 REM
120 REM VARIABLES USED:
130 REM  E = EMPLOYEE NUMBER
140 REM  H = HOURS WORKED BY THE EMPLOYEE
150 REM  T1 = TOTAL HOURS WORKED BY ALL EMPLOYEES
160 REM  T2 = TOTAL TAXES
```

```
170 REM  T3 = TOTAL WAGES
190 REM  W = WAGE OF EMPLOYEE
210 REM  T = TAXES FOR EMPLOYEE
220 REM  R1 = RATE OF PAY FOR COMPANY
230 REM  R2 = WITHHOLDING TAX RATE USED BY COMPANY
240 REM  R3 = FICA TAX RATE
250 REM  N = NET WAGE
260 REM  L = PAGE LINE COUNT
270 REM  I = LOOP INDEX VARIABLE
280 REM
290 REM
300 REM ********************************************************
320 REM INITIALIZE ALL VARIABLES ASSUMED TO HAVE A VALUE
330 T1 = 0
340 T2 = 0
350 T3 = 0
361 L = 56
370 OPEN "HOURS" FOR INPUT AS #1
380 OPEN "LP:" FOR OUTPUT AS #2
390 PRINT "ENTER PAY RATE TO BE USED (XX.XX) [-1 TO END] ";
400 INPUT R1
410 IF (R1 < 0) THEN 2000
402 PRINT "ENTER FEDERAL TAX RATE (XX.XX = 20.00%) ";
430 INPUT R2
440 PRINT "ENTER FICA TAX RATE (XX.XX = 6.70%) ";
450 INPUT R3
460 PRINT "STARTING PAYROLL PROCESS"
470 INPUT #1,E;H
480 IF (E <= 0) THEN 990
490 REM HAVE THE EMPLOYEE RECORD, AND NEED TO START
500 REM CALCULATING THE PAY
510 IF (H > 40) THEN 560
520 REM ** THEN **  CALCULATE REGULAR PAY
530   W = H * R1
540   GOTO 580
550 REM ** ELSE **  CALCULATE OVERTIME PAY
560   W = H * R1 * 1.5
```

F I G U R E H-9 *(continued)*

```
570 REM ** ENDIF **
580 REM
590 REM CALCULATION OF TAXES
600 REM FOR FUTURE GOVERNMENTAL REGULATION CHANGES
610 REM LOOK TO CHANGE THE CALCULATION METHOD HERE
620 T = W * R2
630 T = T + (W * R3)
640 REM A STATE TAX CALCULATION COULD BE INSERTED HERE
770 REM
780 REM  CALCULATE THE NET WAGE
790 N = W - T
830 REM
840 REM  PRINT A PAYROLL REGISTER
850 IF (L <56) THEN 890
860 REM  PRINT A SIMPLE HEADING
870 PRINT #2 "          PAYROLL REGISTER"
880 PRINT #2 "EMP #   GROSS    TAXES      NET"
881 L = 0
890 PRINT #2 USING "##### ####.## ####.## ####.##";E;W;T;N
891 REM INCREMENT THE LINE COUNTER
892 REM L = L + 1
900 REM
910 REM ACCUMULATE TOTALS FOR THE GRAND TOTAL LINE
920 T1 = T1 + H
930 T2 = T2 + T
940 T3 = T3 + W
970 GOTO 470
980 REM
990 REM  PRINT THE GRAND TOTAL LINE
1000 PRINT #2
1010 PRINT #2        "GRAND    TOTALS FOR THIS PAYROLL RUN"
1020 PRINT #2        "GROSS     TAXES        HOURS"
1030 PRINT #2 USING "####.## #####.## ####.##";T3;T2;T1
2000 CLOSE #1
2010 CLOSE #2
2020 END
```

F I G U R E H-9 *(continued)*

H.25 What is a program branch?

H.26 Diagram the logic of the IF-THEN-ELSE-ENDIF "statement."

H.27 What type of statements can the ON-GOTO statement replace?

H.28 According to post office regulations, a package may not be sent first class if its length plus its girth exceeds 100 inches. Write a program that reads the lengths and girths of packages, and for each package prints the length and girth of the package, as well as whether the package may be sent via first class mail.

H.29 A machine part must have a gap of not less than 0.97 millimeters and not greater than 1.03 millimeters. Write a program that reads the size of the gap and prints a message that the part is to be accepted or rejected.

H.30 What is the meaning of each of the following relational operators?
a. $>$
b. $<=$
c. $<>$
d. $=$
e. $==$
f. $>=$
g. $<$

H.31 Write a BASIC program that finds the maximum of three numbers.

H.32 A college graduate agrees to begin working for a company at the extremely modest salary of one penny per week, with the stipulation that his salary will double each week. What is his weekly salary and how much has he earned at the end of six months? at the end of one year? You may assume that a month has four weeks.

H.33 Find the total amount credited to a savings account after ten years if $10 is deposited each month at an annual interest rate of 5.25% compounded monthly.

SUMMARY

Decisions about program execution are constructed using the IF-THEN statement. The format of IF-THEN is

IF (condition) THEN statement

The condition part of the IF statement is built by making a statement that can be answered as either true or false. We build these conditions by expressing constants, variables, or expressions in some sort of relationship. The condition is then evaluated while the program is executing.

GOTO statements unconditionally transfer execution (program control) from the current statement to the statement named in the GOTO. The format of the GOTO statement is:

nnnnn GOTO *nnnnn*

These transfers (often called branches) can be either forward or backward in the program.

We used the IF-THEN statement and the GOTO statement to build another "statement," the IF-THEN-ELSE-ENDIF. This program structure allows the programmer logically to follow the program from the IF statement to the "ENDIF," treating the entire sequence of statements as one logical unit.

Another statement learned was the ON-GOTO statement. This type of GOTO is executed on certain types of conditions. It is often used to replace several IF statements. The format is:

nnnnn   ON condition GOTO nnnnn,nnnnn,nnnnn, . . .

IF statement (IF-THEN statement)	Logical operator
Condition	GOTO statement
Relational operator	ON-GOTO statement
Collating sequence	CONT statement

SECTION 4—LOOPS

Now that you have had the opportunity to work with the decision structure IF, you can look at another very powerful programming tool, the *looping structure*. In this section you will look at the three primary types of looping structures available. First you will look at the iterative FOR-NEXT structure. There is no direct way to implement the other types of looping structures in most versions of BASIC. A few versions do have this capability, and Microsoft's WHILE will be shown. You will then build a DO-WHILE structure and a DO-UNTIL structure.

FOR-NEXT Statement

Let's suppose that you have been asked by a friend (Tim) to write a program to sum the numbers from 1 to 10, and you know nothing about loops in programming. Certainly one solution is the following:

```
10 A = 1
20 B = 2
30 C = 3
40 D = 4
50 E = 5
60 F = 6
70 G = 7
80 H = 8
90 I = 9
100 J = 10
110 S = A + B + C + D + E + F + G + H + I + J
120 PRINT S
130 END
```

You can plainly see that 10 variables have been used (the letters A through J), and that each variable has been assigned a value between 1 and 10 inclusive. Statement 110 adds all of the variables together and places the result in a variable called S. This program is cumbersome, yet straightforward. Now let's assume that Tim is well satisfied with the results of your program. In fact, Tim is so satisfied with your work that he would now like a program that is similar. How similar? Well, everything in the program should remain the same, except that he would like to add the first 100 numbers instead of the first 10. You can see that the job is not too difficult, but you are not really wild about doing the job. After some mumbling, you write a program just like the first example, but for 100 numbers.

As before, the program is relatively easy to understand, but as you are coding the program, you are thinking that there must be a better way. You also begin to wonder if computers are as powerful as you thought they were, and you continue to mumble. After two hours of typing, the program is done, and it looks like everything works.

It doesn't take too much time after you tell your friend that the new program is done before he rushes back absolutely excited. He now wants a program that will add up all the numbers from 1 to 1000! He successfully dodges your punch and runs from the room, not really understanding why you are upset. As you begin to calm down, you recognize that you probably knew enough about programming to do the job in a better way. Yes, you knew that those IF statements could be used to build other logical structures, by using their ability to make decisions.

Statement 80 in the following program uses the variable S to accumulate the sum of the numbers. The statement $S = S + N$ means "Take the current value of S, add the current value of N, and store the result in the variable S." Using the variable S for this purpose is called *accumulating* a total. Accumulating totals is a very common job performed by programs.

Another very common job performed by computers is called counting. Statement 100 in the following program uses the variable N as a counter. Notice that the statement $N = N + 1$ means "Take the current value of the variable N, add 1 to it, and store the result back in the variable N." Every time the statement is executed the value of N increases by 1.

Consider the following BASIC statements to do the job that your friend originally asked for.

```
10 PRINT "ENTER THE LAST NUMBER TO BE ADDED"
20 INPUT L
30 REM USE THE VARIABLE S FOR THE SUM OF ALL NUMBERS
40 REM UP THROUGH AND INCLUDING L
50 S = 0
60 N = 1
70 REM BODY OF THE LOOP STARTS HERE
80 S = S + N
90 REM INCREMENT N SO IT WILL HAVE THE NUMBER VALUE
100 N = N + 1
110 REM NOW DO THE TEST TO SEE IF THE LOOP IS COMPLETE
120 IF (N <= L) THEN 80
130 PRINT "SUM OF THE NUMBERS FROM 1 TO ";L;" IS ";S
140 END
```

You have not used any new statements to do the job, but simply used BASIC statements that you already knew about. The test at line 120 is used to transfer program control (to "loop" back) to statement 80. The loop lies from statement 80 through statement 120, and it is created by a test and branch to a specific statement (in this case 80). If you recall, all statements in BASIC are executed one after another unless they are branched-to by a GOTO, a GOTO in some other form (such as the THEN 80 in statement 120), or by some other control structures that you will learn about later. Note that your friend could ask for a program to add up the numbers from 1 to the largest number your computer could handle, and your program could do the job. Our friend will be pleased, and you will be glad you don't have to write the same program over and over.

What you have done with the program to add up the numbers from 1 to any number is to create the program structure known as a loop. It is called a *loop* because the instructions 80 through 120 are repeated many times in a pattern that resembles a loop. The loop is one of the most powerful structures that you can use on a computer, and the speed of computers makes repeating a sequence of steps feasible to complete a job.

Let's look at the logic behind an *iterative* (counting) *loop*. Most iterative loops have logic that looks like that shown in figure H-10.

The small program that you wrote to add up the numbers from 1 to any number follows this same pattern. In fact every loop must have this pattern (or have logic in which the test occurs between the initialize box and statement box) if the structure is an iterative loop. Every looping pattern must have some sort of test to allow exit from the loop.

The format of the FOR-NEXT pair is as follows:

nnnnn   FOR loop variable = start value TO end value STEP amount
        body of loop
        NEXT loop variable

for example:

```
FOR I = 1 TO 100 STEP 2
   BASIC statements
NEXT I
```

The loop variable represents any valid BASIC variable name, and it is used in both the FOR and corresponding NEXT statements.

The start value is the value of the loop variable with which you want to start the loop. In the case of your friend, you always wanted to add up the numbers from 1 to some number. What happens when you want to add up the numbers from some other number (say 50) to some other number? In the program that you wrote without using the FOR-NEXT pair, you would need to initialize the variable to a value other than 1 at line 60, after you figured out that statement had set the start value. In the FOR-NEXT case, you need only look at the FOR statement to find the start value that must be changed. The FOR instruction needed to add the numbers from 50 to 100 would look like the following:

```
FOR I = 50 TO 100
```

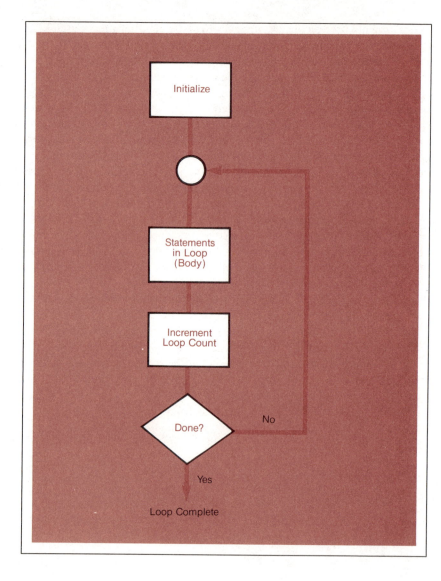

The ending value is the last value you want to process. As your friend makes requests for different ending values, you only need to change the ending value in the FOR statement to process different ending values. Note that, when you wrote the program without using the FOR-NEXT statements, you changed the IF statement test to accommodate the new ending value.

What would happen if you are now asked to add up all the odd numbers between 1 and 100? A simple change in the FOR statement option STEP allows you to change the increment value. If you include the STEP option with an increment of 2, then the computer will add 2 to the value of the loop variable every time the NEXT statement is executed. If we chose 1 as the start value, and 100 as the end value, then the loop variable value would follow the pattern:

1, 3, 5, 7, 9, ..., 97, 99. The BASIC FOR statement to do this job looks like this:

```
FOR I = 1 TO 100 STEP 2
```

To change the start value, ending value, or the increment when using the FOR-NEXT pair, only the FOR statement must change. In the loop that you built using the IF-THEN statement, you must look for the correct statement to change if you want to change the starting value, ending value, or increment. In more complex loops, this job becomes more difficult.

Now that you understand a little more about how the FOR-NEXT pair works, let's write a program to add the numbers from 1 to any number.

```
10 PRINT "ENTER THE LAST NUMBER TO BE ADDED"
20 INPUT L
30 REM USE THE VARIABLE S FOR THE SUM OF ALL NUMBERS
40 REM UP THROUGH AND INCLUDING L
50 S = 0
60 FOR N = 1 TO L
70 REM BODY OF THE LOOP STARTS HERE
80 S = S + N
90 NEXT N
100 PRINT "SUM OF THE NUMBERS FROM 1 TO ";L;" IS ";S
110 END
```

Note that this program is very similar to the earlier program that you wrote using only the BASIC statement IF for control. All the statements are in the same order as the previous example. The logic for initialization is contained in the FOR statement at line 60. The increment of the variable used in the loop (N) is done by the NEXT statement at line 110. The test to see if the loop has reached completion is created for us by the NEXT statement.

Knowing how many times a loop will be executed is often needed by the programmer. The number of times a loop is executed is found by using the following formula:

times executed = INT((End Value − Start Value) / Increment) + 1

The INT (integer) function truncates (drops) any decimal fraction left by the division. For example, in the statement FOR I = 1 to 10 STEP 2, the start value is 1, the end value is 10, and the increment is 2. According to the formula, 10 minus 1 divided by 2 is 4.5. The INT of 4.5 is 4. Adding 1 to 4 gives the result 5 for the number of times that the loop is executed.

Some cautions should be noted on the use of FOR-NEXT. The FOR statement must always have a NEXT statement paired with it. The variable named in the NEXT statement is used to identify which FOR statement started this loop.

Another potential trouble spot is the use of the STEP option. Make sure that the looping operations will end! For example, if you are using the statement

```
50 FOR I = 1 TO 100 STEP -2
   BASIC statements
200 NEXT I
```

this loop will never end, because the ending value of 100 will never be reached by a loop variable pattern that looks like the following: 1, −1, −3, −5, …. On some systems, the loop variable value is not known after leaving the loop. If you are counting on knowing the value of the loop variable upon completion of the loop, assign the loop variable into another variable before exiting the loop. Finally, never change the loop variable value inside the loop. This often causes a loop not to end because the ending condition is never met (similar to the negative STEP above).

DO-WHILE Structure

Often the logic of a program demands that you loop *while* a certain condition is true. BASIC does not have a specific command to do this job for us, but this logic is needed so often that you need to learn how to build a DO-WHILE loop.

The logic of the DO-WHILE structure is shown in figure H-11. The test must be made on a variable that changes within the loop, or else you run the danger of having a never-ending loop (usually called an *infinite loop*). There are usually statements initializing the variables used in the loop before the test. The entire DO-WHILE structure can be treated as a single logical unit. The DO-WHILE is sometimes called a pretest structure, because a test is performed before any statements in the body of the loop are executed.

Let's go back to the problem of adding up the numbers from 1 to some ending number. The problem could be restated as follows: Add up the numbers from 1 to an ending value while the number to be added is less than or equal to the ending value. Did you notice that what the program needs when the problem is stated this way is similar to the first solution you wrote? The modified version follows.

```
10 PRINT "ENTER THE LAST NUMBER TO BE ADDED"
20 INPUT L
```

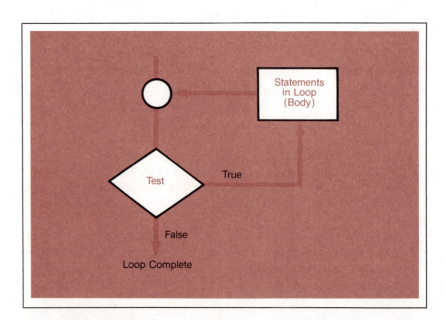

FIGURE H-11

Logic of the DO-WHILE structure

```
30 REM USE THE VARIABLE S FOR THE SUM OF ALL NUMBERS
40 REM UP THROUGH AND INCLUDING L
50 S = 0
60 N = 1
65 IF (N < L) THEN 130
70 REM BODY OF THE LOOP STARTS HERE
80 S = S + N
90 REM INCREMENT N SO IT WILL HAVE THE NUMBER VALUE
100 N = N + 1
110 REM END DO-WHILE
120 GOTO 65
130 PRINT "SUM OF THE NUMBERS FROM 1 TO ";L;" IS ";S
140 END
```

Certain versions of BASIC have the statements available to build the DO-WHILE structure directly. These statements are not included in the ANSI minimal standard. The format of the WHILE instruction is

nnnnn WHILE <expression>

.

.

.

{<loop statements>}

.

.

.

WEND

The program that manually built the WHILE loop could be rewritten as follows.

```
10 PRINT "ENTER THE LAST NUMBER TO BE ADDED"
20 INPUT L
30 REM USE THE VARIABLE S FOR THE SUM OF ALL NUMBERS
40 REM UP THROUGH AND INCLUDING L
50 S = 0
60 N = 1
65 WHILE (N > L)
70 REM BODY OF THE LOOP STARTS HERE
80    S = S + N
90 REM INCREMENT N SO IT WILL HAVE THE NUMBER VALUE
100    N = N + 1
110 REM END DO-WHILE
120 WEND
130 PRINT "SUM OF THE NUMBERS FROM 1 TO ";L;" IS ";S
140 END
```

When the nonstandard BASIC statements WHILE and WEND are used, indentation of the BASIC statements within the loop is recommended for the sake of readability. The indentation shows that it is the programmer's intent that the indented statements are to be thought of as part of a single unit of logic.

DO-UNTIL Structure

There are other times when the logic of a program demands that you loop *until* a certain condition is true. BASIC does not have a specific command to do this job for us, but this logic is needed so often that you need to learn how to build a DO-UNTIL loop.

The logic of the DO-UNTIL structure is as shown in figure H-12. Did you notice that this solution is the solution that you built when you didn't know about the FOR-NEXT statement, and simply used the statements that you did know?

Again, the test must be made on a variable that changes within the loop, or else you run the danger of having a never-ending loop. There are usually statements initializing the variables used in the loop before the test. The entire DO-UNTIL structure can be treated as a single logical unit. The DO-UNTIL is sometimes called a post test structure.

Let's continue to use the problem of adding up the numbers from 1 to some ending number. The problem could be restated as follows: Add up the numbers from 1 to an ending value until the number to be added is greater than the ending value. The program to solve this problem is similar to the DO-WHILE solution. Please note the change in line 120, and note that line 65 is not needed in the DO-UNTIL solution to the problem.

```
10 PRINT "ENTER THE LAST NUMBER TO BE ADDED"
20 INPUT L
30 REM USE THE VARIABLE S FOR THE SUM OF ALL NUMBERS
```

Logic of the DO-UNTIL structure

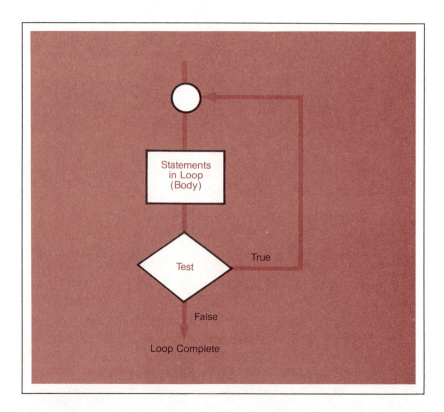

```
40  REM UP THROUGH AND INCLUDING L
50  S = 0
60  N = 1
70  REM BODY OF THE LOOP STARTS HERE
80  S = S + N
90  REM INCREMENT N SO IT WILL HAVE THE NUMBER VALUE
100 N = N + 1
110 REM END DO-UNTIL
120 IF (N <= L) THEN 80
130 PRINT "SUM OF THE NUMBERS FROM 1 TO ";L;" IS ";S
140 END
```

One difference between the DO-WHILE and DO-UNTIL loops is in the location of the test. Review the flowcharts of the logic for each type of loop. Did you notice that the DO-WHILE loop tests the condition before any of the loop body is done? The location of the test makes it possible for the DO-WHILE not to be executed at all. The DO-UNTIL forces the loop body to be executed at least one time before the test is made. The FOR-NEXT is usually a special case of the DO-UNTIL structure but may be implemented as a DO-WHILE on some systems.

H.34 What construct is used for an iterative loop?

H.35 Give the format of the FOR-NEXT statement.

H.36 The DO-WHILE is often called a pretest loop. Why?

H.37 The DO-UNTIL is often called a post test loop. Why?

H.38 Write a program to produce a multiplication table for learning to multiply in a third grade class.

H.39 Write a BASIC program to print a table for converting Fahrenheit temperature to Celsius. The table should list the Fahrenheit temperatures from 32 through 212 degrees in 2-degree increments and the equivalent temperature in Celsius. The formula is

```
C = (5/9) * (F - 32)
```

H.40 Write a program that calculates the product of the odd numbers from 1 to 30.

H.41 Write a program that prints a mortgage amortization schedule. Your program should input P (the original loan amount), I (the annual interest rate), and L (the number of years the mortgage is to run). Compute the monthly payment (P1) according to the following formula:

```
P1 = P * ((I/12)/(1-(1 + I/12)^(-L * 12)))
```

Looping is a very powerful programming tool. You looked at three types of loops in this section: FOR-NEXT, DO-WHILE, and DO-UNTIL.

The FOR-NEXT loop is similar to a loop that you could build using the IF-

THEN and GOTO statements. The logic of FOR-NEXT (iterative loops) is shown in figure H-10. The format of the FOR-NEXT pair is as follows:

nnnnn   FOR loop variable = start value TO end value STEP amount
        body of loop
        NEXT loop variable

The DO-WHILE program construct is built using other BASIC statements, and is not a BASIC reserved word. The logic is shown in figure H-11.

The DO-UNTIL program construct is built using the IF-THEN statement, and is not a BASIC reserved word. The logic is shown in figure H-12.

WORD LIST
(in order of appearance in text)

Looping structure	FOR and NEXT statements
Loop	DO-WHILE structure
Accumulating	Infinite loop
Iterative loop	DO-UNTIL structure

SECTION 5—SUBSCRIPTED VARIABLES AND ARRAYS

Because you store many data values in variables, it would be helpful to have an easy way to reference the variables. In BASIC, you have a tool available to do that job.

One-Dimensional Arrays

Remember your friend who needed numbers added? Consider the following BASIC program, which is cumbersome but does the job for the numbers from 1 through 4. The variable S is used to hold the sum of the numbers.

```
10 A1 = 1
20 A2 = 2
30 A3 = 3
40 A4 = 4
50 S = 0
60 S = S + A1
70 S = S + A2
80 S = S + A3
90 S = S + A4
100 PRINT S
110 END
```

Remembering that variables name locations in storage, you recognize that you have set up four locations for the variables A1 through A4. A1 is a reasonable variable name representing the first value to be added. It would really be convenient if you could choose a variable name and use a number to represent a portion of the name. BASIC allows us to do just that. Compare this new program below with the one just shown:

```
10 A(1) = 1
20 A(2) = 2
30 A(3) = 3
```

```
40 A(4) = 4
50 S = 0
60 S = S + A(1)
70 S = S + A(2)
80 S = S + A(3)
90 S = S + A(4)
100 PRINT S
110 END
```

The only difference is in the way the variables are named. Let's change your program just a bit further.

```
10 FOR I = 1 TO 4
20 A(I) = I
30 NEXT I
50 S = 0
60 FOR I = 1 TO 4
70 S = S + A(I)
80 NEXT I
100 PRINT S
110 END
```

This time the result is still the same, but the program is slightly shorter. The assignment statement at line 20 is saying "Take the current value of the loop index variable I and assign the value into the Ith storage location named by A." In other words, put 1 in A(1), 2 in A(2), 3 in A(3), and 4 in A(4). Figure H-13 diagrams the variables A(1), A(2), A(3), and A(4). Statement 70 is saying "Take the value stored in the Ith location named by A, and add it to the variable S." A special name is given to variables that consist of a letter and a number in parentheses. They are called *subscripted variables*. Subscripted variables are of the format

Variable name (Subscript)

where variable name is any valid variable name. The subscript can be either a constant, variable, or an expression. If the value of the subscript will ever exceed ten, you must let the system know with another special BASIC state-

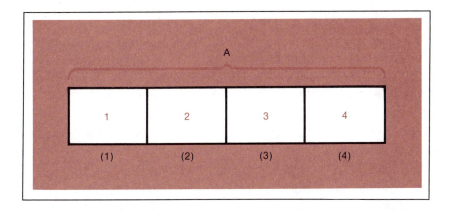

Diagram of a one-dimensional array

ment, the DIM statement. The DIM (which stands for dimension) statement must occur in the program before the first use of the subscripted variable named. The format of the DIM statement is

nnnnn   DIM Variable name (Number needed)

where the variable name is any valid BASIC variable name that is to be used as a subscripted variable. If a variable is named in a DIM statement, most BASIC implementations do not allow the variable name to be used for other purposes in the program. The "number needed" is a number that tells the BASIC interpreter how many storage locations to reserve for the variable. If ten or fewer locations are needed, most BASIC implementations do not require the programmer to have a DIM statement. It is still a good idea to dimension every subscripted variable.

A collection of related data items grouped for ease of reference can be called an *array*. An array must contain data of like nature. For example, if you knew the rainfall amounts for all 50 states in the United States, you might choose to store the data in an array called R. You would need a DIM statement because your array would have more than ten subscripted variables. An individual subscripted variable such as R(1) is often called an element. To define a 50-element array to store rainfall you could use a DIM statement like the following:

```
10 DIM R(50)
```

When only one subscript appears in a subscripted variable, we say that the array has only *one dimension*. Many programs written using arrays require only one dimension.

Two-Dimensional Arrays

Sometimes the logic of the program demands more than one dimension. For example, if you wanted to keep the monthly rainfall for the 50 states, you could require 12 separate arrays, or you could add another "dimension" to your existing array. In effect, you are going to build a table of states and monthly rainfalls. The dimension statement could look like the following:

```
10 DIM R(50,12)
```

This 50 × 12 array is diagrammed in figure H-14. The first number tells us how many rows will be in the table, and the second number tells us how many columns. These two memory aids may be helpful if you are having trouble keeping rows and columns separate.

1. This is no advertisement, but if you can't remember the order in which the subscripts occur, remember "Royal Crown" (RC) cola will always tell you. (Rows will be first and Columns will be second.)

2. Columns on a building run up and down. They do in a table, too.

Arrays can be extremely powerful programming tools if used properly. Recall the earlier example of building an array for the numbers from 1 to 4. Let's add the DIM statement to the beginning of that program, and do the job for the first 1000 numbers. It would look like the following.

```
10 REM PROGRAM TO BUILD AN ARRAY OF 1000 NUMBERS
20 REM PRINT OUT THE SUM AFTER BUILDING THE ARRAY
```

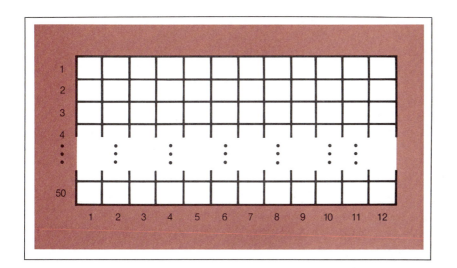

```
30 DIM A(1000)
40 S = 0
50 FOR I = 1 TO 1000
60 A(I) = I
70 S = S + A(I)
80 NEXT I
90 PRINT S
 .
 .
 .
  other statements
 .
 .
 .
400 END
```

As you can see by comparing this program to the earlier program to add four numbers, the logic and the number of written statements are almost the same.

Perhaps another example would be in order here. A program that determines a distribution of grades using the DATA statement should be appropriate. The number of grades in each interval will be stored in G(1), G(2), G(3), and G(4).

```
10 REM DETERMINE THE GRADE DISTRIBUTION OF GRADES
20 REM STORED IN A DATA STATEMENT
21 REM THE SCORES MUST BE > 59 AND < 100
30 DIM G(4)
40 FOR I = 1 TO 4 ⎫
50 G(I) = 0        ⎬ Initialize
60 NEXT I          ⎭
70 READ A                                            ⎫
80 DATA 74,82,91,72,81,96,78,61,73 ⎬ Input
90 DATA 78,68,75,84,-1                               ⎭
```

```
100 IF A = -1 THEN 140
110 J = INT ((A/10)) - 5      Process
120 G(J) = G(J) + 1
130 GOTO 70
140 FOR I = 1 TO 4
150 PRINT G(I);" GRADES FROM";    Output
160 PRINT 50+10*I;"TO";50+10*I+9
170 NEXT I
180 END

RUN

2 GRADES FROM 60 TO 69
6 GRADES FROM 70 TO 79
3 GRADES FROM 80 TO 89
2 GRADES FROM 90 TO 99
```

This program has clearly defined initialization, input, processing, and output sections. When an array is dimensioned, most versions of BASIC will set the variables to zero. It is nonetheless a good idea to initialize variables before they are used. This problem uses the trailer data technique with the value -1. When the value -1 is encountered, it serves as a signal to complete processing. The calculation at line 110 determines which of the four ranges this particular score fits in. The decimal portion of the score is dropped in this particular operation. Once the range has been determined, one is added to the counter of the subscripted variable that represents the range at line 120.

Let's consider a practical application to illustrate the need for arrays. Consider the problem of a wholesaler who provides discounts to customers based on the size of their orders. The amount of the discount is computed as shown in figure H-15.

Now, how can the amount of the discount be determined in a BASIC program? First, consider how the discount is calculated without using arrays. A portion of the program to do this job follows.

```
(The program has already set A to the amount of the
 order. D is set to the amount of the discount.)
210 IF A < 500 THEN 300
220 IF A <= 1000 THEN 320
```

FIGURE H-15

Decision table

| | If the Order Is | |
Greater Than	But Less Than or Equal to	Then the Discount Is
$ 0	$ 500	0%
500	1,000	3%
1,000	5,000	5%
5,000	10,000	7%
10,000	———	10%

```
230 IF A <= 5000 THEN 340
240 IF A <= 10000 THEN 360
250 REM A IS GREATER THAN 10000
260 D = .10
270 GOTO 400
280 D = 0
290 GOTO 400
300 D = .03
310 GOTO 400
320 D = .05
330 GOTO 400
340 D = .07
400 (The program continues from here.)
```

This is an awkward program. It contains a long list of IF statements followed by a list of assignment statements. What happens if the company decides to have more breaks in their discount structure? If, for example, the company had 100 different discount breaks, then there would be 100 IF statements and 100 assignment statements. There is a better way to develop this program.

The following table summarizes the company's discount structure.

Rows	Amount ($)	Columns Discount Rate (%)
1	500	0
2	1,000	3
3	5,000	5
4	10,000	7
5	100,000	10

This table can be used to determine the amount of discount as follows. Compare the amount of the order to the items in the first column. Find the first row that has a value greater than the amount of the order. The discount in this row is the correct discount. Thus, if the amount of the order is 2500, then the first row having an amount greater than this quantity is row 3. The discount is therefore 5%. If the amount is 750, then row 2 has the discount. If the amount is 7500, then row 4 has the correct discount.

Let's set up a table containing the discount rates. your dimension statement could look like the following:

```
20 DIM T(5,2)
```

How can you get values into this table? You could do it with a long string of assignment statements like this:

```
30 T(1,1) = 500
40 T(1,2) = 0
50 T(2,1) = 1000
60 T(2,2) = 3
   and so forth
```

This approach is tedious and would be even more so if the table dimensions were something like 100,100. Also, what if you want to input the values into the table from a terminal? In this case you might code the following:

```
30 PRINT "ENTER MAXIMUM AMOUNT TO BE COVERED BY RATE ";
40 INPUT T(1,1)
50 PRINT "ENTER DISCOUNT RATE (NO '.') ";
60 INPUT T(1,2)
70 PRINT "ENTER MAXIMUM AMOUNT COVERED BY RATE ";
80 INPUT T(2,1)
90 PRINT "ENTER DISCOUNT RATE (NO '.') ";
100 INPUT T(2,2)
   and so forth
```

When statement 40 is executed, the user is expected to provide the value for the maximum amount. The amount will be put into position 1,1 of T. The next prompt at line 60 will retrieve the discount rate to be put in position 1,2.

Examine the last BASIC statements. Notice the pattern in the subscripts? The first subscript is 1 in statement 40, 2 in statement 80, and would have been 3 in the next statement. You can use a variable to represent the first subscript.

For example, the table could be filled by the following statements:

```
10 DIM T(5,2)
20 FOR I = 1 TO 5
30 PRINT "ENTER THE MAXIMUM AMOUNT COVERED BY RATE ";
40 INPUT T(I,1)
50 PRINT "ENTER DISCOUNT RATE (NO '.') ";
60 INPUT T(I,2)
70 NEXT I
```

Here you are using a FOR-NEXT loop to execute the INPUT instruction 5 times. The first time it is executed, I has the value 1, then it has the value 2, then 3, then 4, and finally 5. Changing the size of the table is done by changing the 5 in statements 10 and 20 to the appropriate number needed.

Arrays can be used to store information that has similar characteristics. In the example above, the information stored in the rows are pairs of amounts and rates. The statements needed to do the job are minimized when placed inside a loop type structure. Commercial programmers often use tables to store related information for processing.

A Programming Example

The calculation of wages can be done with a simple test. The additional calculations needed to allow the withholding of voluntary deductions combine the technique of looping from section 4 and the new method of storing data you have learned in this section.

Voluntary deductions are those things an employee wishes to have withheld from his check. Examples include United Way, Christmas clubs, savings bonds, and other employee-desired deductions. This company has chosen to allow up to five deductions. The system could be modified to allow the deductions to

```
10 REM THIS PROGRAM CALCULATES THE PAYROLL FOR A COMPANY
20 REM TO DO THIS JOB, THE FOLLOWING STEPS ARE DONE:
30 REM  1) WAGES ARE CALCULATED
40 REM  2) TAXES ARE CALCULATED
50 REM  3) VOLUNTARY DEDUCTIONS ARE CALCULATED
60 REM  4) A PAYROLL REGISTER IS PRINTED
70 REM
80 REM FILES USED:
90 REM  HOURS IS A FILE CONTAINING THE EMPLOYEE
100 REM NUMBER AND THE HOURS WORKED
110 REM
120 REM VARIABLES USED:
130 REM  E = EMPLOYEE NUMBER
140 REM  H = HOURS WORKED BY THE EMPLOYEE
150 REM  T1 = TOTAL HOURS WORKED BY ALL EMPLOYEES
160 REM  T2 = TOTAL TAXES
170 REM  T3 = TOTAL WAGES
180 REM  T4 = TOTAL DEDUCTIONS
190 REM  W = WAGE OF EMPLOYEE
200 REM  D = ARRAY OF FIVE VOLUNTARY DEDUCTIONS
210 REM  T = TAXES FOR EMPLOYEE
220 REM  R1 = RATE OF PAY FOR COMPANY
230 REM  R2 = WITHHOLDING TAX RATE USED BY COMPANY
240 REM  R3 = FICA TAX RATE
250 REM  N = NET WAGE
260 REM  L = PAGE LINE COUNT
270 REM  I = LOOP INDEX VARIABLE
280 REM
290 REM
300 REM ******************************************************
310 DIM D(5)
320 REM INITIALIZE ALL VARIABLES ASSUMED TO HAVE A VALUE
330 T1 = 0
340 T2 = 0
350 T3 = 0
360 T4 = 0
361 L = 56
```

Modified payroll program

```
370 OPEN "HOURS" FOR INPUT AS #1
380 OPEN "LP:" FOR OUTPUT AS #2
390 PRINT "ENTER PAY RATE TO BE USED (XX.XX) [-1 TO END] ";
400 INPUT R1
410 IF (R1 < 0) THEN 2000
420 PRINT "ENTER FEDERAL TAX RATE (XX.XX = 20.00%) ";
430 INPUT R2
440 PRINT "ENTER FICA TAX RATE (XX.XX = 6.70%) ";
450 INPUT R3
460 PRINT "STARTING PAYROLL PROCESS"
470 INPUT #1,E;H
480 IF (E <= 0) THEN 990
490 REM HAVE THE EMPLOYEE RECORD, AND NEED TO START
500 REM CALCULATING THE PAY
510 IF (H > 40) THEN 560
520 REM ** THEN **  CALCULATE REGULAR PAY
530  W = H * R1
540   GOTO 580
550 REM ** ELSE **  CALCULATE OVERTIME PAY
560  W = H * R1 * 1.5
570 REM ** ENDIF **
580 REM
590 REM  CALCULATION OF TAXES
600 REM  FOR FUTURE GOVERNMENTAL REGULATION CHANGES
610 REM  LOOK TO CHANGE THE CALCULATION METHOD HERE
620 T = W * R2
630 T = T + (W * R3)
640 REM  A STATE TAX CALCULATION COULD BE INSERTED HERE
650 REM
660 REM  VOLUNTARY DEDUCTIONS
670 FOR I = 1 TO 5
680  D (I) = 0
690 NEXT I
700 PRINT "EMPLOYEE"; E; "IS BEING PROCESSED"
710 PRINT "ENTER ANY VOLUNTARY DEDUCTION NEEDED"
720 I = 1
730 PRINT "ENTER VOLUNTARY DEDUCTION (0.00 FOR NONE) ";
```

FIGURE H-16 (continued)

```
740 INPUT D(I)
750 I = I + 1
760 IF (D(I-1) > 0.0)THEN 730
770 REM
780 REM  CALCULATE THE NET WAGE
790 N = W - T
800 FOR I = 1 TO 5
810  N = N - D(I)
820 NEXT I
830 REM
840 REM  PRINT A PAYROLL REGISTER
850 IF (L <56) THEN 890
860 REM  PRINT A SIMPLE HEADING
870 PRINT #2 "          PAYROLL REGISTER"
880 PRINT #2 "EMP #  GROSS   TAXES   DED.      NET"
881 L = 0
890 PRINT #2 USING "##### ####.## ####.## ###.## ####.##";E;W;T;G-T-N;N
891 REM INCREMENT THE LINE COUNTER
892 REM L = L + 1
900 REM
910 REM ACCUMULATE TOTALS FOR THE GRAND TOTAL LINE
920 T1 = T1 + H
930 T2 = T2 + T
940 T3 = T3 + W
950 FOR I = 1 TO 5
960  T4 = T4 + D(I)
960 NEXT I
970 GOTO 470
980 REM
990 REM  PRINT THE GRAND TOTAL LINE
1000 PRINT #2
1010 PRINT #2 "GRAND TOTALS FOR THIS PAYROLL RUN"
1020 PRINT #2 "  GROSS    TAXES    DED. HOURS"
1030 PRINT #2 USING "#####.## #####.## ####.## ####.##";T3;T2;T4;T1
2000 CLOSE #1
2010 CLOSE #2
2020 END
```

F I G U R E H-16 *(continued)*

be entered along with the hours, or the master record could contain this information. We chose not to do this, in order to keep this system simple. See figure H-16.

You should compare this version to the earlier version in figure H-9 and note the additions to the program.

QUESTIONS

H.42 What is a subscripted variable?

H.43 What is an array?

H.44 What is an element of an array?

H.45 What is the dimension statement used for?

H.46 What is a table?

H.47 Write a program that builds a 15-element array that has as its contents twice the subscript. Then transfer the contents of the first array to a second array in the reverse order (element 1 goes into element 15, element 2 goes into element 14, and so forth). Finally, print out both arrays.

H.48 The inventory of different types of cereals in four stores is given by the following table.

Store	Corn Flakes	Cheerios	Puffed Wheat
1	22	12	14
2	13	14	16
3	19	10	3
4	60	18	4

If you used the matrix C to represent this table, what would be the value of the following elements: $C(1,1)$, $C(4,3)$, $C(3,1)$, $C(2,3)$, $C(1,2)$? Write a program to build the array C, and total each cereal type, as well as the different types of cereal by store.

SUMMARY

Subscripted variables allow us to store many similar data values in variables that have an easy way for the programmer to reference them by name. A collection of subscripted variables is often called an array, or table. An array is defined using the DIMension statement. When you are referring to a single subscripted variable, you use the term *element*. When references are made to subscripted variables, the FOR-NEXT loop allows us easily to access many different variables.

WORD LIST

(in order of appearance in text)

Subscripted variable
Array
Element

One-dimensional array
Two-dimensional array

As our programming has become more and more complex, you have probably noticed that sometimes you would like to be able to do a particular piece of programming once in your program, and then avoid the need to write out that same code over and over again. In fact, there are some *routines* (sections of code) that are used so commonly that vendors supply them with the system, so all programs are able to use them. The purpose of this section is to show you how to use subroutines, functions, and library functions.

Subroutines can be useful in many ways. First, they can be used to partition logic into separate independent modules. Subroutines provide a direct way to implement logic written in pseudocode. Because pseudocode is usually written so that the main procedure calls procedures at lower levels, it is often called top-down design. Even if a subroutine is used only once in a program, the separation of logic in a large program is very valuable.

Subroutines can be used to limit the size of very complex routines. Program code can be very hard to understand if it becomes very large. A rule of thumb is that one routine should not exceed 50 lines. If a routine is larger than 50 lines, it is often wise to separate a section of the routine that does a particular job. For example, if a subroutine is to validate an account number, then the BASIC statements needed to look up the number may be broken into a separate subroutine.

Finally, we often want the computer to execute a section of code at any of several points in a program. For example, if we need to calculate the number of days between two dates in several places within the program, we can write a subroutine that finds the difference in days. When the difference is needed, the subroutine can be asked to run (called). After the subroutine has been executed, the difference in the two days will have been produced.

The BASIC language provides us with a pair of statements to implement subroutines. The statements GOSUB and RETURN are used to define sections or modules of code to be used as subroutines. Subroutines can be regarded as sections or modules of code written in BASIC. These sections of code can be used again and again.

An example of a commonly needed subroutine is a subroutine to print headings at the top of reports. Headings generally include a description of the report (title), the company name, a date and time the report was run, a page number, and descriptions of the various columns that will appear on the report. Because of the various information required, many BASIC statements are needed to complete this task. The desired result from the heading subroutine is to do all the steps needed to print headings. The steps needed to print a heading are

1. increment the page counter;

2. build any needed information for the heading (company name, date, page number, etc.);

3. print the needed heading lines;

4. Reset the line counter (which is keeping track of the number of lines on the page).

SECTION 6—SUBROUTINES, FUNCTIONS, AND INTRINSIC FUNCTIONS

Subroutines

We may want to ask for these steps to be done at any of several points in the program. Please note the following example, showing the logic needed to execute a subroutine.

```
       .
       .
       .
 110 GOSUB 260
→120                    Transfers control to line 260
       .
       .
       .
 250 REM  **** HEADING SUBROUTINE ****
 260 P = P + 1
 270 PRINT "EMPLOYEE LIST ", "PAGE ";P
 280 REM  RESET THE LINE COUNTER
 290 L = 0
 300 RETURN
       .
       .
       .
```

The use of the word GOSUB is commonly referred to as a *call*. We will use the word call whenever we are talking about executing a subroutine. The statement GOSUB works like a GOTO, but the computer keeps track of where the subroutine was called from. From the example above, note that at line 110 is a GOSUB statement that refers to line 260. The line number named in the GOSUB is the starting line of the subroutine statements. The RETURN statement at line 300 marks the end of the subroutine. All statements from the beginning of the subroutine to the RETURN statement are executed as if they had been written just after line 110.

The major advantage to writing these statements as a subroutine is that they can be reused by other portions of the program. Another important advantage is that this section of code can be treated as a separate logical unit. The logic in the subroutine is developed separately. This logical unit or module can be assumed to provide a result for us in a "black box" fashion. We ask for a particular job to be done, and the module does that job for us.

Consider the following example, illustrating the flow of a subroutine.

```
 10 REM THIS PROGRAM DEMONSTRATES THE FLOW OF A
 15 REM SUBROUTINE
 20 REM BY USING PRINT STATEMENTS TO SHOW WHERE THE
 30 REM PROGRAM IS CURRENTLY EXECUTING
 40 PRINT "ONE"
 50 GOSUB 110
 60 PRINT "THREE"
 70 PRINT "REPEATING"
 80 GOSUB 110
 90 PRINT "FOUR"
100 GOTO 140
```

```
110 REM BEGINNING OF SUBROUTINE TO PRINT "TWO"
120 PRINT "TWO FROM IN THE SUBROUTINE"
130 RETURN
140 END

RUN

ONE
TWO FROM IN THE SUBROUTINE
THREE
REPEATING
TWO FROM IN THE SUBROUTINE
FOUR
```

The calls made to the subroutine at lines 50 and 80 cause the phrase "TWO FROM IN THE SUBROUTINE" to print. When the call is executed at line 50, program control is transferred to line 110. The PRINT statement at line 120 is executed. Then the RETURN statement at line 130 transfers program control to line 60. The PRINT statements at lines 60 and 70 are executed. The GOSUB at line 80 transfers control back to the subroutine. The PRINT statement at line 120 is executed again. This time the RETURN statement transfers control to the statement following line 80. The PRINT statement is executed at line 90. Finally, a GOTO is used to branch around the subroutine code so it will not be repeated. A common mistake when using subroutines is to allow the normal program flow to "fall into" the subroutine module. This causes the program to execute the subroutine when it is not desired, and sometimes can force the program into an infinite loop.

Note also in the example that the RETURN statement transferred control to two different locations, depending on where the subroutine had been called from. A RETURN statement always transfers control to the statement following the subroutine call. This transfer of control is not to be confused with the way a GOTO works. A GOTO forces flow of control to a specific statement. A RETURN allows the control to go back to where the routine was called from.

A subroutine may contain more than one RETURN statement. This facility is provided because under certain conditions there may be a need to exit from a subroutine before executing all the instructions. For example, if you were attempting to find a rate of speed given the distance and time, you might code your subroutine as follows:

```
350 REM **** FIND THE RATE OF SPEED GIVEN THE DISTANCE
360 REM **** USING THE FORMULA RATE = DISTANCE / TIME
370 REM IF THE TIME IS ZERO, RETURN A RATE OF ZERO
380 R = 0
390 IF T = 0 THEN RETURN
400 R = D / T
410 RETURN
```

The main thing we are trying to avoid in this example is the possibility of dividing by zero. A better (and standard) way to code line 390 would be:

```
390 IF T = 0 THEN 410
```

527

Functions

By not using multiple RETURN statements, we are forcing the subroutine to enter through only one statement and exit through only one statement. This keeps the program logic as simple and understandable as possible.

Functions are very similar to subroutines. Among the differences are these:

1. A function returns only a single value;
2. A function is given a name at the beginning of the function code.

The format of the BASIC statement defining a function is

nnnnn   DEF FN \<name\> [\<(parameter list\>)] = \<function definition\>

Consider the following subroutine that cubes a number:

```
150 GOSUB 430
  .

  .

  .
410 REM **** ROUTINE TO MULTIPLY A NUMBER BY ITSELF 3
420 REM TIMES (COMMONLY KNOWN AS A CUBE)
430 D = L * L * L
440 RETURN
```

The cube subroutine could be expressed as a function in the following code:

```
10 DEF FNC(A) = A * A * A
  .

  .

  .
140 REM *** FUNCTION TO CUBE THE VALUE WILL BE USED
150 D = FNC (L)
```

The net result of using either the subroutine or the function in this case is exactly the same. In each case, the number is multiplied by itself three times, and the result is stored in the variable D. For complex operations that require the return of only a single value, functions are used (the term is invoked). To the programmer, the function reference looks as if the system provided the operation, just as we use the * or / signs. All that we had to do to set up the function was to DEFine it.

Let's look at some of the attributes demonstrated in the example above. Note that the name of the function is FNC. Names of functions must begin with the letters FN and can have one letter following these two. The definition of the function must occur before the first use of the function in the program. This lets the BASIC interpreter know what is meant when the function is invoked by some other BASIC statement in the program. The name is needed so a reference in the program can be made by name. The variables used inside the DEF statement are simply to let the BASIC language know what the format of the operations are to be like; they are not recognized as variables in the program.

The variable named in the function invocation is called an *argument*. In the example, line 430 shows the argument used to be the variable L. The value of L is passed to the function to be evaluated in the format defined by the DEF statement. The value contained in the variable L replaces all occurrences of A in the function. The operations specified in the DEF are performed, and the value is returned from the function.

What the DEF statement does is this. If the function is invoked, the value of the variable named at the point that the function was asked for (in our example, L) is substituted in the formula defined in the DEF statement. The formula in the DEF statement is performed and the resulting value is returned to the invoking statement (where the function was requested). The value returned is then used in place of the function name. If the function invocation was an assignment, as in our example, the value is assigned into the target variable of the assignment statement (in this case D). If the function invocation was part of a more complex expression, the value returned is used like any other value. For example, if the following statement were in our program,

```
120 X = 5 * FNC(L) + 31
```

the current value of L would be cubed, the result would be multiplied by 5, 31 would be added to the result of the multiplication, and the sum would be placed in the variable X.

Intrinsic or Library Functions

Intrinsic (built-in) *functions* are similar to user-defined functions, with one primary exception. Intrinsic functions are provided with the system by being built into the interpreter, whereas user-defined functions must be written with each program. The BASIC interpreter determines when you are asking for a function to be executed and executes that sequence of instructions on the system. On larger systems, the functions are stored on disk, and are retrieved as needed. When functions are available to be used by all programs, they are said to be in a *system library*. The system library is a collection of functions and programs, usually written by the vendor, that do certain jobs. Even the built-in functions of an interpreter can be pictured as residing in a certain section of the interpreter. References in this module will assume that built-in functions reside in a system library.

An example of an intrinsic function is a routine to compute a random number. To use the random number function in your program, you must provide a starting place (seed) for the random-number generator. The variable R serves this purpose in the following program. You could code the following statement:

```
50 X = RND (R)
```

When the BASIC interpreter encountered line 50, it would attempt to find the function defined inside the program. If the program did not contain the function named (in this case RND), an attempt to find the function on the system library would be made. Sometimes the program code is simple, and sometimes it is complex. If you prefer to think of the system library as a set of black boxes that do certain jobs according to certain rules, that is a fair analogy. Figure H-17 lists some typical intrinsic or *library functions,* and the rules for their usage.

The INT(X) function is used to find the greatest integer less than or equal to the value passed. The values of J and K after executing the following statements

Function	Description	Special Considerations
SQR(X)	Square root of X	X must be positive
INT(X)	Greatest integer less than or equal to X	None
ABS(X)	Absolute value of X	None
SGN(X)	Set the answer based on the value of X; if X > 0, the answer is 1; if X = 0, the answer is 0; if X < 0, the answer is −1	None
RND(X)	Produce a random number between 0 and 1	None
TAB(I)	Space to Ith position	No effect if beyond I
EXP(X)	Natural log exponentiation (e^X)	None
LOG(X)	Natural log of X	X > 0
SIN(X)	Sine of X	X in radians
COS(X)	Cosine of X	X in radians
TAN(X)	Tangent of X	X in radians
ATN(X)	Arc tangent of X	Answer given in radians

FIGURE H-17

Common library functions

```
J = INT(-121.1)
K = INT(31.4)
```

are −122 and 31, respectively. The decimal portion of the number is not included after this function is executed because we are producing integers.

The ABS function produces the absolute values of the numbers passed as arguments. This means that any negative number is made positive, and the values of positive numbers are unchanged.

For some systems to produce a different random number each run, the BASIC keyword RANDOMIZE must occur as one of the first statements in the program. This will cause a different seed to be used to generate true random numbers by the intrinsic function RND. Pseudorandom numbers will be produced if the keyword RANDOMIZE is not used. Pseudorandom numbers are still random numbers, but because the seed that is used is always the same, the sequence of random numbers produced is always the same. The function RND will only produce numbers with values between zero and one, including zero. If a larger number is needed—say a value from one to ten—a multiplication and INT function must be used to provide this number. The following statements provide a number between one and ten:

```
10 RANDOMIZE
20 N = RND (R)
30 N = INT (N * 10) + 1
```

String Functions

String functions are another class of functions that are intrinsic. They are used to manipulate string variables. Remember that the ability of computers to manipulate strings is very powerful. All strings are represented internally with a coding scheme known as ASCII. The ASCII scheme is presented in appendix 2. Figure H-18 lists some typical string functions.

Function	Description
ASC(X$)	Returns the numeric value of the ASCII code representing the first character of the string X$
CHR$(I)	Returns a 1-character string containing the character with the ASCII code I
INSTR([I,]X$,Y$)	Searches for the first occurrence of string Y$ in X$, and returns the position in the string where the match is found; the optional offset I sets the starting point for the search
LEFT$(X$,I)	Returns a string comprised of the leftmost I characters of X$; I must be in the range 0 through 255
LEN(X$)	Returns the number of characters in X$
MID$(X$,I[,J])	Returns a string of length J characters from X$, beginning with the Ith character; I and J must be in the range 0 through 255
RIGHT$(X$,I)	Returns the rightmost I characters of X$
SPACE$(X)	Returns a string of X blank-space characters
STR$(X)	Returns a string representation of the value of X; for example, if the value of X is 27, returns the string "27"
STRING$(I,J) or STRING$(I,X$)	Returns a string of length I whose characters all have ASCII code J or are the same as the first character of X$
VAL(X$)	Returns the numerical value of string X$; for example, if the value of X$ is "27," returns the value 27

Common intrinsic string functions

Any of these functions can be used to analyze the contents of strings. For example, if you desire to force all letters to be capital letters, you can check the letters within a string to see if their ASCII value is in the range of capital letters. If they are not, you can then use string functions to change the noncapital letters to capitals.

Be sure to check to see if your system has other intrinsic functions available to make your programming easier.

QUESTIONS

H.48 What two BASIC statements are needed to build a subroutine?

H.49 What four steps are needed to print a heading?

H.50 How are functions different from subroutines?

H.51 What does the DEF statement do?

H.52 What is a system library?

H.53 What is a library function?

H.54 Write a user-defined function that—
   a converts centimeters to inches
   b. converts inches to feet

c. applies a 3% sales tax

d. rounds a number to the nearest cent

H.55 Write a program that will print ten random integers between 60 and 100, inclusive.

H.56 Write a simplified game of 21 (Blackjack). A deck of cards contains many cards numbered from 1 to 10. The computer is to ask how many cards you want. It then deals the cards. If the total is greater than 21, you automatically lose. The computer deals itself 3 cards. You many continue to draw cards as you desire. The player with the highest count less than or equal to 21 wins. Keep track of how many games the computer wins, and how many games you win.

H.57 Print a table that lists the numbers from 1 to 20, listing the square and the square root of each number.

H.58 Write a program to generate 1000 random numbers. In the program, count the values between 0 and 0.1, 0.1 and 0.2, and so forth. Print the totals in each range.

SUMMARY

This section covers the concepts of reusable program code. Subroutines, user-defined functions, and intrinsic functions are all sets of computer instructions that do certain jobs.

Subroutines are created through the use of GOSUB and RETURN statements. The execution of the statement GOSUB is commonly known as a call to the subroutine. A subroutine consists of all statements from the line number named in the GOSUB through the RETURN statement.

Functions are very similar to subroutines. The differences include these: (1) a function returns only a single value, and (2) a function must be given a name. Functions are defined through the use of the DEFine statement. Reference to a function is usually called invoking the function.

Intrinsic functions are similar to user-defined functions. Intrinsic functions are normally supplied by the vendor, and they are kept in the system library. Intrinsic functions perform mathematical as well as string manipulation.

WORD LIST

(in order of appearance in text)

Routine	Argument
Subroutine	Intrinsic function
Call	System library
Function	Library function
Invoke	String function

SECTION 7—FILE INPUT AND OUTPUT

The BASIC language standard is limited. Because of this, advanced input and output on different computer systems is very different. Accept what happens on your system as correct, even if what the text says is not exactly what happens on your system. Represented here are the most-used methods allowed by the most popular versions of BASIC.

File Processing

Every program that we have written up to this point has processed data that either (1) was entered by a user at program run time or (2) was included in the program at the time it was written (or modified). The user/programmer determines how much internal data is available via the READ and DATA statements. The amount of data available via the READ and DATA statements or via assignment statements is usually not a large quantity. Much of the power of computers comes from being able to process large quantities of data. Every computer has a limit on how much data can be stored in main memory at any one point in time. Because of the limits of main memory capacities, the limited space available for internal data, and the slow speed at which a user enters data, data is often kept by the computer system in some other form.

As you have done the programming for this class, you have recognized that the computer has kept your source programs (a form of data) on tape, diskette, or disk. The programs that move your BASIC programs around the system are fairly complex, but you never have to worry about managing the input and output of the source-program files you were using. Don't worry, the system programs will still be responsible for the files used to keep your BASIC source programs. However, we are going to learn in a general sense how to tell our BASIC programs to retrieve data from computer files for processing.

What is a file? A *file* is a collection of similar or related records. That's nice, you say, but what is a record? A *record* is a collection of fields. I'm not playing games with you, but I know your next question has to be "What is a field?" A *field* is a collection of characters, where the characters are the symbols we are used to using in our everyday language. Those symbols are A through Z, 0 through 9, and all the special characters such as $, *, and −. Characters are grouped together in a field because they have a particular meaning. For example, a name field is a collection of characters that, when taken collectively, are recognized as a name. Other examples of fields would be address, city, state, zip code, balance due, and phone number. All of these fields taken together could make up a record. If you had many records (names and addresses in this example), you could collect them together as a file.

We could therefore think of the records to be processed as groups of data to be processed. Under program control, we can read and/or write records of a file. As we process the data, we may be manipulating the data to produce new information.

The files on computers can be accessed in several different ways. There are two main types of files: sequential and direct. Magnetic tapes on reels or cassettes are capable of storing only sequential files. Diskettes and hard disks are capable of storing data in either a sequential or a direct fashion.

Sequential files are organized by placing one record after another, usually in some sort of order. For example, if customers have been assigned account numbers, the name-and-address records in the file are likely to occur in account-number order. The data records that are stored in a sequential file must be read one after another. If you desire the tenth record, you must first read the first nine records. If the files are small, the read time is generally not a problem. When the files become large, the read time can become a factor.

Direct files, on the other hand, are usually organized in some fashion that allows programs to access a single record without reading any of the other records in a file. Direct access often takes place by using a key to find a record. A *key* is a data field or data fields that uniquely define the record. For example, if each employee is assigned an employee number, the records in the payroll file could be organized using the employee-number field as the key.

In general, study of the application will make it obvious which method to choose. The steps needed to use either method are about the same. Every file must be created once. Usually the programmer uses programs supplied with the system (a system utility program) to create a file. Occasionally the program itself will create a new file.

After the file has been created, there are statements in the program instructing the system to access the file. First, a file must be opened to be made available for program access. By *opening* a file, you are letting the system know that you would like access to the file. In some cases, other people are prevented from using the same file at the same time. During the time that you have the file open, you are allowed to read from or write to the file.

Many dialects of BASIC allow input or output to files opened for input. This feature allows one to extend (make larger) an existing data file. This may be done when all of the records in the current file have been "read" to the current end of file.

When you open a file in some systems, you can specify that your access to the file is read-only. *Read-only* means you have only the right to read from the file, not the right to write to the file. If a file is opened as a read-only file, an error will occur if the file does not exist. This correctly prevents processing from proceeding. Opening a file as read-only also prevents accidental updates by a program if a write instruction was incorrectly issued by the program.

After all activity on a file is complete, you must always close the files. *Closing* a file tells the system that you are through using the file, and that any changes that you have made can be preserved. Some systems will close the files for you automatically when your program completes. Allowing the system to close files for you is an unwise practice. As you try to use your programs on systems other than the one you wrote it on, the method of closing files may change, causing unpredictable results.

The procedure for creating a file that will be used as an input file to other programs varies from system to system. Some systems will automatically place *delimiters* (such as commas) between fields as they are written to an output file. Other systems will create the output file exactly as it would have been output to the display. If the delimiters are not written automatically, the user must explicitly add the delimiting commas between the fields. Why are the delimiters needed at all? Remember that the INPUT statement retrieves one field at a time from a user. If the fields are separated by a comma, they are considered separate fields. Because the file input/output is handled using the INPUT instruction, the rules applying to the comma for separating fields still hold.

Because so many systems have so many ways of using files, the following discussion of file usage is broken up into different machine types. The underlying principles of file access will remain the same, regardless of the machine on which the file manipulations are done.

Files on Apple systems are called text files. They are sequential in format. To access the diskette files on an Apple, an extra control character must be included with every PRINT command. This control character is CTRL-D, which is produced by the function CHR$(4). For your own convenience, you should create a variable that contains CHR$(4).

Apple

Remember that the steps in accessing a file are

1. open the file,
2. read from or write to the file, and
3. close the file.

On the Apple, you must tell the computer whether you intend to read from or write to the file, and thereafter the INPUT or PRINT statements function as reads or writes. (There are different versions of BASIC for different models of Apple computers. If the following formats do not work properly, consult your system manual.) The formats of the open, read, write, and close statements on the Apple II Plus follow:

to open: *nnnnn*   PRINT CTRL-D; "OPEN filename"
to read: *nnnnn*   PRINT CTRL-D; "READ filename"
to write: *nnnnn*   PRINT CTRL-D; "WRITE filename"
to close: *nnnnn*   PRINT CTRL-D; "CLOSE filename"

Again, use a variable to which you have assigned the value of CTRL-D, so your coding of these four statements might be a little easier. This example builds a file:

```
10 D$ = CHR$(4)
20 PRINT D$; "OPEN SAMPLE"
30 PRINT D$; "WRITE SAMPLE"
40 PRINT D$; "BASIC"
50 PRINT D$; "FILES"
60 PRINT D$; "ARE"
70 PRINT D$; "FUN"
80 PRINT D$; "CLOSE SAMPLE"
90 END
```

The next example reads data from the same file:

```
10 D$ = CHR$(4)
20 PRINT D$; "OPEN SAMPLE"
30 PRINT D$; "READ SAMPLE"
40 FOR I = 1 TO 4
50 INPUT D$; F$(I)
60 NEXT I
```

```
70 PRINT D$;"CLOSE SAMPLE"
        .
        .
        .
```

In the first example, the open (at line 20) actually creates the file called SAMPLE in the catalog or directory of the disk. The write command at line 30 lets the computer know that any following PRINT commands are to be recorded on the disk. Closing the file saves it for later use. In the second example, because the file already exists, the open command says to find the file that is named and to prepare to use it. The read command (line 30) says that all following INPUT statements are to be read from the disk. The loop builds an array of the four items that we knew to be on the disk.

A file name must begin with a letter, and can have up to 30 characters. There are differences between versions of cassette and disk I/O, so you should consult your manuals or tutorials on this subject.

DEC

File handling on most DEC systems can be done through three different methods. Method 1 is formatted ASCII files; method 2 is virtual storage matrices; method 3 is record I/O.

All types of input/output operations make use of the OPEN and CLOSE commands. The format of these commands and examples follow:

nnnnn　OPEN "filename" FOR (INPUT or OUTPUT) AS FILE #X
nnnnn　CLOSE X

where filename is at most a 6-character name with an appropriate extension such as .DAT (which means data), and where X represents a file number chosen from the range 0 through 12

```
100 OPEN "SAMPLE.DAT" FOR INPUT AS FILE #5
110 OPEN "SAMPLE.DAT" FOR OUTPUT AS FILE #6
900 CLOSE #5
910 CLOSE I FOR I=1 TO 12
```

When we specify that a file is for OUTPUT, this means that the file is a new file and will be added to our disk directory. The OPEN command will delete any existing files with the same name. A file opened for INPUT means that we expect that file to exist. If it doesn't, then we expect an error message.

To use method 1 (formatted ASCII files), the INPUT and PRINT commands are modified slightly. To modify the INPUT statement (for a read) or the PRINT statement (for a write), add the file number specified in the OPEN statement. This directs the computer to use the active file named for I/O operations. (This is one method to route hardcopy printout to special terminals or the system printer. Simply replace the file name with the target-device name. In the example above, replace SAMPLE.DAT with the appropriate device name or with KB: for keyboard). Example: PRINT #5, "THIS IS A LINE OF OUTPUT". The following example builds a file that contains a small message.

```
10 OPEN "SAMPLE.DAT" FOR OUTPUT AS FILE #5
20 FOR I = 1 TO 4
```

```
30 READ M$
40 PRINT #5,M$
50 NEXT I
60 CLOSE #5
70 DATA "BASIC","FILES","ARE","FUN"
80 END
```

This program then builds an array with that message in it for later printing:

```
10 OPEN "SAMPLE.DAT" FOR INPUT AS FILE #5
20 FOR I = 1 TO 4
30 INPUT #5, M$(I)
40 NEXT I
  .
  .
  .
100 FOR I = 1 TO 4
110 PRINT M$(I)
120 NEXT I
  .
  .
  .
160 CLOSE #5
170 END
```

Method 2 is the use of virtual storage matrices (or arrays). Virtual arrays are defined through the use of the DIM statement. The DIM statement equates the files on the disk with the dimensioned arrays, and the program can then treat them as if they were simple, normal program arrays. When you are using virtual arrays, the program may appear simply to be handling arrays. Remember that we are actually reading and writing on disk files. These operations take place at slower speeds than storing and referring to variables in main storage. An additional note about strings stored in virtual arrays: all strings must be the same length. Most systems will assume that the length of the string is 16, but the choices include 1, 2, 4, 8, 16, 32, . . . , 256. The following examples show the OPEN statement and some DIM statements.

```
100 OPEN "DATA.DAT" FOR INPUT AS FILE #2
110 DIM #2, A(1024), B(1024)
120 DIM #8, A$(100)=8, B$(20,20)=64
```

Statement 110 is using file (or channel) 2 for two arrays, A (1024 numbers) and B (1024 numbers). Statement 120 is using file 8 for array A$ (100 strings of length 8) and B$ (a two-dimensional array that is 20 × 20, whose strings are 64 characters long).

Method 3 is the record I/O method. The additional commands of GET, PUT, FIELD, LSET, and RSET are used. In this method, extensive use is made of CVTXX, CHR$, AND ASCII. This is an advanced I/O method that is beyond the scope of this text. DEC has provided in their reference manuals good examples for this method.

537

With these systems, you must use the OPEN and CLOSE commands to establish access to files. The format of these commands and examples follow:

nnnnn   OPEN "filename" FOR (INPUT or OUTPUT) AS FILE #X
nnnnn   CLOSE X

where filename is at most an 8-character name, and where X represents a file number chosen from the range 0 through 12

```
100 OPEN "SAMPLE" FOR INPUT AS FILE #5
110 OPEN "SAMPLE" FOR OUTPUT AS FILE #6
900 CLOSE #5
910 CLOSE #6
```

When we specify that a file is for OUTPUT, this means that the file is a new file and will be added to the directory (catalog) of the disk or diskette. A file opened for INPUT means that we expect that file to exist. If it doesn't, then we expect an error message.

To use files on the Microsoft systems, the INPUT and PRINT commands are modified slightly. To modify the INPUT statement (for a read) or the PRINT statement (for a write), add the file number specified in the OPEN statement. This directs the computer to use the active file named for I/O operations. The following example builds a file that contains a small message.

```
10 OPEN "SAMPLE.DAT" FOR OUTPUT AS FILE #5
20 FOR I = 1 TO 4
30 READ M$
40 PRINT #5,M$
50 NEXT I
60 CLOSE #5
70 DATA "BASIC","FILES","ARE","FUN"
80 END
```

This program then builds an array with that message in it for later printing:

```
10 OPEN "SAMPLE.DAT" FOR INPUT AS FILE #5
20 FOR I = 1 TO 4
30 INPUT #5, M$(I)
40 NEXT I
        .
        .
        .
100 FOR I = 1 TO 4
110 PRINT M$(I)
120 NEXT I
        .
        .
        .
160 CLOSE #5
170 END
```

With these systems, you must use the DOPEN and DCLOSE commands to establish access to files. The format of these commands and examples follow:

nnnnn DOPEN # <file number>,"filename"[,W]
nnnnn CLOSE # <file number>

where filename is at most an 8-character name, and where <file number> is a file number chosen from the range 0 through 12

```
100 DOPEN#5, "SAMPLE"
110 DOPEN#5, "SAMPLE", W
900 DCLOSE#5
```

When we specify that a file is to be used for output, this means that the file is a new file and will be added to the directory (catalog). We are creating a new file. A file opened for input means that we expect that file to exist. If it doesn't, then we expect an error message.

To use files on the PET systems, the INPUT and PRINT commands are modified slightly. To modify the INPUT statement (for a read) or the PRINT statement (for a write), add the file number specified in the DOPEN statement. This directs the computer to use the active file that is named for I/O operations. The following example builds a file that contains a small message:

```
10 DOPEN#5, "SAMPLE", W
20 FOR I = 1 TO 4
30 READ M$
40 PRINT #5,M$
50 NEXT I
60 DCLOSE#5
70 DATA "BASIC","FILES","ARE","FUN"
80 END
```

This program then builds an array with that message in it to be printed later:

```
10 DOPEN#5, "SAMPLE"
20 FOR I = 1 TO 4
30 INPUT #5, M$(I)
40 NEXT I
  .
  .
  .
100 FOR I = 1 TO 4
110 PRINT M$(I)
120 NEXT I
  .
  .
  .
160 DCLOSE#5
170 END
```

With these systems, you must use the OPEN and CLOSE commands to establish access to files. The format of these commands and examples follow:

nnnnn   OPEN "mode", <buffer number>, "filename"
nnnnn   CLOSE <buffer number>

where mode is an I for sequential input or an O for sequential output, where filename is at most an 8-character name, and where <buffer number> is a file number chosen from the range 0 through 15

```
100 OPEN"O", 5, "SAMPLE"
110 OPEN"I", 5, "SAMPLE"
900 CLOSE 5
```

When we specify that a file is to be used for output, this means that the file is a new file and will be added to the directory (catalog). A file opened for input means that we expect that file to exist. If it doesn't, then we expect an error message.

To use files on the TRS-80 systems, the INPUT and PRINT commands must be modified slightly. To modify the INPUT statement (for a read) or the PRINT statement (for a write), add the file number specified in the OPEN statement. This directs the computer to use the active file named for I/O operations. The following example builds a file that contains a small message:

```
10 OPEN"O", 5, "SAMPLE"
20 FOR I = 1 TO 4
30 READ M$
40 PRINT #5,M$
50 NEXT I
60 CLOSE #5
70 DATA "BASIC","FILES","ARE","FUN"
80 END
```

This program then builds an array with that message in it to be printed later:

```
10 OPEN"I", 5, "SAMPLE"
20 FOR I = 1 TO 4
30 INPUT #5, M$(I)
40 NEXT I
    .
    .
    .
100 FOR I = 1 TO 4
110 PRINT M$(I)
120 NEXT I
    .
    .
    .
160 CLOSE #5
170 END
```

H.59 Explain the relationship of files, records, and fields.

H.60 Why are files opened and closed?

H.61 What are the two main types of files?

H.62 What is a key?

H.63 What is a system utility?

SUMMARY

The BASIC language standard is limited. Advanced input and output varies greatly on different computer systems.

File processing also is nonstandard. The concepts supporting file processing are standard, however. There are two major methods of accessing files: sequential and direct. A file is a collection of records. A record is a collection of fields. A field is a collection of characters.

Files must be opened before access is permitted. Reading and/or writing records may take place while the file is open. When access is complete, the file should be closed. Each computer company has its own unique method of accessing files.

WORD LIST
(in order of appearance in text)

File	Key
Record	Opening a file
Field	Read-only access
Sequential file	Closing a file
Direct file	Delimiter

MODULE I

Systems Programs

APPLICATION vs SYSTEMS PROGRAMS

LANGUAGE PROCESSORS
Purpose of Application Programs
Machine Language and Program
   Translation
Program Compilation
Program Interpretation

THE OPERATING SYSTEM
Job Management
Task Management
Data Management

UTILITIES

Systems programs manage the computer's resources and provide services that improve the productivity of the computer. In this module, we will define major categories of systems programs and discuss their function.

APPLICATION vs SYSTEMS PROGRAMS

Application programs satisfy a particular user need. For example, there are application programs to do financial analysis, to keep the general ledger, to account for goods in inventory, to analyze laboratory data, and so forth. Such programs have a specific purpose that relates directly to the needs of the people having the computer. Sources of application programs were defined in chapter 4. To review, they can be obtained *off-the-shelf*, they can be *purchased and altered*, or they can be *custom developed*. When programming is required, it can be done by in-house personnel, or it can be done by personnel who are employed by an outside company. Application programs are generally neither as large nor as complex as systems programs.

Systems programs are more general than application programs. They do not satisfy a particular need like inventory accounting. Rather, they provide an environment in which application programs can be executed; they also make the computer more usable. Systems programs are normally provided by the manufacturer of the computer. They are acquired off-the-shelf, although in rare circumstances an organization will alter a systems program. Because systems programs are complex, and because their development requires in-depth knowledge of hardware, they are almost never developed on a custom basis. They are normally leased from the computer vendor. Prior to 1970, the cost of systems programs was bundled with the cost of the computer. Using organizations paid one price for hardware and necessary systems programs. Today, however, hardware and systems programs are priced separately. The characteristics of systems and application programs are summarized in figure I-1.

Systems programs can be divided into three broad categories. The *operating system* (or *supervisor*, or *executive*) manages the computer's resources. *Utilities* are the second category of systems programs. Utilities provide a commonly needed service. For example, there are utilities to copy a file, to make a duplicate diskette, and to sort a file of data. Utilities save an organization the work of having to write its own programs for these services. The third category of systems programs is the *language processors*. These programs translate instructions coded in languages like BASIC into machine instructions, and they prepare the translated instructions for execution. We will consider the language processors first, then the operating system, and finally the utilities.

LANGUAGE PROCESSORS

The first category of systems programs that we will consider is the language processors. Before discussing these processors, we need to consider what computer programs are and how they relate to hardware.

Purpose of Application Programs

Suppose you own a car rental agency. You charge your customers $25 for each day they rent a car and 20¢ for each mile they drive. You decide that your clerks are making too many errors and that the manual computation of customer bills takes too long. You decide to get a computer to compute bills automatically.

Application Programs	Systems Programs
Solve a particular problem	Are general purpose

Acquired:
    Off-the-shelf
    Altered
    Custom-tailored
	Usually acquired off-the-shelf

Sometimes written in-house	Usually obtained from CPU vendor
Purchased or leased	Usually leased

FIGURE I-1

Characteristics of appliction and systems programs

You approach a group of computer specialists and ask them to build a system to compute your bills. Suppose there is no such thing as a computer program. In this case, the computer people will build a *special-purpose electronic machine* to compute your bills. You will input the number of days of rental and the number of miles driven, and the machine will output the customer charge. This procedure is shown in figure I-2.

Now, before they build this machine, the computer people will ask you for the maximum number of miles and days. Suppose you say 500 miles and 10 days. Given this information, they will then build the electronic equivalent of the table shown in figure I-3. The table will have 5000 entries, one for each combination of miles and days. The machine will have transistors and resistors and other electronic components that cause it to find the right entry for each combination of days and miles.

This is a special-purpose machine; when you have no bills to compute, the machine will be idle. This usage is a waste of the resource. Further, you may not want to have a single-function machine cluttering up your work space. So, although this machine will satisfy your needs (in fact, many such machines exist—in microwave ovens, cars, record changers, etc.), there are other, better ways to solve your problem.

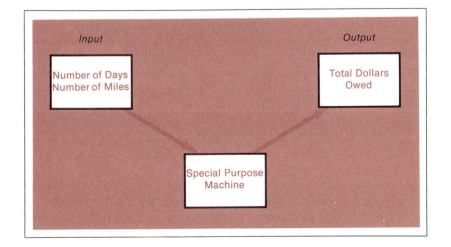

FIGURE I-2

Computing rental charges using special-purpose machine

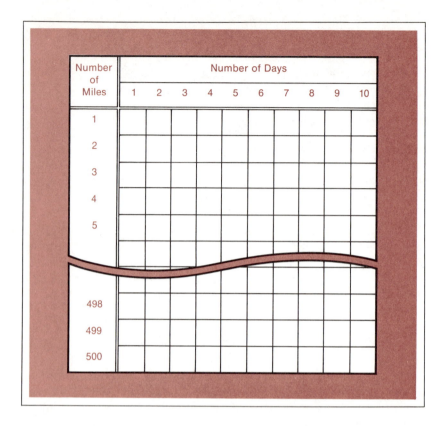

Number of Miles	Number of Days									
	1	2	3	4	5	6	7	8	9	10
1										
2										
3										
4										
5										
498										
499										
500										

FIGURE I-3

Table showing charges for combinations of days and miles

Suppose that, instead of acquiring a special-purpose machine, you buy a calculator that adds and multiplies. You then give your employees the formula:

Total due = $25 * Number of days + 20¢ * Number of miles

You show them how to use the calculator. This approach works, but the calculation of bills is certainly not automatic. In fact, this approach is probably not an improvement over the manual process.

Suppose you buy a calculator that has a *memory* that can hold the sequence of steps necessary to compute a bill. Suppose also that this calculator performs these steps whenever you ask it to. In this case, you have an automatic machine like the one in figure I-2, but it is not a special-purpose machine. You can load different sequences of steps into the machine depending on what you want to do. To see how this computer is different from the special-purpose machine, examine the memory shown in figure I-4.

First, note that this memory is divided into boxes or cells. Each box has a numerical address. The boxes can hold instructions or data. In figure I-4, the boxes in the top of memory hold instructions; those at the bottom hold data; and those in the middle are unused.

The contents of these boxes are groups of binary digits, or *bits*. On most computers, the boxes are called *bytes*. Instructions and data can occupy one or more bytes. In figure I-4, the first two instructions each take 3 bytes, and

1	2	3	4	5	6
Read number of days into 91,92			Read number of miles into 89,90		
7	8	9	10	11	12
Multiply 95,96 × 91,92		Put result in 87,88		Multiply 93,94 × 89,90	
13	14	15	16	17	18
Put result in 85,86		Add 87,88 to 85,86		Put result in 83,84	
19	20	21 If more data, go to 1	22 Stop		
Write 83,84 to CRT					
				83	84
					Amount
85	86	87	88	89	90
Temporary value		Temporary value		Number of Miles	
91	92	93	94	95	96
Number of days		Value is .20		Value is 25.00	

FIGURE I-4

Example of memory with instructions and data

the other instructions each take 2 bytes. The first instruction starts in byte 1, the next in byte 4, the next in byte 7, and so forth.

Bytes 83 through 96 hold data. In this example, each data item takes 2 bytes. This statement is not always true; some data items take more and some take less. Working backwards (for convenience), bytes 95,96 hold the constant 25.00. Bytes 93,94 hold the constant .20. Bytes 91,92 will hold the number of days rented, and bytes 89,90 will hold the number of miles driven. Bytes 87,88, and 85,86 will hold two temporary values. Finally, bytes 83,84 will hold the amount that is computed.

Now, to compute a customer bill, the computer will begin executing the instructions starting at byte 1. It will execute the instructions in sequence. Note that the next to last instruction is conditional. If there is more data, the computer will go to byte 1; otherwise, it will stop.

Now, you may ask, why is this computer with a memory an improvement over the special-purpose machine in figure I-2? There are three reasons. First, the contents of the computer's memory can be changed. Another program can be read into the computer's memory, and the computer will then solve a different problem. Thus, the computer can be used for many different purposes.

Second, the memory requirement for the general-purpose computer, program, and data is much smaller than that for the special-purpose machine. The table in figure I-3 has 5000 entries. Even so, it allows only for cars driven no more than 10 days or 500 miles. The program and data in figure I-4 occupy much less space, and they are far more general. The program is not limited to cars driven only 10 days or 500 miles.

The third reason that the program and general-purpose computer are preferred over the special-purpose machine involves testing. To verify the accuracy of the special-purpose computer, 5000 different entries must be validated. If the machine is built to allow more realistic numbers, say, 90 days and 1000 miles, a total of 90,000 entries must be validated!

For the programmed computer, however, we need only validate the program and its constants to be certain that the amounts to be computed will be accurate. This task may not be easy, especially for a more realistic problem, but it is far less difficult than the one for special-purpose machines.

The term *validation* means to ensure to some level of confidence that the program works as it is supposed to. It is often impossible to *guarantee* that a program works correctly. The point here is that a program is easier to validate than a special-purpose machine. Further, once it is validated, it need not be checked again when inputs change.

To summarize, programmable computers are better than special-purpose machines because they can be used for several tasks, they have smaller memory requirements, and they are more easily tested. The next question is, How do humans put programs into memory?

Machine Language and Program Translation

The boxes in figure I-4 represent bytes that hold groups of binary digits. Thus, the content of a box is a sequence of 0's and 1's, say, 10010110. A difficulty now arises. How can commands like "multiply the contents of location 95,96 by the contents of location 91,92" be represented by 0's and 1's?

The answer is that instructions are represented by codes. Figure I-5 shows a few *binary instruction codes* for large IBM computer systems. *Multiply* is represented by the code 10011100; *divide* is represented by the code 10011101; and so on. The addresses of the locations containing the numbers to be multiplied or divided are also represented in binary format. That representation is beyond the scope of this discussion, however.

In the early days of computing, programmers had to memorize binary instruction codes. Thus, someone might spend an hour or two to produce the following program:

```
110010001000111110101010101011101010111010001111101001010100010101
010100101010111001010101010100000010111101111000111011101111110111
010101011100100100100010111110100111001010101000101010101111110101
010001010101001011111100010101011000011100101001110010011100100010
010101110010101010101001001010101111101011010001011101101001111101
```

Writing such gibberish might be fun for a few hours, but clearly it is no way to spend a lifetime. Further, programs produced by this method often had errors, and the errors were very hard to find and fix. Consequently, people looked for a better way to produce programs.

Instruction	Binary Code
Add	10011010
Divide	10011101
Multiply	10011100
Subtract	10011011
Move	10010010

FIGURE I-5

Examples of binary instruction codes for IBM computers

Program Compilation

These people were computer professionals, so it was natural that they look to the computer for a solution to the problem. Eventually they developed what are known today as *high-level languages*. These are English-like languages in which programmers can express commands. These languages are then translated into machine language (binary form) by the computer.

For example, a programmer might write a program such as:

```
INPUT A, B
C = A + B
PRINT C
```

These English-like statements are translated into a sequence of 0's and 1's that cause the computer to read two numbers, add them together, and print the result.

Figure I-6 illustrates a process called *program compilation*, which is a method of translating programs. The English-like statements that are produced by humans are called *source code*. These statements are input to a translation program called a *compiler*. A binary (0's and 1's) version of the program is produced. This binary version is called *object code*.

There are many programming languages and dialects of programming languages. Each language or dialect has its own compiler. Programs written in BASIC use one compiler. Programs written in COBOL use another.

The compiler is a program. It is *not* a piece of hardware or a special machine. It is a program that resides in main memory and it accepts other programs as its data. As a program, it was written by someone.*

In figure I-6, the object code generated by the compiler is stored on a file. Even though it has been translated, it may not be ready for execution. The program may contain references to other programs. For example, a programmer may write an application program that requires the current time of day to be printed on a report. Although the programmer can write his or her own routine to determine the time, there is probably a routine that determines the time on a *system library*. When the programmer needs the time routine, he or she will

---

*An interesting question now appears. Because the language translators are programs, they need to be translated themselves. What program translates the language translators?

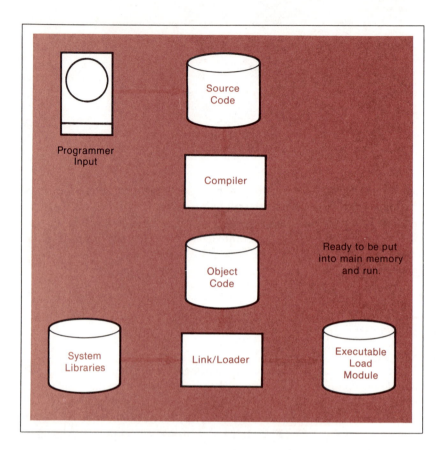

FIGURE 1-6

Example of program compilation and
load process

consult the library documentation to determine the name of such a routine.
Suppose the name of this routine is TIME, and it is used as follows:

```
X = TIME
```

This statement sets the variable X to the current time of day.

Now, when the application program is translated, the compiler will recognize TIME as the name of an external routine. Since the compiler does not have the source code of the TIME routine, it cannot translate it. Instead, the compiler inserts a note into the object code indicating that TIME is an *external reference*. This note means that the TIME routine should be taken from a library.

Now, before the application program object code can be executed, the object code of TIME must be appended to it. This action is done by a program called either a *link/loader*, a *linkage editor*, or some other name. The link/loader searches the libraries for the TIME routine, as well as for any other external programs. These programs are then appended to the object code. The output of this process is an *executable load module*. This module is ready to be read into main memory and executed.

If the program is to be used over and over again, the executable load module is saved. This way, the program need not be compiled and link/loaded every time it is run. For example, a weekly payroll program is not compiled each week. Instead, its load module is saved from week to week. It is only compiled when changes are made to the program.

Thus, every program has three versions or formats. It is written by a human in *source form*, it is compiled (translated) into *object form*, and it is merged with other routines to form an *executable load module*.

Program Interpretation

Figure I-6 shows program compilation. An alternative form of translation is *program interpretation*. The difference between the two processes is that, whereas in compilation the entire program is translated before execution begins, in interpretation the program is translated and executed one line at a time. When interpretation is used, a line is translated and executed, then the next line is translated and executed, and so forth. External references such as the TIME routine are resolved as they are encountered.

Interpretation is more common with small and simple programs, like the ones you are writing in this class. In fact, most BASIC systems use interpretation. In the commercial world, however, compilation is far more commonly used.

Whether translated by a compiler or an interpreter, the program will require other services from the operating system as it executes. Furthermore, computers that are used for data processing are not as simple as the one shown in figure I-4. Usually, more than one program is running at a time, which requires that the activities of several programs be coordinated. These functions are managed by the *operating system*.

THE OPERATING SYSTEM

The three basic functions of the operating system are job management, task management, and data management. Figure I-7 shows the relationships of these three functions. Work to be done is kept on a job queue. The job management

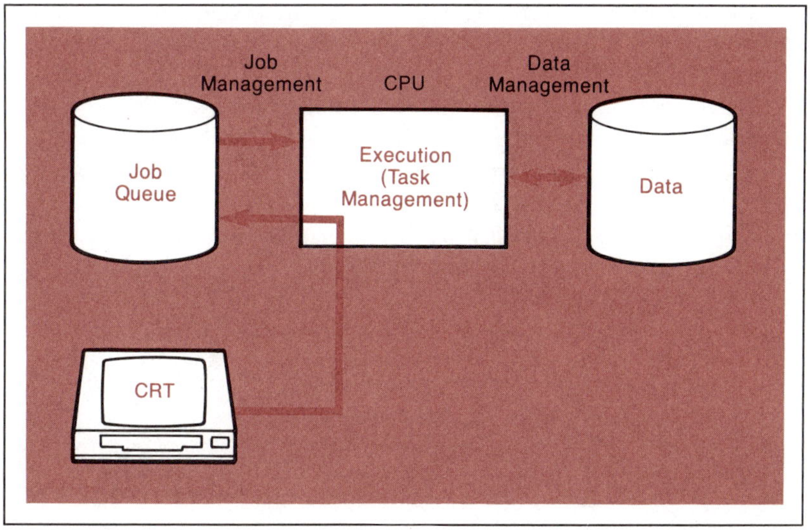

FIGURE I-7

Job, task, and data management

551

Job Management

portion of the operating system selects jobs from the queue and starts them. Once started, a job is controlled by the task management portion of the operating system. Task management assigns CPU time and main memory to jobs and controls the flow of jobs residing in main memory. Data management provides data access services to programs during processing.

A *job* is a sequence of one or more units of work that accomplish a user task. For example, the produce-payroll-checks job might have three units of work, or steps. In the first step, payroll amounts are computed and a new master file is generated. In the second step, a payroll register (list of checks) is printed. Finally, in the third step, the paychecks themselves are printed. Normally, one program (executable load module) is run per step.

The function of the job management portion of the operating system is to schedule jobs and to allocate computer resources to them. There may be many jobs waiting for execution at one time. These jobs will need different types of computer equipment. Job management allocates resources and starts jobs so as to maximize throughput and avoid resource conflicts.

For example, produce-payroll-checks may require three tape drives in its first step and one tape drive in the two remaining steps. If the computer has only three tape drives, this job cannot be started until all of the drives are free. Once the first step is completed, however, other jobs can be started that require only one or two tape drives. Similar conflicts can occur with disk drives, printers, main memory, and other resources.

The function of job management is even more complex because jobs may have differing priorities. Order entry processing is probably more important than producing a summary of last year's sales. If so, the order entry job should receive resources before sales summary. Balancing the needs of jobs and recognizing priorities is difficult. Job management functions are summarized in figure I-8.

If you have run programs only on a microcomputer, you may not realize the need for job management. Most micros are single-user systems. Only one person can use them at a time. However, there are many computers that run dozens of jobs concurrently. For these computers, job management is critical.

Task Management

Task management begins when a job is scheduled for execution. The job is loaded into main memory and the CPU begins to execute the job's instructions. At this point, the job is referred to as a *task*. A task is a unit of work that competes in its own right for CPU time. As soon as the job is started, it may create additional tasks to perform work concurrently. In a sense, the primary task of the job gives birth to additional tasks.

FIGURE I-8

Functions of job management

Select jobs from job queue
Allocate resources
Avoid resource conflicts
Recognize priorities

Each task requires CPU time and main memory. Usually, the CPU is allocated in some type of round-robin fashion. For example, each task may be allocated one-tenth of a second of CPU time. This one-tenth is given to the first task, then to the second, then to the third, and so forth. If there are ten tasks, one second is required to complete the entire cycle. If there are twenty tasks, two seconds are required for a cycle. Sharing the CPU in this way is sometimes called *time slicing*.

CPU time allocation is complex for two reasons. First, the tasks may have different priorities. A task that is doing work for order entry will likely have a higher priority than a task doing work for the sales history report. Thus, the round-robin strategy may have to be modified to give more time to high-priority tasks.

The second reason that time allocation is complex is that tasks may be unable to use all of their allocated time. For example, suppose that the highest priority task needs data before it can continue. If so, data management will be called upon to transfer the data. Data retrieval, however, takes a long time (relative to the speed of the CPU). Therefore, the CPU will go on to other tasks while the data is being transferred. Once the data arrrives, however, the CPU should be assigned to the waiting task (because it has the highest priority).

The reassignment is accomplished via *interrupts*. Whenever events of importance occur within the computer, an interrupt message is sent to task management. Task management can choose to respond to the interrupt or not. In general, task management will respond to interrupts that involve work at a higher priority than the CPU is currently doing. If the interrupt involves work at a lower priority, the interrupt message is saved and processed later.

To return to the example of the highest priority task waiting for data: when the data transfer is complete, an I/O-complete interrupt message will be generated. Task management routines will examine this message and determine that the highest priority task is now ready to continue. The CPU will be reassigned from whatever work it is doing to process the highest priority task.

Interrupts are used for other purposes as well. For example, on some computers, when power fails, a power-failure interrupt is generated. This interrupt has a very high priority. When it is detected, task management sends a death message to every active task. Essentially, this message says, "We're dying— you have 100 milliseconds (or whatever) of CPU time to tidy up your affairs. Write your will, and generate whatever messages you will need in your next life." When power is restored, the tasks are restarted, and they read the messages written at the end of their previous lives. Most likely, these messages will tell them how to resume processing.

Another task management function is to provide *supervisor services*. There are many activities that are too complex or too risky for user tasks to do for themselves. For example, a task may want to send a message to another task. To do so, the task will need to write in the memory space assigned to the other task. In general, however, this activity cannot be allowed; if one task were able to write in another task's memory whenever it wanted, havoc could result. Thus, to send a message to another task, the task must ask task management to send the message. In response, the operating system will send the message, but it will coordinate the message with other processing in the task, and it will be certain to write the message only in the correct memory location. In this way, the message will be safely delivered.

The *allocation of main memory* is the last function of task management that we will discuss. When tasks are initiated, a certain amount of memory is allocated to the task. As the task progresses, more or less memory may be needed. When the task wishes to change the amount of memory it has, it requests the change from task management (changing memory allocation is another supervisor service).

Some computers have *virtual* memory. This term means that the task thinks it has more memory than it actually has. To understand this concept, consider figure I-9, which illustrates the scheme used by one popular virtual memory system. In this figure, memory has been divided into 4K-byte pages (K = 1024). Task A has been assigned pages 1 through 10 and task B has been assigned pages 11 through 20.

In actuality, task A has been assigned only five real pages of memory. When task A is running, any five of the pages 1 through 10 can be in main memory at a time. In figure I-9a, pages 3, 4, 5, 6, and 7 reside in memory. The remaining pages (1, 2, 8, 9, and 10) have been stored, temporarily, on disk. If the task needs an instruction or data located on one of the pages on disk, the operating system will remove one of the pages that is in memory and replace it with the needed page. Thus, in figure I-9b, page 9 was needed. The operat-

FIGURE I-9a

A virtual memory system example

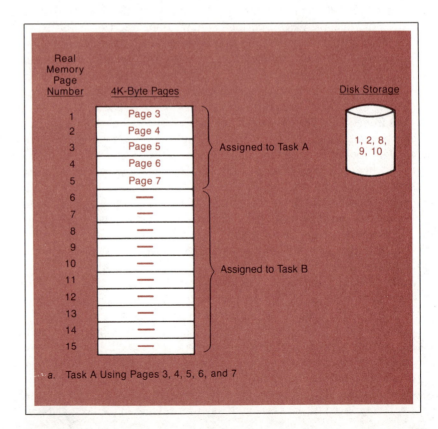

a. Task A Using Pages 3, 4, 5, 6, and 7

ing system removed page 3 and copied page 9 into the place that was held by page 3.

Thus, it appears to task A that it has 10 pages of memory. However, only five of those are resident in memory at once. The task is unaware of the real situation because whenever it needs data, the operating system provides it. The operating system makes it appear to task A that 10 consecutive pages of memory are available.

Using virtual memory, programs can be much larger than the actual main memory size. This is an advantage because main memory is expensive, and, in many large programs, much of the code is unused for long periods of time. For a virtual system, the unused code will be stored on disk until it is needed. Task management functions are summarized in figure I-10. Extended architecture systems have increased the size of virtual memory, providing even greater capacity.

The data management portion of the operating system provides services to create, process, and administer data. For example, when an application program issues a command such as INPUT (in the BASIC language), the data management portion of the operating system processes the command. It determines where the data is located and issues commands to the various hardware components (disk controller, disk drive, etc.) to cause the data to be transmit-

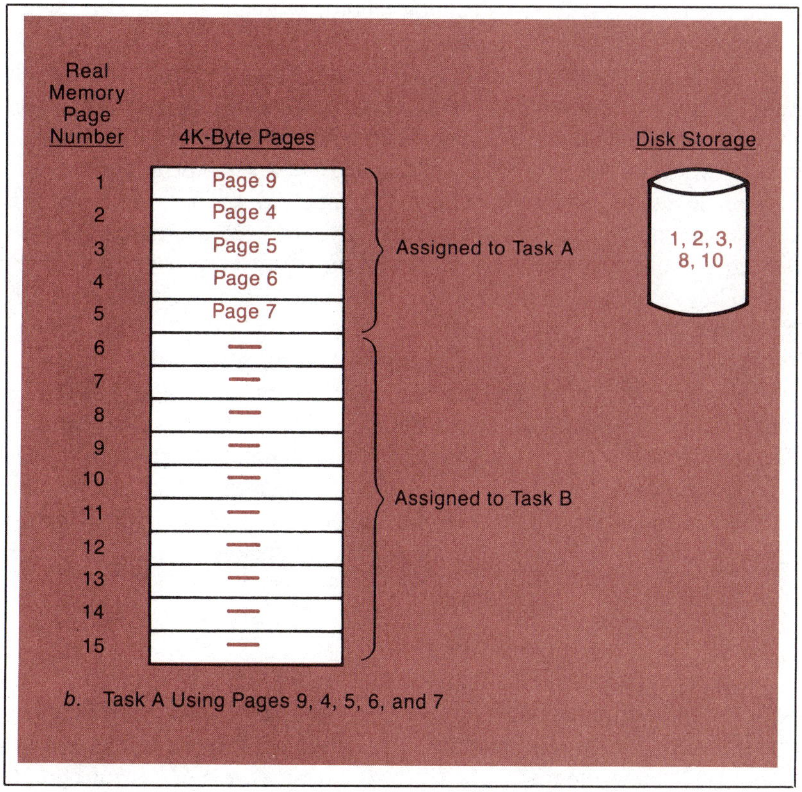

Data Management

FIGURE 1-9b

A virtual memory page change

b. Task A Using Pages 9, 4, 5, 6, and 7

Allocate CPU
Process interrupts
Provide supervisor services
Allocate main memory

ted. When the data arrives, the data management routines ensure that all of the data arrived, and in good condition. If so, data management routines transfer the data to the user. If not, the data management routines take corrective action. Similar actions occur with PRINT (or other commands to create or modify data).

Data management is a large and complex function. There are many services beyond INPUT and PRINT. For example, before data can be INPUT, a file must be created. The structure of the file must be defined and the structure must be physically constructed on the disk or other media. Data management routines do this work in accordance with instructions from the program or other source. The situation is even more complicated when you consider that files can have sequential, indexed sequential, and random organizations. Data management must be able to support all three.

In addition to creation and processing, data management provides services to facilitate *data administration*. In some systems, data management routines maintain a catalog of data. This catalog records who created the data, when it was created, when it was last processed, and so forth.

Data catalogs are useful for managing libraries of data. Consider the problem of a tape library containing thousands of tape volumes. How can operations know which of the tape volumes are needed? If there are tapes that have not been used in several years, are they still needed? To determine this information, operations needs to know who created the data and when. In one large data center, the operations staff did a manual inventory of all their tapes. They called the person responsible for the creation of every tape in their library. Among other surprises, they found 107 tapes that had been issued to someone who had died two years previously.

Some computers have a set of programs that perform *database management*. These programs are called the database management system (DBMS). Database processing is discussed in more detail in chapter 7. For now, realize that the DBMS, if used, is part of the operating system data management function. For some computers, a DBMS is built into the operating system. For others, the DBMS is an optional item. For still others, the DBMS is provided by a completely different vendor. Data management functions are summarized in figure I-11.

UTILITIES

The final category of systems programs that we will discuss is utilities. These programs provide commonly needed services. Examples are sorting data, copying data from one diskette to another, initializing files, and so forth.

Figure I-12 shows the menu of utilities available on a WANG word processing system. When the user selects one of the items on this menu, one of six

Provide facilities to:
    Create data
    Process data
        For sequential, indexed sequential, and direct files
    Administer data
Support database processing

FIGURE I-11

Functions of data management

o Copy document to archive diskette
o File document to archive diskette
o Retrieve document from archive diskette
o Delete document from system diskette
o Delete document from archive diskette
o Prepare archive diskette for processing

FIGURE I-12

Sample menu of utility services

utility programs is executed. This word processing system has two floppy diskettes. One is called the *system diskette* and the other is called the *archive*. The first utility copies a document from the system diskette to the archive diskette. The original copy remains unchanged. The second utility files a document (when it is filed, a document is copied from the system diskette to the archive diskette, and the original is deleted from the system diskette). The third utility retrieves documents from the archive diskette. The fourth and fifth utilities delete documents, and the last utility prepares a new diskette for processing and storing data. During preparation, the diskette is labeled and the basic structure is recorded.

The utilities listed in figure I-12 are typical. Larger systems have more utilities, but they serve the same or similar functions. The point to remember is that utilities are provided with computer systems, and that system evaluations should include consideration of whether necessary utilities are available.

QUESTIONS

I.1 Name and briefly describe the three primary categories of systems programs.

I.2 Explain the purpose of a computer program. Describe three advantages of programmable computers over special-purpose computers.

I.3 Explain the term *byte*. Can an instruction occupy more than one byte? Can data occupy more than one byte?

I.4 What is the purpose of a compiler? Is the compiler a machine? A person? What is it?

I.5 Explain the purpose of a link/loader. How does it integrate programs from a system library with a compiled program?

I.6 Explain the difference between compilation and interpretation.

I.7 Name the three functions of an operating system.

I.8 Describe the functions of job management.

I.9 Describe the functions of task management.

I.10 Describe the functions of data management.

I.11 Explain the term *virtual memory*. Why is virtual memory useful?

SUMMARY

In this module, we discussed program translation, the operating system, and system utilities. Programs are sequences of instructions stored in the main memory of the computer and executed by the computer's CPU. Programs direct general-purpose computers to solve specific problems. Without programs, there would have to be a separate machine for each problem. Such machines would be harder to test than general-purpose computers with programs.

Main memory is divided into boxes with addresses called bytes. Bytes can contain instructions and data. Instructions and data can vary in length; each instruction or data item can occupy one or more bytes.

Programs are written in source code, translated into object code by a compiler, and then formed into executable load modules by the link/loader. A compiler is a program that translates other programs. It is not a piece of hardware or a special machine. There is a separate compiler or compilers for each computer language. When interpretation is used rather than compilation, programs are translated and executed a line at a time.

The operating system is a set of programs that controls use of the computer. These large and complex programs control the computer's resources and manage computer jobs. The operating system has three major parts: job management, task management, and data management. Job management allocates resources and starts jobs. Task management supervises jobs in execution and allocates the CPU and main memory. Data management provides facilities to create, process, and administer data.

Utilities are programs that provide commonly needed services. Examples are programs to copy a diskette and programs to sort a file of data.

WORD LIST

(in order of appearance in text)

Operating system	System library
Supervisor	External reference
Executive	Link/loader
Utilities	Linkage editor
Language processors	Executable load module
Special-purpose machine	Program interpretation
Memory	Job management
Program	Task management
Bit	Data management
Byte	Time slicing
Program validation	Interrupts
Binary instruction code	Virtual memory
High-level language	Page
Source code	Data administration
Compiler	Database management
Object code	

A. Consider the problem of initiating computer jobs. Suppose that a system supports low-, medium-, and high-priority jobs. Further, suppose that the only constraints on jobs are the amount of memory and the number of tape drives. For each job on the job queue, the priority, the amount of memory needed, the number of tape drives needed, and the expected length of the job are recorded. Specify an algorithm for selecting jobs to be executed. Assume that M bytes of memory and T number of tape drives are available.

B. If the compiler is a program, what compiles the compiler?

C. Interview the operations manager of a data center. List and describe the utilities used in operations. Interview a systems and programming manager. List and describe the utilities used for systems development.

M O D U L E   J

Survey of Computer Programming Languages

Ben Katz shook his head in amazement and despair. What were these people talking about, and how important was it? Ben was the General Manager of DEMPCO Enterprises, a position he had assumed two months earlier. Just prior to that time, DEMPCO had been purchased by the company Ben worked for. He was the first manager after the realignment.

In front of Ben were two people from Data Processing. Jay had been a programmer at DEMPCO for 15 years. He was recognized as the person who kept the shop together. Susan was a young systems analyst who seemed to have a lot on the ball. She had worked at DEMPCO for only six months, but she had several years of experience in previous jobs.

The discussion concerned the future direction of programming at DEMPCO. Apparently, most of DEMPCO's programs were written in something called assembler language. *This situation had Susan upset. She felt that these programs should be phased out and gradually replaced by programs written in another language. She seemed to vacillate about what other language should be used.*

Jay thought the assembler language programs were fine. In fact, he thought they were excellent— very efficient, he said (although he never really indicated what he meant by efficient*). Jay believed that programmers at DEMPCO should continue writing assembler language programs because they provided "efficiency" unavailable with other languages.*

The issue had come to a head last Friday in a Data Processing staff meeting. Susan and Jay had had a confrontation about the issue. They had asked Ben for a decision on the company's future direction. Both Susan and Jay were threatening to quit if the wrong decision was made.

If you were Ben, what would you do?

In this module, we will discuss computer languages. More specifically, we will discuss what are known as *procedural programming languages*. Using these languages, the programmer gives instructions to the computer. As these instructions are executed, the computer produces the results desired (one hopes). In module K, we will discuss programming with another kind of language: nonprocedural languages.

In this module, we will consider how languages have been developed. Four types of computer programming problems will then be defined. Languages commonly used for each type of problem will be briefly described. With that knowledge, we will return to the case of DEMPCO Enterprises to see how the language selection issue was resolved.

You would probably be amazed to walk into a forest in the Pacific Northwest and find someone cutting down a 300-foot tree with an ax. Yet, in any middle-sized city, you will find some people writing computer programs with the equivalent of an ax. To understand why, consider how programming languages were developed.

Teaching the Turtle New Tricks:
Schoolchildren Find the Logo Language a Good Way to Start

At the progressive Lamplighter School in Dallas, the students are hard at work at their computer consoles, their faces intent in the reflected greenish light of the video screens. An eight-year-old types instructions that bring forth on the screen a figure of the space shuttle *Columbia,* complete with desert landing strip and disposable booster rockets. A nine-year-old pointedly picks apart the logic of one of his teacher's programs. Three-year-olds who cannot yet speak in complete sentences bang away at their keyboards, conjuring up electronic squiggles and squares.

Like thousands of other students across the country, these children are exploiting the advantages of a new electronic-age language called Logo, which in effect allows them to be their own computer programmers.

Most small computers come supplied with a programming language called BASIC, for Beginner's All-purpose Symbolic Instruction Code. Written in the mid-'60s for Dartmouth College students, BASIC assumes a working knowledge of

algebra and some technical computer jargon as well. Logo, by contrast, was created with grade-school children in mind. To keep things very, very simple for the user, Logo starts off with a handful of English words that the computer recognizes as commands to make it do things. The word PLAY, for instance, tells a properly equipped computer to play a musical note. Another command, SENTENCE, instructs it to put two words together into a sentence. Still more commands direct the movement of a tiny triangular character called the turtle, which crawls across the screen leaving a trace of where it has been. Typing in, say, RIGHT 90, turns the turtle 90° to the right. FORWARD 50 sends it sliding forward about 50 mm. Sitting down at a Logo computer, eight-year-olds can start getting simple results almost immediately. They can also put commands together, like building blocks, to teach the turtle new tricks. With skillful supervision they will be writing their own programs before the first hour is up . . .

"Logo's immediate result is it

establishes a good first impression," says Seymour Papert, 59, the gray-bearded, South African-born M.I.T. mathematician whose theoretical work in the arcane field of artificial intelligence led to Logo. "It convinces the child that he can master the machine. It lets him say, 'I'm the boss.' " Says Dr. Sylvia Weir, a pediatrician who works with the Educational Computing Group at M.I.T.: "People have usually considered the stupid thing in the class-room the child. Now the stupid thing, as it were, is the computer. And the child is the teacher." Giving children this kind of control can sometimes have dramatic effects. In an experimental program at the Cotting School for Handicapped Children in Boston, one 17-year-old suffering from cerebral palsy who could barely hold a pencil, much less write coherent English sentences, blossomed during 2½ years of Logo instruction. He now writes papers at the college freshman level and majors in computer science at the University of Massachusetts.

By PHILIP FAFLICK
Time, October 2, 1982

As stated in module I, the first computers were programmed in binary using 0's and 1's. This process took a long time, and programs written in binary were very hard to change. Consequently, computer specialists looked for better ways to program. In the mid-1950s, the first versions of *high-level languages* were developed. These languages allowed programmers to write instructions that were closer to English than to binary but that could be translated into machine language.

The people who developed these early languages were truly pioneers. They had little theory to go by, and they developed languages by intuition. Some of the languages just grew. People considered the computers they had and the problems they wanted to solve, and they developed the best language they could to solve the problems.

Unfortunately, some of the languages were terrible! They never worked correctly; or they were very hard to use; or they directed the computer inefficiently; or the programs written in them were nearly impossible to read; and so on. Some languages never had enough time or money invested in their development to get a fair trial. All in all, over 1000 languages have been developed in the last 30 years. Of those, not more than 10 are in popular use today.

As languages were implemented, as they were used, and as one language was compared to another, principles of language design were developed. By 1970, many experts had a good idea of the best way to design languages.

A milestone in this process was the discovery in the late 1960s that all programming logic could be represented by three basic instruction patterns or *constructs: sequence, alternation*, and *iteration. Sequence* means that a group of instructions is to be performed in order. *Alternation* means that the sequence of instructions to be performed is selected, depending on some condition. For example:

```
IF A IS LESS THAN B
    THEN
        /execute one or more statements/
    ELSE
        /execute one or more different statements/
END-IF
```

Iteration means that a sequence of instructions is to be performed repeatedly while (or until) some condition is true. For example, the following iteration might be used to calculate the year that some investment exceeds $1 million.

```
DOWHILE PRINCIPAL IS LESS THAN 1000000
    ADD 1 TO YEAR
    COMPUTE NEW PRINCIPAL AT 10 PERCENT
END-DO
```

Alternation and iteration are discussed more fully in modules H and I.

The discovery of these three constructs meant that other instruction patterns were unneeded. It meant that the logic of every program, no matter how complex, could be reduced to these simple building blocks. Some languages that had frills and extras beyond these patterns could be simplified.

Even more important, many languages represented one or more of these three patterns awkwardly. The alternation pattern, for example, is badly represented by several languages. (The BASIC language, alas, is one.) People began to see that programs written in these languages were hard to read, hard to understand, and hard to change.

Other principles were also discovered. These principles helped experts to understand the characteristics of a good programming language.

Unfortunately, by that time, several languages had become firmly entrenched in user organizations. These languages had some good characteristics, but they also had many bad ones. Thousands of programs had been written using them. Companies could not afford to rewrite the programs completely. They could not afford to retrain all of their programming personnel. Many programmers had spent years learning one or more languages. They did not want a new language to come along that would outdate their skills.

Therefore, there was, and is, tremendous economic, political, and personal resistance to new languages. Of the 10 most popular languages in use today, eight were developed before 1970. Seven were designed before 1965.

As you read this survey of languages, keep in mind that every one of them has major defects. However, every one of them also does something well. After all, they are the survivors of the 1000 or so languages that have been developed in the history of computing.

The story of computer languages is not finished. Today we have languages that were created in the pioneering stage. These languages will be improved or replaced. Some people believe that the nonprocedural languages discussed in module K will replace the languages discussed in this module for many, if not most, applications. Others believe that such replacement is unlikely. This debate will be resolved in the course of your business career. You will also deal with computer personnel caught in the agony of this and other, similar dilemmas.

PROGRAMMING APPLICATIONS AND LANGUAGES

In the last 30 years, computer specialists have learned that there is no such thing as a typical computer program. Programs vary considerably; consequently, there is no single best computer language. Some languages are better for one type of processing, and some are better for others. In this section, we will investigate four categories of applications: business, scientific, systems, and special purpose. Each category requires a different type of programming language.

Business Applications and Languages

Business applications typically involve transferring large amounts of data, and business programs often execute many input/output instructions. However, once the data is in main memory, business programs usually perform few mathematical operations on it. Instead, data items are compared to one another, decisions are made, and changes are made to stored data. Structured reports are frequently produced.

Additionally, business applications are often online. There may be many users operating concurrently at many terminals. Users often want to access the same files of data, so program coordination is important. This topic is discussed further in chapter 8.

Business is a dynamic activity, and business programs change frequently. Because the person who wrote a program is often not available to change it, business programs need to be easy to read and understand.

Order entry is a typical business application. When an order is processed, customer, inventory, and production records must be accessed. Data about customer credit, items on hand or in production, shipping addresses, and so forth, is processed to make order approval and shipping decisions.

Hundreds of orders may be processed in a day, so a tremendous volume of data may be transferred to and from the files. However, the processing of this data involves simple arithmetic; there is no need for sophisticated mathematics.

Generally, several order entry clerks process the same files. If their access is not carefully controlled, they can interfere with one another.

These characteristics of business programs mean that a business programming language should have extensive input/output capability. It should be easy to do I/O, and data should be transferred efficiently. Further, the language should have a rich vocabulary for describing records, fields, data types, and so forth.

The logic of business processing is sometimes complex, so the alternation pattern (IF-THEN-ELSE) should be clear and easy to understand. Sophisticated mathematical vocabulary and notation are unimportant.

Because online, concurrent processing is prevalent, the language should have commands for locking and unlocking records and for performing other types of program coordination.

The characteristics of business applications programming are summarized in figure J-1. This figure also lists four languages commonly used for business programming. We will briefly describe each of these.

BASIC   As mentioned in module H, the acronym *BASIC* stands for Beginners' All-purpose Symbolic Instruction Code. BASIC was designed in the late 1960s at Dartmouth College and was intended to introduce students to programming. As its name implies, it is an all-purpose language for beginners.

A simple BASIC program is shown in figure J-2. This program reads accounts receivable records and computes the number of accounts with a zero balance, the number with a positive balance, and the total of the balances. After all records are input, the results are printed. BASIC's primary virtue is that it is simple and therefore easy to learn to use. BASIC has very primitive input/

FIGURE J-1

Summary of business applications programming

Characteristics of Business Applications
Frequent input and output of large amounts of data
Little mathematical manipulation of data
Frequent online processing
Concurrent processing control important
Programs often need to be changed
Programs need to be easy to read
Languages Commonly Used
BASIC
COBOL
PL/I
RPG

```
010 REM        THIS PROGRAM PROCESSES ACCOUNTS RECEIVABLE DATA
020 REM        VARIABLE ASSIGNMENTS ARE:
030 REM        N1 = NUMBER OF ACCOUNTS WITH ZERO BALANCES
040 REM        N2 = NUMBER OF ACCOUNTS WITH POSITIVE BALANCES
050 REM        T  = TOTAL OF BALANCES
060 REM        N$ = NAME OF CUSTOMER
070 REM        B  = AMOUNT OF CUSTOMER BALANCE
100    N1 = 0
150    N2 = 0
200    T  = 0
225 REM        PROCESSING LOOP STARTS HERE
250    INPUT N$, B
300    IF N$ = "END" THEN 650
350    IF B = 0 THEN 550
400    N2 = N2 + 1
450    T = T + B
500    GOTO 250
550    N1 = N1 + 1
600    GOTO 250
625 REM        TERMINATION SECTION
650    PRINT "NUMBER OF ACCOUNTS WITH ZERO BALANCE IS ", N1
700    PRINT "NUMBER OF ACCOUNTS WITH POSITIVE BALANCE IS ", N2
750    PRINT "TOTAL OF BALANCES IS ", T
800    END
```

FIGURE J-2

Sample BASIC program

output capability, and its vocabulary for alternation is clumsy. As shown in module H, iteration structures can be awkward to implement in BASIC.

BASIC is popular because it is simple, and it works well for small problems, such as computing the interest on a mortgage. However, because of its limitations, BASIC is not good for all business applications. When complex programs are written in BASIC, the code is usually hard to read and understand, and therefore it is hard to change.

Actually, BASIC's simplicity has turned out to be a disadvantage. BASIC has been applied to problems for which it is not suited. Beginners have learned BASIC and then never graduated to a language that is harder to learn but more powerful. As the beginner's programming skill improved, he or she took on more complex tasks, but carried BASIC along. After some period of time, a beginner's language is used to accomplish complex tasks. The resulting code is hard to read and otherwise undesirable.

BASIC is offered with many small business computers and microcomputers. Often the computer vendor extends the capabilities of BASIC to allow for the sophisticated input/output needed for business data processing. Such extension of capabilities, however, is a trap. Once a company develops programs using the language extensions, they find it hard to switch to another vendor's computer. If they switched, all of the programs would have to be rewritten to remove the special commands. This modification would be very expensive.

To summarize, BASIC is an easy language for beginners to use when they are learning about programming. The standard language can result in programs that are hard to read and excessively complex. Vendors have augmented the language to give it more power. BASIC is often used with microcomputers.

COBOL The acronym *COBOL* stands for COmmon Business Oriented Language. COBOL was designed by a committee of users and computer manufacturers in the late 1950s. The users wanted a language that would be suited to business problems and that would support sophisticated input and output processing.

COBOL is an old and established language. It is nationally standardized and supported by all major computer manufacturers. Between 60 and 80 percent of all business application programs are written in COBOL.

Figure J-3 shows the accounts receivable problem coded in COBOL. This problem is the same one used to demonstrate BASIC in figure J-2.

Because COBOL was designed with business applications in mind, it has been very successful in the business environment. It has an extensive vocab-

FIGURE J-3

Procedure division of a COBOL program

Note: A COBOL program has four parts, called *divisions*. The IDENTIFICATION DIVISION names the program. The ENVIRONMENT DIVISION describes the files to be used; the DATA DIVISION describes the format of the data. Finally, the PROCEDURE DIVISION describes actions for the computer to take. For simplicity, only the PROCEDURE DIVISION is shown here.

```
PROCEDURE DIVISION.
    PERFORM A10-INITIALIZE.
    PERFORM A20-PROCESS UNTIL EOF-FLAG = 1.
    PERFORM A30-WRAPUP.
    STOP RUN.
A10-INITIALIZE.
    OPEN INPUT DATA-FILE
         OUTPUT PRINT-FILE.
    MOVE 0 TO EOF-FLAG.
    MOVE 0 TO NUM-ZERO-BAL.
    MOVE 0 TO NUM-POS-BAL.
    MOVE 0 TO TOTAL-BAL.
    READ DATA-FILE AT END MOVE 1 TO EOF-FLAG.
A20-PROCESS.
    IF BAL IS GREATER THAN 0
            ADD 1 TO NUM-POS-BAL
            ADD BAL TO TOTAL-BAL
    ELSE
            ADD 1 TO NUM-ZERO-BAL.
    READ DATA-FILE AT END MOVE 1 TO EOF-FLAG.
A30-WRAPUP.
    WRITE PRINT-REC FROM HEADER1.
    WRITE PRINT-REC FROM SUMMARY-DATA.
    CLOSE DATA-FILE PRINT-FILE.
```

ulary for defining files, records, and fields. Its alternation and iteration constructs are much better than BASIC's.

Unfortunately, COBOL has disadvantages, too. It is a large language with many features. Like any committee project, everyone's good ideas were incorporated. Consequently, COBOL is easily misused, and it takes most people a year or so of programming to learn the language well.

Further, COBOL was designed to be *self-documenting*. Many lines of code must be written even for simple problems. A few years ago, someone said that when the weight of the cards containing the COBOL statements exceeds the weight of the computer, then the program is ready to run. Actually, COBOL was designed to solve medium- and large-sized business problems. It is time consuming and frustrating to write small COBOL programs.

COBOL was designed before online processing existed. Therefore, the standardized language does not have any special commands to coordinate concurrent processing. Most manufacturers of computers with online capability have expanded their versions of COBOL to include such commands.

If there is *one* business programming language, COBOL is it. Over the years, COBOL has proven to be amazingly durable. It has the features necessary to handle most business processing problems. You probably do not go one day without handling a document or form that was generated by a COBOL program.

PL/I Programming Language I, or PL/I, was developed by IBM in the mid-1960s as a general-purpose language that could be used for all types of computer processing—business, scientific, and systems.

Figure J-4 shows the accounts receivable problem coded in PL/I. Compare this to the BASIC and COBOL programs shown in figures J-2 and J-3.

PL/I has many similarities to COBOL. The vocabulary for defining files, records, and data items is rich. A wide variety of input/output techniques is available. The constructs for alternation and iteration are excellent. PL/I has all the features necessary for business application programming. Additionally, PL/I has features for scientific and systems programming that make it truly a general-purpose language.

Unfortunately, all of these features mean that PL/I is complex. The PL/I learning period is lengthy. The designers of PL/I attempted to reduce the impact of this complexity by defining levels of the language. The idea was that beginners could easily use a subset of PL/I and never know that other features were available. The implementation of this idea has been only partially successful.

In spite of its excellent features, PL/I has not been readily accepted in the business community. There are several reasons for this rejection. First, for many years, PL/I was only available on IBM computers. Companies that developed programs in PL/I were in effect committing themselves to the use of IBM equipment now and in the future. This commitment was more than most companies wanted to make.

Second, the existing PL/I compilers do not generate efficient object code. Programs written in PL/I occupy more main storage than equivalent programs written in another language. They take more machine time to run.

Finally, although PL/I is an excellent language, it does not appear to have substantial advantages over COBOL for business applications. Therefore, it is

```
ACCT_REC: PROCEDURE OPTIONS(MAIN);

Note: Definitions of variables go here. For simplicity, they are not
      shown in this example.

      ON ENDFILE (AR_FILE) EOF_FLAG = 1;
      EOF_FLAG = 0;
      NUM_ZERO_BAL = 0;
      NUM_POS_BAL  = 0;
      TOTAL_BAL    = 0;
      GET LIST (CUST_NAME, AMOUNT);
      DO WHILE EOF_FLAG = 0;
          IF AMOUNT GT 0
              THEN DO;
                    NUM_POS = NUM_POS + 1;
                    TOTAL_BAL = TOTAL_BAL + AMOUNT;
                    END;
                ELSE NUM_ZERO_BAL = NUM_ZERO_BAL +1;
          GET LIST (CUST_NAME, AMOUNT);
      END;

      PUT PAGE LIST ('NUMBER OF ZERO BALANCES IS ', NUM_ZERO_BAL);
      PUT SKIP(2) LIST ('NUMBER OF POSITIVE BALANCES IS ',
                        NUM_POS_BAL, 'TOTAL OF BALANCES IS ',
                        TOTAL_BAL);
      STOP;
      END;
```

FIGURE J-4

Portion of a PL/I program

not sufficiently better to justify switching languages and possibly becoming dependent on IBM. Consequently, most companies have stayed with COBOL.

RPG   The acronym *RPG* stands for Report Program Generator. RPG is not a programming language like BASIC, COBOL, or PL/I, but it is sometimes called a programming language. Many business reports are generated using RPG, so you should know about it.

To use RPG, a programmer defines the format of input files by naming fields and specifying their lengths and types (numeric, character, etc.). Then, the programmer defines simple operations on fields, such as, "add all order amounts together." He or she then specifies that this total is to be printed on a report.

RPG is well named. It is useful for reading files and producing reports. However, when complex logic is involved, many experienced programmers will choose a programming language like COBOL or PL/I. An example of RPG is shown in figure J-5.

Scientific Applications and Languages

A second category of languages includes those used for *scientific applications*. These applications differ from business applications in that they involve considerably less input/output. Although scientific applications do access stored

```
010F* THIS PROGRAM CALCULATES THE NUMBER OF ACCOUNTS WITH ZERO
020F* BALANCES, THE NUMBER WITH POSITIVE BALANCES,
030F* AND THE SUM OF THE BALANCES
040FPAYROLL IP   F   80   80              READ40
050FREPORT   0   F  133  133        0F   PRINTER
010IPAYROLL AA   01
020I                                            1    20 NAME
030I                                           21   262AMT
010C    01         AMT       COMP  0                    10   20
020C    10         TPOS      ADD   1       TPOS         30
030C    10         TBAL      ADD   AMT     TBAL         82
040C    20         TNEG      ADD   1       TNEG         30
010OREPORT   H   201    0F
0200         OR         1P
0300                                       56 'RECEIVABLE REPORT'
0400         H   2      0F
0500         OR         1P
0600                                       26 'NUMBER OF ZERO BALANCES'
0700                                       61 'NUMBER OF POSITIVE BALANCES'
0800                                       90 'TOTAL OF BALANCES'
0900         T 1        LR
1000              TNEG      15
1100              TPOS      48
1200              TBAL      86 '     ,  $0.   '
```

FIGURE J-5

FIGURE J-5

Sample RPG program

data, this access is much less frequent, and the volume of data transferred is much smaller than for business systems. However, the data that is transferred is heavily processed using complex mathematical and logical algorithms.

Scientific applications are usually batch oriented. Sometimes online processing is used to input data to start a scientific program, but then the program executes autonomously. Few scientific programs are interactive, and few involve concurrent processing.

Statistical analysis is a typical scientific application. To estimate the impact of smoking on cancer, doctors may gather data about the health and smoking habits of 1000 people. This data will be input to programs that compute statistics like the average rates of cancer among smokers and nonsmokers, the correlation of smoking with cancer, and other more sophisticated statistical estimators.

The amount of data read into the program will be small, at least in comparison to a business system like order entry. However, the data will be manipulated in mathematically sophisticated ways. The CPU will be very busy squaring and summing numbers, integrating probability functions, and so forth.

Further, there will be no need for several users to access the data concurrently. The researchers will be content to receive output reports one at a time.

Finally, scientific programs are not changed as frequently as business programs are. When changes do occur, they are usually additions to programs and not rewrites. For example, it is unlikely that a new method will be defined to compute the average or standard deviation of a sample of data. However, changes to order processing in business can and do occur frequently.

We have not defined scientific programs as programs used by scientists. Sometimes scientists use programs from the business category. For example, when scientists have applications involving a great deal of data, they use the computer as a business person would. In this case, the scientist is using business data processing techniques.

Figure J-6 summarizes the characteristics of scientific application programs and lists several languages commonly used. We will summarize these languages.

ADA The newest programming language included in this book is ADA. It was developed through contracts issued by the U.S. Department of Defense. The goal was to develop a scientific and systems language suitable for a national standard, like COBOL.

ADA is not an acronym. This language is named after Lady Ada Augusta Lovelace, who was a pioneer and important figure in computing in the nineteenth century. (See module A for more information.)

ADA was announced in May of 1979 and became operational in early 1980. Although it is too soon to tell how the language will be accepted, early indications are that it is an excellent language and may well receive widespread acceptance. ADA is a derivative of the PASCAL language.

ALGOL ALGOrithmic Language, or *ALGOL*, is one of the oldest programming languages. ALGOL was developed primarily for scientific programming. It has excellent alternation and iteration capability, and programs written in ALGOL tend to be easy to read and understand. ALGOL has limited input/output capability.

FIGURE J-6

Summary of scientific applications programming

Characteristics of Scientific Applications
Less input/output than business programs
Heavy mathematical processing
Primarily batch applications
Little concurrent processing
Change less frequent than with business programs
Languages Commonly Used
ADA
ALGOL
APL
BASIC
FORTRAN
PASCAL
PL/I

Although ALGOL never received much acceptance in North America, it has been widely used in Europe. It is the grandparent of several other programming languages, including PL/I, ADA, and PASCAL (see below).

APL APL is an acronym for A Programmer's Language. This language is oriented toward problem solving at a terminal. It is especially useful for operating on arrays. APL has a host of language-unique commands for array processing.

Because there are many special characters in the APL language, an APL terminal or keyboard is required (see figure J-7). APL is known for its power. Very complex operations can be specified with just a few variables and operators. Unfortunately, this characteristic also makes APL programs hard to read and understand.

FIGURE J-7

Special terminal used for APL programming

573

Although APL has a large and loyal following, it is not as commonly used as languages like COBOL or BASIC. It is *primarily* available on IBM computers. This constraint, combined with the need for a special terminal and the large memory required for the APL compiler, has limited its use. Even still, APL proponents claim that there are few better languages. The introduction of APL on microcomputers may add to the number of users of APL.

FORTRAN   The language *FORTRAN*, or FORmula TRANslator, is an old language that was developed primarily for scientific programming. FORTRAN is a prime example of a language that just grew. It was originally used to translate formulas, but people kept adding to its capability until it became a general-purpose language. Unfortunately, FORTRAN is like an old miner's shack that rooms have been added on to year after year. It has little architectural integrity.

FORTRAN has limited input/output capability. Although its alternation construct is excellent, its iteration constructs are only minimally acceptable. Programs written in FORTRAN tend to be hard to read and understand. Consequently, they are hard to change.

Amazingly, in spite of these disadvantages, more scientific programs have been written in FORTRAN than in any other language. There are many reasons for this strange situation. One is that many programmers didn't know how much better off they could be with other languages. Another reason is economic.

In the late 1950s and early 1960s, there was a battle raging between proponents of FORTRAN and those of ALGOL. IBM was behind FORTRAN, and other, smaller vendors were behind ALGOL. Because IBM sold many more computers than other vendors, FORTRAN became the language most often used. The greater use of FORTRAN occurred in spite of the fact that ALGOL is a much better language.

This awareness, however, is hindsight. In fairness to IBM, few people knew at the time that ALGOL was a better language. When the defects of FORTRAN became apparent, IBM developed PL/I, which had many features similar to ALGOL.

PASCAL   The *PASCAL* language is named after Blaise Pascal, the French mathematician and philosopher. It was developed in the mid-1970s. PASCAL is an excellent language for scientific and systems applications, but has limited input/output capability. The constructs for alternation and iteration are excellent, and complex data formats are easily represented.

PASCAL has received considerable acceptance in computer science and engineering departments at colleges and universities. It has had growing acceptance in industry. PASCAL and ADA are very similar, but ADA has more general input/output capability. Therefore, some experts think ADA will be used more often in industry than PASCAL.

Other Scientific Languages   As figure J-6 indicates, both PL/I and BASIC are used for scientific applications. Recall that PL/I is a rich language that can result in excellent programs. Its chief drawbacks are that it is complex and that the object code tends to be inefficient.

The same remarks can be made about BASIC for scientific applications as were made about BASIC for business applications. It is easily learned and can be effectively used for simple problems. Some professionals would say that it is not suited for major programming efforts.

The third category of programming applications is *systems programs*. These programs belong to the computer itself. The operating system, including compilers and utilities, is one example, and a database management system is another. Programs in this category can be very sophisticated. They contain complex logic; they are often executed concurrently; and they tend to be very large. Further, systems programs run almost continuously, so efficiency is very important.

The operating system is primarily involved with logical operations. These operations include such tasks as selecting the next job; allocating files, main memory, and CPU time; and coordinating input/output operations.

Because relatively little I/O or mathematical processing is involved, these functions are not so important. The major requirement for a system programming language, therefore, is that it easily represent complex logic. The structures used to represent alternation and iteration should be clear and straightforward. Systems programming languages also need to be very efficient.

Figure J-8 lists the characteristics of systems applications. Of the four languages listed, ADA, PASCAL, and PL/I have been discussed already. Actually, PL/I has not been widely used for systems applications; however, its derivatives have. It may also be premature to put ADA on this list. ADA has not been available long enough to be used for major projects, although many people predict that it will be.

The first language listed for systems applications is called *assembler language*. Actually, this is not one language, but a class of languages. Each computer has its own assembler language.

Assembler language is midway between machine language and the higher level languages we have been discussing. It is more like English than machine language, but not as English-like as COBOL or PASCAL.

The basic statement in assembler language is a machine instruction. However, instead of an instruction code like 01011010, the machine instructions

Systems Applications and Languages

Summary of systems applications programming

Characteristics of Systems Applications
Sophisticated and complex logic
Extensive input and output
Concurrent processing frequent
Very large programs
Extensive use—efficiency important

Languages Commonly Used
Assembler
ADA
PASCAL
PL/I and its derivatives

are mnemonic (memory aiding) like ADD A,B or MOVE C,D. An assembler language program is a list of machine instructions written mnemonically. Figure J-9 shows an example of an assembler language program.

The major advantage of assembler language is efficiency. Because assembler language is very close to machine language, the programmer can tailor the application to the machine in a way that is not possible in a higher level language. Further, some sophisticated operations can be performed only in assembler language. When these operations are required by the application (as they sometimes are for systems applications), the program must be written in assembler language.

Unfortunately, assembler language has major drawbacks. For one, it takes longer to program an application in assembler than it does in a higher level language. Assembler language programs are hard to read and understand, and

FIGURE J-9

Sample assembler language program

```
ACCTREC   STM    14,12,12(13)    SAVE THE REGISTERS
          BALR   12,0            ESTABLISH ADDRESSABILITY
          USING  *,12
          ST     13,SAV+4        STORE SAVE AREA ADDRESS
          LA     13,SAV          GET NEW SAVE AREA ADDRESS
          OPEN   (ARDATA,INPUT,PRINTER,OUTPUT)
          SR     3,3             PUT ZERO IN R3
          SR     5,5             PUT ZERO IN NUMBER POSITIVE (R5)
          SR     6,6             PUT ZERO IN TOTAL BALANCES (R6)
          SR     7,7             PUT ZERO IN NUMBER NEGATIVE (R7)
*
*         NOW PROCESS
*
LOOP      GET    ARDATA,BUFFER    READ IN DATA: AMT IS IN BUFFER
          L      4,AMT
          CR     3,4             IS AMOUNT ZERO?
          BC     8,EQUAL         BRANCH IF IT IS.
          LA     5,1(5)          AMOUNT NOT ZERO.ADD 1 TO NUM POS VALUE
          AR     6,4             ADD AMOUNT TO SUM OF BALANCES
          B      LOOP
EQUAL     LA     7,1(7)          ADD 1 TO NUMBER OF ZERO ACCOUNTS
          B      LOOP
*
*         END OF DATA PROCESSING
*
ENDODATA  ST     5,NUMPOS
          ST     6,TBAL
          ST     7,NUMZERO
          PUT    PRINTER,MSG1      MSG1 HAS NUMZERO IN IT
          PUT    PRINTER,MSG2      MSG2 HAS NUMPOS AND TBAL IN IT
          CLOSE  (ARDATA,PRINTER)
          L      13,SAV+4        GET OLD SAVE AREA
          RETURN (14,12)         RESTORE REGISTERS
```

therefore they are hard to fix and change. Finally, assembler language is very system dependent. Each computer has a different assembler language. If a business wants to change computers (especially if it wants to change to a different brand of computer), all of the assembler language programs must be rewritten.

Ten years ago, nearly all systems applications were written in assembler language. Today, this situation is changing. Although major portions of some operating systems are still written in assembler, other operating systems are written in PASCAL, ADA, or a PL/I derivative. Other types of systems applications are also being written more and more in languages other than assembler.

As was mentioned in the DEMPCO case in the beginning of this module, many business applications were at one time written in assembler language. This fact is no longer true. The only assembler language routines around today are those left over from years ago. Assembler language is simply too hard to understand, and applications are too system dependent.

The final category of program applications is the miscellaneous category. These are the *special-purpose applications*, like process control, operations research, computer simulation, and so forth (see chapter 3). Because of the uniqueness of these applications, special languages have been developed for them. These applications account for a small percentage of programs, however, and we will not consider them further here.

Figure J-10 summarizes the languages surveyed in this module. Of these, the languages you are most likely to encounter are COBOL, BASIC, RPG, and PL/I. As you study figure J-10, pay particular attention to their features.

Special-Purpose Applications and Languages

LANGUAGE SELECTION AT DEMPCO ENTERPRISES (continued)

Ben Katz didn't know what to think about the controversy regarding language selection. You know by now that assembler language probably was not the correct language for DEMPCO. Actually, Jay knew that too, but he was being defensive. He was good at coding assembler. He didn't want anyone to diminish his value by eliminating his language. He was also afraid to try to learn a new language. Therefore, almost in spite of himself, Jay was arguing for assembler language. Because Ben didn't know anything about programming languages, he asked one of the data processing supervisors at the parent company to advise him. The supervisor, Ruth Bennett, was known throughout the company as an excellent manager, as well as technically well informed.

It took Ruth about 30 minutes of talking with Jay to understand the situation. She knew assembler was the wrong language. She also knew why Jay was acting the way he was. Without confronting him, she asked Jay and Susan to join her in a committee to determine the best language for DEMPCO in the long run.

Ruth never did confront Jay. She didn't want to, because she thought he was sharp, and she didn't want DEMPCO to lose his skills. She also felt that Jay would make a good decision if language selection could be presented in a nonthreatening way.

Language	Alternation Construct	Iteration Construct	I/O Capability	Primary Uses
ADA	Excellent	Excellent	Good	Systems, Scientific
ALGOL	Excellent	Excellent	Good	Scientific
APL	Excellent	Excellent	Good	Scientific
Assembler	Poor	Poor	Excellent	Systems
BASIC	Poor	Fair	Poor	Education, Simple Programs
COBOL	Excellent	Excellent	Excellent	Business
FORTRAN	Excellent	Fair	Fair	Scientific
PASCAL	Excellent	Excellent	Poor	Education, Systems, Scientific
PL/I	Excellent	Excellent	Excellent	General Purpose
RPG	None	None	Fair	Report Writing

FIGURE J-10

Comparison of programming language features

Consequently, she asked Jay and Susan to consider the most important characteristics for programs at DEMPCO. She also asked them to develop a list of criteria for a programming language. The committee then met to weigh, or rank, the criteria.

Jay and Susan agreed that the most important characteristic of a program is correctness. Therefore, they wanted a language in which it would be easy to write and to correct the programs. On the second characteristic, they disagreed. Susan thought programs should be adaptable. She believed that many aspects of business at DEMPCO would change in the near future, and she wanted a language that would allow programs to be easily changed. Jay thought that programs should be economical. When Susan asked him what he meant by that, he said that they should solve the problem with the minimum amount of CPU time and main memory space.

Because they disagreed, they decided to mention all three characteristics of programs at their meeting with Ruth. They also developed a list of language selection criteria for the meeting.

Ruth was pleased with their work. She thought that it was not important to decide which factor should be second and which should be third. She did point out one fact to Jay: programs can be economical by being efficient, but they can also be economical by being easy to write and test.

The committee used all three characteristics in developing the ranked list of criteria shown in figure J-11. Although ease of learning was considered a criterion, it was not as important as other factors. The most important factors involved ease of use, because the committee felt that a language that was easy to use would be most likely to result in correct programs.

Ease of maintenance (adaptability) and portability were also considered important. However, after some discussion, the committee agreed that programming efficiency was only moderately important. Computers are simply becoming too cheap for that to be a major factor.

After the committee had developed this list of criteria, Ruth asked Susan and Jay to consider which language best fit the overall criteria. She told them to interview programmers who had experience in various languages and to recommend the best language to the committee. Susan and Jay decided to consider assembler, BASIC, COBOL, and PL/I.

It was easy to eliminate one language. Both Jay and Susan believed it was important to maintain as much machine independence as possible. They felt that using PL/I would tie them too much to IBM computers, so they eliminated it from further consideration.

As they investigated BASIC, it became apparent that the BASIC IF statement (see figure J-2) was inconvenient. They believed that it would be difficult to develop complex programs in BASIC, and that it would be easy to make errors with it. Consequently, they eliminated BASIC from consideration.

Now their choices were limited to assembler and COBOL. Ruth arranged for both Susan and Jay to take a one-week COBOL programming course. After this course, Jay changed his mind. He said he believed that the advantages of a high-level language like COBOL would outweigh any programming inefficiencies. (Ruth guessed that he also felt better about changing because he saw that he would be able to learn the new language.) Therefore, Jay and Susan recommended COBOL as the future language for DEMPCO, and Ruth concurred.

Criteria	Level of Importance
Ease of learning	Low
Ease of use	High
Alternation construct	High
Iteration construct	High
Language documentation	High
Ease of maintenance	High
Program readability	High
Standardization	Medium
Portability	High
Program efficiency	Medium

FIGURE J-11

Ranking of language criteria for DEMPCO Enterprises

J.1 Name and describe the three fundamental programming constructs.

J.2 What significance do these three constructs have for programming languages?

J.3 Describe three reasons why some of the older, less desirable languages continue to be used.

J.4 Name five characteristics of business applications.

J.5 Give two advantages and two disadvantages of each of the following languages. Assume that these languages will be used for business processing.
- **a.** BASIC
- **b.** COBOL
- **c.** PL/I

J.6 Is BASIC a good business programming language? Explain why or why not.

J.7 Is COBOL a good business programming language? Explain why or why not.

J.8 What is the significance of COBOL's being a standardized language?

J.9 Approximately what percent of all business application programs are written in COBOL?

J.10 Describe four characteristics of scientific applications.

J.11 If FORTRAN is not considered a good language, why is it so widely used?

J.12 Describe four characteristics of systems applications.

J.13 What are the advantages and disadvantages of assembler language?

J.14 What measures of a good program did the staff at DEMPCO develop?

SUMMARY

Since the advent of the computer, over 1000 different programming languages have been developed. Of these, only about 10 are in popular use today. The need and structure of languages was clarified by the discovery that all programming logic can be represented by three basic instruction patterns: sequence, alternation, and iteration.

There are four categories of language applications: business, scientific, systems, and special purpose. Business applications typically involve large amounts of data with little mathematical processing. Popular business languages are COBOL, BASIC, PL/I, and RPG. Scientific applications usually involve far less data than business applications, but the data is heavily processed. Common scientific languages are ADA, ALGOL, APL, FORTRAN, PL/I, and PASCAL. Systems applications involve large programs that contain complex logic and that are often executed concurrently—assembler language, PASCAL, ADA, or a PL/I derivative. Finally, special-purpose languages are used for applications such as process control, operations research, statistics, and the like. Unique languages have been developed for these applications.

A. What do you think about the way that DEMPCO selected a language? Do you believe they made a good decision? If you worked for DEMPCO, what would you have done differently?

B. Suppose a company is using a language that is inappropriate for its needs. What are the likely results of this situation? Is the company even likely to know that it is using the wrong language? How could a company find out if its application programming language is appropriate?

C. Some people claim that the language that we use limits or constrains the thoughts we have. For example, Sanskrit (an ancient human language) had more than 15 different words for love. Consequently, it is possible to describe nuances of love more specifically in Sanskrit than in English. How does this situation pertain to programming? How does the choice of language impact programmers? Can an inappropriate language constrain programmers? Can an appropriate language liberate them? What impact does choice of language have on companies?

MODULE K

Nonprocedural Programming

Recently, a new class of programming languages has been developed. Languages in this class differ considerably from traditional languages like BASIC, COBOL, or PASCAL. The new languages, called *nonprocedural languages*, enable programmers to increase their productivity tremendously. One major manufacturer reported a programmer productivity improvement of greater than 100 to 1 using SQL (a nonprocedural language), as compared to using PL/I (a procedural language). Additionally, nonprocedural languages are simple and easy to learn. Consequently, it is possible for end users to do some of their own programming with only a few days of training.

PROCEDURAL vs NONPROCEDURAL PROGRAMMING

An easy way to understand the difference between procedural and nonprocedural programming is to consider an example. Figure K-1 shows a file of records about a company's products. Each record has product number, product name, product weight, and other data. The company is considering changing shipping vendors. To make the decision, they need to know the average weight of their products.

Figure K-2*a* shows pseudocode of a procedural algorithm to compute the average product weight. This algorithm simply reads all product records, sums their weights, and divides the total sum by the number of products. Figure K-2*b* shows a BASIC program that implements this algorithm.

Figure K-3 shows a nonprocedural program to compute the average weights. This program is written in SQL (Structured Query Language), a nonprocedural language. Compare the length and complexity of the program in figure K-2*b* with the program in figure K-3 and you can see why productivity improvements of 100 to 1 are possible.

Procedural and nonprocedural languages differ in the way they achieve desired results. With procedural processing, the programmer gives a sequence of instructions to the computer and hopes that, when the computer follows the instructions, the desired output will result. With nonprocedural processing, the programmer gives the computer a description of the desired result and allows the computer to determine a sequence of instructions that will obtain that result. Thus, with procedural processing, the programmer provides *instructions*, whereas with nonprocedural processing, the programmer provides a *description of results*.

There are several nonprocedural languages. Examples are FOCUS, NOMAD, RAMIS, and SQL. These languages have the same goals but differ in vocabulary and syntax. The relationship among these languages is like the relationship among procedural languages, such as BASIC, COBOL, and PASCAL. This module uses SQL for examples, but this use does not imply that SQL is superior to the others.

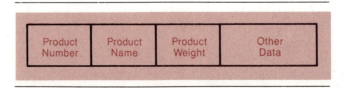

THE COMPUTER INDUSTRY AND CAREERS

Gold Rush of the 1980s

The computer industry is the gold rush of the 1980s—Apple Computer achieves $1 billion in sales in less than 10 years, after two young graduate students build a computer in their garage. IBM exceeds $36 billion in sales. People in their 20s have a bright idea, start a company or write software, and become wealthy overnight. So far, few roadmaps through this golden frontier exist.

HARDWARE, SOFTWARE, AND SERVICES

The computer industry is the gold rush of the 1980s. People in their 20s have a bright idea, start a company, and become millionaires overnight. Apple Computer achieves $1 billion in sales in less than 10 years of existence. IBM exceeds $36 billion in sales.

The computer gold rush involves three types of companies: hardware vendors, software vendors, and service vendors. The characteristics of these vendors vary. Hardware companies have different opportunities and working environments than software vendors. Service organizations are different still. Although most companies specialize in either hardware, software, or services, some companies do provide products from more than one of these categories.

Computer hardware vendors are similiar to traditional manufacturers. They design, develop, manufacture, sell, and support physical products. Some sell computer parts, like chips. Others sell complete components, like terminals and disk units. Still others sell complete computer systems.

Hardware vendors have four basic internal functions. In *product development*, engineers and engineering technicians design new products or changes to existing products. In addition to design, this work may involve research and development into new technologies. In *manufacturing*, the personnel build products according to the designs provided by product development.

A computer hardware vendor uses product development teams of computer scientists and engineers to design new products.

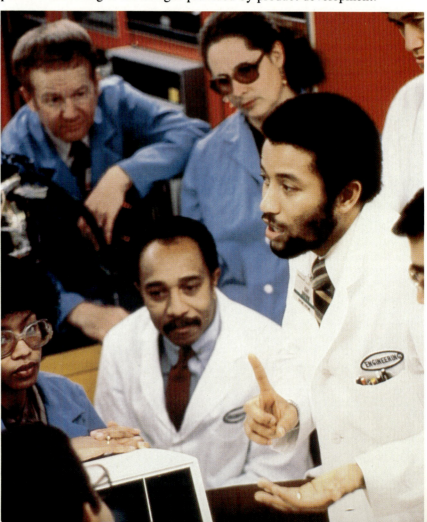

Sales is a third function of hardware vendors. Sales activity varies according to product. The sale of mainframes is usually made directly from the vendor to the customer. Minicomputer sales can be made directly, but they are also made indirectly via third-party companies, called OEMs (original equipment manufacturers). OEMs add value to the minicomputer hardware by adding more hardware, programs, or services. OEMs sell directly to their customers. Microcomputer sales are almost never made directly from manufacturer to customer. They are usually made from retail computer stores, business supply stores, and department stores. Microcomputers are often sold as computer appliances.

The fourth function, *product support*, involves assistance to customers after sales have occurred. Product support personnel provide education in the use and care of equipment. The product support organization also maintains and repairs equipment when necessary. A difficult product support task is to maintain an inventory of spare parts. Over the years, a company may have hundreds of products and variations on products. Knowing which parts are in which versions of which products can be difficult. Keeping a cost-effective inventory of spares can be nearly impossible.

Chip manufacturing and fabrication jobs often require that work be done in dust-free, clean rooms . . .

Almost as clean is a typical computer vendor's maze of office compartments.

HARDWARE, SOFTWARE, AND SERVICES
(continued)

The chart on this page shows projected dollar sales of computer systems from 1981 to 1986, broken down by type. By 1986, total hardware sales are expected to be over $62 billion—an increase of over $6 billion per year between 1981 and 1986. Observe that most of that growth is for minis and micros. Mainframe sales are expected to increase only slightly.

For hardware vendors, manufacturing and distribution can occur all over the world. This IBM plant is in Scotland.

The position of sales representative in the computer industry can offer an excellent income, as well as considerable contact with people.

PROJECTED GROWTH OF THE COMPUTER INDUSTRY, 1981 TO 1986

World-Wide Hardware Sales	1981	1986
Mainframes	$17.4	$24.7
Minis	6.2	15.4
Micros	5.8	22.3
	$29.4 Billion	$62.4 Billion

SOURCE: International Data Corporation

Hardware manufacturers may
manufacture computers or "peripherals,"
such as these printers.

Quality control of their disk surfaces is
important to RCA to assure consistent
storage capability.

Even the seven colors offered in these IBM
terminals must undergo quality control
checking.

Computer system vendors, such as Apple, sell both hardware and software.

Today the most important part of a microcomputer system is its software, and software vendors emerge overnight.

PROJECTED GROWTH OF THE
COMPUTER INDUSTRY, 1981 TO 1986

The second type of computer company in the software vendor. Software vendors are a new phenomenon in business. In a sense, they are manufacturers, but they do not manufacture anything physical. They manufacture programs, which are "thought-stuff." Software vendors are manufacturers of logical poetry.

Once a computer program is developed, the cost of production is very, very low. A computer program to do word processing, for example, may sell for a retail price of $495. The manufacturer may net, say, $250 of this amount. The cost of producing a copy of the program and its documentation may be only $15. This is an incredibly high gross margin.

Software vendors have the same four internal functions that hardware vendors have. The characteristics of the functions are different, however. Product development for software companies consists of the analysis, design, and construction of programs. The vendor identifies a need, determines the requirements for programs to meet that need, designs programs, and builds and tests them. Documentation is also a product development function.

The manufacturing function of a software vendor is simple, at least as compared to hardware manufacturing. Copies of the program are made on floppies or other media, and then the floppy is packaged with documentation—period.

Sales activity for software vendors is similar to sales activity for hardware vendors. For programs to be run on mainframe computers, direct sales to customers are common. For minicomputer programs, both direct and OEM sales strategies are used. Microcomputer program sales are nearly always made via a third party. Microcomputer retail stores, business supply stores, and department stores all sell programs for micros.

Distribution of microcomputer programs is emerging as a new area of the computer industry. Such distributors buy programs from vendors and resell them to retail stores. They provide sales assistance and sales training as well.

Some companies, called *software houses*, develop computer programs on a custom basis. These companies either alter existing programs to meet specific needs, or they design and build entirely new programs.

The chart on this page shows anticipated growth in program sales. In 1981, the great bulk of program revenue was for mainframe applications. By 1986, that is expected to change. More and more program revenues will stem from microcomputer applications.

The third type of computer company provides services. Computer service companies vary widely. Some companies provide computer processing service. This service can be a specific one, such as processing deposits, checks, and teller transactions for credit unions. Such a service provides a complete pack-

World-Wide Software & Services	1981	1986
Time Sharing	$ 7.9	$15.0
Software Packages	3.6	16.3
Professional Services	3.5	10.3
Systems Houses	1.5	5.2
	$16.5 Billion	$46.8 Billion

SOURCE: International Data Corporation

age, including processing hardware, programs, personnel, forms, training, and so forth. Other companies provide less comprehensive service.

Consulting companies provide information as a service. Consultants analyze needs and help their customers to select and acquire hardware, programs, or other resources. They provide education and training. Consultants also serve as advisers to management.

Some consultants, called *EDP auditors*, provide expertise to CPAs in conjunction with annual audits. These consultants evaluate the completeness and effectiveness of controls over accounting systems. They also do an evaluation of emergency and disaster recovery plans.

Customer training for a new computer system is provided by the customer service department.

This IBM service center offers customers product support in a wide variety of forms.

A *consultant* provides analysis and advice to a computer user.

COMPUTER CAREERS

As computer applications have spread throughout society, the number and type of computer-related jobs have increased dramatically. At one time, there were only a few different types of jobs. Today, there are dozens of job titles, and, unfortunately, there are few standard meanings for the titles that exist. The chart below shows computer industry job titles broken down by employer—vendor versus user.

A *computer scientist* at a major university conducts research funded by a hardware vendor in a continuing search for new technology.

COMPUTER INDUSTRY JOB TITLES

Vendors			Users	
Hardware	*Software*	*Service*	*Data Processing Department*	*End Users*
Computer engineer	Software engineer	Consultant	Computer operator	Word processing operator
Electrical engineer	Systems analyst	Computer operator	Data entry operator	Office administrator
Engineering aid	Programmer	Data entry operator	Applications programmer	Architect
Quality assurance technician	Quality assurance technician	EDP auditor	Systems analyst	Product engineer
Industrial engineer	Production supervisor	Technical writer	Data administrator	Graphic artist
Production supervisor	Technical writer	Salesperson	Management	Scientist
Technical writer	Salesperson	Customer service technician		Lawyer
Salesperson	Product support technician	Management		Consultant
Maintenance technician	Management			Liaison with computer personnel
Product support technician				Teacher
Management				

Vendors Hardware vendors employ people to design, produce, sell, and support hardware products. Computer and electrical engineers are the top echelon of their personnel. Other positions in this area are quality control engineer, industrial engineer, and production engineer. In addition, supporting personnel include engineering aids, production assistants, and quality control supervisors. Hardware vendors, like all of the vendor types, also employ technical writers, salespeople, support personnel, and managers.

Software vendors employ people to design, produce, sell, and support programs. Typical job titles include programmer, systems analyst, and software engineer. The latter job title refers to someone who designs, programs, and tests software products. Quality control personnel test programs to verify that they perform according to specifications.

The personnel in a computer service company vary according to the company's products. A processing service company would have computer operators, programmers, systems analysts, salespeople, and account support representatives. Account support personnel serve as a technical liaison between the customer and the service company.

A consulting company employs consultants. These people need to have expertise in one or more specialties. They also need to be superb communicators and good judges of people.

Programmers and systems analysts may spend little time at a computer terminal. Instead, they are involved in designing program solutions to problems, sometimes in small teams.

Computer engineers at Intel design and modify products.

Users   Career opportunities among companies that use computer products can be divided into two categories. The first is traditional data processing. People in operations run the computer equipment and perform limited routine maintenance. Data entry personnel convert computer data into machine-sensible form. Usually, but not always, this process involves operating some type of keyboard device. Systems analysts and programmers build new computer systems or maintain existing systems.

Data administration personnel standardize and protect the usage of computer data. Computer managers plan, organize, and control some aspect of the computer department.

End users are people who use computer-based products to perform their jobs. Word processing systems are used both by secretaries and by professionals, such as attorneys, consultants, authors, and architects. Office administration personnel manage the information resources of an office.

Engineers use computer systems to facilitate design. Products for computer-assisted design and manufacturing (CAD/CAM) and computer-assisted engi-

Data entry clerks key program statements and input data.

Computer operations personnel run and maintain computer center equipment.

neering (CAE) allow engineers to design on computer screens. The designs are stored on computer media. Later, approved designs are input to other computer-based systems that control and operate machinery.

Robots are beginning to be used in manufacturing. Robots perform repetitive work without error and can work in undesirable or dangerous environments. The use of robots has led to a new job title. A *production automation specialist*, with knowledge of manufacturing *and* computing, oversees the application of robots.

Scientists use computers to analyze and store data. Computers are used as sensing devices in laboratories, and they facilitate experiments in other ways. The space program would have been impossible without computers.

Computers are being used in more and more products. They are being used in automobiles, for example, to monitor fuel flow as well as to perform other functions. Talking soda machines have microprocessors, as do microwave ovens and washing machines. Consequently, engineers of all sorts of products increasingly need to understand computer technology.

Systems analysts find that communication skills and knowledge of the organization are as important as technical knowledge.

A *data administrator* standardizes data and develops computer security procedures.

CAREER PLANNING

A *computer department manager* combines technical knowledge with skill in planning, organizing, and controlling.

The chart on this page shows entry-level job titles for college majors in information systems, computer science, and computer engineering. Differences in salary are shown for two- and four-year degree graduates. The salaries shown are estimates of entry-level positions in 1984. Inflation, demand, company size, and local economic conditions greatly influence these salaries.

Because this chart shows only entry-level positions, some computer careers are omitted. Specifically, project leader and other management positions are not shown. Although exceptions occur, such management positions are more readily offered to experienced employees.

Selecting a Job—for You   The computer industry is expected to grow from a $46-billion industry in 1981 to a $99-billion industry in 1986. In an industry growing at such a rate, there are obviously many jobs. Because this is true, you should take some time to decide which of these many jobs will be best for you. With this objective, you can obtain the education most appropriate for the type of job you want.

First, as much as you are able, determine what you want. You are unique, and the best job for you will be different from the best job for someone else. Do you like to be with people? Do you enjoy interaction with your fellow students? Is it hard for you to work for long periods of time on your own? If so, sales, product support, and systems analysis, consulting, and management jobs may be appropriate for you. Each of these jobs will bring you into contact with people, and, in all of them, good communication skills are essential.

JOB TITLES AND ENTRY-LEVEL SALARIES (in $)

		College Major		
		Information Systems (Business)	*Computer Science*	*Computer (Electrical) Engineering*
Two-year Degree	*Vendor*	Programmer (20,000) Product support (18,000) Sales (20,000 +) Technical writer (18,000)	Programmer (20,000) Systems programmer (23,000) Product support (18,000) Technical writer (18,000)	Engineering aid (16,000) Production technician (18,000) Maintenance technician (20,000) Technical writer (18,000)
	User	Programmer (18,000) Junior analyst (23,000) Data administration ass't. (21,000) Computer operator (14,000)	Programmer (18,000) Systems programmer (23,000)	Maintenance technician (18,000)
Four-year Degree	*Vendor*	Programmer (25,000) Product support (23,000) Sales (25,000 +) Consultant (30,000 +) Technical writer (22,000)	Programmer (25,000) Systems programmer (27,000) Software engineer (27,000) Product support (23,000) Technical writer (22,000)	Computer engineer (32,000) Production supervisor (26,000) Support engineer (28,000) Maintenance engineer (28,000) Technical writer (22,000)
	User	Programmer (23,000) Systems analyst (28,000) Data administrator (27,000) Operations manager (24,000)	Programmer (23,000) Software engineer (25,000) Systems programmer (27,000)	Data communications specialist (30,000) Computer facilities maintenance supervisor (27,000)

Partly based on *Infosystems*, June 1983.

If you do not enjoy the company of other people in your work, then you will probably find more solitary jobs satisfying. Programming, operations, engineering, and other technical jobs may be your forte. If you are in the middle of this continuum—if you like people and also enjoy working on your own— then jobs that involve both solitary and group activities may be appropriate. Applications programming, systems analysis, product support, technical writing, and project management are possible jobs for you.

Did this farmer at an Alberta, Canada, wheat cooperative think he would want to learn to use a computer?

Banks and similar businesses may train employees at every level to use the computer.

Offices are becoming more automated as they implement word processing systems.

CAREER PLANNING
(continued)

Women have found the computer industry full of opportunities—perhaps because of the youth of this industry.

Your First Job   The best jobs come to those who actively seek them. Unless you develop a wide reputation and considerable expertise, the perfect job will not come looking for you. Begin to prepare while you're a student. If possible, seek out part-time employment at various jobs. See what you like to do and what you do not. Such part-time employment will also make your résumé more interesting when the time comes to find a job.

When selecting your first job, pick not only the work but also the people with whom you will work. Work for someone from whom you can learn. You may think you learned a lot in school, but, after one year on the job, you'll be amazed at how little you knew when you graduated.

Perhaps the best career advice was offered by a cross-country coach who told his runners, "On the bottom line, running should be fun. If you don't enjoy it, if, at some point, you don't get into it so much that you're not even aware you're running, then you should find another sport." A young product support engineer said that his job was so much fun, he felt guilty getting paid for it. If you can find a job like that for yourself, you'll be good at it, and your career will be exceedingly successful.

Once you find a job, take it seriously. If first impressions are not lasting, they are at least very powerful. When you accept a job, arrange your personal affairs so that you can work just as hard as you must to make an excellent

JOB TITLES BY INTEREST AND DESIRE TO WORK WITH PEOPLE

Area of Interest	Desire to Work with People		
	Low	*Medium*	*High*
Systems/applications orientation (information systems degree recommended)	Applications programming Maintenance programming Computer operations	Applications programming Systems analysis Technical writing Quality assurance Project management	Systems analysis Data administration Sales Customer support Education and training Project management Teaching Data processing management
Technical/software orientation (computer science degree recommended)	Programming Systems programming	Programming Systems programming Technical writing Quality assurance	Sales Customer support Systems analysis Programming/analysis Education and training Project management Teaching
Hardware design orientation (computer engineering degree recommended)	Engineering Engineering support Equipment maintenance Data communications	Engineering Engineering support Customer support Equipment maintenance Quality assurance Technical writing Project management	Sales Customer support Education and training Project management Teaching

impression. If you make that impression, it will carry you through all sorts of ups and downs. Be the last person out of the office four nights out of five. Read documentation, read standards, and learn all you can. Be courteous, helpful, agreeable, ambitious, competent, and sincere. Do more than you are supposed to do. Aim to be the best employee at your level.

If you have mechanical skills and enjoy working by yourself, then engineering technology may be your career.

Word processing skills are in increasing demand for new employees.

If you enjoy working with people, then customer sales and training can be an exciting career.

The spread of microcomputers has greatly expanded the opportunities for computer store retail salespeople.

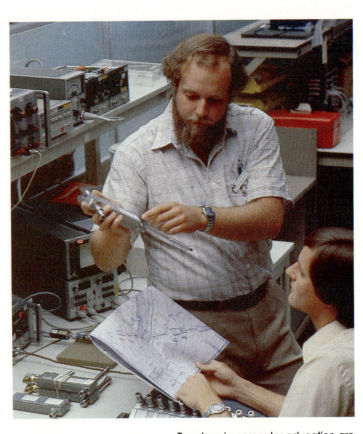

Teachers in computer education are needed in high schools, community colleges, and universities.

QUESTIONS

1. What are the three major segments of the computer industry? Describe differences in these segments.

2. Summarize projected sales growth in the computer industry between 1981 and 1986.

3. Name three job titles to be found in a hardware vendor.

4. Name three job titles to be found in a software vendor.

5. Name three job titles to be found in a services vendor.

6. Think about what you like to do. How important is working with other people? How important is working with hardware, software, or systems? Once you have answered these questions, list three or four jobs that might be appropriate for you.

7. What can you do today to prepare for a job you will like?

```
N     = 0
SUM   = 0
FLG   = 0
READ FIRST PRODUCT RECORD
      AT END SET FLG = 1
DOWHILE FLG = 0
      SUM  = SUM + WEIGHT
      N    = N + 1
      READ NEXT PRODUCT RECORD
            AT END SET FLG = 1
ENDDO
AVG = SUM / N
DISPLAY AVG
```

a. Algorithm to calculate average product weight

```
 10 N = 0
 20 S = 0
 30 F = 0
 40 INPUT N1, N2$, W
 50 IF N1 > 0 THEN 70
 60 F = 1
 70 IF F = 1 THEN 140
 80 S = S + W
 90 N = N + 1
100 INPUT N1, N2$, W
110 IF N1 > 0 THEN 130
120 F = 1
130 GOTO 70
140 A = S / N
150 PRINT " AVERAGE WEIGHT IS ", A
160 END
```

b. BASIC program to implement algorithm in a

FIGURE K-2

Computing average product weight

SQL, and most of the other nonprocedural languages, require that the data that is to be processed be stored as a relational database. Chapter 7 describes relational database processing. Here, we will review the essential concepts.

A relation is a table. The rows of the table correspond to records in a file. Each row contains data about some person, place, document, or thing. For example, the rows could contain data about employees, factories, orders, or automobiles. The columns of the table correspond to fields in a file. Each column contains data that represents some property. For example, the columns might represent employee name, factory location, order number, or auto color.

RELATIONAL DATABASE MANAGEMENT

```
SELECT     AVG(WEIGHT)
FROM       PRODUCT
```

FIGURE K-3

Nonprocedural code to compute average product weight

Reinventing Computer Science

"I think it's clear: There is going to be a real revolution. It's like computer science is starting all over again."

Few men are as qualified to make such a sweeping statement as John Backus. More than a quarter century ago he headed the small group of IBM programmers that invented FORTRAN, still one of the world's most widely used computer languages. And, for the last decade, he has been one of the leading figures in what now appears to be a growing movement to abandon such conventional languages in favor of a much more flexible style of "functional programming." It is the promise of being able to use such powerful new programming languages that has been one of the driving forces in development of advanced computer architectures, particularly "reduction" computers.

Backus is outspoken about his reasons for taking this still controversial position. "The thing we need most in the computing world today," he says with only slight hesitation, "is an order of magnitude reduction in programming costs. We've got all this cheap hardware coming out of our ears, but one program for one of these little computers costs more to develop than the computer does!" The solution, he says, is to build programs that can easily be manipulated and combined for new applications. Today, adapting standard software packages to fit individual requirements usually takes a professional programmer. But, says Backus, functional programming will make it possible for people with very little understanding to create, within a limited area, "programs that will do what they want."

The main problem with conventional programming languages is the way they handle data. In order to multiply one number by another, the central processing unit of a computer must first call them from memory by using their storage addresses, then send the result back to a third address. In his 1977 Turing Award Lecture, Backus dubbed this communications process "the von Neumann bottleneck," and said that the "primitive word-at-a-time style of programming" it engendered has led to development of languages that are now "growing even more enormous, but not stronger." The alternative, he concluded, would be a kind of functional programming in which "combining forms can use high level programs to build still higher level ones in a style not possible in conventional languages."

High Technology, February, 1983

In a relational database, only one entry is allowed in a column. Employees may have only one name, factories may have only one location, and so forth.

Figure K-4 shows a table that has multiple entries in a column and is therefore not a relation. Each row of this table corresponds to a student. The last column of this table has classes in which the student is enrolled. Because students may be enrolled in more than one class, this column can have more than one value.

The table in figure K-4 would not be allowed in a relational database. Rather, the table would need to be decomposed into two tables. This decomposition is shown in figure K-5. The STUDENT table has data about students, and the ENROLLMENT table has data about the correspondence of students and classes. The Grade column contains the grade earned by a particular student. We will use the data in figure K-5 to illustrate SQL commands.

STRUCTURED QUERY LANGUAGE

SQL was developed at the IBM San Jose research facilities in the 1970s. This language has gone through several versions; it was initially called SEQUEL, and it is still known by that name in some circles. SQL has been tested by

SID	Name	Major	Grade_level	Age	Classes		
100	JONES	HISTORY	GR	21	BD445		
150	PARKS	ACCOUNTING	SO	19	BA200		
200	BAKER	MATH	GR	50	BD445	CS250	
250	GLASS	HISTORY	SN	50	none		
300	BAKER	ACCOUNTING	SN	41	CS150		
350	RUSSELL	MATH	JR	20	none		
400	RYE	ACCOUNTING	FR	18	BA200	BF410	CS250
450	JONES	HISTORY	SN	24	BA200		

FIGURE K-4

Variable length table (not relation)

SID	Name	Major	Grade_level	Age
100	JONES	HISTORY	GR	21
150	PARKS	ACCOUNTING	SO	19
200	BAKER	MATH	GR	50
250	GLASS	HISTORY	SN	50
300	BAKER	ACCOUNTING	SN	41
350	RUSSELL	MATH	JR	20
400	RYE	ACCOUNTING	FR	18
450	JONES	HISTORY	SN	24

a. STUDENT Relation

Student_number	Class_name	Grade
100	BD445	A
150	BA200	A
200	BD445	B
200	CS250	A
300	CS150	A
400	BA200	B
400	BF410	A
400	CS250	B
450	BA200	C

b. ENROLLMENT Relation

FIGURE K-5

Student enrollment data as two relations

unsophisticated computer users and has been changed to simplify its structure and use. SQL is a language. There are several implementations of it. The IBM product SQL/DS (Structured Query Language/Data Store) is one implementation of it. The database management system ORACLE [130] is another. The query language used by MicroRIM's RBASE 4000 (a DBMS for micros) [124] is quite similar to SQL.

SQL processes tables. SQL statements take tables for input, transform those tables in accordance with the user's needs, and produce tables as output. In the examples that follow, every result will be a table.

SQL can be used in query/update mode, or SQL statements can be embedded in application programs. When SQL is used in query/update mode, the user types an SQL command via a CRT or other terminal, and the system responds by printing the table that has been generated. If the table is too large to fit on one screen, the first rows of the table are printed. Users can scroll forward to see the rest of the table. We will not consider SQL statements that are embedded in application programs in this book. See [132] for information about application program interfaces.

SQL has commands to define data structure, to query data, to change data, and to control concurrent processing. In this module, we will consider only the commands to query data. See [133] for more information on the other commands.

Querying a Single Table

First, we will consider SQL facilities for querying a single table. To follow custom, all SQL commands will be shown in capital letters. Also, at times, SQL expressions will be indented. This indentation is shown for clarity; in SQL, the position of expressions is arbitrary. Finally, to provide reference

PROFILE

New Class of Information Analysts Predicted

ANAHEIM, Calif.—Application development will likely disappear as a separate DP job category by the '90s, but for the time being, application programmers still have many more employment opportunities than their systems counterparts.

That was the conclusion reached by Gladys Brantley, Interfet Corp.'s vice-president and controller, who spoke at a recent National Computer Conference session dealing with "Career Development in the 1980s."

Brantley predicted the emergence of a new class of systems professionals, which she called information analysts.

Unlike systems employees with traditional programming/analysis backgrounds, information analysts will come primarily from the business rather than the technical ranks, although the majority will boast at least a smattering of formal DP training.

In the not-too-distant future, the advent of this new class of computing professionals will have profound consequences for the application programming job slot as it is traditionally defined, Brantley predicted.

By the '90s, the burden of developing new user software will be borne much more heavily by the emerging information analysts than by conventional application programmers, Brantley said.

One of the main roles of the information analysts will be to develop new applications by "cobbling together off-the-shelf software packages," Brantley predicted.

Because of the rise of the information analyst class, end users soon will no longer have a pressing need for today's typical application programmers, she said.

If application programming fails to vanish from the scene altogether, it will at least shrink substantially or evolve to become an increasingly design- and analysis-oriented function, according to Brantley.

By JEFFRY BEELER
Computerworld, May 30, 1983

numbers for text discussion, each SQL example will be numbered. These numbers are not part of SQL; they are inserted for discussion purposes.

Selecting Columns

Suppose we want to view only a few of the columns. Let's say we want to see only the student number (SID), the student name, and the student major. The following expression will generate an appropriate table:

1.
```
SELECT    SID, NAME, MAJOR
FROM      STUDENT
```

The keywords *SELECT* and *FROM* are always required. The columns to be obtained are listed after SELECT. The table to be used is listed after FROM. The result of this projection for the data in figure K-5*a* is:

```
100  JONES     HISTORY
150  PARKS     ACCOUNTING
200  BAKER     MATH
250  GLASS     HISTORY
300  BAKER     ACCOUNTING
350  RUSSELL   MATH
400  RYE       ACCOUNTING
450  JONES     HISTORY
```

A frustrated private airplane pilot, unable to reach the weather service because of busy phone lines, checks the aviation forecast in another city on his microcomputer. A would-be car buyer quickly retrieves electronically a list of all the magazine articles written about an unusual model. An investor who wants to analyze his stock portfolio but is unwilling to waste half a day poring over paperwork uses a special software package that pulls together all the information he needs on his home computer.

The owners of the almost 3 million personal computers in the U.S. are beginning to find a new solution to their information needs—access to data bases that only big companies could once afford. Without corporate resources, individuals must often take a trip to the library to do research. And even then they must usually settle for out-of-date printed information. But increasing numbers of personal computer owners—business professionals and consumers alike—are using a wide assortment of computerized data bases that are up to the minute, often open 24 hours a day, and as handy as their telephones.

Until now, the major players in this embryonic business have been Dow Jones News/Retrieval, H & R Block's CompuServe, and Source Telecomputing, a Reader's Digest subsidiary. New participants are entering the information market, however, and opening up vast sources of data—ranging from financial and investment news and statistics to magazine indexes of every stripe. And new computer programs on the market automatically organize incoming information just the way the user wants it—allowing computer users to do more with the data once they have obtained it.

Business Week, January 17, 1983

Consider a similar example:

2. SELECT   MAJOR
     FROM   STUDENT

The result of this operation is the following:

```
HISTORY
ACCOUNTING
MATH
HISTORY
ACCOUNTING
MATH
ACCOUNTING
HISTORY
```

As you can see, duplicate rows are printed. SQL does not eliminate duplicates. Such removal can be expensive and in many cases is not desired. If we want duplicate rows to be removed, then the qualifier *UNIQUE* must be specified, as follows:

3. SELECT   UNIQUE MAJOR
     FROM   STUDENT

PROFILE

The leading 'libraries' that a personal computer user can consult

Service	*Hookup cost, charges**	*Number of subscribers*	*Main services offered*	*Startup date*
Dow Jones News/Retrieval	$50, 10¢–$1.20/minute	60,000	Business and economic news, stock quotes, investment information	Nov. 1977
CompuServe Information Service	$20–$40 (depending on software package purchased), $5–$22.50/hour	36,000	Financial information, banking, games, shopping, weather, encyclopedia, newspapers, bulletin boards	July 1979
The Source	$100, $5.75–$29.75/hour	26,000	News and research tools, consumer tips, market quotes, travel, shopping, games, bulletin boards	June 1979
NewsNet	No hookup fee, $18–$24/hour, extra to read newsletters not already subscribed to, up to $96/hour	300	More than 80 newsletters covering many subjects	Apr. 1982
Dialog Information Services Inc.'s Knowledge Index	$35, $24/hour	NA	Descriptive indexes of articles, books, and reports; newspapers	Dec. 1982
DRI-VisiCorp	$250 for VisiLink software package; $10–$125 per data base	NA	58 updated data bases: economic forecasts, foreign exchange, individual industries	Jan. 1983
BRS/After Dark	$50, $6–$15/hour	NA	Abstracted indexes of articles, from science to education	Jan. 1983

*Hookup costs include differing amounts of free time and sometimes are waived in certain promotions. Charges vary according to time of day, data base used, and transmission speed

Data: BW NA = not available

The result of this operation is:

```
HISTORY
ACCOUNTING
MATH
```

Selecting Rows

Suppose we want to specify all of the columns but only for certain rows. Let's say we want to view all of the data for the math majors. The following statements will generate the desired table:

4.
```
SELECT      SID, NAME, MAJOR, GRADE_LEVEL, AGE
FROM        STUDENT
WHERE       MAJOR = 'MATH'
```

The SELECT expression specifies the names of all rows of the table. FROM specifies the table to be used, and the new expression, *WHERE*, provides the conditions for the selection. The format SELECT—FROM—WHERE is the fundamental structure of SQL commands.

```
200   BAKER      MATH     GR    50
350   RUSSELL    MATH     JR    20
```

We can combine the selection of columns and rows as follows:

5.
```
SELECT      NAME, AGE
FROM        STUDENT
WHERE       MAJOR = 'MATH'
```

The result is:

```
BAKER       50
RUSSELL     20
```

Also, several conditions can be expressed in a WHERE clause. For example, we can say:

6.
```
SELECT      NAME, AGE
FROM        STUDENT
WHERE       MAJOR = 'MATH'
        AND AGE > 21
```

The result is the following:

```
BAKER       50
```

The conditions in WHERE clauses can refer to a set of values. For this procedure, the keyword *IN* or *NOT IN* is used. Consider:

7.
```
SELECT      NAME
FROM        STUDENT
WHERE       MAJOR IN ['MATH', 'ACCOUNTING']
```

This expression means, "Present the names of students who have either a math or an accounting major." The result is:

```
PARKS
BAKER
BAKER
RUSSELL
RYE
```

Consider the expression:

8.
```
SELECT      NAME
FROM        STUDENT
WHERE       MAJOR NOT IN ['MATH', 'ACCOUNTING']
```

This expression will cause the names of students other than math or accounting majors to be presented. The result is:

```
JONES
GLASS
JONES
```

The expression *MAJOR IN* means that the value of the Major column can equal *any* of the listed majors. The expression *MAJOR NOT IN* means the value must be different from *all* of the listed majors.

SQL provides five built-in functions to facilitate query processing. They are: COUNT, SUM, AVG, MAX, and MIN. COUNT and SUM sound similar but are different. COUNT computes the number of rows in a table; SUM totals numeric columns. AVG, MAX, and MIN also operate on numeric columns. AVG computes the average value, and MAX and MIN obtain the maximum and minimum values of a column in a table.

Consider the query expression:

9. SELECT   COUNT(*)
    FROM   STUDENT

The number of STUDENT rows will be counted, and this total will be displayed in a table having a single row and single column, as follows:

8

Consider the expressions:

10. SELECT   COUNT(MAJOR)
    FROM   STUDENT

11. SELECT   COUNT(UNIQUE MAJOR)
    FROM   STUDENT

Expression 10 counts all majors, including duplicates. Expression 11 counts only unique majors. The results are:

10. 8

11. 3

The special functions can be used to request a result, as in the above examples. Further, in some versions of SQL, built-in functions can be used as part of a WHERE clause. Consider:

12. SELECT   SID, NAME
    FROM   STUDENT
    WHERE   AGE > AVG(AGE)

The result (the average age is 30.38) is:

```
200        BAKER
250        GLASS
300        BAKER
```

Built-in functions can appear in both SELECT and WHERE clauses:

13. SELECT   COUNT(*)
    FROM   STUDENT
    WHERE   AGE = MAX(AGE)

This operation produces the number of students having the maximum age. Because two rows have the age 50, the result is:

2

To increase the utility of built-in functions, these functions can be applied to groups of rows in a table. Such groups are formed by collecting rows together (logically, not physically) that have the same value in a specified column. For example, students can be grouped by major. This means that one group will be formed for each value of MAJOR. For the data in figure K-5, there will be a group of HISTORY majors, a group of ACCOUNTING majors, and a group of MATH majors.

The SQL keyword *GROUP BY* instructs the system to group rows together that have the same value in a column. Consider:

```
14. SELECT      MAJOR, COUNT(*)
    FROM        STUDENT
    GROUP BY    MAJOR
```

The result of this expression is:

```
HISTORY         3
ACCOUNTING      3
MATH            2
```

The rows of the STUDENT table have been logically grouped by the value of MAJOR. Then, the COUNT function sums the number of rows in each group. The result is a table having two columns, the major name and the count. Thus, for groups, both columns and built-in functions can be specified in the SELECT command.

In some cases, we do not want to consider all of the groups. For example, we might form groups of students having the same major and then wish to consider only those groups that have more than two students. In this case, we use the SQL *HAVING* clause to identify the subset of groups we want to consider.

Suppose we want to know the name and average age of students of all majors having more than two students. The following SQL statements will obtain this result:

```
15. SELECT      MAJOR, AVG(AGE)
    FROM        STUDENT
    GROUP BY    MAJOR
    HAVING      COUNT(*) > 2
```

Here, groups of students having the same major are formed. Then, groups having more than two students are selected. (Other groups are ignored.) The major and the average age of these selected groups are produced. The result is:

```
HISTORY         31.67
ACCOUNTING      26
```

For even greater generality, WHERE clauses can be added as well. Consider the following:

```
16. SELECT      MAJOR, AVG(AGE)
    FROM        STUDENT
```

```
WHERE      GRADE_LEVEL = 'SN'
GROUP BY   MAJOR
HAVING     COUNT(*) > 1
```

The result of this operation will vary depending on whether the WHERE condition is applied before or after the HAVING condition. To eliminate ambiguity, the SQL convention is that WHERE clauses are applied first. Thus, in the above operation, senior students are selected. Then groups are formed, then the groups are selected by the HAVING condition, and then the result is presented. In this case, the result is:

```
HISTORY        37
```

Querying Multiple Tables

In this section, we will extend the discussion of SQL to include operations on two or more tables. The STUDENT and ENROLLMENT data in figure K-5 will be used to illustrate SQL features.

Joining Tables

Examine the data in figure K-5. Suppose someone asked you to produce (by hand) a table having the following rows: student name, class name, and grade. Do you see a problem? Student name is stored in the STUDENT table whereas class name and grade are stored in the ENROLLMENT table. How would you proceed?

Chances are you would look at the first row of STUDENT, obtain the student number (100 in this case), and see if there are any rows in ENROLLMENT for student 100. For the data in figure K-5, the first row of ENROLLMENT is a class taken by student 100. At this point, you would probably write the name of student 100 from STUDENT, and the name of the class and the grade from the first row of ENROLLMENT as the first row in your table. You would proceed similarly for the other rows in STUDENT. As you proceed in this way, you are joining data in STUDENT together with data in ENROLLMENT such that the SID in STUDENT equals the STUDENT_NUMBER in ENROLLMENT.

Joining Tables with SQL

SQL has language to join tables together in this way. The following SQL statements will present student name, class name, and grade of all students:

```
17. SELECT   NAME, CLASS_NAME, GRADE
    FROM     STUDENT, ENROLLMENT
    WHERE    STUDENT.SID = ENROLLMENT.STUDENT_NUMBER
```

The WHERE clause of this statement ensures that only matching rows are joined.

The other SQL facilities can be added to this structure. For example, the following statements present this data for MATH majors:

```
18. SELECT       NAME, CLASS_NAME, GRADE
    FROM         STUDENT, ENROLLMENT
    WHERE        STUDENT.SID = ENROLLMENT.STUDENT_NUMBER
         AND     STUDENT.MAJOR = 'MATH'
```

SQL Summary

In this section, we have presented a short overview of SQL facilities. With just this knowledge, however, you can express a wide variety of queries. If you wish to know more about SQL, consult [132] or [133].

THE APPLICATION OF NONPROCEDURAL PROGRAMMING

Nonprocedural languages have not yet seen widespread acceptance. In fact, there is some evidence to indicate that nonprocedural programming has been better received by end users than by computer professionals [24]. This situation is likely to change in the future for reasons of economics. Like database processing, nonprocedural languages enable humans to be more efficient at the same time that they make computers less efficient. Because the cost of humans is likely to continue to increase in the future, while the cost of hardware is likely to continue to decrease, nonprocedural languages will probably see more and more use.

Impact on Systems Development

Consider the impact of nonprocedural programming on systems development. Assume that it is true that nonprocedural languages provide productivity improvements in the neighborhood of 100 to 1. What does this fact mean? First, program maintenance will be cheaper and easier. For example, when users want a change to a report format, the change can be implemented quickly. Furthermore, because program maintenance is easier, the cost of a mistake in design is less. Using a procedural language, we must be extremely careful during design. Measure twice and cut once is one byword. With nonprocedural languages, mistakes *regarding programs* are easier to correct.

(Do not be misled by this statement, however. Even with nonprocedural languages, data and procedure design are still critical. Mistakes regarding which data to collect or which actions people should take will be no easier to fix with nonprocedural languages than with procedural languages. Only programming mistakes will be easier to correct.)

In addition to shortening design and programming, nonprocedural languages can also shorten and improve the quality of requirements definition. With database management and nonprocedural languages, it becomes possible to build *prototype systems*. A prototype is a test system; it is an experimental system not intended to be the operational system. Using prototype methodology, the systems development personnel interview users and then build the sample, or prototype, system. The users test the prototype and determine how well it meets their needs. The systems development personnel can then adjust the prototype system (quickly, using nonprocedural programming) until the users are satisfied. The prototype then becomes a statement of requirements.

Prototype systems are much easier for users to evaluate than traditional statements of requirements. Many users do not understand written requirements statements. Using the analogy of custom clothing mentioned in chapter 4, having users evaluate traditional requirements statements is like having the buyer of a suit evaluate a garment pattern. The pattern of the shoulder section of a suit has a strange shape. Most of us would not know from this shape how well the suit will fit our shoulder. Users of information systems feel similarly when evaluating requirements documents.

If nonprocedural languages can shorten the programming, design, and requirements stages of systems development, they will appreciably shorten the entire systems development process. In this case, systems will be more easily and readily developed. This improvement will be a great relief to management, and data processing personnel will have a response to management's anguished cry, Why does systems development take so long?

End User Programming

Because of the simplicity of nonprocedural languages, some users have found it possible to do their own programming. Generally, this programming involves query and reporting tasks. For example, users may write SQL statements to obtain new information from a relational database. When it is possible, end user programming greatly reduces the frustrations of users. End users feel that they are able to help themselves, in contrast to the sometimes frustrating process of submitting a change request to data processing and waiting weeks or months for that request to be fulfilled.

Although end user programming has great potential, it must be carefully managed. End users should not expect to do all programming for themselves. Certain programming tasks are so important or critical that they should be left to professionals. Again using the custom-clothing analogy, some clothes can be appropriately constructed at home. Others, such as an astronaut's suit, should be left to professionals.

For example, it is unlikely that end users would be able to program a new online transaction processing system such as that used by airlines. The difficulty of the programming and the need for high performance dictate that the programming be professional. In fact, most experts agree that end users ought not to program systems that change public data (data needed by more than one user). Users can write their own programs to read public or private data, or write their own programs to change their own private data (assuming they are willing to accept the consequences of their mistakes). Writing programs to change public data ought to be left to professionals, however.

QUESTIONS

K.1 Describe the difference between procedural and nonprocedural programming. How do the two approaches differ in the way they achieve desired results?

K.2 Give an example of a relational *table, row*, and *column*.

K.3 Give an example of a table that has repeating entries in a column. Decompose this table into two tables that have no such repeating entries.

K.4 Explain the difference between SQL and SQL/DS.

Questions K.5 through K.7 concern the following relation:

```
CLASS (CLASS_NAME, ROOM, TIME, NUMBER_STUDENTS)
```

K.5 Give example data for the relation CLASS. Use class names that occur in figure K-5.

K.6 Show SQL statements to answer the following queries:

    a. List the names of all classes and the number of students enrolled in each.

    b. List the names of all classes that meet in room SC213.

    c. List the names of all classes that meet in either room SC213 or SC104.

    d. List each room and give the number of classes that meet in that room.

    e. List each room and compute the average number of students attending class in that room.

    f. List each room and give the number of classes that meet in that room. List only rooms that have an average number of students greater than 15.

K.7 Assume a database contains relations STUDENT and ENROLLMENT from figure K-5, as well as relation CLASS. Show SQL statements to answer the following queries:

    a. List the class name, grade, and room number of every class for which a student has enrolled.

    b. List the class names and times for all classes taken by student 100.

    c. List the student number, class name, and time for all classes in room SC213.

    d. Print the class name and room for all math students. (Hint: You must join all three relations to answer this query.)

K.8 What impact does nonprocedural programming have on the programming activity of a systems development project?

K.9 Describe the impact of nonprocedural programming on the design step of systems development. Which design activities will be easier? Which will be no different?

K.10 Define prototyping. What is the role of prototyping in systems development?

K.11 What kinds of applications are appropriate for end user programming? What kinds of applications are inappropriate?

SUMMARY

Nonprocedural languages enable programmers to be considerably more productive. Using a nonprocedural language, a programmer describes *what* is wanted instead of *how* to obtain the desired result. There are several nonprocedural languages. FOCUS, NOMAD, RAMIS, and SQL are examples.

Most nonprocedural languages require that data be stored in a relational database. Relational data is represented as tables. Each row of a table represents an object; each column represents a property of an object. Relational tables (or relations) may not have multiple entries in a column.

Structured Query Language (SQL) is a nonprocedural language. The basic format of SQL statements is SELECT—FROM—WHERE. Built-in functions, as well as GROUP BY and HAVING keywords, can also be used. When data is needed from more than one table, the tables must be joined.

Nonprocedural programming promises to shorten programming, design, and requirements phases of systems development. Nonprocedural programming facilitates prototyping. End user programming of some applications becomes feasible with nonprocedural programming.

Nonprocedural language
Relational database management
Tables
Rows
Columns
Structured Query Language (SQL)
SELECT
FROM
WHERE
COUNT

SUM
AVG
MAX
MIN
GROUP BY
HAVING
Table joining
Prototype systems
End user programming

QUESTIONS TO CHALLENGE YOUR THINKING

A. Locate a company that is using a nonprocedural language. How happy are they with it? Have they found productivity improvements? Have they encountered any special problems? Who uses the language? Do they allow end user programming? If so, how has it worked out?

B. Obtain documentation on FOCUS, NOMAD, MANTIS, or another nonprocedural language. Compare that language to SQL. Answer queries 1 through 18 using the language you have found.

MODULE L

Popular Applications Software

ELECTRONIC SPREADSHEETS

WORD PROCESSING

SPELLING CHECKERS

SYSTEM SOFTWARE

The microcomputer revolution has changed the way that people think about the power of computers. As the price of computer hardware falls, more applications are cost effective to run on computers. More software becomes available, and the software is easier to use. It has reached the point that many people cannot do their jobs without computers.

In the programming modules, we have concentrated our efforts on writing BASIC programs. However, most people don't have the time or inclination to write BASIC programs. What most people want from computers is the ability to perform specific tasks such as word processing, keeping accounts receivable, or forecasting sales. These types of jobs can be done with programs that are readily available for purchase. Most software packages available for microcomputers are very reasonably priced, particularly when compared to the cost of the labor required to write the software from scratch.

The software covered in this module is available for almost any manufacturer's hardware. The concepts covered will remain the same from one software company's package to another company's package. The ideas behind these software packages were thought up by people like you, who not too many years ago had simply seen what computers could do, and then created an idea to use the computer's capabilities.

The software covered will include electronic spreadsheets, word processing, spelling checkers, and the supporting system software. Throughout this module, no endorsement is implied for any product.

ELECTRONIC SPREADSHEETS

The scratch pad is one of the best tools to aid in thinking. Ideas can be jotted down, discussed, mulled over, thought about, rearranged, and worked with until the finished idea is in just the right form. Then a final finished copy can be produced to serve as a working copy and permanent record of the idea.

The electronic spreadsheet works in much the same fashion as a scratch pad. Ideas can be recorded and manipulated on a terminal, using the computer keyboard as the pencil. Any type of data can be manipulated by an electronic spreadsheet.

VISICALC (a registered trademark of Software Arts, Inc.) is a popular spreadsheet software package. An electronic spreadsheet is a large table containing some number of rows and columns. A VISICALC spreadsheet may be up to 63 columns wide and up to 254 rows long. These columns and rows can be used in any way we want to use them. Possible uses include descriptions, fixed amounts, and calculations based on the amounts that reside in other locations in the table.

Budgeting considerations are a good application to run using an electronic spreadsheet. If a budget is calculated manually, the numbers for the respective months and categories are spread out on a large accounting worksheet. The numbers are added up in various fashions to show what income is needed or what expenses should be cut.

Assume that we are running a small preschool and need to make up a budget for the school year. The income is provided by tuition, and there are a limited amount of expenses. The budget may look something like this:

Income
Interest	13.74
Tuition	9042.60

Expenses
Salaries	4588.48
Tax Deposits	1194.74
Unemployment	266.77
Bonuses	200.00
Janitor	159.76
Advertising	26.66
Misc.	459.42
Equipment	0.00
Utilities	182.45

You have probably prepared a similar budget for your own home at one time or another. Budgets always provide a forum for questions. For example, is the income going to be sufficient to cover expenses? What will happen if the utility bills significantly increase? How will the income be affected if three students are added or if two students are lost?

To answer such questions, perhaps it is best to look at what will happen on a month-by-month basis. If we were to write these figures out on paper it could be done as follows:

	Jan	Feb	Mar	. . .	Dec	YEAR
INCOME						
Interest						
Tuition						
EXPENSES						
.						
.						
TOTAL INCOME						
TOTAL EXPENSE						
INCOME – EXPENSE						
CUMULATIVE TOTAL						

As experimentation is done by changing various figures, the budget must be refigured by hand. It may take many attempts to arrive at a workable budget. All of this work can be extremely time consuming if done by hand. These are exactly the type of calculations handled by VISICALC.

Notice that the budget for the preschool needs 18 rows for the different categories and 14 columns to hold the descriptions, monthly totals, and yearly total.

Let's solve this problem using VISICALC. Turn the computer on, just as we have done to write our BASIC programs. Insert the VISICALC diskette and start the system. The VISICALC program will be loaded into the computer's memory. It is a large program, and it takes about 30 seconds to load. There will be a message asking you to wait. When the program is loaded (the diskette drive stops working), depress the ENTER key, and you are ready to use the VISICALC program.

First, we must enter the preschool budget into the table represented by the spreadsheet. Note that the rows and columns are labeled. The rows are labeled with numbers, and the columns are labeled with letters. The program will refer to only one position on the spreadsheet at a time, represented by the cursor. The first line of the display always indicates the current position of the cursor. The cursor is moved by using the arrow keys to move the cursor one position in the direction of the arrow. The command > can be used to go to a specific location. To go to location B6, you would key >B6. The spreadsheet looks like figure L-1.

We must key in the description fields down the left side of the spreadsheet, starting with row 2. All of the descriptions will be in column A. All of the month names will be in row 1, columns B through N. You can correct typing mistakes by using the backspace key.

The word INCOME is entered in position A2, Interest in A3, Tuition in A4, and so forth, until all of the categories have been entered. Using the arrow keys to position the cursor at B1, the month name Jan could be entered in B1, Feb in B2, and so forth, until the word YEAR is entered in N1. After all of the headings are typed in, our spreadsheet should look like figure L-2.

Note that all of the description that was keyed was not displayed. The display was truncated after showing the first few positions. The VISICALC default is to display 7 characters, including a leading space. Each entry will be retained

FIGURE L-1

The initial spreadsheet display

	A	B	C	D	E	F	G	H	I	J
1		Januar	Februa	March	April	May	June	July	August	Septem
2	INCOME									
3	Intere									
4	Tuitio									
5										
6	EXPENS									
7	Salari									
8	Tax De									
9	Unempl									
10	Bonuse									
11	Janito									
12	Advert									
13	Misc.									
14	Equipm									
15	Utilit									
16	TOTAL									
17	TOTAL									
18	NET IN									
19	CUMULA									
20										
21										

FIGURE L-2

Headings entered in spreadsheet

in its entirety (up to the maximum of 125 characters) although the entire field may not display. We can instruct VISICALC to display more of the description by making the column wider. This is done with the /GC command. If /GC20 is typed in, the column width is changed from the default of 7 characters to 20. This is enough to display any description that we have keyed. The spreadsheet would now look like figure L-3.

The budget data could now be entered for each category. We can enter the monthly figures in the January column, and we can use the power of VISICALC to copy these numbers to the other columns.

Remembering that the > command is an easy way to get around in VISICALC, we can use it to position the cursor at the first location where we want to key in monthly budget figures. In this case, the first January figure belongs at B3. Typing >B3 followed by the ENTER key, we position the cursor at B3. The interest for January can be keyed (1.15). Moving the cursor down one position allows us to type in the January tuition (753.55). Continuing in this fashion, we key all the data for January.

The total income for January is the sum of the interest and the tuition. This can be keyed into the spreadsheet by keying

    +B3+B4

The leading + sign tells VISICALC that the entry is a calculation. If this is entered in location B16, the required sum will be calculated by the spreadsheet.

	A	B	C	D
1		January	February	March
2	INCOME			
3	Interest			
4	Tuition			
5				
6	EXPENSES			
7	Salaries			
8	Tax Deposits			
9	Unemployment			
10	Bonuses			
11	Janitor			
12	Advertising			
13	Misc.			
14	Equipment			
15	Utilities			
16	TOTAL INCOME			
17	TOTAL EXPENSE			
18	NET INCOME			
19	CUMULATIVE TOTAL			
20				
21				

FIGURE L-3

Spreadsheet display after increasing
column width

To add the expenses, the locations B7 through B15 must be added. This could be entered as shown above, but VISICALC provides a shortcut. After positioning the cursor at location B17, the statement

```
@SUM(B7.B15)
```

could be keyed. This statement instructs VISICALC to add the values found in the locations named.

The entry in B17 will then be calculated as the sum of B7 through B15. The entry for B18 is +B16−B17. The entry that reflects the cumulative total is the same as B18, so in B19 we may key +B18. The column for January is now complete.

To complete the column for February, we do not have to go through all the steps that we did for January. We know that the entries are the same, and VISICALC has a feature that allows you to replicate any sequence of entries. To replicate column B, key in

```
/R
```

followed by the ENTER key. You will then see a prompt at the top of the screen that says

```
Replicate: Source Range or Enter
```

VISICALC is asking us what we wish to copy. We are interested in copying column B from row 2 through 15. Type in

```
B2.B15
```

followed by the ENTER key. VISICALC will respond with

```
Replicate: Target Range
```

Respond with the columns that you want to duplicate. Remember that you are trying to copy the January column into the February through December columns. The command is

```
C2.M2
```

followed by the ENTER key. The letter C corresponds to the February column, and the letter M corresponds to the December column. VISICALC will copy all corresponding columns, and will give you the opportunity to change those columns where a formula was used. As VISICALC reaches a formula, you will be given the opportunity to copy the formula exactly, or to change the formula to make it work for this particular column. A change for the new column is made relative to the new position. For example, when the program reaches position B16, the following message will be displayed.

```
B16:  +B2+B3
Replicate: N=No Change R=Relative
```

Your response should be either N or R. A response of N duplicates the formula exactly. A response of R would cause the formula to be duplicated as +C2+C3 in column C and +D2+D3 in column D, and so forth.

We have now filled in all of the columns of the spreadsheet except for column N, the year-to-date totals. After positioning the cursor to position N2, we can sum up the values contained in row 2 by using the command @SUM(B2.M2).

This formula needs to be replicated down column N. The source range is N2.N2, and the target range is N3.N19. The formula must be relative to its position. This will fill the last column.

The cumulative totals in the final row must now be filled in. The entry at C19 should be +B19+C18. This formula says to take the previous cumulative total and add the month's total. The result is placed in the cumulative total. This formula can be replicated in a relative fashion, as were the month columns or the year-to-date rows.

Saving and loading of VISICALC files are done with the commands /SS to save and /SL to retrieve the file from diskettes. The command to save the preschool budget is

```
/SS BUDGET
```

Entries may be modified in the budget, and the formula entries will be recalculated to reflect the correct totals.

VISICALC has many more features, which include the ability to print what has been entered. In addition, some companies have done the necessary steps to set up the contents of the VISICALC table. These products are called overlays for VISICALC. For example, overlays can be purchased that reflect current government tax forms. The limitations for the use of VISICALC are bounded only by your imagination.

Other products that perform the same type of tasks include Multi-Plan, SuperCalc, and Lotus 1-2-3.

WORD PROCESSING

Another popular application for commercial software on microcomputers is word processing. Word processing is the ability to key and manipulate text data. Word processors function much like a typewriter, but they have the added feature of extremely easy error correction and text movement. Word processors retrieve, display, edit, print, and store text information.

Microcomputers function similarly to a typewriter when used for word processing. As text is typed, it appears on the CRT display. You are accustomed to seeing text displayed while you type your programs. The power of the word processor is not easily seen when text is being entered. The real power is seen when editing takes place.

The editing functions provided by a word processor include the deletion or insertion of characters, words, or paragraphs. These commands are executed by pushing a program function key, or a combination of keys. Of course, the software package being used makes a difference in how the program functions. A popular word processing program is WordStar (distributed by MicroPro International Corporation).

WordStar is driven by a menu system. The program is loaded by the system or by keying of the program name, WS. When the program is loaded, the No-file or Opening menu will be displayed. The Opening menu provides commands to communicate with the system. Options are available to list data files that are on diskette, and the ability is also provided on this menu to print, rename, copy, or delete a file.

Options are also provided on the Opening menu that allow you to run other programs, return control to the system, or to run additional support such as spelling checkers or mailing-preparation programs.

Reading the menu carefully will provide you with the ability to do any of the functions listed on the menus. In WordStar, selecting the option that allows us to create a file takes us to the main menu.

The main menu provides the editing functions needed while using the word processor. Cursor movement on the screen can be controlled in any direction, as can screen scrolling. *Scrolling* is the up or down movement of the text that appears on the screen. Additional menus that provide printing capabilities, more powerful but less commonly used editing functions, and control of the on-screen editing capabilities are commonly provided.

While you are editing, the CRT serves as a window into the entire text. The text can become extremely large, and you may view any portion at any time. Commands can be inserted into the text to provide certain characteristics at the time the text is printed. For example, these characteristics could include underlining, centering, and pagination.

Typewriters are likely to become obsolete as word processors become more powerful and less expensive. This entire book was prepared using word processing. Other products that do word processing include EDIX/WORDIX and Multi-Mate.

SPELLING CHECKERS

In conjunction with word processors, there are software packages that can check the spelling of words contained in edited files. The programs that check spelling are simple in concept and easy to run. Typically the program is loaded by program name, or as a selection from a word processing menu.

The spelling checker scans a word processing file, notes all occurrences of a word, and then checks the spellings of the words in the word processing file against a dictionary. The dictionary is usually supplied with the spelling checker. Thirty to forty thousand words are contained in the typical vendor-supplied dictionary. As could be expected, however, all the words that are used in your particular environment may not be contained in the vendor-supplied dictionary. For example, a doctor, architect, or musician will have a vocabulary unique to the particular profession. Most spelling checkers provide the option to build an auxiliary dictionary of words. Whenever the spelling checker is run, the standard dictionary and the auxiliary dictionary are checked.

Once the file has been checked, the misspelled or bad words can be displayed. Many spelling checkers provide additional capabilities at this point. You may have the choice of interactively correcting words in the word processing file. Another choice may be to mark the misspelled words in the word processing file with a special character, so that it is easy to locate them in a later word processing session. New words that were reported as bad, that are in fact not bad, can be added to the auxiliary dictionary during this process.

SYSTEM SOFTWARE

Some of the advances in system software for microcomputers in the past few years have been astounding. Supporting all of the application software that you have been using is the system software.

There are two very popular operating systems in widespread use on micros. They are DOS and CP/M. These programs provide a relatively simple and straightforward operating system for the microcomputer. The essential functions needed to control physical devices and to support disk files are contained in the software.

The CP/M operating system is divided into three parts: the console command processor (CCP), the basic disk operating system (BDOS), and the basic input/output system (BIOS). The CCP reads commands from the operator's console. Built-in commands are processed internally by the CCP. For commands that cannot be processed internally, the CCP loads the appropriate transient application programs. An example of a command that would not be processed internally is a file copy. The BDOS supervises the internal activities of the operating system. The BIOS module executes all I/O operations for the CCP and the BDOS modules. All of this happens behind the scenes, and the end user need not even consider the implications.

Perhaps the most significant aspect of CP/M is that the system provides a universal run-time environment for applications software. A first-time user may select the new system according to its hardware capabilities and obtain programs to suit his needs from third-party vendors. Broadening the choice of software packages clearly benefits the computer user. The same statements apply to DOS.

Also available are packages to provide database support. These packages provide a standard interface to files that can be easily used by programs. Many of these software packages provide the ability to inquire against data files without writing programs. Some packages are available that allow word processing files to be treated as data files. Integrating all of the data on a microcomputer by using database technologies will change our view of micro-computers even more in the next few years. Products for database processing include dBase II, MicroRim's Rbase, and BPI's Information Management.

Other packages are available that provide the ability to build and manage display screens. In the past when software has been written, building the image that is seen on the screen required a major effort. The new software packages that aid in screen generation will decrease new application development time even more.

Software development will continue to change radically in an attempt to catch up with the rapidly changing hardware technologies. Microcomputers were introduced in the early 1970s and have revolutionized the way computers are used.

Computers shall continue to become more user friendly. End users will be able to develop their own software easily by using new development tools. You can be assured also that hardware development will not slow down.

QUESTIONS

L.1 Prepare the preschool budget outlined in the text.

L.2 Prepare your own budget using a spreadsheet.

L.3 What is an electronic spreadsheet?

L.4 Think of three uses for an electronic spreadsheet.

L.5 Explain why word processing is beneficial.

L.6 Write a letter to your family using a word processing program.

L.7 What is the purpose of the auxiliary dictionary in a spelling checker?

SUMMARY

Electronic spreadsheets can be regarded as a replacement for a scratch pad. They are organized in rows and columns that can process data as entered by the user, and can manipulate the data under user command.

Word processors provide the capability of manipulating text. Retrieving, displaying, editing, printing, and storing text is handled by the word processing software. Generation of error-free documents is made much easier. The functions performed are similar to those of a typewriter, with electronic cut-and-paste added.

Spelling checkers can scan files, comparing the words contained in the file to a known dictionary. Errors are reported and correction is often allowed.

The system software provided for microcomputers is changing rapidly. The operating systems DOS and CP/M have had many development tools written to support application development using these systems. The new technologies include database support, screen generation, and integration of all data process-ing activity.

Spreadsheet
Word processing
Scrolling

Spelling checker
System software
Database software

APPENDIX 1

Answers to Selected Questions

F.1 Beginners's All-purpose Symbolic Instruction Code.

F.2 A set of instructions written for a computer.

F.3 Source code is the statements that a programmer writes in some computer language such as BASIC. Object code is the translated instructions that the computer system can execute.

F.4 Programs are translated by either an interpreter or a compiler. An interpreter looks at a source statement, determines what needs to be done by the computer, and constructs the machine-executable instructions needed. Then the computer executes them. Thus each line of a program is translated on a one-at-a-time basis. A compiler translates all of the statements at one time, producing an object code module. Interpreted code has syntax checking done at entry time. Compiled code does not have to be translated every time the program is run.

F.5 Examples:
  a. Input devices—CRT, diskette drive, card reader, hard disk drive, tape drive
  b. Output devices—printer, diskette, tape drive, or hard disk drive, CRT
  c. Secondary-storage devices—diskette drive, tape drive, hard disk drive

F.6 The marker used on a CRT to show the current or active typing position. It is typically shown with a box or underline.

F.7 It directs the computer to print out what is named.

F.8 Type the line number with the new BASIC statement.

F.9 Type the line number of the statement to be deleted, with nothing following the number.

F.10 Use a PRINT statement with no items to print.

F.11 Any valid alphabetic, numeric, or alphanumeric data.

F.12 Commas force the PRINT statement to use the tab stops that are located at column 1, 16, 31, ... This function is very similar to the tab on a typewriter.

F.13 Semicolons instruct the computer to print immediately without spacing.

F.14 This allows for the printing of a sign. If the number is positive, the plus sign doesn't print. If the number is negative, then there would be room for the minus sign.

F.15 The INPUT statement allows the user to enter data while the program is executing.

F.16 Any programs, no matter how simple, can possibly have errors.

MODULE H

H.1 A named location used by the computer. It can change as the program executes.

H.2 Numeric variables are named by using one letter from the alphabet (A through Z) or by using one letter from the alphabet followed by a single digit (0 through 9). Alphanumeric (string) variables are named by using one letter from the alphabet followed by the character "$".

H.3 Alphabetic (A-Z), numeric (0-9), or a special character.

H.4 A collection of alphanumeric characters.

H.5 An operator is a symbol that represents an operation (a function to be performed).

H.6 The order of operations: see figure H-1.

H.7 It provides the ability to use again data that has been destroyed in calculations within the program.

H.13 The work area can be regarded as the scratch pad where all system commands have their effect. Secondary storage is where a BASIC source program can be kept on a long-term basis. Programs can be SAVEd from the work area to secondary storage and LOADed to the work area from secondary storage.

H.14 System commands direct the computer system to perform a particular task. For example, listing of a program in the work area is done by using the system command LIST.

H.15 NEW and RUN.

H.16 SAVE and LOAD.

H.17 Depends on system.

H.22 It allows decisions to be made about program execution at runtime.

H.23 Logic of the IF-THEN statement: see figure H-7.

H.24 The GOTO statement allows for unconditional transfer. This allows modification of program execution.

H.25 A change in the order of program execution. Also known as a transfer of control.

H.26 Logic of the IF-THEN-ELSE-ENDIF "statement": see figure H-8.

H.27 IF statements.

H.34 The FOR-NEXT.

H.35 Format of the FOR-NEXT statement:

nnnnn   FOR loop variable = start value TO end value STEP amount
            body of loop
            NEXT loop variable

H.36 Because the test in the logic of the loop occurs before any other part of the loop.

H.37 Because the test is made last in the logic of the loop.

H.42 A variable that consists of a letter and number within parentheses and that references a particular storage location.

H.43 A collection of similar data elements that can be referenced easily by their name.

H.44 An element of an array is a single data value out of an array.

H.45 It defines the number of elements in an array.

H.46 A special kind of an array that has two dimensions. It often keeps data that is related in two ways.

H.48 GOSUB and RETURN.

H.49 Steps needed to print a heading:
   a. increment the page counter,
   b. build any needed information for the heading,
   c. print the needed heading lines,
   d. reset the line counter.

H.50 Functions return only a single value, and functions are named.

H.51 Defines the operations to be performed by a function statement while naming the function.

H.52 A collection of support functions/programs, usually supplied by the vendor.

H.53 A library function is a routine that produces a certain result. Examples include random-number generation, trigonometric functions, and square roots.

H.59 A file is a collection of records. A record is a collection of fields. A field is a collection of characters.

H.60 To signal to the system that the file is being used.

H.61 Random and sequential.

H.62 A unique identifier of a record.

H.63 A program that is usually vendor supplied and does some task (such as copying a file).

MODULE L

L.3 An electronic spreadsheet is a scratch pad that is divided into rows and columns. This scratch pad can be used to manipulate data using formulas involving other locations in the spreadsheet.

APPENDIX 2

ASCII Character Codes

ASCII Code	Character	ASCII Code	Character	ASCII Code	Character	ASCII Code	Character
000	NUL	030	RS	060	<	099	c
001	SOH	031	US	061	=	100	d
002	STX	032	SPACE	062	>	101	e
003	ETX	033	!	063	?	102	f
004	EOT	034	"	064	@	103	g
005	ENQ	035	#	065	A	104	h
006	ACK	036	$	066	B	105	i
007	BEL	037	%	067	C	106	j
008	BS	038	&	068	D	107	k
009	HT	039	'	069	E	108	l
010	LF	040	(	070	F	109	m
011	VT	041	)	071	G	110	n
012	FF	042	*	072	H	111	o
013	CR	043	+	073	I	112	p
014	SO	044	,	074	J	113	q
015	SI	045	–	075	K	114	r
016	DLE	046	.	076	L	115	s
017	DC1	047	/	086	V	116	t
018	DC2	048	0	087	W	117	u
019	DC3	049	1	088	X	118	v
020	DC4	050	2	089	Y	119	w
021	NAK	051	3	090	Z	120	x
022	SYN	052	4	091	[	121	y
023	ETB	053	5	092	\	122	z
024	CAN	054	6	093	]	123	{
025	EM	055	7	094	^	124	|
026	SUB	056	8	095	<	125	
027	ESCAPE	057	9	096	'	126	}
028	FS	058	:	097	a	127	DEL
029	GS	059	;	098	b		

ASCII codes are in decimal notation
LF=Line Feed, FF=Form Feed, CR=Carriage Return, DEL=Rubout

APPENDIX 3

Comparison of Micro BASICs

SYSTEM COMMANDS/EDITING

Description of Command	APPLE II Applesoft (disk)	PET (cassette)	TRS-80 Model III d = disk c = cassette	HP-2000	Atari 400/800	MicroSoft (IBM, MS-DOS, CP/M)
Loads a program	LOAD NAME	LOAD "NAME"	dLOAD "NAME" cCLOAD "N" a one letter name	GET-NAME	dLOAD "D:NAME" cCLOAD	LOAD "NAME"
Saves a program	SAVE NAME	SAVE "NAME"	dSAVE "NAME" cSAVE "N"	SAVE	dSAVE "D:NAME" cCSAVE "N"	SAVE "NAME"
Names a program	Automatic. Done when saving program	Automatic. Done when saving program	Automatic. Done when saving program	NAME-NAME	Automatic. Done when saving program	✔
Executes the current program	RUN	✔	✔	✔	✔	✔
Loads and executes a program	RUN NAME	Shifted RUN STOP (key). Loads and executes next program	dRUN "NAME"	EXE-NAME	dRUN "D:NAME"	RUN "NAME"
Executes current program starting at line 500	RUN 500	✔	✔	RUN-500	GO TO 500	✔
Halts a program or listing	Control C (2 keys)	Stop (key)	Break (key)	Break (key)	Break (key) or Ctrl 1 (2 keys)	✔
Continues program execution halted by the previous command or key(s)	CONT	✔	✔	na	Ctrl 1 (2 keys)	✔
Deletes current program in memory. (Sets all variables to zero and strings to null)★	NEW ★	✔ ★	✔ ★	SCR	✔ ★	✔ ★
Checks for recording errors after a program is saved.	na	VERIFY "NAME"	cCLOAD? "N"	na	na	CLOAD "N"
To place multiple statements on a line	:	✔	✔	na	✔	✔
Lists the entire program	LIST	✔	✔	✔	✔	✔

Description of Command	APPLE II Applesoft (disk)	PET (cassette)	TRS-80 Model III d = disk c = cassette		Atari 400/800	Microsoft (IBM, MS-DOS, CP/M)
LISTS program lines from line X to line Y	LIST X-Y	✔	✔	LIST-X,Y	LIST X,Y	✔
Display program line X (used for editing)	LIST X	LIST X	EDIT X	LIST-X,Y	✔	✔
Deletes program lines from line X to line Y	DEL X,Y	na	DELETE X-Y	DEL-X,Y	na	DELETE X-Y
Deletes the whole (specified) program from the storage device	DELETE NAME	record over old program	[d]KILL NAME [c]record over old program	PUR-NAME	[c]record over old program	KILL "NAME"
Clears the screen and puts cursor at top left	HOME	CLR (key)	CLS	Shift Clear (2 keys)	Shift Clear (2 keys)	HOME
Resets all variables to zero	CLEAR	CLR (key)	CLEAR	na	CLR	CLEAR
Returns amount of memory still available to use	FRE (0)	FRE (0)	PRINT MEM	na	PRINT FRE (0)	FRE (0)
Deletes one character line being typed and moves cursor one space to left	—	DEL (key)	—	Ctrl H (2 keys)	Delete Back S (key)	DEL (key)
Cancels line currently being typed	Control X (2 keys)	go to next line; type previous line number and press RETURN key	Shift—will restart current line, or use Break (key)	Control X (2 keys)	Shift Delete (2 keys)	Control U

BASIC STATEMENTS

Description of Command	APPLE II Applesoft (disk)	PET (cassette)	TRS-80 Model III d = disk c = cassette		Atari 400/800	Microsoft (IBM, MS-DOS, CP/M)
For writing program comments (ignored by computer)	REM	✔	✔	✔	✔	✔
For writing on line comments	:REM	✔	:REM OR:'	na	✔	:REM OR :
Assigns the value of Y to the variable X	X = Y	✔	✔	✔	✔	✔
Puts a ? on the screen and waits for the user to type a string value for A$	INPUT A$	✔	✔	✔	✔	✔
Establishes a list of data elements that can be used by READ statements	DATA 5, "Y", 12	✔	✔	✔	✔	✔
Assigns the next data element to A$	READ A$	✔	✔	✔	✔	✔
Starts READing from first data element again	RESTORE	✔	✔	✔	✔	✔
Prints string X = and then the value of the variable X	PRINT "X" = "; X (or ? means PRINT)	✔ (or ? means PRINT)	✔ (or ? means PRINT)	✔	✔	✔
Concentrates printed items (allows no space between strings)★	: no space after numbers and ★	✔ one space after numbers and ★	✔ one space after number and ★	★	✔	✔ one space after number and ★
Separates items into Tab fields	, 3 Tab fields of 16,16,8	✔ 4 Tab fields of 10,10,10,10	✔ 4 Tab fields of 16,16,16,16	✔ 5 Tab fields of 15,15,15,15,15	✔ Default Tab positions at 7,15,23,31,39	✔ 5 Tab fields of 14,14,14,14,14

Description of Command	*APPLE II Applesoft (disk)*	*PET (cassette)*	*TRS-80 Model III d = disk c = cassette*	*HP-2000*	*Atari 400/800*	*Microsoft (IBM, MS-DOS, CP/M)*
(only in PRINT statement) Moves cursor to position X	TAB (X)	TAB (X-1)	TAB (X)	TAB (X)	na (uses TAB key)	TAB (X)
(conditional branch) If the assertion X = 5 is true, execute the rest of the line. If the assertion is false, ignore the rest of the statement and jump to the next numbered line (Instead of a line number, any reasonable BASIC statement may follow THEN)★	IF X = 5 THEN 20 ★	✓ ★	✓ ★	✓	✓ ★	✓ ★
Branches to line 400 (unconditional branch)	GO TO 400	✓	✓	✓	✓	✓
Executes all statements between the FOR statement and the corresponding NEXT, initially with X = 1, then with X = 5, X = 9, etc., until X = 20 at which time execution jumps to the line number after the NEXT statement. STEP size is one if not specified.	FOR X = 1 TO 20 STEP 4 . . . NEXT X		✓	✓	✓	✓
BRANCHES to the subroutine at line 1000	GOSUB 1000	✓	✓	✓	✓	✓
Marks the end of the subroutine; returns to statement following most recent GOSUB	RETURN	✓	✓	✓	✓	
Halts execution (indicates in which program line)★	STOP ★	✓ ★	✓ ★	✓	✓	✓ ★
Halts execution with no message	END	✓	✓	✓	✓	✓

DEFINING VARIABLES AND THEIR RELATIONSHIPS

Negation	−	✓	✓	✓	✓	✓
Exponentiation	^	|	|	^or**	^	✓
Multiplication	*	✓	✓	✓	✓	✓
Division	/	✓	✓	✓	✓	✓
Addition	+	✓	✓	✓	✓	✓
Subtraction	−	✓	✓	✓	✓	✓
Equal	=	✓	✓	✓	✓	✓
Not equal	<>	✓	✓	<> or #	✓	✓
Less than	<	✓	✓	✓	✓	✓
Greater than	>	✓	✓	✓	✓	✓
Less than or equal to	<=	✓	✓	✓	✓	✓

Description of Command	*APPLE II Applesoft (disk)*	*PET (cassette)*	*TRS-80 Model III d = disk c = cassette*	*HP-2000*	*Atari 400/800*	*MicroSoft (IBM, MS-DOS, CP/M)*
Greater than or equal to	>= ✔	✔	✔	✔	✔	✔
Logical "NOT"	NOT	✔	✔	✔	✔	✔
Logical "AND"	AND	✔	✔	✔	✔	✔
Logical "OR"	OR	✔	✔	✔	✔	✔
Real Variables (range: approx ± 9.99999999 E + 37) [precision]★ Let A and B represent any letter. Let 1 represent any digit.	AB or A1 [9 digit]★	✔ [9 digit]★	✔ [7 or 16 digit]★	A or A1 [6 digit]★	✔ [9 digit]★	A or A1 [9 digit]★
Integer Variables (range ±32767)	AB% or A1%	✔	✔	na	na	✔
String Variables (range 0 to 255 characters)★	AB$ or A1$ ★	✔ ★	✔ ★	A$	✔	✔ ★

DEBUGGING AIDS

Branches to the Xth line number in the list (i.e., if X = 2, branches to line 100)	ON X GOTO 300, 100, 500	✔	✔	GOTO X OF 300, 100, 500	✔	✔
Branches to subroutine at the Xth line number in the list	ON X GOSUB 400, 100, 900	✔	✔	GOSUB X OF 400, 100, 900	✔	✔
(In error-handling routine) Causes return to the statement where error occurred	RESUME	na	✔	na	TRAP 4000 GOTO PEEK (186) + PEEK (187)*256	✔
Subsequent errors cause branch to error-handling routine at line 500 instead of message and program halt (i.e., if you think an error may occur, it branches to the error-handling routine	ONERR GOTO 500	na	ON ERROR GOTO 500	IF ERROR THEN 500	TRAP 500	ON ERROR GOTO 500
Lists each line number as it is executed	TRACE	na	TRON (shifted @ causes pause)	na	na	TRON
Turns off previous command	NO TRACE	na	TROFF	na	na	TROFF
Returns the contents of memory location	PEEK (location)	✔	✔	na	✔	✔
Changes the value of the memory location (ml) to 33	POKE ml, 33	✔	✔	na	✔	✔

ARRAYS

Description of Command	APPLE II Applesoft (disk)	PET (cassette)	TRS-80 Model III d = disk c = cassette	HP-2000	Atari 400/800	Microsoft (IBM, MS-DOS, CP/M)
Sets maximum subscripts for A; reserves memory space for $(X + 1)*(Y + 1)*(Z + 1)$ real elements starting with A(0,0,0)	DIM A(X,Y,Z)	✔	✔	DIM A(X,Y) (NO A(0,0))	✔	✔
Sets maximum subscripts for A$, which may contain $(X + 1)*(Y + 1)$ string elements, each up to 255 characters	DIM A$(X,Y)	✔	✔	na DIM A$(20) sets aside 20 spaces for characters to be stored in A$. No subscripted string variables allowed.	na	✔

FUNCTIONS

Description of Command	APPLE II Applesoft (disk)	PET (cassette)	TRS-80 Model III d = disk c = cassette	HP-2000	Atari 400/800	Microsoft (IBM, MS-DOS, CP/M)
Defines a function FNA. In later use, the argument used with FNA will be substituted for X in the defined expression [i.e., FNA (5) returns 15].	DEF FNA(X) = X + 2*X	✔	d ✔ c na	✔	na	✔
Returns sine cosine of X radians tangent	SIN (X) COS (X) TAN (X)	✔	✔	✔	✔ in degrees or radians	✔
Returns arctangent of X in radians	ATN(X)	✔	✔	✔	✔	✔
Returns − 1 if X < 0, 0 if X = 0, 1 if X > 0	SGN(X)	✔	−	✔	✔	✔
Returns absolute value of X	ABS(X)	✔	✔	✔	✔	✔
Returns positive square root of X	SQR(X)	✔	✔	✔	✔	✔
Returns e (2.718289) to the power X	EXP(X)	✔	✔	✔	✔	✔
Returns natural logarithm of X	LOG(X)	✔	✔	✔	✔	✔
Returns largest integer less than or equal to X	INT(X)	✔	✔	✔	✔	✔
Returns random real numbers from 0 to 0.99999999 each time used	RND(1)	✔	RND(0)	✔	RND(0)	✔
Returns number of characters in A$	LEN (A$)	✔	✔	✔	✔	✔
Returns number value of X, converted to string	STR $(X)	✔	✔	CONVERT X TO X$	✔	✔
Returns A$, up to the first non-numeric character, as a numeric value	VAL (A$)	✔	✔	CONVERT X$ TO X	✔	✔
Returns leftmost X characters of A$	LEFT$(A$,X)	✔	✔	A$(1,X)	A$(1,X)	✔
Returns rightmost X characters of A$	RIGHT$(A$,X)	✔	✔	A$(LEN(A$) − X + 1,LEN(A$))	A$(LEN(A$) − X + 1,LEN(A$))	✔

Description of Command	APPLE II Applesoft (disk)	PET (cassette)	TRS-80 Model III d = disk c = cassette	HP-2000	Atari 400/800	Microsoft (IBM, MS-DOS, CP/M)
Returns Y characters of A$, starting at character X	MID$(A$,X,Y)	✔	✔	A$(X,X + Y)	A$(X,X + Y)	✔
Operator used to concatenate strings	+	✔	✔	A$(LEN(A$) + 1) = B$	A$(LEN(A$) + 1) = B$	✔
Return ASCII code for first character of A$	ASC (A$)	✔ Has its own code for graphics	✔ Has special code for special graphics	NUM (A$)	✔ Has special code for special graphics	✔ Has special code for special graphics
Returns ASCII character whose code is X	CHR $(X)	✔ Has its own code for graphics	✔	✔	✔ Has special code for special graphics	✔ Has special code for special graphics

624

APPENDIX 4

Electronic Spreadsheet Command Summary

COMMANDS

Symbol	Name	Purpose
/B	the Blank command	Blank a single entry.
/C	the Clear command	Clear the entire sheet, Y confirms.
/D	the Delete command	Delete a row or column.
	R	Delete a row.
	C	Delete a column.
/F	the Format command	Format a single entry.
	D	Default
	G	General
	I	Integer
	L	Left-justified
	R	Right-justified
	$	Dollars and cents
	*	Graph
/G	the Global command	Globally affect the sheet.
	C	Column width
	O	Order of recalculation
	R	Rowwise
	C	Columnwise
	R	Recalculation
	A	Automatic
	M	Manual
	F	Format
	D	Default
	G	General
	I	Integer
	L	Left-justified
	R	Right-justified
	$	Dollars and cents
	*	Graph
/I	the Insert command	Insert a row or column.
	R	Insert a row
	C	Insert a column
/M	the Move command	Move a row or column.
/P	the Print command	Print all or part of the sheet to a device.
/R	the Replicate command	Replicate an entry, row, or column onto another area of the sheet.

COMMANDS *(continued)*

Symbol	Name	Purpose
/S	the Storage command	Access storage.
	L	Load a sheet
	S	Store a sheet
	D	Delete a stored sheet
	I	Initialize a diskette
	Q	Quit
	#	Access a file in the Data Interchange Format (DIF, a trademark of Software Arts, Inc.)
	L	Load a DIF file
	S	Save a DIF file
/T	the Title command	Freeze titles in place.
	H	Horizontally
	V	Vertically
	B	Both
	N	Neither
/V	the Version Number command	Display the version number.
/W	the Window command	Affect the window display.
	H	Horizontal split
	V	Vertical split
	1	1 (one) window
	S	Synchronized scrolling
	U	Unsynchronized scrolling
/-	the Repeating Label command	Repeat part of a label throughout a single entry.

BUILT-IN FUNCTIONS

@ABS(argument)	The absolute value
@ACOS(argument)	The arccosine
@ASIN(argument)	The arcsine
@ATAN(argument)	The arctangent
@AVERAGE(argument1,argument2,...)	The average
@COS(argument)	The cosine
@COUNT(argument1, argument2,...)	Count how many
@ERROR	The error function and error value
@EXP(argument)	e to a power
@INT(argument)	Integer
@LN(argument)	Natural logarithm
@LOG10(argument)	Logarithm, base 10
@LOOKUP(argument1,argument2)	Look up a value in a table
@MAX(argument1,argument2,...)	The maximum value
@MIN(argument1,argument2,...)	The minimum value
@NA	Not available
@NPV(argument1,argument2)	The net present value
@PI	Value of (pi)
@SIN(argument)	The sine
@SQRT(argument)	The square root
@SUM(argument1,argument2,...)	Sum the values
@TAN(argument)	The tangent

APPENDIX 5

Word Processing Software Summary

WORD PROCESSING SYSTEM

	Applewriter II and III	Easywriter II	Screenwriter II	Spellbinder	Superscript	WordStar
Micro	Apple II Apple II + Apple III	IBM PC IBM PC XT	Apple II +	All Micros with these op systems	Radio Shack	All Micros with these op systems
Operating system	Apple IIDOS Apple IIIDOS	DOS	Apple IIDOS	CP/M, MP/M, C/DOS, IBM, PC/DOS, Most, Oasis	TRS/DOS	CP/M, MS DOS
Display lines/ columns	AppII 12×40 AppIII 24×80	25×80	21×40 21×70	screen dependent	16×66	22×80
Merge capability	Yes	With EasyFiler (extra)	Yes	Yes	Yes	With **MailMerge** (extra)
Records processing	With MailList Manager (extra)	With EasyFiler (extra)	Sort—no Select—yes	Sort—yes Select—no	With ProfileIII (extra)	With SuperSort (extra)
Column/tabs	Tabs	Tabs, decimal alignment	Tabs, decimal alignment	Move and insert columns, tabs, decimal alignment	Tabs, decimal alignment	Move and insert columns, tabs, decimal alignment
Program control keys	No	No	Yes	Yes	10 user-defined keys	Yes
Global search	Yes	By page	Yes	Yes	Yes	Yes
Comments	Training Pak available; split screen; saves deleted text	Bold and underline show on screen	Proportionate spacing; footnoting; indexing; full print enhancements	Proportionate spacing; help menus; five fonts; variable line spacing	Audio training available; full print enhancements; proportionate spacing; user-created special print codes	Training guide; **help** menus; horizontal scrolling; special page formatting; full print enhancement
Added hardware needed	II needs 80-column board	Two disk drives	None	None	Model I needs two disk drives	Apple needs 80-column board

627

APPENDIX 6

Hardware / Software Vendors

Apple Computer, Inc.
10260 Bradley Drive
Cupertino, California 95014

Atari, Inc.
1265 Borregas Avenue
Sunnyvale, California 94086

Commodore Business Machines
487 Devon Park Drive
Wayne, Pennsylvania 19087

Cromemco, Inc.
280 Bernardo Avenue
Mountain View, California 94040

Digital Equipment Corp.
146 Main Street
Maynard, Massachusetts 01754

Fortune Systems Corp.
1501 Industrial Road
San Carlos, California 94070

Hewlett-Packard
1820 Embarcadero Road
Palo Alto, California 94303

IBM Information Systems
Post Office Box 1328
Boca Raton, Florida 33432

Information Unlimited Software
(EasyWriter II)
281 Arlington Avenue
Berkeley, CA 94707

Kay-Comp
Non-Linear Systems, Inc.
Post Office Box N
Del Mar, California 92014

Lexisoft
(Spellbinder)
Box 1378
Davis, California 95617
(916) 758-3630

Lifetree Software
(VolksWriter for IBM)
177 Webster Street
Suite 342
Monterey, California 93940

MicroPro International
(WordStar and other software)
1229 Fourth Street
San Rafael, California 94901
(415) 457-8990

Morrow Designs
P.O. Box 5755
San Leandro, California 94577

NEC Home Electronics
1401 Estes Avenue
Elk Grove Village, Illinois 60007

North Star Computers, Inc.
14440 Catalina Street
San Leandro, California 94577

Oasis Systems
(The WORD and The WORD Plus)
2765 Reynard Way
San Diego, California 92103
(714) 291-9489

Olivetti Corp.
155 White Plains Road
Tarrytown, New York 10591

Osborne Computer Corp.
26500 Corporate Avenue
Hayward, California 94545

Otrona Corp.
2500 Central Avenue
Boulder, Colorado 80301

Peachtree Software
(PeachText and other software)
3 Corporate Square, Suite 700
Atlanta, Georgia 30329
(404) 325-8533

Perfect Software, Inc.
(Perfect Writer)
1400 Shattuck Avenue
Berkeley, California 94709

Screenplay Systems
(Scriptor)
211 East Olive Avenue, Suite 203
Burbank, California 91502
(213) 843-6557

Sierra On-Line, Inc.
(Screenwriter II)
36575 Mudge Ranch Road
Coarsegold, California 93614

Silicon Valley Systems
(WordHandler)
1625 El Camino Real, #4
Belmont, California 94002

Sinclair Research
50 Staniford Street
Boston, Massachusetts 02114

Tandy Corp.
Radio Shack
One Tandy Center
Fort Worth, Texas 76102

Texas Instruments, Inc.
Post Office Box 73
Lubbock, Texas 79408

Vector Graphic, Inc.
500 N. Ventu Park Road
Thousand Oaks, California 91320

Victor Business Products
3900 North Rockwell
Chicago, Illinois 60018

Xerox Office Products
1341 Mockingbird Lane
Dallas, Texas 75247

Zenith Data Systems
1000 Milwaukee Avenue
Glenview, Illinois 60025

APPENDIX 7

Start-up Instructions for Specific Systems

The following sections are machine-specific instructions. Choose the section that fits, or most closely resembles, your system.

APPLE

Apple computers were among the earliest microcomputers on the market. Because of their early entry, they made some pioneering decisions about screen formats and the supported BASIC statements. In fact, Apple's Integer BASIC does not meet the ANSI minimal standard. Another dialect of BASIC called Applesoft BASIC is available on the Apple. There are many different models of Apple computers available.

All of the pieces of hardware must have the power turned on for the computer to function properly. The CRT is a separate device, so it has a separate power switch. The power switch for the Apple is on the left back of the sloping keyboard package. Housed inside this small unit are the CPU and all of the attachments for your system. Make sure that you place the diskette with the DOS (disk operating system) on it in the primary diskette drive. The DOS is a very sophisticated program that will control the operation of the system. The disk drive will start to make a noise in an attempt to read the system diskette. If everything has been done properly, the computer will respond with the] character as a prompt waiting for your command.

DEC

Digital Equipment Corporation (DEC) is one of the larger minicomputer companies. Minicomputers are similar to large computers; they are generally more sophisticated than microcomputers. They operate at faster speeds and generally have more main memory available. Hard disk drives are also very common. Normally the system software is run by a computer center of some type, and there typically are a few computer specialists around whose job is to keep the system functioning properly. The system will have a sequence of steps to be followed to get on (log on) and off (log off) of the computer. Your system will be unique depending on the type of operating system being used. Please ask your instructor or computer center for specific directions.

There generally will be an account number assigned to control your access to the computer. The system will monitor any activity by a user and respond to the request. Most DEC systems have passwords to prevent unauthorized users from using the computer system. The passwords will not appear on the terminal as they are typed in. When the computer is ready for you to proceed, it responds with the word READY or with a prompt symbol such as % or $.

The terminal power switch is usually on the back side of the terminal. The power switch will usually be of the toggle variety. After the power for the CRT is on, there are several things that could happen, depending on your system.

1. Pressing the RETURN key could activate the account number prompt.

2. Typing in the word HELLO followed by the RETURN key may be necessary to activate the system request for your account number.

3. Holding down the key labeled CTRL while simultaneously pressing the key for the letter C (CTRL-C or ^C) may ask the system to service your terminal. You may then type in the word LOG and proceed through the account number, password questions.

DEC has introduced microcomputers that can use common operating systems. These machines work most like a CP/M machine.

IBM with DOS or CP/M

The IBM personal computer (PCjr., PC, or PC XT) has power switches on the right back side of the logic unit. The monitor and diskette drives are controlled by the power switch on the back of the PC itself. IBM has different versions of BASIC, including the modified version of Microsoft BASIC supplied with the computer. The different versions of BASIC are available to give different capabilities in handling input and output, compilation, and program statements. The PC also has different operating systems available. If you are using MS DOS (Disk Operating System) or CP/M (Control Program for Microprocessors), you will need to insert the diskette containing these programs in the left-hand drive (drive A) before turning on the power. If you do not have a diskette in drive A, the PC will begin functioning using the built-in Cassette BASIC.

As soon as your operating system has been loaded by the computer (booted), the computer will ask for the date. When you have responded with the date, the system will respond with a message, and "A>". The A> is the system prompting you for your next action. Since we want to run BASIC, we type in the word BASIC, and the system responds with "OK". We are ready to begin programming.

Remember to use the function keys on the left side of the keyboard to save some typing strokes. The meanings of these keys are displayed on the bottom of the monitor.

MORROW DESIGNS with CP/M

The Micro Decision computer produced by Morrow Designs has power switches on the right back side of the logic unit, and one on the front of the monitor. The diskette drives are controlled by the power switch on the back of the computer itself. Morrow Designs has different versions of BASIC, including the modified version of Microsoft BASIC supplied with the computer. Different versions of BASIC are available to give different capabilities in handling input and output, compilation and program statements. The CP/M diskette must be inserted in the left-hand drive (drive A) before turning on the power. If you do not have a diskette in drive A, the computer will ask you to insert the CP/M diskette in drive A.

As soon as your operating system has been loaded by the computer (booted), the computer will display a list of programs that may be selected (menu). We want to run BASIC, so we type in the option for BASIC, and the system responds with Ready. We are ready to begin programming.

VIC, PET, or CBM

The Commodore VIC or Commodore 64 computers are the first of another new wave of microcomputers. The computer is contained in a keyboard that can use a television as a monitor. The system documentation is written so that inexperienced users can easily discover how the system works.

The PET and CBM (Commodore Business Machines) are very similar. The power switches are on the back left-hand side of the machines. After the power has been turned on, you will receive a system message and a system response using the word READY. This signals that the system is ready for you to use.

If you are using a cassette PET system, the system commands are like those covered in section 7 of module H. The program names must be inside quote marks (") for the SAVE and LOAD commands.

If you are using a diskette system (floppy disk), the SAVE and LOAD commands are preceded by the letter D. You must also specify the drive that is to be used if you have more than one drive. Therefore a disk save of a program called SAMPLE would look like this:

```
DSAVE "SAMPLE",D1
```

if you want to save the program on drive 1. If you want to use drive 0, the ",D1" is not needed. If the program already exists on the drive, you must include the @ sign in the SAVE command.

```
DSAVE "@SAMPLE",D1
```

Loading a program is done in a similar fashion. Again use the ",D1" when you want drive 1, otherwise leave it off and the program will be loaded from drive 0.

```
DLOAD "SAMPLE",D1
```

Remember to use these commands in place of SAVE and LOAD when you read section 2 of module H.

TRS-80

Each of the three models of the TRS-80 from Radio Shack (Tandy Corporation) functions differently. The Model III or Model IV are the most self-contained units. The older Model I functions very similarly. If you have trouble following the instructions in the modules, refer to the manuals for these machines. The manuals are written for inexperienced users.

The power switch is under the keyboard on the right-hand front side of the computer. Insert the system diskette in the primary drive, and power the system on. The system messages will be displayed, and "TRSDORS Ready" will be displayed. You can then enter BASIC system commands.

APPENDIX 8

Summary of BASIC Statements

Keywords	Purpose	Examples	Text Reference (page)
Assignment Statement			
LET	Optional keyword for assignment statement. Assign a value to a variable.	60 C = 99 90 D = A 170 B = 141.0 190 W$ = "PAM"	470
Data Entry Statements			
INPUT	Accepts input data from user.	20 INPUT A	476
DATA	Used to store internal data for program.	20 DATA 21.0, 80.0	478
READ	Used to retrieve internal data.	10 READ A, B	478
RESTORE	Resets data pool pointer for internal data.	50 RESTORE	479
Data Output Statements			
PRINT	Prints numeric or string data for user.	30 PRINT "FIRST VALUE", "SECOND VALUE" 40 PRINT A, B	472
PRINT USING	Print output data according to a specified format.	70 PRINT USING "##"; I	473
Control Statements			
FOR	Iterative loop control.	40 FOR I = 1 TO 100 STEP 2 (BASIC statements)	507
NEXT	End of FOR..TO..STEP iterative loop.	90 NEXT I	507
GO TO	Unconditional transfer to another statement.	50 GOTO 10	497
GOSUB	Subroutine call.	110 GOSUB 260	526

Keywords	Purpose	Examples	Text Reference (page)
RETURN	Signifies the end of a subroutine.	130 RETURN	526
IF-THEN	Decision-making statement	100 IF (H * 3 > 41) THEN 40 110 IF (D <= 0.0) THEN 70	493
STOP	Stops program without closing files.	80 STOP	481
Other BASIC Statements			
REM	Remark statement for programmer's comments.	90 REM VARIABLES USED: 100 REM P THE TOTAL POINTS	480
DIM	Dimensions numeric or string arrays.	10 DIM R(50)	516
DEF	User-defined function.	10 DEF FNC(A)=A * A * A	499
ON..GOTO	Calls subroutine based on expression.	70 ON X GOTO 150, 210, 250	499
ON..GOSUB	Transfers control based on expression.	80 ON X GOSUB 150, 210, 250	500
RANDOMIZE	Force different random-number generation with each program run.	10 RANDOMIZE	530
END	Signifies program end, closes files.	210 END	481
File Statements			
OPEN	Request use of file from the system.	10 OPEN "SAMPLE.DAT" FOR INPUT AS FILE #5	476
CLOSE	Tells the system that the file is no longer needed.	60 CLOSE #5	476
INPUT#	Acquire input data from file.	30 INPUT #5, M$(I)	534–540
PRINT#	Write output data to file.	40 PRINT #5,M$	476
Other Needed Information			
Defining variables			468
System commands			487
Arithmetic operators			470
String functions			530
Numeric functions			531
Designing programs			447, 465
Building DO-WHILE or DO-UNTIL			510, 512

Bibliography

1. Ackoff, Russell L. "Management Misinformation Systems." *Management Science,* Vol. 14, No. 4, pp. 147–156.
2. Alter, S. L. "How Effective Managers Use Information Systems." *Harvard Business Review,* November-December, 1976, pp. 97–104.
3. Carlson, Eric D. "An Approach for Designing Decision Support Systems." *Data Base,* Vol. 10, No. 3, Winter, 1979, pp. 3–22.
4. *Datapro Reports.* Delran, N. J.: Datapro Research Corporation, 1983.
5. Donelson, William S. "MRP—Who Needs It?" *Datamation,* Vol. 25, No. 5, May, 1979, pp. 185–194.
6. Drucker, Peter. "Drucker's Anatomy." *Concepts,* Vol. 6, No. 4, Autumn, 1982, pp. 2–7.
7. Eliason, Alan, and Kent D. Kitts. *Business Computer Systems and Applications.* Chicago: Science Research Associates, 1979.
8. Freedman, David H., and Roy Friedman. "Bar-code and Voice Recognition Ease Data-entry Problems." *Mini-Micro Systems,* Vol. 16, No. 7, June, 1983, pp. 239–246.
9. Fu, King-sun. "Robotics and Automation." *IEEE Computer,* Vol. 15, No. 12, December, 1982, pp. 13–14.
10. Jaffe, Merle. "Decision Support Systems for Manufacturing." *Infosystems,* Vol. 30, No. 7, July, 1983, pp. 112–114.
11. Kenealy, Patrick. "Market Overview: Minicomputer Line Printers." *Mini-Micro Systems,* Vol. 16, No. 1, January, 1983, pp. 131–140.
12. ———. "Product Profile: Small-business Systems." *Mini-Micro Systems,* Vol. 16, No. 7, June, 1983, pp. 151–192.
13. Leeson, Marjorie. *Computer Operations.* Chicago: Science Research Associates, 1983.
14. Lucas, H. J., Jr. *Why Information Systems Fail.* New York: Columbia University Press, 1975.
15. Mallender, Ian H. "Color Non-impact Printers Hit the Market." *Mini-Micro Systems,* Vol. 16, No. 7, June, 1983, pp. 217–224.
16. McLeod, Raymond, Jr. *Management Information Systems,* 2nd ed. Chicago: Science Research Associates, 1983.
17. Mehlmann, Marilyn. *When People Use Computers.* Englewood Cliffs, N.J.: Prentice-Hall, 1981.
18. Poppel, Harvey L. "The Information Revolution: Winners and Losers." *Harvard Business Review,* January-February, 1978.
19. Rubin, Charles. "Some People Should Be Afraid of Computers." *Personal Computing,* Vol. 7, No. 8, August, 1983, pp. 55–57.

Part One: Introduction

637

20. Scharer, Laura L. "User Training: Less is More." *Datamation,* Vol. 29, No. 7, July, 1983, pp. 175–182.
21. Stone, Harold, ed. *Introduction to Computer Architecture,* 2nd ed. Chicago: Science Research Associates, 1980.
22. Verity, John W. "1982 Mini-micro Survey." *Datamation,* Vol. 28, No. 12, November, 1982, pp. 34–48.
23. Williams, Gregg. "The Lisa Computer System." *Byte,* Vol. 8, No. 2, February, 1983, pp. 33–50.
24. Whol, Amy, and Kathleen Carey. "We're Not Really Sure How Many We Have." *Datamation,* Vol. 28, No. 12, November, 1982, pp. 106–109.

Part Two: Fundamental Computer Systems

25. Boehm, Barry W. *Software Engineering Economics.* Englewood Cliffs, N.J.: Prentice-Hall, 1981.
26. Bohl, Marilyn. *Information Processing,* 3rd ed. Chicago: Science Research Associates, 1980.
27. Bohl, Marilyn. *Introduction to IBM Direct Access Storage Devices.* Chicago: Science Research Associates, 1981.
28. Brechtein, Rick. "Comparing Disk Technologies." *Datamation,* Vol. 24, No. 1, January, 1978, pp. 139–150.
29. Burch, John G., Felix R. Strater, and Gary Grudnitski. *Information Systems: Theory and Practice.* New York: John Wiley, 1979.
30. Carlson, Robert D., and James A. Lewis. *The Systems Analysis Workbook,* 2nd ed. Englewood Cliffs, N.J.: Prentice-Hall, 1979.
31. Cortada, James W. *EDP Costs and Charges.* Englewood Cliffs, N.J.: Prentice-Hall, 1980.
32. *Data World.* Pennsauken, N.J.: Auerbach Publishers, 1980.
33. Freedman, Daniel P., and Gerald M. Weinberg. *Walkthroughs, Inspections, and Technical Reviews,* 3rd ed. Boston: Little, Brown, and Company, 1982.
34. Glass, Robert L., and Ronald A. Noiseux. *Software Maintenance Guidebook.* Englewood Cliffs, N.J.: Prentice-Hall, 1981.
35. Kindred, Alton R. *Data Systems and Management.* Englewood Cliffs, N.J.: Prentice-Hall, 1973.
36. Moritz, Frederick G. "Conventional Magnetic Tape Equipment." *Modern Data,* Vol. 8, No. 3, March, 1975, pp. 51–55.
37. Orr, Kenneth T. *Structured Systems Development.* New York: Yourdon Press, 1977.
38. Page-Jones, Meilir. *The Practical Guide to Structured Systems Design.* New York: Yourdon Press, 1980.
39. Rubin, Martin, ed. *Documentation Standards and Procedures for On-line Systems.* New York: Van Nostrand Reinhold, 1979.
40. Weinberg, Victor. *Structured Analysis.* New York: Yourdon Press, 1978.
41. Yourdon, Edward, and Larry L. Constantine. *Structured Design.* New York: Yourdon Press, 1978.

Part Three: Advanced Computer Systems

42. Abrams, Marshall, Robert P. Blanc, and Ira W. Cotton, eds. *Computer Networks.* IEEE Tutorial #JH3 100-5, 1978.

43. Bingham, John E., and Garth W. P. Davies. *Planning for Data Communications*. New York: John Wiley, 1977.

44. Booth, Grayce M. *The Distributed Systems Environment*. New York: McGraw-Hill, 1981.

45. Bowerman, Robert. "Relational Database Systems for Micros." *Datamation,* Vol. 29, No. 7, July, 1983, pp. 128–134.

46. Chen, Peter P., ed. *Entity-Relationship Approach to Information Modeling and Analysis*. Saugus, Calif.: ER Institute, 1981.

47. Chu, Wesley, and Peter B. Chen, ed. *Centralized and Distributed Data Base Systems*. IEEE Tutorial #EHO 154-5, 1979.

48. Codd, E. F. "Relational Database: A Practical Foundation for Productivity." *Communications of the ACM,* Vol. 25, No. 2, February 1982, pp. 109–117.

49. *Communications Solutions*. Delran, N.J.: Datapro Research Corporation, 1978.

50. *Data Communications Management*. Pennsauken, N.J.: Auerbach Publishers, 1979.

51. *Data Communications Primer—Student Text*. IBM manual GC20-1668, While Plains, New York.

52. Date, Chris J. *An Introduction to Database Systems*. Reading, Mass.: Addison-Wesley, 1981.

53. Davis, Dwight B. "Pioneering Vendors Attempt to Develop Infant Broadband Local Net Market." *Mini-Micro Systems,* Vol. 16, No. 1, January, 1983, pp. 81–92.

54. *Executive Guide to Data Communications*. New York: McGraw-Hill, 1977.

55. Klee, Kenneth, John W. Verity, and Jan Johnson. "Battle of the Networkers." *Datamation,* Vol. 28, No. 3, March, 1982, pp. 115–127.

56. Kroenke, David. *Database Processing,* 2nd ed. Chicago: Science Research Associates, 1983.

57. Lefkovits, David. *File Structures for On-line Systems*. New York: Spartan Books, 1969.

58. Liebowitz, Burt H., and John H. Carson, ed. *Distributed Processing,* 2nd ed. IEEE Tutorial, #EHO 127-1, 1978.

59. Lim, Pacifico Amarga. *CICS/VS Command Level with ANS COBOL Examples*. New York: Van Nostrand Reinhold, 1982.

60. Martin, James. *Computer Data-Base Organization*. Englewood Cliffs, N.J.: Prentice-Hall, 1977.

61. Martin, James. *Telecommunications and the Computer.* Englewood Cliffs, N.J.: Prentice-Hall, 1976.

62. McQuillan, John M., and Vinton G. Cerf. *A Practical View of Data Communication Protocols*. IEEE Tutorial #EHO 137-0, 1978.

63. McQuillan, John M., and David C. Walden. "The ARPA Network Design Decisions." *Computer Networks,* Vol. 1, No. 5, August, 1977.

64. Rothfeder, Jeffrey. "Networking the Workplace." *Personal Computing,* Vol. 7., No. 6, June, 1983, pp. 79–87.

65. Sanders, Ray. "Managing Data Communications." *Datamation,* Vol. 24, No. 11, November, 1978, pp. 43–47.

66. Tanenbaum, Andrew S. *Computer Networks*. Englewood Cliffs, N.J.: Prentice-Hall, 1981.
67. Thierauf, Robert J. *Distributed Processing Systems*. Englewood Cliffs, N.J.: Prentice-Hall, 1978.
68. Weitzman, Cay. *Distributed Micro/Minicomputer Systems*. Englewood Cliffs, N.J.: Prentice-Hall, 1980.
69. White, Wade, and Morris Holmes. "The Future of Commercial Satellite Telecommunications." *Datamation,* Vol. 24, No. 7, July, 1978, pp. 94–102.

Part Four: Special Computing Topics

70. Bonner, Paul. "Communicating with Presentation Graphics." *Personal Computing,* Vol. 7, No. 7, July, 1983, pp. 110–119.
71. Bonner, Susan, and Kang G. Shin. "A Comparative Study of Robot Languages." *IEEE Computer,* Vol. 15, No. 12, December, 1982, pp. 82–96.
72. Burch, John G., and Joseph L. Sardinas. *Computer Control and Audit.* New York: John Wiley, 1978.
73. *Computer Crime: Criminal Justice Resource Manual.* Washington, D.C.: Bureau of Justice Statistics, 1979.
74. Dorf, Richard C. *Computers and Man.* San Francisco: Boyd and Fraser, 1977.
75. Framer, Dale F. "Confessions of an EDP Auditor." *Datamation,* Vol. 29, No. 7, July, 1983, pp. 193–198.
76. Harris, Larry R. "Fifth Generation Foundations." *Datamation,* Vol. 29, No. 7, July, 1983, pp. 148–156.
77. Hearn, Donald, and M. Pauline Baker. *Microcomputer Graphics.* Englewood Cliffs, N.J.: Prentice-Hall, 1983.
78. Holoien, Martin O. *Computers and Their Societal Impact.* New York: John Wiley, 1977.
79. Kling, Rob. "EFTS: Social and Technical Issues." *Computers and Society,* Fall, 1976, pp. 3–10.
80. ———. *Passing the Digital Buck: Unresolved Social and Technical Issues in Electronic Funds Transfer Systems.* Public Policy Research Organization, Report Number ICS-TR #87, University of California, Irvine, 1976.
81. Krauss, Leonard I., and Aileen MacGahan. *Computer Fraud and Countermeasures.* Englewood Cliffs, N.J.: Prentice-Hall, 1979.
82. Mair, William C., Donald R. Wood, and Keagle W. Davis. *Computer Control and Audit.* Wellesley, Mass.: QED, 1978.
83. McCauley, Carole Sperrin. *Computers and Creativity.* New York: Praeger, 1974.
84. McCorduck, Pamela. *Machines Who Think.* San Francisco: W. H. Freeman, 1979.
85. McKibbin, Wendy Lea. "Who Gets the Blame for Computer Crime?" *Infosystems,* Vol. 30, No. 7, July, 1983, pp. 34–36.
86. McKnight, Gerald. *Computer Crime.* London/ Michale Joseph, 1973.
87. Minsky, M. L. "Artificial Intelligence." *Scientific American,* September, 1966, pp. 142–148.

88. Morrison, Philip, and Emily Morrison, eds. *Charles Babbage and His Calculating Engines*. New York: Dover Publications, 1961.

89. Morton, A. S., and M. L. Ernst. "The Social Impacts of Electronic Funds Transfer." *IEEE Transactions on Communications,* October, 1975, pp. 1148–1155.

90. Mueller, Robert E., and Erik T. Mueller. "Would an Intelligent Computer Have a Right to Life?" *Creative Computing,* Vol. 9, No. 8, August, 1983, pp. 149–153.

91. Negroponte, Nicholas. "The Computerized Global Village." *Concepts,* Vol. 7, No. 1, Winter, 1983, pp. 8–11.

92. Parker, Donna B. *Crime by Computer.* New York: Charles Scribner's Sons, 1976.

93. *Personal Privacy in an Information Society.* U.S. Government Printing Office, No. 052-003-00395, July, 1977.

94. Rhodes, Wayne L., Jr. "Office of the Future, Fact or Fantasy?" *Infosystems,* March, 1980, pp. 45–54.

95. Rhodes, Wayne L., Jr., and Raymond S. Winkler. "Twenty-fifth Annual DP Salary Survey." *Infosystems,* Vol. 30, No. 6, June, 1983, pp. 40–44.

96. Roberts, Jerome J. "Computer-generated Evidence," *Data Management,* November, 1974, pp. 20–21.

97. Rothman, Stanley, and Charles Mosmann. *Computers and Society,* 2nd ed. Chicago: Science Research Associates, 1976.

98. Ryan, Frank B. "The Electronic Voting System for the United States House of Representatives." *Computer,* November-December, 1972, pp. 32–37.

99. Sanders, Donald H. *Computers in Society,* 2nd ed. New York: McGraw-Hill, 1977.

100. Shannon, Daniel. "Copycatting in the Software Patch." *New York Times,* May 9, 1982, p. F–17.

101. Staples, Betsy. "Computer Intelligence: Unlimited and Untapped." *Creative Computing,* Vol. 9, No. 8, August, 1983, pp. 164–166.

102. Tapscott, Don. "Investigating the Electronic Office." *Datamation,* Vol. 28, No. 3, March, 1982, pp. 130–138.

103. Turning, A. M. "Can a Machine Think?" *Mind,* 1950, pp. 2099–2123.

104. Ware, Willis H. "Handling Personal Data." *Datamation,* Vol. 23, No. 10, October, 1977, pp. 83–87.

105. Weizenbaum, Joseph, *Computer Power and Human Reason: From Judgement to Calculation.* San Francisco: W. H. Freeman, 1976.

106. Wiener, Norbert. "Some Moral and Technical Consequences of Automation." *Science,* Vol. 131, May, 1960, pp. 1355–1358.

107. Yasaki, E. K. "Bar Codes for Data Entry." *Datamation,* Vol. 21, No. 5, May, 1975, pp. 63–68.

Part Five: Programming

108. Ageloff, Roy, and Richard Mojena. *Applied BASIC Programming.* Belmont, Calif.: Wadsworth, 1980.

109. Arjani, K. A. *Structured Programming Flowcharts.* New York: Collegium, 1978.

110. Bernstein, M. K. "Hardware Is Easy—It's Software That's Hard." *Datamation*, Vol. 24, No. 11, November, 1978, pp. 32–36.

111. Bien, Darl, and Gregory A. Cook. *BASIC Programming with Quantative Methods in Business*. New York: Petrocelli Charter, 1975.

112. Bohl, Marilyn. *A Guide for Programmers*. Englewood Cliffs, N.J.: Prentice-Hall, 1978.

113. ———. *Tools for Structured Design*. Chicago: Science Research Associates, 1978.

114. Bosworth, Bruce, and Harry L. Nagel. *Programming in BASIC for Business*. Chicago: Science Research Associates, 1977.

115. Brooks, Frederick P., Jr. *The Mythical Man-Month*. Reading, Mass.: Addison-Wesley, 1975.

116. Dijkstra, Edsger W. *A Discipline of Programming*. Englewood Cliffs, N.J.: Prentice-Hall, 1976.

117. ———. "The Humble Programmer." *Communications of the ACM*, Vol. 15, No. 10, October, 1972, pp. 859–866.

118. Dolan, Kathy. *Business Computer Systems Design*. Santa Cruz: Mitchell Publishing, 1983.

119. Gries, David, ed. *Programming Methodology*. New York: Springer-Verlag, 1978.

120. Hughes, Joan K. *PL/I Structured Programming,* 2nd ed. New York: John Wiley, 1979.

121. Johnston, Randolph P. *BASIC Using Microcomputers*. Santa Cruz: Mitchell Publishing, 1983.

122. McCracken, Daniel D. "The Changing Face of Applications Programming." *Datamation*, Vol. 24, No. 11, November, 1978, pp. 25–30.

123. ———. *A Simplified Guide to COBOL Programming*. New York: John Wiley, 1976.

124. *MicroRIM Users Manual*. Bellevue, Wash.: MicroRIM Corporation, 1983.

125. Mills, Harlan D. "Top-Down Programming in Large Systems," ed. R. Rustin. *Debugging Techniques in Large Systems*. Englewood Cliffs, N.J.: Prentice-Hall, 1971.

126. Myers, Glenford J. *The Art of Software Testing*. New York: John Wiley, 1979.

127. Noll, Paul. *The Structured Programming Cookbook*. Fresno, Calif.: Mike Murach and Associates, 1978.

128. ———. *Structured Programming for the COBOL Programmer.* Fresno, Calif.: Mike Murach and Associates, 1978.

129. Orr, Kenneth T. *Structured Systems Development*. New York: Yourdon Press, 1977.

130. *ORACLE Users' Guide*. Menlo Park, Calif.: Relational Software Incorporated, 1981.

131. Sammet, Jean E. *Programming Languages: History and Fundamentals*. Englewood Cliffs, N.J.: Prentice-Hall, 1969.

132. *SQL/Data System Application Programming*. IBM Corporation Document SH24-5018-1, 1982.

133. *SQL/Data System General Information*. IBM Corporation Document GH24-5012-0, 1981.

134. Weinberg, Gerald M. *The Psychology of Computer Programming*. New York: Van Nostrand Reinhold, 1971.

135. Welburn, Tyler. "Toward Training the Compleat COBOL Programmer." *Interface,* Vol. 1, No. 2, Spring, 1979, pp. 40–42.

136. ———. *Advanced Structured COBOL*. Palo Alto, Calif.: Mayfield, 1983.

137. ———. *Structured COBOL*. Palo Alto, Calif.: Mayfield, 1981.

138. Yourdon, Edward, and Larry L. Constantine. *Structured Design*. New York: Yourdon Press, 1978.

Glossary/Index

Baud *(continued)*
per second. Line speed in baud is less than or equal to line speed in bits per second. 252

Billing system, 15–17, 77

Binary A number system having two symbols, 0 and 1. Place values are based on powers of two. Binary is used by computers because 0's and 1's are easily represented electronically. 31, 346–349

Binary instruction codes, 548

Bit A binary digit. Bits have either of the values 0 or 1. 31, 146, 546–548

Bit pattern, 31

Bits per second A measure of the speed of a communications line which describes how many bits can be transmitted across the line in one second. 252

Blake Records and Tapes, 4–11

Block A group of records on a file that are read or written together, as a unit. Records are grouped into blocks to reduce wasted space on tape or disk and to improve input/output processing speed. 153–155

BPI, see bytes per inch.

BPS, see bits per second.

Buffer An area of main memory used as a temporary holding place for data during input and output. 154

Business applications and languages, 565–570

Byte The collection of bits necessary to form one character. Some computers have 8 bits per byte; others have 6 bits per byte. 33, 34, 146, 546–548

Bytes per inch A term used to describe the recording density of magnetic tape. Common tape densities are 800, 1600, and 6250 bytes per inch. 152

Capital expenditure analysis, 80

Case statement A multi-branch structure in pseudocode. Useful when different actions are to be taken depending on the value of a variable. 193

Cash planning, 80, 81

Cashless society A society in which all financial transactions take place electronically. Paychecks and other income would be deposited electronically, and all purchases would be made via check or electronic transaction. There would be no need for cash. 386

Cathode-ray-tube, see CRT

CCP, see communications control program

Central processing unit The portion of the computer hardware that executes program instructions. As defined in this text, it contains a control unit, main memory, and the arithmetic and logic unit. Some definitions do not include main memory as part of the CPU. 22, 46, 428.

Centralized processing, 250

Centralized data Data that is stored in only one location in a distributed processing system. 307–309

Change report, 74

Character A single letter, digit, or special sign (like #,$). Characters are represented by bytes in computer storage. 32–35

Character printer A printer that writes a full character. Contrast with dot-matrix printer. 46

Characteristics of financial computer systems, 79

Check digits A digit that is added to a field to help verify correctness. 161

Checkless society A society in which all transactions take place electronically. All paychecks would be deposited electronically, and all purchases would be made by electronic means. There would be no need for checks. 386

Checks and balances A situation that exists when the authority and/or ability to perform an action is divided among two or more employees. 378

Class enrollment system, 30, 31, 36, 50, 56, 59, 60

Clientele, of system The people for whom a system exists. The consumers of the systems services. The clientele of the class enrollment system is students. Clientele for an airline reservation system is airline passengers. Contrast with users. 63

COBOL language COmmon Business Oriented Language. The most commonly used programming language for business applications. COBOL was developed by a committee of users and manufacturers in the late 1950s. 25, 26, 568, 569, 578

Code conversion The process of converting character codes used by one hardware component to those used by a different hardware component. Needed in teleprocessing and distributed systems in which hardware from different manufacturers is used. 264, 265, 305

Colleague relationship among computers, 289, 290

Colleagues, 297–299

Common carriers, 256

Communication subnetwork, 300

Communications control program, 268, 304, 305

Communications controllers, 266

Communications lines, 252–255

Compiler A program that translates source program language statements into object code. Computer manufacturers provide a compiler for each language to be used on their computer. 549

Complement addition The process by which machines subtract in binary. 348, 349

Complex network In a database, a many-to-many relationship among records in which the parents of a record can be of the same type. 218, 220

Components of a business computer system There are five: See hardware, programs, data, procedures, and personnel.

Computer committee at Horizon, 121–123

Computer crime
definition, 364, 365
prevention, 369–378
through programming, 437
types of, 364, 368, 369

Computer operators, 28

Computer system A collection of computer hardware, programs, data, procedures, and trained personnel that interact to satisfy a need. 22, 70

Computers
business impact, 382–387
in the health professions, 387
in the legal professions, 390, 391
in politics, 391–393
negative impact on society, 397–401

Concentrator A computer used to process messages in a teleprocessing system. A concentrator combines/distributes messages from/to terminals, it conducts polling, performs character conversion, and handles other communications functions. A concentrator does not do applications processing. It is physically remote from the applications processing computer. 264–266, 270, 271

Conceptual view The complete, organizational view of a database. 219

Concurrent processing The process by which the CPU executes several programs. For example, it may allocate a short amount of time (say 10 milliseconds) to each program in round-robin fashion. Portions of the programs are executed sequentially, but the process occurs so fast it appears to humans that the programs are executed simultaneously. 276, 277, 552–555

Concurrent update problem Difficulties that occur when concurrently executing programs attempt to access and modify the same data. 277

Condition symbol, 55

Construction, 110
at Horizon, 139, 140

Consultant, 122, 123